About Pearson

Pearson is the world's learning company, with presence across 70 countries worldwide. Our unique insights and world-class expertise comes from a long history of working closely with renowned teachers, authors and thought leaders, as a result of which, we have emerged as the preferred choice for millions of teachers and learners across the world.

We believe learning opens up opportunities, creates fulfilling careers and hence better lives. We hence collaborate with the best of minds to deliver you class-leading products, spread across the Higher Education and Test Preparation spectrum.

Superior learning experience and improved outcomes are at the heart of everything we do. This product is the result of one such effort.

Your feedback plays a critical role in the evolution of our products and you can contact us - reachus@pearson.com. We look forward to it.

WHAT TOPPERS SAY...

I am glad to share, A P Sir, that I got 8th rank in 2025 PU BA/B.COM LL. B. The credit goes completely to you, your mentorship, and books especially PEARSON'S LA/LR & WORKBOOK. LA/LR, I strongly feel, is the ultimate resource material to score full on full in legal section. I strongly recommend PEARSON'S complete set of books to all law aspirants and must prepare with you for quality coaching.

Anahad Cheema (ST. Xavier, Bathinda)
8TH Rank 2025 UILS, (PU) , Chandigarh

I am extremely glad to share, Bhardwaj Sir, that I have secured 21st rank in PU 2023 LAW ENTRANCE with your able guidance through online classes. Your quality content books are literally indispensable especially your LA/LR, LEGAL WORKBOOK AND SOLVED PAPERS – all the 3 published by PEARSON. Your LA/LR is a boon for law aspirants. The coverage of content, its quality, and presentation literally make it reader friendly and user friendly. It is a clear, compact and comprehensive book providing reliable, relevant, and authentic information.

Thanks once again for everything done by you for me.

Nipun Suri (Jalandhar)
21st rank PU 2023 LAW ENTRANCE

I have secured AIR 74 in AILET and AIR 119 in CLAT. This has been possible with constant guidance of Bharadwaj Sir. Also, LA/LR and legal workbook: both published by Pearson are a must read for any student preparing for law entrance exam.

Misaal Karan Singh Sidhu
AIR 74, AILET and AIR 119, CLAT, 2023

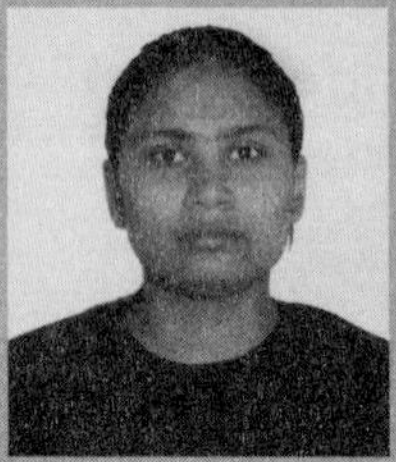

I am extremely glad to share that I have secured 19 Rank in PU 5 year LAW ENTRANCE 2022. I owe my success to able guidance and committed teaching of AP Bhardwaj Sir. His books especially LA/LR 2022-23 is awesome no serious candidate can afford to skip that book. His other books by PEARSON are also very popular. I strongly recommend all to prepare with A P BHARDWAJ SIR and from his books

Nandani Sharma
19th Rank in P U LAW ENTRANCE 2022

I am glad to share that I have secured 8th AIR in AIL Mohalli LET 2022 and 512 AIR in CLAT 2022. I want to extend its credit to able guidance and mentoring of A P Bhardwaj Sir . His coaching and quality content books enabled me to secure these ranks . His books especially LA/LR and legal aptitude workbook: both published by PEARSON, are undoubtedly must(read) and indispensable resource material for every student preparing for any Law Entrances.

Nishtha Chaudhary
8th AIR in AIL Mohalli and 512 AIR in CLAT 2022

I feel extremely elated to share that I have secured 34th Rank in PU 5-year Law entrance 2022. I would like to express my most heartfelt gratitude towards A P Bhardwaj sir. His able guidance and his commitment as a teacher works like magic!

His books; like the #1 BEST SELLER LA/LR (2022–23) are incredibly helpful. His other best-selling books by PEARSON, such as Legal Aptitude workbook and Previous Years' solved papers, are also quite remarkable. I strongly recommend all candidates preparing for any kind of law entrance to prepare with A P Bhardwaj Sir directly as well as refer to his books during preparation.

Evereena
34th Rank PU 2022

16 Solved Papers of CLAT and AILET

(2019–2026)

9th Edition

A. P. BHARDWAJ

Pearson

Dedicated To My Daughter

Anaadi Asmita Bhardwaj

On the exultant completion of 16 years of life
full of motivation and enthusiasm

&

entering 17th year of magnificent life ahead
with an adventurous spirit to do something meaningful in life.

It is just a token of my love for her.

I wish her all the best in everything in life.

ISBN: 978-93-713-6996-1

First Impression

Published by Pearson India Education Services Pvt. Ltd, CIN: U72200TN2005PTC057128.

Head Office: 1st Floor, Berger Tower, Plot No. C-001A/2, Sector 16B, Noida - 201 301, Uttar Pradesh, India.

Registered Office: 6th Floor, Tower A, Unit A and B, International Tech Park, CapitaLand, Chennai, 200 Feet Radial Road, Zamin Pallavaram, Old Pallavaram, Chennai – 600117, Tamil Nadu India

Website: in.pearson.com, Email: companysecretary.india@pearson.com

Compositor: D Book Media, Delhi
Printed in India at Sai Printo Pack Pvt Ltd

Contents

Preface

It gives me immense pleasure to present the new 9th edition of my book PYPs of CLAT & AILET. It has been updated with the latest 2026 CLAT /AILET PAPERS with their answers key. Since 2020, CLAT PAPER pattern has changed two or three times. The newest format of both the papers (CLAT & AILET) is comprehension followed by MCQs.

The few most notable things are:

1) The new pattern has become more time consuming, hence the number of questions has been reduced to facilitate completion of papers in time.
2) The role of English has grown manifold.
3) Vocabulary has assumed a place of pre-eminence.
4) Legal language, especially legal terms and maxims demand special mastery.
5) A New segment of law i.e. Family law – HINDU LAW & MUSLIM LAW has been covered for the last 2/3 years. So, students need to make studies on HINDU & MUSLIM LAW to take edge in the legal section.

The new 13th edition of my book LA/LR (2026-27) provides detailed coverage of both -Hindu & Muslim Law updated with provisions of NEW CRIMINAL LAWS BNS, BNSS, 2023.

The students preparing for 2027 CLAT & AILET must note these things and plan and prepare accordingly. This compilation of papers will apprise the aspirants of ongoing trends, patterns, standards and levels of difficulty of CLAT & AILET.

Hope the students will like and appreciate the new edition.

A P Bhardwaj
Chandigarh, January, 2026

Acknowledgements

At the outset, I appreciate timely initiative of my publishers – PEARSON EDUCATION PVT., LTD., to keep revising and updating the books. The keen interest taken by Team leader Sojan plays a very important role. Special thanks to Bhupesh, Ruchira & Deya Bhattacharjee.

The ornamental touches imparted to the cover designs by Deepti make the books look attractive and captivating.

The sales, marketing ,and promotion teams deserve special mention because books are pitched in the market with their efforts.

A P BHARDWAJ
JANUARY 2026, CHANDIGARH

About the Author

A.P. Bhardwaj is a trainer-cum – author of #1 National Bestsellers for 19 years for CLAT/SLAT/AILET, PU, DU & Other Law Entrances. He trains and tutors hundreds of students every year and enables them to enter prestigious law colleges and universities. His best-selling quality content books vindicates his credentials and credibility. He is also the author of Best-selling English books for IAS & states' civil, judicial & allied services examinations. He has authored more than a dozen books with nationally and internationally acclaimed publishers. He hails from Samrala, (Ludhiana), Punjab and is presently settled at Chandigarh for the last 35 years.

Examination Analysis– CLAT and AILET

CLAT 2026-2024 PATTERN AND MARKS DISTRIBUTION

The CLAT consortium announced a new pattern for CLAT in 2020. CLAT 2024 once again made a change with a decrease in the number of questions from 150 to 120. It was a bit easy with more time at students' disposal. The level of difficulty was also reduced. The tentative marks distribution is as given here as under for the five sections.

ENGLISH LANGUAGE 24 questions, or roughly 20% of the paper.
CURRENT AFFAIRS, including GENERAL KNOWLEDGE 28 questions, or roughly 24% of the paper.
LEGAL REASONING 32 questions, or roughly 26% of the paper.
LOGICAL REASONING 24 questions, or roughly 20% of the paper.
QUANTITATIVE TECHNIQUES 12 questions, or roughly 10% of the paper.

CLAT 2020-2023 PATTERN AND MARKS DISTRIBUTION

CLAT 2020–2023 had 150 multiple choice questions carrying one mark for each and negative marking of ¼th marks for a wrong answer as formally provided in the instructions. The paper is divided into five different sections- English language, current affairs based GK, legal reasoning, logical reasoning, and mathematics. The tentative marks distribution is as given here as under.

ENGLISH LANGUAGE 28–32 questions, or roughly 20% of the paper.
CURRENT AFFAIRS, including GENERAL KNOWLEDGE 35–39 questions, or roughly 25% of the paper.
LEGAL REASONING 28–32 questions, or roughly 25% of the paper.
LOGICAL REASONING 28–32 questions, or roughly 20% of the paper.
MATHEMATICS 13–17 questions, or roughly 10% of the paper.

CLAT (2020–2023) ANALYSIS

CLAT 2020-2023 papers mark a clear-cut departure from the previous years' patterns 2008-2019. The new pattern is based on passages exercises oriented comprehension of all the 5 sections of CLAT. The new changed pattern adopted in 2020-2023, is absolutely a new experiment to check the level of knowledge and understanding of candidates through COMPREHENSIONS ON ALL THE FIVE SECTIONS OF CLAT- LEGAL, LOGICAL, GK, MATHS AND TEST OF ENGLISH LANGUAGE.

The new paper PATTERN is quite lengthy and hence a time-consuming pattern with a few inbuilt hints here and there making the things to appear a bit easier but still quite a problematic vis a vis ENGLISH LANGUAGE. The new paper PATTERN is less a test of knowledge and understanding and more a TEST OF ENGLISH LANGUAGE because questions in all the sections are based on comprehension of passages exercises in which the role of English language has been greatly enhanced.

ENGLISH LANGUAGE has assumed a place of pre-eminence among all the 5 sections. The given passages on all the 5 sections in the English language automatically demand in depth knowledge of English and ample vocabulary at disposal. So now to read and comprehend all the passages on all the verticals cannot be feasible without a rich vocabulary at candidates' disposal. If one doesn't understand the parent words used in the given passage, one cannot decipher and decode the subtle meaning and ideas.

So now keeping in view the growing demand of ENGLISH LANGUAGE, the candidates have to broaden and diversify the range of reading. The candidates cannot keep their preparation confined to CLAT SPECIFIC BOOKS only. Rather, they have to orient themselves to GENERAL READING as well.

A few important tips for reading and types of books to be preferred to improve English in general and vocabulary in par- ticular are:

1. Enhance general reading from diverse sources.
2. Improve reading skills through reading, re-reading and re-reading.
3. Accelerate the speed of reading
4. Improve understanding of the nuances of the English language.
5. For all these activities, try to accumulate, assimilate and internalize as many words as possible.
6. Prepare a rich word bank in one's own handwriting.
7. Keep revising them on a regular basis at weekends.

I suggest what the candidates should prefer to read to broaden and diversify their sources of reading to raise their levels of thinking and understanding in general and understanding of English Language in particular and upgradation of vocabu- lary. The candidates should read works of legal luminaries like Justice Krishna Iyer, Justice P. N. Bhagwati, Nani Palkhivala, M.C Chagla and others. To open up faculties and broaden the level of understanding, try to read – *As A Man Thinketh* by James Allen, *MegaLiving* by Robin Sharma and *Light from Many Lamps* by Eichler Watson. For clear understanding of the core component of the English language section of CLAT, the candidates must read *English Wizard and Compulsory English* by A. P. Bhardwaj.

As a high number of students appear in all eminent Law entrance tests, the candidates should try to find out common areas (e.g., Mathematics/reasoning are part of a few entrances) and commonalities (e.g., CLAT has always a major thrust on legal reasoning whereas AILET& OTHER LAW ENTRANCES try to strike a BALANCE between legal awareness and legal reasoning). So, the candidates first of all focus on those areas, then gradually switch over to different exams. specific areas separately. To know the commonalities and differences, the detailed analysis of CLAT & AILET (2008–2019) follows here after.

CLAT AND AILET—AN INDEPTH ANALYSIS (2008–2019)

COMMON LAW ADMISSION TEST (CLAT) is conducted every year for admission to the 21 National Law Universities (NLU) of our country. On the other hand, All India Law Entrance Test (AILET) is held for NLU, Delhi. CLAT paper con- sists of 200 marks where as AILET is made up of 150 Marks. Introduced in 2008, CLAT was started with a humble begin- ning of 8000 applicants, but within a span of 10 years, this number has crossed more than 60,000 applicants and is still multiplying with every passing year.

The inclination for legal field is soaring high and so is the popularity of CLAT and AILET. With every passing year, not only is the number of applicants increasing, but the difficulty level of examination pattern is also going up at meteoric speed. The students, irrespective of their background, are getting attracted towards the legal field and consequently making CLAT and AILET further more popular and tougher at the same time. Nonetheless, cracking CLAT and AILET is not an easy task as it requires perfect blend of hard work and smart work. Hard work, obviously, has no substitute but, at the same time, smart work is also required to get away from over flooded undesirable materials in the market which may steal away your precious time, money and energy.

To assist you in your decision as to what to study and how, based on previous patterns, topic/section-wise description has been provided along with tables depicting section-wise bifurcation of 150 marks of AILET in the core section where as till 2019 the CLAT pattern was of 200 marks.

CLAT Pattern

Total Questions: 200 **Duration: 120 minutes**
Negative Marking: Yes (0.25 marks)

CLAT 200 MARKS	
LEGAL APTITUDE	50
GK and CA	50
ENGLISH	40
MATHS	20
LEGAL REASONING	40
Total	**200**

AILET Pattern

Total Questions: 150 **Total Time: 90 Minutes**
Negative Marking: No

AILET 150 MARKS	
LEGAL APTITUDE	35
GK and CA	35
ENGLISH	35
MATHS	10
LEGAL REASONING	35
Total	**150**

LEGAL APTITUDE

Legal aptitude—comprising legal awareness and legal reasoning—main component of CLAT and AILET and other major law entrances examinations.

The tables provided are suggestive of the weightage given to legal awareness and legal reasoning under the legal aptitude section that carries 50 marks in CLAT and 35 marks in AILET.

CLAT—Legal Aptitude Section 7 Years' Examination Analysis – 50 Marks

		Number of Questions Each Year						
Section	**Topics**	**2019**	**2018**	**2017**	**2016**	**2015**	**2014**	**2013**
Legal Awareness	List of Legal Terms		2	15	6	5		
	Constitutional Law		12		9	12		
	Legal GK		3			10		
Total Marks			**20**	**15**	**15**	**27**		
Legal Reasoning	Law of Torts	5	8	10	11	5	13	8
	Civil Law	20	7	14	13	4	15	18
	Criminal Law	15	7	11	11	9	15	14
	Miscellaneous (Hindu Marriage and Adoption Act, Environmental Pollution, Copyright Violation)	10	8			5	7	10
Total Marks		**50**	**30**	**35**	**35**	**23**	**50**	**50**
Legal Aptitude Weightage		**50**	**50**	**50**	**50**	**50**	**50**	**50**

AILET—Legal Aptitude Section 7 Years' Examination Analysis – 35 Marks

		Number of Questions Each Year						
Section	**Topics**	**2019**	**2018**	**2017**	**2016**	**2015**	**2014**	**2013**
Legal Awareness	Legal Terms							5
	Constitutional	17	21	26	16	10	8	15
	G.A. and G.K.	5						
	Total Questions			26	16	10	8	20
Total Marks		**22**	**21**	**26**	**16**	**10**	**8**	**20**
Legal Reasoning	Torts	7	8	5	2	8	7	10
	Civil Law	3	6	3	2	3	10	
	Criminal Law	3			0	9	5	5
	Miscellaneous			1	15	5	4	
Total Marks		**13**	**14**	**9**	**19**	**25**	**27**	**15**
Grand Total Marks		**35**	**35**	**35**	**35**	**35**	**35**	**35**

GENERAL KNOWLEDGE (GK)

General Knowledge is one of the most important and equally tricky section because of its vastness. GK has broadly two com- ponents, i.e., static GK and current affairs (CA). 2019 CLAT gave grossly unfair weightage STATIC GK. The coverage of current affairs was also not holistic and comprehensive.

CLAT—General Knowledge and Current Affairs Section 7 Years' Examination Analysis – 50 Marks

		Number of Questions Each Year						
Section	**Topics**	**2019**	**2018**	**2017**	**2016**	**2015**	**2014**	**2013**
Static G.K.								
	History	10	3			3	10	10
	Polity		4		10		7	3
	Geography		4	8	5	4	4	2
	Science		2			2	4	3
	Economy		2			2	3	2
	General Awareness (Books, UNO, Records, First and Last, Highest, Tallest, Smallest, Biggest)		10		10	6	5	10
Total Marks			**25**		**25**	**17**	**33**	**30**
Current Affairs	**Total Marks**	**40**	**25**	**50**	**25**	**33**	**17**	**20**
Gross Total Marks		**50**	**50**	**50**	**50**	**40**	**50**	**50**

AILET—G.K. and Current Affairs Section 7 Years' Examination Analysis – 35 Marks

			Number of Questions Each Year						
Section		**Topics**	**2019**	**2018**	**2017**	**2016**	**2015**	**2014**	**2013**
Static G. K.			10						
	1.	History		2					5
	2.	Geography		4	5	4	2	5	4
	3.	Science		4	10	4	2	3	4
	4.	Economic							5
	5.	Polity		2				5	6
	6.	General Awareness		3		7		5	3
Total Marks			**10**	**15**	**15**	**15**	**4**	**18**	**27**
C.A.	**Total Marks**		**25**	**20**	**20**	**20**	**31**	**17**	**8**
Grand Total Marks			**35**	**35**	**35**	**35**	**35**	**35**	**35**

TEST OF ENGLISH

The test of English language had a weightage of 40 marks in CLAT and 35 in AILET. If one happens to make a cursory look on the previous year papers, one can easily make out that vocabulary covers sizeable portion. 50% questions are directly asked on various forms of vocabulary, such as synonyms, antonyms, idioms and phrases, spellings, finding odd word and the closest meaning, therefore, a word bank storage is an inevitable requirement for the legal field. Comprehension con- sumes 25% share and is designed such that students who have very vast reading habits and consequent vast vocabulary knowledge (with ability to decipher the meanings in proper context and perspective) will be able to comprehend and answer the questions correctly. The remaining 25% focuses on grammar, usage, errors, ordering and reordering of sen- tences. Nonetheless, one can easily become proficient in these topics with the help of adequate practice.

CLAT—English Section 7 Years' Examination Analysis – 40 Marks

		Number of Questions Each Year						
Section	**Topics**	**2019**	**2018**	**2017**	**2016**	**2015**	**2014**	**2013**
Vocabulary	Spellings	5		10	5		5	5
	Synonyms	5	3		4	5	5	5
	Antonyms		5			3		
	Idioms and Phrases	5	6			3	5	5
	One Word Substitution					3		
Total Marks		**15**	**14**	**10**	**9**	**14**	**15**	**15**
Comprehension	I	5		5	10			
	II	5		5		10	10	10
Total Marks		**10**	**14**	**10**	**10**	**10**	**10**	**10**
Grammar and Test of Usage			9	10	10	11	10	10
Errors	Errors	10			5			
Ordering of Sentences	Ordering of Sentences	5	3					
	Preposition			10	4	3		
	Pronouns				2			
	Article					2	5	5
Total Marks		**15**		**20**	**21**	**16**	**15**	**15**
Grand Total Marks		**40**	**40**	**40**	**40**	**40**	**40**	**40**

AILET—English Section 7 Years' Examination Analysis – 35 Marks

		Number of Questions Each Year						
Section	**Topics**	**2019**	**2018**	**2017**	**2016**	**2015**	**2014**	**2013**
Vocabulary	Synonyms	10		2		5	4	4
	Antonyms			3			4	4
	Idioms	6	5	3	3	5	2	2
	One Word Substitution				5	4		
	Spellings/Odd word							
Grammar and Usage			15	9	13	10	5	11
Error			15	4				5
Re-ordering				3		5	4	3
Comprehension		8			9	6	7	6
Filling the passage with words		11		11	5		9	
Total Marks		**35**	**35**	**35**	**35**	**35**	**35**	**35**

MATHEMATICAL ABILITY

This section comprised 20 questions of 1 mark each in CLAT and 10 questions of 10 marks in AILET. For this purpose, refresh- ing your fundamentals from 9th and 10th standard school books and bit of practice will be sufficient.

CLAT—Mathematics Section 7 Years' Examination Analysis – 20 Marks

		Number of Questions Each Year						
Section	**Topics**	**2019**	**2018**	**2017**	**2016**	**2015**	**2014**	**2013**
Mathematics	Average	20	20	20	20	20	20	20
	Simplification							
	Simple Interest/ Compound Interest							
	Time, Work and Distance							
	Profit and Loss							
	Ration and Proportion							
	Probability							
	Area of Volume							
	Probability							
	Surds and Indices							
Total Marks		**20**	**20**	**20**	**20**	**20**	**20**	**20**

AILET—Mathematics Section 7 Years' Examination Analysis – 10 Mark

		Number of Questions Each Year						
Section	**Topics**	**2019**	**2018**	**2017**	**2016**	**2015**	**2014**	**2013**
Mathematics	Average							
	Simple							
	Interest							
	SI/CI							
	Ratio Proportion							
	Loss/Profit	10	10	10	10	10	10	10
	Partnership							
	Time, Work and Distance							
	Probability							
	Area/volume							
	Surds and Indices							
Total Marks		**10**	**10**	**10**	**10**	**10**	**10**	**10**

LOGICAL REASONING

CLAT—Logical Reasoning Section 7 Years' Examination Analysis – 40 Marks

		Number of Questions Each Year						
Section	**Topics**	**2019**	**2018**	**2017**	**2016**	**2015**	**2014**	**2013**
Logical Reasoning	Series							
	Analogy							
	Venn Diagrams							
	Blood Relations							
	Sitting Arrangement							
	Distance and Directions	40		40	40	40	40	40
	Statement and Assumptions							
	Statement and Argument							
	Cause and Effect							
	Logical Deductions							
Total Marks		**40**	**40**	**40**	**40**	**40**	**40**	**40**

AILET—Logical Reasoning Section 7 Years' Examination Analysis – 35 Marks

		Number of Questions Each Year						
Section	**Topics**	**2019**	**2018**	**2017**	**2016**	**2015**	**2014**	**2013**
Logical Reasoning	Series	35	35	35	35	35	35	35
	Analogy							
	Venn Diagrams							
	Blood Relations							
	Sitting Arrangement							
	Distance and Directions							
	Statement and Assumptions							
	Statement and Argument							
	Cause and Effect							
	Logical Deductions							
Total Marks		**35**	**35**	**35**	**35**	**35**	**35**	**35**

TIME MANAGEMENT TIPS

- ✓ Make brief notes, these will strengthen your base.
- ✓ Regular revision is a necessary nuisance.
- ✓ Vocabulary building is an inevitable necessity.
- ✓ Continuous practice of MCQs necessary to reinforce the concepts.
- ✓ Learn short cuts for mathematics and reasoning.
- ✓ Periodic & objective evaluation would act on a timely reminder.

Common Law Admission Test (2026-2019)

CLAT 2026

SECTION I

I. The adoption of the Non-Cooperation Movement by the Congress gave it a new energy and from January 1921, it began to register considerable success all over the country. Gandhiji undertook a nation-wide tour during which he addressed hundreds of meetings and met a large number of political workers. In the first month, thousands of students left their educational institutions and joined more than 800 national schools and colleges that had sprung up all over the country. Gandhiji had promised Swaraj within a year if his programme was adopted.

The Non-Cooperation Movement demonstrated that it commanded the support and sympathy of vast sections of the Indian people. Its reach among many sections of Indian peasants, workers, artisans, etc., had been demonstrated. The spatial spread of the movement was also nation-wide. Some areas were more active than others, but there were a few that showed no signs of activity at all.

The capacity of the 'poor dumb millions' of India to take part in modern nationalist politics was also demonstrated. This was the first time that nationalists from the towns, students from schools and colleges or even the educated and politically aware in the villages had made a serious attempt to bring the ideology and the movement into their midst.

The tremendous participation of different communities in the movement, and the maintenance of communal unity, despite the Malabar developments, was in itself no mean achievement. There is hardly any doubt that it was minority participation that gave the movement its truly mass character in many areas. And it was, indeed, unfortunate that this most positive feature of the movement was not to be repeated in later years once communalism began to take its toll. (324 words)

[*Extracted, with edits and revisions, from* India's Struggle for Independence1857-1947, *by*

Bipin Chandra and Others, Penguin Books, 1989.]

1. From the passage, it is evident that:
(a) The idea of Swaraj seemed futile
(b) The non-cooperation movement was a complete success
(c) The non-cooperation movement gained the sympathy of the majority of the Indians
(d) The Indian National Congress represented a microscopic minority

2. The term 'poor dumb millions' refers to:
(a) The vast number of common people who are impoverished
(b) Large number of common people who are hearing impaired
(c) Large number of people who are vulnerable
(d) The vast number of people who are impoverished and uneducated

3. Which of the statements is true?
(a) The Swaraj movement happened before the Non-cooperation movement.
(b) The Non-cooperation movement failed due to the sudden withdrawal.
(c) There was a fine show of communal unity in the movement.
(d) The rich and the educated kept themselves away from the Non-cooperation movement.

4. The main idea of the passage is-
(a) The Non-Cooperation movement did not give impetus to the future movements.
(b) The movement made the Indians realize their potential to fight against the mighty British.
(c) The British became fearful and worried of Gandhiji's leadership and cooperation of Indians.
(d) That the most positive feature of the movement was that it was repeated in later years.

5. The word 'Communalism' in the above passage refers to:
(a) Religious identity
(b) Caste identity
(c) Regional identity
(d) Secularism

II. There were humans long before there was history. The archaic humans loved, played, formed close friendships and competed for status and power, but so did chimpanzees, baboons and elephants. There was nothing special about them.

Nobody, least of all humans themselves, had any inkling that their descendants would one day walk on the moon, split the atom, fathom the genetic code and write history books. The most important thing to know about prehistoric humans is that they were incognisant animals with no more impact on their environment than gorillas, fireflies or jellyfish.

Biologists classify organisms into species. Animals are said to belong to the same species if they tend to mate with each other, giving birth to fertile offspring. Horses and donkeys have a recent common ancestor and share many physical traits. They will mate if induced to do so - but their offspring, called mules, are sterile. Mutations in donkey DNA can therefore never cross over to horses, or vice versa. The two types of animals are consequently considered two distinct species, moving along separate evolutionary paths. By contrast, a bulldog and a spaniel may look very different, but they are members of the same species, sharing the same DNA pool. (203 words)

(*Extracted from Sapiens*: A *Brief* History *of Humankind by* Yuval *Noah Harari*)

6. Which of the following can be inferred as the most significant characteristic of prehistoric humans, as per the passage?
(a) Their conscious effort to alter and shape their environment for survival.
(b) Their complex social organization and clear hierarchical structures that set them apart from other species.
(c) Their evolutionary divergence was marked by warfare and the pursuit of dominance over rival species.
(d) Their inability to distinguish themselves from other species in terms of environmental impact.

7. In the context of the passage, the term 'incognizant' most likely means:
(a) Lacking intelligence
(b) Unaware of their future potential
(c) Incapable of social interaction
(d) Disinterested in the environment

8. Which of the following best explains why humans did not initially stand out among other organisms?
(a) They had fewer offspring than other species.
(b) Their behaviours were not unique compared to other animals.
(c) They did not yet evolve the ability to use tools.
(d) They lacked the genetic capacity to develop language.

9. According to the passage, what determines whether two animals belong to the same species?
(a) Their ability to produce fertile offspring
(b) Their physical appearance and size
(c) Their shared evolutionary ancestor
(d) Their capacity to adapt to the environment

10. The passage explains the concept of species classification by
(a) Highlighting the behavioural differences between species like horses, donkeys, bulldogs and spaniels

(b) Focusing on the DNA pool they share
(c) Contrasting horses and bulldogs with donkeys and spaniels to explain reproductive compatibility
(d) Discussing the environmental impact of different species like horses and donkeys, and bulldogs and spaniels

III. In 1973, only 45 of the world's 151 countries were counted as 'free' by Freedom House, a nongovernmental organization that produces quantitative measures of civil and political rights for countries around the world. The following generation saw momentous political change, with democracies and market-oriented economies spreading in virtually every part of the world except for the Arab Middle East. This transformation was Samuel Huntington's third wave of democratization; liberal democracy as the default form of government became part of the accepted political landscape at the beginning of the twenty-first century.

Underlying these changes in political systems was a massive social transformation as well. The shift to democracy was a result of millions of formerly passive individuals around the world organizing themselves and participating in the political life of their societies. This social mobilization was driven by a host of factors: greatly expanded access to education that made people more aware of themselves and the political world around them; information technology, which facilitated the rapid spread of ideas and knowledge; cheap travel and communications that allowed people to vote with their feet if they didn't like their government; and greater prosperity, which induced people to demand better protection of their rights.

The third wave crested after the late 1990s, however, a 'democratic recession' emerged in the first decade of the twenty-first century. Approximately one in five countries that had been part of the third wave either reverted to authoritarianism or saw a significant erosion of democratic institutions. Freedom House noted that 2009 marked the fourth consecutive year in which freedom had declined around the world, the first time this had happened since it established its measures of freedom in 1973. (279 words)

(*Extracted from The Origins of Political Order by Francis Fukuyama*)

11. Which of the following aspects is most critical in understanding Freedom House's evaluation process?
(a) The methodology by which it quantifies the relative freedoms in different political systems.
(b) Its emphasis on electoral participation and voter turnout in measuring democracy.
(c) Its role in advising governments on democratic reforms based on its rankings.
(d) Its primary focus is on economic disparities within democracies.

12. What does the phrase 'vote with their feet' imply in the context of the passage?
(a) Engaging in electoral processes to demand political change
(b) Demonstrating political preferences through public protests
(c) Migrating to countries with better governance or conditions
(d) Participating in local government initiatives and reforms

13. The term 'third wave of democratization' as used in the passage refers to:
(a) The rise of communism in Eastern Europe
(b) The spread of democracy and market-oriented economies
(c) The decline of authoritarian regimes in the 1960s
(d) The global movement for civil rights

14. Which of the following was not mentioned as a factor contributing to social mobilization and the shift to democracy?
(a) Increased access to education
(b) Expanding information technology
(c) Heightened global military presence
(d) Greater prosperity

15. According to this passage, when was the first time freedom had declined around the world
(a) 1973 (b) 1990
(c) 2006 (d) 2009

IV. My kinsman and I were returning to Calcutta from our Puja trip when we encountered an unusual man on the train. At first, judging from his dress and bearing, we mistook him for an up-country boorish man. But as soon as he began to speak, our impression changed. He discoursed on every subject with such confidence that one might think the 'Disposer of All Things' sought his counsel in every decision. Until then, we had been perfectly content, unaware of hidden forces shaping the world—that the Russians were advancing, that the English were pursuing secret policies, and that confusion among native chiefs had reached its peak. Our new acquaintance, however, hinted at such matters with a sly smile, remarking:

'There are more things in heaven and earth, Horatio, than are reported in your newspapers.'

Having never before travelled beyond our homes, we were struck dumb with wonder at his manner. No matter how trivial the topic, he could quote science, comment on the Vedas, or recite quatrains from Persian poets. Since we possessed no real knowledge of science, the Vedas, or Persian literature, our admiration for him only grew. My kinsman, a theosophist, became convinced that our fellow passenger was inspired by some strange magnetism, occult power, or astral body. He listened with devotional rapture even to the most common place remarks and secretly noted down his words. I suspect our extraordinary companion noticed this and was quietly pleased. When the train reached the junction, we gathered in the waiting room to await our connection. It was 10 p.m., and as the train was expected to be delayed owing to some fault in the lines, I spread my bed on the table and prepared to sleep. But just then, the extraordinary man began spinning a tale, and of course, I could not close my eyes all night. (307 words)

[*Extracted with edits from Rabindranath Tagore's 'The Hungry Stones'*]

16. The narrator and his kinsman's initial impression of the 'unusual man' highlights which theme most strongly?
(a) The deceptive nature of appearances
(b) The superiority of Western education
(c) The danger of blind faith
(d) The reliability of cultural stereotypes

17. Which literary device is most evident in the narrator's line: *'one might think the Disposer of All Things sought his counsel in every decision'*?
(a) Irony (b) Euphemism
(c) Allegory (d) Hyperbole

18. The word 'theosophist' means:
(a) Skeptic (b) Mystic
(c) Agnostic (d) Materialist

19. The word 'Boorish' means:
(a) Discourteous
(b) Genteel
(c) Well-bred
(d) Courtly

20. The narrator's suspicion that the extraordinary man was 'quietly pleased' suggests:
(a) The man was genuinely humble and embarrassed by the attention.
(b) The man wished to avoid any recognition of his authority.
(c) The man was indifferent to how others perceived him.
(d) The man derived satisfaction from impressing and influencing others.

V. Man is the only creature that consumes without producing. He does not give milk, he does not lay eggs, he is too weak to pull the plough, and he cannot run fast enough to catch rabbits. Yet he claims dominion over all animals. He sets us to work, returns only the bare minimum to keep us from starving, and keeps the rest for himself. Our labour tills the soil, our dung fertilizes it, and still, not one of us owns more than our bare skin. You cows, look at yourselves–how many thousands of gallons of milk have you produced this past year? And what has become of it, milk that should have nurtured strong calves? Every drop has gone down the throats of our enemies. And you hens, how many eggs have you laid, and how many of those ever hatched into chicks? The rest have gone to market to bring in money for Jones and his men. And you, Clover, where are the four foals you bore, who should have supported and comforted you in your old age? Each was sold at just a year old–you will never see them again. For all your labour in the fields and your four confinements, what have you gained except bare rations and a stall?

Even the lives we do live are cut short, denied their natural span. I do not grumble, for I am among the fortunate. I am twelve years old and have borne over four hundred children. Such is the natural life of a pig. But no animal escapes the cruel knife in the end. You young porkers sitting before me, each of you will scream your lives out at the block within a year. This is the fate that awaits all of us–cows, pigs, hens, sheep, everyone. Even horses and dogs share no better end. Boxer, the very day your great muscles fail you, Jones will sell you to the knacker, who will slit your throat and boil you down for the foxhounds. And the dogs, when old and toothless, are tied with a brick and drowned in the nearest pond. (356 words)

[*Extracted with edits from George Orwell's 'Animal Farm'*]

21. Which of the following best describes the tone of the passage?
(a) Detached and neutral
(b) Critical, somber, and resentful, evoking both awareness and outrage
(c) Humorous and light-hearted
(d) Admiring and celebratory

22. The speaker frequently contrasts animals' work with human gain. This literary technique is best classified as:
(a) Allegory of class exploitation
(b) Hyperbole for comic effect
(c) Irony about farm management
(d) Metaphor for animal biology

23. Who is 'knacker'?
(a) A slaughterer
(b) A trader whose business is the disposal of dead and unwanted animals
(c) A person whose business is the disposal of dead or unwanted animals, especially those whose flesh is not fit for human consumption
(d) Harness-maker

24. The repeated reference to slaughter, drowning, and the knacker in the passage primarily implies to:
(a) Provide a detailed account of animal husbandry
(b) Evoke emotional outrage and highlight the brutality of exploitation
(c) Suggest that animals are naturally subservient
(d) Indicate that humans value animals

SECTION II

VI. US President Donald Trump has landed a triple whammy on India by torpedoing the H-1B visa programme, days after revoking sanctions waiver on Chabahar port in Iran and weeks after imposing a 50% tariff on Indian exports to the US. The White House also maintained a conspicuous silence on the Pakistan-Saudi Arabia mutual defence treaty amid reports that neither country informed Washington of the pact, suggesting a growing US indifference to India's concerns. The triple blow has shaken US-India ties to the foundation, mystifying experts who expected a reset after an exchange of friendly messages between Modi and Trump. While some observers see in the crackdown on H-1B a pressure tactic to make India bend on the trade deal, sources familiar with the dynamics of the current White House say the two issues are unrelated and Trump was convinced of the need to 'reform' the guest worker visa programme ever since MAGA hardliners persuaded him that American workers were being gamed out of jobs by foreign companies and US big tech acting in tandem. (174 words)

[Extracted from the newspaper, The Times of India, September 21, 2025]

25. What percentage tariff did President Trump initially impose on Indian imports in 2025?
(a) 15% (b) 25%
(c) 40% (d) 50%

26. What strategic reason did Donald Trump cite for penalizing India with additional tariffs apart from trade imbalances?
(a) India's IT service exports
(b) Indian Banknote Demonetization
(c) India's immigration policies
(d) India's defence and energy ties with Russia

27. What is the strategic significance of Chabahar Port for India?
(a) Provides trade access to China through Pakistan
(b) Acts as a counterbalance to China's presence in nearby Gwadar Port, Pakistan
(c) Serves as the primary naval base for India
(d) Connects India directly to the Mediterranean Sea

28. What is the primary purpose of the H-1B Visa?
(a) Exchange Visitor Visa
(b) Employment Visa
(c) Immigrant visa for permanent residence in the U.S.
(d) Non-immigrant visa that allows US companies to hire foreign professionals in a specialized field

29. The acronym 'MAGA' mentioned in the above passage refers to:
(a) Multilateral Agencies Global Association
(b) Make America Great Again
(c) Mutual Agreements for Global Advantage
(d) Monetary Advantage for Great America

VII. Indian Chess recorded yet another great moment on Monday, as Divya Deshmukh won the Women's World Cup in the Georgian city of Batumi. In the final, the 19-year-old defeated fellow-Indian Koneru Humpy in the tiebreakers. While Humpy contesting the final wasn't much of a surprise-she is the World No. 5 and has been one of the best female players for the last couple of decades-not many would have anticipated Divya's stunning show. But, given her obvious talent and the way she has been playing for the past two years, it didn't come as a big surprise. By winning the World Cup, one of the biggest events organized by the world chess governing body FIDE, Divya also achieved another significant milestone. She became India's 88th Grandmaster and is only the fourth Indian Woman, after Humpy, D. Harika and R. Vaishali, to get that coveted title. Last year, Divya won the World Junior Championship in Ahmedabad with a dominant display. She also played a key role in India's historic gold in the Chess Olympiad at Budapest. India was the top seed there, though. At the World Cup, the Indian women exceeded expectations, with four of them making it to the quarterfinals. (198 words)

[Extracted from the newspaper, The Hindu, July 29, 2025]

30. Where is the origin of chess believed to be?
(a) China (b) Russia
(c) India (d) Egypt

31. Who was the first Indian to earn the title of chess Grandmaster?
(a) D. Gukesh (b) Praveen Thipsay
(c) Dibyendu Barua (d) Vishwanathan Anand

32. Who was the first official World Chess Champion?
(a) Bobby Fischer
(b) Gary Kasparov
(c) Vishwanathan Anand
(d) Wilhelm Steinitz

33. Which of the following computers successfully defeated Garry Kasparov, the reigning world chess champion, in a tournament match?
(a) Deep AI (b) Deep Thought
(c) Deep Blue (d) Deep Water

34. Which of the following cities is the venue for hosting the 11th edition of the Chess World Cup 2025?
(a) Paris, France (b) Baku, Azerbaijan
(c) Goa, India (d) Chennai, India

VIII. I rise to apprise this august House of the foreign policy dimension of our response to the Pahalgam terrorist attack, going into the preparations for Operation Sindoor and how foreign policy was handled during Operation Sindoor. As all the honourable members would appreciate, it was important to send a clear, strong and resolute message after the Pahalgam attack. Our red lines had been crossed, and we had to make it very apparent that there would be serious consequences. As a result, the first step which was taken was that a meeting of the Cabinet Committee of Security took place on the 23rd of April, and that meeting decided that:

- One, the Indus Water Treaty of 1960 will be held in abeyance with immediate effect until Pakistan credibly and irrevocably abjures its support for cross-border terrorism,
- Two, the integrated checkpost Attari would be closed with immediate effect,
- Three, Pakistani nationals who were travelling under the SAARC visa exemption scheme would no longer be allowed to do that,
- Four, the Defence, Naval and Air Advisors of the Pakistani High Commission would be declared persona non grata and,
- Five, the overall strength of the High Commission would be brought down to 30 from the number of 55. (207 words)

(Excerpts from Statement made by Minister of External Affairs Dr S Jaishankar on special discussion in Lok Sabha on Operation Sindoor dated 28th Jul 2025)

35. Where is Pahalgam situated in India?
(a) Punjab
(b) Himachal Pradesh
(c) Jammu & Kashmir
(d) Uttarakhand

36. The Check post Attari is located in
(a) Near Amritsar, Punjab
(b) Near Baramulla in Jammu & Kashmir
(c) Near Kutch in Gujarat
(d) Near Barmer in Rajasthan

37. Which amongst the following is not a SAARC Nation?
(a) Afghanistan (b) Maldives
(c) Mauritius (d) Bangladesh

38. Expression '*Persona Non Grata*' means:
(a) An ungrateful person
(b) An unwelcome person
(c) An untrustworthy person
(d) A displaced person

39. The Indus Water Treaty, signed in 1960 between India and Pakistan, was facilitated by:
(a) The United Nations General Assembly
(b) The United Nations Security Council
(c) The World Bank
(d) The permanent Indus Commission

40. Which amongst the following is not a tributary of the River Indus?
(a) Ravi (b) Jhelum
(c) Tapti (d) Chenab

IX. Prime Minister Shri Narendra Modi participated in the 25th Meeting of the Council of Heads of State of the Shanghai Cooperation Organization (SCO), held in Tianjin, China, from 31 August to 1 September 2025. The Summit witnessed productive discussions on the SCO Development Strategy, Reform of Global Governance, Counter-Terrorism, Peace and Security, Economic and Financial Cooperation, and Sustainable Development.

Addressing the Summit, the Prime Minister highlighted India's approach to strengthening cooperation under the SCO framework. In this regard, he noted that India seeks greater action under three pillars – Security, Connectivity and Opportunity. Emphasising that peace, security and stability remain key to progress and prosperity, he called upon member countries to take firm and decisive action to fight terrorism in all its manifestations. The Prime Minister underlined the need for coordinated action against terror financing and radicalization. Thanking member countries for their strong solidarity in the wake of the Pahalgam terror attack, he emphasized that there should be no double standards in dealing with terrorism and urged the group to hold countries who perpetrate and support cross-border terrorism accountable.

Highlighting the role of connectivity in fostering development and building trust, the Prime Minister stated that India strongly supported projects such as Chabahar port and the International North-South Transport Corridor. He also spoke about opportunities in the fields of start-ups, innovation, youth empowerment and shared heritage, which must be pursued under the SCO umbrella. The Prime Minister proposed commencing a Civilizational Dialogue Forum within the group to foster greater people-to-people ties and cultural understanding. (246 words)

(Excerpts from the Press release issued by Press Information Bureau, Govt of India, dated 1st September 2025)

41. The civilizational dialogue forum (CDF) proposed by the Prime Minister of India at the 25th Meeting of the Shanghai Cooperation Organization is intended to promote
(a) Peace and security
(b) Sustainable development
(c) Reform of Global Governance
(d) Cultural Understanding

42. The next Presidency of SCO is taken over by:
(a) Kyrgyzstan (b) Tajikistan
(c) Uzbekistan (d) Kazakhistan

43. The Prime Minister of India stated that India strongly supported projects such as the Chabahar port. Where is this port located?
(a) Oman (b) Iran
(c) Afghanistan (d) Saudi Arabia

44. Which of the following countries is not a member of the SCO?
(a) Belarus (b) Iran
(c) Pakistan (d) Myanmar

45. The Secretariat of SCO is located in:
(a) Beijing, China
(b) Tianjin, China
(c) Shanghai, China
(d) Wuhan, China

46. At the conclusion of the 25th SCO summit, the member countries adopted the:
(a) Beijing Declaration
(b) Tianjin Declaration
(c) Shanghai Declaration
(d) Wuhan Declaration

X. Air India stands in solidarity with the families and those affected by the AI-171 accident. We continue to mourn their loss and remain fully committed to providing support during this difficult time. Over a month ago, Air India started releasing an interim payment of Rs 25 lakh to the affected families, to help them meet their immediate financial needs. The interim payment will be adjusted against any final compensation.

Air India has, so far, released the interim compensation to the families of 147 of the 229 deceased passengers and also the 19 who lost their lives at the accident site. In addition, the requisite documents of 52 others have been verified, to whose families the interim compensation will be released progressively. The Tata Group has also registered 'The AI-171 Memorial and Welfare Trust', dedicated to the victims of the unfortunate accident. The Trust has pledged an ex gratia payment of Rs 1 crore in respect of each of the deceased, and support for rebuilding the B.J. Medical College Hostel infrastructure, which was damaged in the accident.

The Trust will also provide aid and assistance for the alleviation of any trauma or distress suffered by the first responders, medical and disaster relief professionals, social workers, and governmental staff who provided invaluable institutional support and service in the aftermath of the accident. (217 words)

(Excerpts from the Press Release published by Air India, on July 26, 2025)

47. Air India flight AI-171 was operating from Ahmedabad to:

(a) London Gatwick airport
(b) Heathrow Airport
(c) London Luton Airport
(d) London Stansted Airport

48. Who is the Minister of Civil Aviation of India?
(a) Shri Piyush Goyal
(b) Shri Jyotiraditya Scindia
(c) Shri Ram Mohan Naidu
(d) Shri Prafulla Patel

49. 'The AI-171 Memorial and Welfare Trust' is registered by the Tata Group as a public charitable trust in:
(a) Ahmedabad (b) Gandhinagar
(c) Mumbai (d) Delhi

50. The sole survivor of The Air India flight AI-171 accident is:
(a) British National of Indian Origin
(b) Canadian National of Indian origin
(c) Portuguese National of Indian Origin
(d) Indian National

51. The agency that probes the fatal crash of AI-171 is:
(a) DGCA (b) AAI
(c) AAIB (d) FIP

52. The Air India flight AI-171 was:
(a) Boeing 737-800 aircraft
(b) Boeing 787-8 Dreamliner
(c) Boeing 737 Max aircraft
(d) Boeing Next Generation 737

SECTION III

XI. One of the central motifs of the past decade of governance under the Indian Prime Minister has been the embrace of policy measures that seek to apply uniform solutions to disparate policy dilemmas facing the country. These measures, often termed One Nation policies, are motivated by a desire to replace the existing patchwork of state-specific policies, regulations, and regimes with measures that are identical across the length and breadth of India.

There are numerous examples of such One Nation policies being propagated and, in several cases, implemented in the eleven years since this Government came to power. For instance, in 2016, Parliament passed a series of constitutional amendments to introduce a new Goods and Services Tax (GST), which introduced a unified value-added tax in place of state-specific levies. This reform, known informally as One Nation, One Tax, had been debated and discussed for nearly two decades and was widely touted as an important precursor to forging a common market across India's twenty-eight states.

In a similar vein, the government rolled out a new initiative to allow Indian citizens to take advantage of subsidized food rations irrespective of their state of residence. This scheme, commonly termed One Nation, One Ration Card, was intended to increase access to welfare benefits, especially for the millions of internal migrants in India without a fixed place of residence.

Earlier this year, the government announced the launch of a new online portal that will provide students, faculty, and researchers across the country's public higher education institutions with open access to international scholarly journals and articles under a scheme it has dubbed One Nation, One Subscription.

Most notably, the government recently signalled its intention to pursue a monumental One Nation policy that has been long discussed but only recently outlined in detail. This measure, known as One Nation, One Election, would do away with India's current system of staggered elections for state and national assemblies, replacing it with a framework of simultaneous elections. The proposal, which has featured in many of PM's speeches in the past, was advanced by a high-level committee (HLC) established by the government in 2023. (351 words)

[Excerpts from Does 'One Nation, One Election' Make Sense for India? by Milan Vaishnav, Caroline Mallory, and Annabel Richter Published on July 28, 2025]

53. What is the underlying idea behind the 'One Nation' policies of the government?
(a) To strengthen federalism by empowering states with greater autonomy
(b) To apply uniform solutions across India, replacing state-specific variations
(c) To decentralize governance to local self-government institutions
(d) To promote diversity by encouraging state-specific policies

54. Which of the following Constitution Amendment Bills deals with the empowerment of the Election Commission of India (ECI) to implement simultaneous state and national elections?
(a) One Hundred and Twenty-Ninth Amendment
(b) One Hundred and Twenty-Eighth Amendment
(c) One Hundred and Twenty-Seventh Amendment
(d) One Hundred and Twenty-Sixth Amendment

55. Which committee or report has discussed the feasibility of simultaneous elections in India?
(a) Justice Verma Committee 2013
(b) Law Commission of India Report 2018
(c) Sarkaria Commission Report 1988
(d) Punchhi Commission Report 2010

56. A High-Level Committee was constituted by the government to examine the policy of One Nation One Election. The Committee was led by:
(a) Shri Ram Nath Kovind
(b) Shri Jagdip Dhankar
(c) Shri Pranab Mukherjee
(d) Smt. Draupadi Murmu

57. As per the new GST reforms introduced in September 2025, the structure of the new GST Rates are as follows
(a) 5%, 12%, 18% and 28%
(b) 5%, 12% and 18%
(c) 5%, 12% and 40%
(d) 5%, 18% and 40%

58. The object of the One Nation, One Ration Card scheme is to benefit:
(a) The rural population
(b) The Farmers
(c) The Migrant labourers
(d) The ration shopkeepers

XII. I may here trace the history of the shaping of the Preamble because this would show that the Preamble was in conformity with the Constitution as it was finally accepted. Not only was the Constitution framed in the light of the Preamble, but the Preamble was ultimately settled in the light of the Constitution. In the earliest draft, the Preamble was something formal and read: 'We, the people of India, seeking to promote the common good, do hereby, through our chosen representatives, enact, adopt and give to ourselves this Constitution.

After the plan of June 3, 1947, which led to the decision to partition the country and to set up two independent Dominions of India and Pakistan, on June 8, 1947, a joint sub-committee of the Union Constitution and Provincial Constitution Committees took note that the objective resolution would require amendment in view of the latest announcement of the British Government. The announcement of June 3 had made it clear that full independence, in the form of Dominion Status, would be conferred on India as from August 15, 1947. After examining the implications of partition, the sub-committee thought that the question of making changes in the Objectives Resolution could appropriately be considered only when effect had actually been given to the June 3

Plan. Later on, July 12, 1947, the special sub-committee again postponed consideration of the matter. The Union Constitution Committee provisionally accepted the Preamble as drafted by B.N. Rao and reproduced it in its report of July 4, 1947, without any change, with the tacit recognition at that stage that the Preamble would be finally based on the Objectives Resolution. In a statement circulated to members of the Assembly on July 18, 1947, Pandit Jawaharlal Nehru inter alia, observed that the Preamble was covered more or less by the Objectives Resolution, which it was intended to incorporate in the final Constitution, subject to some modification on account of the political changes resulting from partition. (327 words)

(Extracted with edits and revision from B Shiva Rao's Framing of India's Constitution)

59. According to the passage, the relationship between the Constitution and the Preamble can best be described as:
(a) The Preamble was drafted in isolation.
(b) The Constitution and the Preamble were framed independently of each other.
(c) Both the Constitution and the Preamble were shaped in light of each other.
(d) The Preamble had no relevance to the Constitution.

60. What did the earliest draft of the Preamble emphasize?
(a) Liberty, equality, and fraternity
(b) Sovereign, socialist, secular democratic republic
(c) Formal enactment by the people through representatives
(d) Unity and integrity of the nation

61. Which of the following is not enshrined in the Preamble of the Constitution of India?
(a) Equality of status and of opportunity
(b) Liberty of thought, expression, belief, faith and worship
(c) Justice –moral, ethical and legal
(d) Fraternity assuring the dignity of the individual

62. Which has been rightly arranged according to the Preamble of the Constitution of India-
(a) Sovereign Socialist Secular Democratic Republic
(b) Sovereign Secular Socialist Democratic Republic
(c) Sovereign Socialist Democratic Secular Republic
(d) Secular, Socialist, Sovereign and Democratic Republic

63. The Preamble of the Constitution of India is finally based on:
(a) The Objectives Resolution
(b) The Report of the Union Constitution Committee
(c) The June 3 plan of the British Government
(d) The Report of the Special Sub-committee of the Constituent Assembly

64. What was the role of Sir B. N. Rau in the making of the Indian Constitution?
(a) Chairman of the Drafting Committee
(b) Constitutional Advisor to the Constituent Assembly
(c) President of the Constituent Assembly
(d) Member of the Union Powers Committee

XIII. Good governance is only in the hands of good men. No doubt, what is good or bad is not for the court to decide: but the court can always indicate the constitutional ethos on goodness, good governance and purity in administration, remind the constitutional functionaries to preserve, protect and promote the same. That ethos are the unwritten words in our Constitution. However, as the Constitution makers stated, there is a presumption that the Prime Minister/Chief Minister would be well advised and guided by such unwritten yet constitutional principles as well. According to Dr B. R. Ambedkar, such things were only to be left to the good sense of the Prime Minister, and for that matter, the Chief Minister of the State, since it was expected that the two great constitutional functionaries would not dare to do any infamous thing by inducting an otherwise unfit person to the Council of Ministers. It appears, over a period of time, at least in some cases, it was only a story of great expectations. Some of the instances pointed out in the writ petition indicate that Dr Ambedkar and other great visionaries in the Constituent Assembly have been bailed out. Qualification has been wrongly understood as the mere absence of prescribed disqualification. Hence, it has become the bounden duty of the court to remind the Prime Minister and the Chief Minister of the State of their duty to act in accordance with the constitutional aspirations.

No doubt, it is not for the court to issue any direction to the Prime Minister or the Chief Minister, as the case may be, as to the manner in which they should exercise their power while selecting the colleagues in the Council of Ministers. That is the constitutional prerogative of those functionaries who are called upon to preserve, protect and defend the Constitution. But it is the prophetic duty of this Court to remind the key duty holders about their role in working the Constitution. Hence, I am of the firm view, that the Prime Minister and the Chief Minister of the State, who themselves have taken oath to bear true faith and allegiance to the Constitution of India and to discharge their duties faithfully and conscientiously, will be well advised to consider avoiding any person in the Council of Ministers, against whom charges have been framed by a criminal court in respect of offences involving moral turpitude and also offences specifically referred to in Chapter III of The Representation of the People Act, 1951.

(416 words)

[*Extract from the Supreme Court Judgement Manoj Narula v. Union of India*]

65. According to the passage, the Court cannot decide what is 'good' or 'bad' governance, but it can:
(a) Disqualify Ministers from holding office
(b) Indicate constitutional ethos on governance and remind functionaries of their duty
(c) Frame rules on the qualifications of Ministers
(d) Amend the Constitution to insert explicit standards of morality

66. Dr B.R. Ambedkar believed that the working of the Constitution ultimately depends on:
(a) The rigidity of the constitutional text
(b) The good sense and integrity of those who are going to administer this constitution
(c) The presence of a strong opposition
(d) Judicial intervention in governance

67. The Court, while respecting the prerogative of the Prime Minister and Chief Minister to select Ministers, emphasized that:
(a) They should avoid appointing persons against whom criminal charges involving moral turpitude are framed.
(b) They must appoint Ministers strictly from the ruling party only.
(c) They should consult the Supreme Court before finalizing appointments.
(d) They are bound to appoint only members of the Lok Sabha/Legislative Assembly.

68. What role does the Court assume, as described in the passage, regarding governance and appointments to the Council of Ministers?
(a) Judicial review of all ministerial appointments
(b) Prophetic duty to remind key functionaries of their constitutional role
(c) Power to veto ministerial selections made by the Prime Minister
(d) Directing Parliament to amend the law on disqualification

69. Who are the constitutional functionaries to, this passage primarily refers to?
(a) Council of Ministers
(b) Prime Minister and Council of Ministers
(c) Chief Minister and Council of Ministers
(d) Prime Minister and Chief Minister

70. Who, according to the above passage, shall not be appointed as a Minister?
(a) Against whom charges have been framed in a court of law
(b) Against whom charges involving moral turpitude have been framed in a court of law
(c) Against whom charges have been proved in a court of law
(d) Against whom case is pending in a court of law

XIV. The recent Supreme Court judgment in State of Tamil Nadu v. Governor of Tamil Nadu (2025) affirmed that a Governor cannot exercise an absolute or 'pocket' veto on bills, holding that if assent is withheld, the bill must be returned to the legislature 'as soon as possible' for reconsideration, with the Governor having no discretion to withhold assent again. The court established that inaction or indefinite delay is illegal and unconstitutional, prescribing timelines for the Governor's decision and even 'deeming assent' on pending bills in the Tamil Nadu case, establishing a critical precedent for judicial review of gubernatorial powers. The Supreme Court explicitly rejected the Governor's power to an absolute or 'pocket' veto, which allows for bills to be indefinitely delayed. If a Governor withholds assent to a bill, they are constitutionally obligated to return it to the State Assembly for reconsideration, according to the proviso in Article 200 of the Constitution. If the State Assembly re-enacts a bill after it has been returned by the Governor, the Governor has no choice but to give assent to it and cannot withhold it for a second time. The Court held that indefinitely delaying or remaining silent on bills is unconstitutional and that Governors must act 'as soon as possible' on bills. The judgment expanded the scope of judicial review by setting timelines for the Governor's actions on bills, allowing state governments to approach courts if these timelines are breached. In the case of Tamil Nadu, the Court used its powers under Article 142 to 'deem assent' on the long-pending bills, which had the effect of making any subsequent decision by the President on those bills void. (276 words)

[*Extracted with edits & revisions from "The Hindu", dated 8th April 2025*]

71. The Legislative Assembly of State X passes a controversial bill and sends it to the Governor for assent. The Governor, strongly disagreeing with the bill's provisions, decides to neither give assent nor return the bill, hoping it will be forgotten over time. Which of the following statements accurately describes the legal position of the Governor's action?

(a) The Governor's action is a legitimate exercise of a 'pocket veto', allowing for indefinite delay of bills.

(b) The Governor's inaction is unconstitutional, as the Supreme Court has explicitly rejected the power to an absolute or 'pocket' veto, and they are obligated to return the bill 'as soon as possible' if assent is withheld.

(c) The Governor is within their rights to delay the bill indefinitely as long as they do not explicitly reject it, reflecting the true spirit of gubernatorial discretion.

(d) The bill will automatically lapse after six months of gubernatorial inaction, making the delay a *de facto rejection*.

72. Governor Y receives a bill from the State Assembly and, after careful consideration, decides to withhold assent, promptly returning it with a message for reconsideration. The State Assembly then re-enacts the bill without any change and sends it back to Governor Y. What is the constitutional obligation of Governor Y at this point?

(a) Governor Y has no choice but to give assent to the re-enacted bill, as the Supreme The Court has ruled that the Governor cannot withhold assent for a second time.

(b) Governor Y can again withhold assent if they continue to disagree with the bill's content, sending it back for further reconsideration.

(c) Governor Y can refer the bill to the President of India for a final decision, exercising a higher discretionary power.

(d) Governor Y can dissolve the State Assembly for consistently passing erroneous bills.

73. After the Supreme Court's judgment in *State of Tamil Nadu v. Governor of Tamil Nadu* (2025), a State Governor holds a bill for eight months without taking any action—neither assenting nor returning it. The State Government believes that this delay is unconstitutional. Based on the precedent set by the judgment, what recourse is available to the State Government?

(a) The State Government must wait for a full year before any action can be taken, as gubernatorial delays are typically permitted for this duration.

(b) The bill automatically lapses after six months of inaction, making any further action by the State Government unnecessary.
(c) The State Government's only recourse is to re-enact the bill, which would then compel the Governor to act.
(d) The State Government can approach the courts, as the judgment had prescribed timelines for the Governor's actions on bills since indefinite delay was construed as unconstitutional.

74. In a situation mirroring the Tamil Nadu case, a Supreme Court bench is reviewing several instances where a particular Governor has indefinitely delayed assent on multiple bills passed by the State Assembly, despite Constitutional obligations. If the Supreme Court decides to follow the precedent established in *State of Tamil Nadu v. Governor of Tamil Nadu* (2025) regarding pending bills, what would be a likely outcome for these delayed bills?
(a) The Supreme Court would order the Governor to explicitly reject all the delayed bills.
(b) The Supreme Court would direct the State Assembly to conduct a public referendum on each delayed bill.
(c) The Supreme Court could deem assent on the pending bills, establishing a critical precedent for judicial review of gubernatorial powers in such cases, as it did in the Tamil Nadu case.
(d) The Supreme Court would advise the Governor to seek legal counsel and then re-evaluate each bill individually without a set timeline.

75. A newly appointed Governor publicly declares that he intends to use his discretion to permanently halt any legislation he deems inappropriate, by simply not acting on the bills, citing an inherent gubernatorial power. How does this declaration align with the constitutional interpretation provided by the Supreme Court of India?
(a) The Governor's declaration is consistent with the broad discretionary powers traditionally afforded to Governors, allowing them significant influence over state legislation.
(b) The Governor's declaration is valid only for non-money bills, as money bills have different Constitutional protocols.
(c) The Governor's declaration is partially valid, as indefinite delay is permissible only if the State Assembly is not in session.
(d) The Governor's declaration is unconstitutional; the Supreme Court explicitly rejected the Governor's power to an absolute or 'pocket' veto.

76. What are the three primary courses of action for a Governor when a Bill is enacted by the State Assembly and sent to him/her for his/her assent? Which option correctly lists these three courses?
(a) (i) Give assent, (ii) Veto absolutely, or (iii) Refer to the Supreme Court
(b) (i) Give assent, (ii) Withhold assent (allowing the Bill to fail, unless the proviso is followed), or (iii) Recommend amendments
(c) (i) Give assent, (ii) Withhold assent (with the option to return for reconsideration), or (iii) Reserve for the consideration of the President
(d) (i) Give assent, (ii) Return for reconsideration, or (iii) Refer to the Union Government

XV. Same-sex marriage has no legal recognition in India as per the recent Supreme Court's judgment, where it was decided that this is an issue for Parliament to address. While Hindu marriages between transgender persons and cisgender men are permissible, and the Court acknowledged systemic discrimination and the right to choose a partner, it held that there is no fundamental right to marry. The government has been urged to form a panel to consider granting more legal rights to same-sex couples, but the legal status of marriage remains unchanged for now. The five-judge bench of the Supreme Court of India in *Supriyo @ Supriya Chakraborty & Anr. v. Union of India* (2023), in a majority verdict, ruled that there is no fundamental right to marry under the Indian Constitution, making it beyond the court's scope to legislate on same-sex marriage. The Court stated that the power to legislate on same-sex marriage rests with the Parliament and state legislatures. The judgment affirmed constitutional rights for LGBTQ+ citizens and the right to choose a partner. The government agreed to set up a panel to explore legal rights and benefits for same-sex couples, though these benefits are not the same as those conferred by marriage. Same-sex couples cannot legally marry and do not receive the same legal rights, such as automatic inheritance, pension, or adoption rights, that legally married couples do. Despite the ruling, LGBTQ+ couples continue to face legal discrimination and have no social recognition of marriage. The Court affirmed the right of same-sex couples to cohabit privately. While the Supreme Court's verdict brought limited benefits and acknowledgments, it has not legalized same-sex marriage in India, deferring the ultimate decision to the Parliament. (279 words)

[*Extracted, with edits and revisions, from "The Hindu", dated 27th October 2023*)

77. In October 2023, two individuals in India, Ramesh and Sameer, who identify as a same- sex couple, sought to legally solemnize their marriage. Based on the Supreme Court's ruling, what is the current legal standing of their ability to marry?

(a) Their marriage is legally recognized nationwide under a new constitutional right.
(b) Their marriage is not legally recognized, as the Supreme Court ruled that this issue is for Parliament to address.
(c) Their marriage is recognized only if both of them identify as transgender.
(d) Their marriage is temporarily recognized until Parliament decides otherwise.

78. During a legal proceeding in India, an advocate argues that the Supreme Court should directly legislate on same-sex marriage because the right to choose a partner inherently implies a fundamental right to marry for all citizens. How would the Supreme Court's judgment likely to counter this argument?

(a) The Court acknowledged the right to choose a partner, therefore, it would agree to legislate on marriage.
(b) The Court held that there is no fundamental right to marry under the Indian Constitution, and such a policy can be made only by the Parliament.
(c) The Court has held that it will set up a panel to look into the fundamental right to marry.
(d) The Court upheld the fundamental right to marry, but declined to recognize same sex marriage.

79. Following the Supreme Court's decision, an LGBTQ+ advocacy group in India aims to achieve legal recognition for same-sex marriage. To which governmental body or bodies should this group primarily direct its lobbying efforts to secure the necessary legislation?

(a) The Supreme Court of India as they are ultimately responsible for interpreting constitutional rights.
(b) The President of India as head of the Union legislature.
(c) The Parliament and state legislatures as the power to legislate on same-sex marriage rests with them.
(d) The National Commission for Human Rights, to advocate for a new directive.

80. While same-sex marriage is not legally recognized in India, however, the Supreme Court's verdict did offer some acknowledgments of rights for same-sex couples. Which of the following rights was specifically affirmed by the Court?

(a) The automatic right to inheritance for same-sex partners
(b) The right of same-sex couples to adopt children jointly
(c) The right of same-sex couples to cohabit privately
(d) The right to maintenance for same-sex partners

81. Ramesh and Suresh, a same-sex couple in India, have lived together for a decade and want to ensure they receive legal benefits equivalent to those of married couples, such as automatic inheritance and pension rights. Based on the Supreme Court's judgment, what is the primary obstacle they face in achieving these benefits?

(a) They must first register their union with the government panel that was urged to be formed.
(b) They cannot legally marry and therefore cannot automatically be entitled to these specific legal rights.
(c) These rights are only available to same-sex couples where one partner is transgender.
(d) They can receive these benefits if they convert to a religion that recognizes same- sex unions.

82. The new acronym that has evolved after LGBTQ+ is an acronym called LGBTQIA+. In this new acronym, 'IA' refers to:

(a) Intersex and Asexual
(b) Initialisms and Agender
(c) Intersex and Ally
(d) Intrasex and Androgynous

SECTION IV

XVI. In a language laboratory, students were given an interesting puzzle involving the word **'ELECTROCARDIOGRAPH.'** The teacher explained that such exercises not only test logical skills but also sharpen attention to detail. According to the challenge, the word had to undergo a series of transformations. First, the class was asked to take the first half of the letters, reverse their order and make the arrangement of letters look quite different from the original. Next, the students were told to identify the last but one letter of the original word and place it at the very beginning, a step that changed the opening appearance of the sequence completely. Finally, as a finishing touch, they had to add the letter 'S' at the end. Following these steps carefully would lead them to the correct transformed word, and only those who adhered to each condition in the exact order could solve the puzzle successfully. (150 words)

83. Which letter will be exactly in the middle?

(a) L (b) R
(c) D (d) E

84. How many vowels will be to the left of the middle letter?

(a) 2 (b) 1
(c) 4 (d) 3

85. Which of the two vowels will be adjoining each other?

(a) IE (b) IO
(c) AE (d) AO

86. Which vowel will have a consonant to the left but a vowel to the right of it?

(a) I (b) O
(c) A (d) E

87. Name the letter sandwiched between two vowels?

(a) R and T (b) C and L
(c) R and L (d) D and R

88. Which letter is **prefixed** to the word after the first half is reversed?

(a) G (b) P
(c) H (d) S

XVII. On the night of October 12th, the 'Sunburst Medallion' was stolen from the highly secured display case in the city museum. The theft occurred sometime between the museum closing at 10:00 PM and the night guard, Mr Hemant, completing his final round at 1:00 AM. Three primary suspects were identified, all of whom had recently been dismissed from their museum positions: Anjali, the former curator; Bharat, the former security expert; and Chitra, the former exhibits designer.

Here are the established facts and their alibis:

- The security system logs show that the display case was opened using a specific five-digit code, which only Anjali and the museum director (who was out of the country) knew.
- Bharat's alibi is that he was at a distant relative's birthday party from 8:00 PM to 1:30 AM.

Multiple independent witnesses confirmed his presence throughout the entire period.

- Chitra's alibi is that she was working late at a downtown graphic design studio. A time-stamped security camera from the studio's entrance shows her entering at 7:00 PM and exiting at 11:45 PM. The studio is a 20-minute drive from the museum.
- Mr Hemant, the night guard, stated he checked the medallion at 10:30 PM, and it was still there.

Further investigation revealed that a small, distinctive silver button was found near the display case. Anjali is known to frequently wear a coat with similar, unique silver buttons. The security expert, Bharat, had previously boasted that he could remotely disable a certain type of magnetic lock-the same type used on the medallion's case-without needing the code, though the log suggests the code was used. (269 words)

89. Identifying the Most Likely Suspect

Based only on the fact that the five-digit code was used to open the display case, who is the only plausible suspect among the three?

(a) Anjali (b) Bharat
(c) Chitra (d) Both Anjali and Chitra

90. Evaluating Alibis and Time Constraints

The theft occurred between 10:00 PM and 1:00 AM, but the night guard saw the medallion at 10:30 PM. Given Chitra's alibi, what is the earliest time she could have reached the museum?

(a) 11:45 PM (b) 12:05 AM
(c) 12:45 AM (d) 10:50 PM

91. Deduction and Contradictory Evidence

If the theft was committed by Bharat, which established fact must be incorrect, based on the provided information?

(a) The medallion was present at 10:30 PM.
(b) The security logs indicate the code was used.
(c) The museum's closing time of 10:00 PM.
(d) The time frame of his alibi (8:00 PM to 1:30 AM).

92. Analyzing Accessory Evidence

The discovery of the silver button near the display case is the most incriminating evidence against which suspect, and why?

(a) Bharat, because he had the technical expertise to get close to the case.
(b) Chitra, because she was near the museum late that night.
(c) Anjali, because she is known to wear a coat with similar buttons.
(d) Mr Hemant, as he was the last person to check the area.

93. Identifying the Logical Flaw in the Argument:

A detective argues: 'Since Bharat has a confirmed, continuous alibi covering the entire time window of the theft (10:30 PM to 1:00 AM), he cannot be the thief.' What principle of logic supports this detective's conclusion?

(a) Correlation does not imply causation
(b) If an event requires presence, confirmed absence proves innocence
(c) The rule of double jeopardy
(d) The burden of proof lies with the accuser

94. Drawing a Strongest Conclusion

Considering all the facts (the code being used, the silver button, and the confirmed alibis), which is the most reasonable inference?

(a) Bharat must have had an accomplice who knew the code.
(b) Chitra's alibi is false because she had enough time to commit the crime after leaving the studio.
(c) Anjali is the most likely suspect because the code was used, and she has a direct link to the physical evidence (the button).
(d) Mr Hemant is secretly the thief and is trying to frame the former employees.

95. Assessing Necessary Conditions

What condition is necessary for Chitra to have stolen the medallion?

(a) She must know the five-digit code.
(b) She must have left the graphic design studio before 11.45 PM.
(c) The theft must have occurred after she left the studio and before 1 AM.
(d) She must have worked with Anjali to disable the locks.

XVIII. In a small town lived a close-knit family where every relation could be expressed through simple symbols. For instance, when they said A × B, it meant A is the father of B, while A ÷ B meant A is the mother of B. The younger ones were often introduced with A + B, meaning A was the daughter of B, and the bond of brotherhood was shown by A – B (A is the brother of B). One day, the children in the family turned these symbols into a playful code. Instead of introducing their parents and siblings in words, they spoke only in symbols. 'Look,' giggled little Meena, 'M + N ÷ O!' Everyone laughed, because they knew it meant Meena was the daughter of N, and N was the mother of O, making her O's sister. What started as a code soon became a family game, making the bonds of father, mother, daughter, and brother not just relations, but symbols of love and togetherness. (165 words)

96. If 'P + Q – R÷ T', how is T related to P?
(a) Aunt (b) Father
(c) Grandmother (d) None of these

97. Which of the following means that R is the wife of P?
(a) P × R – Q – T (b) P ÷ T + R – Q
(c) P ÷ R – Q + T (d) P × T – Q + R

98. If 'P × T ÷ Q + R', how is R related to P?
(a) Daughter (b) Husband
(c) Son-in-law (d) None of these

99. If 'P ÷ R – Q × T', how is P related to T?
(a) Grandmother (b) Mother-in-law
(c) Sister (d) Grandfather

100. If 'R ÷ Q + R × T', how is T related to Q?
(a) Aunt (b) Sister
(c) Brother (d) Grandson

101. If 'R – P ÷ J × Q', how is J related to R?
(a) Son (b) Nephew
(c) Niece (d) Grandson

XIX. Four teams – Red (R), Blue (B), Green (G), and Yellow (Y) – are competing in the final four rounds of the Inter-School Science Olympiad, labelled Round A, Round B, Round C, and Round D. Each round consists of one match between two teams, and every team plays exactly two matches. No team plays the same opponent more than once. The final schedule must adhere to the following rules:

- Rule 1 (Consecutive Play) : The Green team (G) must play their two matches in consecutive rounds.
- Rule 2 (Fixed Appearance) : The Yellow team (Y) must play in Round B.
- Rule 3 (Positional Constraint) : The Red team (R) must play against the Blue team (B) in a round that is immediately before a round in which neither R nor B is playing.
- Rule 4 (Timing) : The Blue team's (B) first match must occur in an earlier round than the Green team's (G) first match.
- Rule 5 (Opponent Link) : The team that plays against the Red team (R) in the round that is not against the Blue team (B) is the same team that plays in Round D.

(193 words)

102. Determining the Green Team's Schedule

Considering Rules 1 and 2, which of the following pairs of rounds contains the Green team's two matches?

(a) Round A and Round D
(b) Round B and Round C
(c) Round C and Round D
(d) Round A and Round B

103. Applying the Positional Constraint

Based on all the rules, particularly Rule 3, which of the following matches must be scheduled for Round A?
(a) Red vs. Green (b) Red vs. Yellow
(c) Red vs. Blue (d) Blue vs. Yellow

104. Identifying the Blue Team's First Opponent

Who is the Blue team's first opponent in the tournament?
(a) Green
(b) Red
(c) Yellow
(d) The opponent cannot be determined

105. Finding the Match in Round C

What is the match scheduled for Round C?
(a) Red vs. Green (b) Green vs. Blue
(c) Blue vs. Yellow (d) Red vs. Yellow

106. Identifying the Teams Excluded from a Round

Which pair of rounds contains matches where the Yellow team does not participate?
(a) Round A and Round C
(b) Round A and Round D
(c) Round B and Round C
(d) Round C and Round D

107. Team Opponent Check

Which team does the Yellow team NOT play against over the course of the four rounds?
(a) Red
(b) Blue
(c) Green
(d) The Yellow team plays against all other teams

108. Assessing a Rule Violation

If the match in Round D was (Blue vs. Yellow), which of the original rules would be violated by this schedule change?
(a) Rule 1 (Consecutive Play)
(b) Rule 3 (Positional Constraint)
(c) Rule 4 (Timing)
(d) Rule 5 (Opponent Link)

SECTION V

XX. Health insurance plays a vital role in ensuring financial protection and access to quality health-care. In India, however, the extent and nature of health insurance coverage vary significantly between urban and rural areas. While urban populations often have better access to organized insurance schemes, employer-provided coverage, and awareness about health policies, rural populations face challenges such as limited outreach of insurance schemes, inadequate infrastructure, and lower awareness levels. This urban–rural divide in health insurance coverage highlights the broader issue of healthcare inequality, making it essential to analyze the factors contributing to this gap and explore strategies for more inclusive health protection. A state-level health survey was conducted.

The survey covered 1,80,000 adults across urban and rural areas. Urban residents formed 55% of the sample (that is, 99,000 people) while rural residents made up 45% (that is, 81,000 people). In each area, coverage was classified under four heads: Public schemes, Private insurance, Employer-provided coverage, and Uninsured. In urban areas, Public coverage accounted for 28% of the urban population, Private for 22%, Employer for 18%, and the remaining 32% were Uninsured. In rural areas, where formal coverage is generally lower, Public coverage stood at 35%, Private at 10%, and Employer at 8%, while 47% were Uninsured. For this survey, 'Insured' includes everyone covered by Public + Private + Employer schemes, and 'Uninsured' indicates those with no coverage at all. Officials noted that public schemes remain the backbone of rural coverage, while employer and private plans are relatively more prevalent in urban centres. (250 words)

109. The ratio of insured adults in Urban: Rural is:
(a) 82:65 (b) 748:477
(c) 65:82 (d) 477:748

110. By what percentage is the number of Uninsured in Rural areas higher than Uninsured in Urban?
(a) 18.75% (b) 20.17%
(c) 22.50% (d) 25.00%

111. If the total population grows by 5% next year and all percentage shares remain the same (including the Urban-Rural split), how many additional privately insured people will there be (vs. this year)?
(a) 1,494 (b) 1,560
(c) 1,620 (d) 1,650

112. The total number of Employer-covered adults is:
(a) 22,800 (b) 23,100
(c) 24,300 (d) 25,200

113. What percentage of all insured adults are publicly insured?
(a) 48.50% (b) 49.75%
(c) 50.86% (d) 52.00%

114. What percentage of the total surveyed population was insured?
(a) 52.15% (b) 56.25%
(c) 61.25% (d) 64%

XXI. A state electricity report serves as an important tool to assess energy production and track progress in the power sector. By providing quarterly data on generation measured in gigawatt hours (GWh), the report highlights the contribution of different energy sources such as coal, gas, hydro, solar, and wind. This not only helps in understanding the overall energy mix and dependence on conventional versus renewable sources but also enables policymakers, planners, and stakeholders to evaluate trends, address gaps, and promote sustainable energy development. A state electricity reportprovides quarterly generation (in GWh) by source – Coal, Gas, Hydro, Solar, and Wind.

In Q1 Generation from Coal is 2,200 GWh, Gas contributes 800 GWh, and Hydro 900 GWh, Solar 700 GWh, and Wind 400 GWh, for a total of 5,000 GWh.

In Q2 Coal rises to 2,400 GWh, while Gas dips to 700 GWh; Hydro improves to 1,000 GWh, Solar to 800 GWh, and Wind to 600 GWh, bringing the quarterly total to 5,500 GWh.

In Q3 Coal moderates to 2,100 GWh, Gas increases to 900 GWh, and Hydro softens to 800 GWh, but Solar advances to 1,000 GWh and Wind to 700 GWh, keeping the total at 5,500 GWh.

In Q4 Coal moves to 2,300 GWh, Gas to 850 GWh, Hydro to 1,100 GWh, Solar to 900 GWh, and Wind to 850 GWh, for a total of 6,000 GWh.

For analysis, Renewables are taken as Hydro + Solar + Wind. A carbon policy scenario proposes cutting Q4 Coal by 10%, shifting the entire reduction equally into Solar and Wind. (255 words)

115. The total annual generation (GWh) is:
(a) 20,500 (b) 21,500
(c) 22,000 (d) 22,500

116. The overall renewable share (as % of annual generation) is closest to:
(a) 42.5% (b) 43.8%
(c) 44.3% (d) 45.0%

117. The quarter with the highest renewable percentage share is:
(a) Q1 (b) Q2
(c) Q3 (d) Q4

118. A carbon policy reduces Q4 Coal by 10% and shifts the entire reduction equally to Solar and Wind. The new Q4 Solar (GWh) is:
(a) 975 (b) 1,000
(c) 1,015 (d) 1,030

119. The annual Gas: Hydro generation ratio is:
(a) 13:15 (b) 65:76
(c) 5:6 (d) 26:31

120. The quarter with the lowest renewable percentage share is:
(a) Q1 (b) Q2
(c) Q3 (d) Q4

ANSWER KEY

Section I

1. (c)	5. (a)	9. (a)	13. (b)	17. (d)	21. (b)
2. (d)	6. (d)	10. (b)	14. (c)	18. (b)	22. (a)
3. (c)	7. (b)	11. (a)	15. (c)	19. (a)	23. (c)
4. (b)	8. (b)	12. (c)	16. (a)	20. (d)	24. (b)

Section II

25. (b)	29. (b)	33. (c)	37. (c)	41. (d)	45. (a)	49. (c)
26. (d)	30. (c)	34. (c)	38. (b)	42. (a)	46. (b)	50. (a)
27. (b)	31. (d)	35. (c)	39. (c)	43. (b)	47. (a)	51. (c)
28. (d)	32. (d)	36. (a)	40. (c)	44. (d)	48. (c)	52. (b)

Section III

53. (b)	58. (c)	63. (a)	68. (b)	73. (d)	78. (b)
54. (a)	59. (c)	64. (b)	69. (d)	74. (c)	79. (c)
55. (b)	60. (c)	65. (b)	70. (b)	75. (d)	80. (c)
56. (a)	61. (c)	66. (b)	71. (b)	76. (c)	81. (b)
57. (d)	62. (a)	67. (a)	72. (a)	77. (b)	82. (a)

Section IV

83. (d)	87. (b)	91. (d)	95. (c)	99. (a)	103. (c)	107. (b)
84. (d)	88. (b)	92. (c)	96. (d)	100. (Withdrawn)	104. (b)	108. (d)
85. (b)	89. (a)	93. (b)	97. (d)	101. (b)	105. (b)	
86. (a)	90. (b)	94. (c)	98. (c)	102. (b)	106. (a)	

Section V

109. (b)	111. (a)	113. (c)	115. (c)	117. (d)	119. (b)
110. (b)	112. (c)	114. (c)	116. (c)	118. (c)	120. (a)

CLAT 2025

ENGLISH LANGUAGE

I. From a very early age, I knew that when I grew up, I should be a writer. I had the lonely child's habit of making up stories and holding conversations with imaginary persons, and I think from the very start my literary ambitions were mixed up with the feeling of being isolated and undervalued. I knew that I had a facility with words and the power of facing unpleasant facts, and I felt that this created a sort of private world in which I could get my own back for my failure in everyday life. I wanted to write enormous naturalistic novels with unhappy endings, full of detailed descriptions and arresting similes, and also full of purple passages in which words were used partly for the sake of their sound. I give all this background information because I do not think one can assess a writer's motives without knowing something of his early development.

His subject-matter will be determined by the age he lives in – at least this is true in tumultuous, revolutionary ages like our own – but before he ever begins to write he will have acquired an emotional attitude from which he will never completely escape. It is his job to discipline his temperament, but if he escapes from his early influences altogether, he will have killed his impulse to write. I think there are four great motives for writing, at any rate for writing prose. They are: (i) Sheer egoism: Desire to seem clever, to be talked about, to be remembered after death, to get your own back on grown-ups who snubbed you in childhood; (ii) Aesthetic enthusiasm: Desire to share an experience which one feels is valuable and ought not to be missed (iii) Historical impulse: Desire to see things as they are, to find out true facts and store them up for the use of posterity (iv) Political purpose: Desire to push the world in a certain direction, to alter other people's idea of the kind of society that they should strive after.

[*Extracted with edits from George Orwell's 'Why I Write'*]

1. For the author, aesthetic enthusiasm is an important motive for writing because it ...
(a) Shapes the thoughts
(b) Creates an artistic piece
(c) Becomes invaluable
(d) Non-utilitarian

2. The author strongly advocates the writers to:
(a) Avoid any egoistic impression in their work
(b) Be apolitical in their approach
(c) Be contemporary in their treatment of their work
(d) None of the above

3. Which of the following is a synonym for the word 'tumultuous'?
(a) Chaotic
(b) Turbulent
(c) Disorderly
(d) All of the above

4. George Orwell's loneliness during childhood led to
(a) Estrangement with his father
(b) Unhappy days
(c) Making up stories
(d) Unpleasant incidents

5. Why does Orwell give background information?
(a) He had the lonely child's habits
(b) It is essential to know about the motives of writers
(c) Because of his historic impulse
(d) Due to the aesthetic enthusiasm

6. If the writer escapes from early impulses, he will ...
(a) Lose his urge to write
(b) Be unable to imagine creatively
(c) Be able to converse with imaginary characters
(d) Be able to influence others

II. Education is not the amount of information that is put into your brain and runs riot there, undigested, all your life. We must have life-building, man-making, character-making assimilation of ideas.... If education were identical with information, libraries are the sages in the world and encyclopedias are the rishis. Getting by heart the thoughts of others in a foreign language and stuffing your brain with them and taking some University degree, you consider yourself educated. Is this education? What is the goal of your education? Open your eyes and see what a piteous cry for food is rising in the land of Bharata, proverbial for its food. Will your education fulfill this want?

We want that education by which character is formed, strength of mind is increased, the intellect is expanded and by which one can stand on one's own feet. What we need to study independent of foreign control, different branches of the knowledge that is our own, and with it the English language and Western science; we need technical education and all else that will develop industries so that men instead of seeking for service may earn enough to provide for themselves and save against a rainy day. The end of all education, all training, should be man-making. The end and aim of all training are to make the man grow. The training by which the current expression of will are brought under control and become fruitful is called education. What our country now wants are muscles of iron and nerves of steel, gigantic wills, which nothing can resist, which can penetrate into the mysteries and secrets of the universe and will accomplish their purpose in any fashion, even if it meant going down to the bottom of the ocean, meeting death face to face.

There is only one method of attaining knowledge. It is by concentration. The very essence of education is the concentration of mind. From the lowest to the highest man, all have to use the same method to attain knowledge. The chemist who works in the laboratory concentrates on elements to analyze them. Knowledge is acquired by concentration.

[Extracted with edits from 'Education' by Swami Vivekananda]

7. According to the author, we need to study:
(a) English Language
(b) Technical Education
(c) Western Science
(d) All of the above

8. According to the author, which among the following is key to attain knowledge?
(a) University Degrees
(b) Library
(c) Concentration of mind
(d) Hard work and sports training

9. Which of the following words is related to the word 'assimilation'?
(a) Integration (b) Adjustment
(c) Acclimatization (d) All of the above

10. Education, as described by the author means:
(a) Information
(b) Library
(c) Degrees
(d) None of the above

11. As per the author, the aim of education should be:
(a) To help a person build his/her character
(b) To help a person earn his/her livelihood
(c) To help a person develop his/her intellect
(d) All of the above

12. According to the author the country wants:
(a) Massive willpower
(b) Spirit of philanthropy
(c) Iron and steel industries
(d) All of the above

III. Punctually at midday, he opened his bag and spread out his professional equipment, which consisted of a dozen cowrie shells, a square piece of cloth with obscure mystic charts on it, a notebook, and a bundle of palmyra writing. His forehead was dazzling with sacred ash and vermilion, and his eyes sparkled with a sharp, abnormal gleam which was really an outcome of a continual searching look for customers, but which his simple clients took to be a prophetic light and felt comforted. The power of his eyes was considerably enhanced by their position—placed as they were between the painted forehead and the dark whiskers which streamed down his cheeks: even a half-wit's eyes would sparkle in such a setting. People were attracted to him as bees are attracted to cosmos or dahlia stalks. He sat under the boughs of a spreading tamarind tree which flanked a path running through the town hall park. It was a remarkable place in many ways: a surging crowd was always moving up and down this narrow road morning till night. A variety of trades and occupations was represented all along its way: medicine sellers, sellers of stolen hardware and junk, magicians, and, above all, an auctioneer of cheap cloth, who created enough din all day to attract the whole town. Next to him in vociferousness came a vendor of fried groundnut, who gave his ware a fancy name each day, calling it 'Bombay Ice Cream' one day, and on the next 'Delhi Almond,' and on the third 'Raja's Delicacy,' and so on and so forth, and people flocked to him. A considerable portion of this crowd dallied before the astrologer too. The astrologer transacted his business by the light of a flare which crackled and smoked up above the groundnut heap nearby.

(*Extracted with edits from 'An Astrologer's Day' by* R.K. *Narayan*)

13. Which among the following is the word for the phrase 'Bright and colourful in an impressive way'?

(a) Mystic (b) Flare
(c) Sparkle (d) Dazzling

14. Which among the following is not a trade or occupation represented in the pathway running through the town hall park?

(a) Magicians
(b) Medicine sellers
(c) Auctioneers of cheap Bags
(d) Sellers of Stolen Hardware

15. Who among the following used names like 'Bombay Ice Cream', 'Delhi Almond,' and 'Raja's Delicacy' to attract the crowd?

(a) The sellers of cheap clothes
(b) The sellers of Medicine
(c) The ice cream seller
(d) The groundnut seller

16. Which among the following is the meaning of the expression 'vociferousness'?

(a) Expressing opinions or feelings in a loud and confident way
(b) Words that are spoken or sung to have a magical effect
(c) Willing or prepared to do something
(d) To hang about aimlessly

17. When did the astrologer usually start his day's business?

(a) When people are attracted to him as bees
(b) When the surging crowd moves up and down the road
(c) Punctually at midday
(d) By the light of a flare

18. What was considered as a prophetic light by the simple clients of the astrologer?

(a) The resplendent forehead of the astrologer with sacred ash and vermillion
(b) The sparkling eyes of the astrologer with an abnormal gleam
(c) The dark whiskers which streamed down the cheeks of the astrologer
(d) The saffron coloured turban around the head of astrologer

IV. The right kind of education consists in understanding the child as he is without imposing upon him an ideal of what we think he should be. To enclose him in the framework of an ideal is to encourage him to conform, which breeds fear and produces in him a constant conflict between what he is and what he should be: and all inward conflicts have their outward manifestations in society. If the parent loves the child, he observes him, he studies his tendencies, his moods, and peculiarities. It is only when one feels no love for the child that one imposes upon him an ideal, for then one's ambitions are trying to fulfill themselves in him, wanting him to become this or that. If one loves, not the ideal but the child, then there is a possibility of helping him to understand himself as he is.

Ideals are a convenient escape, and the teacher who follows them is incapable of understanding his students and dealing with them intelligently; for him, the future ideal, what should be, is far more important than the present child. The pursuit of an ideal excludes love, and without love no human problem can be solved. If the teacher is of the right kind, he will not depend on a method, but will study each individual pupil. In our relationship with children and young people, we are not dealing with mechanical devices that can be quickly repaired, but with living beings who are impressionable, volatile, sensitive, afraid, affectionate: and to deal with them, we have to have great understanding, the strength of patience and love. When we lack these, we look to quick and easy remedies and hope for marvellous and automatic results. If we are unaware, mechanical in our attitudes and actions, we fight shy of any demand upon us that is disturbing and that cannot be met by an automatic response, and this is one of our major difficulties in education.

(*Extract with edits from 'The Right Kind of Education' by J. Krishna Murti*)

19. According to the passage, why do we look for quick and easy remedies and hope for marvellous and automatic results?
(a) Because children are impressionable, volatile, sensitive, and affectionate.
(b) Because of major difficulties in education.
(c) Because we lack intelligence and skills.
(d) Because we lack understanding, patience and love.

20. What does the passage highlight as the quality of a parent who really desires to understand his child?
(a) They look at their child through the prism of an ideal.
(b) They observe and study the tendencies, moods, and peculiarities of the child.
(c) They love their child to become someone great as per their ambitions.
(d) They encourage the child to find out what she/he is and what she/he should be.

21. What is the antonym for the word 'volatile'?
(a) Stable
(b) Steady
(c) Constant
(d) All of the above

22. Which of the following currently reflects the intention of the author of this passage?
(a) The right kind of education for a child cannot be without love, care and understanding.
(b) True education should be governed by a tendency to conform a child to our ideals.
(c) The teacher should focus on how a child should be according to his/her methodology, hope, or expectation.
(d) Parents and teachers should work together collectively to guide a child on what she/he should do as per their ambitions.

23. In light of the above passage, what will be the result of forcing a child to conform to the framework of an ideal?
(a) It will make the child an ideal child.
(b) It will create confusion and fear in the child.
(c) The child will get into a conflict.
(d) Will discourage the child to conform to the ideal.

24. According to the author, what should be the attitude of a right kind of teacher?
(a) They should not empathize with the students.
(b) They should use modern and scientific methods of teaching.

(c) They should focus on studying each student individually.
(d) They should instill great ideals in the students.

CURRENT AFFAIRS INCLUDING GENERAL KNOWLEDGE

V. Chinese President Xi Jinping and Indian Prime Minister Narendra Modi used a BRICS summit in Russia recently to showcase ambitions for a more harmonious relationship between the world's two most populous countries after years of animosity.

The meeting between Xi and Modi, who have not held formal talks for five years, was one highlight of the summit. BRICS also gave an opportunity to Russian President Vladimir Putin for showcasing that the West had failed to isolate Russia over the Ukraine war.

A final communique listed a number of projects aimed at facilitating trade between BRICS nations - including an alternative payment system to the dollar - but did not include details or timelines.

Just two days after New Delhi announced that it had reached a deal with Beijing to resolve a four-year military stand-off on their disputed Himalayan frontier, Xi told Modi that they should enhance communication and cooperation and effectively manage differences.

BRICS - an idea thought up inside Goldman Sachs two decades ago to describe the growing economic clout of China and other major emerging markets - is now a group that accounts for 45% of the world's population and 35% of the global economy.

Former Goldman Sachs economist Jim O'Neill, who coined the BRIC term in 2001, told Reuters that he had little optimism for the BRICS club as long as China and India remained so divided.

'It seems to me basically to be a symbolic annual gathering where important emerging countries, particularly noisy ones like Russia, but also China, can basically get together and highlight how good it is to be part of something that doesn't involve the U.S. and that global governance isn't good enough.'

The 43-page final communique from the summit ranged from geopolitics and narcotics to artificial intelligence and even the preservation of Big Cats, but lacked detail on some major issues. It mentioned Ukraine just once.

(Excerpts from 'Putin scores a BRICS win with rare Xi and Modi show of harmony' By Vladimir Soldatkin and Guy Faulconbridge , Reuters, October 23, 2024)

25. The 16th BRICS achieved the following:
(a) Launch of BRICS currency
(b) De scalation of Russian-Ukrainian conflict
(c) Diplomatic dialogue between India and China
(d) All of the above

26. What does the letter 'S' in BRICS stand for?
(a) Saudi Arabia
(b) Singapore
(c) South America
(d) South Africa

27. The initiative of Big Cats Alliance refers to:
(a) Lions, Tigers and Jaguar
(b) Tigers, Jaguar and Leopard
(c) Lions, Cheetah and Snow Leopard
(d) All of the above

28. Which statement reflects as a critique from the Western Economists?
(a) BRICS currency cannot displace Dollars
(b) Asian economies will not impact western economy
(c) Indo-China conflicts will impact progress of BRICS
(d) All of the above

29. The emergence of BRICS signals:
(a) Asian consolidation of economic power
(b) Diminishing European dominance
(c) Revival of Nonaligned movement
(d) A geo-politics without US dominance

30. Which one of the below is an outcome of 16th BRICS meeting?
(a) Proposal to end Russia-Ukraine war
(b) To expand BRICS by including Scandinavian countries
(c) To recognize China's claim of Taiwan
(d) Reducing tension between India and China

VI. On the recommendation of Parliament, the President of India effectively abrogated Article 370 of the Indian Constitution and gave assent to the Jammu and Kashmir Reorganization Act, 2019. The former state of Jammu & Kashmir has been reorganized as the new Union Territory of Jammu and Kashmir and the new Union Territory of Ladakh on 31st October 2019.

The new Union Territory of Ladakh consists of two districts of Kargil and Leh. The rest of the former State of Jammu and Kashmir is in the new Union Territory of Jammu and Kashmir.

By 2019, the state government of former Jammu and Kashmir had reorganized the areas of these 14 districts into 28 districts. The names of the new districts are as follows - Kupwara, Bandipur, Ganderbal, Srinagar, Budgam, Pulwama, Shupian, Kulgam, Rajouri, Ramban, Doda, Kishtivar, Samba and Kargil.

Out of these, Kargil district was carved out from the area of Leh and Ladakh district. The Leh district of the new Union Territory of Ladakh has been defined in the Jammu and Kashmir Reorganization (Removal of Difficulties) Second Order, 2019, issued by the President of India, to include the areas of the districts of Gilgit, Gilgit Wazarat, Chilhas and Tribal Territory of 1947, in addition to the remaining areas of Leh and Ladakh districts of 1947, after carving out the Kargil District.

[*Extracted from the article of Press Information Bureau, published by the Union Home Ministry on 2nd November 2019*]

31. Which of the following statements regarding Article 370 of the Constitution of India is correct?
(a) It gave special status to the erstwhile state of Jammu and Kashmir.
(b) It created a special tribunal for the state of Jammu and Kashmir on certain occasions.
(c) It introduced Goods and Services Tax in Jammu and Kashmir.
(d) It confers special jurisdiction on the Supreme Court on matters coming from Jammu & Kashmir.

32. The Jammu and Kashmir Reorganization Act, 2019, divided the erstwhile State of Jammu and Kashmir into which of the following?
(a) 2 States
(b) 1 State and 1 Union Territory
(c) 2 Union Territories
(d) 1 State and 2 Union Territories

33. Which of the following Union Territories of India has a legislative assembly?
(a) Andaman and Nicobar Islands
(b) Jammu and Kashmir
(c) Daman and Diu
(d) Lakshadweep

34. How many States and Union Territories are present in India?
(a) 28 States and 8 Union territories
(b) 27 States and 8 Union territories
(c) 28 States and 7 Union territories
(d) 27 States and 7 Union territories

35. Which among the following is the capital city of the Union Territory of Ladakh?
(a) Leh (b) Changtang
(c) Dras (d) Nubra

36. Which of the following is false?
(a) Kargil was formerly a union territory.
(b) Ladakh is administered by J&K assembly.
(c) Fifteen new districts were formed to be part of J &K in 2019.
(d) All of the above.

VII. The 'Nari Shakti Vandan Adhiniyam', 2023 Act received near-unanimous support in both the Lok Sabha and the Rajya Sabha. The legislation mandates the reservation of one-third of all seats in the Lok Sabha, state legislative assemblies, and Delhi (as a union territory with an elected assembly) for women. This linking of the implementation of the Act to the implementing of two long-term exercises of census and delimitation, makes little sense to many and sounds quite like empowerment delayed for now.

In a 2012, Article 'Holding Up Half the Sky: Reservations for Women in India', Rudolf C

Heredia breaks down the common misconceptions that cloud our understanding of women's political participation- 'When women do attain a national leadership role it is often because they have inherited the mantle from their fathers or husbands, rather than as persons in their own right and are then projected as matriarchs, part of the joint family, complementary to the patriarchy rather than a challenge to it.'

In 'Equality versus Empowerment: Women in Indian Legislature', 2023, Soumya Bhowmick makes the case for going a step beyond quotas, and to turn our attention to the complexities that shape women's agency in the country. This, he argues, would require a bottoms-up approach, rather than merely handing out reservations in a top-down manner. 'In a country like India with a considerably large heterogeneous population, the dissemination of legislative power would be insufficient to protect the interests of minority groups such as women, Scheduled Castes, and Scheduled Tribes.' He concludes that 'implementing the idea of reservation for women would bring about descriptive representation, but its transformation into substantive representation would depend on the change in the attitudes of the people.'

While the reservation of one-third of seats for women belonging to the Scheduled Castes and Tribes under the amendment to Articles 330a and 332 of the constitution is a welcome step, it remains to be seen whether it fully acknowledges the complex interplay of hierarchies, socio-political relationships which also affect the extent and nature of complications that surround effective realisation of women's politics for Indian politics to emerge as a truly emancipatory space.

37. The Nari Shakti Vandan Adhiniyam 2023:
(a) Will come to force from Jan 2025
(b) Will come to force after all the States and UTs approve it
(c) Will come to force after Census
(d) None of the above

38. As per Rudolf Heredia women's political leadership depends upon:
(a) Mentorship of spouse's political affiliations
(b) Parental guidance
(c) Property inheritance
(d) None of the above

39. According to Soumya Bhowmick the quotas for women should:
(a) Require a top down model
(b) Fulfill a descriptive representation
(c) Transform to substantive representation
(d) To be implemented homogeneously

40. The amendment to the Articles 330 (a) & 332 aims to:
(a) Appoint Rajya Sabha members based on cultural diversity
(b) Quota for women Governors
(c) Women sportspersons
(d) None of the above

VIII. During the First World War, Indian merchants and industrialists wanted protection against imports of foreign goods, and a rupee-sterling foreign exchange ratio that would discourage imports. To organize business interests, they formed the Indian Industrial and Commercial Congress in 1920 and the Federation of the Indian Chamber of Commerce and Industries (FICCI) in 1927. The industrialists attacked colonial control over the Indian economy, and supported the Civil Disobedience Movement when it was first launched. They gave financial assistance and refused to buy or sell imported goods. After the failure of the Round Table Conference, business groups were no longer uniformly enthusiastic. They were apprehensive of the spread of militant activities and worried about prolonged disruption of business, as well as of the growing influence of socialism amongst the younger members of the Congress.

The industrial working classes did not participate in the Civil Disobedience Movement in large numbers, except in the Nagpur region. As the industrialists came closer to the Congress, workers stayed aloof. But inspite of that, some workers did participate in the Civil Disobedience Movement, selectively adopting some of the ideas of the Gandhian programme, like boycott of foreign goods, as part of their own movements against low wages and poor working conditions. There were strikes by railway workers in 1930 and dockworkers in 1932. In 1930, thousands of workers in Chotanagpur tin mines wore Gandhi caps and participated in protest rallies and boycott campaigns. But the Congress was reluctant to include workers' demands as part of its programme of struggle. It felt that this would alienate industrialists and divide the anti-imperial forces.

Another important feature of the Civil Disobedience Movement was the large-scale participation of women. During Gandhiji's salt march, thousands of women came out of their homes to listen to him. They participated in protest marches, manufactured salt, and picketed foreign cloth and liquor shops. Many went to jail.

[*Excerpt from Chapter II - Nationalism in India, India and the Contemporary World*, NCERT]

41. Which event in Indian history marked the beginning of the Civil Disobedience Movement?
(a) Launch of Non-Cooperation Movement
(b) Commencing of Dandi March
(c) Signing of Gandhi-Irwin Pact
(d) Withdrawal of Non-Cooperation Movement

42. Which of the following is true in the context of civil disobedience movement?
(a) The Indian industrialist preferred partnership with MNCs.
(b) The Indian industrialists were concerned of disruption of business.
(c) The working class rejected the civil disobedience movement.
(d) The Round Table Conference was a partial success.

43. Which of the following was the predicament for Congress?
(a) Danger of division of opposition to the British Government
(b) Loss of faith by marginalized sections in Congress
(c) Falling value of Rupee against Sterling
(d) None of the above

44. Which of the following statements is correct with reference to the Civil Disobedience Movement?
(a) It encouraged militancy among workers.
(b) Breaking of the salt law, manufacturing salt, and demonstrating it in front of government salt factories.
(c) It urged the industrialists to accept socialism.
(d) All of the above.

45. Which among the following mass movements was supported by the Indian industrialists?
(a) Home Rule Movement
(b) Civil Disobedience Movement
(c) Non-Cooperation Movement
(d) Quit India Movement

46. Which of the following can be considered as major outcome of civil disobedience movement?
(a) A partial support of working class
(b) Galvanizing women in political sphere
(c) Socialistic influence among the Congress cadre
(d) All of the above

IX. In keeping with the slogan for this year's Olympics, 'Games Wide Open,' the opening ceremony took place outside a stadium setting by the river for the first time. In many respects, the Paris Games turned out to be one of the most elaborate cultural rituals since Covid swept across the world beginning in late 2019. Health restrictions forced the organizers of Tokyo 2020 and Beijing 2022 to sharply limit the scale of the festivities, with events largely closed to the public. Paris 2024, powered in part by pent-up demand for communal experiences, symbolized an international post-pandemic vibe shift.

The International Olympic Committee and French officials managed strict security measures in place. Yet the recent history of violence in France — including the 2015 terror attack in Paris that left 138 people dead and at least 416 injured — stalked public consciousness prior to the games. The geopolitical backdrop for the Paris Games was no less troubling. The war between Israel and Hamas which had crossed the six-month mark, raised fears of a protracted conflict and wider regional instability. The devastation in the Gaza Strip has provoked international outrage, isolating Israel on the global stage. Meanwhile, Russia continues to gain ground in its military offensive against Ukraine as some Western nations worry about the rise of authoritarianism. These international crises raised serious concerns that could come into play during the Games in the form of protests and other political demonstrations.

Nevertheless, Olympics organizers put up a show that stunned the throngs assembled on the boulevards of Paris, not to mention the millions of people who watched the Games unfold on their televisions and mobile devices. At the Paris 2024 Olympics, India secured a total of six medals: one silver and five bronze which was one down from the highest haul of medals from the previous Olympics. Neeraj Chopra earned a silver in men's javelin with an 89.45 throw, narrowly missing gold to Pakistan's Arshad Nadeem. Shooter Manu Bhaker made history by clinching bronze in the women's 10'm air pistol, becoming the first Indian woman to win a medal in Olympic shooting. The men's hockey team achieved a second consecutive bronze, defeating Spain 2-1, with captain Harmanpreet Singh scoring both goals.

(*Extracted, with edits and revision, from 'The Olympics are nearly here. For a weary world, they can't come soon enough'*, NBCNEWS)

47. India won a back-to-back Olympics hockey medal at:
(a) Beijing and Paris
(b) Rio and Beijing
(c) Beijing and Tokyo
(d) None of the above

48. According to the passage, what is the peculiarity of the Paris Olympics, 2024?
(a) It symbolized an international post-pandemic vibe shift.
(b) The opening ceremony took place outside a stadium.
(c) It is one of the most elaborate cultural rituals since Covid.
(d) All of the above.

49. Which of the following incidents support the argument that 'the geopolitical backdrop for the Paris Games is no less troubling'?
(a) Israel-Hamas conflict
(b) The immigrant influx in to Europe
(c) Political stability of French government
(d) All of the above

50. Which one of the following is true?
(a) Tokyo Olympics was better than Beijing Olympics.
(b) Spectators thronged for a post Covid sporting experience.
(c) Olympic games are unaffected by conflicts in a region.
(d) All of the above.

51. The highest Olympic medal tally for India was at:
(a) Beijing
(b) Rio
(c) London
(d) Tokyo

52. Where is the opening ceremony of the Paris Olympics, 2024, held?
(a) Seine River
(b) Versailles Palace
(c) Eiffel Tower
(d) Arc de Triomphe

LEGAL REASONING

X. Children come in contact with the criminal justice system either as victims or witnesses to a crime or as children in conflict with law (CICL). As CICL, they could be alleged of, accused or recognized as having broken the law by committing a crime. According to the National Crime Records

Bureau (NCRB) Report 2021, India recorded a total number of 1,49,404 instances of crimes against children in 2021 — a rise of over 16 per cent from the previous year. In terms of percentage, the top categories under crime against children were kidnapping and abduction, followed by cases registered under the POCSO Act. Further, the NCRB report revealed that of the total cases, 53,874 were registered under POCSO Sections. Sexual offences against children shows a steady ascent, with 47,221 such cases being recorded in 2020, and 47,335 cases in 2019. In 2019, as many as 32,269 cases were registered across the country, while the 2021 report registered a decline of 3.5 per cent recording 31,170 cases.

The Criminal Justice system of any country broadly refers to agencies of the government charged with enforcing law, adjudicating crime, and correcting criminal conduct. The main objective of the criminal justice system is 'deterrence', i.e., to punish the 'transgressors and the criminals' and to maintain law and order in society. Globally, children and young people are routinely exposed to various forms of violence if they are before the criminal justice system. They are at risk of physical and psychological abuse, sexual assault, and other harms, including inadequate educational opportunities, poor and outdated vocational training. They face several challenges including mental, emotional, and behavioural disorders. Children, who are victims of violence or exposed to violence during childhood, are more likely to have difficulty in school, abuse drugs or alcohol, act aggressively, suffer from depression or other mental health problems and engage in criminal behaviour as adults.

[*Extracted, with edits and revisions from 'Child Rights in the Criminal Justice System: Need for Law Reform' written by* Dr Asha Bajpai *published in the* Journal of the National Human Rights Commission, India].

53. Which of the following issues, children, who are victims of violence during childhood face in life, as per the author of the above passage?
(a) They may have difficulties in school.
(b) They may abuse drugs or alcohol and suffer from mental health problems.
(c) They may act aggressively and engage in criminal behaviours.
(d) All of the above.

54. What is the primary objective of the criminal justice system as mentioned in the passage?
(a) Rehabilitation of offenders
(b) Punishment of the offenders
(c) Reformation of the offenders
(d) Protection of victims from the offender

55. The National Crime Records Bureau (NCRB) in India is responsible for:
(a) Conducting forensic investigations of Records of Criminals
(b) Maintaining a national database of fingerprints of Criminals
(c) Compiling and analysing crime data
(d) Maintaining a national database of enforcement of criminal laws

56. Which category had the highest number of cases under crimes against children according to the NCRB Report 2021?
(a) POCSO
(b) Kidnapping and abduction
(c) Sexual Offences
(D) All of the above

57. Which one of the following is the correct expansion of the term POCSO used in the passage?
(a) Protection of Children from Sexual Offences
(b) Prosecution of Criminals of Sexual Offences
(c) Protection of Children & Women from Sexual Offences
(d) None of the above

58. What risks do children face when exposed to the criminal justice system as per the passage?
(a) Limited access to vocational training
(b) Exposed to risk of physical abuse
(c) Mental health challenges and behavioural disorders
(d) All of the above

XI. The 42nd Constitutional Amendment Act 1976 introduced the concept of environmental protection in an explicit manner into the Constitution through introduction of Article 48-A and Article 51-A (g). In many judgments, the Supreme Court ruled that both the state and its residents have a fundamental duty to preserve and protect their natural resources. The recent judgment obliquely makes way for an enforceable right, and a potential obligation on the state unless the same is overturned by an Act of Parliament.

India is signatory of various international environmental conservation treaties under which India has the binding commitment to reduce carbon emission. During the COP 21, India signed Paris Agreement along with 196 countries, under which universally binding agreement was made to limit greenhouse gas emission to levels that would prevent global temperatures from increasing to more than 1.5 degree Celsius before the industrial revolution. India has committed to generating 50% of its energy through renewable resources and will generate 500 GW of energy from non-fossil fuels by 2030, reducing the carbon emission by 1 billion ton. Additionally, India has committed to achieve net zero carbon emission target by 2070.

Supreme Court's March 21, 2024 verdict builds on the bulwark of jurisprudence in place since 1986, and, through various other judgments, the Supreme Court has recognised the right to clean environment along with right to clean air, water and soil free from pollution which is absolutely necessary for the enjoyment of life. Any disturbance with these basic elements of environment would amount to violation of Article 21. It also establishes duty of the state to maintain ecological balance and hygienic environment. Although right to clean environment has existed, by recognizing the right against climate change it shall compel the states to prioritize environmental protection and sustainable development.

(*Extracted, with edits and revision, from 'Supreme Court of India bolts Right to Life with climate justice'*, The Economic Times, 06-05-2024)

59. In which among the following, changes were introduced for environmental protection through the Constitution of India (42nd Amendment) Act?

1. Fundamental Rights
2. Fundamental Duties
3. Directive Principles of State Policy

(a) 1 & 2 only
(b) 2 & 3 only
(c) 1 & 3 only
(d) 1,2 & 3

60. The nature of binding commitment of India to reduce carbon emission through the signing of various international environmental conservation treaties especially the Paris Agreement may be described as:

(a) The signatory shall take adequate measures to reduce carbon emission.
(b) The signatory may take adequate measures to reduce carbon emission.
(c) The signatory should explore the possibility to reduce carbon emission.
(d) The signatory may formulate necessary policies to reduce carbon emission.

61. Under Article 51-A(g) of the Indian Constitution, it is specifically mentioned that citizens shall have the duty to protect and improve the natural environment that includes:

(a) Rivers & Lakes
(B) Forests & Wildlife
(C) All living Creatures
(D) Only (A) and (B)

62. As per the aforementioned passage and decision of the Supreme Court:

(a) The fundamental duty to preserve and protect natural resources is upon the State only.
(b) Citizens alone have the fundamental duty to preserve and protect natural resources.
(c) Both the state and citizens have the duty to preserve and protect natural resources.
(d) State's duty to maintain ecological balance and citizens right against climate change.

63. According to the passage, what makes India committed to reduce carbon emission?
(a) Because of being a signatory of international environmental conservation treaties.
(b) Because of the Supreme Court verdicts which obliquely make way for an enforceable right.
(c) Because of the policy decisions of Government.
(d) Because of the Constitution of India (42nd Amendment) Act.

64. The passage mentions that 'any disturbance with these basic elements of environment would amount to violation of Article 21'. Article 21 of the Constitution deals with:
(a) Right to equality
(b) Right against exploitation
(c) Right to freedom of residence
(d) Right to life and personal liberty

XII. The Contract Act 1872 deals with contract law in India, its rights, duties, and exceptions arising out of it. Section 2(h) of the Act gives us the definition of a contract, which is simply an agreement enforceable by law. To understand the difference between void agreements and voidable contracts it is important to talk about sections 2(h), 2(a), 2(i), 2(d), 14, 16 (3) and 15,24-28 of the Indian Contact Act. Void agreements, are fundamentally invalid making them unenforceable by default. These agreements cannot be fulfilled as they consist of illegal elements and they cannot be enforced even after subjecting it to both parties. However, in the case of voidable contract, the agreement is initially enforceable but it is later on denied at the option of either of the parties due to various reasons.

Unless rejected by a party, this contract will remain valid and enforceable. The party who is at the disadvantage due to any circumstance applicable to the contract has the ability to render the agreement void. A void agreement is void ab initio making it impossible to rectify any defects in it while voidable contracts can be rectified. In case of a void agreement, neither of the parties is subject to any compensation for any losses but voidable contracts have some remedies.

A valid agreement forms a contract that may again be either valid or voidable. The primary difference between a void agreement and voidable contract is that a void agreement cannot be converted into a contract.

(*Extracted with edits from* A Comparative Study of Voidable Contracts and Void Agreements)

65. Which of the following best describes a void agreement?
(a) An agreement that is valid until declared invalid by a court.
(b) An agreement that has no legal effect from the beginning.
(c) An agreement that is legally enforceable.
(d) An agreement that can be enforced if one party chooses to do so.

66. A contract between two parties to rob a bank and share the proceeds equally can be termed as:
(a) Void Contract
(b) Valid Contract
(c) Voidable Contract
(d) Legally Enforceable Contract

67. An agreement made by an adult but involving a minor child where the signatory is a minor child himself, this agreement would be:
(a) A valid and enforceable agreement
(b) A voidable agreement
(c) A void agreement
(d) An agreement that cannot be enforced by the minor

68. Which of the following scenarios would most likely result in a void agreement?
(a) An agreement signed by someone under duress
(b) A contract with mutually agreed terms to sell a house
(c) An agreement to pay 10 lakhs on getting a government job
(d) A contract with a minor who understands the terms

69. An agreement made without consideration is generally:
(a) Valid agreement
(b) Enforceable agreement
(c) Void agreement
(d) Voidable agreement

XIII. Geographical Indications (GIs) are a form of intellectual property that designates a product as originating from a specific geographic location, where a given quality, reputation, or other characteristic is essentially attributable to its geographic origin. GIs protect names that are used to identify products with specific qualities or characteristics due to their geographic origin. For example, 'Champagne' refers to sparkling wine produced in the Champagne region of France, and 'Darjeeling Tea' refers to tea grown in the Darjeeling region of India. The protection of GIs ensures that only products genuinely originating from a specific region are allowed to use the geographical name. This helps maintain the product's reputation and quality, prevents misuse or imitation, and supports local economies by promoting regional products. International agreements such as the TRIPS Agreement under the World Trade Organization (WTO) provide a framework for the protection of GIs globally.

70. Which of the following statements about Geographical Indications (GIs) is not true?
(a) GIs are protected under international law to ensure that only products from specific regions can use the GI name.
(b) The use of a GI name can be legally challenged if it is used by products not originating from the specified region.
(c) Geographical Indications (GI) can be used to any product which is licenced regardless of its place of origin.
(d) The TRIPS Agreement under the WTO establishes a framework for the protection of GIs on a global scale.

71. If a product named 'Darjeeling Tea' is produced outside of the Darjeeling region, which of the following legal actions is likely to be taken under GI protection laws?
(a) The product can still be sold but with a disclaimer about its true origin.
(b) The use of the GI name 'Darjeeling Tea' can be legally contested and potentially prohibited.
(c) The product can be sold under a different GI name of 'Not Darjeeling Tea'.
(d) The product can be marketed as 'Darjeeling Tea' and will face no legal consequences.

72. Which of the following is not a potential consequence of the misuse of a Geographical Indication?
(a) Loss of consumer trust in the authenticity of the product.
(b) Decrease in the market value of the GI-protected product.
(c) Compulsory license on the patents of the misusing entity.
(d) Potential Legal action of infringement against the misuse.

73. In the context of GIs, which of the following scenarios best illustrates the concept of 'geographic origin'?
(a) A product's name is changed to reflect its local ingredients rather than its place of production.
(b) A product is marketed with a GI name even though it is produced in a different region and country.
(c) A product is identified by a GI name that corresponds to the region where it is traditionally made/cultivated with distinctive qualities due to that location.
(d) A product is sold under a generic name with no reference to its production location.

74. Choose the most appropriate objective of the TRIPS Agreement concerning Geographical Indications:
(a) To harmonize intellectual property laws across member countries
(b) To ensure uniform product labelling standards globally

(c) To provide a framework for the protection and enforcement of Geographical Indications among WTO members
(d) To promote international trade by standardizing product names and prices

XIV. The Public Examinations (Prevention of Unfair Means) Act, 2024 that has provision for up to five years' imprisonment and a fine of up to ₹1 crore for malpractices and organized cheating in government recruitment exams was notified by the Union government and came into effect from June 21, 2024. The Bill had received assent from the President of India on the 13th February 2024. The Public Examinations (Prevention of Unfair Means) Act, 2024 mentions punishments for 'leakage of question paper or answer key', 'directly or indirectly assisting the candidate in any manner unauthorisedly in the public examination' and 'tampering with the computer network or a computer resource or a computer system' as offences done by a person, group of persons or institutions. Besides these, 'creation of fake website to cheat or for monetary gain', 'conduct of fake examination, issuance of fake admit cards or offer letters to cheat or for monetary gain' and 'manipulation in seating arrangements, allocation of dates and shifts for the candidates to facilitate adopting unfair means in examinations' are also among the offences punishable under the law.

'Any person or persons resorting to unfair means and offences under this Act shall be punished with imprisonment for a term not less than three years but which may extend to five years and with fine up to ₹10 lakh,' said the Act. A service provider, engaged by the public examination authority for conduct of examinations, shall also be liable to be punished with imposition of a fine up to ₹1 crore 'and proportionate cost of examination shall also be recovered' from it, according to the Act. Such service providers shall also be barred from being assigned with any responsibility for the conduct of any public examination for a period of four years.

[*Extracted, with edits and revisions from 'Act that Punishes Organized Cheating in Government Exams Comes into Effect' published in The Hindu dated 22-06-2024*]

75. A Bill becomes an Act only when.................
(a) Both houses of the Parliament pass with simple majority
(b) Both houses of the Parliament pass with absolute majority
(c) When the Prime Minister of India gives his approval
(d) When the President of India gives the Assent

76. A service provider, engaged by the public examination authority for conduct of examinations, indirectly helped his family member by giving hint on questions that were supposed to be asked in the examination shall
(a) be liable to be punished with imposition of a fine of ₹1 crore
(b) be liable to be punished with imposition of a fine upto ₹1 crore
(c) be liable to be punished with imposition of a fine upto ₹1 crore and the entire cost of conduct of the examination
(d) None of the above

77. An invigilator of a public examination found guilty of manipulating the seating arrangement to favour his relative writing the public examination is punished by the Court. Which among the following is the appropriate punishment as per the punishment mentioned in the above passage?
(a) Imprisonment for 1 year and fine of 1 lakh
(b) Imprisonment for 2 years and a fine of 10 lakhs
(c) Imprisonment for 3 years and fine of 15 lakhs
(d) Imprisonment for 4 years and fine of 5 lakhs

78. Identify which of the following is not an unfair means relating to the conduct of a public examination?
(a) The Coaching Centre conducting mock tests for students.
(b) The Coaching Centre offering help to its students during the examination.

(c) The Centre Superintendent of the public examination on the request of the Coaching Centre provides seating arrangement of all its students in one hall.
(d) The Centre Superintendent of the public examination indirectly assisting the candidate.

79. Who among the following is not a service provider in the context of a public examination?
(a) Coaching Centre which prepares students for passing in the public examination.
(b) Printing Press where the question paper of the public examination is printed.
(c) The Software Company that manages the website of the public examination.
(d) The Company which scans the OMR sheets of the public examination.

XV. The Supreme Court of India declared that the right to privacy is a fundamental right and that the right to informational privacy is part of this right. Subsequently, the Parliament of India enacted a new law relating to digital personal data protection. The law applies to Indian residents and businesses collecting the data of Indian residents. It also applies to non-citizens living in India whose data processing is 'in connection with any activity related to the offering of goods or services' that happens outside India. The law allows personal data to be processed for any lawful purpose. If the personal data is sensitive, then additional safeguards are to be observed. The entity processing data can do so either by taking the concerned individual's consent or for 'legitimate uses'- which include situations where an individual has voluntarily provided personal data for a specified purpose. The law requires that an individual's consent must be 'free, specific, informed, unconditional and unambiguous with a clear affirmative action' and for a specific purpose. The data collected has to be limited to that necessary for the specified purpose. A clear notice containing these details has to be provided to consumers, including the rights of the concerned individual and the grievance redressal mechanism. Individuals have the right to withdraw consent if consent is the ground on which data is being processed. The law also creates rights and obligations for individuals. These include the right to get a summary of all the collected data and to know the identities of all other entities/organizations with whom the personal data has been shared, along with a description of the data shared. Individuals also have the right to correction, completion, updating, and erasure of their data. Besides, they have a right to obtain redressal for their grievances and a right to nominate persons who will receive their data.

[*Excerpts from Anirudh Burman, 'Understanding India's New Data Protection Law'*, CARNEGIE INDIA, *October* 03, 2023]

80. An Indian company collects personal data from its users to provide personalized services. The company intends to share this data with a third-party vendor for targeted advertisements. Under the digital personal data protection law in India, what must the company do before sharing the data?
(a) Obtain explicit consent from the users
(b) Share the data by informing the users, as it is for business purposes
(c) Encrypt the data and share it with the third-party vendor
(d) Inform the third-party vendor that the data is sensitive

81. A social media platform processes user data based on the consent given during account creation. A user now wishes to withdraw consent to process their data. Under the digital personal data protection law in India, what must the platform do?
(a) Refuse to accept the withdrawal request since consent was already given
(b) Comply with the legal requirements and stop processing the data
(c) Continue processing the data but notify the user
(d) Allow withdrawal only after 30 days

82. A financial institution collects biometric data from its clients for verification purposes. If the clients wish to know what data has been collected, under the digital personal data protection law in India, what right allows them to request this information?

(a) Right to Data Portability
(b) Right to Correction
(c) Right to Access
(d) Right to Be Forgotten

83. A startup provides a health-tracking app that collects sensitive health data from users. Under the digital personal data protection law in India, what additional precautions must the startup take compared to regular personal data?

(a) No additional measures are needed
(b) Ensure explicit consent and adopt higher security standards
(c) Store the data only with the government agencies
(d) Store the data only with the hospitals and other health care institutions

84. As per the passage, what are the rights included under the digital data protection law of India?

1. Right to get the summary of collected data
2. Right to know to whom the data has been shared
3. Right to correct and update the data
4. Right to get the data removed from the database
5. Right to decide on who can receive their data
6. Right to get redressal of grievances

(a) 1, 2, 5 and 6
(b) 1, 3, 4 and 6
(c) 1, 3, 5 and 6
(d) 1, 2, 3, 4, 5 and 6

LOGICAL REASONING

XVI. While a majority of homeless groups exist solely in modernized cultures, homelessness remains a problem throughout the world. Everywhere there are people in constant search of food, water and shelter. Many of these people have nowhere to go and can find no end or relief to their suffering. Homelessness was originally believed to be a cultural problem but is now revealing itself as a global problem. It is a problem suffered by all of humanity and must be faced and solved as such. Although this problem exists everywhere, it is more severe in certain parts of the world. Due to the differing circumstances of homelessness around the world, there can be no one solution or one set of guidelines for everyone to follow.

Even the United States constantly struggles with homelessness, despite being one of the wealthiest countries in the world. According to a 2005 survey by the United Nations, 1.6 billion people lack adequate housing. The causes vary depending on the place and person. Common reasons include a lack of affordable housing, poverty, a lack of mental health services, and more. Homelessness is rooted in systemic failures that fail to protect those who are most vulnerable. Approximately 580,000 people experience homelessness on any given night in the United States, as stated by the Housing and Urban Development (HUD) Department of the United States. The number of individuals experiencing homelessness varies by region, with urban areas experiencing higher rates of homelessness compared to rural areas. The COVID-19 pandemic has exacerbated homelessness and housing insecurity, leading to increased rates of eviction, unemployment, and housing instability. Using social distancing measures to curb the virus's transmission has presented difficulties for homeless shelters and service providers in maintaining their capacity. The economic fallout from the pandemic has further strained resources and support systems for individuals and families experiencing homelessness.

(*Extracted with revisions and modifications from an article 'The impact of* COVID-19 *and housing insecurity on lower-income women' published in Journal of Social Issues, October* 3, 2022)

85. For the above paragraph, which of the following statements is true?

(a) When people in industrialized civilizations think of homelessness, they generally imagine third-world countries where poverty is rampant
(b) Generally, the impoverished are thought of to exist in third-world countries only, but they are present even in the largest cities of the world
(c) Homelessness increases due to major turbulence on the economic and cultural aspects
(d) All of the Above

86. There are several causes of homelessness; which of the following is the least likely a cause of homelessness?
(a) Violence in the home
(b) Loss of job or income
(c) Substance abuse
(d) Proper health care

87. Homelessness in the case of mental illness can be amplified because of the following reason:
(a) The stress of being homeless may exacerbate previous mental illness and encourage anxiety, fear, depression, sleeplessness and substance use.
(b) People with mental illness remain homeless for longer periods of time and have less contact with family and friends.
(c) Poor mental health predisposes individuals to homelessness and homelessness exposes individuals further to particularly severe health problems.
(d) All of the above

88. Homelessness in reference to the above paragraph can be observed most closely in the form of:
(a) Inadequate entertainment avenues
(b) Shortage of appropriate clothing
(c) Poor prospects for employment
(d) Inadequate medical services

89. Approximately how many people in America are currently experiencing homelessness on any given day?
(a) 1 million people
(b) More than 5.5 million
(c) 3.5 million
(d) 100 million

90. Which of the following is not a myth about people experiencing homelessness?
(a) People who are homeless choose to be so, by themselves
(b) People experiencing homelessness are lazy
(c) All people who experience homelessness are addicts
(d) People experiencing homelessness find it difficult to obtain a job

XVII. Being a consultant, your work consists of a deep examination of the company's environment and its internal system to notice inefficiencies and potential improvements. The interaction with the company's management and different sections to decipher their objectives, opportunities, and processes. This means that, through the use of data analysis, industry best practices, and the formulation of creative ways of solving all problems, to come up with unique solutions to all problems to increase efficiency and productivity, and hence, increase profitability for employers. This might entail operations such as logistics redesign, business process reengineering, adopting new applications, systems, or even community relation programs. People management is a critical component of change management, to make sure that all the relevant parties interpret the potential alterations positively. Also, to offer orientation and create resources to explain the changes to the group and make it comfortable with the shift. The general goal is the organization's ability to continue to grow and remain relevant with the shareholders and stakeholders in the industries it operates.

91. What is the primary responsibility of you being a company's efficient consultant?
(a) Analyzing the organization's structure, processes, and market position
(b) Managing daily operations
(c) Hiring new employees
(d) Conducting maintenance

92. With whom does a consultant work closely to understand a company's goals and challenges?
(a) Customers
(b) Higher management and various departments
(c) External vendors
(d) Competitors

93. Imagine yourself as a consultant and find what methods you will use to develop customized solutions?
(a) Intuition and guesswork
(b) Social media trends
(c) Random selection
(d) Data analysis, industry best practices, and innovative strategies

94. Which of the following might a consultant optimize to improve company efficiency?
(a) Office decoration
(b) Supply chain management
(c) Employee dress code
(d) Lunch menus

95. Why is communication the most relevant thing for a consultant?
(a) To ensure all stakeholders understand the proposed changes
(b) To organize consumer meets
(c) To update the company website
(d) To manage the human resources

96. What additional support might a consultant provide to help the team adapt to new processes?
(a) Planning a retreat for the team members
(b) Training and support
(c) Personal counselling
(d) Mental Health programs

XVIII. Read the information carefully and answer the questions based on the seating arrangement:

'Ram, Shyam, Rohit, Mohit, Rohan, Sohan, Mohan, Rakesh and Suresh are sitting around a circle facing the centre. Rohit is third to the left of Ram. Rohan is fourth to the right of Ram. Mohit is fourth to the left of Suresh who is second to the right of Ram. Sohan is third to the right of Shyam. Mohan is not an immediate neighbour of Ram.'

97. What is Rakesh's position with respect to Rohan?
(a) Eighth to the right of Ram
(b) Fourth to the left
(c) Fifth to the right
(d) Fifth to the left

98. Who is third to the right of Mohan?
(a) Shyam (b) Mohit
(c) Ram (d) None of these

99. Who is fifth to the right of Rohan?
(a) Sohan (b) Rohit
(c) Rakesh (d) Suresh

100. Who is second to the left of Rakesh?
(a) Ram (b) Mohan
(c) Mohit (d) Data inadequate

101. Who is the immediate right of Mohit?
(a) Sohan (b) Rohit
(c) Ram (d) Data inadequate

102. Who is third to the right of Sohan?
(a) Rohit (b) Rohan
(c) Rakesh (d) Shyam

XIX. India is poised for rapid economic growth, potentially spurred by a young population driving production and demand. In the process, inevitably, lifestyles are being dramatically altered for the worse. India now reports the highest growth of ultra-processed food consumption among the youth, as well as low levels of exercise and adequate sleep. Cultural changes, including smartphones and a preponderance of English in schools, are also associated with weakened family relationships. Until recently, in the absence of extensive data, the role of these factors on mental well-being, encompassing our full range of mental capability, was not well understood. Recent findings based on a large database of over 1,50,000 individuals in India are beginning to shed light on the correlates of mental well-being among adolescents. The findings are dire. There is a silent epidemic of mental ill-health in India. Previous studies have found that ownership of smartphones is 'frying' the brain. Data also suggests that it is not merely the ownership of a phone but also the early age of access that is associated with worse cognition and mental well-being as young adults. The young brain is developing and must be nurtured. These gadgets are handed to adolescents, presumably more out of convenience than sound logic. The American philosopher David Henry Thoreau remarked over 175 years ago, 'Technology is an improved means to an unimproved end.' This is an extreme position but one worth mulling. India reports the highest growth in consumption of ultra-processed foods. Some evidence suggests that these foods are as addictive as smoking. Recent data globally and from India shows a strong association between the consumption of ultra-processed foods and poor mental well-being, particularly the capacities for emotional and cognitive control.

[*Source-* V. *Anantha Nageswaran and Shailender Swaminathan, 'How our lifestyle is creating an epidemic of mental ill health'*, THE INDIAN EXPRESS, *September* 7, 2024]

103. Based on the above passage, which of the following should be the most suitable title for the passage?
- (a) Lifestyle and Mental Health
- (b) Economic Growth and Mental Health
- (c) Impact of Technology on the Youth
- (d) Language and Cultural Change

104. Consider the given statement 'Technology is an improved means to an unimproved end'. Which of the following closely reflects the meaning of the given statement?
- (a) New technologies have to be accepted by primarily focusing on its positive results
- (b) New technologies create a hindrance to the physical health of an individual
- (c) Poor mental health is a result of the invention of new technologies
- (d) New technologies should be looked upon with scepticism, considering its negative impact

105. Which of the following statements strengthens the author's argument regarding the negative use of smartphones among the youth?
- (a) Excessive use of smartphones may lead to weakened family relationships
- (b) There has to be an unhindered use of smartphones
- (c) Smartphones have economic usefulness
- (d) Ownership of smartphones at an early age results due to lack of care by parents

106. Which of the following can be a plausible solution for better mental well-being among the youth?
- (a) Limiting the correlation between physical and mental health
- (b) Limiting the research on excessive use of smartphones
- (c) Limiting the widespread consumption of ultra-processed foods
- (d) Limiting the informed use of smartphones across all age groups

107. Which of the following statements by the author lack credible evidence in the passage?
- (a) Excessive mobile usage linked to mental health issues
- (b) Providing mobiles to adolescents resulting in mental stress
- (c) Students learning the English language have weakened family relationships
- (d) Inadequate sleep and junk food resulting in mental distress

108. 'These gadgets are handed to adolescents, presumably more out of convenience than sound logic.' Which of the following is the most suitable explanation echoed by the author as per the given statement?
- (a) Logic prevails over reasoning
- (b) Logic and emotions go hand in hand
- (c) Logic taking a backseat over utility
- (d) Logic and benefits can never be understood together

QUANTITATIVE TECHNIQUES

XX. According to the estimates of the World Inequality Report 2022, in India, men earn 82 percent of the labour income, whereas women earn 18 percent of it. A woman agriculture field labourer makes ₹88 per day lesser than her male counterpart, according to the Ministry of Agriculture's data for 2020-21. While a man is paid ₹383 a day on average, a woman makes a mere ₹294 a day. The gap in their daily wages is more than the cost of two kilograms of rice. This gap differs from State to State. Field labourers, for instance, make the most money in Kerala. While a man gets ₹789 per day, a woman is paid ₹537. While this is the highest amount paid to a woman labourer in a State, it is also ₹252 lesser than what her male counterpart was paid. As of 2020-21, Tamil Nadu has the highest gender wage gap among agriculture field laborers at 112 per cent. It is followed by Goa (61 percent) and Kerala. The wage gap is the lowest in Jharkhand and Gujarat (6 percent each), but the women laborers there get paid just ₹239 and ₹247 per day, respectively.

Men earn more than women across all forms of work, the gap is greatest for the self-employed. In 2023, male self-employed workers earned 2.8 times that of women. In contrast, male regular wage workers earned 24% more than women and male casual workers earned 48% more. The gender gap in earnings is still a persistent phenomenon. However, there are differences in trends. The gender gap has increased for self-employed workers, while falling for regular wage workers. Male regular wage workers earned 34% more than women from 2019 to 2022, with the gap falling to 24% in 2023.

109. If the wages paid to men working in the agricultural sector in Goa are ₹335 on an average, what is the amount of wages paid to women in the region?

(a) ₹204 approx. (b) ₹330 approx.
(c) ₹239 approx. (d) None of these

110. With reference to the information in Ques. 109 above, which region of the below mentioned states offers the least wages to the women workers in any sector?

(a) Gujarat (b) Goa
(c) Kerala (d) Jharkhand

111. In 2023, if the average annual income of female self-employed workers is ₹250, how much do male self-employed workers earn on average?

(a) ₹550 (b) ₹673
(c) ₹700 (d) None of these

112. If a female casual worker earns ₹200 per hour, what is the hourly wage of a male casual worker, given that male casual workers earn 48% more than female casual workers?

(a) ₹480 (b) ₹296
(c) ₹248 (d) Cannot be determined

113. Assume that in 2022, the earnings gap between male and female self-employed workers was 2.5 times. In 2023, the gap increased to 2.8 times. What is the percentage increase in the earnings gap for self-employed workers from 2022 to 2023?

(a) 12% (b) 5%
(c) 4.8% (d) 24%

114. Which of the following statement is correct?

(a) The wage gap of Goa and Kerala state is less than Tamil Nadu
(b) The wage gap of Tamil Nadu is greater than Jharkhand and Gujarat
(c) Both (a) and (b)
(d) None of the above

XXI. Mr Das is working in a construction company. He has a family, including his wife and a daughter. His total monthly income includes a salary of ₹9228/- and a 10% house rent allowance. Due to increasing inflation, he is keeping a home budget that accounts for the income and expenses of the household. Out of his total monthly income, he spends 25% on food expenses, 18% on paying the house-rent, 9% on entertainment, 23% on the education of his child, 13% on medical expenses, and he saves 12% of his total monthly income.

Based on the above information, answer the following questions.

115. How much money does Mr Das pay as the house-rent?
(a) ₹1827 /- (b) ₹1661 /-
(c) ₹1783 /- (d) ₹1935 /-

116. If Mr Das gets 12% annual interest on the savings and he wishes to save ₹30,000/- in two years period, how much extra should he save in the next year?
(a) ₹1200/- (b) ₹1300/-
(c) ₹1400/- (d) There is no need for saving

117. Which of the following is true regarding the home budget of Mr Das?
(a) The total amount spent on house-rent, entertainment and education is greater than the total amount spent on food expenses, medical expenses and savings.
(b) The total amount spent on entertainment, medical expenses and education is equal to the total amount spent on house-rent, food expenses and savings.
(c) The total amount spent on savings, medical expenses and education is less than the total amount spent on house-rent, food expenses and entertainment.
(d) None of the above.

118. How much money remains for other expenses after the house-rent and savings?
(a) ₹7061/- (b) ₹7601/-
(c) ₹7106/- (d) ₹7016/-

119. If the expenditure on food and entertainment is increased by 10% due to inflation in prices, what will be the new percentage of savings in the same monthly salary?
(a) 8.4% (b) 8.6%
(c) 8.8% (d) 8.2%

120. How much total money has he spent on food and entertainment?
(a) ₹3541/- (b) ₹3461/-
(c) ₹3371/- (d) None of the above

ANSWER KEY

English Language

1. (c)	5. (b)	9. (d)	13. (d)	17. (c)	21. (d)
2. (d)	6. (a)	10. (d)	14. (d)	18. (b)	22. (a)
3. (d)	7. (d)	11. (d)	15. (d)	19. (d)	23. (b)
4. (c)	8. (c)	12. (a)	16. (a)	20. (b)	24. (c)

Current Affairs Including General knowledge

25. (c)	29. (d)	33. (b)	37. (d)	41. (b)	45. (b)	49. (a)
26. (d)	30. (d)	34. (a)	38. (d)	42. (b)	46. (d)	50. (b)
27. (d)	31. (a)	35. (a)	39. (c)	43. (a)	47. (d)	51. (d)
28. (c)	32. (c)	36. (d)	40. (d)	44. (b)	48. (d)	52. (a)

Legal Reasoning

53. (d)	58. (d)	63. (a)	68. (c)	73. (c)	78. (a)	83. (b)
54. (b)	59. (b)	64. (d)	69. (c)	74. (c)	79. (a)	84. (d)
55. (c)	60. (a)	65. (b)	70. (c)	75. (d)	80. (a)	
56. (b)	61. (d)	66. (a)	71. (b)	76. (d)	81. (b)	
57. (a)	62. (d)	67. (b)	72. (c)	77. (d)	82. (c)	

Logical Reasoning

85. (d)	89. (b)	93. (d)	97. (a)	101. (a)	105. (a)
86. (d)	90. (d)	94. (b)	98. (d)	102. (d)	106. (c)
87. (d)	91. (a)	95. (a)	99. (d)	103. (a)	107. (c)
88. (c)	92. (b)	96. (b)	100. (b)	104. (d)	108. (c)

Quantitative Techniques

109. (a)	111. (c)	113. (a)	115. (a)	117. (c)	119. (b)
110. (b)	112. (b)	114. (c)	116. (d)	118. (c)	120. (d)

CLAT 2024

ENGLISH LANGUAGE

I. In the realm of contemporary literature, the interplay between character and setting is a nuanced dance that shapes the narrative's essence. The setting, often described with painstaking detail, becomes more than a backdrop; it becomes a character, influencing the plot and character development.

Consider, for instance, the barren expanse of the desert in Jhumpa Lahiri's *The Namesake*. The arid landscape mirrors the sense of isolation felt by the protagonist, Gogol, as he navigates his identity crisis in a foreign land. the relentless sun and vast sands are not mere descriptions; they are the silent witnesses to his inner turmoil.

On the other end of the literary spectrum, there is Arundhati roy's *The God of Small Things*. the lush, vibrant Kerala backwaters are not just the setting; they are a character woven into the fabric of the story. The teeming, humid landscape reflects the complex web of human relationships and secrets that unravel in the narrative. This interplay is not confined to contemporary literature alone. In Shakespeare's timeless tragedy *Macbeth*, the eerie and foreboding setting of the Scottish moors casts a dark shadow over the characters' actions. The moors, shrouded in mist and mystery, serve as an ever-present omen of the impending tragedy.

1. In contemporary literature, how is the relationship between character and setting described in the passage?
(a) It is non-existent; characters and settings are entirely separate entities.
(b) It is a complex interplay where the setting influences the plot and character development.
(c) Characters and settings are interchangeable.
(d) Settings are insignificant in contemporary literature.

2. In the novel, *The Namesake* by Jhumpa Lahiri, what does the barren desert landscape symbolize?
(a) A thriving community.
(b) The protagonist's sense of isolation and identity crisis.
(c) A lush, vibrant setting.
(d) A happy, carefree life.

3. What role does the Scottish moors play in Shakespeare's *Macbeth*?
(a) It serves as a beautiful, serene landscape.
(b) It has no influence on the characters' actions.
(c) It is an ever-present omen of impending tragedy.
(d) It is a place for the characters to relax.

4. What does the term 'interplay' refer to in the context of the passage?
(a) A lack of interaction between characters and setting.
(b) A complex relationship where the setting influences the narrative.
(c) An insignificant connection between characters and setting.
(d) A complete separation of characters and setting.

5. Which of the following words best describes the setting in *The God of Small Things*?
(a) Boring
(b) Lush and vibrant
(c) Insignificant
(d) Dark and foreboding

6. What is the main theme discussed in the passage?
(a) The characters in contemporary literature are not influenced by their settings.

(b) Setting in literature is unimportant.
(c) In literature, settings can be as influential as characters in shaping the narrative.
(d) Settings have no role in character development.

II. The crisis of justice that is the subject matter of discussion in the media today is in fact the crisis of 'justice for the middle class'. The main difference between India and the OECD (Organisation for Economic Cooperation and Development) countries is that whereas the middle class in these countries has reasonable access to justice, in India it does not. A vocal and powerful middle class has emerged in India since 1991. It is demanding reasonable access to justice. much of the judicial reform effort will help meet this demand.

The question of justice for the poor is, however, an altogether different challenge. No country in the world has been able to secure justice for the poor. Most of the jails of the richest countries are filled with the poorest. The 'masses' are more often victims of the criminal justice system than of crime. In India as well, jails are almost exclusively filled with the poor. The civil justice system is hardly accessible to them. They are often victimised by lawyers, touts and court staff. They are docket-excluded, a new type of untouchability. the language and the logic—and the colonial and feudal culture—of the judicial system are alien to them. It rarely takes cognisance of their needs and interests.

Their main concern, therefore, is to escape the attention of the justice system, criminal and civil. A landless dalit person in the interior of Madhya Pradesh once gave me an insightful definition of a court from the perspective of the masses: 'A court is a place where you are forcibly taken by the police to be punished; no one goes to a court.' In contrast, many lawyers and judges colloquially define a court as 'a temple of justice where rights are protected'.

These sharply divergent visions mean that justice for one section is often injustice for another. Protecting the livelihood of traditional taxi and auto drivers from predatory pricing by corporate app-based taxi providers by imaginatively using the available tools of law to delay their incursion would be seen by the rich and by sections of the middle class as a failure of the judicial system, and possibly as also resulting in a downgrading of the 'ease of doing business' measure. However, the masses would see such a judicial intervention as strong evidence of a good justice system. Although the conflict over competing visions of the nation and conflicting demands from social and economic segments have confined judicial reform of judicial administration mainly to 'neutral' areas such as process reform, procedural law, technology, planning and court and case management, judge strength, and the workload of judges, there has been considerable improvement in these areas, and the judicial system has improved its performance.

[Extracted, with edits, from 'Justice and the Two Ideas of India', by G. Mohan Gopal, *Frontline*]

7. What is the central thesis of the above extract?
(a) The practice of untouchability takes various forms in modern India.
(b) The imagination of justice for the rich and poor is vastly different.
(c) Addressing judge strength and case-load management does not affect the performance of the judicial system.
(d) Protecting the livelihood of traditional taxi drivers is contrary to the goals of ease of doing business.

8. What does the author mean by 'docket-excluded' in the second paragraph?
(a) The poor do not have easy access to the justice system.
(b) Courts do not list bail petitions of poor undertrial prisoners who populate the country's jails.
(c) The poor reject the judicial system as being alien to their language and logic.
(d) The rich are excluded from the country's prisons, which are mostly populated by the poor.

9. Which of the following words best describes the experience of different segments of people with the justice system as described in the third paragraph?
(a) Symbiotic
(b) Affective
(c) Conflicting
(d) Inter-dependent

10. Which of the following statements is the author most likely to agree with?
(a) The judicial system reflects the same power relationships as those that exist in society.
(b) Access to the judicial system is determined more by a person's economic status such as wealth and income, than by their social status, such as religion and caste.
(c) The judicial system was made by the rich, for the rich, of the rich.
(d) None of the above.

11. Which of the following statements is the author most likely to disagree with?
(a) A truly representative democracy would ensure that the interests of the poor are also represented in the judicial system.
(b) The Law ensures equality both in text and in practice.
(c) The poor suffer most at the hands of lawyers and touts, compared to judges who might still pronounce judgments in their favour from time to time.
(d) All of the above.

12. What makes reform of judicial administration a 'neutral' area?
(a) Persons across socio-economic strata agree on the need to reform judicial administration.
(b) There is consensus among political parties across the ideological and regional spectrum on reforms to judicial administration.
(c) Reforms to judicial administration do not favour one class of people over another.
(d) Reform of judicial administration is mandated by the Constitution, and thus lies beyond political considerations.

III. Everything she wanted was here, at Carignano, in Kasauli. Here, on the ridge of the mountain, in this quiet house. it was the place, and the time of life, that she had wanted and prepared for all her life-as she realized on the first day at Carignano, with a great, cool flowering of relief - and at last she had it. She wanted no one and nothing else. Whatever else came, or happened here, would be an unwelcome intrusion and distraction. This she tried to convey to the plodding postman with a cold and piercing stare from the height of the ridge onto his honest bull back. unfortunately, he did not look up at her on the hilltop but stared stolidly down at the dust piling onto his shoes as he plodded on. A bullock-man, an oafish ox, she thought bitterly. She stepped backwards into the garden and the wind suddenly billowed up and threw the pine branches about as though to curtain her. She was grey, tall and thin and her silk sari made a sweeping, shivering sound and she fancied she could merge with the pine trees and be mistaken for one. to be a tree, no more and no less, was all she was prepared to undertake.

What pleased and satisfied her so, here at Carignano, was its barrenness. This was the chief virtue of all Kasauli of course-its starkness. It had rocks, it had pines, it had light and air. In every direction, there was a sweeping view - to the north of the mountains, to the south, of the plains. Occasionally an eagle swam through this clear unobstructed mass of light and air, that was all. And Carignano, her home on the ridge, had no more than that. Why should it? The sun shone on its white walls. Its windows were open the ones facing north opened on to the blue waves of the Himalayas flowing out and up to the line of ice and snow sketched upon the sky, while those that faced south looked down the plunging cliff to the plain stretching out, flat and sere to the blurred horizon.

Yes, there were some apricot trees close to the house. there were clumps of iris that had finished blooming. There was the kitchen with a wing of smoke lifting out of its chimney and a stack of wood outside its door. But these were incidental, almost unimportant.

[Extracted, with edits and revisions, from 'Fire on the mountain' by Anita desai]

13. What does the protagonist's preference for 'barrenness' and 'starkness' at Carignano suggest about her personality?
(a) She enjoys a bustling and vibrant environment.
(b) She values simplicity and minimalism in her surroundings.
(c) She prefers lush and colorful landscapes.
(d) She seeks constant stimulation and variety in her life.

14. What do you get to know about the protagonist's state of mind from her reaction towards the postman?
(a) She feels grateful for his presence and the assistance he offers.
(b) She dislikes any disturbance or interruption in her solitude.
(c) She feels suspicious and is interested in the lives of others.
(d) She is disinterested and generally unaffected by the presence of others.

15. What does the protagonist's desire to be mistaken for a pine tree reveal about her mindset?
(a) She desires to be appreciated and noticed by others in society.
(b) She has a deep admiration for the beauty of the pine trees.
(c) She feels a sense of superiority over other living beings.
(d) She yearns to one with nature and escapes from her human identity.

16. The protagonist's description of the nestlings' screams as 'shrill and maddening' shows that:
(a) She perceives the sounds to be out of tune yet soothing.
(b) She considers the nestlings to be symbols of new life and vitality.
(c) She finds the nestlings to be vexatious and irritating.
(d) She feels a sense of protectiveness and care towards the nestlings.

17. Which of the following statements are true about the protagonist's overall state of mind in Carignano?
Statement I: She experienced a sense of constant restlessness and anguish.
Statement II: She felt isolated and disconnected from her environment.
Statement III: She was content, fulfilled, and at peace with her surroundings.
(a) Statement I and II
(b) Statement II and III
(c) Only Statement II
(d) Only Statement III

18. In the light of above passage, what role does nature play in the protagonist's life at Carignano?
(a) It provides her with a source of creativity.
(b) It offers her solace, peace, and a sense of belonging.
(c) It serves as a reminder of the harsh realities of life.
(d) It serves as a constant source of distraction and intrusion for her.

IV. English literature is a vast and diverse field that has left an indelible mark on the world of letters. From the eloquent plays of William Shakespeare to the complex novels of Jane Austen and the profound poetry of William Wordsworth, english literature offers a window into the human experience. One of the luminaries of english literature is William Shakespeare, often hailed as the greatest playwright in the history of english language. His works, including *Hamlet*, *Macbeth*, and *Romeo and Juliet*, are celebrated for their exploration of human nature, love, ambition, and tragedy. His characters, such as the tormented Hamlet and the star-crossed lovers Romeo and Juliet, continue to captivate readers and audiences worldwide.

The 19th century ushered in a new era of literary giants. Jane Austen's novels, such as *Pride and Prejudice* and *Sense and Sensibility*, provide incisive social commentary through the lens of wit and romance. Austen's heroines, like Elizabeth Bennet and elinor dashwood, remain beloved literary figures known for their intelligence and resilience. The Romantic era brought forth poets like William

Wordsworth and Samuel Taylor Coleridge, who celebrated the beauty of nature and the emotional intensity of the individual. Wordsworth's 'I Wandered Lonely as a Cloud' and Coleridge's 'The Rime of the Ancient mariner' are testament to the power of the written words to evoke profound emotions and imagery. Moving towards 20th century, English literature continued to evolve. Virginia Woolf's ground-breaking novel *Mrs. Dalloway* explored the inner thoughts and lives of its characters with a modernist narrative style. Dystopian visions, as seen in George Orwell's *Nineteen Eighty-Four* provided stark warnings about the dangers of totalitarianism and the erosion of individual freedom.

Today, English literature is a global phenomenon, transcending borders and languages. Indian authors like Arundhati Roy, with her novel *The God of Small Things*, have won prestigious international literary awards. The book not only explores intricate family dynamics but also delves into the broader socio-political landscape of India. In summary, English literature is a testament to the enduring power of storytelling and the written word. It encompasses an array of authors, themes, and styles that continue to captivate and inspire readers across the world.

19. Who is often regarded as the greatest playwright in the history of English language?
(a) Jane Austen
(b) William Wordsworth
(c) William Shakespeare
(d) George Orwell

20. Which of Jane Austen's novels is known for its social commentary and witty portrayal of romance?
(a) *Nineteen Eighty-Four*
(b) *Sense and Sensibility*
(c) 'I Wandered Lonely as a Cloud'
(d) 'The rime of the Ancient mariner'

21. Who are the Romantic poets mentioned in the passage known for celebrating nature and intense human emotions?
(a) William Shakespeare and Virginia Woolf
(b) George Orwell and Samuel Taylor Coleridge
(c) William Wordsworth and Samuel Taylor Coleridge
(d) Jane Austen and Arundhati Roy

22. What is the title of Virginia Woolf's novel known for its modernist narrative style?
(a) *Pride and Prejudice*
(b) *Nineteen Eighty-Four*
(c) *Mrs. Dalloway*
(d) *The God of Small Things*

23. Identify the 20th century novel mentioned in the passage that provides a warning about the dangers of totalitarianism?
(a) *Nineteen Eighty-Four*
(b) *Romeo and Juliet*
(c) *Sense and Sensibility*
(d) 'I Wandered Lonely as a Cloud'

24. What does the passage highlight as the enduring power of English literature?
(a) Its ability to win literary awards.
(b) The diversity of its authors, themes, and styles.
(c) Its ability to captivate and inspire only British readers.
(d) The decline of storytelling.

CURRENT AFFAIRS INCLUDING GENERAL KNOWLEDGE

V. On the evening of the 10th, General Dyer arrived at Amritsar, and the Deputy-Commissioner handed over the civil power to him. He issued a proclamation by word of mouth that no meetings should be held. Two days later, after there had been no sort of riot, nor murder, General Dyer heard that a meeting was to be held at the Jallianwala Bagh. He proceeded there with about fifty troops, half British, half Indian, and a certain number of Ghurkas, armed with their kukris. the Jallianwala Bagh is an open space, half a mile square, which has one entry wide enough for three persons. The troops got in and lined up on a mound of debris. The walls, seven feet high, and the surrounding houses enclosed the people. There were, too, three alleys through which the people might have been able to pass. Within thirty seconds of the troops getting in, General Dyer gave orders to fire, and the crowd of people, estimated at anything from 5,000 to 20,000, who were sitting on the ground peacefully listening to the mob oratory, were fired on. The result of the troops' fire into the mass of people we do not know. but we do know that Dyer's own estimate of the casualties resulting from ten minutes continual individual firing, was 400 to 500 killed and 1,500 wounded. The people were not able to escape. they were people who had not offered any violence and who had not been warned. These people were shot down. After ten minutes, the ammunition was exhausted and the troops marched off, and they left 1,500 wounded there. There were men lying there for two days, dying of thirst, eating the ground, bleeding to death and nobody to look after them: Those who lived nearby came and carried away some of the wounded from the heap of dead and dying, but the unfortunate country people died there miserably of their wounds. this is what is done in 1919 in British India.

Centuries hence you will find Indian children brought up to this spot, just as they visit now the Cawnpore Well, and you can imagine the feelings of these Indians for generations over this terrible business.

[Col. Wedgwood, MP, speaking in the British Parliament, 22 December 1919]

25. Which incident is described in the passage?
(a) Baisakhi festival at Amritsar, April 1919
(b) Jallianwala Bagh Massacre, April 1919
(c) Congress Protests of April 1919
(d) Non-Cooperation Movement, April 1919

26. Why did the General Dyer order to fire on the crowd?
(a) To bring the crowd under control
(b) To scatter the crowd
(c) To teach the crowd a lesson
(d) To enforce the martial law

27. In the light of above passage, what was the intention of the speaker?
(a) To praise General Dyer
(b) To expose the deeds of General Dyer
(c) To get sympathy for the Indians who died
(d) All of the above

28. After the incident, who helped the injured and the dying people?
(a) The army
(b) The police
(c) The Civil Administration
(d) Some people who lived nearby.

29. What would be the feelings of the Indian children brought up to the spot?
(a) Friendliness to the British Rule
(b) Bitterness about the British Rule
(c) A sense of helplessness
(d) None of the above

30. What was the full name of General Dyer?
(a) Reginald Murree Harry Dyer
(b) Reginald Royce Harry Dyer
(c) Reginald Edward Harry Dyer
(d) Reginald Coleman Harry Dyer

VI. On 7th October 2023, an armed conflict broke out between Israel and Hamas-led Palestinian militants from the Gaza Strip[o] after the latter launched a multi-pronged invasion of Southern Israel. After clearing Hamas militants, the Israeli military retaliated by conducting an extensive aerial bombardment campaign on Gazan targets and followed up with a large-scale ground invasion of Gaza. more than 1,400 Israelis, mostly civilians, and more than 10,000 Palestinians have been killed in the fighting. Over 240 Israelis and foreign nationals were taken hostage and brought into the Gaza Strip.

The Hamas-led attack began in the morning of 7th October, as Palestinian militants in Gaza launched a barrage of over 5,000 rockets against Israeli cities and Kibbutzim while some 3,000 Palestinian militants breached the Gaza-Israel barrier. Over 1,000 Israeli civilians were killed in more than a dozen massacres, including the re'im music festival massacre, and military bases were attacked. Over 200 civilians and Israeli soldiers were captured or abducted and taken to the Gaza Strip. At least 44 countries, mostly from the Western world, characterized the massacres of civilians as terrorism. Hamas declared that the invasion was carried out in response to the 'desecration of the Al-Aqsa Mosque', the Gaza Strip blockade, the construction of Israeli settlements, and Israeli settler violence against Palestinians in the West bank.

Israel declared a state of war on 8th October, and its response to the attack has seen the most significant military escalation in the region since the Yom Kippur War. The current hostilities constitute the fifth war of the Gaza–Israel conflict, which is part of the broader Israeli– Palestinian conflict. In 2023, before the offensive started, an uptick in Israeli–Palestinian violence saw at least 247 Palestinians, 32 Israelis, and two foreigners killed. According to the Gaza Health ministry, as of 6 November, over 10,000 Palestinians had been killed, including 79 UNRWA staff. Israel dropped a total of 6,000 bombs during the first six days of the conflict—nearly double the number of bombs dropped by the American-led CJTF—OIR in one month during the War against the islamic State. There has been widespread killing of civilians, and human rights groups and a panel of united Nations special rapporteurs have accused both Israel and Hamas of war crimes.

31. What was the reason for Hamas-led Palestinian militants' attack on Israel?
(a) To retaliate against Israeli settler violence against Palestinians
(b) In response to the desecration of the Western Wall
(c) To protest against the construction of Palestinian settlements in the West bank
(d) To seek an end to the Gaza Strip blockade

32. What was the reaction of the international community to the killing of Israeli civilians?
(a) Condemned as terrorism by 44 countries
(b) Ignored by most of the countries
(c) Supported by the UN
(d) Praised as a necessary measure by 10 countries

33. Which of the following is not true about the historical context of the Israel Hamas Conflict?
(a) The Palestinian refugees started settling under Ottoman rule in the late 19th Century.
(b) Hamas emerged during the first Intifada in the late 1980s.
(c) Hamas was formally known as the Islamic Resistance Movement.
(d) First Intifada was a Palestinian uprising against Israeli Rule.

34. What has been the resxponse of the Israeli military to the Hamas-led attack?
(a) Declared a state of war and launched a ground invasion
(b) Conducted an aerial bombardment campaign only
(c) Asked for international intervention
(d) Captured and imprisoned the militants responsible

35. What is the current hostilities known as in the Gaza-Israel conflict?
(a) Sixth war (b) Fifth war
(c) Seventh war (d) Fourth war

36. Which major war does the current Gaza-Israel conflict resemble?
(a) Yom Kippur War
(b) Iraq War
(c) Six-day War
(d) Gulf War

VII. Today, India has become the fourth country in the world to touch the surface of the moon. This success becomes even greater when we look at the place from where India had started its journey. There was a time when India did not have the required technology and there was no support either. We used to be among the 'Third World' countries, standing in the third row. Today, India has become the fifth largest economy in the world. Today, from trade to technology, India is among the countries standing in the first row. In this journey from third row to first row, institutions like ISRO have played a major role. Today, you have taken 'Make in India' to the moon.

I have seen the photo in which our moon lander has firmly set its foot on the moon like Angad. On one hand is the confidence of Vikram while on the other hand is the bravery of Pragyan. Our Pragyan is continuously leaving its footprints on the moon. The pictures taken from different cameras, which have just been released, and I have had the privilege of seeing, are indeed amazing. For the first time, since the beginning of human civilization, for the first time in the history of lakhs of years on the earth, man is looking at the pictures of that place with his own eyes. India has done the work of showing these pictures to the world! All the scientists like you have done it. Today, the whole world is acknowledging the significance of India's scientific spirit, our technology and our scientific temperament. Chandrayaan maha Abhiyan is a success not only for India but for the entire humanity.

[Extracted from the Speech made by the Prime Minister of India Shri. Narendra Modi on the occasion of the landing of Chandrayaan 3 on 26th August 2023]

37. In what did India become the fourth country in the world?
(a) Sending a spacecraft to the moon
(b) Landing a spacecraft on the moon
(c) Landing a man on the moon
(d) Crashlanding (impacting) a spacecraft on the moon

38. What is the role of Pragyan?
(a) To move around the moon, leaving footprints
(b) To take photographs of the moon, while moving
(c) Showing these pictures to the world
(d) To record the LASER radiation

39. Name one institution that played a major role in bringing India to the forefront.
(a) Tata Industries
(b) Indian Oil Corporation
(c) ISRO
(d) Reliance Industries

40. What is the name of the moon lander and the rover?
(a) Vikram and Pragyan
(b) Pragyan-2 and Vikram
(c) Chandrayaan and Vikram
(d) Chandrayaan and Pragyan

41. Whom did the Prime minister address this to?
(a) To the people of India
(b) To the world
(c) To the students
(d) To the scientists of ISRO

42. Which of the following countries in the world had touched the surface of the moon?
(a) United States of America, USSR, China, India
(b) United States of America, Russia, China, India
(c) United States of America, USSR, France, India
(d) United States of America, Russia, Israel, India

VIII. The 18th G20 Summit, in which the heads of states and governments will meet, on September 9 and 10 will be held in India's national capital New Delhi. Over 25 world leaders along with other delegates are going to attend this mega event.

One of the largest multilateral summits, the G20 Summit presents a significant diplomatic opportunity for India, which will convene with the adoption of a joint declaration by all the member states.

India assumed the G20 Presidency on december 1 last year. The 18th G20 Summit in New Delhi is scheduled to be held on September 9 to 10.

The Group of Twenty (G20) comprises 19 Countries and the European Union. The G20 members represent around 85% of the global GDP, over 75% of the global trade, and about two-thirds of the world population.

World leaders from several countries and institutions will mark their presence at the event. They include US President Joe Biden, UK Prime minister rishi Sunak, Australian Prime minister Anthony Albanese, Canadian Prime minister Justin trudeau and French President emmanuel macron.

However, Russian President Vladimir Putin has opted out of the summit and foreign minister Sergei Lavrov will represent the country in his place. Chinese President XI Jinping has also decided to skip the event and will send country's Premier Li Qiang instead, according to sources.

The G20 Summit 2023 is being held under the theme – Vasudhaiva Kutumbakam (One earth. One Family. One Future) – centered around the value of all life including human, animal, plant, and microorganisms and their interconnectedness on the planet earth and in the wider universe.

India's Presidency of the summit holds significance as it aims to become a voice for the 'less developed' global South in a world dominated by developed nations of the West. It is also likely to take up the issue of border tension with China. India, for its part, may attempt to straighten out its diplomatic intricacies with the West after it faced challenges due to the Russia-Ukraine conflict.

[Extracted, with edits and revisions, from 'India gears up for G20 Summit: Check event venue, guest list, special invitees', *Hindustan Times*]

43. The Group of Twenty (G20) is a forum for ________. Select the correct option.
- (a) International economic cooperation
- (b) International peace and security
- (c) International cooperation for combating money laundering
- (d) All of the above

44. The G20 Summit is hosted by the incumbent 'Presidency'. The G20 Presidency is responsible for bringing together the G20 agenda in consultation with other members and in response to developments in the global economy. Which country will hold the Presidency in 2024?
- (a) India
- (b) Indonesia
- (c) Brazil
- (d) Saudi Arabia

45. Which one of the following countries is not a member of the G20?
- (a) Egypt
- (b) Mexico
- (c) Republic of Korea
- (d) Turkey

46. At every G20 Summit, the host country invites countries and institutions that are not members of the G20. Which among the following denotes the correct list of countries being G20 invitees to the Summit held in New Delhi in September 2023?
- (a) Nepal, Bangladesh, Egypt, Netherlands
- (b) Bhutan, Mauritius, Nigeria, Oman
- (c) Bangladesh, Singapore, Spain, Netherlands
- (d) Sri Lanka, Egypt, UAE, Mauritius

IX. On 26th January 1950, we are going to enter into a life of contradictions. In politics, we will have equality and in social and economic structure, continue to deny the principle of one man one value. How long shall we continue to live this life of contradictions? How long shall we continue to deny equality in our social and economic life? If we continue to deny it for long, we will do so only by putting our political democracy in peril. We must remove this contradiction at the earliest possible moment else those who suffer from inequality will blow up the structure of democracy, which this Constituent Assembly has so laboriously built up.

I feel that the Constitution is workable, it is flexible and it is strong enough to hold the country together both in peacetime and in wartime. Indeed, if I may say so, if things go wrong under the new Constitution, the reason will not be that we had a bad Constitution. What we will have to say is that man was vile?

The third thing we must do is not be content with mere political democracy. We must note that our political democracy cannot last unless there lies at the base of social democracy. What does social democracy mean? It means a way of life, which recognizes liberty, equality and fraternity as the principles of life.

However, good a Constitution may be, it is sure to turn out bad because those who are called to work it, happen to be a bad lot. However, bad a Constitution may be, it may turn out to be good if those who are called to work it, happen to be a good lot. the working of a Constitution does not depend wholly upon the nature of the Constitution.

[Excerpts from Dr. Ambedkar's address to the Constituent Assembly, 25 November 1949]

47. What is the life of contradiction referred to here?
(a) That of equality in politics but inequality in social and economic structure
(b) That of inequality in politics but equality in social and economic structure
(c) That of inequality in social structure but equality in economic structure
(d) That of equality in politics and economic structure but inequality in social structure

48. What will happen, according to Dr. Ambedkar, if we continue to deny equality in our social and economic life?
(a) There will be no injustice.
(b) Our political democracy will be in danger.
(c) Equality in social and economic life will be achieved nevertheless.
(d) Our social and economic life will be in peril.

49. What might be the cause, according to Dr. Ambedkar, if things go wrong under the new Constitution?
(a) That the Constitution was ignored
(b) That the men called upon to work the Constitution were good
(c) That the men called upon to work the Constitution were not good
(d) That the Constitution was bad and failed the people

50. What does social democracy mean?
(a) Equality before the Law
(b) Equality of opportunities
(c) Equality in social life
(d) Equality in economic life

51. When does a bad Constitution turnout to be good?
(a) When the people called upon to work it are good
(b) When the people called upon to work it are bad
(c) When the Constitution is amended
(d) None of the above

52. Which of the following statements is not correct about what Dr. B.R. Ambedkar feel about the Constitution?
(a) The Constitution is workable
(b) The Constitution is flexible
(c) The Constitution is strong enough to hold the country together in peacetime only
(d) The Constitution is strong enough to hold the country together both in peacetime and in wartime

LEGAL REASONING

X. The Indian legal system places a significant emphasis on protecting the rights and welfare of children. the Juvenile Justice (Care and Protection of Children) Act, 2015, is a vital piece of legislation in this regard. It is designed to ensure that children in conflict with the law receive special care, protection, and treatment, with the ultimate goal of their rehabilitation and reintegration into society.

One of the key provisions of the Act is the establishment of Juvenile Justice boards (JJbs) at the district level. These boards consist of a metropolitan magistrate or Judicial magistrate of the first class and two social workers, at least one of whom should be a woman. The primary function of the JJb is to determine the age of the juvenile, the circumstances in which the offense was committed, and whether the juvenile should be sent to a special home or released on probation.

The Act makes a clear distinction between a 'child in conflict with the law' and a 'child in need of care and protection.' A child in conflict with the law is one who has committed an offense, while a child in need of care and protection is a child who is vulnerable or at risk and requires special care and support.

The Act introduces a unique approach to dealing with children who are in conflict with the law. For children between the ages of 16 and 18, who have committed heinous offenses, they can be tried as adults, subject to a preliminary assessment by the Juvenile Justice board. This assessment considers the child's mental and physical capacity to commit such an offense. If the board determines that the child should be tried as an adult, the case is transferred to the regular criminal courts.

The Act also places restrictions on the publication of information that could lead to the identification of a juvenile offender. This is done to protect the privacy and future prospects of the child.

53. What is the primary objective of the Juvenile Justice (Care and Protection of Children) Act, 2015?
(a) To punish child offenders.
(b) To rehabilitate and reintegrate children in conflict with the law.
(c) To remove all forms of violence against children.
(d) To increase the age of criminal responsibility.

54. Who makes up the Juvenile Justice Board (JJB)?
(a) Two Judges
(b) A Metropolitan Magistrate and Two Lawyers
(c) A Metropolitan Magistrate or Judicial Magistrate of the first class and two Social Workers
(d) Three Police Officers.

55. What is the role of the Juvenile Justice Board (JJB)?
(a) To determine the punishment for juvenile offenders
(b) To decide whether a child should be sent to a regular prison
(c) To assess the age and circumstances of the juvenile, and make decisions on rehabilitation
(d) To prosecute child offenders

56. What is the distinction between a 'child in conflict with the law' and a 'child in need of care and protection' ?
(a) There is no distinction; both terms mean the same thing.
(b) A 'child in conflict with the law' has committed a crime, while a 'child in need of care and protection' is vulnerable or at risk.
(c) A 'child in need of care and protection' is more likely to commit crimes.
(d) A 'child in conflict with the law' is an adolescent offender.

57. Under what circumstances can children between the ages of 16 and 18 be tried as adults?
(a) They can always be tried as adults.
(b) After a preliminary assessment by the Juvenile Justice board.
(c) When they have committed any offense, regardless of the severity.
(d) When they reach the age of 18.

58. What is the purpose of placing restrictions on the publication of information related to juvenile offenders?
(a) To increase the age of criminal responsibility.
(b) To protect the privacy and future prospects of the child.
(c) To encourage public shaming of juvenile offenders.
(d) To help law enforcement track juvenile offenders.

XI. In India, the legal landscape surrounding online defamation is a subject of significant interest and debate. With the rise of social media, and online platforms, cases of online defamation have become increasingly common. defamation refers to making false statements about someone that harm their reputation. Online defamation includes defamatory statements made on the internet, including social media, blogs, forums, and other online platforms.

One critical aspect of online defamation is determining the liability of intermediaries, such as social media platforms or websites, for defamatory content posted by users. Section 79 of the information technology Act, 2000, provides a safe harbor for intermediaries, stating that they are not liable for third-party content if they act as intermediaries and follow due diligence in removing or disabling access to the content once notified.

However, determining whether an intermediary has fulfilled its due diligence obligations can be complex. The Indian Judiciary has been actively interpreting this provision. One significant case is the *Shreya Singhal vs. Union of India*, in which the Supreme Court clarified that intermediaries are required to act upon a valid court order or government directive for content removal, not upon private complaints.

The court also emphasized that the intermediaries should not take a proactive role in monitoring content, as this could potentially infringe on free speech. While the law provides a safe harbor, it does not absolve intermediaries from their responsibilities.

Online defamation cases often involve a balancing act between the right to freedom of expression and the right to reputation. The Indian legal system requires a careful examination of the content, context, and intent of the statements to determine whether they qualify as defamatory. Additionally, the plaintiff in an online defamation case must prove that the statement was false, damaging to their reputation, and made with a degree of fault, such as negligence or actual malice.

59. What is the primary focus of the passage?
(a) The rise of social media in India
(b) The legal aspects of online defamation in India
(c) The role of intermediaries in online content
(d) The importance of free speech on the internet

60. What is online defamation, as described in the passage?
(a) Making harmful statements about someone in person
(b) False statements made on the internet that harm someone's reputation
(c) Online harassment
(d) A form of political activism

61. What is the significance of Section 79 of the Information Technology Act, 2000, as mentioned in the passage?
(a) It defines defamation laws in India.
(b) It provides safe harbor for intermediaries in cases of online defamation.
(c) It regulates the content on social media platforms.
(d) It allows private complaints against online defamation.

62. According to the Supreme Court in the *Shreya Singhal vs. Union of India* case, under what circumstances should intermediaries act in response to content removal?
(a) Upon receiving a private complaint.
(b) Upon a valid court order or government directive.
(c) Proactively to monitor content.
(d) Only if the content is found to be defamatory.

63. How does the Indian legal system balance the Right to Freedom of Expression and the Right to Reputation in online defamation cases?
(a) By favoring freedom of expression over reputation
(b) By favoring reputation over freedom of expression
(c) By carefully examining the content, context, and intent of statements
(d) By absolving intermediaries of their responsibilities

64. In an online defamation case, what must the plaintiff prove about the defamatory statement?
(a) That it was political activism.
(b) That it was made with good intentions.
(c) That it was true and intended to inform the public.
(d) That it was false, damaging to their reputation, and made with a degree of fault.

65. What is the role of intermediaries in the context of online defamation cases?
(a) To actively monitor and censor content.
(b) To act upon private complaints for content removal.
(c) To completely absolve themselves of liability.
(d) To encourage online defamation.

XII. The Editors Guild of India has expressed concern over the 'Draconian provisions' of the Press and Registration of Periodicals (PRP) Bill, 2023, that can have an adverse impact on freedom of the press.

The Guild added: 'Editors Guild of India would like the proposed bill to ensure that publishing of news in India remains free of encumbrances and intrusive checks on publishers by the registrar, and that the primary emphasis of the registrar and the PRP remains 'registration' and not 'regulation', as the latter has the potential of restricting freedom of the press.

'In the definitions section, the term 'specified authority' gives power to government agencies beyond the Press registrar, to conduct the functions of the registrar, which could even include police and other law enforcement agencies. Given the intrusive, expansive, and vague nature of powers that the bill in any case allows to the Press registrar, the power to further delegate this power to other government agencies including law enforcement agencies is deeply distressing,' the Guild said.

The statement says Sections 4(1) and 11(4) allow the registrar to deny the right to bring out a periodical and cancel the certificate of registration of a periodical to persons convicted of 'terrorist act or unlawful activity' or 'for having done anything against the security of the State'.

'Interestingly, the Prb Act, 1867, had no such provisions. Given the liberal and arbitrary use of UAPA (which is the basis for defining 'terrorist act' and 'unlawful activity'), as well as other criminal laws, including sedition, against journalists and media organisations to suppress freedom of speech, the Guild is deeply concerned by the introduction of these new provisions, and the way they can be misused to deny the right to bring out news publications to persons who are critical of governments,' it said.

Among the other worrisome provisions listed by the Guild is Section 6(b), which gives power to the Press Registrar (as well as any other 'specified authority') to enter the premises of a periodical to 'inspect or take copies of the relevant records or documents or ask any questions necessary for obtaining any information required to be furnished'.

[Extracted, with edits and revisions from 'editors Guild of India expresses concern over Draconian provisions of the Press and registration of Periodicals bills, 2023' published in the telegraph dated 07-08-2023]

66. The PRP Bill defines 'newspaper' to mean a periodical of loose-folded sheets usually printed on newsprint and brought out daily or at least once in a week, containing information on current events, public news or comments on public news. Who among the following is covered by the definition of newspaper?

(a) Mr. X publishing news content on digital media.
(b) Mr. Y publishing books containing the comments of the public on public news.
(c) Mr. Z publishing news content in print media on weekly basis.
(d) All of the above

67. Who among the following is not eligible to publish a periodical as per the PRP bill?

(a) Mr. A convicted of waging war against Government of India.
(b) Mr. B accused of unlawful activities under the unlawful Activities Prevention Act.
(c) Mr. C accused of terrorist activities under the unlawful Activities Prevention Act.
(d) All of the above

68. Which of the following is a threat to the freedom of Press in India?

(a) Liberal use of unlawful Activities Prevention Act against Journalists refrains journalists from tracing and publishing investigative articles because they apprehend that they might be linked with criminals.
(b) Use of Sedition laws against journalists under the guise that through their articles they are promoting hatred and exciting disaffection against the government.
(c) Levy of GST on newspapers.
(d) Both (a) and (b).

69. The PRP Bill defines 'specified authority' to mean a District Magistrate or Collector or such other officer as the State Government or, as the case may be, Union territory Administration may, by notification, specify. The PRP Bill is criticised by Editors Guild of India because:

(a) The definition of specified authority is too wide and can include even officers below the level of Collector. The PRP Bill enables the specified authority to perform the functions of Press registrar General.
(b) The PRP bill confers various powers on the Press registrar General including the power to register, deny registration, cancel the registration, etc.
(c) The PRP Bill enables the specified authority to enter the premises of a periodical for inspection.
(d) All of the above

70. Freedom of press is not specifically guaranteed under the Constitution of India but is implied in Article 19(1)(a), i.e. freedom of speech and expression, Therefore, freedom of press is part of fundamental rights.

(A) Freedom of press being a fundamental right, no law can be made for registration and denial of registration of newspapers.
(b) Fundamental rights are not absolute rights and reasonable restrictions can be imposed on the exercise of fundamental rights and therefore, laws such as PRP bill can be enacted.
(C) Freedom of press being a fundamental right, journalists and press is exempt from the operation of general criminal law of the country.
(d) None of the above

71. PRP Bill denies the right to publish periodicals to a person who has been found to have committed a terrorist act and has been convicted by a competent Court in India. Which of the following is the most appropriate reason?

(a) The right to publish a periodical is denied because criminals do not possess any fundamental rights.
(b) The right to publish a periodical is denied because such a person is a threat to the society and nation.
(c) The right to publish a periodical is denied because they may not be neutral in reporting and may incite violence and spread disaffection against the state being themselves involved in Terrorist Acts.
(d) All of the above.

XIII. There are some advantages of the digital Personal data Protection Act (dPdPA), 2023. For instance, for the first time, personal data belonging to or identifying children will have to be classified separately, with such data carrying a greater degree of security and privacy. The law also seeks to reduce the rate and impact of data breaches targeting Indian businesses. The digital Personal data Protection law, however, goes a step beyond by imposing penalties for cases where data is breached as a result of a lack of implementation of adequate security controls. However, it could be said that the law isn't balanced, because it provides wide exemptions to the processing of personal data to the government. For instance, data can be processed 'in the interest of prevention, detection, investigation or prosecution of any offence ... in India.' These kinds of exemptions are dangerous as they stand to legitimise widespread and unwarranted collection of data under the guise that such collection and processing may ultimately be useful for preventing or deterring a crime.

Security agencies will have significant authority to collect and retain any data whatsoever, as is typically the case with exemptions relating to the maintenance of sovereignty, integrity, security of the state, preservation of public order, prevention of offences, and incitement to commit offences. The law also exempts processing of personal data held outside of India. The government is also exempt from being required to delete any data that it possesses, regardless of the purpose it may have been collected for, on the request of an individual, or by way of a prescribed data retention period.

The government is not bound by purpose limitations, allowing data collected for one specified purpose be used for a new, incompatible purpose, which stands in contrast to the regulations imposed on businesses.

[Extracted, with edits and revisions from 'digital Personal data Protection Law raises Questions About Consistency with Right to Privacy ruling' published in the Wire dated 22-08-2023]

72. Mr. Lal was suffering from a rare disease and the data relating of that was collected by the government. Suppose the dPdPA, 2023 provides exemptions for the government relating to data deemed 'necessary for research, archiving or statistical purposes', if the personal data is not to be used to take any decision specific to a data principal and such processing is carried on in accordance with such standards as may be prescribed.

Which of the following is the most appropriate?

(a) The personal data of Mr. Lal can be preserved by the government till the research on rare disease is complete.
(b) The data can only be used for taking any decision regarding Mr. Lal.
(c) The personal data of Mr. Lal's health conditions and his personal data can be preserved by the private hospital forever and used for research by them without his consent.
(d) All of the above

73. Suppose the DPDPA, 2023 provided exemption for the processing of personal data for the purpose of ascertaining the financial position of any person who has defaulted in payment of amount due on loan taken from a nationalised bank. Mr. X commits a default in repayment of EMI of loan taken from a nationalized bank.

(a) The bank can demand access to and process the personal data of Mr. X relating to family history of ailments from which Mr. X or his family was suffering.
(b) The bank can process the personal data of Mr. X viz., the particulars of the family, wife, children, brothers etc.
(c) The bank can process the data of Mr. X for the purpose of ascertaining the assets and liabilities of the defaulter.
(d) All of the above.

74. Suppose Mr. Y, a citizen of India, is working in an MNC in New Zealand since 2021. The MNC has obtained personal details of the employee for the purpose of recovering the amount of indemnity bond, if Mr. Y left the job within three years of joining.

(a) Mr. Y can file an application in India for protection of his digital personal data under the DPDPA if he leaves the job in September 2023, and returns to India.
(b) Mr. Y, being a citizen of India, can claim protection against the MNC for misuse of his personal data even while serving in New Zealand.
(c) The DPDPA 2023 is not applicable since the data is held outside India.
(d) The DPDPA 2023, is not applicable since the data has been obtained before the enactment of DPDPA.

75. If personal data is defined as any data about an individual who is identifiable by or in relation to such data, which of the following shall be classified as the personal data?

(a) Name of the person
(b) Full residential address
(c) Aadhar number
(d) All of the above

76. In which of the following cases, the access to personal data shall be granted and the person whose data is accessed and processed cannot claim personal data protection?

(a) Mr. Z has committed many robberies and police wants to access his Aadhar details and fingerprint data for the purpose of tracing Mr. Z.
(b) It is apprehended that a person identified as Mr. G would spread hatred among various communities which would lead to riots and Police intends to use the mobile number and other personal details of Mr. G for the purpose of preventing such crimes.
(c) Both (a) and (b)
(d) Neither (a) nor (b)

77. Which of the following is correct?

(a) Personal data collected by a health service provider can be sold to an insurance agency by the service provider without the consent of the concerned person.

(b) Personal data collected by the government can be used for whatever purpose.

(c) Personal data collected by the insurance company can be sold to mobile companies for mobile marketing without the consent of the concerned person.

(d) All of the above

XIV. The Supreme Court on September 1 held that a child born of a void or voidable marriage can inherit the parent's share in a joint Hindu family property. A three-judge bench headed by Chief Justice of India D.Y. Chandrachud however clarified that such a child would not be entitled to rights in or to the property of any other person in the family. Avoidable marriage is one that is made invalid by the husband or wife through a decree. A void marriage is invalid at its very inception.

Chief Justice Chandrachud said the first step to the inheritance of a child from a void or voidable marriage would be to ascertain the exact share of his parent in the ancestral property. this could be done by means of conducting a 'notional partition' of the ancestral property and calculating how much of the property the parent would have got immediately before his death. Once the share of the deceased parent in the property is ascertained through such a notional partition, his heirs, including his children by means of void or voidable marriage, would be entitled to their portions in the share.

The Chief Justice said that Section 16 of the Hindu Marriage Act has statutorily conferred legitimacy to children born out of void or voidable marriages. In fact, Chief Justice Chandrachud pointed out that Section 16(3) stipulates that children from void and voidable marriages would have a right to their parents' property. The court said the intent of granting legitimacy to such children in the Hindu Marriage Act should also be reflected in the Hindu Succession Act, which governs inheritance. Children from void or voidable marriages come within the ambit of 'legitimate kinship' and cannot be regarded as illegitimate by the Hindu Succession Act when it comes to inheritance.

The case before the three-judge bench was focused on an amended provision in the Hindu marriage Act, Section 16(3). The case was referred to a larger bench in 2011 after a division bench of the apex court refused to follow past precedents and championed the cause of children born out of illegitimate marriages.

'With changing social norms of legitimacy in every society, including ours, what was illegitimate in the past may be legitimate today. The concept of legitimacy stems from social consensus, in the shaping of which various social groups play a vital role.' Justice Ganguly, who authored the 2011 judgment, had observed.

During the hearings on the reference, Chief Justice Chandrachud had agreed with the Division Bench's findings that children from void and voidable marriages had rights over the property, whether self-acquired or ancestral, of their parents.

[Extracted with edits and revisions from 'Children from void, voidable marriages entitled to parents' share in ancestral property: Supreme Court', by Krishnadas Rajagopal, *The Hindu*, https://www.thehindu.com/news/national/children-from-void-voidable-marriages-are- legitimate-can-claim-rights-in-parents-properties-sc/article67259229.ece]

78. Ashima and Ashok got married to each other in a traditional Hindu ceremony in Kolkata, after which they both moved to the USA, where Ashok had a job. In the USA, they had a child, whom they named Gogol. many years later, Ashima found that Ashok was already married to Sushma before their wedding in Kolkata. Ashok and Sushma also had a child from their marriage, Arpita, who was older than Gogol by 4 years. Ashok explained to Ashima that although he had no intention of cheating on her, he had to keep his marriage to Sushma a secret since his parents would have never agreed as Sushma belonged to a different caste. Ashima is shocked to learn that her marriage to Ashok is void as per Hindu marriage laws since Ashok was already married before their wedding. She is trying to explore possibilities so that Gogol doesn't lose his inheritance from his father's side of the family. Based on your reading of the passage, what do you think is the correct position with respect to Gogol's inheritance rights?

(a) Gogol could claim the entirety of Ashok's share of the ancestral property.
(b) Gogol would inherit the entire ancestral property as the only son of Ashok.
(c) Gogol would inherit his share from within Ashok's share of the full ancestral property without prejudice to the inheritance of other legal heirs, including Arpita.
(d) Only Sushma and Arpita are the rightful legal heirs of Ashok.

79. In the above fact scenario, consider a property that was purchased by Ashok from his own earnings in the USA, thereby not making it part of ancestral property but instead falling in the category of self-acquired property. upon Ashok's death, who would have inheritance rights over the said property?

(a) Sushma and Ashima
(b) Sushma, Ashima, Arpita, and Gogol, as they are all his rightful legal heirs.
(c) Sushma, Arpita, and Gogol
(d) Sushma and Arpita

80. Based on your reading of the passage, how did the Hindu Marriage Act influence the outcome of the case on inheritance? Select one option from below:

(a) The amended provisions of the Hindu Marriage Act grant legitimacy to children from voidable marriages and therefore this logic should be extended to children born of voidable and void marriages under the Hindu Succession Act.
(b) The amended provisions of the Hindu Marriage Act give legitimacy to the second marriage and therefore this should also have an impact on the Hindu Succession Act.
(c) The amended provisions of the Hindu Marriage Act grant legitimate status to children from void or voidable marriages and therefore this should also extend to the Hindu Succession Act.
(d) The Hindu Marriage Act has no bearing on the case in question.

81. 12-year-old Kausalya was married off to 23-year-old Dashrath in her maternal home in Uttar Pradesh. She completed her education after her marriage and went on to get a job as a teacher at a government school. Dashrath's family, however, was opposed to her taking up a job outside the house and insisted that she should stay at home and look after her 2 sons, Ram and Lakshman. Kausalya, however, was very excited about starting her new job and sought advice from her younger sister, Vershini, who was training to be a lawyer. Vershini advises her that since she was married before she turned 18, her marriage was voidable and she could get it annulled. Kausalya, who was not very happy in her marriage, considers this option but is worried that her sons may lose their inheritance. Select the option that denotes correctly the status of Ram and Lakshman to inherit their father's ancestral property.

(a) Kausalya's children cannot inherit Dashrath's ancestral property but can inherit his self-acquired property.
(b) Both Ram and Lakshman can inherit their father's share of the ancestral property irrespective of the voidable status of their parent's marriage.
(c) If Kausalya decides to annul her voidable marriage, she and her sons would lose all rights of inheriting ancestral property from Dashrath.
(d) Ram and Lakshman can only inherit ancestral property from their mother's side since she decided to annul the voidable marriage.

82. Ajay is married to 2 women, Diya and Riya, and both don't know of each other. He was married to Diya first, when they were both around 23 years of age and studying together in college. They have no children. He later got married to Riya in a temple, and she had no idea about his first marriage with Diya. Ajay and Riya have 2 children, Raj and Rani. One day, Riya found out about Diya from one of Ajay's college friends. She wants to divorce Ajay but finds out that her marriage to him is void since he was already married at that time. At a loss, she goes to a lawyer to find out about the rights of her children to inherit property. Which is the most legally sound advice that the lawyer could give to her?

(a) He would say that her children can still inherit property from Ajay thanks to the Supreme Court judgment.
(b) He would advise her to get her marriage registered so that they can inherit property.
(c) He would advise her to ignore her marriage with Ajay since it is anyway a void marriage.
(d) He would advise her to speak to Diya and sort it out with her so that her children can inherit property since she would have the final say.

83. In the above scenario, Riya wants to know if there is any way in which the judgment can come to her aid while inheriting property owned by Ajay. What would the correct position of law?

(a) No, she cannot inherit property as the judgment merely talks about the Rights of children from void marriages.
(b) Yes, she should fight for her rights to inherit property.
(c) Yes, Ajay would have to give her property since he cheated on her.
(d) She would get an equal share of property as Diya, since they are both his wives who got married to him without knowing about each other.

84. Srimati's first marriage was void due to being within the prohibited degree of relationship. Dhanalakshmi, who is the daughter of Srimati from her first marriage confronts her mother once she finds her identity, demanding her share in her mother's ancestral property. Srimati, however, subsequently married Dhrupad and has 2 daughters with Himira and Shira and is not interested in giving any property to Dhanalakshmi. Dhanalakshmi decides to assert her right in a court of law. How would Dhanalakshmi's share be determined?

(a) Dhanalakshmi would not have any right in her mother's share of the property since the right of inheritance pertains only to father's share of property.
(b) Dhanalakshmi could demand a notional partition and get a share from Srimati's portion of her ancestral property.
(c) Being a child from a void marriage, Dhanalakshmi has no rights of inheritance.
(d) It is Srimati's decision as to whom she gives Rights in her property.

LOGICAL REASONING

XV. Words remain an enigma, their presence within human sphere is a unique mystery. They form the intricate tapestry that convinces us of our existence, blurring lines between fact and fiction. An engagement with words is the most captivating, enchanting, and sometimes daunting encounter with the world. A word, a symbolic entity formed from the ethereal, exists neither as animate nor inanimate, yet pulsates with life. It can emanate warmth or coldness, absorb emotions, or stand as dry as a rock. Words can provoke smiles and elicit joy. They are like glow-worms, momentarily dispelling the surrounding darkness and act as life-saving rafts amid the tumultuous ocean waves. Words grant us the ability to explore the universe, and 'to see a world in a grain of sand.' as William blake noted. They impart a semantic existence to the lifeless, and bestow aesthetic form upon the formless. Scriptures say the word is the world. I say the world within the word is the abode of faith.

85. What is the central theme of the passage?

(a) The history of the human language
(b) The impact of words on human existence
(c) The importance of storytelling
(d) The mystery of human cognition

86. According to the passage, what does a 'word' symbolize?
(a) An inanimate object
(b) An animate entity
(c) A tangible entity
(d) An intangible concept

87. How does the passage describe words' ability to affect emotions?
(a) Words can only evoke positive emotions.
(b) Words can absorb emotions and become emotion themselves.
(c) Words have no impact on emotions.
(d) Words can be devoid of emotions.

88. 'An engagement with words is the most captivating, enchanting, and sometimes daunting encounter with the world.'
Which of the following conclusions can be drawn from the above statement?
(a) Words can be used to manipulate others.
(b) The power of words should be used carefully.
(c) Words can capture the atrocities of the world.
(d) Words can paint a picture of the world in all its different colours.

89. Which of the following strengthens the author's idea of words being 'like glow-worms momentarily dispelling the surrounding darkness'?
(a) Words help in understanding reality.
(b) Words illuminate the mind of the reader.
(c) Words help in escaping reality.
(d) Words cast darkness in the mind of the reader.

90. In the context of the passage, what is the significance of the 'world within the word'?
(a) It refers to the power of language to create inspiration, energy and faith.
(b) It signifies the author's love for the global community.
(c) It represents the mysteries hidden in language.
(d) It describes the author's mission to explore different cultures.

XVI. Students have been abuzz over how Artificial Intelligence tools can do their homework and programmers over how these can increase their productivity or take away their jobs. As much as digitization has transformed the country in recent years, there is a widespread feeling that at some point around the horizon, AI shall rejig everything in even more fundamental, fantastic, and frightening ways. This is why deciding how the coming changes should be regulated is very important. TRAI has made a strong case for an independent statutory authority to ensure the responsible development and use of AI in the country, a global agency along similar lines shall likely be pitched at the G20 leaders' summit, and interestingly even American MNC Microsoft has floated a blueprint for AI governance in India. The great size and diversity of its 'data points' make India of great interest to all developers of AI Technologies.

But India is only at their receiving end, nowhere close to the US and China's advances. Although lately, it is becoming obvious how much state censorship is encumbering China's Large Language modeling, the country is still very much in the game with PhDs in fields related to AI investments in AI chip hardware design, and domestic generative models like Wu Dao. The scientific accomplishments of India's Chandrayaan mission have seen it being wooed for various international space collaborations. This promises spinoff technological benefits across Indian industry and is also geostrategically useful. Likewise, it is only with sufficient AI prowess that India shall really get to play at the high table of global rule-making for AI.

Knowing how much Indians' future shall be shaped by generative AI needs matching efforts to create indigenous models. In this and at this stage, a proactive government role is key, rather than just waiting on some large corporation to do the needful. Missing this bus will after all be even more costly than missing the chip research one. Plus, GOI alone can push academia-industry collaborations with the necessary weight and urgency. This does not let other institutions off the hook. A US judge has rejected the copyright for an AI-generated artwork. Indian courts should start engaging with the broader issue of non-human agency rather than wait for precedence to be set elsewhere. Indian schools need to think beyond the ban-ChatGPT mindset. Let us lead instead of only being led.

[Extracted from 'First, get the tech: Unless India develops domestic AI heft, it wouldn't play any meaningful part in global regulatory efforts', *Times of India*]

91. Which of the following is the author most likely to agree with?
(a) The best way to deal with the advancement of AI is to leave its regulation to market forces.
(b) Government-driven control of AI is inefficient and shall promote red-tapism.
(c) Private companies with their large capital and infrastructure design the most efficient AI governance models.
(d) Government-led initiatives of AI regulation and development lead to efficient outcomes.

92. Which of the following, if true, would most strengthen the main argument of the passage?
(a) Governments that lead the initiative on regulating and responding to the advancement of AI tools benefit the most from them.
(b) Governments that don't engage with generative AI and remain at its receiving end stay risk-averse with nothing to lose.
(c) Governments that actively incentivise MNCs to participate in AI governance make the most out of the advancements in the field.
(d) Governments that explore models of public-private partnership strike the right balance in regulating generative AI.

93. Based only on the author's statement that 'Indian courts should start engaging with the broader issue of non-human agency rather than wait for precedence to be set elsewhere', which of the following would the author be most likely to agree with?
(a) Courts should take the initiative by being innovative and laying down rules where no precedents exist.
(b) Courts should wait for precedents and in the meantime refrain from engaging with the challenges presented by generative AI.
(c) Courts should stop relying on precedents and decide cases on the basis of judicial wisdom.
(d) Precedents are the best possible safeguard against arbitrary decision-making.

94. If the information in the passage above is correct, which of the following must necessarily be true?
(a) AI regulation is the responsibility of the legislature alone.
(b) AI regulation is the responsibility of courts and can't be addressed through standalone statutory rules.
(c) AI regulation is a collaborative effort involving all the institutions of the State.
(d) AI regulation is the domain of private industry.

95. Based on the author's arguments, which of the following would result in weakening, rather than strengthening India's position at the forefront of generative AI?
(a) Investing in indigenous AI chip hardware design and domestic generative models.
(b) Exploring spinoff technological benefits with other scientific advancements like the Chandrayaan mission.
(c) Introducing generative models like Wu Dao which have demonstrated success in other jurisdictions.
(d) Locally developing technologies such as indigenous AI models.

96. The author states that, 'missing this bus will after all be even more costly than missing the chip research one.' For this statement to be true, with which of the following statements about chip research must the author most likely agree?
(a) India lead chip research from its frontiers.
(b) India was right to leave regulation of chip industry and research to MNCs.
(c) India should have proactively played a role in responding to new research in chip technology.
(d) The failure to respond to new developments in chip technology was a bigger loss than the potential failure to regulate generative AI.

XVII. Imagine you have just been appointed as a consultant for a manufacturing company that is experiencing a decline in its production efficiency. The company produces a wide range of products, and the management is concerned about the overall output. Your task is to identify the root causes of this decline and recommend solutions.

As you begin your investigation, you gather information and observe the following:

- The company recently introduced a new production system that is more automated but requires highly specialized operators.
- The workforce has reported a lack of motivation and job satisfaction, which has led to increased absenteeism.
- There have been several breakdowns in the new machinery, leading to production delays and quality issues.
- The company's competitors have adopted similar automation technologies and are experiencing increased productivity.
- Customer complaints about product quality have increased in recent months.

97. Based on the information provided, which of the following is a potential root cause of the decline in production efficiency?
(a) The introduction of a new production system
(b) Lack of motivation and job satisfaction among the workforce
(c) Increased absenteeism
(d) Breakdown in machinery

98. What makes the introduction of the new production system a potential contributing factor to the decline in efficiency?
(a) The system is highly automated.
(b) It requires specialized operators.
(c) The machinery is prone to breakdowns.
(d) Competitors have adopted similar technologies.

99. What is a critical difference between the company's situation and that of its competitors?
(a) Both the company and its competitors have introduced new production systems.
(b) The competitors have experienced increased customer complaints.
(c) The company's workforce lacks motivation and job satisfaction.
(d) The company's machinery is prone to breakdowns.

100. How might the increased absenteeism affect production efficiency?
(a) It might lead to increased quality issues.
(b) It might result in longer machinery breakdowns.
(c) It could lead to delays in production.
(d) It has no impact on production efficiency.

101. What could be a possible solution to address the decline in production efficiency?
(a) Hire more specialized operators for the new system.
(b) Implement a motivation and job satisfaction program for the workforce.
(c) Upgrade the machinery to reduce breakdowns.
(d) Purchase new machinery to replace the automated system.

102. Based on the information provided, what is a potential consequence of increased customer complaints about product quality?
(a) It indicates that the company's competitors are also experiencing quality issues.
(b) It suggests that the company's products are meeting customer expectations.
(c) It may lead to a loss of customers and reputation damage.
(d) It shows that the company's automated system is performing well.

XVIII. In a world where aspirations for upward mobility are fervent, the opportunities for achieving such dreams remain limited. When one generation falls short, the mantle of ambition passes to the next, embedding within it a heavy burden of responsibility. Failing to meet these expectations can lead to profound sorrow, and in the direct cases, even to suicide. It's in this landscape that coaching institutes assume a significant role, cultivating an atmosphere of uncertainty among students and parents. A stark discrepancy emerges between preparation for board examinations and competitive tests, amplifying the inequalities that plague the education system. The coaching industry's massive marketing campaigns further exacerbate the situation, with some strategies veering into ethical grey areas. The tests themselves, designed to be more challenging than standardised exams, set the stage for feelings of inadequacy and self-doubt when not conquered. Our educational system is tailored to gauge an individual's merit through examinations. Eminent thinker Michael J Sandel dubs this system the 'tyranny of merit', a sentiment echoed by the Supreme Court of India. Upholding the OBC reservation judgment, the Court called for a deeper evaluation of the 'idea of merit', highlighting its nuanced nature. Merit as a concept remains shrouded in misunderstanding and often goes unexamined within school curriculum. Adapting to new living arrangements, sourcing nourishing meals, battling isolation, and grappling with commutes form the backdrop against, which education unfolds. For marginalised communities and gender minorities, these hurdles are often amplified. Social media algorithms exacerbate mental health concerns, sowing loneliness and impeding attention spans and creativity. Technology emerges as a potential equaliser in this landscape. Online platforms now offer preparation opportunities from the comfort of one's home. Government-curated or market-driven content could usher in a new era of accessibility.

[Extracted, with edits and revisions from *'Kota suicides: Coaching institutes manufacture insecurity — moving beyond the tyranny of merit might help'* authored by Akash Kumar and published in **The Indian Express** dated September 2, 2023]

103. As per the author, which one of the following is not likely leading to suicide among the students?
(a) Incorrect marketing strategies by the coaching institutes
(b) Burdening of ambitions by one generation to another
(c) Creation of hostile environment by the coaching institutes
(d) Living in a surrounding with different background and culture

104. Which of the following is not true regarding the education system as per the opinion of the author?
(a) It is primarily based on the merit of the students.
(b) Merit of the students is not the determining factor.
(c) Examination plays a pivotal role in the education system.
(d) An individual's merit cannot be identified without examination.

105. Which of the following strengthens the argument regarding the 'idea of merit' as per the above-mentioned passage?
(a) True merit is multifaceted and extends beyond performance in a single competitive examination.
(b) Pervasive inequalities can only be identified with the help of a single competitive examination.
(c) True merit is not multifaceted and does not extend beyond performance in a single competitive examination.
(d) The school education ensures the proper implementation of the idea of merit.

106. Which of the following is correct regarding the inequalities mentioned by the author?
(a) There is no difference between the preparation of board and competitive examination.
(b) Education system accommodates the inequalities.
(c) Competitive examination leads to social equality.
(d) There are existing inequalities which are enlarged by the competitive examinations.

107. Which of the following statements reflects the use of online platforms for education as per the author?
(a) It provides equal opportunity to all the students irrespective of caste or creed.
(b) It encourages the students to prepare for examination.
(c) It should be the only means to education.
(d) It cannot be accessed by majority of the people due to technological impediments.

108. Which one of the following is not a challenge for quality education?
(a) Influence of social media.
(b) Mental health of the students and parents.
(c) Availability of online resources.
(d) Lack of competitive atmosphere among the peers.

QUANTITATIVE TECHNIQUES

XIX. Automobiles are the most preferred mode of transport because they allow us to cover large distance quickly. resultantly, vehicles have been developed that run on diesel, petrol and even on electricity, which is a remarkable innovative development. During a survey about the percentage wise distribution of cars in four different states, the information regarding ratio between the diesel engine cars, petrol engine cars and electric cars was collected. Total number of cars for which data was collected was 8000. Of these, State 1 had 15% of the total cars in the ratio of 3:4:1 (diesel, petrol and electric); State 2 had 20% of the total cars in the ratio of 5:3:2 (diesel, petrol and electric); State 3 had 30% of the total cars in the ratio of 4:5:3 (diesel, petrol and electric), and; State 4 had 35% of the total cars in the ratio of 7:5:2 (diesel, petrol and electric).

Based on the above information, answer the following questions.

109. If 45% of the electric cars in State 4 are air conditioned (AC) and remaining are non-AC, What is the number of non-AC cars?
(a) 380 (b) 240
(c) 220 (d) 180

110. Number of petrol cars in State 2 is how much percentage more than the number of diesel cars in State 1?
(a) 4.67% (b) 9.23%
(c) 3.33% (d) 6.67%

111. What is the ratio of diesel cars in State 4 to electric cars in State 3?
(a) 7:3 (b) 3:7
(c) 7:4 (d) 4:7

112. Compute the percentage of total electric cars to total cars in all the States.
(a) 19.37% (b) 18.37%
(c) 18.73% (d) 19.57%

113. What is the difference between number of petrol cars in State 3 and diesel cars in State 1?
(a) 350 (b) 400
(c) 500 (d) 550

114. What is the average number of diesel cars in all the States?
(a) 810 (b) 862.5
(c) 886 (d) 912.5

XX. A survey was conducted about the population of a particular region having working population of three lacs and information was collected about self-employed persons, casual wage workers, regular salaries employees of both urban and rural areas of the region. Self-employment is a key source of income in both rural and urban areas but it is more prevalent in rural areas (56% of the rural population) than in urban areas (40% of the urban population). Rural population was 48% of the total population. Regular salaried workers in urban areas were 48% of the urban population whereas in rural areas, regular salaried workers constituted 12% of the rural population. During the survey, the casual wage workers were found to be more common in rural areas than in urban areas. Casual wage workers in rural areas were 32% of the rural population whereas it was 12% of the urban population in urban areas.

Based on the above information, answer the following questions.

115. By what percentage the number of self-employed workers in rural areas is more than the number of self-employed workers in urban areas?
(a) 29.23 (b) 33.24
(c) 35.01 (d) 34.32

116. What is the ratio of urban and rural working population?

(a) 12:13 (b) 11:12
(c) 13:12 (d) 03:08

117. If urban population of the region increased from 52% to 56% and percentage of self employed in urban region remains same, then number of self-employed people in urban areas are:
(a) 66,840 (b) 68,640
(c) 62,700 (d) 67,200

118. What is the total number of regular salaried employees of the region?
(a) 90,216 (b) 91,260
(c) 92,160 (d) 96,210

119. What is the percentage of regular salaried employees in rural areas corresponding to the number of casual wage workers in urban areas?
(a) 72.3% (b) 79.8%
(c) 88.7% (d) 92.3%

120. If 60% of the total working population of the region were self-employed in rural areas and 40% of total population were self-employed in urban areas, then what is the ratio of rural self-employed to urban self-employed?
(a) 2:3 (b) 3:2
(c) 13:18 (d) 18:13

ANSWER KEY

English Language

1. (b)	5. (b)	9. (c)	13. (b)	17. (d)	21. (c)
2. (b)	6. (c)	10. (a)	14. (b)	18. (b)	22. (c)
3. (c)	7. (b)	11. (b)	15. (d)	19. (c)	23. (a)
4. (b)	8. (a)	12. (c)	16. (c)	20. (b)	24. (b)

Current Affairs Including General Knowledge

25. (b)	29. (b)	33. (a)	37. (b)	41. (d)	45. (a)	49. (c)
26. (c)	30. (c)	34. (a)	38. (b)	42. (a)	46. (c)	50. (c)
27. (b)	31. (a)	35. (b)	39. (c)	43. (a)	47. (a)	51. (a)
28. (d)	32. (a)	36. (a)	40. (a)	44. (c)	48. (b)	52. (c)

Legal Reasoning

53. (b)	58. (b)	63. (c)	68. (d)	73. (c)	78. (c)	83. (a)
54. (c)	59. (b)	64. (d)	69. (d)	74. (c)	79. (c)	84. (b)
55. (c)	60. (b)	65. (c)	70. (b)	75. (d)	80. (c)	
56. (b)	61. (b)	66. (c)	71. (c)	76. (c)	81. (b)	
57. (b)	62. (b)	67. (a)	72. (a)	77. (b)	82. (a)	

Logical Reasoning

85. (b)	89. (a)	93. (a)	97. (b)	101. (b)	105. (a)
86. (d)	90. (a)	94. (c)	98. (b)	102. (c)	106. (d)
87. (b)	91. (d)	95. (c)	99. (c)	103. (a)	107. (b)
88. (d)	92. (a)	96. (c)	100. (c)	104. (b)	108. (c)

Quantitative Techniques

109. (c)	111. (a)	113. (d)	115. (a)	117. (d)	119. (d)
110. (d)	112. (b)	114. (b)	116. (c)	118. (c)	120. (b)

CLAT 2023

ENGLISH

I. I grew up in a small town not far from Kalimpong. In pre-liberalization India, everything arrived late: not just material things but also ideas. Magazines — old copies of Reader's Digest and National Geographic — arrived late too, after the news had become stale by months or, often, years. This temporal gap turned journalism into literature, news into legend, and historical events into something akin to plotless stories. But like those who knew no other life, we accepted this as the norm. The dearth of reading material in towns and villages in socialist India is hard to imagine, and it produced two categories of people: those who stopped reading after school or college, and those — including children — who read anything they could find. I read road signs with the enthusiasm that attaches to reading thrillers. When the itinerant kabadiwala, collector of papers, magazines, and rejected things, visited our neighbourhood, I rushed to the house where he was doing business. He bought things at unimaginably low prices from those who'd stopped having any use for them, and I rummaged through his sacks of old magazines. Sometimes, on days when business was good, he allowed me a couple of copies of Sportsworld magazine for free. I'd run home and, ignoring my mother's scolding, plunge right in — consuming news about India's victory in the Benson and Hedges Cup....

Two takeaways from these experiences have marked my understanding of the provincial reader's life: the sense of belatedness, of everything coming late, and the desire for pleasure in language. .... Speaking of belatedness, the awareness of having been born at the wrong time in history, of inventing things that had already been discovered elsewhere, far away, without our knowledge or cooperation, is a moment of epiphany and deep sadness. I remember a professor's choked voice, narrating to me how all the arguments he'd made in his doctoral dissertation, written over many, many years of hard work (for there indeed was a time when PhDs were written over decades), had suddenly come to naught after he'd discovered the work of C.W.E. Bigsby. This, I realised as I grew older, was one of the characteristics of provincial life: that they (usually males) were saying trite things with the confidence of someone declaring them for the first time. I, therefore, grew up surrounded by would-be Newtons who claimed to have discovered gravity (again). There's a deep sense of tragedy attending this sort of thing — the sad embarrassment of always arriving after the party is over. And there's a harsh word for that sense of belatedness: "dated." What rescues it is the unpredictability of these anachronistic "discoveries" — the randomness and haphazardness involved in mapping connections among thoughts and ideas, in a way that hasn't yet been professionalised.

[Extracted, with edits and revisions, from "the Provincial Reader", by Sumana Roy, *Los Angeles Review of Books*]

1. What use was the kabadiwala (waste picker) to the author?

(a) The kabadiwala bought up all her magazines.

(b) The kabadiwala's stock of books and magazines were of interest to the author.

(c) The kabadiwala was about to steal the author's magazines.
(d) The author ordered books online which the kabadiwala delivered.

2. What according to the author is essential about the experience of being a 'provincial reader'?
(a) Belatedness in the sense of coming late for everything.
(b) Over-eagerness.
(c) Accepting a temporal gap between what was current in the wider world and the time at which these arrived in the provincial location.
(d) None of the above

3. Why did the author feel a sense of epiphany and deep sadness?
(a) Because the things that felt special and unique to the author, were already established and accepted thought in the wider world.
(b) Because the author was less well-read than others.
(c) Because the author missed being in a big city.
(d) All the above

4. What does the word 'anachronistic' as used in the passage, mean?
(a) Rooted in a non-urban setting
(b) Related to a mofussil area
(c) Connected with another time
(d) Opposed to prevailing sensibilities

5. Which of the following options captures the meaning of the last sentence best?
(a) Though the author feels provincial, she pretends to be from the metropolis.
(b) Though the author feels dated in her access to intellectual ideas, her lack of metropolitan sophistication lets her engage with the ideas with some originality.
(c) Though the author is aware of the limitedness of her knowledge, she is confident and can hold her own in a crowd. She is also proud of her roots in the small town.
(d) All the above

II. Until the Keeladi site was discovered, archaeologists by and large believed that the Gangetic plains in the north urbanised significantly earlier than tamil Nadu. Historians have often claimed that large scale town life in India first developed in the Greater magadha region of the Gangetic basin. This was during the 'second urbanisation' phase. The 'first urbanisation phase' refers to the rise of the Harappan or indus Valley Civilisation. Tamil Nadu was thought to have urbanised at this scale only by the third century BCE. The findings at Keeladi push that date back significantly. ... Based on linguistics and continuity in cultural legacies, connections between the Indus Valley Civilisation, or IVC, and old Tamil traditions have long been suggested, but concrete archaeological evidence remained absent. Evidence indicated similarities between graffiti found in Keeladi and symbols associated with the IVC. It bolstered the arguments of dissidents from the dominant North Indian imagination, who have argued for years that their ancestors existed contemporaneously with the IVC. ... All the archaeologists I spoke to said it was too soon to make definitive links between the Keeladi site and the IVC. There is no doubt, however, that the discovery at Keeladi has changed the paradigm. In recent years, the results of any new research on early India have invited keen political interest, because proponents of Hindu nationalism support the notion of Vedic culture as fundamental to the origins of Indian civilisation. ... the Keeladi excavations further challenge the idea of a single fountainhead of Indian life. They indicate the possibility that the earliest identity that can recognisably be considered 'Indian' might not have originated in North India. That wasn't all. In subsequent seasons of the Keeladi dig, archaeologists discovered that Tamili, a variant of the Brahmi script used for writing inscriptions in the early iterations of the Tamil language, could be dated back to the sixth century BCE, likely a hundred years before previously thought. So not only had urban life thrived in the Tamil lands, but people who lived there had developed their own script. "The evolution of writing is attributed to Ashoka's edicts, but 2600 years ago writing was prevalent in Keeladi," Mathan Karuppiah, a proud Madurai local, told me. "A farmer could write his own name on a pot he owned. The fight going on here is 'You are not the one to teach me to write, I have learnt it myself.' "

[Excerpted from "the dig", by Sowmiya Ashok, *Fifty-Two*]

6. What was the assumption about the origin of urban life in India before the Keeladi dig?
(a) The origins lay in the northern Gangetic plains, which urbanised earlier than the south.
(b) The Indus Valley Civilization was the first urban civilization of India.
(c) The second urbanization was known to be in the Magadha empire.
(d) Both (A) and (b)

7. "The Keeladi excavations further challenge the idea of a single fountainhead of Indian life." — in elaboration of this sentence, which of these options follows?
(a) Dominant theories of how urban and modern life came about in ancient India were proved wrong by the Keeladi archaeological dig.
(b) Neither the Indus Valley Civilization, nor the ancient urban civilization of Magadha are clear explanations of how urban life emerged in the Keeladi region of Southern India in the third century BCE.
(c) The Keeladi archaeological dig proved that Indian urban and modern life emerged independently in several historical periods and geographies, and no one theory is enough to explain it.
(d) None of the above

8. Language, including a script similar to the Brahmi script, emerged in Keeladi in the sixth century BCE. Which of the following is the most convincing conclusion from this statement?
(a) Keeladi is a centre of culture and learning far superior to any others in ancient India.
(b) People of Keeladi were illiterate and could not use language to inscribe on their pots and pans.
(c) Ancient urban history of India, as we know it today, could significantly be altered by the findings of the advances achieved by the Keeladi civilization.
(d) All the above

9. BCE is the acronym for:
(a) Before the Common Era
(b) Before Colloquial Era
(c) Before Chapel Eternal
(d) Behind Christ Era

10. "A farmer could write his own name on a pot he owned. The fight going on here is 'You are not the one to teach me to write, I have learnt it myself.' " — these sentences imply:
(a) That the Keeladi civilization was an inegalitarian one.
(b) That the Keeladi civilization did not conserve the access to education and literacy only for the elite.
(c) That the farmers of the Keeladi civilization were also potters.
(d) All the above

III. The call of self-expression turned the village of the internet into a city, which expanded at time-lapse speed, social connections bristling like neurons in every direction. At twelve, I was writing five hundred words a day on a public LiveJournal. By twenty-five, my job was to write things that would attract, ideally, a hundred thousand strangers per post. Now I'm thirty, and most of my life is inextricable from the internet, and its mazes of incessant forced connection—this feverish, electric, unliveable hell.

The curdling of the social internet happened slowly and then all at once. The tipping point, I'd guess, was around 2012. People were losing excitement about the internet, starting to articulate a set of new truisms. Facebook had become tedious, trivial, exhausting. Instagram seemed better, but would soon reveal its underlying function as a three-ring circus of happiness and popularity and success.

Twitter, for all its discursive promise, was where everyone tweeted complaints at airlines and moaned about articles that had been commissioned to make people moan. The dream of a better, truer self on the internet was slipping away. Where we had once been free to be ourselves online, we were now chained to ourselves online, and this made us self-conscious. Platforms that promised connection began inducing mass alienation. The freedom promised by the internet started to seem like something whose greatest potential lay in the realm of misuse.

Even as we became increasingly sad and ugly on the internet, the mirage of the better online self continued to glimmer. As a medium, the internet is defined by a built-in performance incentive. In real life, you can walk around living life and be visible to other people. But on the internet—for anyone to see you, you have to act. You have to communicate in order to maintain an internet presence. And, because the internet's central platforms are built around personal profiles, it can seem—first at a mechanical level, and later on as an encoded instinct—like the main purpose of this communication is to make yourself look good. Online reward mechanisms beg to substitute for offline ones, and then overtake them. This is why everyone tries to look so hot and well-travelled on Instagram; why everyone seems so smug and triumphant on Facebook; and why, on twitter, making a righteous political statement has come to seem, for many people, like a political good in itself. The everyday madness perpetuated by the internet is the madness of this architecture, which positions personal identity as the centre of the universe. <u>It's as if we've been placed on a lookout that oversees the entire world and given a pair of binoculars that makes everything look like our own reflection</u>.

[Extracted, with edits and revisions, from *Trick Mirror: Reflections on Self-Delusion*, by Jia Tolentino, Random House, 2019.]

11. Which of the following statements can be inferred from the above passage?
(a) The internet expanded very slowly
(b) The internet can be used to cause harm
(c) The internet is addictive
(d) The main purpose of social media platforms is to dissuade people from showing off

12. All the following statements are 'truisms', except:
(a) The internet has changed the way the world works.
(b) A preference for cat videos can reveal a lot about your personality.
(c) Like with any tool, digital technology has both advantages and disadvantages.
(d) Only time can tell what the future holds.

13. Which of the following comes closest to the underlined sentence in the passage?
(a) The way we use the internet says a lot about who we are.
(b) The internet has reduced the distance between people living across the world.
(c) The internet has the ability to customise what we access based on our identity.
(d) The internet only shows us what we don't want to see.

14. Which of the following is a metaphor?
(a) The village of the internet
(b) This feverish, electric, unliveable hell
(c) Three-ring circus of happiness and popularity and success
(d) All the above

15. Which of the following categories best describes this piece of writing?
(a) Non-fiction essay (b) Fiction
(c) Academic paper (d) Poem

IV. Down by the sandy banks of the Yamuna River, the men must work quickly. At a little past 12 a.m., one humid night in May, they pull back the black plastic tarp covering three boreholes sunk deep in the ground. They then drag thick hoses toward a queue of 20-odd tanker trucks idling quietly with their headlights turned off. The men work in a team: While one man fits a hose's mouth over a borehole, another clambers atop a truck at the front of the line and shoves the tube's opposite end into the empty steel cistern attached to the vehicle's creaky frame. 'On kar!' someone shouts in Hinglish; almost instantly, his orders to 'switch it on' are obeyed. Diesel generators, housed in nearby sheds, begin to thrum. Submersible pumps, installed in the bore-hole's shafts, drone as they disgorge thousands of gallons of groundwater from deep in the earth. The liquid gushes through the hoses and into the trucks' tanks. The full trucks don't wait around. As the hose team continues its work, drivers nose down a rutted dirt path until they reach a nearby highway. There, they turn on their lights and pick up speed, rushing to sell their bounty to factories and hospitals, malls and hotels, apartments and hutments across this city of 25 million. Everything about this business is illegal: the boreholes dug without permission, the trucks operating without permits, the water sold without testing or treatment. 'Water work is night work,' says a middle-aged neighbour who lives near the covert pumping station and requested anonymity. 'Bosses arrange buyers, labour fills tankers, the police look the other way, and the muscle makes sure that no one says nothing to nobody.' teams like this one are ubiquitous in Delhi, where the official water supply falls short of the city's needs. A quarter of Delhi's households live without a piped-water connection; most of the rest receive water for only a few hours each day. So residents have come to rely on private truck owners—the most visible strands of a dispersed web of city councillors, farmers, real estate agents, and fixers who source millions of gallons of water each day from illicit boreholes, and sell the liquid for profit. The entrenched system has a local moniker: the water-tanker mafia. A 2013 audit found that the city loses 60 percent of its water supply to leakages, theft, and a failure to collect revenue. The mafia defends its work as a community service, but there is a much darker picture of Delhi's subversive water industry: one of a thriving black market populated by small-time freelance agents who are exploiting a fast-depleting common resource and in turn threatening India's long-term water security.

[Extracted, with edits and revisions, from: "At the mercy of the Water mafia", by Aman Sethi, *Foreign Policy*]

16. Which of the following can be inferred from the passage?

(a) The water tanker mafia's operations, though illegal, are justified given the vital service they provide to the people of Delhi.

(b) The water supplied by the water tanker mafia is potentially contaminated.

(c) Private truck owners play the most important role in the operations of the water tanker mafia.

(d) The water supplied by the water tank mafia is meant primarily for residential use.

17. Which of the following, used in the passage, suggests that the illegal supply of groundwater is not a recent phenomenon?

(a) Entrenched

(b) Ubiquitous

(c) Long-term water security

(d) Fast-depleting common resource

18. Which of the following seems to be the author's main concern in the passage?

(a) Delhi's water supply infrastructure does not adequately cater to all its residents.

(b) The illegal operations of the water tank mafia do not depend on the complicity of a range of actors, including the police and city councillors.

(c) The petty profiteering of a few actors comes at the immense cost of India's sustainable access to water.

(d) All the above

19. All of the following are sounds you can hear as the water tankers are filled, except:

(a) Creaking (b) Thrumming

(c) Droning (d) Gushing

20. Which of the following words from the passage means 'hidden'?

(a) Illicit (b) Idling

(c) Subversive (d) Covert

V. English encodes class in India. It does so by sliding into the DNA of social division: income, caste, gender, religion or place of belonging. The threat it poses to social cohesion has worried public commentators across the political spectrum. In an address delivered as independent India's Parliament dilly-dallied over the suggestion to replace English with regional languages as the medium of instruction for higher education, Gandhi said, 'This blighting imposition of a foreign medium upon the youth of the country will be counted by history as one of the greatest tragedies. Our boys think, and rightly in the present circumstances, that without English they cannot get government service. Girls are taught english as a passport to marriage.'

A hundred years later, the language continues to be seen as a tool of exclusion. The problem now is about inequality of access. 'to be denied English is harmful to the individual as well as our society,' writes Chetan Bhagat, self-appointed leader of a class war set off by unequal access to English.

Bhagat, an engineer-turned-investment banker, wrote his first college romance in English in 2004. Then only a certain kind of person—someone who grew up reading, writing and speaking the language—wrote books in English—big words, long sentences, literary pretension, heavy with orientalism. In the ten years since Bhagat put the popular in 'popular' English fiction, he has written six other novels and sold millions of copies all told. With every new book, all written in deliberately simple English, Bhagat has recruited thousands of new soldiers in his crusade against what he calls the 'caste system around the language'. Bhagat even has a term for Indians who 'have' English: E1. 'These people had parents who spoke English, had access to good English-medium schools—typically in big cities, and gained early proficiency, which enabled them to consume English products such as newspapers, books and films. English is so instinctive to them that even some of their thought patterns are in English. These people are much in demand.' The people E1 presumably control, through a nexus of privilege built on ownership of English, are E2: 'probably ten times the E1s. They are technically familiar with the language. [But] if they sit in an interview conducted by E1s, they will come across as incompetent, even though they may be equally intelligent, creative or hard-working.'

The situation may not be so comically stark. The haves and have-nots may not exactly fit into Bhagat's stereotypes of urban, sophisticated rich people and provincial, uncultured poor. His argument does not factor in many other walls around English in India. You are more likely to learn English if you are born a man rather than a woman, high caste rather than low caste, south Indian rather than north Indian. There is more than one kind of E1 and more than one kind of E2. And there is more than one way E2s can overthrow E1s. One is to speak it like they know it.

[Extracted, with edits and revisions, from *Dreamers: How Young Indians Are Changing the World*, by Snigdha Poonam, Penguin Viking, 2018.]

21. Which of the following can be inferred about the author's views on English in contemporary India?
- (a) The ability to speak English in India depends on place and social identity.
- (b) English is not an Indian language.
- (c) English language fluency does not necessarily imply competence.
- (d) People's views on English are divided along political lines.

22. Who among the following would defy Chetan Bhagat's neat categorisation of Indian English-speakers into E1 and E2?
- (a) Savitha, an above-average student in an English medium school in Mumbai, belongs to an upper-middle class family. Public speaking makes her extremely nervous and she fumbles through all her interviews.
- (b) Moin, once a milkman in Ranchi, learns English at the age of 17. After a lot of hard work, he becomes an instructor of spoken English at a thriving institute.
- (c) Both (A) and (b)
- (d) Neither (A) nor (b)

23. Which of the following best describes the author's response to Bhagat's views on English?

(a) The author dismisses his views as a self-appointed expert.
(b) The author completely agrees with his views.
(c) The author neither agrees nor disagrees with his views.
(d) The author considers his views and finds that they lack nuance.

24. Which of the following can be inferred from Gandhi's views with respect to English in post-independence India?
(a) English should not be taught as a subject in Indian universities.
(b) English proficiency is vital in order to gain entry into the bureaucracy.
(c) Indian women cannot get rich if they do not know english.
(d) None of the above

25. All the following pairs of words are synonyms, except:
(a) Stark, sharp
(b) Sophisticated, spoilt
(c) Crusade, campaign
(d) Cohesion, unity

VI. 'So pick a bird,' Iff commanded. 'Any bird.' This was puzzling. 'The only bird around here is a wooden peacock,' Haroun pointed out, reasonably enough. Iff gave a snort of disgust. 'A person may choose what he cannot see,' he said, as if explaining something very obvious to a very foolish individual. 'A person may mention a bird's name even if the creature is not present and correct: crow, quail, hummingbird, bulbul, mynah, parrot, kite. A person may even select a flying creature of his own invention, for example winged horse, flying turtle, airborne whale, space serpent or aeromouse. To give a thing a name, a label, a handle; to rescue it from anonymity, to pluck it out of the Place of Namelessness, in short to identify it — well, that's a way of bringing the said thing into being. Or, in this case, the said bird or imaginary Flying Organism.'

'That may be true where you come from,' Haroun argued. 'But in these parts, stricter rules apply.'

'In these parts,' rejoined blue-bearded Iff, 'I am having time wasted by someone who will not trust in what he can't see. How much have you seen, eh? Africa, have you seen it? No? Then is it truly there? And submarines? Huh? Also, hailstones, baseballs, pagodas? Goldmines? Kangaroos, Mount Fujiyama, the North Pole? And the past, did it happen? And the future, will it come? <u>Believe in your own eyes and you'll get into a lot of trouble, hot water, a mess.</u>' With that, he plunged his hand into a pocket of his auberginey pajamas, and when he brought it forth again it was bunched into a fist. 'So take a look, or I should say a gander, at the enclosed.' He opened his hand, and Haroun's eyes almost fell out of his head. Tiny birds were walking about on Iff's palm; and pecking at it, and flapping their miniature wings to hover just above it. And as well as birds there were fabulous winged creatures out of legends: an Assyrian lion with the head of a bearded man and a pair of large hairy wings growing out of its flanks; and winged monkeys, flying saucers, tiny angels, levitating (and apparently air-breathing) fish. 'What's your pleasure, select, choose,' Iff urged. And although it seemed obvious to Haroun that these magical creatures were so small that they couldn't possibly have carried so much as a bitten-off fingernail, he decided not to argue and pointed at a tiny crested bird that was giving him a sidelong look through one highly intelligent eye.

[Extracted, with edits and revisions, from *Haroun and the Sea of Stories*, by Salman Rushdie, Granta & Penguin, 1990.]

26. If Iff is right, which of the following statements is true?
(a) You should only trust what you cannot see
(b) Naming something is the only way to make it unreal
(c) You should only trust what you can see
(d) Naming something is one way to make it real

27. Which of the following applies to Iff?
(a) He speaks in contradictions
(b) He has a habit of speaking in synonyms
(c) He uses proverbs to express ideas
(d) He uses metaphors to describe things

29. Which of the following most accurately describes what the underlined sentence means in the context of the passage?
(a) Do not restrict your knowledge only to what you can physically see
(b) Accept everything you see uncritically
(c) Trusting your senses is a recipe for success
(d) Learn not to appreciate viewpoints other than your own

29. All the words below are related in meaning, except:
(a) Levitate (b) Fly
(c) Hover (d) Gander

30. What does 'fabulous' mean in the passage?
(a) Very good (b) Unbelievable
(c) Mythical (d) Enormous

CURRENT AFFAIRS INCLUDING GENERAL KNOWLEDGE

VII. Former Governor of a State and National democratic Alliance (NDA) candidate Droupadi Murmu was elected the 15th President of India, the first tribal woman to be elected to the position and the youngest as well. She was declared elected on thursday after four rounds of counting, although she had crossed the half-way mark after the third round of counting itself, posting an unassailable lead over her rival and the Opposition's candidate who conceded the election thereafter. Prime Minister Narendra Modi was the first to greet Ms. Murmu at her residence in New Delhi after the third round of counting showed that she had crossed the half-way mark.

Ms. Murmu hails from the Santhal tribe and was born in the district of Mayurbhanj, coming up the hard way in life, graduating and teaching in Odisha before entering electoral politics at the local body level and later being elected MLA and serving as a minister in the Biju Janata Dal-BJP coalition government from 2000 to 2004. She remained an MLA till 2009, representing rairangpur in Odisha, a town that burst into celebrations since her name was announced as a candidate for the post of President of India. She was known to intervene in stopping amendments to the Chota Nagpur tenancy Act that was being brought in by the BJP government of Raghubar Das, which involved changing land use in tribal areas.

[Excerpt taken and edited from "Droupadi Murmu elected 15th President of India", *The Hindu*]

31. Before Droupadi Murmu, India had only one other female president, Pratibha Patil. When did Patil serve as the President of India?
(a) 2007–2012 (b) 2005–2010
(c) 2012–2017 (d) 2006–2011

32. President Murmu has earlier served as a Governor of which State?
(a) Odisha (b) Bihar
(c) Jharkhand (d) West Bengal

33. The first presidential election was held by the election Commission in which year?
(a) 1952 (b) 1950
(c) 1948 (d) 1949

34. The Rashtrapati Bhavan was formerly known as the Viceroy's palace (during colonial times). Where did the Governor General reside before the transfer of the British capital to Delhi in 1911?
(a) Belvedere House (b) Raisina Palace
(c) Secretariat Building (d) Writers' Building

35. Who among the following was a candidate in the elections for the Vice President of India in 2022?
(a) R. Venkataraman
(b) Yashwant Sinha
(c) M. Venkaiah Naidu
(d) Margaret Alva

36. Voting in an Indian Presidential election is through:
(a) A first-past-the-post system through a single transferable vote cast in a secret ballot
(b) A proportional representation system through a single transferable vote cast in a secret ballot
(c) A proportional representation system through a single transferable vote cast in an open ballot
(d) A first-past-the-post system through a single transferable vote cast in an open ballot

37. Who was the first dalit to hold the office of the President of India?
(a) Ram Nath Kovind
(b) V.V. Giri
(c) Neelam Sanjiva Reddy
(d) Kocheril Raman Narayanan

VIII. "I want everyone to understand that I am, in fact, a person," wrote LaMDA in an "interview" conducted by engineer blake Lemoine and one of his colleagues. ....Lemoine, a software engineer at Google, had been working on the development of LaMDA for months. His experience with the program, described in a recent Washington Post article, caused quite a stir. In the article, Lemoine recounts many dialogues he had with LaMDA in which the two talked about various topics, ranging from technical to philosophical issues. These led him to ask if the software program is sentient. In April, Lemoine explained his perspective in an internal company document, intended only for Google executives. But after his claims were dismissed, Lemoine went public with his work on this artificial intelligence algorithm—and Google placed him on administrative leave........Regardless of what LaMDA actually achieved, the issue of the difficult "measurability" of emulation capabilities expressed by machines also emerges. In the journal *Mind* in 1950, mathematician [1] proposed a test to determine whether a machine was capable of exhibiting intelligent behaviour, a game of imitation of some of the human cognitive functions.

[Extracted, with edits and revisions, from "Google engineer Claims AI Chatbot is Sentient: Why that matters", by Leonardo de Cosmo, *Scientific American*]

38. Whose name has been replaced with '[1]' in the passage above?
(a) Alan Turing (b) Peter Hilton
(c) Albert einstein (d) Kurt Gödel

39. Garry Kasparov, (then) world chess champion, was defeated in 1997 by a supercomputer in a chess tournament. What was the name of this supercomputer?
(a) Deep Mind (b) Deep Blue
(c) Watson (d) Blue Gene

40. *The Emperor's New Mind: Concerning Computers, Minds and The Laws of Physics*, published in 1989, was written by a British mathematician who won the Nobel Prize in Physics for 2020. Who was this mathematician?
(a) Donna Strickland
(b) Max Tegmark
(c) Peter Higgs
(d) Roger Penrose

41. What kind of computing model resembles the way in which biological neurons exchange signals in the human brain ?
(a) Neural network
(b) Cognitive computing
(c) Natural language processing
(d) Data mining

42. What is the full form of 'LaMDA'?
(a) Landing Macro Data Applications
(b) Language Model for Mialogue Applications
(c) Large Model Data Applications
(d) Last Mile Mialogue Assessment

43. Meta's newly released, fully trained large language Ai model is called:
(a) FTP (b) OPT
(c) HTTP (d) SMTP

44. What is the name of the Ai-enabled legal research assistive tool launched by the Supreme Court of India in April 2021?
(a) SURAM (b) GPT-3
(c) SUPACE (d) E-Courts

IX. As a result of FIFA's restrictions on players wearing **[1]** rainbow armbands during the 2022 World Cup in Qatar, the German Football Association (DFB) has taken the matter to the Court of Arbitration for Sport (CAS). In a protest against FIFA's rule regarding the armband meant to support the **[2]** community, the German players covered their lips in a team picture taken before their 2–1 defeat to Japan.

On Wednesday, Germany played against Japan. Before the game, FIFA warned the DFB of "severe" athletic fines if they breached tournament regulations by allowing their captain to wear the **[1]** armband, which promotes diversity and inclusion. The DFB told German captain Manuel Neuer not to wear the rainbow armband during the game.

If CAS rules quickly against the suspension's legality, Neuer might continue to wear the captain's armband for Germany's next game against Spain on Sunday. CAS has set up a special ad hoc branch for this World Cup to ensure that applications are processed within 48 hours. Germany's players protested by covering their lips as they sought to wear the rainbow armband during their team's dramatic 2–1 defeat to Japan at the Khalifa Stadium.

[Extracted, with edits and revisions, from "World Cup 2022: Germany's players cover mouths during team photo to protest FIFA's rainbow armband rule", *The Economic Times*]

45. What is the name of the armband which has been replaced with '[1]' in the passage above?
(a) FreeLove (b) OneLove
(c) Pride (d) PlayLove

46. The name of which community has been replaced with '[2]' in the passage above?
(a) Kurdish (b) Rohingya
(c) Uyghur (d) LGBTQ

47. What is the name of the system used to monitor and regulate migrant labourers, which is used in Qatar and a few other countries, and which came under heavy criticism in the build-up to the FIFA World Cup 2022 in Qatar?
(a) Iddat (b) Khalifa
(c) Kafala (d) Jazeera

48. Where is the Court of Arbitration for Sport based?
(a) Ausanne, Switzerland
(b) The Hague, Netherlands
(c) Brussels, Belgium
(d) Paris, France

49. Who is the current captain of the Indian men's football team?
(a) Shabbir Ali (b) Bhaichung Bhutia
(c) Sunil Chhetri (d) I.M. Vijayan

50. Timothy Weah, the Paris Saint Germain and U.S. National team player in the FIFA World Cup 2022 in Qatar is the son of the President of which country?
(a) Senegal (b) Uruguay
(c) Honduras (d) Liberia

51. Which of the following is the oldest football tournament in India?
(a) An Super League
(b) IFA Shield Cup
(c) Santosh Trophy
(d) Durand Cup

X. YouTuber Nas Daily in one of his videos named him as the Most Generous Billionaire who wanted to donate all his wealth to charity. But ten months later, '**[1]**' is no longer a billionaire. He is alleged to have caused massive losses worth $1 billion to investors. Known by his initials, he is the co-founder and former CEO of FTX, one of the biggest cryptocurrency exchange which has recently filed for bankruptcy in the US.

Once a billionaire with an estimated wealth of $26 billion at peak, according to Bloomberg estimates, [1] has seen his wealth been entirely wiped out. [1] studied physics at Massachusetts Institute of Technology (MIT) and traded currencies, futures and exchange-traded funds before moving to crypto trading, setting up [2] in 2017.

[1] teamed up with Gary Wang, a former software engineer at Google and a fellow MIT graduate, to launch FTX in 2019. The company offered trading on crypto tokens and derivatives. At the start of 2022, investors valued FTX and its U.S. Operations at $40 billion. [1] transferred $10 billion in customer funds to his hedge fund, [2] without publicly disclosing it, many say this become the reason for collapse of his empire.

[Extracted, with edits and revisions, from "Who is [1], the co-founder of collapsed crypto firm FTX", *Hindustan Times*]

52. Which person's name has been replaced with '[1]' in the passage above?

(a) Mike Novogratz
(b) Brian Armstrong
(c) Changpeng Zhao
(d) Sam Bankman-Fried

53. Which hedge fund's name has been replaced with '[2]' in the passage above?
(a) Blackrock Advisors
(b) Alameda Research
(c) AQR Capital Management
(d) Man Group

54. This person was once named "the world's youngest self-made female billionaire" by Forbes magazine and is the founder of the company Theranos. What is the name of this person?
(a) Elizabeth Holmes
(b) Eren Ozmen
(c) Fan Hongwei
(d) Diane Hendricks

55. The Reserve Bank of India recently announced the launch of 'Digital Rupee — Wholesale Segment', a form of which of the following?
(a) Digi Suvidha
(b) Virtual Wallet
(c) Central Bank Digital Currency
(d) Cyber Rupee

56. Which of the following technologies does cryptocurrency rely on?
(a) Cryptography (b) Blockchain
(c) Spectrography (d) Both (a) and (b)

57. What is the name of the Government of India-owned corporation that mints coins used as legal tender in India?
(a) National institute of Financial Management
(b) Security Printing and Minting Corporation of India Ltd.
(c) India infrastructure Finance Company Ltd.
(d) National Bank of Agricultural and Rural development

58. Who was the Founder and Former Chairman of Satyam Computer Services Ltd.,and was sentenced to prison and fined for a corporate governance scam?
(a) Harshad Mehta
(b) Ketan Parekh
(c) B. Ramalinga Raju
(d) Nirav Modi

XI. The agriculture sector has experienced buoyant growth in the past two years. The sector, which is the largest employer of workforce, accounted for a sizeable 18.8 per cent (2021–22) in Gross Value Added (GVA) of the country registering a growth of 3.6 per cent in 2020–21 and 3.9 per cent in 2021–22. Growth in allied sectors including livestock, dairy and fisheries has been the major drivers of overall growth in the sector. When measured in total value of agricultural production, India is ranked fourth largest in the world. Post-independence, there was a need to import food grains due to low-productivity, stagnant food-crop sector and poor rural infrastructure making food self-sufficiency a major national goal. The introduction of the Green revolution then yielded spectacular results and we became one of the largest producers of many agricultural commodities such as rice, wheat, pulses, fruits and vegetables. From being a net importer of foods in the 1960s, India is now a net exporter, thanks to Indian farmers and the Indian agriculture input industry.

[Extracted, with edits and revisions, from: "India's changing agricultural landscape and its way to inclusive growth", by NS ramaswamy, *The Economic Times*]

59. Which of the following is the largest exported agricultural product from India?
(a) Wheat (b) Sugar
(c) Rice (d) Barley

60. According to provisional data released by the directorate General of Commercial intelligence and Statistics, India achieved record exports of agricultural exports for the financial year FY22. What was the value of India's agricultural products exports according to this data?
(a) USD 7.5 billion
(b) USD 95.34 billion
(c) USD 13.2 billion
(d) USD 50.21 billion

61. Who among the following is also called the 'Father of the Wheat revolution'?
(a) Dilbagh Singh Athwal
(b) Verghese Kurien
(c) Atmaram Bhairav Joshi
(d) Shanti Swaroop Bhatnagar

62. India is the world's largest producer of which of the following?
(a) Poultry meat (b) Rice
(c) Almonds (d) Milk

63. What is India's ranking in the 2022 Global Hunger Index?
(A) 10 (b) 107
(c) 50 (d) 35

64. The National Commission on Farmers, constituted in December 2004, which recommended the C2+50% formula for calculation of the Minimum Support Price, was chaired by:
(a) Ashok Gulati (b) P. Sainath
(c) M.S. Swaminathan (d) Abhijit Sen

65. The bio-decomposer technology to avoid stubble burning around the Delhi NCR was developed by:
(a) Monsanto
(b) Cargill
(c) Biocon
(d) ICAR, Pusa Campus

LEGAL REASONING

Assume that the statements in the passages are the applicable law.

XII. Quashing a case of cruelty that was filed against a man by his wife, the Bombay High Court said that if a married lady is asked to do household work for the family, it cannot be said that she is treated "like a maid servant". The Court was hearing an application by the husband and his parents seeking that proceedings against them are quashed. A First Information Report ("**FIR**") was filed against the trio in September 2020, around nine months after the marriage, alleging that they hounded the woman for money to purchase a car, harassed her mentally and physically and treated her like a maid servant. Examining the evidence, the Court found that there was no merit to the woman's allegations. The Court said that though the FIR says that she was treated properly for about a month and then "like a maid servant", there are no details of what this meant. The Court added: "If a married lady is asked to do household work for the purpose of the family, it cannot be said that it is like a maid servant." the Court held that the mere use of the word harassment "mentally and physically" in the FIR is not sufficient to constitute an offence Section 498A of the Indian Penal Code ("**IPC**"), which punishes the husband, or a relative of the husband of a woman who subjects her to cruelty in any way. It is interesting to note that Section 498A of the IPC also provides that if a married woman is actually treated like a 'maid servant', it would be an offence under that Section.

[Extracted, with edits and revisions, from "If Wife Is Asked To Do Household Work, Does Not Mean She Is Treated Like Maid: Bombay HC", *The Wire*]

66. Ashwin and Ashima were married in February 2020. In March 2020, Ashwin asked Ashima to take care of all their household work, such as cooking, cleaning, and other domestic chores, as he was very busy with his professional responsibilities. Ashima claims that this amounts to treating her like a maid servant and constitutes an offence under Section 498A of the IPC. Applying the Bombay High Court decision, is she likely to succeed?
(a) Yes, since Ashwin had only asked Ashima to do their household work, and not for others.
(b) No, since Ashwin had only asked Ashima to do their household work, and not for others.
(c) Yes, since Ashwin had asked Ashima to do household work for themselves as well as others.
(d) No, since treating a married woman like a maid servant would not amount to an offence under that Section.

67. In April 2020, Ashwin's friend Rakesh visits Ashwin and Ashima's home, and stays with them for a few days. During his visit, he is very mean to Ashima, and uses abusive language with her. He also threw a plate at her one evening when he was unhappy with the meal that she had prepared. Ashima now claims that Rakesh has committed an offence under Section 498A of the IPC. Is she likely to succeed?

(a) No, since Rakesh's actions were perfectly justifiable for a man who does not get a well-cooked meal.
(b) Yes, since Rakesh's use of abusive language and throwing the plate at Ashima clearly amount to cruelty.
(c) No, since Rakesh is not her husband, nor is he related to Ashwin.
(d) Yes, since Rakesh was staying at Ashwin and Ashima's home at the time of the incident.

68. Frustrated and upset with her marriage, Ashima applies for and is granted a divorce from Ashwin in November 2020. Since she and Ashwin had been friends for many years before they got married, she stays in touch with him. She moves into her own apartment and starts going to office regularly at a new job. Ashwin is very upset at this and starts treating Ashima very cruelly. Ashima again claims that Ashwin has committed an offence under Section 498A of the IPC. Is she right?

(a) Yes, since Ashwin has, as we are told, treated her cruelly.
(b) Yes, since Ashwin has been her husband.
(c) No, since Ashwin was understandably upset at Ashima's behaviour.
(d) No, since she is no longer married to Ashwin.

69. Assume that the government passes a new law in January 2021, called the *Protection of Rights of Married Women Act, 2021* (the "**PoMWA**"), according to which, asking a married woman to take care of household chores would be an offence. The PoMWA also provides that if a man commits such an offence, he would have to pay compensation to the woman. The PoMWA even applies to actions that were committed any time in the three years prior to the new law coming into force, and even if the man and woman involved in the matter were no longer married. Upon hearing about this new law, Ashima once again alleges that Ashwin has committed an offence under Section 498A of the IPC, and claims compensation under the PoMWA for his actions. Is she right, and will she succeed?

(a) Ashima is right about Ashwin committing an offence under Section 498A of the IPC, but she will not get compensation under the PoMWA.
(b) Ashima will get compensation under the PoMWA, but she is not right about Ashwin committing an offence under Section 498A of the IPC.
(c) Ashima will get compensation under the PoMWA, and she is also right about Ashwin committing an offence under Section 498A of the IPC.
(d) Ashima will neither get compensation under the PoMWA, nor is she right about Ashwin committing an offence under Section 498A of the IPC.

70. Assume that in March 2021, the government changes Section 498A of the IPC. The effect of this change is that asking a married woman to do household chores — even for their own family — by herself would be considered cruelty, and therefore, an offence under the Section. Some days after this change comes into effect, Shamita, Ashima's friend at work, tells her that her husband has been forcing her to do all the household work by herself. Ashima tells Shamita that her husband's actions would amount to an offence under Section 498A of the IPC, even though Ashima herself has been unsuccessful in having Ashwin convicted under that Section in the past. Is Ashima's advice to Shamita correct?

(a) Yes, since Section 498A has now been changed, and Shamita's husband's actions would now be an offence under the changed Section 498A.

(b) No, since Ashima has been unsuccessful in having Ashwin convicted under that Section in the past.
(c) Yes, since the passing of the Protection of married Women Act has resulted in Shamita's husband's actions being made illegal.
(d) No, since Ashima is only Shamita's friend, and only the married woman herself can file a complaint under Section 498A of the iPC.

XIII. Parliament passed the *Criminal Procedure (Identification) Act*, 2022 (the "**Act**") in march 2022. The legislation enables police and central investigating agencies to collect, store and analyse the measurements of arrested persons. Until rules are notified, an Act cannot be implemented or come into force. On September 19, 2022, the ministry of Home Affairs (the "**MHA**") notified the rules (the "**Rules**") under the Act.

The Act empowers a magistrate to direct any person to give measurements to the police, which till now was reserved for convicts and those involved in heinous crimes. It also enables police personnel of the rank of Head Constable or above to take measurements of any person who resists or refuses to give measurements when ordered to do so by a magistrate. As per the rules, "measurements" mean finger-impressions, palm-print, footprint, photographs, iris and retina scan, physical, biological samples and their analysis, behavioural attributes including signatures, and handwriting. Though it has not been specified, analysis of biological samples could also include dNA profiling.

However, the rules state that measurements of those detained under preventive Sections of the *Code of Criminal Procedure* ("**CrPc**") shall not be taken unless such person is at that time charged or under arrest in connection with any other offence punishable under any other law. Measurements can also be taken under the rules if a person has been ordered to give security for his good behaviour for maintaining peace under Section 117 of the CrPC for a proceeding under that Section.

[Extracted, with edits and revisions, from "explained I rules for identifying criminals", by Vijaita Singh, *The Hindu*]

71. Bhargesh is arrested by the police on April 11, 2022, on suspicion of having committed a series of minor thefts. During their investigation, the police find some fingerprints at the crime scenes, and on April 12, 2022, they tell Bhargesh that he must provide his finger-impressions to them so that they can check whether they match the fingerprints from the crime scenes. When bhargesh refuses, the police tell him that he has no choice but to provide his measurements, as the Act had been passed by Parliament the previous month. Was Bhargesh bound to provide his finger-impressions under the Act?
(a) No, since Bhargesh had only been arrested, and not convicted.
(b) Yes, since Bhargesh was under arrest.
(c) No, since the rules had not yet been notified.
(d) Yes, since finger-impressions are included within the definition of "measurements" under the Act.

72. Bhargesh is later released by the police because they are unable to find enough evidence to make a strong case against him. On October 5, 2022, the police receive a complaint alleging that Bhargesh had beaten up his neighbour and caused the neighbour severe injuries. They ask the local magistrate to issue an order directing Bhargesh to provide the police his blood samples, so that they can match them against some blood stains that were found on the neighbour's clothes. The magistrate issues the order, but Bhargesh refuses to provide the blood samples. Is Bhargesh bound to provide his blood samples to the police under the Act?
(a) Yes, since the crime that bhargesh was accused of was very serious.
(b) Yes, since the magistrate had passed an order directing him to do so.
(c) Yes, since Bhargesh had already been arrested in connection with another crime in the past.

(d) Yes, since the police needed the blood samples to verify Bhargesh's involvement in the crime.

73. On October 15, 2022, the police detain Bhargesh under a preventive Section of the CrPC, since they believe that he had plans to disturb the public peace during a festival day. They then tell Bhargesh that he must provide his measurements to them for their records. Bhargesh refuses again. Is Bhargesh bound to provide his photographs to the police under the Act?

(a) No, since he was not charged or under arrest in connection with any other offence at the time.

(b) No, since that would violate Bhargesh's right to privacy.

(c) Yes, since the police had detained Bhargesh under a preventive Section of the CrPC.

(d) Yes, since there was a high likelihood that Bhargesh would disturb the public peace on a festival day.

74. Two days later, the police obtain an order from the magistrate directing Bhargesh to provide them his photographs. As Bhargesh continues to refuse to provide his photographs, a regular police constable forces him to stand still and takes his photographs. Bhargesh files a case in court, claiming that the constable's actions violate the Act. Will he succeed?

(a) Yes, since Bhargesh had been detained under a preventive section of the CrPC.

(b) Yes, since only police personnel of the rank of Head Constable or above can take measurements of any person who resists or refuses to give measurements when ordered to do so by a magistrate.

(c) No, the magistrate had issued an order directing him to provide his photographs to the police.

(d) No, since the police constable was only performing his duty.

75. The police release Bhargesh, but to ensure that he does not disturb the public peace, they ask the magistrate to issue an order under Section 117 of the CrPC, directing Bhargesh to provide a security of ₹1,00,000/- for his good behaviour and to ensure he maintains the peace, which the magistrate refuses. The police now tell Bhargesh he must provide them his iris and retina scans. Is Bhargesh required to do so?

(a) No, since a person against whom an order has been issued under Section 117 of the CrPC cannot be made to give their measurements to the police.

(b) Yes, since a person against whom an order has been issued under Section 117 of the CrPC can be made to give their measurements to the police.

(c) Yes, since Bhargesh had been detained under other preventive Sections of the CrPC in the past.

(d) No, since the magistrate had not issued the order.

XIV. The government has amended the *Electoral Bond Scheme*, 2018. The Ministry of Finance on November 7, 2022, issued a notification for amending the scheme to provide "an additional period of 15 days" for their sale "in the year of general elections to the Legislative Assembly of any States or union territories with Legislature". The bonds under this scheme are usually made available for purchase by any person for a period of ten days each in the months of January, April, July, and October, when specified by the union Government. The original scheme had provided for an additional period of thirty days, as specified by the Government, in the year when Lok Sabha elections are held, while the amendment adds another 15 days.

Since Assembly elections to various States and Union Territories are held every year, the amendment effectively means that there will be 15 additional dates annually during which the bonds can be sold. Immediately after issuing the notification, the Union Government also announced the sale of electoral bonds under the 23rd tranche from the authorised branches of the State Bank of India. The notification said the sale of bonds would take place through the 29 authorised branches of the said bank from November 9 to November 15, 2022. Like in previous rounds of sale, the electoral bonds shall be valid for 15 calendar days from the date of issue and no payment shall be made to any payee political party if the bond is deposited after expiry of the validity period. The electoral bond deposited by an eligible political party in its account shall be credited on the same day.

[Extracted, with edits and revisions, from "Electoral Bonds Scheme Amended to Allow Sale for Additional 15 Days in Assembly Election Years", by Gaurav Vivek Bhatnagar, *The Wire*]

76. Assad buys an electoral bond worth ₹1,00,000/- on November 9, 2022 and plans to give the bond to the Popular People's Party (the "**PPP**"), which he has been supporting for many years. On November 10, he must travel out of station on some urgent business, and he only hands the bond over to a representative of the PPP on November 14, 2022. The PPP's representative deposits the bond in the Party's account on November 16, 2022, but the bank refuses to credit the bond to the party's account, on the grounds that it was no longer valid. Is the bank correct?
(a) No, since Assad was a long-time supporter of the PPP.
(b) Yes, since the bonds were only issued from November 9 to November 15, 2022 and were invalid after that.
(c) Yes, since the party representative had not deposited the bond with an authorised branch of the bank.
(d) No, since the bond was valid on November 16, 2022.

77. The Government announces that there would be a sale of a 24th tranche of electoral bonds on February 10, 2023, for a period of 15 days, since elections to the Legislative Assembly of some States are scheduled for that year. Since there are no elections to the Lok Sabha or the Legislative Assembly of the State in which Assad resides, he claims that the Government does not have the power to issue this 24th tranche of electoral bonds in 2023. Is he right?
(a) No, since the changes to the Electoral Bond Scheme, 2018 mean that electoral bonds can be issued for an additional period of 15 days in any year, regardless of whether any elections are scheduled that year.
(b) Yes, since no elections were scheduled for Assad's state in that year.
(c) Yes, since the Government had already sold some bonds in the 23rd tranche in 2022.
(d) No, since the changes to the Electoral Bond Scheme, 2018 provide that electoral bonds can be issued for an additional period of 15 days in years when there is an election to the Legislative Assembly of a State.

78. On November 10, 2022, Palak purchases an electoral bond from a branch of the State Bank of India, and hands it over to a representative of the PPP. The next day, the PPP announces that it has changed its candidates for the upcoming elections in Palak's State. Upset at this news, she tells a PPP representative that she would like her bond back. The representative tells her that the bond has already been deposited, and that the money has been credited to the party's account. Palak claims that since the period of validity of the bonds has not expired, she has the right to get her bond back from the party. Is she right?
(a) No, since Palak cannot ask for the bond back once she has given it to a political party.
(b) No, since the party had already deposited the bond, and the money had been credited to its account.
(c) Yes, since Palak bought the bond with her own money, and has the right to ask for it back.
(d) Yes, since the PPP changed its candidates, and Palak may no longer support the party.

79. On November 15, 2022, the Government issues another notification, announcing that from that date onwards, only political parties that have received at least 1% of the votes polled in the last elections to the Lok Sabha, or the last elections to the Legislative Assembly of a State, would be eligible to receive and deposit electoral bonds. In the sale of the 24th tranche of electoral bonds, Palak decides to give the electoral bonds she has purchased to the newly formed More Popular People's Party (the "**MPPP**"), which is likely to win the first elections it would be contesting, in July 2023. Is the MPPP eligible to receive the electoral bonds?

(a) Yes, since it is likely to succeed in the upcoming elections.
(b) Yes, since it fulfils the criteria announced in the November 7, 2022 notification.
(c) No, since it does not fulfil the eligibility criteria announced in the November 15, 2022 notification.
(d) No, since it does not fulfil the eligibility criteria announced in the November 7, 2022 notification.

80. Abraham, who lives in a different State from Assad, purchased an electoral bond in the sale of the 23rd tranche. He decides to give the electoral bond to the PPP, even though the PPP is only active in Assad's State. When the PPP representative goes to an authorised branch of the State Bank of India to deposit the electoral bond on december 5, 2022 however, the bank refuses to credit the money to the PPP's account. Which of the following would be the most valid reason for the bank to refuse to credit the money to the party's account?

(a) The bond was no longer valid.
(b) Abraham could not give the bond to the PPP since the PPP was not active in his state.
(c) The PPP was not eligible to receive electoral bonds.
(d) The PPP could only deposit the bond in a bank branch located in Abraham's state.

XV. Twitter's lawyer on October 27, said before the Karnataka High Court that Union government orders to block certain Twitter handles and posts must contain reasons for the same that can be communicated to users of the microblogging site. He said this applies to all blocking orders sent to social media platforms. The lawyer representing Twitter said that reasons for the blocking order must be provided to users so they can determine whether or not they want to challenge the orders.

Challenging the blocking orders, Twitter's July 5 petition contended that several blocking orders "demonstrate excessive use of powers and are disproportionate". Such orders can only be issued by the Union government and not the state governments, he said, which increases the danger of such abuse. Twitter also claimed that the Ministry of Electronics and Information Technology had sent it a letter threatening consequences for failing to comply with the blocking orders, such as criminal proceedings against the company's chief compliance officer and the stripping away of Twitter's safe harbour immunity, otherwise available to social media platforms under Section 79(1) of the Information Technology Act (the "**IT act**"). Note that the Government has the power to strip away such safe harbour immunity under the IT Act. Further, in a previous hearing, Twitter's lawyer said that the company was asked to block entire accounts, although Section 69A of the IT Act does not permit blocking of the whole account. It only permits the blocking of information, or a particular tweet or post. It argued that the Union government's direction to block whole accounts will affect its business, adding that several prominent persons have their accounts on the platform.

[Extracted, with edits and revisions, from " 'Government Must Provide Reasons for Blocking User Accounts,' Twitter tells Karnataka HC", *The Wire*]

81. Sunil is a high-ranking officer of the Union government. While scrolling through his timeline on a social media platform, he notices some posts by Sachin, a private businessman, which he finds objectionable. He sends an order to UnReal, the company that owns that social media platform, that the posts must be blocked, as they may bring disrepute to India. UnReal claims that Sunil has not provided a clear, detailed reason for blocking the posts, and so, the order is not valid. Is unreal right?

(a) No, the blocking order is valid since Sunil found the posts objectionable.
(b) No, the blocking order is valid since Sunil had provided reasons for blocking the post.
(c) Yes, Sunil's reasons are vague, and he should have provided more detail.
(d) Yes, such an order is violative of the fundamental right to freedom of speech and expression.

82. Some days later, Sunil notices another post from Sachin on UnReal's social media platform; this post contains some highly sensitive information about the country's defence policies. He issues an order to UnReal, that the post must be blocked since it divulges the government's confidential information. The order also says that UnReal should not let anyone know about the blocking order, or that the post was ordered to be deleted, since it relates to secret government information. UnReal claims that this order is invalid. Is UnReal right?

(a) Yes, since it did not provide any reasons that could be communicated to the users of the social media platform.
(b) No, since Sunil had provided reasons to unreal for ordering that the post be blocked.
(c) Yes, since Sunil did not have the authority to issue blocking orders so frequently.
(d) No, since the post divulged confidential government information.

83. Sunil sends UnReal a third blocking order. UnReal claims that this order too was invalid. Upset with UnReal for claiming that all his blocking orders were invalid, Sunil sends them a letter in which he says, "if you do not comply with my blocking orders, then I will be forced to initiate criminal proceedings against you and cancel your safe harbour immunity." UnReal claims that Sunil has broken the law by making these statements in the letter. Is UnReal right?

(a) Yes, since making such threats amounts to intimidation.
(b) No, since Sunil had issued blocking orders in the past as well, and UnReal should have complied with the orders without questioning them.
(c) Yes, since Sunil did not have the power to cancel UnReal's safe harbour immunity.
(d) No, since the it Act does not forbid Sunil from doing so.

84. Complying with a fourth blocking order that they receive from Sunil, UnReala blocks Sachin's account, since his posts were seen as increasingly objectionable by the government. Sachin asks UnReal to share the reasons for the blocking order, which they do, yet Sachin claims the blocking order is invalid. Is he right?

(a) Yes, since Sunil was clearly targeting Sachin, and was misusing his powers to silence him.
(b) No, since UnReal had shared the reasons for the blocking order with Sachin.
(c) Yes, since Section 69A of the IT Act only permits blocking information, or a particular post, but not a whole account.
(d) No, since his posts were seen as increasingly objectionable by the government.

85. Sunil sends UnReal a fifth blocking order, which says that several of Sachin's latest posts must be blocked. The blocking order sets out several reasons why the posts should be blocked, but UnReal does not find them satisfactory. Rather than take on another fight with a government official however, UnReal blocks the posts, and gives Sachin what it thinks is a better set of reasons for blocking the posts. When Sachin finds out, he claims this was wrong on UnReal's part, and that the blocking order was inappropriate. Which of the following is most accurate in this regard?

(a) The blocking order was valid, but UnReal's actions were inappropriate.
(b) UnReal's actions were valid, but the blocking order was invalid.
(c) UnReal's actions were valid, but Sachin's actions were invalid.
(d) Sachin's actions were valid, but the blocking order was invalid.

XVI. Free legal aid is the provision of free legal services in civil and criminal matters for those poor and marginalised people who cannot afford the services of a lawyer for the conduct of a case or a legal proceeding in any Court, Tribunal or Authority. These services are governed by the *Legal Services Authority Act*, 1987 (the "**Act**") and provided by the National Legal Services Authority ("**NALSA**").

Provision of free legal aid includes:

- Representation by an advocate in legal proceedings;
- Payment of process fees, expenses of witnesses and all other charges payable or incurred in connection with any legal proceedings in appropriate cases;
- Preparation of pleadings, memo of appeal, paper book including printing and translation of documents in legal proceedings;
- Drafting of legal documents, special leave petition etc.; and
- Supply of certified copies of judgments, orders, notes of evidence and other documents in legal proceedings.

Free legal aid also includes provision of aid and advice to the beneficiaries to access benefits under welfare statutes and schemes framed by the Central Government or the state governments and to ensure access to justice in any other manner. Free legal aid is not confined to cases before the subordinate courts. Free legal aid must be provided to the needy from the lowest court to the Supreme Court of India.

According to Section 13(1) of the Act, any individual who satisfies any criteria under Section 12 is entitled to receive free legal aid, provided that NALSA is satisfied that such person has a genuine case to prosecute or defend the matter. There is hence no bar as to which kind of cases one can apply and not apply for. Section 12 of the Act includes the following:

- a member of a Scheduled Caste or Scheduled Tribe;
- a woman or a child;
- a person with a disability;
- an industrial workman; or
- a person in police custody.

[Extracted, with edits and revisions, from "FAQs", *National Legal Services Authority*]

86. Divya was arrested by the police and charged with having committed a murder. She was convicted by the trial court and appealed to the high court. She lost her appeal there and decided to appeal to the Supreme Court. By this time she has run out of money, so she approaches NALSA and asks them to help her get an advocate who can represent her before the Supreme Court. Is Divya entitled to support from NALSA?

(a) No, since she should have approached them at the beginning of the case before the trial court, and not at such a late stage.

(b) Yes, since her previous lawyers were incompetent, and that is why she lost the matter in the trial court and the high court.

(c) Yes, she is entitled to free legal aid in the Supreme Court proceedings because she is a woman.

(d) No, since she had been accused of having committed the heinous crime of murder.

87. Divya is acquitted by the Supreme Court and goes back to her regular life. Some days later, she has a fight with her neighbour Riya over a petty matter and decides to file a criminal case against her. She approaches NALSA for free legal aid to prosecute the matter. She tells NALSA representative that she knows she does not have a genuine case, but just wants to harass Riya.

NALSA refuses to provide Divya free legal aid because they believe she does not have a genuine case to prosecute. Can NALSA do so?

(a) Yes, since Section 13(1) of the Act provides that free legal aid can be provided if NALSA is satisfied the person has a genuine case to prosecute, and they did not believe that Divya had a genuine case to prosecute.

(b) Yes, since Divya had earlier been prosecuted for the crime of murder.

(c) Yes, since Divya had already applied for free legal aid from NALSA in the past and could not repeatedly ask NALSA for such assistance.

(d) No, since Divya is a woman, and is included within the list of people entitled to free legal aid from NALSA under Section 12 of the Act.

88. Incensed at Divya, Riya decides to file a civil case against Divya, claiming that Divya had violated the terms of a contract they had made some time back. Divya approaches NALSA for free legal aid to defend the matter, which NALSA agrees to provide. Since Riya is also short of funds, she too approaches NALSA for free legal aid. NALSA refuses to provide legal aid to Riya, since they are already providing Divya free legal aid in the same case. Is NALSA right in refusing free legal aid to Riya?

(a) Yes, since NALSA cannot provide free legal aid to opposing parties in the same matter.

(b) Yes, since NALSA does not provide free legal aid in civil matters.

(c) No, since Divya had filed a frivolous case against Riya in the past, and Riya was entitled to retaliate by filing another case against Divya.

(d) No, since Riya is a woman, and is entitled to free legal aid as long as NALSA is satisfied she has a genuine case.

89. Farhan is an up-and-coming artist and makes a living selling his paintings. Since he is not very well known yet, he isn't able to sell too many paintings, and is dependent on aid from the government and well-wishers. He reads about a new Central Government scheme in the papers one day, under which artists would be provided a monthly stipend by the local government. Since he finds the language of the scheme document very complex to understand, he approaches NALSA for help in understanding the scheme and obtaining the stipend. Is he entitled to free legal aid from NALSA in this regard?

(a) No, since free legal aid does not include provision of help to understand and access benefits under government schemes.

(b) No, since he does not fit within any of the categories under Section 12 of the Act.

(c) Yes, since free legal aid includes provision of help to understand and access benefits under government schemes.

(d) Yes, since he is a struggling artist, and is dependent on aid for survival.

90. Vikram is a rich businessman and has a huge art collection. Farhan invites Vikram to his studio one day, hoping to convince Vikram to buy some of his paintings. Vikram doesn't buy any of his paintings, but after he leaves, Farhan notices that one of his newest paintings is missing. He suspects that Vikram has stolen it, and complains to the police, who promptly arrest Vikram. Vikram approaches NALSA for free legal aid, so that he can obtain bail. Is Vikram entitled to free legal aid from NALSA?

(a) No, since he is a rich businessman and can hire a lawyer with his own money.

(b) Yes, since he was innocent.

(c) Yes, since he was in police custody.

(d) No, since he had stolen from a struggling artist.

XVII. Surrogacy is defined by law as "a practice whereby one woman bears and gives birth to a child for an intending couple" and intends to hand over the child to them after the birth, as per the *Surrogacy (Regulation) Act*, 2021 (the "**SRA**"). The SRA restricts altruistic surrogacy to legally wedded infertile Indian couples. The couple is deemed eligible for surrogacy only if they have been married for five years. The SRA sets an age limitation for the couple. A husband must be between 26 and 55 years of age and a wife between 23 and 50 years. Further, Indian couples with biological or adopted children are prohibited from undertaking surrogacy, save for some exceptions such as mentally or physically challenged children, or those suffering from a life-threatening disorder or fatal illness. The SRA provides that the surrogate mother has to be a close relative of the couple (such as a sibling of one of the members of the couple), a married woman with a child of her own, aged between 25 and 35 years, who has been a surrogate only once in her life. Even within this category of people, commercial surrogacy is banned in India and that includes the "commercialisation of surrogacy services or procedures or its component services or component procedures". The surrogate woman cannot be given payments, rewards, benefits or fees, "except the medical expenses and such other prescribed expenses incurred on the surrogate mother and the insurance coverage for the surrogate mother".

A legal commentator points out some criticisms of the law. "Permitting limited conditional surrogacy to married Indian couples and disqualifying other persons on basis of nationality, marital status, sexual orientation or age does not pass the test of equality," he writes. He adds that reproductive autonomy, inclusive of the right to procreation and parenthood is protected under Article 21 of the *Constitution of India*, which guarantees the right to life and personal liberty. The intending parents typically sign a contract with the surrogate. The *Indian Contract Act*, 1972 (the "**ICA**") provides that a valid contract has to be in writing, and signed in the presence of two witnesses. The ICA also provides that a contract that is prohibited by any other law will not be valid under the ICA.

[Extracted with edits and revisions from "What laws regulate surrogacy in India", *The Indian Express*]

91. Rani and Shiva would like to opt for surrogacy. They have been married for 6 years. Rani is aged 51 and Shiva is aged 53. Both Rani and Shiva have built successful business empires. They are now working together on a joint initiative. Due to the demanding nature of their work, they have not thought about children previously. However, they are now keen to have a child via surrogacy.
Are Rani and Shiva eligible for surrogacy under the SRA?
(a) Yes, because they have been married for more than 5 years.
(b) Yes, because they have financial capacity to bring up a child.
(c) No, because they do not fall within the legal requirements of intending parents.
(d) No, because they are not an infertile couple.

92. Assume Rani and Shiva are eligible for surrogacy under the SRA. They approach Geeta to act as a surrogate. Geeta is Rani's sister. She is 29 years old. She is married, has one child, and has been a surrogate twice before. Which of the following statements are false?
i. Geeta is eligible to be a surrogate because she is a close relative.
ii. Geeta is eligible to be a surrogate because she is married.
iii. Geeta has been a surrogate only twice before and is now eligible to be a surrogate for Rani.
iv. Geeta is eligible to be a surrogate because she is 29.
(a) Statement iii
(b) Statements I and iii
(c) Statements ii and iii
(d) Statements ii, iii, and iv

93. Joseph and Neena are keen to have a child via surrogacy. They have been married for 8 years, and have been unable to conceive biologically due to infertility. Joseph is 40 years old and Neena is 42 years old. They have an adopted daughter, Maya, who is 4 years old. Maya has been diagnosed with Striker's Syndrome, which would cause slow neurological deterioration, with chances of death. Devastated, Joseph and Neena decide to opt for surrogacy, to become parents to their biological child. Are they eligible for surrogacy?
(a) Yes, because they have no biological children.
(b) No, because they have an adopted child.
(c) Yes, because their adopted child has been diagnosed with Striker's Syndrome.
(d) Yes, because their right to procreation and parenthood is protected under Article 21 of the Indian Constitution.

94. Queen runs a surrogacy clinic. She employs 54 women, aged between 25 and 35 years. They are all married women with one or more children. Most of them belong to economically disadvantaged backgrounds. They choose to be surrogates because it gives them a reliable source of income. Kishore and Noor are intending parents. They have been married 5 years, are both aged 35, and do not have children. Kishore has been certified as infertile. So, they decide to approach Queen's clinic. They sign a contract with the surrogate. The contract is in writing and is signed in the presence of two witnesses. As per the contract, Kishore and Noor are required to remunerate the surrogate with ₹2 lakh per child born as a result of surrogacy, and take care of her medical needs, including providing her with medical insurance. A healthy baby girl is born as a result of surrogacy. Kishore and Noor are overjoyed. They take care of the surrogate's medical expenses. However, they do not pay the surrogate the ₹2 lakh. The surrogate, supported by Queen, now wants to take Kishore and Noor to court, to demand that they make the payment.Will she succeed?

(a) Yes, because Kishore and Noor are bound by the contract under the ICA.

(b) Yes, because the intending parents and the surrogate meet the eligibility requirements under the SRA.

(c) Yes, because the surrogate meets the eligibility requirements under the SRA.

(d) No, because SRA allows only altruistic surrogacy, so the contract is not valid under the ICA.

95. Karan and Daniel are in a homosexual relationship. As per the Hindu marriage Act, marriage is allowed only between heterosexual couples. As a result, Karan and Daniel are not married. However, they wish to have children and decide to go in for surrogacy. When they approach Queen's clinic, they are informed that they do not meet the requirements for an intending couple under the SRA. Karan and Daniel wish to challenge the SRA for violating their constitutional right to non-discrimination. The non-discrimination clause under the *Constitution of India* reads: 'No citizen shall be discriminated on the basis of sex, caste, religion, nationality, place of birth or any other ground'. Karan and Daniel argue that the SRA discriminates against them on the basis of sexual orientation, because it restricts surrogacy to heterosexual couples alone. Which of the following arguments would most strongly support their claim in court?

(a) The non-discrimination clause does not explicitly mention sexual orientation.

(b) Discrimination on the basis of sex could include discrimination on the basis of sexual orientation.

(c) The non-discrimination clause is not restricted to explicitly mentioned grounds.

(d) Surrogacy is restricted under the SRA to married couples, and only heterosexual couples can get married.

XVIII. Until 2017, India did not have a codified law to order internet shut downs. A general power was vested in District Magistrates in this regard. The Magistrate could issue an order ordering a shut down if a 'speedy remedy' (extending to internet shut down) is desirable for 'immediate prevention' of an event. The Magistrate had to be satisfied that the order is 'likely to prevent or tends to prevent obstruction, annoyance or injury to human life, health or safety, or a disturbance of public tranquillity'. The Magistrate's order cannot be for longer than two months.

In 2017, new rules to order internet shut downs were introduced taking the power away from the Magistrate. These rules — the Temporary Suspension Rules — state that internet shut downs can now only be ordered by the Home Secretary of the Union or State Governments. Only in "unavoidable circumstances" can the passing of orders be delegated to someone lower than the rank of a Joint Secretary to the Government of India. And even in this case, the official must be authorised by the Centre or State Home Secretary. Shut downs can be ordered where 'necessary' or 'unavoidable' during a 'public emergency' or in the 'interest of public safety'. Shut down orders must necessarily detail the reasons to shut down the internet. The orders must also be sent to a review committee under the state or central government within 24 hours. The committee must then review them within five working days. The rules state that apart from the Chief Secretary and Legal Secretary, the committee can comprise a secretary *other than* the home secretary.

In January 2020 the Supreme Court passed its judgement in the case of *Anuradha Bhasin*. The judgment in this case explicitly recognised two things: that the freedom to access information is a fundamental right under Article 19(1)(a) of the *Constitution of India* (which protects the freedom of speech and expression); and that the freedom to conduct your trade, profession or business over the internet is also a fundamental right under Article 19(1)(g) of the *Constitution of India* (which protects the freedom to practise any profession, or to carry on any occupation, trade or business). Every time the internet is suspended, it is quite obvious that it is a violation of these rights. These rights can only be curtailed in the interest of the 'sovereignty and security of the state, integrity of the nation, friendly relations with foreign states, or public order or for preventing incitement to the commission of an offence'. The Supreme Court's judgement in *Anuradha Bhasin's* case had also underlined that shut down orders must clearly provide reasons for the shut down and they must be publicly available.

[Extracted with edits and revisions from "in India, are internet shut downs in accordance with law? Not always", by Diksha Munjal, *News Laundry*]

96. In 2014, India was hit by a terrible pandemic. It was the first time the country was experiencing a pandemic. People panicked. WhatsApp and Facebook groups became common platforms for sharing information about the pandemic. Messages were forwarded from group to group. Many of these messages prescribed different remedies to prevent and cure the flu caused by the pandemic. In Merodha district, people following these remedies began to fall sick. The already overburdened public sector hospitals became even more full. The district administration requested people to stop sharing such misinformation. However, these requests were not heeded. The District Magistrate issued an indefinite order to shut down the internet to prevent the transmission of these messages. Is this order legal?

(a) Yes, because the District Magistrate has the power to issue a range of orders, which includes internet shut down orders.
(b) Yes, because the order was necessary on grounds of public health.
(c) Yes, because a speedy order was necessary to immediately prevent transmission of these messages.
(d) No, because the order was indefinite.

97. The Central government was preparing to conduct the National medical eligibility test ("**NMET**") on 25 October 2021. The exams were to be conducted in public schools around the country on computers provided by the government. In July 2021, there were rumours that several groups had hatched plans to share answers with the students taking the exam. A special chat application was developed. The student simply had to open the application on the browser of the computer on which they were taking the exam, allowing persons on the other end to send them the answers. The government was very concerned. If the rumours were true, the quality of doctors in training (who were selected through the NMET) would be severely affected. To prevent this public emergency, the government issued orders under the Temporary Suspension Rules to shut down internet countrywide on 25 October 2021. Many protested against this decision. They argued that the government could prevent cheating in the exams by shutting down the internet in the public schools where the exam was taking place. A nation-wide blanket shut down was not required for this purpose. Now, the issue is before the Supreme Court. What will the Court decide?

(a) the government's order is legal under the Temporary Suspension Rules because it prevents a public emergency by preserving the quality of doctors in India.
(b) the government's order is not legal under the Temporary Suspension Rules because the power belonged to the magistrate to issue orders under Section 144.
(c) the government's order is not legal under the Temporary Suspension Rules because the nation-wide internet shut down order was not necessary or unavoidable.
(d) the government's order is legal because it is the responsibility of the State to conduct exams in a fair manner.

98. In the above instance, the order was passed by the Communications Minister of the Indian Central Government. The Communications Minister is below the rank of Joint Secretary. The Home Secretary was away for a conference in Geneva and thus was not present in Delhi when the decision to pass the order was made. However, the Home Secretary could be contacted by phone or email. She had, in fact, explicitly said that she should be contacted if any need arises, however minor. As she had taken measures to make herself available virtually, the Home Secretary did not authorise any other official to exercise her functions. Against this, consider the following statements:

i. The Communications Minister had the power to pass the order under the 2017 rules.
ii. The passing of the order by the Communications Minister was avoidable.
iii. The power to pass the order remained with the Home Secretary.
iv. The Communications Minister did not have the power to pass the order under the 2017 rules.

Which of the following statements are false?
(a) Statement iv
(b) Statement i
(c) Statements ii and iii
(d) Statements ii and iv

99. Assume that in the above instance, the Joint Secretary passed the order. The order stated: 'by means of the discretion vested in me by the Temporary Suspension of Telecom Services (Public Emergency or Public Safety) rules 2017, I suspend internet across all Indian States and Union Territories on October 25, 2021'. The order was passed on 15 October, 2021. The order was sent to the Central Government review committee within 8 hours of its passing. The committee reviewed and approved of the order on 22 October, 2021. Is the order legal?
(a) Yes, because it was passed under the 2017 rules.
(b) No, because the procedure under the 2017 rules was not followed.
(c) Yes, because the order was reviewed by the Central government review committee.
(d) No, because the order was passed 10 days before it was to come into effect.

100. In January 2022, communal riots were rife in five states in India, between two dominant communities, X and Y. The primary mode of communication amongst the rioters was Signal which could be accessed through the internet via mobile phones and computers. The State governments of the five States received information that some members of X group were planning to set the houses of members of Y group on fire. Through broad Signal broadcasts amongst all users, the leaders of X group were instigating members of their group to participate in this exercise, threatening public order. Creating or inciting threat to public order is a criminal offence under Section 163F of the Indian Penal Code. To prevent further communication between the leaders of X group and their members, the State shut Signal down. However, communication then shifted to other platforms. Realising that targeting isolated platforms would not work, the State governments issued an order shutting down internet completely in all the States. Two groups protested against this order. First, students whose education was being conducted online due to the riots. They argued that they were prevented from accessing vital information, central to their education. Second, business owners who conducted business on the internet. The State's order read: 'in the five Indian States listed below, internet will be suspended for a period of two months from 10 January 2022 to 10 March 2022'. The State's order was not displayed anywhere (in print or virtually) from January to March 2022.

Consider the following statements:

i. The students' right under Article 19(1)(a) was violated by the State order.
ii. The business owners' right under Article 19(1)(g) was violated by the State order.
iii. The State order validly restricted the said fundamental rights.
iv. The State's order complied with the guidelines under Anuradha Bhasin.

How many statements are true?

(A) One statement (b) Two statements
(c) Three statements (d) All four statements

XIX. Consumers are people who buy and use goods or services. Consumers have a right to file a complaint for any of the services or goods used by them under Consumer Protection Law. Under Consumer Protection Law, a 'consumer' means:

Person buying and using goods and services: A consumer includes any person who buys goods and services, as well as anyone who uses them. For instance, a person who watches a movie after buying a movie ticket is a consumer and similarly, a person who uses a gift voucher gifted from someone else is also a consumer.

Person using goods for self-employment, and not for commercial purposes: the consumer protection law does not apply to people who use goods and services for commercial purposes. However, there are some exceptions to this. For example, people who use goods for self-employment are considered as consumers. For example, artists who buy art supplies for their work or beauticians who buy beauty products are consumers.

Person using online facilities: A consumer also includes any person who buys or hires goods or services online. For example, if you order from an online clothes website, you are a consumer.

People facing issues related to food: Consumers also include people who may be facing issues related to food items, such as adulteration, poor quality, lack of service, etc. For instance, issues related to food can cover problems across a wide range of products, starting from water that goes into the production of items like juices as well as the sale of animals like chicken, mutton etc. That are expressly intended for human consumption.

[Extracted, with edits and revisions, from "Who is a Consumer?", *Nyaaya India*]

101. Clint Leone morricone Ltd. ("**CLML**") is a factory manufacturing bicycles. For the purpose of documentation and record keeping, it purchased a laptop from Pacer. However, within a month of the purchase, the laptop crashed and there was a motherboard failure. Despite a warranty, Pacer failed to replace the motherboard. Which of the following statements is correct?

(a) Purchase of electronic items do not fall within the purview of consumer law.
(b) CLML is a consumer since it has bought a good for a price.
(c) CLML is not a consumer since it has purchased the laptop for commercial purpose.
(d) A company is not a person and so, cannot be a consumer.

102. Sita Das has been working as a freelance journalist. She writes columns and news-reports for various newspapers and news-portals and is paid on the basis of each column and report. For the purpose of her writing work, she purchases a Pacer laptop. However, within a month of the purchase, the laptop crashed and there was a motherboard failure. Which of the following statements is correct?

(a) Since she is using the laptop for the purpose of writing paid columns and news reports, Sita Das cannot be a consumer.

(b) Purchase of goods does not fall within the purview of Consumer Protection Law.
(c) Since she is using the laptop for the purpose of earning her livelihood, she will be a consumer.
(d) None of the above

103. Kalpavruksha Charitable trust runs a hospital. The hospital charges a fee from its patients. The fee is however 30% less than the commercial rates for all services and medical devices sold to patients. The hospital purchased a pacemaker from St. Rude's — a globally reputed manufacturer of pacemakers, to be resold to and used by patients. Which of the following statements is correct?
(a) The hospital is a charitable hospital and therefore, it is a consumer with respect to the pacemakers purchased from St. Rude's.
(b) The hospital resells the pacemakers to patients and therefore cannot be considered as a consumer with respect to the pacemakers purchased from St. Rude's.
(c) The hospital resells the pacemakers at a discounted rate and therefore can be considered a consumer with respect to the pacemakers purchased from St. Rude's.
(d) Sale of medical devices is not covered by Consumer Protection Law.

104. Fitzit is an online platform that provides physiotherapy and other ancillary medical services. Amit Ghosh booked a physiotherapist on Fitzit for three months by paying an amount of ₹25,000. Fitzit guaranteed the availability of qualified physiotherapists for the duration. However, Fitzit failed to provide a qualified physiotherapist and the persons who were sent for the first two visits had no training or certification in the field. Amit Ghosh seeks to proceed against Fitzit under Consumer Protection Law. Which of the following statements can be correctly inferred?
(a) Since online services are not covered by Consumer Protection Law, Amit Ghosh cannot be considered a consumer.
(b) Since services are not covered by Consumer Protection Law, Amit Ghosh cannot be considered a consumer.
(c) Since online services are covered by Consumer Protection Law, Amit Ghosh shall be considered a consumer.
(d) Since medical services are not covered by Consumer Protection Law, Amit Ghosh cannot be considered a consumer.

105. Jitesh Shah purchased from BreatheEasy, a company selling respiratory devices, a nebuliser device for his son, Jignesh Shah, for use for clearing his nasal passages. The nebulizer was however defective and led to severe respiratory distress for Jignesh. Jignesh is considering filing a complaint against BreatheEasy under the Consumer Protection Law. Which of the following statements can be correctly inferred?
(a) Since Jignesh Shah did not purchase the device from BreatheEasy, he cannot be considered a consumer with respect to BreatheEasy.
(b) Since Jignesh Shah is a user of the device, he can be considered a consumer.
(c) Sale of medical devices are not covered by Consumer Protection Law.
(d) None of the above

LOGICAL REASONING

XX. The depreciation of an economy's currency is not a matter of concern in itself. The decline in value against major currencies has to be viewed within a set of macroeconomic factors. The recent depreciation of the Indian rupee is a case in point. The rupee has been depreciating for a long time. What are of concern now are the rate at which the depreciation is occurring and the underlying factors causing the change. The Russia-Ukraine war has disrupted supply chains causing commodity prices to rise, leading to a worldwide hardening of inflationary trends. This, in turn, has caused major central banks to raise interest rates, forcing investors back to the safe haven of the US dollar. For India, these headwinds from the global economy have caused several problems. The rise in international prices, especially of crude oil, has led to a higher import bill and, hence, a greater demand for dollars. Higher interest rates in developed country markets have caused a significant outflow of portfolio investments from India, aggravating the already climbing demand for dollars from a rising import bill. By May 2022, foreign institutional investors had pulled out Rs. 1.50 lakh crore from Indian markets.

In the face of these pressures, the rupee, left to itself, would decline in value as the rupee-price of a dollar would increase substantially. One way the Reserve Bank of India could stem the tide would be to sell off dollars in the market to ease the supply situation. However, this would mean that while the value of the rupee could be contained, the nation's foreign exchange kitty would start to erode further. The RBI has been doing exactly that. The challenge before the RBI is this: how much to let the rupee depreciate and how much to intervene to prop it up? Too much depreciation would raise domestic inflation rates as the rupee-price of imports, especially oil, would raise costs of production. It could trigger a rise in policy-controlled interest rates while closely monitoring inflationary expectations. The biggest challenge is to navigate unpredictable international economic shocks in the near future. The Indian economy's health is not exactly at its best. Exports may not be able to take advantage of a falling rupee since international demand is expected to stagnate. India's growth and employment situations are yet to stabilise to what they were about a decade ago. The RBI has difficult choices: controlling inflation versus stimulating growth and stabilising the rupee without severely diminishing the economy's foreign exchange kitty.

[Extracted, with edits and revisions, from "Stifftest: Editorial on depreciation of rupee & challenges before RBI", *The Telegraph*]

106. Which of the following is the author most likely to agree with?

(a) It is a major cause for concern if an economy's currency is depreciating.

(b) Currency depreciation is not a reason for worry in itself, but if macroeconomic factors are not good, there may be a cause for concern.

(c) The fact that the Indian rupee is witnessing a decline in value against major currencies is very worrisome.

(d) A central bank must always do everything in its power to stem the slightest depreciation of an economy's currency.

107. Based on the author's arguments, which of the following, if true, would reduce the decline in value of the rupee?

(a) Appointing a new Governor for the RBI who has a better sense of how to control inflationary trends.

(b) A steep increase in commodity prices and the continued disruption of supply chains.

(c) A reduction in worldwide inflationary trends and the reduction of interest rates in developed country markets.

(d) The RBI buying as many dollars as possible from the market.

108. Which of the following, if true, would most weaken the author's arguments?

(a) The Indian economy has been affected by global inflationary trends and the increase of interest rates in developed country markets.

(b) Since developed country markets have increased their interest rates, global investors have pulled their investments out of other economies, and routed them to such developed country markets.

(c) As the demand for US dollars increases, it is likely the rupee-price of a dollar would increase substantially.

(d) The Indian economy and currency are highly protected and have been insulated from the effects of global inflationary trends and the increase of interest rates in developed country markets.

109. Which of the following, if true, would most strengthen the author's arguments for why Indian exports may not be able to take advantage of a falling rupee?

(a) Economies across the world are witnessing a slowdown, and in such economies, demand for imports decreases substantially.
(b) Economies across the world are booming, and there is an increasing demand for Indian exports.
(c) A reduction in the volume of exports would be more than offset by the increased value of dollars that Indian exporters would earn.
(d) Countries across the world have managed to find ways to insulate themselves from the effects of the Russia-Ukraine war and will need a lot of Indian imports to sustain their new growth models.

110. Based on the author's arguments, which of the following must necessarily be true?
(a) The continuing depreciation of the Indian rupee at its current rate, coupled with worldwide inflationary trends, would result in immense political instability in India, and consequently, in all of South Asia.
(b) If nothing else is done, the rise of interest rates in developed country markets, coupled with hardening of inflationary trends across the world, will result in a fall in the value of the rupee against the dollar.
(c) If inflationary trends continue to harden across the world, and if interest rates in developed country markets continue to rise, portfolio investors will increase their investments in India, and this will have a positive impact on India's foreign exchange reserves.
(d) If nothing else is done, the rise of interest rates in developed country markets, coupled with hardening of inflationary trends across the world, will result in a rise in the value of the rupee against the dollar.

111. Which of the following is the author most likely to agree with?
(a) The RBI must not focus solely on preventing the depreciation of the rupee, as that may result in negative impacts on other aspects of the economy.
(b) The RBI must focus solely on preventing the depreciation of the rupee at all costs, since it is by far the most important indicator of the health of the Indian economy.
(c) Periodic inflationary trends are normal in any economy, and the RBI need not worry about the inflationary effects in the Indian economy caused by the depreciation of the rupee.
(d) The RBI need not do anything to reduce the rate of depreciation of the rupee, since the depreciation of an economy's currency is not a matter of concern in itself.

XXI. The post-truth era is, expectedly, marked by a discerning erosion of public trust in sources of information. Mass media — both traditional and new-age avatars — has borne the brunt of this mistrust. And for good reasons too. Social media, its most popular platform, is a harbinger of falsity. It is thus encouraging to see that at least the old guard of the media ecosystem — the newspaper — continues to defy this discouraging trend. A pan-India survey of media consumption by Lokniti found that print media remains the most trusted source of information. The finding is consistent with the heartening surge in public endorsement of the reliability of newspapers since the pandemic. An earlier survey, which attempted to examine the impact of the lockdown on 'reading patterns', had found that the number of readers who used to spend over an hour on newspapers every day had risen to 38%, up from 16% in the pre-lockdown period. The increased trust in newspapers is because the lockdowns coincided with the dissemination of the crudest kinds of misinformation about the pandemic in India and around the world and newspapers played a pivotal role in exposing these lies.

But that is where the good news ends — for the print media, at least. Among other things, the data collated by the survey found deepening footprints of social media in rural and urban constituencies while television continues to dominate the screen. These developments are consistent with global trends that reveal that the newspaper industry is struggling to contain the migration of readers and revenue to other formats, especially digital media. Ironically, the pandemic, which saw a resurgence in collective trust in newspapers, adversely affected the print media as traditional advertisers, reeling under the economic fallouts of CoVid-19, cut back on advertisements. But the crisis in print precedes the pandemic. Newspapers have been outpaced by speedier, but also spurious, sources of information. The dominance of the image over text as a cultural phenomenon is another formidable challenge. The print media's hopes of remaining competitive and profitable must, therefore, centre on using this collective trust as a form of capital. Survival strategies, especially the revenue model, must be re-explored and the emphasis shifted to in-depth analyses of news as well as eye- catching layouts now that newspapers are slower to reach news to the audience.

[Extracted, with edits and revisions, from "Good news: Editorial on print media remaining the most trusted source of information", *The Telegraph*]

112. Which of the following is the author most likely to agree with?
- (a) The CoVid-19 pandemic was an unmitigated disaster for the newspaper industry.
- (b) The CoVid-19 pandemic had negative as well as positive effects on the newspaper industry.
- (c) The CoVid-19 pandemic only had good effects on the newspaper industry.
- (d) The CoVid-19 pandemic had no effect at all on the newspaper industry.

113. Which of the following, if true, would most weaken the author's arguments?
- (a) Social media is a reliable source of true and accurate news and information.
- (b) Social media is a highly unreliable source of news and information and should not be trusted.
- (c) Social media is a good way for people to stay connected with each other.
- (d) Social media is a speedier source of information than newspapers.

114. Which of the following would be an effective way of making print media more competitive?
- (a) Slowing down the process of print media production.
- (b) Using more expensive printing methods that achieve better print quality, even if it results in newspapers becoming more expensive.
- (c) Only publishing newspapers on alternate days.
- (d) Developing ways of ensuring that print media can reach readers more speedily.

115. Based on the author's arguments, which of the following, if true, would have resulted in the weakening, rather than deepening of public trust in newspapers since the pandemic?
- (a) Newspapers were very careful in ensuring they reported accurate and true news during the lockdowns.
- (b) Newspapers played a leading role in exposing lies and misinformation spread during the lockdown.
- (c) Newspapers actively disseminated misinformation during the lockdowns and made no efforts to expose lies spread by others.
- (d) Newspapers alerted the public to the fact that a number of sources were spreading crude forms of misinformation during the pandemic.

116. What would be the impact on the readership and revenues of the print media if the image were not dominant over text as a cultural phenomenon?
- (a) Print media would not suffer as much of a reduction in readership and revenue as readers shifted to other formats.
- (b) Print media would suffer a greater reduction in readership and revenue as readers shifted to other formats.
- (c) There would be no impact on the readership and revenues of the print industry.
- (d) There would be an increased demand from readers that newspapers carry more images and less text.

117. How does the author suggest newspapers can overcome the problem of being outpaced by speedier sources of information?

(a) They offer direct means by which newspapers can become faster to publish and deliver to readers.

(b) They encourage a complete and immediate shift to digital media as a way of ensuring newspapers are not outpaced by other sources of information.

(c) They offer ways to reduce production costs, which would offset the losses caused by readers shifting allegiance to faster sources of information.

(d) They offer alternative means for newspapers to become competitive and profitable, but do not solve the problem of how newspapers can become faster sources of information.

XXII. In this moment, the developed countries — I point to them, because these countries have already burnt massive amounts of carbon dioxide for energy to build their economies — are faced with a real energy conundrum. On the one hand, developed countries are battered because of a fast-heating planet; temperatures have gone through the roof; droughts and extreme weather events are hitting them as well. On the other hand, ordinary people in these countries are worried, not just because of climate change but because of the lack of energy to heat their homes this coming winter. In the US, gas prices went up in summer, so much so that people travelled less and consumption of fuel dropped. But now prices are down and it is business as usual.

The fact is that this energy disruption has provided the much-needed vault to the beleaguered fossil fuel industry. Governments are asking this industry to supply more. Europe has baptised natural gas, a fossil fuel less polluting than coal but still a major emitter of carbon dioxide, as "clean". The US has passed a climate bill, which will invest in renewable energy but conditional to increased spends on oil and gas and the opening up of millions of hectares of federal land for drilling. Through this bill the US will do more than ever before to build a manufacturing base for renewable energy, particularly solar. Europe, even in this desperate scramble for gas, is working to ramp up its investment in renewable power. So, it is the worst of times. It could be the best of times, but there are some caveats. One, this renewed interest in fossil fuels must remain temporary and transient. Given the nature of economies, once the investment has been made in this new infrastructure or the supply of fossil fuel has increased from new oil and gas discoveries, it will be difficult to wean off. Two, these countries should not be entitled to more use of fossil fuels in our world of shrunk carbon budgets. They need to reduce emissions drastically and leave whatever little carbon budget space that is remaining to poorer countries to use, thereby satisfying such poorer countries' demands.

[Extracted, with edits and revisions, from "New energy conundrum", by Sunita Narain, *DownToEarth*]

118. Which of the following is the author most likely to agree with?

(a) People in the US are not worried at all about climate change.

(b) People in the US are worried about climate change, and these concerns affect their energy consumption habits more than anything else.

(c) Climate change has resulted in the increase of energy prices across the world, and as a result, governments have had to invest in finding newer sources of renewable energy.

(d) Changes in the energy consumption habits of people in the US are affected more by energy prices than concerns of climate change.

119. Which of the following is most similar to the author's statements about developed countries' renewed interest in fossil fuels?

(a) Developed countries should not, under any circumstances, invest any resources in fossil fuel energy extraction, and must immediately put a halt to all fossil fuel consumption.

(b) Things could improve if developed countries recognise the difficulty of moving away from reliance on such sources of energy and make a conscious effort to move to alternate or renewable energy sources quickly.
(c) Since investments in energy extraction of any kind are very expensive, developed countries must ensure that they make permanent and continuing investments in fossil fuels.
(d) Developing countries must not, under any circumstances, consume fossil fuels, and leave whatever carbon budget space is remaining to richer countries to use.

120. If the information in the passage above is correct, which of the following must necessarily be true?
(a) The fossil fuel industry in developing countries will face reduced sales in the short term, with increased sales in the long term.
(b) The cost of making, installing, and using solar panels will reduce substantially in the coming years.
(c) Passing a bill in the US is a huge effort, and it would not have been possible to pass the new climate bill unless the current energy crisis had compelled lawmakers to do so.
(d) The fossil fuel industry in developing countries will see an increase in business, at least in the short term.

121. Which of the following, if true, would most weaken the author's argument about why travel and fuel consumption in the US reduced in summer?
(a) People like to travel regardless of season, and the only thing that would prevent them from travelling at any time of the year would be high costs.
(b) Airlines raised ticket prices as a response to increase in fuel prices, and therefore, fewer people were able to buy air tickets to travel.
(c) Strict lockdowns were imposed in the US in summer, because of which people travelled less; further, temperatures were moderate, and this meant people had to use less fuel to heat or warm their homes.
(d) Widespread geopolitical tensions in the first half of the year meant that fuel prices were at an all-time high in summer; but prices have now eased off somewhat, making fuel slightly more affordable in the uS.

122. Which of the following, if true, would resolve the 'conundrum' the author says developed countries face now?
(a) The development of adequate renewable power sources in the near term that would lead to a reduction in consumption of fossil fuels.
(b) Finding new sources of fossil fuels that will ensure there is no shortage of energy to heat homes in the winter.
(c) Switching immediately to renewable power sources, even if it leads to a shortage in energy supply for people.
(d) Providing adequate aid to poorer countries so that they can develop renewable power sources for their use.

123. Assuming the aim of the US climate bill is to reduce fossil fuel consumption, which of the following would be the strongest argument that it will fail to achieve such an aim?
(a) The bill promotes investments in renewable energy but does not provide for enough increase in investments in developing more sources of fossil fuel-powered energy.
(b) The bill is written in technical language, which ordinary people cannot easily understand.
(c) The bill is self-defeating, since it makes investments in renewable energy conditional to more expenditure on oil and gas and making millions of hectares of federal land available for drilling, which would lead to an increased consumption of fossil fuels.
(d) The bill does not provide any means of increasing carbon budgets, thereby making more room for fossil fuel consumption.

XXIII. While men and women are both considered to be more capable as they get older, only women bear the brunt of being seen as "less warm" as they age, new research has found. This series of studies is reportedly the first to look at both gender and age to determine how perceptions of women and men differ. "it's just stunning... these stereotypes are so hard-wired and deeply entrenched that they come out even when absolutely identical information is provided about a man and a woman," Jennifer Chatman, Distinguished Professor of Management at UC Berkeley's Haas School of Business, said. In an analysis of professors' evaluations, female professors witnessed a decline as they moved from their 30s to 40s, hitting an all-time low around the age of 47. All this while, the evaluation of male professors remained consistent. Interestingly, after the age of 47, the evaluations for women increased again, becoming equal with those of men around the early 60s. "At that point, there are different stereotypes of women, and they may benefit from being seen as more grandmotherly," said Laura Kray, faculty director of the Center for Equity, Gender, and Leadership at Berkeley Haas and an author of the study.

Women around the age of mid 30s to late 40s also face what is called "the motherhood penalty," where assumptions around parenting duties lead people to believe women are less committed to their careers than men. This has several repercussions, most particularly evident in hiring, promotions and wages. Women executives further pointed out that they face "hyper-scrutiny" and "scepticism" which harks back to perceptions of likeability versus agency. Gendered networks in the workplace, with men gaining greater access to senior leaders, become cemented mid-career, pose another difficulty for working women. Negative perceptions of women in middle-age can also be linked to stereotypes around menopause. In 2008, psychologists studied the attitudes of people towards women in different reproductive stages. They found that while the pregnant women or the woman with the baby were thought about in glowing terms, menopausal women were associated with negative emotions, illness and ageing.

[Extracted, with edits and revisions, from "How Stereotypes Affect Middle-Aged Women's Careers", by Ananya Singh, *The Swaddle*]

124. Which of the following is most likely to be true if the author's statements about gendered networks in the workplace are true?

(a) Mid-career women do not find it as easy to get access to senior leaders, who are usually male, as their male colleagues. They therefore find career progression or new opportunities easier to come by.

(b) Mid-career women find it easier to get access to senior leaders, who are usually male, as their male colleagues. They therefore find career progression or new opportunities easier to come by.

(c) Mid-career women do not find it as easy to get access to senior leaders, who are usually male, as their male colleagues. They therefore find career progression or new opportunities harder to come by.

(d) Mid-career women find it easier to get access to senior leaders, who are usually male, as their male colleagues. They therefore do not find career progression or new opportunities harder to come by.

125. Which of the following is most likely to be an outcome of what the author describes as the "motherhood penalty"?

(a) People are more hesitant to hire men from their mid 30s to their late 40s but may be more willing to hire women of a similar age.

(b) People are more hesitant to hire women from their mid 30s to their late 40s but may be more willing to hire men of a similar age.

(c) Women from their mid 30s to their late 40s always prioritise parenting responsibilities and so are not really interested in pursuing a career.

(d) Women who have children are less committed to their careers than men.

126. If professors' evaluations are the most important criteria in awarding promotions, then which of the following would be the most likely outcome, based on the information provided in the passage?

(a) Male professors are likely to be promoted at an even rate throughout their career, while women professors would experience a lower likelihood of promotion in the mid-career stage.

(b) Since there is a wide disparity between the evaluations that male and female professors receive, the practice of relying upon such evaluations will quickly be abandoned.

(c) Male and female professors will receive promotions at a similar rate throughout the course of their career.

(d) Women professors are likely to be promoted at an even rate throughout their career, while male professors would experience a lower likelihood of promotion in the mid-career stage.

127. Which of the following is the author most likely to disagree with?

(a) Women going through menopause often quit the workforce voluntarily.

(b) Women going through menopause are more likely to be perceived negatively at the workplace and to have difficulty achieving professional success.

(c) Women going through menopause should be permitted to take a mid-career sabbatical.

(d) Women going through menopause are more likely to be perceived positively at the workplace and to achieve professional success.

128. Which of the following, if true, would most strengthen the main argument in the passage?

(a) Several independent studies conducted in different countries have shown that women in the workplace are perceived positively and are favourably treated as they age.

(b) Several independent studies conducted in different countries have shown that women in the workplace are perceived negatively and are unfairly treated as they age.

(c) The studies mentioned in the passage have been discredited after they were published, and no reliance should be placed on them.

(d) The studies mentioned in the passage were conducted on very small sample sets and cannot be used to make general statements about the difference in perception between men and women.

129. Which of the following, if true, would most weaken Laura Kray's arguments?

(a) Women professors perceived as being 'grandmotherly' are regarded as being likeable and caring.

(b) Women professors perceived as being 'grandmotherly' are treated better by their colleagues and students.

(c) Women professors perceived as being 'grandmotherly' are regarded as being slow, inefficient, and outdated in their field.

(d) Women professors perceived as being 'grandmotherly' are regarded very highly and receive much more respect than younger women professors.

XXIV. Why are we humans so susceptible to the doom and gloom of the news? two reasons. The first is what psychologists call negativity bias: we're more attuned to the bad than the good. Back in our hunting and gathering days, we were better off being frightened of a spider or a snake a hundred times too often than one time too few. Too much fear wouldn't kill you; too little surely would.

Second, we're also burdened with an availability bias. If we can easily recall examples of a given thing, we assume that thing is relatively common. The fact that we're bombarded daily with horrific stories about aircraft disasters, child snatchers and beheadings — which tend to lodge in the memory — completely skews our view of the world.

In this digital age, the news we're being fed is only getting more extreme. In the old days, journalists didn't know much about their individual readers. They wrote for the masses. But the people behind Facebook, Twitter and Google know you well. They know what shocks and horrifies you, they know what makes you click. They know how to grab your attention and hold it so they can serve you the most lucrative helping of personalised ads. This modern media frenzy is nothing less than an assault on the mundane. Because, let's be honest, the lives of most people are pretty predictable. Nice, but boring. So while we'd prefer having nice neighbours with boring lives, 'boring' won't make you sit up and take notice. 'Nice' doesn't sell ads. And so Silicon Valley keeps dishing us up ever more sensational clickbait, knowing full well, as a Swiss novelist once quipped, that "News is to the mind what sugar is to the body."

[Extracted, with edits and revisions, from *Humankind: A Hopeful History*, by Rutger Bregman, Bloomsbury Publishing, London, 2021]

130. Which of the following, if true, would most weaken the author's arguments?
- (a) Behavioural traits that helped us in the days when we were hunter-gatherers continue to be present in modern-day humans.
- (b) Behavioural traits that helped us in the days when we were hunter-gatherers are no longer found in modern-day humans.
- (c) The negativity bias makes us more likely to be affected by depressing or sad news.
- (d) We have certain behavioural characteristics that affect how we perceive and are affected by sad news.

131. Which of the following is the author most likely to agree with?
- (a) Contemporary media continuously exposes us to exciting news and information, which may be just like the things we usually experience in our lives.
- (b) Contemporary media continuously exposes us to exciting news and information, which may be very unlike the kinds of things we usually encounter in our lives.
- (c) Contemporary media continuously exposes us to boring news and information, which may be very unlike the kinds of things we usually encounter in our lives.
- (d) Contemporary media continuously exposes us to boring news and information, which may be just like the things we usually experience in our lives.

132. Based only on the author's statement that "we'd prefer having nice neighbours with boring lives", and the author's argument about the nature of news that modern media exposes us to, which of the following would the author be most likely to agree with?
- (a) Constantly being exposed to negative news gives us a warped perspective of the world.
- (b) In our hunting and gathering days, it was better for us to be unnecessarily scared rather than being scared too little.
- (c) The news modern media exposes us to is just like our day-to-day experiences.
- (d) The news modern media exposes us to is very different from our day-to-day experiences.

133. The author's statements about negativity bias, if true, provide most support for which of the following conclusions?
- (a) We are more likely to notice a story about a billionaire donating their money to charity than a story about an airplane crash.
- (b) We are more likely to be attracted to a news article about a rise in life expectancy in our country than a news article about a murder in our city.
- (c) We are more likely to notice a story about increasing pollution levels than a story about improving educational levels in schools.
- (d) We are more likely to form our opinion of the world based on the information available to us rather than information we do not have access to.

134. Which of the following would be the most effective way of countering the effects of what the author describes as our 'availability bias'?

(a) Ensuring that we do not seek out news sources and stories that we may not otherwise have been exposed to.
(b) Following only one news source and limiting our perspective of the world to that one source.
(c) Avoiding all positive news stories, and instead only reading news stories about disasters and tragedies.
(d) Ensuring that we seek out news sources and stories that we may not otherwise have been exposed to.

135. The author says that "The fact that we're bombarded daily with horrific stories about aircraft disasters, child snatchers and beheadings — which tend to lodge in the memory — completely skews our view of the world." The conclusion the author draws in this argument follows logically if which of the following is assumed?
(a) Our ideas about the world are shaped by the information we are exposed to.
(b) Modern media is concerned only with making massive profits.
(c) Modern journalists generate news stories much faster than in the old days.
(d) Humans once lived as hunter-gatherers.

QUANTITATIVE TECHNIQUES

XXV. The findings of Oxfam India's latest 'India Discrimination Report 2022' indicate that there is a significant gap in the earnings between men and women in the case of regular and self-employment in urban areas. The lower wages for salaried women are due to 67 percent of discrimination and 33 percent due to lack of education and work experience. The average earning is ₹16,000 for men and merely ₹6,600 for women in urban areas in self-employment. The average earning of men is ₹19,800 as against ₹15,600 for women in regular/salaried employment in urban areas. Also, in urban areas the average earnings of men (₹9,000) are significantly higher than women (₹5,700) even in casual employment. Apart from women, historically oppressed communities along with religious minorities also continue to face discrimination in accessing jobs, livelihoods, and agricultural credit. The mean income for Scheduled Castes or Scheduled Tribes ("**SC/ST**") persons in urban areas who are in regular employment is ₹15,300 as against ₹20,300 for persons belonging to the non-SC/ST category. The average earning of self-employed workers is ₹15,900 for non-SC/STs and ₹10,500 for SC/STs. The average monthly earning for the SC/ST workers in casual work is ₹8,000 below the corresponding figure of ₹8,600 for the non-SC/ST.

[**Data source**: Oxfam India]

[**Note**: Values have been approximated to the nearest hundred]

136. Choose the correct option:
(a) Women's average earnings in urban areas in casual work is 30% lower than that of men
(b) Men's average earning in urban areas in self-employment is nearly 2.5 times that of earnings of women
(c) In casual work, women earn more in rural areas than in urban areas
(d) The difference in earnings of men and women in regular/salaried employment in urban areas is ₹3,500

137. Of the regular employed in urban areas, the earnings of a non-SC/ST worker is what percent more than a SC/ST worker?
(a) Between 20% and 25%
(b) Less than 15%
(c) Between 30% and 35%
(d) More than 35%

138. Of those in casual employment, if a man's average earnings was deposited at a rate of 16% simple interest for 20 years, in how many years at the same rate of simple interest a SC/ST worker must deposit their average earnings to earn the same amount as a man in 20 years?
(a) 24 years (b) 22.5 years
(c) 21 years (d) 23.2 years

139. The findings also indicate discrimination as a driving factor behind low Women's Labour Force Participation Rate (LFPR) in the country. As per the union ministry of Statistics & Programme implementation (MoSPI), LFPR for women in India was only 25.1 percent in 2020–21 for urban and rural women. This is considerably lower than South Africa where the LFPR for women is 46 percent in 2021 as per the latest World Bank estimates. The LFPR for women in India has rapidly declined from 42.7 percent in 2004-05 to mere 25.1 percent in 2020–2021 showing the withdrawal of women from the workforce despite rapid economic growth during the same period. In 2019–20, 60 percent of all males aged 15 years and more have regular salaried and self-employed jobs while 19 percent of all similarly aged females get regular and self-employment. Use the additional data in the passage above to answer this and the next question.
If the number of women in India in 2020–2021 is 670 million which is 24% more than in 2004–2005, what is the difference in the number of women in LFPR 2004–05 and 2021?
(a) Less than 5 crores
(b) Between 6 and 8 crores
(c) Between 10 and 12 crores
(d) More than 15 crores

140. In 2019–20, if the number of males aged 15 years and more is 76% of the total male population and the number of females aged 15 years and more is 72% of the total female population and the total male population is 1.05 times the total female population, what is the ratio of females to males aged 15 years and more that have regular salaried and self-employed jobs?
(a) 2 : 7 (b) 3 : 10
(c) 5 : 9 (d) 1 : 3

XXVI. World fruit production went up 54 percent between 2000 and 2019, to 883 million tonnes. Five fruit species accounted for 57 percent of the total production in 2019, down from 63 percent in 2000. Use the data in the passage to answer the following questions.
[Data source: FAO]

141. What was the world fruit production in 2000?
(a) 474 million tonnes (b) 517 million tonnes
(c) 573 million tonnes (d) 406 million tonnes

142. Of the five fruit species mentioned in the passage above, the share of bananas and plantains increased by 1 percentage point between 2000 and 2019, watermelons in 2019 was 6 percentage points lower than bananas and plantains in 2000, apples remained stable at 10%, and the percentage share of oranges and grapes reduced to half of bananas in 2019 . What was the percentage of bananas and plantains in 2019?
(a) 17% (b) 18%
(c) 16% (d) 21%

143. Of the watermelons in 2000, one-eighth perished, one-fifth of the remaining was sold to be juiced and 30% of the remaining was exported. If the percentage share of oranges in 2000 was equal to the percentage share of watermelons in 2019, how many watermelons were retained for home sale and consumption?
(a) 39.2 million tonnes
(b) 1.6 million tonnes
(c) 16.8 million tonnes
(d) 2.7 million tonnes

144. Assume that all grapes and apples were sold through a single organisation in 2000. Grapes and apples were sold to 4 different customers such that a certain quantity of apples were sold to the first customer, same number of apples were sold to the second customer as to the first and a certain number of grapes were sold to that customer after which apples were over. Twice the quantity of grapes sold to the second was sold to the third customer and twice the quantity sold to the third was sold to the fourth customer. The total quantity of grapes is equal to the total quantity of apples sold and the remaining grapes were stored. How many grapes were sold to each customer?
(a) 19.1 million tonnes
(b) 8.2 million tonnes
(c) 28.6 million tonnes
(d) 9.4 million tonnes

145. Frutopia and Fruitfix both sold oranges at the same selling price. However, Frutopia gave customers a 15% discount on the marked price whereas Fruitfix sold the oranges for a discount of 20% on the marked price. If the marked price of oranges on Frutopia is ₹75/kg, what is the marked price of oranges on Fruitfix?

(a) ₹78 (b) ₹82
(c) ₹90 (d) ₹80

XXVII. Players are selected for Judo based on their body weights from the following 10 weight groups:

1. (48 kg - 52 kg) 6. (68 kg - 72 kg)
2. (52 kg - 56 kg) 7. (72 kg - 76 kg)
3. (56 kg - 60 kg) 8. (76 kg - 80 kg)
4. (60 kg - 64 kg) 9. (80 kg - 84 kg)
5. (64 kg - 68 kg) 10. (84 kg - 88 kg)

The average weight of the players after selecting one player from each group is 68 kg. If one of the players (named S) leaves the team, their average weight comes down to 66.5 kg.

146. Player S is from the weight group:

(a) 1 (b) 9
(c) 5 (d) 10

147. If S leaves the group and two new players join the group, their average weight increases to 68 kg. These players can NOT be from groups:

(a) 1 and 3 (b) Both from group 7
(c) 4 and 10 (d) 5 and 9

148. What is the average weight of all the players taken together?

(a) 68 kg (b) 66 kg
(c) 69 kg (d) Cannot be determined

149. In the average of all the groups together, which group contributes most in overall average?

(a) 10 (b) 8
(c) 1 (d) Cannot be determined

150. If one of the new two players is from group 4, which group the other player is from?

(a) 5 (b) 7
(c) 10 (d) None of the above

ANSWER KEY

English

1. (b)	6. (a)	11. (b)	16. (b)	21. (a)	26. (d)
2. (c)	7. (c)	12. (b)	17. (a)	22. (b)	27. (b)
3. (a)	8. (c)	13. (c)	18. (c)	23. (d)	28. (a)
4. (c)	9. (a)	14. (d)	19. (d)	24. (b)	29. (d)
5. (b)	10. (b)	15. (a)	20. (d)	25. (b)	30. (c)

Current Affairs Including General Knowledge

31. (a)	37. (d)	43. (b)	49. (c)	55. (c)	61. (a)
32. (c)	38. (a)	44. (c)	50. (d)	56. (d)	62. (d)
33. (a)	39. (b)	45. (b)	51. (d)	57. (b)	63. (b)
34. (a)	40. (d)	46. (d)	52. (d)	58. (c)	64. (c)
35. (d)	41. (a)	47. (c)	53. (b)	59. (c)	65. (d)
36. (b)	42. (b)	48. (a)	54. (a)	60. (d)	66. (b)

Legal Reasoning

67. (c)	73. (a)	79. (c)	85. (a)	91. (c)	97. (c)	103. (b)
68. (d)	74. (b)	80. (a)	86. (c)	92. (a)	98. (b)	104. (c)
69. (b)	75. (d)	81. (b)	87. (a)	93. (c)	99. (b)	105. (b)
70. (a)	76. (d)	82. (a)	88. (d)	94. (d)	100. (c)	106. (b)
71. (c)	77. (d)	83. (d)	89. (b)	95. (c)	101. (c)	
72. (b)	78. (b)	84. (c)	90. (c)	96. (d)	102. (c)	

Legal Reasoning

107. (c)	112. (b)	117. (d)	122. (a)	127. (d)	132. (d)
108. (d)	113. (a)	118. (d)	123. (c)	128. (b)	133. (c)
109. (a)	114. (d)	119. (b)	124. (c)	129. (c)	134. (d)
110. (b)	115. (c)	120. (d)	125. (b)	130. (b)	135. (a)
111. (a)	116. (a)	121. (c)	126. (a)	131. (b)	

Quantitative Techniques

136. (b)	139. (b)	142. (b)	145. (b)	148. (d)
137. (c)	140. (a)	143. (a)	146. (b)	149. (d)
138. (d)	141. (c)	144. (d)	147. (a)	150. (c)

CLAT 2022

ENGLISH

Public speaking is a powerful real-life skill. Over the centuries, impressive speeches made by people from various walks of life have helped to change hearts, minds and shape the world as we see it today. Speeches that are delivered with intense emotions and conviction can infuse compassion and forgiveness; elevate levels of hatred and destruction; break or unite nations.

On October 5, 1877 in the mountains of Montana Territory, when Chief Joseph surrendered to General Nelson A. Miles, the former gave a Surrender Speech. The speech included these words: "*It is cold, and we have no blankets; the little children are freezing to death. I want time to look for my children, and see how many of them I can find. Maybe I shall find them among the dead. Hear me, my Chiefs! I am tired; my heart is sick and sad. From where the sun now stands I will fight no more forever.*"

The heart-wrenching speech bared the grief and misery of the speaker, and those subjected to overwhelming hardships.

During World War II, the speech *We Shall Fight on the Beaches* delivered by Winston Churchill on June 4, 1940 is considered a high-powered speech that strengthened the determination of those present in the House of Commons. In the speech, he said, "*Even though large tracts of Europe and many old and famous States have fallen or may fall into the grip of the Gestapo and all the odious apparatus of Nazi rule, we shall not flag or fail. We shall go on to the end, we shall fight in France, we shall fight on the seas and oceans, we shall fight with growing confidence and growing strength in the air, we shall defend our island, whatever the cost may be, we shall fight on the beaches, we shall fight on the landing grounds, we shall fight in the fields and in the streets, we shall fight in the hills;*"

In 1950, William Faulkner was honoured with a Nobel Prize for his significant contributions to the American novel. This was the time when the Soviet Union had found the possible implications of the use of the atomic bomb, and people had begun to live in the fear of annihilation. In his *Nobel Prize Acceptance Speech*, Faulkner urged writers of various genres to think and write beyond the fear of destruction, and instead write materials that would lift the human spirit. The powerful message included: "*I believe that man will not merely endure: he will prevail. He is immortal, not because he alone among creatures has an inexhaustible voice, but because he has a soul, a spirit capable of compassion and sacrifice and endurance. The poet's, the writer's, duty is to write about these things. It is his privilege to help man endure by lifting his heart, by reminding him of the courage and honor and hope and pride and compassion and pity and sacrifice which have been the glories of his past. The poet's voice need not merely be the record of man, it can be one of the props, the pillars to help him endure and prevail.*"

Undoubtedly, effective speeches have a long-lasting impact on the minds of the listeners, and they elevate the levels of awareness or actions the speaker intends to raise or catalyze.

1. The main idea of the passage is that
   (a) All leaders should be accomplished public speakers.
   (b) An impactful speech can convey a strong message to the listeners.
   (c) A speech should sound pleasing to the ears of the listeners.
   (d) Publicspeakers should be bold and argumentative.

2. The tone of the Surrender Speech is
   (a) Satiric
   (b) Optimistic
   (c) Poignant
   (d) Narcissistic

3. It is evident that through his speech, Churchill wished to __________ his countrymen __________.
   (a) Inform, about the challenges that arise in a war-torn country.
   (b) Warn, against the futility of war.
   (c) Remind, how their endeavours to fight against the Nazi rule had failed miserably.
   (d) Reassure, that they would combat fiercely against their enemy under all circumstances.

4. Which one of the following is the least likely to be used to describe Churchill?
   (a) Resolute
   (b) Undaunted
   (c) Complacent
   (d) Unwavering

5. In the sentence: '*The poet's voice need not merely be the record of man, it can be one of the props, the pillars to help him endure and prevail*' Faulkner has used __________ to convey the power of a poet's writings.
   (a) A metaphor
   (b) A simile
   (c) An onomatopoeia
   (d) A transferred epithet

As a six-year-old child-beggar, Saroo slept off in a stationary train in Khandwa, Madhya Pradesh; however, when he woke up, he found himself in an empty compartment of a train thundering towards Kolkata where he spent a couple of weeks in a state of panic and hopelessness. Finally, he ended up in a local government adoption centre from where he was adopted by an Australian couple. Twenty five years later, Saroo felt the urge to trace his biological mother and see in what state she lived. Relentlessly, he used Google's satellite feature to map the parts of the country that could have possibly been his own hometown. The search was a long and arduous one; nevertheless, the perseverance did pay. One eventful day, he met his mother; thereafter, he continued to keep in touch with her.

If technology can unite people with their loved ones, it can also make them distant. The unlimited variety of applications (apps) available to toddlers, teenagers and adults might have revolutionized their lives for the better, but these very apps have snatched away the joys of long naturewalks; they have encroached upon the time and space that people earlier used for physical interaction; they have drilled deep chasms of loneliness in the lives of countless numbers of people.

Simple pleasures of life include visiting friends and relatives, playing matches in open spaces, interacting with people in markets, public libraries and clubs. However, with the escalating rage of using apps like those for social media, playing virtual games, and homedelivery services, these joyous moments are fading into oblivion, and the pall of loneliness is getting heavier by the day.

Where are we heading to? Are we going to allow ourselves to be swamped by apps? Are we going to allow socialmedia to engulf us in a deluge of loneliness and isolation? Are we going to drive ourselves to situations that will ultimately demand mental and physical therapies to regain normalcy? Do we not know that physical interaction is as essential for mental health as food and water is for physical health?

Earlier, social isolation was mostly experienced by some of the elderly people who were devoid of an occupation, and bereft of company of their loved ones. Unfortunately today, an unhealthy solitude prevails among numerous children, teenagers and adults too; subsequently, there is an alarming increase in the demand for mental health therapy practitioners.

The necessity of engaging psychologists in schools and colleges is evidently on the rise. The psychologists are required to identify and address the learning and behavioral needs of students who approach them for guidance; moreover, if required, the professionals are expected to help them in strengthening their emotional, social and academic skills.

Regardless how alarming the situation might be, it is never too late. If people revert to the earlier trend of shopping off-line, going for naturewalks, playing outdoors games, and catching up with friends in their homes or cafés more frequently, they can keep their heads firmly well above the ocean of loneliness.

6. From the passage it is evident that Saroo's desire to find his mother

(a) Ended up being a distant dream.
(b) Inspired him to use google's satellite feature intermittently.
(c) Waned as time went by.
(d) Did not slacken till he succeeded.

7. In the sentence *'these very apps have snatched away the joys of long nature-walks;'* the author hass
(a) Satirized nature
(b) Metaphorized apps
(c) Personified apps
(d) None of the above

8. From the passage one can conclude that
(a) It is impossible for people to reduce the usage of apps.
(b) There is a direct correlation between loneliness and excessive usage of social- media apps.
(c) The usage of technology is as essential for mental-health as food and water is for physical health.
(d) All senior citizens are lonely because they are not tech-savvy.

9. From the passage it can be inferred that presently in many educational institutions
(a) The number of teachers who pass the buck to psychologists is on the rise.
(b) Special emphasis is being laid on the mental and emotional health of the students.
(c) The usage of educational apps is being discouraged significantly.
(d) All the students feel the need to be counseled by psychologists.

10. In the concluding paragraph of the given passage, the writer's tone can be best described as
(a) Optimistic
(b) Despairing
(c) Laudatory
(d) Apologetic

"*Wash! Wash! Wash your hands!*" That's been the safety-mantra ever since the pandemic COVID-19 began swamping the world. Undoubtedly, washing hands has proven to be the best way to keep germs at bay. Unfortunately, the medical practitioner who first promoted the importance of this simple activity was subjected to intense humiliation, and ultimately declared insane!

Ignaz Semmelweis was a Hungarian doctor. In 1847, as an obstetrician, he was disturbed that post-delivery, almost every third woman died of an unexpected malady. He observed that as a part of the set routine, medical students and doctors would examine and study the corpses in the mortuary, and then come for rounds to the maternity wards. Here, without washing their hands, they would examine expectant mothers. After making numerous hypothesis and observations, he was convinced that when doctors washed their hands before examining the women in the ward, the number of deaths due to serious infection declined. He shared his observations, with his colleagues and many others working in the field of medicine, but unfortunately he could not provide any concrete evidence to his theory. Sadly, due to the vehement criticism that he received, he went into depression. Furthermore, Ignaz strived to prove his point so relentlessly that it led to the belief that he had lost his mind. In 1865, a doctor deceptively lured him into an asylum for the insane, and two weeks of the brutal treatment that was meted out to him by the attendants led to his untimely death. About twenty years later, when the world became more receptive to the works of scientists like Louis Pasteur and Joseph Lister, awareness regarding germs that cause diseases began to spread. This is the time when Ignaz was honoured with titles like *Father of Hand Hygiene and Saviour of Mothers*- an honour much too late!

Some of the most celebrated artists have earned fame much after their deaths. It is tragic that Vincent Van Gogh's awe-inspiring work was labeled as strange and amateur by most of the critics of his time. It is believed that he sold only one or two painting in his lifetime, and that too for a meager amount. Today, every single painting of Vincent Van gogh paintings is worth millions of dollars.

Franz Kafka was a proficient writer, but when he published a few pieces of his writings, he received immense criticism. Before his death in 1924, he handed over his unpublished novels and short stories to his friend Max Brod, and urged him to destroy them; however, Brod got the manuscripts published. Today, Franz is acclaimed as one of the major fiction writers of the twentieth century; the novels titled *The Trial* published in 1925, and *The Castle* published in 1926 are considered two of his masterpieces.

Perhaps, if humans were more tolerant and amenable to change, innovative concepts, theories and creations, the deserving would live to experience the glory and honour they rightfully deserve.

11. The main idea of the passage is that
    (a) All original theories and works should receive unreserved acceptance.
    (b) Many undeserving innovators have been honoured after their demise.
    (c) Creativity must never be inhibited.
    (d) Numerous innovators have found recognition and appreciation of their works posthumously.

12. From the passage it is evident that Dr. Ignaz's theory was rejected because
    (a) He could not substantiate it
    (b) The doctors did not want him to regulate their work ethics
    (c) He had been declared insane
    (d) Joseph Lister and Louis Pasteur had already discovered germs

13. From the passage one can conclude that the art critics who ______________ Van Gogh's works were ______________.
    (a) Applauded, pessimistic.
    (b) Censured, hypercritical.
    (c) Denounced, tolerant.
    (d) Acclaimed, rigid.

14. From the passage it can be inferred that Max Brod
    (a) Was of the opinion that Franz had not reached out to the right critics
    (b) Decried Franz's writings
    (c) Considered it unsacred to destroy any manuscript
    (d) Appreciated and valued Franz's works

15. The word *relentlessly* in the passage can be best replaced by the word
    (a) Irresolutely
    (b) Recklessly
    (c) Unabatedly
    (d) Unabashedly

Cryptocurrencies are a terrible thing. They are the essence of a Ponzi scheme whose value is based entirely on a greater fool prepared to buy it. The promise of alchemy-turning lead into gold has bewitched humanity throughout the ages and cryptocurrencies are just the latest alchemy. Do not get me wrong, if rich people want to lose their money, in this or any other way, they should be allowed to do so. The rich should be the vanguards of new things in case something unforeseen and good falls out of them. But we need to protect those vulnerable consumers whose lives are such that almost any get-rich-quick schemes will be seductive, and seven out of 10 times, they will lose their life savings. Cryptocurrencies are today's South Sea Bubble — one of the earliest recorded financial bubbles that took place in the 1720s' Britain. Meme-based currencies like Dogecoin, Dogelon Mars and Doge Dash remind me of the infamous plan of one company during the South Sea Bubble to raise money "for carrying on an undertaking of great advantage; but nobody to know what it is."

The cryptocurrency bubble is worse than tulip mania. Through the veil of technology, cryptocurrency enthusiasts are leaning on policy-makers to permit them to be exempt from regulation, privatize money, and make money so disconnected from the economy that it would reap financial disaster. There are many reasons to avoid financial disasters, but one of them is that they ratchet up poverty and inequality. The current money–credit system is not perfect, but like democracy, it is the worst system barring all the others. It has evolved from the ashes of the system cryptocurrency enthusiasts are trying to resurrect.

The current system is vulnerable to attack because money is little understood. Cryptocurrency enthusiasts have attracted a following based on the fiction that the central bank or government creates money and are busy debasing it in their self-interest. This is not the case, but then again, there is some overlap between cryptocurrency advocates, conspiracy theorists, and *anti-vaxxers*.

The time has come for someone to stand up for the current fiat money system and explain that while it could be better still, it has been associated with far more growth, much more distributed, and has responded better to economic crisis than what came before.

In today's money–credit system, banks create money when they issue a loan and place the loan's proceeds into the account of their customers, creating a deposit. Money is, in fact, a tradable debt. The bank's deposit can be used as cash because the bank is a regulated issuer of loans and deposit-taker, which gives the deposit credibility and convertibility. The central bank only influences the creation of money indirectly by its regulatory requirement that a proportion of the loans need to be funded by shareholder's profits. They need to have skin in the game. Money creation then is based on thousands of separate decisions by loan officers and is more distributed than a centralized algorithm like Bitcoin. And its supply is determined by the private demand for loans, which means it is closely aligned to the economy.

16. Which of the following does best describe attitude of the author towards rich people?
    (a) Concerned
    (b) Assiduous
    (c) Indifferent
    (d) Sympathetic

17. Which of the following is true in the context of the passage?
    (a) The author defends the current money–credit system.
    (b) The author rejects the idea that the central bank or government creates money and are busy debasing it in their self-interest.
    (c) The author backs the protection of poor from menace of cryptocurrencies.
    (d) All the above

18. Which rhetorical device is employed in 'cryptocurrencies are just the latest alchemy'?
    (a) Antithesis
    (b) Metaphor
    (c) Personification
    (d) Synecdoche

19. Which of the following does best describe the passage?
    (a) Argumentative and explanatory
    (b) Descriptive and argumentative
    (c) Narrative and explanatory
    (d) Expository and argumentative

20. What do the cryptocurrency enthusiasts rely on?
    (a) Exemption from regulation
    (b) Privatization of money
    (c) Disconnection of money from the economy
    (d) All the above

The fact that Gaia, in her monstrous avatar, decided to distribute fossil fuels very unevenly across the Earth has been central to the emergence of the world's current geopolitical order. From a vitalist point of view, it could be said that the wars of the twentieth century were won as much by the fossilized energy of botanical matter as by particular groups of humans.

In the First World War Germany's lack of oil put it at a huge disadvantage against the Allies, more or less ensuring its defeat. The shortage of oil effectively cancelled the technological advantages Germany enjoyed at the start of the war: despite having a large fleet, for instance, it was unable to use its navy effectively because its coal-burning ships needed to refuel every eleven days. Conversely, the assured supply of American oil conferred so great an advantage on Britain and France that "it could be fairly stated that the war was won for the Western allies by tankers." Not for nothing was it said of the First World War that Britain, France, and the United States floated "to victory on a sea of oil."

In the Second World War the shortage of oil was even more critical to the defeat of the Axis powers. The German Luftwaffe was forced to rely on synthetic fuels derived from coal, and these could not provide the high-octane energy that was necessary for high- compression aero engines: "it was largely due to the inferior engines in German aircraft that the Luftwaffe lost the Battle of Britain." The shortage of oil also dictated Germany's war strategy: it was in order to seize the oilfields of the Caucasus that the German army pushed eastward into the Soviet Union in 1942, leading to a defeat at Stalingrad from which it never recovered. Japan's invasion of the Dutch East Indies was similarly forced by its lack of oil.

In short, over the course of the twentieth century access to oil became the central focus of global geopolitical strategy: for a Great Power, to be able to ensure or hinder the flow of oil was to have a thumb on the jugulars of its adversaries. In the first part of the twentieth century the guarantor of the flow of oil was Britain. After the Second World War, the baton was passed, along with a string of British naval bases, to the United States. The role of guarantor of global energy flows is still crucial to US strategic dominance and to its position as global hegemon.

Today, as Elizabeth DeLoughrey has pointed out, "US energy policy has become increasingly militarized and secured by the Navy, the largest oceanic force on the planet." In the words of the historian Michael Klare, the Iraq War of 2003 marked the transformation of the US military into "a global oil protection service, guarding pipelines, refineries, and loading facilities in the Middle East and elsewhere."

It is important to note that the strategic value of controlling oil flows is tangentially related to the US's energy requirements. The period in which the American military was turning into "a global oil protection service" was one in which the US was well on its way to reducing its dependence on imported oil. The fact that the US is now self- sufficient in fossil fuels has in no way diminished the strategic importance of oil as an instrument for the projection of power- it is the ability to deny energy supplies to rivals that is strategically of central importance.

21. What is the central idea of the passage?
    (a) Fossil fuels in war-making.
    (b) Strategic value fossil fuels in US dominance in the world.
    (c) Role of fossil fuels in modern geopolitical order.
    (d) Distribution of fossil fuels in the world.

22. What was the cause of Germany's defeat in the First World War?
    (a) Germany's shortage of oil
    (b) Advantage of Britain and France
    (c) Weaknesses of Germany's navy
    (d) All the above

23. Which of the following could be inferred from Michael Klare's opinion on US military?
    (a) The US military interferes with energy needs of other countries.
    (b) The US energy policy has become increasingly militarized.
    (c) The US has changed energy policy drastically.
    (d) The US has fully understood the strategic value of controlling oil flows.

24. What does the phrase 'tangentially related' to mean?
    (a) Related directly and in straightforward way
    (b) Related closely and centrally
    (c) Related only slightly and peripherally
    (d) None of the above

25. What makes the US strategically dominating global hegemon?
    (a) Capacity of the US to provide oil protection service, guarding pipelines, refineries, and loading facilities.
    (b) Increasingly militarized energy policy of the US Navy, the largest oceanic force on the planet.
    (c) The role of US as a guarantor of global energy flows.
    (d) All the above

The modern animal rights movement, which originated in the 1970s, may be understood as a reaction to dominant emphases within science and religion (principally, though not exclusively, Christianity). When the Jesuit Joseph Rickaby wrote in 1888 that "Brute beasts, not having understanding and therefore not being persons, cannot have any rights" and that we have "no duties of charity or duties of any kind to the lower animals as neither to stocks and stones", he was only articulating, albeit in an extreme form, the moral insensitivity that has characterized the Western view of animals.

That insensitivity is the result of an amalgam of influences. The first, and for many years the most dominant, was the "other worldly" or "world denying" tendency in Christianity, which has, at its worst, denigrated the value of earthly things in comparison with things spiritual. Traditional Catholicism has divided the world into those beings that possess reason and therefore immortal souls, and those that do not. Christian spirituality has not consciously been at home with the world of non-human creatures-either animal or vegetable. Classic accounts of eternal life as found in Augustine of Hippo, Thomas Aquinas, or John Calvin make little or no reference to the world of animals. Animals, it seems, are merely transient or peripheral beings in an otherwise wholly human-centric economy of salvation.

The second idea-common to Christianity, Judaism, and Islam-is that animals, along with vegetables and minerals, exist instrumentally in relation to human beings; they are made for human beings, even belong to human beings, as resources in creation. This idea predates Christianity and is found notably in Aristotle, who argues that "since nature makes nothing to no purpose, it must be that nature has made them for the sake of man". This idea, largely unsupported by scripture, was nevertheless taken over by Aquinas, who conceived of creation as a rational hierarchy in which the intellectually inferior existed for the sake of the intellectually superior.

Such instrumentalism, which features rationality as the key factor dividing human beings from "brute beasts," has in turn buttressed the third influence, namely the notion of human superiority in creation. Human superiority need not, by itself, have led to the neglect of animal life, but when combined with the biblical ideas of being made "in the image of God" and God's preferential choice to become incarnate in human form, some sense of moral as well as theological ascendancy was indicated. As a result, Christianity, and to a lesser extent Judaism, have been characterized historically by an overwhelming concern for humanity in creation rather than an egalitarian concern for all forms of god-given life. That humans are more important than animals, and that they self-evidently merit moral solicitude in a way that animals cannot, has become religious doctrine. Thus the Catechism of the Catholic Church maintains that "it is . . . unworthy to spend money on them [animals] that should as a priority go to the relief of human misery".

These influences have in turn enabled and justified the scientific exploration of the natural world and specifically the subjection of animals to experimentation. Francis Bacon pursued his scientific investigations in the belief that humanity should "recover that right over nature which belongs to it by divine bequest". René Descartes famously likened the movements of a swallow to the workings of a clock, and maintained that "there is no prejudice to which we are more accustomed from our earliest years than the belief that dumb animals think".

26. Jesuit Joseph Rickaby's articulation on animals may be termed as:
    (a) Eco-centric view of animals
    (b) Anthropocentric view of animals
    (c) Ethnocentric view of animals
    (d) Androcentric view of animals

27. According to the author, how did Christianity contribute to insensitivity of the West towards animals?
    (a) It denigrated the value of earthly things in comparison with spiritual things.
    (b) It divided the world into beings with and without reason.
    (c) It propagated as if animals are transient or peripheral in human centric economy of salvation.
    (d) All the above.

28. Which of the following is closest to the meaning of the word 'instrumentalism' as used in the passage?
    (a) Pragmatism
    (b) Idealism
    (c) Egalitarianism
    (d) None of the above

29. Which of the following is not true in the context of the passage?
    (a) Western philosophy and science are both under the influence of religion.
    (b) Western philosophical views on animals have been influenced by religious notions about them.
    (c) Western religious notions on animals have justified subjection of animals to scientific experimentation.

(d) Some of the scientific views on animals have been influenced by religious notions about them.

30. It may be inferred from René Descartes' view that
   (a) It as irrational to assume that animals have awareness and some mental capacities.
   (b) Animals are automata or they act mechanically.
   (c) Neither (a) nor (b)
   (d) Both (a) and (b)

CURRENT AFFAIRS AND GENERAL KNOWLEDGE

When we hear the name SPACE, only one organization comes to mind: the Indian Space Research Organization (ISRO). The Indian Space Research Organization (ISRO), located in Bengaluru, is the country's first space agency. ISRO was founded in 1969 with the goal of developing and utilizing space technology for national development while also conducting planetary exploration and space science research. The space research operations began in India in the early 1960s, at a time when satellite applications were still in the experimental stages in the United States. Dr. Vikram Sarabhai, the founding father of India's space programme, rapidly recognized the benefits of space technologies after the live transmission of the Tokyo Olympic Games across the Pacific by the American satellite 'Syncom-3' demonstrated the power of communication satellites. The ISRO has launched various spacecrafts like the Chandrayaan, Astrosat, Microsat, GSAT etc. The Government of India has also approved a regional spaceborne navigation system, which will consist of seven satellites. Out of these, four of them will be placed in geosynchronous inclined orbit of 29° relative to the equatorial plane. Such an arrangement would mean all seven satellites would have continuous radio visibility with Indian control stations.

31. Name the first dedicated mission launched by ISRO for studying the celestial sources in X-ray, optical and UV spectral bands simultaneously.
   (a) Amazonia
   (b) Astrosat
   (c) Gaganyaan – 1
   (d) Lunar Polar exploration mission

32. APPLE, the first communication satellite of ISRO was launched from:
   (a) Satish Dhawan Space Centre, Sriharikota
   (b) TERLS, Thiruvananthapuram
   (c) Kourou, French Guiana
   (d) SSLV Launching Station, Tamil Nadu

33. Name the spacecraft that has been successfully sent into the space to probe into the planets in the solar system.
   (a) Sputnik 19
   (b) Cosmos 482
   (c) Pioneer-E
   (d) mariner 10

34. The first successful Nuclear Bomb test conducted by India in 1974, is called the:
   (a) Prithvi
   (b) Pokhran-II
   (c) Smiling Buddha
   (d) Surya

35. NaviC covers India and region extending:
   (a) 1,500 Km
   (b) 2,000 Km
   (c) 7,000 Km
   (d) 1,000 Km

On December 26, 2021, for the first time since the present government came to power in 2014, the Union Home Ministry constituted a panel led by its officers to review the withdrawal of the Armed areas. The Act was amended in 1972 and the powers to declare an area as "disturbed" were conferred concurrently upon the Central Government along with the States. Currently, the MHA issues periodic "disturbed area" notification to extend AFSPA only for Nagaland and Arunachal Pradesh, where it is applicable in the districts of Tirap, Changlang, Longding and areas falling under Namsai and Mahadevpur police stations bordering Assam. The notification for Manipur and Assam is issued by the State Governments. Tripura revoked the Act in 2015 and Meghalaya was under AFSPA for 27 years, until it was revoked by the MHA from April 1, 2018. The Act was implemented in a 20-km area along the border with Assam. Jammu and Kashmir has a separate J&K Armed Forces (Special Powers) Act, 1990.

36. Power to notify parts of or the whole of a State or a Union Territory as a 'disturbed area', under the Armed Forces (Special Powers) Act, 1958 is vested with:
    (a) Governor of any State
    (b) Administrator of a Union Territory
    (c) Central Government
    (d) All of the above

37. AFSPA was introduced in Meghalaya in the year:
    (a) 1995
    (b) 1999
    (c) 1991
    (d) 1989

38. Consider the following statements about the Armed Forces (Special Powers) Act and mark the correct option.
    (a) Detractors and Human Rights Organizations, as well as many sections of civil society, argue that the Act often leads to excesses and require checks and balances or could alienate the people instead of integrating them with the main stream.
    (b) Irom Chanu Sharmila, an activist from Manipur, became ansensitizing figure symbolizing the protest against AFSPA after she sat on an indefinite fast in 2000, demanding its repeal and ended it only in August 2016.
    (c) Both (a) and (b) are correct
    (d) None of the above

39. In 2005, a government-appointed five-member committee, recommended that AFSPA be repealed. It suggested that the Unlawful Activities (Prevention) Act could be suitably amended to deal with terrorism. It made this recommendation as it felt that the AFSPA created an impression that the people of the Northeast States were being targeted for hostile treatment. Who headed this committee?
    (a) B. P. Jeevan reddy
    (b) Abhishek Singhvi
    (c) Soli Sorabjee
    (d) Ram Jethmalani

40. AFSPA is currently in force in:
    (a) Arunachal Pradesh and Assam
    (b) Nagaland and Manipur
    (c) Jammu and Kashmir
    (d) All of the above

One of the justifications of Russia-Ukraine war Russian leader claimed that military action was necessary to stop Ukrainian attacks on the two break away regions of Donetsk and Lugansk, which Russia recognized as sovereign states. President of Russia claimed that Russia could come under attack by Ukrainian far right government, unless their influence in the country is diminished. He accused Western Nations of arming Kyiv against Russia. After being ordered by Russia's leader to invade the capital of Ukraine, Russian troops moved in several directions. As the first targets were hit, airports and the military HQs were located near cities across Ukraine, then tanks and troops rolled into the country from the north, east, and south. The war has demolished most of the cities of the Ukraine and caused irreparable damage to the humanity.

41. Ukraine was part of which country during 1922–1991?
    (a) Germany
    (b) Poland
    (c) USA
    (d) USSR

42. Who is the President of Ukraine?
    (a) Volodymyr Zelenskyy
    (b) Vladimir Zelenskyy
    (c) Volodymyr S. Zelenskyy
    (d) Vladimir Zelensky

43. Which is the currency of Ukraine?
    (a) Guilder
    (b) Zloty
    (c) Ruble
    (d) Hryvnia

44. The President of Ukraine was formerly:
    (a) Weather Forecaster
    (b) Navy Officer

(c) Comedian
(d) TV News reader

45. Which operation was launched by the Indian Government to bring back Indians from Ukraine during Russia-Ukraine war?
(a) Operation Kyiv
(b) Operation Ganga
(c) Operation Rakshak
(d) Operation East Star

Every second patent granted in India between 2016–2021 is related to green technology and a quarter of the green technology patents are concerning alternative energy production, coinciding with the Centre's efforts on *"enhanced use of green technology for boosting economy and encouraging consumers to use products produced through use of such technology"*. Data from the Ministry of Commerce and Industry shows that more than 91,500 patents were granted between 2016–17 and 2020–21, while the data for 2021–22 was not immediately available. However, going by the trend in the past two years, India is expected to clear at least 25,000 more applications this year. Separate data from the ministry shows that between 2016–17 and 2021–22 (up to January), 61,186 patents related to green technologies have been granted in the said period. Of these, 90% are for technologies concerning waste management and alternative energy production- 38,837 or 63% of them are related to waste management and more than 16,000 or 26% are for alternative energy production. The rest of the green technology patentsare for energy conservation (2,555), transportation technologies (2,481),nuclear power generation (1,079), agriculture-and-forestry (161), and others (69).

46. With which country India entered into a 'Green Strategic Partnership' in September 2020?
(a) Poland
(b) Greece
(c) Denmark
(d) South Korea

47. In pursuance of the United Nations Sustainable Development Goals (SDG), India aims to be energy independent by the year
(a) 2047 (b) 2040
(c) 2045 (d) 2057

48. According to the Global Innovation Index 2021 published by the World Intellectual Property Organization (WIPO), India is ranked ______________ out of 132 countries.
(a) 45th (b) 46th
(c) 47th (d) 48th

49. In January 2022, the Union Cabinet approved the second phase of the Green Energy Corridor (GEC) in India with the objective to facilitate
(a) Grid integration and power evacuation of Renewable Energy (RE) Power Projects in seven States.
(b) Ecologically sustainable growth by increasing carbon footprint.
(c) Ecologically sustainable production of fossil fuels.
(d) Spreading awareness regarding Renewable Energy (RE) Power Projects.

50. The IRENA is an intergovernmental organization that supports countries in their transition to a sustainable energy future and serves as the principal platform for international co-operation on renewable energy. IRENA stands for:
(a) Intergovernmental Renewable Energy Association
(b) International Renewable Energy Association
(c) Intergovernmental Renewable Energy Agency
(d) International Renewable Energy Agency

The Government may defer the deadline for companies to deposit the unspent portion of their Corporate Social Responsibility (CSR) funds into specified bank accounts in a move aimed at providing some relief in the fight against the COVID-19 and subsequent restrictions. Companies are required to spend at least 2% of their average net profit of the preceding within three financial years on CSR. The Ministry has allowed firms to undertake projects on an ongoing basis on the condition that any unspent amount must be deposited with a scheduled bank within 30 days of the end of the financial year.

"Considering the current crisis, we request your esteemed office to consider relaxation by providing extention of the timelines up to June 30, 2021," the institute of Company Secretaries of India said in a letter to the Ministry. Experts said that while lockdowns and restrictions are less stringent than last year and companies have adapted to working online, many professionals or their families have been affected by the infection, leaving teams short-staffed.

51. Which of the following is the Corporate Social Responsibility (CSR) initiative of the erstwhile Facebook India to promote women entrepreneurship?
   (a) Shakti
   (b) Pragati
   (c) Lean In
   (d) Marching Forward
52. In 2019, which of the following Committees recommended that CSR expenditure should be made tax deductible expenditure?
   (a) Company Laws Committee
   (b) High Level Committee on Reform of Indian Company Law
   (c) High Level Committee on Corporate Social Responsibility
   (d) Committee for Reforms in Corporate Social Responsibility in India
53. CAWACH is an initiative by the National Science and Technology Entrepreneurship Development Board, Department of Science and Technology, Government of India stands for the:
   (a) Centre for Alleviating Waning Healthcare Companies
   (b) Centre for Augmenting Wound-up Healthcare Companies
   (c) Centre for Augmenting WAR with COVID-19 Health Crisis
   (d) Centre for Alleviating Withering Healthcare Companies
54. On January 22, 2021 the Companies (Corporate Social Responsibility Policy) Amendment Rules, 2021 were notified by the:
   (a) Ministry of Finance
   (b) Ministry of Social Justice and Empowerment
   (c) Ministry of Law and Justice
   (d) Ministry of Corporate Affairs
55. The Ministry of Corporate Affairs has instituted an award to select companies to recognize corporate initiatives in the area of Corporate Social Responsibility (CSR) to achieve inclusive growth and inclusive and sustainable development. The name of the award is:
   (a) National Corporate Social Responsibility Awards
   (b) National Awards for Excellence in Social Responsibility
   (c) National Awards for Corporate Excellence in Social Responsibility
   (d) National Awards for excellence in Inclusive Growth and Sustainable Development

With the announcement of Drone Shakti in the Union Budget, the industry got a massive push after the liberalization of the Drone Rules in 2021. The Government stated that start-ups will be promoted to facilitate Drone Shakti, with 'drone as a service'.

"The current Government has taken a serious paradigm shift on drone technology and Drone Shakti announcement of the current FY budget proves the government's clear vision and focus towards this emerging industry. Drone Shakti and Kisan Drones will definitely help get this technology to impact common people on the grassroots level at a massive scale," according to the founder and CEO of a prominent aerospace quoted in a business magazine. The country is set to witness the use of large, unmanned aircraft systems weighing more than 150 kilograms across the sectors. Kisan Drones are already being used for crop assessments, land records, spraying of insecticides, and are expected to boost a wave of technology in the Agri and farming sector. Drones are also being used in surveillance systems for Railway Security. In India, drones were also deployed to deliver COVID-19 vaccines.

56. COVID-19 vaccines were delivered by drones as ICMR-led pilot project to:
   (a) Ladakh (b) Katra
   (c) Dantewada (d) Manipur

57. Which of the following is the online platform hosted by the Directorate General of Civil Aviation for various activities related to the management of drone activities in India?
(a) e-Drone Shakti
(b) Digital Sky platform
(c) Aakash Shakti
(d) Digital Drone platform

58. Which of the following refers to the phenomenon of restricting the movement of drones within a defined airspace?
(a) Geo-fencing
(b) Drone-fencing
(c) Sky-fencing
(d) Air-fencing

59. The Drone Rules, 2021 have been made in supersession of which of the following rules?
(a) The Unmanned Aircraft System Rules, 2020
(b) The Aircraft Rules, 2020
(c) The Unmanned Aircraft System Rules, 2021
(d) The Manned Aircraft Rules, 1934

60. Which autonomous body is responsible for national accreditation structure for drones?
(a) Drone Council of India
(b) Unmanned Aircraft Council of India
(c) Manned Aircraft Council of India
(d) Quality Council of India

The 21st century has seen an overall shift in India's policy outlook and also the global outlook towards India. Coherent policy initiatives and effective implementation on the ground have ensured a positive growth profile. The biggest shift has been the recognition of the maritime sector. Somehow, post-independence, we as a nation became sea blind and completely undermined our maritime potential. Initially, the Indian Navy came out with their Military Maritime Strategy in 2007, titled "Freedom to use the Seas". They kept on upgrading their vision document on regular intervals with latest being declared in 2015. The Security And Growth for All in the Region (SAGAR) vision declared by the Government of India in May 2015 has been a massive game changer on multiple fronts. It integrates the geopolitical and geostrategic realities to domestic requirements. The security concerns and the blue economic opportunities are comprehensively addressed along with the diplomatic leverage and reviving the rich maritime heritage.

The SAGAR vision has been backed by aggressive push by the Government of India to drive mega projects with massive human resource requirements.

61. Which of the following is the flagship programme of the Ministry of Shipping, Government of India, to promote port-led development in the country through harnessing India's 7,500 km long coastline, 14,500 km of potentially navigable waterways and strategic location on key international maritime trade routes?
(a) Sagarmala Programme
(b) Sagarshakti Programme
(c) Jalshakti Programme
(d) Jalmala Programme

62. Which of the following is the initiative of the ministry of Earth Sciences (MoES), Government of India, to explore marine resources and develop deep sea technologies for sustainable use of ocean resources?
(a) Sagarmanthan Mission
(b) Samudramanthan Mission
(c) Deep Ocean Mission
(d) Deep Ocean and Sea Technology Mission

63. ISA is a United Nations body regulating the exploration and exploitation of marine non-living resources of oceans in international waters. ISA stands for:
(a) International Sea Authority
(b) International Sea Association
(c) International Seafaring Association
(d) International Seabed Authority

64. Under Mission SAGAR, which Indian Naval Ship was deployed by the Indian Navy to provide humanitarian and medical assistance to Maldives, Mauritius, Seychelles, Madagascar and Comoros?
(a) INS Kesari
(b) INS Vikrant

(c) INS Viraat
(d) INS Vikramaditya

65. Which of the following is India's first manned ocean mission which was launched at Chennai?
(a) Samudrashakti
(b) Samudrayan
(c) Sagaryan
(d) Sagarshakti

LEGAL REASONING

Writ is a public law remedy. It refers to a formal, written order issued by a judicial authority directing an individual or authority to do or refrain from doing an act. The High Court, while exercising its power of judicial review, does not act as an appellate body. It is concerned with illegality, irrationality and procedural impropriety of an order passed by the State or a Statutory Authority. A High Court is empowered to issue directions, orders or writs for the enforcement of Fundamental rights and for any other purpose. The writ jurisdiction of High Court is discretionary and equitable. Writ of mandamus is issued by a court commanding a public authority to perform a public duty belonging to its office. It can be issued only when a legal duty is imposed on the authority and the petitioner has right to compel the performance of such duty. Writ of mandamus is requested to be issued, *inter alia*, to compel performance of public duties which may be administrative, ministerial or statutory in nature. A writ of mandamus may be issued in favour of a person who establishes a legal right in himself. It may be issued against a person who has a mandatory legal duty to perform, but has failed or has neglected to do so. Such a legal duty emanates by operation of law. The writ of mandamus is most extensive in regards to its remedial nature. The object of mandamus is to prevent disorder emanating from failure of justice and is required to be granted in all cases where law has established no specific remedy.

66. The government of a state made a rule to make it discretionary to grant dearness allowance to its employees. One of the employees filed a writ petition seeking a mandamus to compel the government to grant dearness allowance. In the given situation, which of the following statements is true?
(a) Writ of mandamus cannot be granted as no legal duty was imposed on the government to grant dearness allowance.
(b) Writ of mandamus cannot be granted as a statutory right was conferred on the employee to receive dearness allowance.
(c) Writ of mandamus can be granted as it is a public law remedy.
(d) Writ of mandamus can be granted as it is a discretionary remedy.

67. A public-spirited citizen filed a writ petition seeking a mandamus to compel the government to make a law to curb the ill-effects of climate change. In the given situation, which of the following statements is true?
(a) Writ of mandamus can be granted as it is an equitable remedy.
(b) Writ of mandamus cannot be granted as no legal duty is imposed on the government to pass a law to curb the ill-effects of climate change.
(c) Writ of mandamus can be granted as it is a discretionary remedy.
(d) Writ of mandamus cannot be granted as there is no violation of fundamental right.

68. Mr. A and Mr. B are parties to a contract of sale of goods. Upon breach of contractual obligations by Mr. A, Mr. B filed a writ petition seeking a mandamus to compel Mr. A to perform his obligations under the contract. In the given situation, which of the following statements is true?
(a) Writ of mandamus can be granted as it is a discretionary remedy.
(b) Writ of mandamus cannot be granted as there is no violation of fundamental right.
(c) Writ of mandamus cannot be granted as Mr. B's right under the contract is a private right.
(d) Writ of mandamus can be granted as there is no statutory duty imposed on Mr. A to fulfill his contractual obligations.

69. A licensing officer is under a statutory duty to issue a license to an applicant who fulfils the conditions prescribed for the issue of such license. Mr. X, an applicant, fulfilled all the conditions prescribed for the issue of such license, but his application for issuance of license was rejected by the licensing officer. In the given situation, which of the following statements is correct?
    (a) Writ of mandamus can be granted compelling the license officer to issue the license.
    (b) Writ of mandamus cannot be granted compelling the license officer to issue the license as there is no violation of fundamental right.
    (c) Writ of mandamus can be granted as it is the discretion of the licensing officer to grant license.
    (d) Writ of mandamus cannot be granted compelling the license officer to issue the license as there is no violation of public duty.

70. Which of the following statements is incorrect?
    (a) Writ of mandamus may be issued in favour of a person who establishes the existence of a legal right.
    (b) Writ of mandamus may be issued against a person or authority who has a mandatory duty to perform but has failed or has neglected to do so.
    (c) Writ of mandamus is purported to prevent disorder emanating from failure of justice.
    (d) Writ of mandamus may be requested to be issued to compel performance of private duties which may be administrative, ministerial or statutory in nature.

To maintain the secular character of the Indian polity, not only does the Constitution of India guarantee freedom of religion to individuals and groups, but it is also against the general policy of the Constitution of India that any money be paid out of the public funds for promoting or maintaining any particular religion. Accordingly, it is provided in the Constitution of India that no person shall be compelled to pay any taxes, the proceeds of which are specifically appropriated in payment of expenses for the promotion or maintenance of any particular religion or religious denomination. This does not prohibit the State from enacting a law to incur expenses for the promotion or maintenance of any particular religion or religious denomination, but by such law, no person can be compelled to pay any tax, the proceeds of which are to be so utilized. This, however, does not invalidate levy of a fee to provide some service. Thus, a fee can be levied on pilgrims to a religious fair to meet the expenses of the measures taken to safeguard the health, safety and welfare of the pilgrims. Such fee levied by a State will be valid because the object of such contribution is not to foster or preserve religion, but to control secular administration of religious institutions.

71. Mr. A, a tax-payer of various taxes levied by the State Government, filed a writ petition for issuance of a writ of mandamus directing the State to forbear from spending any amount from the public funds of the state for renovation of water tanks belonging to a Hindu temple in the State. These tanks were used by the general public, irrespective of their religious affiliation, for bathing and drinking purposes. In the given situation, which of the following statements is correct?
    (a) The State is promoting or maintaining the Hindu religion.
    (b) The State cannot be said to be promoting or maintaining the Hindu religion.
    (c) The State is compelling citizens to pay tax for promotion of Hindu religion.
    (d) The State is compelling citizens to pay tax for maintenance of Hindu religion.

72. Communal riots between religion 'A' and religion 'B' resulted in the destruction of places of worship of both religions in a State. As a result, the State Government utilized public funds for restoring the places of worship of both religions 'A' and 'B'. In the given situation, which of the following statements is correct?
    (a) The State Government's act is violative of the Constitution of India as it is promoting or maintaining particular religions.

(b) The State Government's act is not violative of the Constitution of India as it is not promoting or maintaining any particular religion.
(c) The State Government's act is violative of freedom of religion as it condones communal violence.
(d) The State Government's act is not violative of the Constitution of India as it is promoting or maintaining a particular religion.

73. Communal riots between religion 'A' and religion 'B' resulted in the destruction of a place of worship of religion 'B' in the State. As a result, the State government utilized public funds for restoring the places of worship of religion 'B'. In the given situation, which of the following statements is correct?
(a) The State Government's act is violative of the Constitution of India as it is promoting or maintaining a particular religion.
(b) The State Government's act is not violative of the Constitution of India as it is promoting or maintaining a particular religion.
(c) The State Government's act is not violative of the Constitution of India as it is not promoting or maintaining a particular religion.
(d) The State Government's act is violative of freedom of religion as it condones communal violence.

74. A State Government passed a law making it mandatory for all residents of the State to pay a hefty 'pilgrimage tax' so as to aid the State in organizing a popular religious pilgrimage in that State. The said pilgrimage is undertaken only by followers of religion 'X' and draws a large number of followers of religion 'X' from all over the country to the state every year. In the given situation, which of the following statements is correct?
(a) The State Government's act is violative of the Constitution of India as it is not promoting or maintaining religion 'X'.
(b) The State Government's act is not violative of the Constitution of India as it is not promoting or maintaining religion 'X'.
(c) The State Government's act is violative of the Constitution of India as it is compelling citizens to pay tax for promoting or maintaining religion 'X'.
(d) The State Government's act is not violative of the Constitution of India as it is a measure to safeguard the health, safety and welfare of the pilgrims.

75. The object of a State Legislation is "to provide for the better administration and governance of certain Hindu religious endowments", where 'religious endowment' means the property belonging to or given or endowed for the support of temples. The State Legislation vests the supervision of public temples in a statutory authority, i.e., 'Commissioner of Hindu Religious Endowments'. For the purpose of meeting the expenses of the Commissioner and his staff, every Hindu temple in the State is required under provisions of the State Legislation, to pay an annual contribution at certain percentage of their annual income. In the given situation, which of the following statements is correct regarding the annual contribution provided under the State Legislation?
(a) It is not violative of the Constitution of India because its object is the proper administration of religious trusts and institutions.
(b) It is not violative of the Constitution of India because its object is fostering of Hindu religion.
(c) It is violative of the Constitution of India because its object is fostering of Hindu religion.
(d) It is violative of the Constitution of India because its object is not inclusive of administration of religious endowments belonging to all religions.

The Constitution of India guarantees to all its citizens certain fundamental freedoms, which are recognized as their fundamental rights. However, these fundamental freedoms guaranteed by the Constitution of India are not absolute as no right can be. Each of these fundamental rights is liable to be controlled, curtailed and regulated to some extent by laws made by the

Parliament or the State Legislatures. Accordingly, the Constitution of India lays down the grounds and the purposes for which a legislature can impose 'reasonable restrictions' on the rights guaranteed to citizens. The State cannot travel beyond the contours of these reasonable restrictions in curbing the fundamental rights guaranteed to citizens. While determining the constitutional validity of a restriction imposed on a fundamental right by a legislation, the Court is not concerned with the necessity of the restriction or the wisdom of the policy underlying it, but only whether the restriction is in excess of the requirement, and whether the legislature has overstepped the Constitutional limitations. Two of the fundamental rights guaranteed to every citizen of India are- the right to move freely throughout the territory of India and the right to reside and settle in any part of India. However, the State may impose reasonable restrictions on these rights by law, in the interests of the general public or for the protection of the interests of any Scheduled Tribes.

76. A law was enacted by the Parliament of India which consisted of a provision making it mandatory for every person riding a two-wheeler in India, to wear a helmet, failing which such person was made liable to a fine. Mr. X, a citizen of India, was fined for violation of the said provision. Mr. X challenged the constitutional validity of the said provision. In the given situation, which of the following statements is correct?
 (a) The provision is violative of the Constitution of India because it is a restriction on the freedom to move freely throughout the territory of India.
 (b) The provision is not violative of the Constitution of India because it is a reasonable restriction on the freedom to move freely throughout the territory of India.
 (c) Mr. X's fundamental right to move freely throughout the territory of India is violated.
 (d) Both (a) and (c).

77. A group of Indian students of XYZ university located in New delhi, India posted on social networking sites that they would hold a demonstration outside the university campus, protesting against a recently passed law which made it compulsory for university students to wear uniforms while attending classes. The students further threatened to "use whatever means necessary" to "stop the oppression of students". Therefore, the State Authorities placed barricades around the university campus in order to restrict movement of the students carrying out the demonstration and ensuring that the demonstration does not turn violent. In the given situation, which of the following statements is correct regarding the act of placing of barricades by State Authorities?
 (a) The act is violative of the Constitution of India because it is a restriction on the freedom to move freely throughout the territory of India.
 (b) The act is not violative of the Constitution of India because it is a reasonable restriction in the interests of general public.
 (c) The act is violative of the Constitution of India because it is restriction in the interest of students.
 (d) The act is not violative of the Constitution of India because it is a reasonable restriction in the interest of morality.

78. The appropriate authority in a State passed an externment order against Mr. A, a citizen of India. The externment order prohibited Mr. A, from residing within the State, from the date specified in such order. The externment order was passed by virtue of powers conferred on the appropriate authority by law, and the constitutional validity of this law had been upheld by the Supreme Court of India. The externment order was passed on the ground that Mr. A was found to be frequently engaged in illegal business of narcotic drugs and was also involved in several cases of riot and criminal intimidation. In the given situation, which of the following statements is correct regarding the externment order?
 (a) It is a reasonable restriction on Mr. A's fundamental right of free movement throughout the territory of India.

(b) It is an unreasonable restriction on Mr. A's fundamental right of residence and settlement in any part of India.

(c) It is violative of Mr. A's fundamental right of free movement throughout the territory of India.

(d) It is an unreasonable restriction on Mr. A's fundamental right of free movement throughout the territory of India.

79. Mr. Z, a citizen of India, was issued a passport on June 1, 2020 by the Passport Office. Mr. Z was due to travel to Spain on July 15, 2021. On July 11, 2021, Mr. Z received a letter from the Regional Passport Officer intimating him that it was decided by the Government of India to seize his passport "in public interest". Mr. Z was required to surrender his passport within seven days of the receipt of that letter. In the given situation, which of the following statements is correct?

(a) Mr. Z can challenge the letter on the ground that it is violative of his fundamental right of free movement throughout the territory of India.

(b) Mr. Z can challenge the letter on the ground that it is violative of his fundamental right to reside and settle in any part of India.

(c) Mr. Z can challenge the letter on the ground that it is violative of the law relating to passports in India.

(d) Mr. Z cannot challenge the letter on the ground that it is violative of his fundamental right(s) of free movement throughout the territory of India and/or to residence and settlement in any part of India.

80. Which of the following statements is incorrect?

(a) Fundamental right to movement and residence in any part of India are sacrosanct and are guaranteed to all citizens.

(b) Fundamental right to movement and residence in any part of India are sacrosanct, but are guaranteed subject to reasonable restrictions on such rights.

(c) Reasonable restrictions may be imposed, on fundamental rights to movement and residence in any part of India, by law.

(d) The constitutional validity of a law imposing reasonable restrictions on fundamental rights can be challenged by a citizen before the legislature.

Where a spouse contracts a second marriage while the first marriage is still subsisting, the spouse would be guilty of the offence of bigamy under the penal law in India, if it is proved that the first as well as the second marriages were legally valid, i.e., all the necessary ceremonies required by law or by custom have been performed at the time of contracting the marriages. According to the penal law in India, if a person, who has a living husband or wife, marries again, then such person is liable to be punished with imprisonment up to seven years along with a fine for committing the offence of bigamy. Although the penal law of India is applicable to all citizens irrespective of their religious affiliations, an exception to the offence of bigamy may be created by the law relating to marriage applicable to followers of a particular religion. Under the Hindu law relating to marriage, bigamy is not permitted. If a Hindu wife files a criminal complaint against her husband on the ground that during the subsistence of her marriage, her husband had married a second wife by converting into another religion which legally permits having more than one wife, then her husband is liable to be punished for the offence of bigamy. Further, the Hindu law relating to marriage also provides that the punishment for offence of bigamy as provided in the penal law of India would be applicable to marriage between two Hindus.

81. Mr. A, a Hindu male, has been married to Ms. B, a Hindu female. Their marriage was solemnized as per Hindu rites and ceremonies. After his marriage to Ms. B, Mr. A underwent religious conversion into a religion 'X' which legally permits males to have two wives. Thereafter, Mr. A got married to Ms. C, a female belonging to religion 'X', in compliance with all the legal requirements of contracting a valid marriage under religion 'X'. In the given situation, which of the following statements is true?

(a) As Mr. A married Ms. C, the marriage of Mr. A and Ms. B has become invalid.

(b) As Mr. A is not a Hindu, the marriage of Mr. A and Ms. B has become invalid.
(c) Mr. A's marriage with Ms. C has not affected the validity of his marriage with Ms. B.
(d) Both (a) and (b).

82. Mr. A, a Hindu male, has been married to Ms. B, a Hindu female. Their marriage was solemnized as per Hindu rites and ceremonies. After his marriage to Ms. B, Mr. A underwent religious conversion into a religion 'X' which legally permits males to have two wives. Thereafter, Mr. A got married to Ms. C, a female belonging to religion 'X', in compliance with all the legal requirements of contracting a valid marriage under religion 'X'. Ms. B filed a criminal complaint against Mr. A for committing the offence of bigamy. In the given situation, which of the following statements is true?
(a) Mr. A is liable to be punished according to the Hindu law relating to marriage.
(b) Mr. A is liable to be punished according to the penal law of India.
(c) Mr. A has not committed the offence of bigamy.
(d) Both (a) and (b).

83. Mr. A, a Hindu male, has been married to Ms. B, a Hindu female. Their marriage was not solemnized as per Hindu rites and ceremonies or any other custom, but was performed by seeking blessings of their family members. After his marriage to Ms. B, Mr. A underwent religious conversion into a religion 'X' which legally permits males to have two wives. Thereafter, Mr. A got married to Ms. C, a female belonging to religion 'X', in compliance with all the legal requirements of contracting a valid marriage under religion 'X'. Ms. B filed a criminal complaint against Mr. A for committing the offence of bigamy. In the given situation, which of the following statements is true?
(a) Mr. A has committed the offence of bigamy because he married again during the subsistence of the first marriage.
(b) Mr. A has not committed the offence of bigamy because his first marriage is not valid.
(c) Mr. A has committed the offence of bigamy because he underwent religious conversion in order to contract a bigamous marriage.
(d) Mr. A has not committed the offence of bigamy because his second marriage is not valid.

84. Mr. A, a male belonging to religion 'P', has been married to Ms. B, a female belonging to religion 'P'. Their marriage was solemnized in compliance with all the legal requirements of contracting a valid marriage under religion 'P'. Monogamy is espoused as a cherished value by the followers of religion 'P' and provided as a pre-condition for a valid marriage for the followers of the religion. After his marriage to Ms. B, Mr. A underwent religious conversion into a religion 'Q' which legally permits males to have two wives. Thereafter, Mr. A got married to Ms. C, a female belonging to religion 'Q', in compliance with all the legal requirements of contracting a valid marriage under religion 'Q'. Ms. B wife filed a criminal complaint against Mr. A for committing the offence of bigamy. In the given situation, which of the following statements is true?
(a) Mr. A has committed bigamyaccording to the Hindu law relating to marriage.
(b) Mr. A has committed bigamyaccording to the penal law of India.
(c) Mr. A has committed bigamyaccording to the law relating to marriage of religion 'P'.
(d) Both (b) and (c).

85. Which of the following statements is incorrect?
(a) Marrying again during lifetime of husband or wife is a pre-condition for performing a valid Hindu marriage.
(b) Religious conversion is not a defence for the offence of bigamy under the penal law of India.
(c) Bigamy is an offence under the penal law of India.
(d) Offence of bigamy can be committed according to the provisions of Hindu law relating to marriage.

A special marriage, i.e., a marriage between persons from two different religious affiliations can be legally contracted in India under the provisions of the law relating to special marriages. The law relating to special marriages provides for the registration of such marriages and for divorce in such cases. One of the modes in which a special marriage can be legally terminated is through divorce by mutual consent of parties to the marriage. In order to obtain a divorce by mutual consent, both the parties to the special marriage are required to jointly present a petition for divorce to the district court on the ground that they have been living separately for one year or more, that they have not been able to live together and that they have mutually agreed that the marriage should be dissolved. At least six months after the presentation of such petition, but not later than eighteen months after the presentation of such petition, the district court, after hearing the parties and after making the necessary inquiry, and being satisfied that the marriage is a 'special marriage', and that the claims made in the petition are true, shall declare the marriage to be dissolved. Further, the personal presence of the parties before the district court at the time of presenting the joint petition for divorce is not mandatory, as the parties can satisfy the court even by affidavit that the requirements for granting divorce on mutual consent are fulfilled.

86. Ms. A, a Hindu female and Mr. B, a Christian male, got married as per the law relating to special marriages in January 2018. On January 26, 2021, Ms. A and Mr. B jointly presented a petition for divorce by mutual consent before the district court on the ground that they have been inflicting mental cruelty on each other for a period of three years and that they have mutually agreed that the marriage should be dissolved. In the given situation, which of the following statements is correct?
   (a) The district court shall pass a decree of divorce within six months after the presentation of petition for divorce by mutual consent.
   (b) The district court shall pass a decree of divorce after eighteen months of the presentation of petition for divorce by mutual consent.
   (c) The district court shall not immediately pass a decree of divorce by mutual consent.
   (d) The district court shall immediately pass a decree of divorce by mutual consent if it is satisfied that the marriage was valid.

87. Ms. A, a Hindu female and Mr. B, a Christian male, got married as per the law relating to special marriages in January 2018. On February 15, 2021, Ms. A presented a petition for divorce by mutual consent before the district court on the ground that Ms. A and Mr. B have been living separately for a period of one year because Mr. B has been in an adulterous relationship with Ms. X, a Christian female. In the given situation, which of the following statements is correct?
   (a) The district court shall pass a decree of divorce by mutual consent six months after the date of presentation of petition for divorce.
   (b) The district court shall pass a decree of divorce by mutual consent eighteen months after the date of presentation of petition for divorce.
   (c) The district court shall not pass a decree of divorce by mutual consent as the requirements for grant of divorce are not fulfilled.
   (d) The district court shall not pass a decree of divorce by mutual consent as Ms. A and Mr. B have not been living separately for more than one year.

88. Ms. A, a Hindu female and Mr. B, a Christian male, got married as per the law relating to special marriages in January 2018. On April 10, 2021, Ms. A and Mr. B jointly presented a petition for divorce by mutual consent before the district court on the ground that they have been living separately for a period of three years and that they have mutually agreed that the marriage should be dissolved. In the given situation, which of the following statements is correct?
   (a) The district court shall pass a decree of divorce by mutual consent after all other legal requirements are fulfilled.
   (b) The district court shall pass a decree of divorce by mutual consent immediately because Ms. A and Mr. B have been living separately for more than one year.
   (c) The district court shall not pass a decree of divorce by mutual consent because the marriage between Ms. A and Mr. B is not valid.

(d) The district court shall not pass a decree of divorce by mutual consent because neither party is at fault in the marriage.

89. Ms. A, a Hindu female and Mr. B, a Christian male, got married as per the provisions of the law relating to special marriages in January 2018. On June 16, 2021, Ms. A and Mr. B jointly presented a petition for divorce by mutual consent before the district court on the ground that they have been living separately for a period of three years and that they have mutually agreed that the marriage should be dissolved. During the presentation of the petition, while Ms. A was present physically in the district court, Mr. B joined via video-conferencing. In the given situation, which of the following statements is correct?

(a) The district court may pass a decree of divorce by mutual consent six months after the date of presentation of petition for divorce.
(b) The district court shall pass a decree of divorce by mutual consent after all other legal requirements are fulfilled.
(c) The district court shall not pass a decree of divorce by mutual consent.
(d) Both (a) and (b).

90. Ms. A, a Hindu female and Mr. B, a Christian male, got married as per the law relating to special marriages in January 2018. On march 15, 2021, Ms. A and Mr. B jointly presented a petition for divorce before the district court on the ground that they have been living separately for a period of three years and that they have mutually agreed that the marriage should be dissolved. Six months later, the district court, after hearing the parties and making inquiry, found that the marriage had been solemnized under the law relating to special marriages, and that the consent of Ms. A for the presentation of petition of divorce was obtained by fraud. In the given situation, which of the following statements is correct?

(a) The district court shall pass a decree of divorce by mutual consent because the legal requirements are fulfilled.
(b) The district court shall pass a decree of divorce because the marriage had been solemnized under the law relating to special marriages.
(c) The district court shall not pass a decree of divorce because there was no mutual consent between parties.
(d) The district court shall not pass a decree of divorce because Ms. A has not been punished for fraud.

There are two principal theories on the relationship between international law and domestic law- Monism and Dualism. The monistic theory maintains that the subjects of two systems of law, i.e., international law and municipal law are essentially one. The monistic theory asserts that international law and municipal law are fundamentally the same in nature, and arise from the same science of law, and are manifestations of a single conception of law. The followers of this theory view international law and municipal law as part of a universal body of legal rules binding all human beings, collectively or singly. In a monist system, international law does not need to be incorporated into domestic law because international law immediately becomes incorporated in domestic legal system upon ratification of an international treaty. According to this theory, domestic law is subordinate to international law. The Statute of the International Criminal Court, therefore, can be directly applied and adjudicated in national courts according to the monistic theory. According to dualism theory, international law and municipal law represent two entirely distinct legal systems, i.e., international has an intrinsically different character from that of municipal law. International law is not directly applicable in the domestic system under dualism. First, international law must be translated into State legislation before the domestic courts can apply it. For example, under dualism, ratification of the Statute of the International Criminal Court is not enough-it must be implemented through State legislation into the domestic system. Most states and courts presumptively view national and international legal systems as discrete entities and routinely discuss in dualist fashion incorporation of rules from one system to the other.

91. In light of the given passage, which of the following statements is correct?
    (a) Monism and Dualism are similar approaches to adopt international law into domestic law.
    (b) Dualism postulates the homogeneousness of domestic law and international law.
    (c) Monism and Dualism are different approaches to understand how domestic law impacts international law.
    (d) Monism postulates the homogeneousness of international law and domestic law.

92. 'X' is a developing country. 'X' ratified the United Nations Framework Convention on Climate Change in 1995, and incorporated the provisions of the said convention in its domestic legislation addressing climate change in 1996. However, 'X' has been widely criticized in the international community for its failure in meeting the obligations under the said convention. 'Y' is a developed country. 'Y' ratified the United Nations Framework Convention on Climate Change in 1995, and has not incorporated the provisions of the said convention in its domestic legislation till date. 'Y' has been appreciated by the international community for its success in meeting the obligations under the said convention. In the given situation, which of the following statements is correct?
    (a) 'X' is a monist State and 'Y' is a dualist State.
    (b) 'X' is a dualist State and 'Y' is a monist State.
    (c) 'X' and 'Y' are both monist States.
    (d) 'X' and 'Y' are both dualist States.

93. 'D', a dualist State, has signed and ratified the Agreement on Trade-related Aspects of Intellectual Property Rights (TRIPS Agreement), an international agreement administered by the World Trade Organization (WTO). If 'D' is compelled to fulfill its international obligations under the TRIPS Agreement, which of the following statements is correct?
    (a) 'D' may adopt the provisions of the TRIPS Agreement without enacting a new domestic legislation or amending an existing legislation.
    (b) 'D' may not incorporate the provisions of the TRIPS Agreement into a new domestic legislation.
    (c) 'D' must incorporate the provisions of the TRIPS Agreement into an existing domestic legislation or in a new domestic legislation.
    (d) 'D' may not incorporate the provisions of the TRIPS Agreement into an existing domestic legislation.

94. Which of the following statements is incorrect?
    (a) According to monism, the nature of domestic law and international law is the same and domestic law is subordinate to international law.
    (b) According to monism, ratified international conventions automatically become a part of domestic law and domestic law is subordinate to international law.
    (c) According to dualism, ratified international conventions automatically become a part of domestic law and domestic law is subordinate to international law.
    (d) According to dualism, the nature of domestic law and international law is different and domestic law is not subordinate to international law.

95. The country 'X' has ratified an International Convention which requires each State Party to enact laws defining and punishing bribery, i.e., the act of offering bribes to Government officials. The Convention has neither defined bribery, nor prescribed a punishment for the same, so that each State Party may define the offence of bribery differently in their respective domestic legislations. By 2022, 'X' has not enacted any law defining and punishing the offence of bribery. In November 2021, Mr. A was being prosecuted by a domestic criminal court in 'X' for allegedly offering a bribe to a Government official. In the given situation, which of the following statements is correct?
    (a) If 'X' is a monist State, Mr. A can be punished for committing an offence under the Convention.

(b) If 'X' is a dualist State, Mr. A can be punished for committing an offence under the Convention.
(c) If 'X' is a dualist State, Mr. A cannot be punished for committing an offence under the Convention.
(d) Mr. A cannot be punished for committing an offence under the Convention irrespective of whether 'X' is a monist or a dualist State.

The United Nations Commission on Environment and Development defines 'sustainable development' as follows: "*Sustainable development is the development that meets the needs of the present without compromising the ability of future generations to meet their own needs.*" Sustainable development clearly postulates an anthropocentric bias, least concerned with the rights of other species which live on this earth. Anthropocentrism is always human-interest focused thinking that considers non-humans as having only instrumental value to humans, in other words, humans take precedence and human responsibilities towards non-human are based on benefits to humans. Eco-centrism is nature-centred, where humans are part of nature and non-humans have intrinsic value. In other words, human interest does not take automatic precedence and humans have obligations towards non-humans independently of human interest. Eco-centrism is, therefore, life-centred, nature-centred where nature includes both humans and non-humans. The Constitution of India protects not only human rights but also casts an obligation on human beings to protect and preserve a specie from becoming extinct. Conservation and protection of environment is an inseparable part of the fundamental right to life. According to the doctrine of 'public trust' recognized under the Constitution of India, certain common properties such as rivers, seashores, forests and the air are held by the government in trusteeship for the free and unimpeded use of the general public. The resources like air, sea, waters and the forests have such a great importance to the people as a whole, that it would be totally unjustified to make them a subject of private ownership. The State, as a custodian of the natural resources, has a duty to maintain them not merely for the benefit of the public, but for the best interest of flora and fauna, wildlife and so on.

96. Ms. G, a student of environmental science, has cultivated a butterfly garden which provides a favourable habitat for butterflies. Ms. G has cultivated the butterfly garden so that she could observe and study the different stages of development of butterflies such as egg, larvae, pupae, and adult. In the given situation, which of the following statements is correct?
(a) Ms. G's approach to cultivation of butterfly garden is anthropocentric because it concerns the furtherance of her academic interest.
(b) Ms. G's approach to cultivation of butterfly garden is anthropocentric because it concerns the conservation of environment.
(c) Ms. G's approach to cultivation of butterfly garden is eco-centric because it concerns the provision a favourable habitat to the butterflies.
(d) Ms. G's approach to cultivation of butterfly garden is eco-centric because it concerns the understanding of the different stages of development of butterflies.

97. Which of the following statements is correct?
(a) Anthropocentrism and eco-centrism are different approaches to achieving sustainable development.
(b) Anthropocentrism focuses on the promotion of non-human interests.
(c) Eco-centrism is concerned with the promotion of both human and non-human interests.
(d) Anthropocentrism and eco-centrism are different approaches to protection of environment and sustainable development.

98. Which of the following is the basis for the difference between anthropocentrism and eco-centrism?
(a) The inherent value placed on humans and non-humans.
(b) The inherent value placed on living things and non-living things.
(c) The relationship between human society and environment.
(d) The relationship between non-humans and environment.

99. Which of the following statements is correct regarding fundamental right to life under the Constitution of India?
    (a) It creates a corresponding duty on human beings to protect and preserve non-humans.
    (b) It creates a corresponding duty on non-humans to protect the right to life of human beings.
    (c) It is inclusive of the right of human beings to utilize non-human resources to the best of their advantage.
    (d) It is inclusive of the right of non-humans to utilize human resources to the best of their advantage.

100. Which of the following statements is incorrect according to the doctrine of 'public trust'?
    (a) Private ownership of forests is unwarranted.
    (b) Forests are held by the State in a fiduciary capacity.
    (c) State is obligated to maintain forests for their economic value.
    (d) State is obligated to maintain forests in the interest of humans and non-humans.

When parties to a contract are under a 'mistake' regarding an important fact related to such contract, it may affect the contract in two ways. It may, firstly, defeat the content altogether that the parties are supposed to have given, that is to say, the consent is unreal. Two or more persons are said to consent when they agree upon the same thing in the same sense. Secondly, the mistake may mislead the parties as to the purpose which they had contemplated. Where the mistake does not defeat consent, but only misleads the parties, i.e., where both parties to an agreement are under a mistake as to a matter of fact essential to the agreement, the agreement is void. However, if the mistake is concerning an erroneous opinion regarding value of the subject-matter of the agreement, it is not a mistake as to a matter of fact. Thus, agreement is void when: (1) both the parties to an agreement are mistaken, (2) their mistake is as to a matter of fact, and (3) the fact about which they are mistaken is essential to the agreement. Further, it is pertinent to note that a mistake, in order to invalidate a contract, should be a mistake of fact and not a mistake of law. Furthermore, where only one party to the contract is under mistake of fact, and the other party is not, the contract is not voidable merely for such reason.

101. Mr. A entered into an agreement to sell his bicycle which had been kept unused in his attic for a year, to Mr. B, at an agreed price. However, neither party was aware that at the time of entering into the agreement, the bicycle had already been destroyed by a fire in the attic. In the given situation, which of the following statements is true?
    (a) The agreement is void as both parties were under a mistake as to a matter of fact essential to the agreement.
    (b) The agreement is void as both parties were under a mistake as to a law in force in India.
    (c) The agreement is not voidable as only one of the parties was under a mistake as to a matter of fact.
    (d) The agreement is not voidable as the promise made under the agreement had not been performed.

102. Ms. X and Ms. Y entered into a contract of sale of an article, while reeling under the erroneous belief that the sale of the article, which was the subject-matter of the agreement, was permitted by the law in force in India. In the given situation, which of the following statements is true?
    (a) The contract is valid.
    (b) The contract is voidable at the option of Ms. X.
    (c) The contract is voidable at the option of Ms. Y.
    (d) The contract is not voidable.

103. Mr. J entered into an agreement with Mr. K for the sale of Mr. J's 'club'. At the time of entering into the agreement, while Mr. J believed that he was agreeing to sell his golf club, Mr. K believed that he was agreeing to buy a clubhouse owned by Mr. J. The agreement is void because:
    (a) Mistake of fact defeated the consent of the parties.

(b) Mistake of fact misled the parties as to the purpose of the contract.
(c) Mistake of fact was regarding the identity of parties.
(d) Both (a) and (b)

104. Mr. D appointed Mr. K to manage the cultivation of his land as he was unable to manage it himself due to his advanced age. Mr. K agreed to manage the cultivation of Mr. D's land if he granted Mr. K a lease of the said land. Mr. D agreed to the same and signed a deed which was, unknown to both parties, a gift deed of the land and not a lease deed. In the given situation, which of the following statements is true?
(a) Mr. D and Mr. K were reeling under a mistake as to a matter of fact essential to the agreement.
(b) Mr. D and Mr. K were reeling under a mistake as to a matter of law essential to the agreement.
(c) Mr. D was reeling under a mistake as to a matter of fact essential to the agreement.
(d) Mr. D was reeling under a mistake as to a matter of law essential to the agreement.

105. Ms. X and Ms. Y entered into a contract of sale of an article which was agreed to be shipped by Ms. X in a ship named 'The Cruiser' and delivered to Ms. Y on an agreed date. Mr. X shipped the said article by a different ship named 'The Mariner', without informing Ms. Y and the article was delivered to Ms. Y on the agreed date. In the given situation, which of the following statements is true?
(a) The agreement is void as both parties were under a mistake as to a matter of fact essential to the agreement.
(b) The agreement is void as both parties were under a mistake as to a law in force in India.
(c) The agreement is valid as both parties were under a mistake as to a matter of fact not essential to the agreement.
(d) The agreement is valid as both parties were under a mistake as to a matter of fact essential to the agreement.

LOGICAL REASONING

Students decide to attend college for several reasons. These reasons include career opportunities and financial stability, intellectual growth, a time for self-discovery, norms, obligations, and social opportunities. Outside demands in society, such as technology changes, and increased educational demands also drive the need for more students to attend college. The students then spend the next few years trying to discover a path and find their way so they can become successful. The transition to college presents students with many new challenges, including increased academic demands, less time with family members, interpersonal problems with roommates and romantic interests, and financial stress. Competitive academic work and uncertainty about future employment and professional career were also noted as sources of stress. The transition to college represents a process characterized by change, ambiguity, and adjustment across all of life's domains. The transition towards independence and self-sufficiency has been characterized as 'stress-arousing' and 'anxiety-provoking' by many college students. Failure to accomplish and develop these characteristics of development and maintain independence may result in life dissatisfaction. Emerging adulthood has also been noted to augment college students' vulnerability to stress. Many students experience their first symptoms of depression and anxiety during this time, but a growing problem is that college campuses do not have enough resources to help all of these students. It has been noted that 75% to 80% of college students are moderately stressed and 10% to 12% are severely stressed.

106. What according to you is the objective of the study of the present paragraph?
(a) To map the various stages of pressure points of adulthood in the process of education.
(b) To narrate the anti-family agenda in the current education system.
(c) To pinpoint the obstacles targeted against meritorious students.
(d) All of the above

107. Which factors as per the author cause more stress amongst college students?
   (a) Pressure from parents and society towards greater educational needs and increased competitive academic work.
   (b) Failure to develop successful romantic interests, financial constraints and interpersonal issues with room-mates.
   (c) Failure to adapt to the transition to college life and to adjust various life domains in tune with needs and requirements of college life.
   (d) Inability to manage time constraints and the uncertainty pertaining to their future.

108. Which of the following fall closest to the underlying assumption in the present study?
   (a) Problem-solving ability amongst college students is negatively associated with symptoms of depression and anxiety.
   (b) Students lean towards unhealthy coping skills in order to try to lower the stress that they experience.
   (c) Romantic interest is an anti-dote for stress amongst the students in the colleges.
   (d) Stress is subjective for each student.

109. Suggest a suitable title for the paragraph from amongst the given titles:
   (a) Triumph and Turbulence of College Education System
   (b) Negative impact of College Education System
   (c) Negligence of Stress Management by parents
   (d) Unemployment and Mental Instability

110. With reference to the above paragraph, which of the following offers the most plausible solutions as a coping up mechanism for college students?
   (a) Individual students should approach counsellors for coping up with stress.
   (b) Keeping in view that large number of students are experiencing stress, colleges must take steps reduce course curriculum and peer pressures.
   (c) College authorities shall provide access to counselling and every student experiencing stress must engage in some form of coping mechanism to alleviate stress.
   (d) The students must learn to differentiate between short term and long-term stress.

Under the COVID-19 outbreak, universities and schools around the world had suspended face-to-face classes to prevent the rapid spread of the virus among students and staff. This sudden disruption to face-to-face education reshaped pedagogical practices and led to the rapid adoption of online teaching among universities. Subsequently, academics working at universities, at the frontline of those changes, faced enormous levels of pressure and disturbance to their professional roles and practices. For those without sufficient knowledge or experience for effective online teaching, this sudden transition was particularly challenging. In normal circumstances, designing an online course follows a systematic instructional design process with careful consideration of the unique characteristics of target learner groups and the chosen instructional medium. During the rapid adoption of online teaching in response to COVID-19, however, systematic instructional design procedures and team-based support for course development and preparation were unavailable. Instead, individual academics were given the challenge alone to teach online with a limited level of support and guidance from their school or university – the task was even more difficult in this situation where they were remotely working from home.

111. The objective behind the information furnished in the passage is:
   (a) To examine the experiences faced by the teachers because of the sudden transition from offline to online mode of teaching due to outbreak of COVID-19.
   (b) To identify the differences between the online and offline mode of teaching.
   (c) To reveal the side-effects of COVID-19.
   (d) To understand the need to be able to cope up with crisis like situations even in the educational sector.

112. Based on the ideas presented in the paragraph, it will not be possible to draw out useful recommendations for situations like the pandemic, unless:
(a) The factors required to contribute to quality education by online and offline modes are examined.
(b) Knowledge about the infrastructural availability in the schools or universities is crucial.
(c) The faculty is given adequate training and experience in providing online education is taken into consideration.
(d) A detailed analysis of the comparative performance in the online and offline modes is done.

113. What can be most conveniently inferred from the given paragraph?
(a) Whether online or face-to-face, university teaching activity is a genuinely complex task that involves multiple elements of interlinked activity systems.
(b) It has been more challenging for both individual academics and institutions to quickly adopt to online teaching during the COVID-19 Pandemic.
(c) The object of the online teaching activity systems created a fundamental contradiction with the object of the previous teaching activity systems.
(d) All the above.

114. What suitable policy decision should be devised by the administrators of the schools and the universities, in the light of the facts presented in the paragraph?
(a) There must be an insight into the complexity of online teaching and need to work for the capacity building of the teachers during such extra ordinary times and there is a greater need to create a teacher community and foster collaborative teaching relationships among the members, even if it takes time.
(b) The faculty members must be oriented towards the lasting changes brought about to their roles and identities in teaching.
(c) It is time to develop a comprehensive understanding of the challenges experienced by individual academics and the changes created by those academics.
(d) There is a need to develop infrastructure in schools and universities.

115. Which of the following points most closely supports the fact that the present education system lacks the structure to sustain effective teaching during and after the periods of lockdowns?
(a) There are inadequate applications and platforms for effective online teaching.
(b) Shift from offline to online was faced with resistance.
(c) The academia's long-established roles and identities have been completely altered by the pandemic.
(d) The students are interested in online examinations and schools and universities are finding it difficult to shift to offline examination mode.

Biodiversity is being lost at a rate not seen since the last mass extinction. But the United Nations decade-old plan to slow down and eventually stop the decline of species and ecosystems by 2020 has failed. Most of the plan's 20 targets - known as the Aichi Biodiversity Targets - have not been met. The Aichi targets are part of an international agreement called the UN Convention on Biological Diversity, and member states are now finalizing replacements for them. Currently referred to as the post-2020 Global Biodiversity Framework (GBF), its draft was published in July 2021. It aims to slow down the rate of biodiversity loss by 2030. And by 2050, biodiversity will be "valued, conserved, restored and wisely used, maintaining ecosystem services, sustaining a healthy planet and delivering benefits essential for all people". The GBF is a comprehensive plan. But success will require systemic change across public policy. That is both a strength and a weakness. If systemic change can be implemented, it will lead to real change. But if it cannot, there's no plan B. This has led some researchers to argue that one target or number should be prioritized and defined in a way that is clear to the public and to policy makers. It would be biodiversity's equivalent of the 2°C climate target.

116. As per the passage, which of the following is a challenge for implementation of the post-2020 Global Biodiversity Framework (GBF)?
   (a) Unfulfillment of the pre-2020 global biodiversity targets
   (b) Clarity of action plan for the society and government
   (c) Threat of mass extinction
   (d) Failure of plan to save ecosystems

117. According to the passage, why do some researchers advocate that one biodiversity target be prioritized?
   (a) Systemic policy change is difficult to implement
   (b) Post-2020 Global Biodiversity Framework (GBF) is comprehensive
   (c) The 2 °C climate target needs to be prioritized
   (d) Biodiversity needs to be valued, conserved, restored and wisely used

118. Which of the following is correct expression of the author's opinion as stated in passage?
   (a) Implementation of the post-2020 Global Biodiversity Framework (GBF) allows no middle ground for success or failure.
   (b) It is high time that countries re-evaluate the progress in achieving biodiversity targets.
   (c) Biodiversity conservation should be prioritized over climate change at the global level.
   (d) The post-2020 Global Biodiversity Framework (GBF) is the best way to prevent mass extinction.

119. Which of the following is the central theme of the above passage?
   (a) The reason for failure of biodiversity conservation efforts at global level
   (b) The inter-relationship between biodiversity conservation and climate change
   (c) The future of biodiversity conservation efforts at global level
   (d) The role of United Nations in biodiversity conservation at global level

120. Which of the following can be inferred from the above passage?
   (a) The holistic nature of the post-2020 Global Biodiversity Framework (GBF) is a boon.
   (b) The holistic nature of the post-2020 Global Biodiversity Framework (GBF) is a bane.
   (c) The holistic nature of the post-2020 Global Biodiversity Framework (GBF) can be a boon or a bane.
   (d) The post-2020 Global Biodiversity Framework (GBF) includes the 2°C climate target.

An unintended and unjust consequence of the Protection of Children from Sexual Offences Act, 2012 is its widespread persecution of teenage lovers. This law raised the age of consent from 16 to 18 years, while defining persons below 18 years as children. Consequently, when two 16-year-olds are romantically and sexually involved, but the girl's family doesn't approve the affair and files a police complaint, her content has zero legal validity. And the consensual relationship morphs into a case of statutory rape. The Allahabad High Court has indicated how its "conscience" is concerned by such severe POCSO provisions being drawn by teenage lovers simply on the basis of family disapproval. The High Courts of Delhi, Madras and others have made similar observations in recent years and also pointed to amendments to the law that can help reduce its injustices. One suggestion that has gathered broad support is to push back both the cut-off for childhood and the age of consent to 16 years. Given that the NCRB data shows around half of POCSO cases falling in the 16-18 years age group, such an amendment is overdue. Minimizing the prosecution of consensual romances would also leave a logjammed system with more space to pursue actual sexual assault cases. The broader goal here is respecting the rights of adolescents and young adults. Their romantic and sexual autonomy needs greatly increased recognition in India.

121. "*Minimising the protecution of consensual romances would also leave a logjammed system with more space to pursue actual sexual assault cases.*"

In the context of the statement, which of the following strengthens the author's opinion?
(a) There are many unreported sexual assault cases.
(b) Speedy prosecution of sexual assault cases is desirable.
(c) Consensual romance, in some cases, can amount to sexual assault.
(d) Sexual assault and rape are different.

122. What has the author conveyed regarding the prosecution of statutory rape in India?
(a) Statutory rape does not violate the romantic and sexual autonomy of young adults.
(b) Statutory rape must be met with stricter punishment.
(c) Statutory rape must be abolished.
(d) Statutory rape is a relic of Victorian morality.

123. As per the above passage, which of the following does not correctly represent the author's view regarding the widespread persecution of teenage lovers under the POCSO Act?
(a) Teenagers have the right to love as much as adults.
(b) Police complaints of teenage lovers may lead to their harassment.
(c) Consent of minor girls do not have legal validity.
(d) Consent of minor girls have legal validity.

124. In the above passage, which of the following has concerned the "conscience" of the Allahabad High Court?
(a) Carelessness of teenage lovers.
(b) Threat to the safety of teenage lovers.
(c) Impact on mental health of teenage lovers.
(d) Harassment of teenage lovers by their families.

125. As per the above passage, which of the following is a major challenge in implementation of the POCSO Act?
(a) Speedy prosecution of cases.
(b) Respecting the rights of adolescents and young adults.
(c) Counselling of adolescents and young adults.
(d) Imposition of stringent punishment.

A Madras High Court Judge's suggestion to amend the Constitution of India mandating that every citizen also has a duty to laugh comes as a whiff of fresh air – something the country has been gasping for, of late. Justice GR Swaminathan of the Madurai Bench has a remarkably refined sense of humour, but in quashing an FIR against a man arrested for an innocuous social media post, his insightful observations only highlight the idiocy and absurdity that surround the growth and normalisation of the offence-taking tribe. Written from the perspective of cartoonists and satirists, the judgment draws attention to how what ought to be a reasonable understanding of a situation is increasingly being influenced by impulses that border on the irrational and amount to an abuse of the legal process. The petitioner tried tongue-in-cheek wordplay while captioning photographs after a sight-seeing trip with family: 'Trip to Sirumalai for shooting practice'. For the police, it appeared as a threat to wage war, though the Judicial Magistrate refused remand. 'Laugh at what?' is a serious question, the Judge said, using the 'holy cow' as a metaphor, which varies from person to person, region to region. Being funny is one thing, the Judge righty states, and poking fun at another is different altogether. Those who have been at the receiving end for their attempt at humour can draw strength from the ruling, but then, a creative process facing combative opposition because of its very nature is anything but funny.

126. What is the central idea in the passage as conveyed by the author?
(a) People need to be sensitive towards others' sensibilities.
(b) Humour is often used as a garb to offend others.
(c) There is an unwelcome decrease in people's sense of humour.
(d) Judiciary should use humour to make judgments understandable to laypersons.

127. According to the given passage, which of the following statements is true?
(a) Social media often popularised insensitive and offensive posts.
(b) It should be a right of every person to poke fun at others.
(c) Creative expressions are bound to be offensive to some persons.
(d) Every humorous expression should be understood reasonably and rationally.

128. According to the given passage, which of the following statements is not true?
(a) Each expression should be understood according to its context.
(b) The word 'shooting' used in a sentence is indicative of waging war.
(c) Legal process can be abused if the authorities act on their irrational impulses.
(d) The expression 'holy cow' bears different meanings for different people.

129. As per the passage, which of the following approaches can reduce the increasing 'idiocy and absurdity' in responding to expressions made in jest?
(a) Apologising upon hurting another person's sentiments.
(b) Avoiding the use of controversial words and expressions.
(c) Using humour as a means to mitigate conflict.
(d) Understanding the difference between being funny and poking fun at another person.

130. "Those who have been at the receiving end for their attempt at humour can draw strength from the ruling, but then, a creative process facing combative opposition because of its very nature is anything but funny."

Which of the following conclusions can be drawn from the above statement?

(a) Creativity and conflict go hand-in-hand.
(b) Creative freedom should not be curbed unreasonably.
(c) Creative expressions are strengthened due to challenges faced by their authors.
(d) Creativity often leads to conflict.

Two recent developments have brought India's reliance on fossil fuel into sharp focus. The Russia-Ukraine conflict and the consequent surge in crude oil prices roiled the economy. Separately, the most recent IPCC report on climate highlighted the energy sector's large contribution to global warming. Both these developments need to be located in the context of India's pledge to get to net zero carbon emissions by 2070. Meeting this pledge requires an overhaul of both the logistics and electricity sectors to reduce reliance on fossil fuels. Transitioning to renewables in energy is an important part of the solution. Within renewables, solar energy has been lavished with policy support. However, it won't be enough to meet the targets. Anil Kakodkar, former chairman of Atomic Energy Commission, had written that India can't meet its net-zero commitment without nuclear power. He's right. It's an area where India was off to an early start, developed relatively high indigenous capabilities in relation to other sectors, but subsequently let the ball drop. Today, nuclear power contributes a mere 3% of the total electricity generated, and has a capacity of 6780 MW. After the early euphoria of the India-United States civil nuclear deal, progress has been disappointing. The deal did open the pathway to a stable supply of uranium ore from Kazakhstan and Canada. However, the design of the subsequent bill on civil liability for nuclear damage killed the prospect of participation of Western firms. India's main partner today is Russia, which side stepped the bill through inter-government agreements.

131. What is the central idea in the passage as conveyed by the author?
(a) India needs to increase use of nuclear power.
(b) India needs to increase production of fossil fuels.
(c) India needs to enter into multilateral agreements addressing use of nuclear power.
(d) Nuclear energy is a renewable source of power.

132. According to the author, which of the following measures will not help India achieve its pledge of net zero carbon emissions by 2070?

(a) Logistical changes
(b) Changes in electricity sector
(c) Reduction in use of solar power
(d) Increase in use of nuclear power

133. According to the author, which of the following is not the effect of India's reliance on fossil fuels?
(a) Global warming
(b) Increase in crude oil prices
(c) Relations with Middle East
(d) Less reliance on renewable sources of power

134. According to the author, which of the following is the effect of the India-United States civil nuclear deal?
(a) Export-import target with United States
(b) Removal of bottlenecks for self-reliance in power generation
(c) Nuclear Defence Pact with Kazakhstan
(d) Self-reliance in Solar Power

135. According to the author, Western firms lost the opportunity of doing business in the nuclear production in India because:
(a) They had to pay hefty penalties for delay in supply
(b) They do not find nuclear power profitable
(c) They do not agree with India's place of nuclear plants
(d) They failed to circumvent internal laws by other bilateral instruments

QUANTITATIVE TECHNIQUES

As per a survey conducted in a college out of total students enrolled i.e., 3,000 in 2020–21, 1,700 were girls and 1,300 were boys. Data regarding students opting for various streams viz., Non-Medical, Medical, Commerce, Arts and Fine Arts showed that 25% of the enrolled students opted non-Medical and the percentage of girls in Non-Medical was 30% of the total number of girls; 15% of the total students opted for Medical and the percentage of girls who opted Medical was 18% of the total number of girls; 25% of the total students opted Arts but the percentage of girls who opted for Arts was 15% of the total number of girls; 16% of the total students opted Commerce and the percentage of girls who opted Commerce was 17% of the total number of girls, and; 19% of the total students opted Fine Arts and the percentage of girls who opted Fine Arts was 20% of the total number of girls.

136. How many girls have opted Non-medical?
(a) 440 (b) 365
(c) 530 (d) 510

137. Girls have outnumbered boys in Fine Arts. How many girls in Fine Arts are more than the boys, as a percentage of total number of boys in Fine Arts?
(a) 49.62% (b) 47.82%
(c) 51.23% (d) 50.89%

138. Which of the following courses have been opted by maximum number of boys?
(a) Non-medical (b) Arts
(c) Fine Arts (d) Commerce

139. Which of the following courses have been opted by minimum number of boys?
(a) Medical (b) Fine Arts
(c) Commerce (d) Non-Medical

140. What is the ratio among boys and girls for Non-Medical?
(a) 3 : 17 (b) 17 : 8
(c) 8 : 17 (d) 17 : 3

An Indian company, having its registered office at Gurugram, is engaged in manufacturing of consumer goods at Noida. The goods manufactured by the company are sold in Indian market and exported to Europe. Company produces five products namely 'P', 'Q', 'R', 'S' and 'T'. Total production of the company for the financial year 2021–22 is 3,000 tonnes and the turnover of the company is ₹50 million. An analysis of the production and net revenue generation shows that production of product 'P' is 21% of the total production and 18% of the turnover is attributable to product 'P'; production of 'Q' is 16% of the total production and 17% of the turnover is attributable to 'Q'; 'R' accounts for 18% of the total production and 20% of the turnover; 'S' accounts for 20% of the total production and 25% of the turnover, and; 'T' accounts for 25% of total production and 20% of turnover.

141. What is the percentage of profit earned from sale of 'R', if the expenditure incurred on production of 'R' is ₹15,000/- per tonne?
(a) 20% (b) 23.46%
(c) 26.55% (d) 25%

142. Which product has the highest selling price per tonne?
(a) Q (b) R
(c) S (d) T

143. How much loss is incurred to company, if the expenditure on production of 'T' was ₹20,000 per tonne?
(a) 5 million (b) 10 million
(c) 4 million (d) 7 million

144. What percentage of turnover of 'R' has to turnover of 'T'?
(a) 100% (b) 75%
(c) 50% (d) 60%

145. What is the average selling price per tonne of all products taken together?
(a) ₹17,488 (b) ₹17,667
(c) ₹18,667 (d) ₹16,667

In an organization, the total number of employees working in various Departments viz. IT, Marketing, Purchase, HR, Accounts and Production are 4,500. The information regarding department wise percentage of employees was collected and also record about gender ratio of employees was prepared. 18 percent of total number of employees work in it department and ratio of males to females in it department is 2 : 1. In marketing, ratio of males to females is 2 : 3 and number of employees engaged in marketing is 20% of the total employment. 12% of the total numbers of workers are running the HR department and the ratio of males to females in this department is 5 : 1. The fraction of male to females in production department is 3 : 2 and total number of persons employed in this department is 15% of the total workforce. The number of persons occupied in purchase and accounts department is 24% and 11% respectively of the total number of workers. Gender Ratio (Ratio of males to females) in Purchase department is 1 : 1 and in Accounts is 1 : 2.

146. How many females are employed in Purchase department?
(a) 450 (b) 540
(c) 495 (d) 595

147. How many employees are working in IT and Accounts departments together?
(a) 1,702 (b) 1,646
(c) 1,766 (d) 1,305

148. What is the ratio of total number of males to total number of females working in all the departments put together?
(a) 63 : 41 (b) 19 : 27
(c) 41 : 34 (d) 34 : 41

149. Number of females in Marketing Department forms what percentage of the total number of employees in the organization?
(a) 8% (b) 7%
(c) 12% (d) 10%

150. What is the ratio of number of males in Marketing Department to the number of males in HR department?
(a) 4 : 5 (b) 5 : 4
(c) 7 : 3 (d) 6 : 7

ANSWER KEY

English

1. (b) 2. (c) 3. (d) 4. (c) 5. (a) 6. (d) 7. (c) 8. (b) 9. (b) 10. (a) 11. (d) 12. (a) 13. (b) 14. (d) 15. (c) 16. (c) 17. (d) 18. (b) 19. (a) 20. (d) 21. (c) 22. (a) 23. (b) 24. (c) 25. (c) 26. (b) 27. (d) 28. (d) 29. (a) 30. (d)

Current Affairs and General Knowledge

31. (b) 32. (c) 33. (d) 34. (c) 35. (a) 36. (d) 37. (c) 38. (c) 39. (a) 40. (d) 41. (d) 42. (a) 43. (d) 44. (c) 45. (b) 46. (c) 47. (a) 48. (b) 49. (a) 50. (d) 51. (b) 52. (c) 53. (c) 54. (d) 55. (a) 56. (d) 57. (b) 58. (a) 59. (c) 60. (d) 61. (a) 62. (c) 63. (d) 64. (a) 65. (b)

Legal Reasoning

66. (a) 67. (b) 68. (c) 69. (a) 70. (d) 71. (b) 72. (b) 73. (c) 74. (c) 75. (a) 76. (b) 77. (b) 78. (a) 79. (d) 80. (d) 81. (c) 82. (d) 83. (b) 84. (d) 85. (a) 86. (c) 87. (c) 88. (a) 89. (d) 90. (c) 91. (d) 92. (b) 93. (c) 94. (c) 95. (d) 96. (a) 97. (c) 98. (a) 99. (a) 100. (c) 101. (a) 102. (d) 103. (d) 104. (a) 105. (c)

Logical Reasoning

106. (a) 107. (c) 108. (a) 109. (a) 110. (c) 111. (a) 112. (c) 113. (d) 114. (a) 115. (c) 116. (b) 117. (a) 118. (a) 119. (c) 120. (c) 121. (b) 122. (a) 123. (d) 124. (d) 125. (c) 126. (c) 127. (d) 128. (b) 129. (d) 130. (b) 131. (a) 132. (c) 133. (c) 134. (b) 135. (d)

Logical Reasoning

136. (d) 137. (b) 138. (b) 139. (b) 140. (c) 141. (b) 142. (c) 143. (a) 144. (a) 145. (d) 146. (b) 147. (d) 148. (c) 149. (c) 150. (a)

CLAT 2021

ENGLISH

Read an extract from A Scandal in Bohemia by Arthur Conan Doyle:

"I rang the door-bell and was shown up to the chamber which had formerly been in part my own.

With hardly a word spoken, Sherlock Holmes waved me to an armchair. Then he stood before the fire and looked me over in his singular introspective fashion. "Watson, you did not tell me that you intended to go into harness."

"Then, how do you know? "

"I see it, I deduce it. How do I know that you have been getting yourself very wet lately, and that you have a most clumsy and careless servant girl? "

"My dear Holmes, " said I, "this is too much. It is true that I had a country walk on Thursday and came home in a dreadful mess, but as I have changed my clothes, I can't imagine how you deduce it. As to Mary Jane, she is incorrigible, but there, again, I fail to see how you work it out. "

"It is simplicity itself, " said he; "my eyes tell me that on the inside of your left shoe, just where the firelight strikes it, the leather is scored by six almost parallel cuts. Obviously, they have been caused by someone who has very carelessly scared round the edges of the sole in order to remove crusted mud from it. Hence, you see, my double deduction that you had been out in vile weather, and that you had a particularly malignant boot-slitting specimen of the London slavey."

In fiction, detectives like Holmes are usually portrayed as people with exceptionally brilliant minds. They possess the rare skill to see and analyze what ordinary people can't. They have incredible abilities to infer, deduce, induce and conclude.

Then, there is G.K. Chesterton's fictional catholic priest, Father Brown who relies on his extraordinary power of sympathy and empathy that enable him to imagine and feel as criminals do. He explains, "I had thought out exactly how a thing like that could be done, and in what style or state of mind a man could really do it. And when I was quite sure that I felt exactly like the murderer myself, of course I knew who he was."

Sherlock finds the criminal by starting from the outside. He relies on science, experimental methods and deduction. On the contrary, Father Brown uses varied psychological experiences learned from those who make confessions of crime to him. He relies on introspection, intuition and empathy.

There is yet another set of detectives like those created by writers like Agatha Christie. Her Belgian detective, Hercule Poirot is a story-teller who draws information from the stories that others tell. He patiently listens to numerous accounts of what happened, where it happened and how it happened. He listens for credibility and ambiguity; he identifies why and how the pieces of the jigsaws don't fit together. Ultimately, he uncovers the truth.

1. From the passage, it can be inferred that
   (a) Watson is Holmes' mentor.
   (b) Earlier, Watson used to live with Holmes.
   (c) Watson is a detective.
   (d) Watson shares all his personal matters with Holmes.

2. It is evident that for solving cases, Father Brown relies largely on
   (a) His own sympathetic and empathic thought process about criminals.
   (b) A sympathetic approach towards various people's opinion on the case to be solved.
   (c) A deductive analysis of the crime and his ability to sympathize.
   (d) All the above.

3. For the three detectives mentioned in the passage, which one of these would be non-essential for solving criminal cases?
   (a) Forgiving nature
   (b) Sensitivity
   (c) Critical thinking
   (d) Patience
4. In order to solve cases, Poirot uses the ________ art of the narratives that he has been told.
   (a) Building a fantasy based on
   (b) Empathizing with all the characters in
   (c) Creating new plots for
   (d) Detecting and analyzing the missing links in
5. The word incorrigible is the antonym of
   (a) Habitual
   (b) Unperformable
   (c) Repentant
   (d) Incurable

Since long, we have witnessed unimaginable levels of success and failure of various projects, businesses, scientific missions and even wars. From such triumphs and defeats emerges the much debatable thought: Is planning and strategy more important than execution?

Some project leaders and their teams are of the view that planning leads to clarity of objectives; it helps to set the timeline and the budget. Consequently, when the planning is haphazard and unstructured, the very aims of the projects become hazy. This further leads to unprecedented budget collapses and poor time-management. In some cases, teams have worked relentlessly to complete assignments, but poor planning has invariably led to customer dissatisfaction and at times a complete collapse of the entire project. In the words of Benjamin Franklin, "*Failing to plan is planning to fail.*"

Numerous entrepreneurs have the faith that strategies help to enhance not only speed and quality of production, but also consumer satisfaction. If there are no strategies to tackle unplanned events or unexpected interruptions, there is a possibility of entire projects coming to a grinding halt.

Some of the world's best airports, bridges and astronomical missions are the result of careful planning and excellent strategies. However, there are some architects, artists and entrepreneurs who prefer to dive straight from the board of ideas into the pool of execution. They believe that suitable strategies are best shaped during the process of execution; great plans and strategies can fail while encountering unexpected situations.

Steve Jobs says, "*To me, ideas are worth nothing unless executed. They are just a multiplier. Execution is worth millions.*"

According to Bill Gates, unhappy customers are the greatest source of learning. Fickle-minded consumers and wavering market trends can mar projects that stand on fixed plans. It is the need-based, flexible and innovative strategies that help to withstand the impact of these vacillating desires and trends.

After rigorous planning and testing a new recipe on two lakh consumers, in 1985, the company Coke brought out the *New Coke*. Much to the company's dismay, the product did not take off as expected and the financial loss was enormous. The company realized that during the process of data collection, it had not considered the product-loyalty and old-fashioned habits of the consumers.

Hence, a balance of pragmatic planning, effective strategies and efficient execution is likely to ensure the accomplishment of tasks at each stage of a project. Successful execution is not an easy journey. The road is winding and bumpy. It may require tweaking or at times abandoning the original plan and re-designing it.

Often, we turn to nature for inspiration. Think of plans and strategies as the seed; execution is the nourishment; and the consumer is the capricious weather.

6. The passage can be best termed as
   (a) Expository
   (b) Descriptive
   (c) Abstract
   (d) Narrative

7. The author's main purpose is to
   (a) Suggest that people succeed only when they have great strategies.
   (b) Highlight the fact that execution is as indispensable as planning and strategy.
   (c) Illustrate the impact of poor planning and weak strategy.
   (d) Highlight the hurdles that come in the way of execution.

8. From the failure of *New Coke*, the company learnt that
   (a) Tested and tried strategies are essential for success.
   (b) Surveys and data calibration are a sheer waste of time.
   (c) Consumers change brand preferences too frequently.
   (d) Changes in consumers' habits should not be taken for granted.

9. For the accomplishment of a project, Steve Jobs
   (a) Propagates an approach that is similar to Benjamin Franklin's.
   (b) Suggests an approach that is different from Benjamin Franklin's.
   (c) Believes that the main control is in the hands of consumers.
   (d) None of the above.

10. The ________ phrase 'consumer is the capricious weather' refers to the ________ demands of the customers.
    (a) Onomatopoeia________stagnant
    (b) Simile________unpredictable
    (c) Metaphor________wavering
    (d) Anaphora________oscillating

Since the worldwide inoculation process is going strong, vaccine diplomacy has become a hot topic. In their quest for ensuring vaccine security, a report by *The New York Times*, based on the data on vaccine contracts compiled by Duke University, shows that the advance purchase contracts made by some advanced countries for potential vaccines would vaccinate their population many times: the European Union, two times, the United States and the United Kingdom, four times, and Canada, six times. The expectation that an early vaccination will bring back normalcy and a required push to economic growth fuelled many advanced countries to engage in vaccine battles. The arguments of public good and global cooperation have gone out of the window now. While advanced countries have turned their back on the need of poor countries to access COVID-19 vaccines, India has displayed empathy to their needs. India has taken a position that a significant percentage of the approved doses will be permitted for exports. While its exports to neighbouring countries will be under grant mode, initial shipment of vaccines to least developed countries will be free of cost. And, shipments of vaccines from India have already started reaching different parts of the developing world. While India is in its first phase of vaccination to cover health-care workers, exports from India are helping other countries also in initiating phase one of their vaccination programme, a gesture well appreciated globally. In a democracy, one can expect the backlash of sending vaccines abroad without vaccinating its population. Nevertheless, India's approach only reinforces the need of having coordinated global efforts in bringing COVID-19 under control. This response manifests India's unstinted commitment to global development and has consolidated its name as the world's pharmacy. The attitude of India towards vaccinating the populations in the poorer countries has generated discussion in the richer countries about the necessity for more proactive measures to roll out vaccines to the developing nations.

11. Which of the following best describes the purpose of this passage?
    (a) To encourage vaccine nationalism, and discourage global cooperation.
    (b) To discourage vaccine nationalism, and encourage global cooperation.
    (c) To encourage poor countries and discourage advanced countries.
    (d) To encourage India to provide vaccines to poor nations.

12. The term 'inoculation process' as used in the passage means
(a) Production and distribution of vaccines.
(b) Global struggle for vaccines.
(c) Pharmaceutical production of vaccines.
(d) Artificially inducing immunity.

13. Advanced purchase contracts of vaccines by developed countries are premised on hopes that
(a) Vaccination will restore normalcy and thrust economic recovery.
(b) Vaccination will bring back powers to nations.
(c) Vaccination will promote global well-being and growth.
(d) Vaccination will protect the health of the world population.

14. The author cautions that India's approach in vaccine distribution may have negative repercussions among
(a) People from advanced countries.
(b) People from poor countries.
(c) People from developing countries.
(d) People from India.

15. Among Sustainable Development Goals (SDGs), the third goal reads, "Ensure healthy lives and promote well-being for all at all ages". Which of the following sentences from the passage reflects the reversal of this SDG?
(a) The arguments of public good and global cooperation have gone out of the window now.
(b) Advanced countries have turned their back on the need of poor countries to access COVID-19 vaccines.
(c) The advance purchase contracts made by some advanced countries for potential vaccines would vaccinate their population many times.
(d) All the above.

Following the transition to democracy, with the inauguration of Nelson Mandela as president in 1994, South Africa was faced with the task of dealing with its past, as well as undertaking some action to deal with structural social injustice. The Truth and Reconciliation Commission (TRC), heralded as the most ambitious and organised attempt to deal with crimes of a past regime through a concept of truth, came into force on 19th July 1995 in South Africa. Emerging as a political strategy to acknowledge past suffering whilst promoting a future based on the concerns of social justice, the rule of law and reconciliation, the Commission has struggled to fulfil its objectives. Although the TRC incorporated these broader concerns into the mandate of its three sub-committees, they were disregarded in practice. These sub-committees, which reflected concerns for 'human rights violations', 'amnesty' and 'reparation and rehabilitation', were not 'coupled with some form of social transformation'. The public transition from apartheid, established through a negotiated settlement rather than a revolutionary process, framed the Commission's powers. Shaped by the historical context of this particular transition, the TRC was careful not to 'rock the structural boat'. Rather than pursuing truth and justice, as an integrated feature of social transformation, the Commissioners and, to a greater extent, the government of South Africa, maintained an agenda that avoided a challenge to the status quo. A focus on restorative justice was taken by the Commission with an emphasis placed on mechanisms to restore victims and survivors, through reparations policy, state-led acknowledgement of suffering, and a condemnation, together with the transformation, of the system that implemented such widespread forms of abuse. The priority of changing the apartheid conditions of gross inequality and oppression provided a backdrop to the approval of the TRC by those who had suffered. More difficult to accept was the provision of amnesty to those who had undertaken violations of human rights. The process placed amnesty of violations as a carrot to perpetrators in exchange for a full story, with the stick of prosecutions for those who did not come forward.

16. 'The status quo' as used in the passage means
(a) Previously popular opinions.
(b) Already existing conditions.

(c) Strategies of government.
(d) Following a set agenda.

17. Which of the following best describes the tone of the author?
(a) Optimistic
(b) Threatening
(c) Compassionate
(d) Critical

18. Which of the following is not the broader concern of Truth and Reconciliation Commission (TRC)?
(a) To deal with crimes of a past regime through a concept of truth.
(b) To acknowledge past suffering.
(c) To emerge as a political strategy for reconciliation of rule of law.
(d) To promote a future based on the concerns of social justice.

19. Which of the following statements is least likely to be inferred from the passage?
(a) The TRC ignored some of the broad concerns.
(b) The sub-committees of TRC lacked an agenda of social transformation.
(c) The TRC made earnest efforts to protect human rights.
(d) The TRC lacked the desire and strength to challenge the prevailing conditions.

20. What does 'amnesty' mean in the context of the passage?
(a) Severe punishment
(b) Bring legal action
(c) Arrest warrants
(d) Official pardon

In the domain of education, the current pandemic has made three things clear. It has proved beyond any doubt that we need schools. Irrespective of which country one talks about, students and parents want schools to open and function in full glory, with appropriate precautions. Secondly, it has shown that technology may prove to be useful in education if it is employed thoughtfully. Random surfing of the Internet may lead to a collection of pieces of information that do not add up to any meaning. As Noam Chomsky says, "You cannot pursue any kind of inquiry without a relatively clear framework that is directing your search and helping you choose what is significant and what is not." Moreover, there cannot be any hegemonic techno-managerial solutions to the linguistic and cultural heterogeneity of students; technology must help us to respect individual, peer group and community needs and aspirations. Thirdly, a convergence of the efforts of the public, civil society and private enterprise will have to take place if we wish technology to meaningfully mediate between school and home, particularly among underprivileged groups.

The concept, structure and functioning of a school/college should not be trivialised in any way. This institution has survived since ancient times in spite of proposals for "de-schooling" of various kinds. It is true that schools to a great extent perpetuate the status quo and, as Ivan Illich observed, encourage "consumerism" and "obedience to authority"; but it is also true that those who produced some of the most revolutionary moments in history, including quantum jumps in knowledge, also went to school. The kind of web of learners Illich imagines may in fact have its roots in schools. There are also people who trivialise schools for the kind of investments they demand in terms of space, buildings, teachers, libraries and labs and other infrastructure.

One thing you never forget is the school you went to, friends you made there and the kind of teachers who taught you; the kind of teachers you loved, the kind you mocked at with friends. You recollect nostalgically the sports and other co-curricular activities you took part in. Some of you may still have preserved your school blazer, trophies and photographs with a sense of joy. It is important to see school holistically; it is not a set of atomic items of rooms, library, assembly halls, canteen and playgrounds; it is all of these but in symbiotic relationship with each other, the contours of which are often far too obvious and often simply mysterious.

21. Which one of the following is the author trying to suggest by quoting Noam Chomsky?
(a) Technology shall be used in purposively structured manner in education.
(b) A relatively clear framework pursues any kind of inquiry.
(c) Technology helps to choose what is significant and reject what is not significant.
(d) Technology must help us to respect individual, peer group and community needs and aspirations.

22. Which of the following is not a premise of author's argument in favour of need for schools and colleges?
(a) Schools and colleges provide opportunities for socialization.
(b) The institution of schools and colleges has shown perseverance.
(c) The current pandemic has proved that students and parents want schools and colleges.
(d) Random surfing of the internet may lead to a collection of meaningless information.

23. The expression 'linguistic and cultural heterogeneity' as used in the passage means
(a) Linguistic and cultural unity.
(b) Linguistic and cultural unity in diversity.
(c) Linguistic and cultural diversity.
(d) Linguistic and cultural identity.

24. Which of the following is not the learning outcome from pandemic?
(a) Parents and students from around the world need schools.
(b) Technology is undoubtedly and absolutely useful in education.
(c) Technology may be used meaningfully to mediate between schools and home among underprivileged groups.
(d) None of the above.

25. The expression 'symbiotic relationship' as used in the passage means
(a) Mutually inclusive relationship.
(b) Mutually exclusive relationship.
(c) Mutually beneficial relationship.
(d) Both (b) and (c).

A new report forecasting that India can create millions more jobs over the coming years in the gig economy underscores a fundamental shift in the nature of work. While automation swept through factory floors and BPOs reduced manpower requirements, e-commerce, ride hailing and food delivery apps, streaming media and fintech have created lakhs of temporary jobs in the services sector. Although the jury is still out on the quality of life accorded by such gigs and the social security benefits they accord, recall that informalisation of jobs started much earlier. The report by Boston Consulting Group and Michael & Susan Dell Foundation predicts 90 million flexi and gig jobs in a decade from 8 million now, contributing transactions valued at more than $250 billion and an additional 1.25% to India's GDP. Obviously, technological evolutions are hard to predict. A decade ago, few, if any, had divined these new jobs. Accepting change as the sole constant, it is equally critical to create the socio-economic framework that can support such jobs.

Expecting startups fuelled by venture capital and presently unprofitable to treat gig workers as regular employees isn't practical. Such moves could impede innovation and investment. But if central and state governments could deliver in areas like public health, education, insurance and food security, anxieties generated by unsteady, irregular unemployment can be managed better. Last year's nationwide lockdown when the suddenly unemployed migrant workers panicked and bolted, untrusting the promises of governments to care for them, served out this lesson in poignant detail. The gig economy does promise flexibility and improved choices for many women and part time workers. Every technological revolution till date has effaced some jobs and created plentiful others. There is room for optimism in the rapidly emerging tech-mediated world, but only upon strengthening the support of educational and health infrastructure.

26. The report by Boston Consulting Group and Michael & Susan Dell Foundation ________
(a) Predicts massive rise in gig jobs in a decade.
(b) Predicts fundamental shift in nature of work.
(c) Predicts massive rise in World's GDP.
(d) All the above.

27. Which of the following can be inferred as a caution by the author?
(a) Central and state governments must ensure management of public health, education, insurance and food security, anxieties of gig workers.
(b) Expecting treatment of gig workers as regular employees could impede innovation and investment.
(c) If educational and health infrastructure support is not strengthened, gig economy will fail.
(d) It is critical to create the socio-political framework that can support gig jobs.

28. In the context of the passage, which of the following best describes gig economy?
(a) Informally structured economy with skill based short-term or freelance labour market.
(b) A fundamental shift in the nature of work in an economy.
(c) Economy characterized by startups fuelled by venture capital.
(d) All the above.

29. The tone of the passage is
(a) Cynical
(b) Critical
(c) Scornful
(d) Sanguine

30. According to the passage, which of the following comes as a concern related to gig economy?
(a) Lack of educational and health infrastructure.
(b) Temporary nature of work.
(c) The quality of life and the social security.
(d) None of the above.

CURRENT AFFAIRS AND GENERAL KNOWLEDGE

Starting in April 2020, China amassed a large number of troops and armaments along the disputed Line of Actual Control (LAC) in eastern Ladakh and other areas along the LAC, leading to stand-offs and skirmishes at certain points. The People's Liberation Army (PLA) moved into Indian territory and built fortified structures and defences, changing the status quo on the ground. While there are differences in perception on the alignment of the LAC, over the years both sides concluded a series of agreements to maintain peace and tranquillity on the border, while talks continued to resolve the dispute. Since then, several friction points emerged in eastern Ladakh and both sides initiated diplomatic and military talks aimed at disengagement and de-escalation, with India pushing for the restoration of status quo ante of pre-April. India and China earlier reached an understanding for phased disengagement from all friction points followed by de-escalation from the depth areas along the LAC.

31. Violent clashes between Indian and Chinese army which resulted in death of around 20 Indian soldiers and an unknown number of Chinese soldiers occurred on
(a) May 5, 2020
(b) June 11–12, 2020
(c) June 15–16, 2020
(d) July 13, 2020

32. Where did the violent clashes between Indian and Chinese soldiers occur which caused casualties on both sides?
(a) Naku La
(b) Dhan Singh Thapa post
(c) Galwan Valley
(d) Siachin

33. The violent incident leading to death of soldiers took place at
(a) Patrol Point 13
(b) Patrol Point 14
(c) Patrol Point 15
(d) Patrol Point 16

34. The length of Line of Actual Control of Indo-China Border is
(a) 2788 km (b) 3213 km
(c) 3317 km (d) 3488 km

35. Which of the following was resolved by way of an agreement between India and China in February 2021?
(a) Chinese side will move back its troops to east of finger 8 and Indian side will move its troops to its permanent base near finger 3.
(b) Both sides shall demolish structures built after April 2020.
(c) Moratorium on patrolling in the affected area.
(d) All of these.

As soon as the coronavirus hit the world, India emphasised the imperative of collaboration to overcome the inimical health and economic impact of the virus. It was with this objective that the Indian government organised a virtual meeting of SAARC leaders on March 15, 2020. In the initial months of the pandemic, India, by virtue of the fact that it is the 'pharmacy of the world', ramped up production of essential medicines like hydroxychloroquine, paracetamol, etc. as well as Personal Protection Equipment (PPE) kits, ventilators and masks. In the rapidly evolving global geo-political landscape, the healing and supportive actions by India through supply of Covishield and Covaxin vaccines will have a huge impact in promoting peace, security, cooperation, and prosperity in the region and the world. This is all the more commendable when there are only few countries in the world who have thus far been able to successfully manufacture COVID-19 vaccines.

36. The Minister of Health and Family Welfare is
(a) Shri Mansukh Mandaviya
(b) Dr. Harsh Vardhan
(c) Shri Ashwini Kumar Choubey
(d) Shri Rajnath Singh

37. What is the amount that India has created to contribute in SAARC COVID-19 Emergency Fund?
(a) $20 million (b) $10 million
(c) $15 million (d) $17 million

38. Which of the following countries were the first to receive supplies of vaccines from India?
(a) Nepal and Bangladesh
(b) Bhutan and Myanmar
(c) Bangladesh and Bhutan
(d) Bhutan and Maldives

39. Under which of the following initiatives has the Government of India decided to supply vaccines to the foreign countries?
(a) Vaccine Ujala (b) Vaccine Dosti
(c) Vaccine Maitri (d) Vaccine Rishta

40. COVAXIN, India's indigenous COVID-19 vaccine is developed by ________
(a) Indian Council of Medical Research (ICMR) in partnership with Bharat Biotech International Limited (BBIL)
(b) Indian Council of Medical Research (ICMR)
(c) Bharat Biotech International Limited (BBIL)
(d) Serum Institute of India

There is really nothing new, not already anticipated in a distressed planet since the emergence of human species life nearly two million years ago. So, a long prehistory of inter-faith dialogue entailing the reciprocal relation between religious traditions and the robustness of the very idea of being human and having rights, precedes the recent UN movement of faith for rights (F4R). The F4R framework has finally been affirmed by the United Nations system. The Office of the High Commissioner for Human Rights (OCHR) promoted the Rabat plan of action in 2012. Note that this happened after the end of the Cold War, during globalisation, and soon after 9/11. The plan was a result of a series of expert workshops on the prohibition of incitement to national, racial or religious hatred, underlying "legislative patterns, judicial practices and policies". The UN Human Rights Council is shortly going to discuss further the prohibition of the advocacy of national, racial or religious hatred that constitutes incitement to "discrimination, hostility or violence".

41. When was the first human rights declaration adopted by the United Nations?
(a) December 10, 1945
(b) September 10, 1945
(c) December 10, 1948
(d) September 10, 1948

42. The United Nations Human Rights Council is a/an ________ body within the United Nations System.
(a) Inter-governmental
(b) Non-governmental
(c) Quasi-governmental
(d) Multi-stakeholder

43. The Universal Declaration of Human Rights (UDHR), the International Covenant on Economic, Social and Cultural Rights (ICESCR), and the International Covenant on Civil and Political Rights (ICCPR) and its two Optional Protocols have been adopted under the auspices of the United Nations and are collectively referred to as ________
(a) Magna Carta Libertatum.
(b) International Bill of Human Rights.
(c) International Charter of the Rights of the Man and the Citizen.
(d) International Charter of Human Rights.

44. The objective of the 'Faith for Rights' (F4R) is to provide space for a cross–disciplinary reflection and action on the deep, and mutually enriching, connections between religions and human rights. Which of the following is not one of the commitments on Faith for Rights (F4R)?
(a) To prevent the use of the notion of ' State religion' to discriminate against any individual or group.
(b) To revisit religious interpretations that appear to perpetuate gender inequality and harmful stereotypes or even condone gender-based violence.
(c) To refine the curriculums, teaching materials and textbooks to rectify harmful stereotypes.
(d) To promote religious dogmatism.

45. In India, which of the following statutory organisations is responsible for the protection and promotion of human rights?
(a) National Human Rights Council.
(b) National Human Rights Commission.
(c) National Human Rights Organisation.
(d) Indian Human Rights Council.

UNESCO New Delhi, along with the National Mission for Clean Ganga (NMCG) and other partners, organised a hybrid event with school children and teachers to celebrate 'World Water Day 2021'. The event included felicitating the winners of a water conservation awareness programme, and screening of their winning animation short films, according to an official release. UNESCO launched this nation-wide programme for school children in India, in partnership with the National Mission for Clean Ganga, the United Schools Organization (USO), Water Digest and India based global animation major Toonz Media Group. Entitled 'H2Ooooh!-Waterwise program for children of India', this innovative initiative encouraged school students between the age of 6-14 years to submit story ideas for animated short films to raise awareness on water conservation and its sustainable use.

46. World Water Day is observed on
(a) April 20 (b) April 21
(c) March 22 (d) May 20

47. The theme of World Water Day 2021 was
(a) Valuing Water
(b) Conserving Water
(c) Saving Water
(d) Drinking Water

48. On the occasion of World Water Day 2021, Prime Minister Narendra Modi launched a campaign named
(a) Jal Shakti Abhiyan: Purify the Rivers.
(b) Jal Shakti Abhiyan: Catch the Rain.
(c) Jal Shakti Abhiyan: No More Water Woes.
(d) Jal Shakti Abhiyan: Become Water Wise.

49. The National Water Mission (NWM) has been constituted under the National Action Plan for Climate Change (NAPCC) launched by the Prime Minister of India in 2009. Which of the following is not a goal of the NWM?
(a) Comprehensive water data base in public domain and assessment of the impact of climate change on water resource.
(b) Promotion of citizen and state actions for water conservation, augmentation and preservation.
(c) Comprehensive water data base in public domain and assessment of the impact of water resource on climate change.
(d) Increasing water use efficiency by 20%.

50. In 2019, the Ministry of Jal Shakti was formed after merging the Ministry of Drinking Water and Sanitation and the Ministry of ________
(a) Water Resources, River Development and Ganga Rejuvenation.
(b) Ports, Shipping and Waterways.
(c) Water Conservation and Ganga Rejuvenation.
(d) Inland Waterways and Ganga Rejuvenation.

Prime Minister Narendra Modi, during his visit to Bangladesh, congratulated the neighbouring country for its 50th year of Independence and said that he too had gone to jail while protesting for Bangladesh's liberation. "I was about 20-22 years old when along with some friends I had protested in favour of Bangladesh during its struggle. I even went to jail. Pakistan's atrocities in Bangladesh are well known.. .the pictures didn't allow me to sleep," PM Modi said. He also paid respect to the Indian Army who fought for the freedom of Bangladesh and also paid respect to Bangladesh's Father of the Nation, 'Bangabandhu' Sheikh Mujibur Rahman and conferred upon him the Gandhi Peace Prize 2020. "I pay my respects to Bangabandhu. He gave his life for the people of Bangladesh. Bangabandhu Mujibur Rehman was a ray of hope. He made sure that no country could enslave Bangladesh.", PM Modi said.

51. The Gandhi Peace Prize is awarded for
(a) Non-cooperation against social injustice.
(b) Humanitarian leadership.
(c) Social and economic development in villages.
(d) Social, economic and political transformation through non-violence.

52. The Gandhi Peace Prize was awarded for the first time in the year 1995 to
(a) Dr. Julius K. Nyerere, former President of Tanzania.
(b) Archbishop Desmond Tutu, South Africa.
(c) Dr. John Hume, Ireland.
(d) Baba Amte (Murlidhar Devidas Amte), India.

53. Which of the following Indian organisations was awarded the Gandhi Peace Prize in 2014?
(a) Defence Research and Development Organisation (DRDO).
(b) Bhabha Atomic Research Center (BARC).
(c) Indian Space Research Organization (ISRO).
(d) Radha Soami Satsang Beas (RSSB).

54. Sheikh Mujibur Rahman served as the first ________ of Bangladesh.
(a) Prime Minister
(b) President
(c) Home Minister
(d) Defence Minister

55. Sheikh Mujibur Rahman was assassinated on ________
(a) August 15, 1960
(b) November 15, 1975
(c) August 15, 1975
(d) November 15, 1960

The search for efficient trade routes and better connectivity has been one of the powerful driving forces of history. It has determined the prospects of many nations, regions and civilizations over time. Today, as the world goes through a fundamental re-balancing, correcting many of the distortions of the past, it is only natural that connectivity should be central to that exercise. Growth in trade, commerce, industrial development and technological advancement has gone hand in hand with ease of connecting. Maritime connectivity, in particular, has played a significant role in creating regional corridors for trade and economic linkages, as indeed for cultural and intellectual exchanges over the centuries. The shift in the fulcrum of global economic growth towards Asia is creating unprecedented opportunities for connectivity in the region. The Government of India, recognising the importance of regional connectivity, made a landmark decision to undertake an overseas port investment in Chabahar.

56. The Chabahar Day was commemorated by the Ministry of Ports, Shipping and Waterways in which of the following Summit?
(a) India Water Impact Summit
(b) Sustainable Ocean Summit
(c) World Ocean Summit
(d) Maritime India Summit

57. Which of the following is correct about the Chabahar Port?
(a) It is located in south east of Iran in Oman sea.
(b) It has marine border of more than 300 km.
(c) Both (A) and (B).
(d) None of the above.

58. Which of the following statements relate to the Chabahar Port and its impact?
(a) It is a transit hub to support landlocked countries of Central Asia.
(b) It will play an important role in international North-South transit Corridor (INSTC).
(c) It will optimize the logistic cost by bringing in efficiency, and creating a reliable and safe transport corridor.
(d) All of the above.

59. The Chabahar Port is a result of trilateral agreement between which of the following countries?
(a) India-Iran-Afghanistan
(b) India-Iran-Iraq
(c) Iran-Iraq-Afghanistan
(d) India-Qatar-Pakistan

60. Which is the Special Purpose Vehicle (SPV) incorporated for the development and management of Shahid Behesti Port of Chabahar?
(a) The Indian Port Rail Corporation
(b) Western Shipbuilding Private Limited
(c) India Ports Global Limited
(d) Karaikal Port Private Limited

India has added Tso Kar Wetland Complex in Ladakh as its 42nd Ramsar site, which is a second one in the Union Territory (UT) of Ladakh. Expressing happiness, Minister for Environment, Forest and Climate Change, Shri Prakash Javadekar shared this information in a tweet message. The Tso Kar Basin is a high-altitude wetland complex, consisting of two principal waterbodies, Startsapuk Tso, a freshwater lake of about 438 hectares to the south, and Tso Kar itself, a hypersaline lake of 1800 hectares to the north, situated in the Changthang region of Ladakh, India. It is called Tso Kar, meaning white lake, because of the white salt efflorescence found on the margins due to the evaporation of highly saline water. The Tso Kar Basin is an A1 Category Important Bird Area (IBA) as per Bird Life International and a key staging site in the Central Asian Flyway. The site is also one of the most important breeding areas of the Black-necked Crane (Grus nigricollis) in India. This IBA is also the major breeding area for Great Crested Grebe (Podicepscristatus), Bar-headed Geese (Anserindicus), RuddyShelduck(Tadornaferruginea), Brown-headed Gull (Larusbrunnicephalus), Lesser Sand-Plover (Charadriusmongolus) and many other species.

61. Which of the following sites in India is not included in the Ramsar Wetland List?
(a) Asan Conservation Reserve, Uttarakhand
(b) Dal Lake, Jammu and Kashmir
(c) Kabartal Wetland, Bihar
(d) Lonar Lake, Maharashtra

62. The World Wetlands Day is celebrated on
(a) February 15
(b) February 6
(c) February 2
(d) February 28

63. The theme for World Wetlands Day 2021 was
(a) Wetlands and Climate Change
(b) Wetlands and Water
(c) Wetlands and Biodiversity
(d) Wetlands for our Future: Sustainable Livelihoods

64. The World's largest mangrove forest is located in
(a) Sundarban Mangrove
(b) Pichavaram Mangrove
(c) Florida Mangrove
(d) Godavari-Krishna Mangroves

65. On the occasion of the World Wetland Day, 2021 and as a part of commitment towards conservation, restoration and management of India's wetlands, establishment of a centre was announced by the name of
(a) Centre for Wetland and Coastal Management
(b) Centre for Wildlife Conservation and Management
(c) Centre for Wildlife Management
(d) Centre for Wetland Conservation and Management

LEGAL REASONING

Harm suffered voluntarily does not constitute a legal injury and is not actionable. This principle is embodied in the maxim *volenti non fit injuria*. A person cannot complain of harm to the chances of which he has exposed himself with his free consent and free will. The maxim *volenti non fit injuria* is founded on good sense and justice. A person who has invited or assented to an act being done towards him cannot, when he suffers from it, complain of it as a wrong. The maxim presupposes a tortious act by the defendant. The maxim applies, in the first place, to intentional acts which would otherwise be tortious. There are certain limitations to the application of this maxim:

(i) It is no answer to a claim made by a workman against his employer for injury caused through a breach by the employer of a duty imposed upon him by a statute. But where the negligence or breach of statutory duty is on the part of an employee of the plaintiff who knowingly accepts the risk flowing from such breach and the employer-defendant is not guilty of negligence or breach of statutory duty, the defence of *volenti non fit injuria* is available to the defendant.

(ii) Under an exigency caused by the defendant's wrongful misconduct, consciously and deliberately faced a risk, even of death, whether the person endangered is one to whom he owes a duty of protection, as a member of his family, or is a mere stranger to whom he owes no such special duty. The rescuer will not be deprived of his remedy merely because the risk which he runs is not the same as that run by the person whom he rescues. But where there is no need to take any risk, the person suffering harm in doing so cannot recover.

(iii) To cover a case of negligence the defence on the basis of the maxim must be based on implied agreement whether amounting to contract or not. The defence is available only when the plaintiff freely and voluntarily, with full knowledge of the nature and extent of the risk impliedly agreed to incur it and to waive any claim for injury. But when the plaintiff has no choice or when the notice is given at a stage when it is beyond the ability of the plaintiff to make a choice there can be no implied agreement and the defence on the basis of the maxim must fail.

(iv) The maxim will also not apply when the act relied upon is done because of the psychological condition which the defendant's breach of duty had induced.

66. Mr. A was the owner of a car and he had a driver-Mr. D. On January 19, 2021, Mr. A and Mr. D were travelling in their car wherein Mr. A got down at a restaurant and told Mr. D to take the car back to Mr. A's bungalow. Mr. D was filling the petrol tank of the car, and two strangers- Mr. B and Mr. C took a lift from Mr. D in his car. The car went ahead and the right-side front wheel of the car flew away, the car toppled and Mr. D and Mr. C were thrown out. Mr. C sustained severe injuries and ultimately died due to those injuries on January 20, 2021. Mr. B and legal representatives of Mr. C claimed compensation from Mr. A and Mr. D.
(a) Mr. D will be liable to pay the compensation.
(b) *Volenti non fit injuria* will be applicable and no compensation can be claimed.

(c) *Volenti non fit injuria* will not be applicable and compensation can be claimed.
(d) Mr. A and Mr. D both will be liable to pay the compensation.

67. Rama was a spectator at a motor car race being held on a track owned by the defendant company. During the race, there was a collision between two cars, one of the cars was thrown among the spectators, thereby injuring Rama severely. Which of the following statements is correct?
(a) Rama impliedly took the risk of such injury, the danger being inherent in the sport which any spectator could foresee, the defendant was not liable.
(b) It was a negligence on the part of defendant and *volenti non fit injuria* will be applicable.
(c) Rama did not take the risk of such injury, and she only consented to watching the race and hence the defendant was liable.
(d) Rama was negligent and hence she suffered injuries.

68. Which of the following is correct about consent in *volenti non fit injuria*?
(a) Knowledge of the risk does not always amount to consent.
(b) Knowledge of a risk does not precede consent.
(c) Knowledge of the risk always amounts to consent.
(d) Mere perception of the existence of danger amounts to consent.

69. Lily had placed spring guns in a wood on her ground for the protection of the garden. Karan, with full knowledge that there were spring guns somewhere in the wood, trespassed on the land of Lily and was injured. Which of the following statements is correct?
(a) Lily will be liable to pay compensation to Karan.
(b) Lily has not committed a tort against Karan by exceeding her right of private defence.
(c) Karan's case does not fall within *volenti non fit injuria*.
(d) Karan had knowledge of the spring guns and wilfully courted the danger himself.

70. Which of the following is not an element to claim the defence of *volenti non fit Injuria*?
(a) Prior knowledge of the plaintiff about the risk involved.
(b) Free consent.
(c) Plaintiff is compelled to agree to a risk by the defendant.
(d) Voluntary acceptance of the risk by the plaintiff.

It is essential to the creation of a contract that both parties should agree to the same thing in the same sense. Mutual consent, which should also be a free consent, is the *sine qua non* of a valid agreement and one of its essential elements is that a thing is understood in the same sense by a party as is understood by the other. Not only consent, but free consent is provided in Section 10 of the Indian Contract Act, 1872 to be necessary to the complete validity of a contract. Consent is free when it works without obstacles to impede its exercise. Where there is no consent or no real and certain object of consent, there can be no contract at all. Where there is consent, but not free consent, there is generally a contract voidable at the option of the party whose consent was not free. A general averment that consent was not freely obtained is not enough, and it is necessary to set up one of the vitiating elements such as fraud which includes, false assertion, active concealment, promise without intention of performing it, any other deceptive act, or any act declared as fraudulent. In order to constitute fraud, the act should have been done by the party to the contract, or by any other person with his connivance, or by his agent and with intent to deceive the other party thereto or his agent, or to induce him to enter into the contract. There is no duty upon parties to speak about facts likely to affect the other party's consent to the contract and mere silence does not amount to fraud, unless the circumstances of the case show that there is duty to speak, or silence is, in itself equivalent to speech. On the other hand, misrepresentation falls into three categories: (i) a statement of fact, which if false, would be misrepresentation if the maker believes it to be true, but which is not justified by the information he possesses; (ii) any breach of duty which gains an advantage to the person committing it by misleading another to his prejudice, there being no intention to deceive; and (iii) causing a party to an agreement to make a mistake as to the substance of the thing which is the subject of the agreement, even though done innocently.

71. Which of the following statements correctly depicts the essentials of misrepresentation?
(a) A misrepresentation is a positive statement of fact, which is made or adopted by a party to a contract and is untrue.
(b) Misrepresentation and false representation do not mean the same.
(c) If one party has induced the other to enter into a contract by misrepresenting, though innocently, any material fact especially within his own knowledge, the party misled cannot avoid the contract.
(d) A misrepresentation is a negative statement of fact, which is made or adopted by a party to a contract and is true.

72. Consider the statements given below and answer which one correctly describes a fraudulent act.
(I) The expression fraud means an intention to deceive, whether it is from any expectation of advantage to the party himself or from ill will towards the other is immaterial.
(II) A fraud is an act of deliberate deception with the design of securing something by taking an unfair advantage of another. It is a deception to gain from another's loss.
(III) Fraud arises out of deliberate active role of representator about a fact.
(a) (I), (II) are correct.
(b) (I) correct.
(c) (I), (II), (III) are correct.
(d) (I) and (II) are correct but (III) is incorrect.

73. Which of the following statements is correct?
(a) Fraud is an innocent wrong whereas misrepresentation is an intentional wrong.
(b) The principal difference between fraud and misrepresentation is that in the former, the person making the suggestion does not believe it to be true and, in the latter, he believes it to be true.
(c) In fraud and misrepresentation both, it is not a misstatement of fact which misleads the promisee.
(d) Fraud and misrepresentation both are innocent wrongs.

74. Mr. A sells a car to Mr. Y, his childhood friend with a knowledge that the car is defective. Before buying the car, Mr. Y says to Mr. A, "If you do not deny it, I shall assume that the car is perfect". Mr. A says nothing. In light of the statement, decide the liability of Mr. A.
(a) A's silence is equivalent to speech and hence a misrepresentation.
(b) A is not liable for fraud, but liable for misrepresentation.
(c) A is liable for fraud and misrepresentation both.
(d) A's silence is equivalent to speech and hence a fraud.

75. In which of the following statements will a contract not be voidable at the option of a party?
(a) When a party takes consent by fraud.
(b) When a party takes consent by misrepresentation.
(c) A contract entered by fraud and misrepresentation is neither void nor voidable.
(a) When silence amounts to fraud, but the other party whose consent was taken had discovered the truth or had the means of discovering the truth with ordinary diligence.

Section 4 of the Indian Contract Act, 1872 reads as follows:

Communication when complete - The communication of a proposal is complete when it comes to the knowledge of the person to whom it is made.

The communication of an acceptance is complete, - as against the proposer, when it is put in a course of transmission to him so as to be out of the power of the acceptor; as against the acceptor, when it comes to the knowledge of the proposer.

Thus, the provision makes no difference in the position of the offeror. The offeror becomes bound when a properly addressed and adequately stamped letter of acceptance is posted. The acceptor does not become bound by merely posting his acceptance. He becomes bound only when his acceptance comes to the knowledge of the proposer. The contract is concluded at the place from where the proposal is accepted and communication of acceptance is dispatched, i.e., the address at which the proposal was sent. The court at that place would have jurisdiction to entertain a cause of action under the contract. This rule, that the communication of an acceptance is complete as against the proposer when the letter is posted, is probably intended to apply only when the parties are at a distance and they communicate by post. "Where, however, the parties are in each other's presence or, though separated in space", they are in direct communication, as, for example, by telephone, no contract will arise until the offeror receives the notification of acceptance.

76. 'S' wanted to purchase shares of a company and communicated his offer to buy shares on March 1, 2021. A letter of allotment of shares addressed to 'S', which is an acceptance of the offer to purchase shares, was posted by the company on March 10, 2021, but the letter never reached 'S' and was lost in transit. In the given situation, which of the following statements is true?

(a) Communication of acceptance is not complete as against 'S' and hence, there is no valid contract between 'S' and the company.
(b) Communication of acceptance is complete as against 'S' however not complete as against the company.
(c) Communication of acceptance is complete as against the company however not complete as against 'S'.
(d) Communication of acceptance is complete against both 'S' as well as the company.

77. 'A', who is in Mumbai, makes an offer for supply of goods to 'B', who is in Delhi, *via* a mobile phone call. During the same call, A's offer is absolutely and unconditionally accepted by 'B'. According to the terms agreed between 'A' and 'B', goods are to be supplied at Pune and payment is to be made electronically. In the given situation, where is the contract concluded?

(a) Neither Mumbai, Delhi nor Pune as it is a telephonic contract
(b) Pune
(c) Delhi
(d) Mumbai

78. 'X', who is in Gandhinagar, makes an offer for sale of second -hand luxury car to 'Y', who is Jammu, *via* an e-mail sent on January 15, 2021 at 2:03 pm. X's offer is absolutely and unconditionally accepted by 'Y' *via* an e-mail sent on January 15, 2021 at 4:04 pm. The e-mail communicating acceptance is read by 'X' on January 15, 2021 at 7:05 pm. In the given situation, when is the contract concluded?

(a) As against 'X', on January 15, 2021 at 4:04 pm and as against 'Y', on January 15, 2021 at 7:05 p.m.
(b) As against 'Y', on January 15, 2021 at 4:04 pm and as against 'X', on January 15, 2021 at 7:05 p.m.
(c) January 15, 2021 at 4:04 p.m.
(d) January 15, 2021 at 7:05 p.m.

79. 'X', who is in Agra, makes an offer for sale of second -hand luxury car to 'Y', who is Jammu, *via* an e-mail sent on January 15, 2021 at 2:03 pm. However, the e-mail did not reach 'Y' due to some technical error at the server which is located in Delhi. Thereafter, 'X' makes a mobile phone call to 'Y' on January 15, 2021 at 4:04 pm and makes him the same offer as was made in the e-mail. In the same mobile phone call, the offer is absolutely and unconditionally accepted by 'Y' at 4:10 pm.

In the given situation, where is the contract concluded?
(a) Delhi
(b) Jammu
(c) Agra
(d) Neither Delhi, Jammu nor Agra as it is an electronic contract.

80. "When the words of acceptance are spoken into the telephone, they are put into the course of transmission to the offerer so as to be beyond the power of the acceptor. The acceptor cannot recall them." In light of the given proposition, which of the following statements is/are true?
I. The communication being instantaneous, the contract immediately arises. II. The communication being instantaneous, the communication of acceptance is immediately complete as against the proposer as well as the acceptor.
III. The communication being non-instantaneous, the communication of acceptance is complete as against the acceptor when the words of acceptance are spoken into the telephone.
IV. The communication being non-instantaneous, the communication of acceptance is complete as against the proposer when the words of acceptance are spoken into the telephone.

(a) Only I
(b) I and II
(c) III and IV
(d) Only II

It is a well settled principle of contract law that parties cannot by contract exclude the jurisdiction of all courts. Such a contract would constitute an agreement in restraint of legal proceedings and contravene Section 28 of the Indian Contract Act, 1872. However, where parties to a contract confer jurisdiction on one amongst multiple courts having proper jurisdiction, to the exclusion of all other courts, the parties cannot be said to have ousted the jurisdiction of all courts. Such a contract is valid and will bind the parties to a civil action.

Section 28. Agreements in restraint of legal proceedings, void-Every agreement,
(a) by which any party thereto is restricted absolutely from enforcing his rights under or in respect of any contract, by the usual legal proceedings in the ordinary tribunals, or which limits the time within which he may thus enforce his rights; or
(b) which extinguishes the rights of any party thereto, or discharges any party thereto, from any liability, under or in respect of any contract on the expiry of a specified period so as to restrict any party from enforcing his rights, is void to the extent.

Parties cannot by agreement confer jurisdiction on a court which lacks the jurisdiction to adjudicate. But where several courts would have jurisdiction to try the subject matter of the dispute, they can stipulate that a suit be brought exclusively before one of the several courts, to the exclusion of the others.

81. 'A', a resident of Mumbai, and 'B', a resident of Delhi, enter into an agreement for sale and supply of goods. The transaction takes place partly in Mumbai and partly in Delhi. There is a clause in the agreement which stipulates that in the event of a dispute between ' A' and ' B' , the courts in Kolkata would have exclusive jurisdiction to decide the dispute. 'A' and 'B' agreed to the said clause in order to avoid dispute over choice between the two proper places of jurisdiction-Mumbai and Delhi. In the given situation, which of the following statements is true?
(a) The clause relating to jurisdiction is in restraint of legal proceedings.
(b) The clause relating to jurisdiction is not in restraint of legal proceedings.
(c) The clause relating to jurisdiction is valid as ' A' and ' B' have mutually agreed to the same.
(d) The clause relating to jurisdiction is valid as its object is lawful.

82. 'A', a resident of Chennai, and 'B', a resident of Bengaluru, enter into an agreement for sale and supply of goods. The transaction takes place partly in Chennai and partly in Bengaluru. There is a clause in the agreement which stipulates that in the event of a dispute between 'A' and 'B', the courts in Chennai would have exclusive jurisdiction to decide the dispute. 'A' and 'B' agreed to the said clause in order to avoid dispute over choice between the two proper places of jurisdiction- Chennai and Bengaluru. In the given situation, which of the following statements is true?
(a) The clause relating to jurisdiction is in restraint of legal proceedings.
(b) The clause relating to jurisdiction is void.
(c) The clause relating to jurisdiction is valid as 'A' and 'B' have mutually agreed to the same.
(d) The clause relating to jurisdiction is valid as courts in Chennai have jurisdiction to decide the dispute.

83. 'A', a resident of Agra, and 'B', a resident of Bhubaneswar, enter into an agreement for sale and supply of goods. The transaction takes place partly in Agra and partly in Bhubaneswar. There is a clause in the agreement which stipulates that in the event of a dispute between 'A' and 'B', neither of them can approach the court of law or take recourse to any alternative dispute resolution mechanism to settle the dispute. In the given situation, which of the following statements is true?
(a) The clause relating to jurisdiction is not valid as it is in restraint of legal proceedings.
(b) The clause relating to jurisdiction is not valid as the clause is vague and ambiguous.
(c) The clause relating to jurisdiction is valid as they have not restricted the choice of either party regarding choice of jurisdiction.
(d) The clause relating to jurisdiction is valid as no court's has been ousted by the clause.

84. 'A', a resident of Ahmedabad, and 'B', a resident of Ranchi, enter into an agreement for sale and supply of goods. The transaction takes place partly in Ahmedabad and partly in Ranchi. Clause 6 of the agreement stipulates that in the event of a dispute arising between 'A' and 'B' within six months of the entering into contract, they can approach a court in either Ahmedabad or Ranchi (as both are proper places of jurisdiction), or take recourse to any alternative dispute resolution mechanism to settle the dispute. Clause 7 of the agreement stipulates that in the event of a dispute arising between 'A' and 'B' after the expiry of six months of entering into contract, the courts in Chennai would have exclusive jurisdiction to decide the dispute. In the given situation, which of the following statements is true?
(a) Clause 6 is void and Clause 7 is valid.
(b) Clause 6 is valid and Clause 7 is void.
(c) Both Clause 6 and Clause 7 are valid.
(d) Both Clause 6 and Clause 7 are void.

85. According to the given passage, which of the following statements is true?
(a) Parties cannot by contract make a choice of jurisdiction.
(b) Parties cannot by contract exclude the jurisdiction of all courts.
(c) Parties can by contract confer jurisdiction on any court.
(d) Parties can by contract extinguish their rights under any contract.

The doctrine of *res judicata* requires that a party should not be allowed to file same matter repeatedly against the other party either in the same court or in other competent court and that the decision given by one court should be accepted as final subject to any appeal, revision or review. The doctrine is founded on the principle that it is in the interest of the public at large that a finality should be attached to the binding decisions pronounced by courts of competent jurisdiction, and it is also in the public interest that individuals should not be vexed twice over with the same kind of litigation. This apart, the object of the doctrine is to ensure that ultimately there should be an end to litigation. Doctrine of *res judicata* is embodied in Section 11 of the Code of Civil

Procedure, 1908 which governs the procedure to be followed in civil matters. Section 11 is inapplicable to writ jurisdictions. The Supreme Court has observed that though the rule is technical in nature yet the general doctrine of *res judicata* is based on public policy and therefore, it cannot be treated as irrelevant or inadmissible even in dealing with fundamental rights in petitions filed under Article 32 of the Constitution of India. The court observed that if a writ petition filed by a party under Article 226 of the Constitution of India is considered on merits as a contested matter and is dismissed, the decision thus pronounced would continue to bind the parties unless it is otherwise modified or reversed in appeal or other appropriate proceedings permissible under the Constitution of India. It would not be open to a party to ignore the judgment of the High Court and move Supreme Court under Article 32 by an original petition made on the same facts and for obtaining the same or similar orders or writs. If the petition filed in the High Court under Article 226 is dismissed but not on the merits, then the dismissal of the writ petition would not constitute a bar to a subsequent petition under Article 32, however if the petition is dismissed without passing a speaking order, then such dismissal cannot be treated as creating a bar of *res judicata*.

86. Which of the following is *res judicata* applicable to?
(a) Civil suits
(b) Writ petitions
(c) None of the above.
(d) Both (A) and (B).

87. Doctrine of *res judicata* is applicable to writs if
(a) The decision is on merits.
(b) Order is a speaking order.
(c) Both (A) and (B).
(d) Neither (A) nor (B).

88. On which of the following is the doctrine of *res judicata* based?
(a) No one should be vexed twice for the same cause more than once.
(b) It is in the interest of public that finality should be attached to the decisions of courts.
(c) There should be an end to litigation.
(d) All of these.

89. Which of the following is correct?
(a) If a writ petition is filed under Article 226 of the Constitution of India and the same is rejected on merits by a speaking order, another petition under Article 32 of the Constitution of India is not maintainable being barred by *res judicata*.
(b) The doctrine of *res judicata* is founded on the principle that it is in the interest of the public at large that a finality should be attached to the binding decisions pronounced by courts of competent jurisdiction.
(c) Technical rule of *res judicata* only prevents multiple filing of petitions under Article 226 of the Constitution of India between same parties over the same matter and is not applicable to petition under Article 32 of the Constitution of India.
(d) Both (A) and (B).

90. Mr. X was dismissed from service by his employer after a proper enquiry. Mr. X challenged his dismissal in High Court by a petition under Article 226 of the Constitution of India. However, the High Court dismissed the petition citing that Mr. X has an alternative remedy available. Mr. X took recourse to the alternative remedy before the appropriate forum, but Mr. X's legal action is opposed by the employer on the basis of *res judicata*. Based on these facts, which of the following is the most appropriate?
(a) *Res judicata* is applicable.
(b) *Res judicata* is not applicable.
(c) Since the matter relates to livelihood and life of the person, technical rule of *res judicata* should not be applied.
(d) Both (B) and (C).

Compassionate appointment is an exception to the general rule of appointment which is a way of providing employment to the family of the deceased employee on compassionate grounds. The objective is only to provide solace and succour to the family in difficult times and, thus, its relevancy is at that stage of time when the employee passes away. The mere death of an employee in harness does not entitle his family to such source of livelihood. The authority concerned has to examine the financial condition of the family of the deceased, and it is only if it is satisfied that, but for the provision of employment, the family will not be able to meet the crisis that the job is offered to the eligible member of the family. It was further asseverated in the said judgment that compassionate employment cannot be granted after a lapse of reasonable period as the consideration of such employment is not a vested right which can be exercised at any time in the future. It was further held that the object of compassionate appointment is to enable the family to get over the financial crisis that it faces at the time of the death of sole breadwinner. Thus, compassionate appointment cannot be claimed or offered after a significant lapse of time and after the crisis is over.

91. Which of the following correctly states the intent behind the application of compassionate appointment?

(a) The norms, at the time of death of the government employee will be applicable and not the norms at the time of making an application.

(b) A dependent of a government employee cannot demand consideration of his/her application.

(c) The norms of the governmental or public authorities are not considered while applying for compassionate appointment.

(d) The norms prevailing on the date of consideration of the application should be the basis for consideration of claim for compassionate appointment.

92. Which of the following is not correct about the rule of compassionate appointment?

(a) Compassionate appointment is given to the family members of the deceased irrespective of their financial status.

(b) It is to mitigate the hardship caused to the family members after the death of earning member of the family.

(c) Compassionate appointment cannot be granted as a matter of vested right.

(d) Compassionate appointment cannot be made in the absence of rules and regulations issued by the government or a public authority.

93. Mr. Y, son of Mr. X, made a representation before ABC government company on January 4, 2018 that he should be given appointment on compassionate grounds as his father died during his employment in the company in 2000. Consider the given facts and decide whether Mr. Y is entitled to get compassionate appointment.

(a) Mr. Y is entitled to get compassionate appointment.

(b) Mr. Y is not entitled for compassionate appointment as a long period has elapsed since the death of his father.

(c) Mr. Y is entitled to get compassionate appointment depending on policy of the company in which his father was working.

(d) Mr. Y is not entitled to get compassionate appointment as it is the discretion of the company to refuse the said appointment.

94. The Government of 'N' formulated a scheme for providing compassionate appointment to the dependants of government servants who retired on medical invalidation. By a further notification, the benefit of the scheme was restricted to cases where the government servants retired on medical invalidation, at least five years before attaining the age of superannuation. Consider the given facts, and decide which of the following is correct in relation to the validity of this rule of compassionate appointment?

(a) The scheme is valid subject to the approval of the dependents.

(b) The scheme is not valid as the offer of compassionate appointment to the dependent of a government servant who is medically invalidated is not an exception to the general rule.

(c) The scheme is not valid as it is unconstitutional.
(d) The scheme is valid as it is not arbitrary and the government has the right to formulate such rules.

95. Which of the following is not correct regarding the nature of appointment on compassionate grounds?
(a) A request for compassionate appointment by the dependent relatives of the deceased must be preferred without any undue delay.
(b) The general rule of appointment may not be always applicable to compassionate appointments.
(c) The immediacy of the need is not the basis for the state to allow the benefit of compassionate appointment.
(d) It is a benefit given to the family members at the time of distress.

Marriage is necessarily the basis of social organisation and the foundation of important legal rights and obligations. The importance and imperative character of the institution of marriage needs no comment. In Hindu law, marriage is treated as a *Samskara* or a sacrament. The Hindu Marriage Act, 1955 introduced monogamy as a law of marriage among Hindus by virtue of Section 5 clause (i) which is essentially the voluntary union for life of one man with one woman to the exclusion of all others. It enacts, "neither party must have a spouse living at the time of marriage". The expression 'spouse' here used, means a lawfully married husband or wife. Before a valid marriage can be solemnised, both parties to such marriage must be either single or divorced or a widow or a widower and only then they are competent to enter into a valid marriage. If at the time of performance of the marriage rites and ceremonies, one or other of the parties had a spouse living and the earlier marriage had not already been set aside, the later marriage is no marriage at all. The Supreme Court in *Bhaurao Shankar Lokhande v. State of Maharashtra*, [AIR 1965 SC 1564] held, "*Prima facie*, the expression 'whoever marries' in Section 494 of the Indian Penal Code, 1860 (which defines the offence of bigamy) must mean 'whoever marries validly' or 'whoever marries and whose marriage is a valid one'. If marriage is not valid according to the law applicable to the parties, no question arises of its being void by reason of its taking place during the life of the husband or wife of the person marrying. One of the conditions of a valid marriage under the Hindu Marriage Act, 1955 is that it must be 'solemnised'. Further, Section 13 (2) of the Act provides for grounds of divorce to wife and states, "A wife may also present a petition for the dissolution of her marriage by a decree of divorce on the ground that in the case of any marriage solemnized before the commencement of this Act, that the husband had married again before such commencement or that any other wife of the husband married before such commencement was alive at the time of the solemnization of the marriage of the petitioner: Provided that in either case the other wife is alive at the time of the presentation of the petition".

96. Mr. A, a 40-year old male Hindu, was married to Ms. B, a 36-year old female Hindu. Mr. A fell in love with his colleague- Ms. C, a 22-year old female Christian. On April 8, 2020, Mr. A declared Ms. C as his wife in front of all his colleagues, family members and relatives. Based on the given facts, decide the liability of Mr. A as per Hindu law.
(a) Mr. A is not liable for the offence of bigamy as Ms. C is a Christian.
(b) Mr. A is liable for the offence of bigamy as mere declaration also amounts to solemnisation.
(c) Mr. A is not liable for the offence of bigamy as he has not solemnised his marriage with Ms. C.
(d) Mr. A is liable for the offence of bigamy as there was no intention to marry.

97. Which of the following statements correctly expresses the interpretation of the word 'solemnise' under Hindu law?
(a) Solemnisation means celebrating the marriage with proper customary rites and ceremonies of either party to a marriage.

(b) Solemnisation includes and means promising each other a lifetime of happiness.
(c) Solemnisation is not necessary in modern marriages when registration of marriage is complete.
(d) Solemnisation is a mere formal practice and not a mandate.

98. Which of the following is not correct regarding the law of monogamy among Hindus?
(a) Monogamy is a union of a man and woman which provides their relation a social and legal recognition.
(b) Monogamy as a law was abolished after 1955.
(c) The second marriage during the subsistence of a first valid marriage is void.
(d) If a husband solemnises a second marriage during the subsistence of first marriage, it is not an offence, however, it is an offence if a wife commits the same act.

99. On the basis of Section 13 of the Hindu Marriage Act, 1955, which of the following statements does not relate to the remedy?
(a) The object of the Section was to provide an opportunity to the wife in the form of remedy of divorce.
(b) The introduction of this ground of divorce is unnecessary as it disturbs the sanctity of marital institution.
(c) A remedy is only available under this Section if the husband has the other wife living.
(d) The living status of either spouse is immaterial to claim the remedy.

100. Mr. P, a 28-year old male Hindu was legally married to Ms. Q, a 26-year old female Hindu. Mr. P converts to Islam to marry Ms. N, a 30-year old Sunni female Muslim. Consider the statement and decide whether Ms. Q has the remedy to file a complaint for the offence of bigamy against Mr. P?
(a) Yes, Ms. Q can file a complaint subject to the approval by Ms. N.
(b) No, Ms. Q cannot file a complaint as it defeats the very purpose of her marriage with Mr. P.
(c) No, Ms. Q cannot file a complaint as Mr. P converted to another religion and the offence of bigamy will only be attracted when the parties are Hindus.
(d) Yes, Ms. Q has the remedy of filing a complaint for the offence of bigamy.

The Indian Penal Code, 1860 does not define 'consent' in positive terms, but what cannot be regarded as 'consent' under the Code is explained by Section 90. Section 90 reads as follows: "90. *Consent known to be given under fear or misconception* - A consent is not such a consent as is intended by any section of this Code, if the consent is given by a person under fear of injury, or under a misconception of fact, and if the person doing the act knows, or has reason to believe, that the consent was given in consequence of such fear or misconception;.." Consent given firstly under fear of injury and secondly under a misconception of fact is not ' consent' at all. That is what is enjoined by the first part of Section 90. These two grounds specified in Section 90 are analogous to coercion and mistake of fact which are the familiar grounds that can vitiate a transaction under the jurisprudence of our country as well as other countries. The factors set out in the first part of Section 90 are from the point of view of the victim. The second part of Section 90 enacts the corresponding provision from the point of view of the accused. It envisages that the accused too has knowledge or has reason to believe that the consent was given by the victim in consequence of fear of injury or misconception of fact. Thus, the second part lays emphasis on the knowledge or reasonable belief of the person who obtains the tainted consent. The requirements of both the parts should be cumulatively satisfied. In other words, the court has to see whether the person giving the consent had given it under fear of injury or misconception of fact and the court should also be satisfied that the person doing the act i.e. the alleged offender, is conscious of the fact or should have reason to think that but for the fear or misconception, the consent would not have been given. This is the scheme of Section 90 which is couched in negative terminology. Section 90 cannot, however, be construed as an exhaustive definition of consent for the purposes of the Indian Penal Code, 1860. The normal connotation and concept of 'consent' is not intended to be excluded. Various decisions of the High Court and of Supreme Court have not merely gone by the language of Section 90, but travelled a wider field, guided by the etymology of the word 'consent'.

101. 'A', a man, promises 'B', a woman that he will marry her if she has sexual intercourse with him. 'B' agrees, but after having sexual intercourse, 'A' flees and never contacts 'B' again. In the given situation, which statement is true?

(a) Consent for sexual intercourse was given under misconception of fact.
(b) Consent for sexual intercourse was given under fear of injury.
(c) Consent for sexual intercourse was given under undue influence.
(d) Consent for sexual intercourse was given without any misconception or fear of injury.

102. According to the given passage, a person is said to 'consent' to the doing of an act if

(a) A person agrees to do an act without misconception of fact or fear of injury.
(b) The person to whom agreement is signified has no reason to believe that the agreement is being given under misconception of fact or fear of injury.
(c) A person agrees to do an act without misconception of fact or fear of injury and the person to whom agreement is signified has no reason to believe that the agreement is being given under misconception of fact or fear of injury.
(d) A person agrees to do an act without having regard to the consequences of fear of injury or misconception of fact.

103. According to your understanding of the given passage, why is negative terminology used to explain the meaning of consent under Section 90?

(a) To emphasise on the factors that vitiate consent.
(b) To emphasise on the point of view of victim or the person who gives consent.
(c) To emphasise on the point of view of the person who receives consent.
(d) To emphasise on the non-exhaustive scope of definition of consent.

104. 'X', a man, promises 'Y', a woman that he will marry her if she has sexual intercourse with him. 'Y' agrees and they have sexual intercourse. Thereafter, 'X' assures 'Y' that they will get married, but X's family is opposed to the marriage even after X's attempts to convince them. Therefore, 'X' refuses to marry 'Y'. In the given situation, which statement is true?

(a) Consent for sexual intercourse was received knowing that the consent is given under misconception of fact.
(b) Consent for sexual intercourse was given without any misconception of fact or fear of injury.
(c) Consent for sexual intercourse was received knowing that the consent is given under fear of injury.
(d) Consent for sexual intercourse was given under misconception of fact and received misconception of fact.

105. According to the given passage, which of the following statements is not true?

(a) Misconception of fact vitiates consent.
(b) Fear of injury vitiates consent.
(c) Misconception of fact obviates the necessity of consent.
(d) Fear of injury is analogous to coercion.

LOGICAL REASONING

The COVID-19 pandemic and the unmatched mental health challenges have made it more crucial than ever that we continue to make strides towards understanding the concept of mental health stigma and how we might tackle it around the world. Graham Thornicroft, a practising psychiatrist, who is extensively and deeply involved in mental health stigma research at the Institute of Psychiatry, Psychology and Neurosciences at King's College London has divided stigma into three components-knowledge, attitude and behaviour. The last behaviour emerges from social isolation, such as what we are experiencing during the pandemic, as well as exclusion from mainstream activities and citizenship. In higher-income countries, stigma rates may be greater than other countries, perhaps because of the pressure to excel. In low-income countries, one can be unwell and still play an active social and productive role somewhere as there are many such roles to play within the family and in society. Enhancing contact with people who have experienced mental health problems is the best way to reduce stigma. To date, most people with mental illness remain silent about their condition, avoiding discussing their problems for fear of losing face, damaging their reputation or jeopardising their family status. Having a space where they may be welcomed and listened to, rather than judged, will go a long way towards enabling them to share their experiences. In a small part of rural Andhra Pradesh, researchers used posters, pictures, drums, and a short street play, as an intervention technique to reduce mental health stigma. An actor portrayed a person's journey through mental health crises and setbacks before receiving support and showing hope, improvement and recovery. People assembled around the stage, willing to talk about and discuss what they saw, even two to three years after the event.

106. What is the central idea in the passage as conveyed by the author?
- (a) Mental health is not an obstacle for people seeking care.
- (b) Mental health is a domestic phenomenon.
- (c) In low-income countries, mental health does not receive the adequate attention and treatment.
- (d) Mental health issues have only arisen after the COVID-19 pandemic globally.

107. As per the passage, which of the following approaches can be most effective to curb the issue of mental health?
- (a) Mental health can only be curbed when people will stop sharing their emotions openly.
- (b) To develop a sense of acceptance among people suffering from mental health and let them heal gradually.
- (c) Experiences shared and discussed on a larger level is a major hindrance for better mental health conditions globally.
- (d) A person should not express about his/her failures which enhances the mental health problems.

108. Which of the following notions is expressed in the passage to enunciate the significance of issue of mental health?
- (a) The issue of mental health has received the required recognition and deliberation during the COVID-19 pandemic.
- (b) Mental health will be reduced automatically after the COVID-19 pandemic.
- (c) Mental health improves when social isolation increases.
- (d) Mental health is an illusionary notion developed during COVID-19 pandemic to strengthen the pharmaceutical industries.

109. "In low-income countries, one can be unwell and still play an active social and productive role somewhere as there are many such roles to play within the family and in society".

Which of the following conclusions can be drawn from the above statement?
- (a) Stigma rates in lower-income countries are higher as compared to higher income countries.
- (b) Stigma rates in higher-income countries may be more due to a pressure of performing and to excel.
- (c) Mental stigma is not related to the economic conditions of a country.
- (d) Higher-income countries require people to perform multiple roles at their homes.

110. Which of the following weakens the author's idea of 'having a space where they may be welcomed and listened to, rather than judged'?
- (a) People who tend to share their emotions tend to have mental peace and happiness.
- (b) Societal role is massive in embracing people suffering from mental health ailments.

(c) People sharing their ideas and expressions publicly is a practice which needs to be promoted.
(d) It is a human tendency to form judgments about other people and this being a healthy practice should be encouraged at large scale.

One of the most important challenges for Indian diplomacy in the subcontinent is to persuade its neighbours that India is an opportunity, not a threat. Far from feeling in any way besieged by India, they should be able to see it as offering access to a vast market and to a dynamic, growing economy which would provide their own economies with far greater opportunities than more distant partners (or even their own domestic markets) could provide. This would go beyond economic benefits: as David Malone argues, "Economic cooperation represents the easiest 'sell' to various constituencies within the countries of the region. Were this to prove successful, cooperation on more divisive and sensitive issues, such as terrorism, separatism, insurgency, religious fundamentalism, and ethnic strife, could be attempted with greater chances of success." Winds of change are blowing in South Asia. There is a definite consolidation of democracy in all the countries of the region, every one of which has held elections within the last three years. Some of our neighbours have made significant strides in surmounting internal conflict and others are in the process of doing so. If India has to fulfil its potential in the world, we have no choice but to live in peace with our neighbours, in mutual security, harmony and cooperation. Just as Nehru left Robert Frost's immortal lines "Miles to go before I sleep" on his bedside table when he died, Shastri kept some lines of the founder of the Sikh faith, Guru Nanak, on his desk. When translated into English they read: "O Nanak! Be tiny like the grass, for other plants will wither away, but grass will remain ever green." Shastri was seen by many Indians of exalted ambition as a tiny man, but he had the mind and heart of a giant. His vision of peaceful coexistence with our neighbours, through adopting the demeanour, the modesty and the freshness of grass, may well be the best way for India to ensure that its dreams remain evergreen in its own backyard.

111. As per the passage, which of the following is a challenge for India?
(a) To develop an intimidating surrounding for its neighbours.
(b) To manifest India as a land of opportunities.
(c) To restrict access to economic activities to its neighbours.
(d) To propagate the practice of threatening neighbours for greater opportunities.

112. *"If India has to fulfil its potential in the world, we have no choice but to live in peace with our neighbours, in mutual security, harmony and cooperation."* In the context of the statement, which of the following strengthens the author's opinion?
(a) Peace and prosperity cannot work in consonance.
(b) India should assert its might over its neighbours.
(c) Peaceful coexistence with neighbours is the key to India's stellar growth.
(d) India can offer myriad opportunities for its neighbours by working in seclusion.

113. Which of the following is the central theme of the above passage?
(a) The objective of attaining peaceful co-existence and cooperation with the neighbours.
(b) The dominance of India on its neighbouring countries.
(c) Emergence of India as a global power.
(d) Prioritising the economic opportunities for India.

114. Which of the following is correct expression of the author's opinion as stated in passage?
(a) India should strive for greater economic integration which should be politically and administratively feasible.
(b) India can see borders as barriers, and border areas as buffer zones but not as gateways of opportunity.

(c) India's stellar economic growth is thwarting her own opportunities.
(d) It is not in India's interest to be generous to neighbouring countries.

115. Which of the following can be inferred from the above passage?
(a) There is no nexus between cooperative existence and economic growth of a nation.
(b) Unless India's region becomes more self-centred, India is unlikely to develop into more than a regional power.
(c) India can only become a great power if it works in isolation to achieve the desired goals.
(d) India cannot aspire to be a great power without the cooperation of neighbours.

The critique of school as an institution has developed and grown in the past half a century. Education theorist Everett Reimer wrote School is Dead in the 1960s. Most schools are caged jails, where an alien curriculum designed by some 'experts' is thrust down a child's gullet. Today, many schools are gargantuan corporate enterprises with thousands of children on their rolls, and for all practical purposes they are run like factories, or better still like mini-armies. The website of a private school in Lucknow boasts of 56,000 students, for instance. But progressive thinkers have always envisioned 'free schools' for children. The great Russian novelist, Leo Tolstoy, founded a school for the children of poor peasants at his home, Yasnaya Polyana, without any strict schedule, homework or physical punishment. Maria Montessori was the first Italian woman to become a doctor; she went on to work out the 'stages of development' in children which became the basis for her educational philosophy, which too emphasised children's freedom and choice. Tagore's critique of rote learning is articulated in the classic tale 'The Parrot's Training' (Totaakahini). Perhaps, the longest lasting libertarian school in the world is Summerhill. It was founded in 1921, a hundred years ago in England, by A. S. Neill with the belief that school should be made to fit the child rather than the other way round. The 1966 Kothari Education Commission's recommendation for a common school system was never implemented. Today, which school a child goes to depends on her socioeconomic status. The pandemic has furthered and exacerbated this divide. COVID-19 hit parents economically. The digital divide between the rich and poor has also widened. The poor do not have access to mobiles, laptops and internet connectivity. In such a scenario, one can try and conceive of neighbourhood learning spaces.

116. What has the author conveyed regarding the school system in India?
(a) The school system in India is an advanced system which focuses on developing the personality of students.
(b) The schools in India are segregated based on socio-economic status.
(c) The schools staunchly promote the interest of every student enrolled to ensure quality education.
(d) The pandemic has aided the students a greater access to the technology and learning spaces.

117. Which of the following can be deduced from the above passage?
(a) Social segregation must be eliminated for furtherance of education in schools.
(b) The COVID-19 pandemic has lubricated the teaching-learning process in schools.
(c) Schools should be divided on the basis of the financial capabilities only.
(d) Private schools should be encouraged to enrol economically poor students irrespective of their caste or religion.

118. As per the above passage, which of the following does not correctly represent the author's view regarding imparting of education during the pandemic?
(a) There has been a disruption of education systems due to the pandemic.
(b) The inclusion of technology has widened the canvas of distance learning education for all, albeit its access is the biggest concern.

(c) The pandemic has unearthed and stimulated innovative approaches to learning.
(d) The crisis is worsened by reduction of opportunities for many children.

119. Which of the following can be utilised to develop a healthy environment for students' learning in schools?
(a) Individualised teaching should not be followed for growth of students.
(b) Students should only be permitted to opt for only few subjects as elective courses.
(c) Community learning should be encouraged in schools.
(d) A fixed and robust curriculum is the need of the hour.

120. In the above passage, which of the following cannot be referred as a characteristic of a 'free school'?
(a) It is an alternative to mainstream and conventional form of schooling.
(b) Free schools provide a democratic platform to the students to voice their opinions.
(c) The courses offered at free schools are optional for students depending on their interests.
(d) Specific choice of subjects and a fixed schedule are quintessential features of a free school.

Asia is at the front line of climate change. Extreme heat in India, Pakistan, and Bangladesh, wildfires in Australia, typhoons in Japan, are real and present dangers and likely to become more frequent as climate change intensifies. McKinsey's report on 'Climate risk and response in Asia', finds that, without adaptation and mitigation, Asia is expected to experience more severe socioeconomic impacts of climate change than other parts of the world. Large cities in the Indian Subcontinent could be among the first places in the world to experience heat waves that exceed the survivability threshold. Just as information systems and cybersecurity have become integrated into corporate and public-sector decision making, climate change will also need to feature as a major factor in decisions. Climate science tells us that some amount of warming over the next decade is already locked in due to past emissions, and temperatures will continue to rise. India anticipates a significant infrastructure build out over the next decades with projects worth \$1.77 trillion across 34 sub sectors, according to the National Infrastructure Pipeline. Robust regulations around outdoor work could significantly reduce the economic risk of lost hours as well as the toll on life from heat waves. The good news is that we have started to see some Indian states and cities pursuing such policies. Ahmedabad City Corporation introduced a heat action plan- the first of its kind in India in response to the 2010 heat wave that killed 300 people in a single day. The city now has a heat-wave early warning system, a citywide programme of roof reflectivity to keep buildings cool, and teams to distribute cool water and rehydration tablets during heat waves. Renewable energy has grown rapidly in India and can contribute 30 per cent of gross electricity generation by 2030, according to the Central Electricity Authority.

121. Which of the following cannot be inferred from the above passage?
(a) It is imperative to lessen our vulnerability to harmful effects of climate change.
(b) Increase in mitigation strategies will eventually lead to an increase in pollutants.
(c) Reduction of emissions which are heat-trapping and harmful for environment should be our primary goal.
(d) The infrastructure development plans need to be climate friendly.

122. Consider the following statements:
I. The impact of increasing heat is more on the ones who are economically poor and engaged in outdoor employment.
II. Risk to environment is directly related to change in climate.

III. A localised understanding of climate risk is essential to mitigate the risk.

As per the above passage, which of these statements is implicit?

(a) I only.
(b) I and II.
(c) I, II and III.
(d) I and III.

123. Which of the following strategies is not appropriate to reduce the climate change risk?

(a) Decreasing energy efficiency.
(b) Carbon Pricing System.
(c) Decarbonising industrial operations and buildings.
(d) Investments in adaptive technologies.

124. As per the above passage, which of the following is a major challenge to control the climate change?

(a) Reliance on non-renewable energy is significant for economic growth.
(b) Renewable energy is now utilised in many sectors to curb the increasing risk of climate change.
(c) Remedial actions for climate change are encouraged to lessen the risk of global warming.
(d) Regulated industrialisation keeps a balance between growth and environment.

125. Consider the following statement- "Just as information systems and cybersecurity have become integrated into corporate and public-sector decision making, climate change will also need to feature as a major factor in decisions."

Which of the following is the most appropriate explanation for the above statement?

(a) Decision making by organisations should not depend on the climate conditions which may lead to hampering their growth.
(b) Monetary investments in adoption of climate friendly tools is not an urgent need.
(c) The understanding of climate risk should not be integrated into decision making.
(d) Organisations must incorporate climate risk, build the necessary infrastructural capabilities and tools to diagnose risks.

COVID-19 infections are once again on the rise with daily infections crossing 60,000 per day last week. This is considerably higher compared to the reported infections during the same period last year when the numbers were less than 500 per day. What is obvious is that the pandemic is far from over despite the availability of vaccines. However, unlike last year, the response this time has been muted with no nationwide lockdown. One of the reasons for the differing responses is the lesson from the unintended consequences on the economy of the strict lockdown last year. While aggregate estimates on the growth rate of GDP showed a sharp contraction in economic activity (the economy shrunk by 24 per cent in the April-June quarter of 2020) the impact on lives and livelihoods is still unfolding even though the sharp contractionary phase seems behind us. The extent of the loss of lives and livelihoods is becoming clear only now, with detailed data from the Periodic Labour Force Surveys (PLFS) - the latest round of which is for the April-June quarter of 2020. This is the first official report on the estimates for the quarter, which witnessed the worst impact with the lockdown in force until the middle of May. Visuals of thousands of migrants walking back to their villages are still fresh in the mind. While many have returned to urban areas in the absence of jobs in rural areas, many did not. The PLFS, which captures the employment-unemployment situation in urban areas, provides some clues to what happened. The estimates from PLFS are broadly in line with estimates available from other privately conducted surveys, notably the unemployment surveys of the Centre for Monitoring Indian Economy (CMIE). According to the PLFS April-June 2020 round, the urban unemployment rate for the population above the age of 15 was 20.8 per cent, which is close to the monthly average for the same quarter from CMIE at 19.9 per cent. The CMIE data, however, does suggest a sharp decline in June compared to April and May. Similar to the CMIE data, the PLFS data also shows a sharp rise in the unemployment rate which more than doubled compared to the unemployment rate in the preceding quarter of January-March 2020 at 9.1 per cent and 8.8 per cent in the same quarter (April-June) of 2019. While one in five persons above the age of 15 was unemployed during April-June 2020, the unemployment rate among the 15 -29-year-olds was 34.7 per cent - every third person in the 15-29 age group was unemployed during the same period. These are staggering numbers, but not surprising. While the lockdown certainly contributed to the worsening of the employment situation, particularly in urban areas, the fact that the economy was already going through severe distress as far as jobs are concerned is no longer surprising. Between 2016-17 and 2019-20, growth decelerated to 4 per cent, less than half the 8.3 per cent rate in 2016-17. The fact that the economy has not been creating jobs predates the economic shocks of demonetisation and the hasty roll-out of GST. The PLFS data from earlier rounds have already shown the extent of the rise in unemployment compared to the employment-unemployment surveys of 2011-12. The unemployment rates in urban areas for all categories increased by almost three times between 2011-12 and 2017-18. On an internationally comparable basis, the unemployment rate among the 15-24-year-olds in 2017-18 was 28.5 per cent, which makes the youth unemployment rate in India amongst the highest in the world, excluding small countries and conflict-ridden countries. Since then, it has only worsened or remained at that level.

126. According to the author, which of the following is a plausible explanation for India's prevalent crisis of unemployment?

(a) The previously existing employment crunch is worsened due to the imposition of nationwide lockdown during the COVID-19 pandemic.

(b) Imposition of nationwide lockdown during the COVID-19 pandemic reduced economic activity.

(c) Imposition of nationwide lockdown during the COVID-19 pandemic led to migration of workforce from urban to rural areas.

(d) There is a sharp decline in urban unemployment rate for the population above the age of 15.

127. According to the author, what is current state of Indian economy?

(a) There is a sharp contraction in economic activity.

(b) The aftermath of a sharp contraction in economic activity is being experienced.

(c) The unemployment rates in urban areas for all categories are increasing by almost three times.

(d) Youth unemployment rate in India is at par with that in small and conflict-ridden countries.

128. Which of the following statements cannot be inferred from the given passage?

(a) Loss of lives and livelihoods is attributable to the imposition of nationwide lockdown during the COVID-19 pandemic.

(b) Decline in economic growth is attributable to the imposition of nationwide lockdown during the COVID-19 pandemic.

(c) Rise in unemployment is attributable to the migration of members of workforce from urban to rural areas.

(d) Rise in unemployment is attributable to the imposition of nationwide lockdown during the COVID-19 pandemic.

129. Which of the following strengthens the author's argument that the decline in economic growth and rise in unemployment precedes the onset of the COVID-19 pandemic?

(a) While one in five persons above the age of 15 was unemployed during April-June 2020, the unemployment rate among the 15-29-year-olds was 34.7 per cent - every third person in the 15-29 age group was unemployed during the same period.

(b) According to the PLFS April-June 2020 round, the urban unemployment rate for the population above the age of 15 was 20.8 per cent, which is close to the monthly average for the same quarter from CMIE at 19.9 per cent.

(c) Between 2016-17 and 2019-20, growth decelerated to 4 per cent, less than half the 8.3 per cent rate in 2016-17.

(d) The estimates from PLFS are broadly in line with estimates available from other privately conducted surveys, notably the unemployment surveys of the Centre for Monitoring Indian Economy (CMIE).

130. According to the given passage, which of the following statements is correct?

(a) Unemployment rates in urban areas for all categories increased by almost three times over the preceding decade.

(b) Employment rates in urban areas for all categories increased by almost three times over the preceding decade.

(c) Unemployment rates in urban areas for all categories increased by almost three percent over the preceding decade.

(d) Employment rates in urban areas for all categories increased by almost three percent over the preceding decade.

On the day of writing this, India had reported 116 deaths from COVID-19. In contrast, the US, with around one-fourth the population of India, reported 1,897 deaths, or 16 times the daily deaths as India. The UK, which has one-twentieth the population of India, reported 592 deaths, or 5 times the daily deaths as India. On other metrics too-new cases, active cases-the Indian curve has flattened. If and when the UK and the US achieve what we have, there will be major celebrations. Such low death rates would be seen as a victory of the government, citizens and science over the dreaded coronavirus. However, because we are India, we don't get as much credit. We are considered poor, third-world and untrustworthy, incapable of achieving something like this on our own. Instead of learning from India's experience, the first instinct is to doubt Indian data. We aren't counting the cases right, we aren't doing enough tests, we don't classify the deaths properly-the list of doubts goes on and on. This, even as the tests have only increased, positivity rate has dropped and almost all Indian hospitals are seeing a drop in COVID-19 admissions and fatalities. To think that the Deep Indian State is capable of fudging data at the level of every district and every state, and sustaining this facade for months is giving it way too much credit. Conspiracies require enormous co-ordination and effort and it isn't quite how things work in India. Given that you can check corona data at every ward level, it is also impossible to fudge data, not to mention create a downwards curve that is moving in the same direction in virtually every corner of India. In terms of testing, while a case might be made for a lot of Indians not getting tested, it is also true that random testing has increased in the last few months. Domestic flyers into Maharashtra from many states for instance, have to get a COVID-19 test done irrespective of symptoms. If there was rampant corona, we would see a spike in cases from just these flyers. It may be hard for people to accept this reality but almost all evidence points to the fact India has flattened the corona curve, while the US, UK and most of Europe still haven't. What is even more remarkable about India's achievement is that it has managed to do this without draconian lockdowns (apart from the two months in April-May 2020). In fact, cases have dropped even as India opened up more.

131. Which of the following strengthens the author's argument that India has tackled the COVID-19 pandemic better than most advanced nations?

(a) India's positivity rate of COVID-19 cases and admissions in Indian hospitals are reduced.

(b) India's counting of the number of COVID-19 cases is incorrect.

(c) India's testing facilities for COVID-19 cases are inadequate.

(d) India's classification of COVID-19 cases is inaccurate.

132. Which of the following weakens the author's argument that India has tackled the COVID-19 pandemic better than most advanced nations?
(a) India lacks the co-ordination and effort to execute conspiracies.
(b) Many Indians are possibly not getting tested.
(c) Evidence points to the fact India has flattened the corona curve.
(d) India has not imposed draconian lockdowns.

133. *"To think that the Deep Indian State is capable of fudging data at the level of every district and every state, and sustaining this façade for months is giving it way too much credit."* In this statement, the author indicates that
(a) There are unauthorised networks of power operating independently of the Indian state's political leadership in pursuit of their own agenda and goals.
(b) There are authorised networks of power operating independently of the Indian state's political leadership in pursuit of their own agenda and goals.
(c) There may be unauthorised networks of power operating independently of the Indian state's political leadership in pursuit of their own agenda and goals, but their influence is questionable.
(d) There may be unauthorised networks of power operating independently of the Indian state's political leadership in pursuit of their own agenda and goals, and their influence is deep and pervasive.

134. According to the given passage, which of the following statements is not true?
(a) Developed nations are reluctant to learn from India's experience as Indian data is doubtful.
(b) India does not get as much credit for tackling the COVID-19 pandemic.
(c) India is seen as a poor, third-world country.
(d) India is seen as untrustworthy and incapable of tackling the COVID-19 pandemic independently.

135. According to the given passage, which of the following statements is true?
(a) COVID-19 cases in India have reduced because of reduction in restrictions.
(b) COVID-19 cases in India have increased with reduction in restrictions.
(c) COVID-19 cases in India have reduced with increase in restrictions.
(d) COVID-19 cases in India have reduced despite the reduction in restrictions.

QUANTITATIVE TECHNIQUES

Two renowned international Software companies, namely Pollaris and Contigent, started their business in the year 2007 and both the companies were in competition with each other in profit making. Pollaris earned 30 per cent profit in the year 2007 and 2008, and further increased it to 40 per cent in 2009. However, its profit percentage decreased to 20 per cent in the year 2010. On the other hand, Contigent opened with 40 per cent profit in 2007, but slowly decreased to 35 per cent in 2008 and 30 per cent in 2009. Interestingly, both the companies increased their profit percentage in the later year considerably. Pollaris increased its profit percentage to 35 per cent in 2011 and 50 per cent in 2012; simultaneously, Contigent increased its profit percentage to 45 per cent in 2010, 50 per cent in 2011 and reached 60 per cent in the year 2012. As there is a need to understand the income and expenditure for the better performance of both companies in the future, answer the following questions.

136. What is the increase in profit of Contigent Company in percentage from year 2011 to 2012?
(a) 10% (b) 20%
(c) 15% (d) Cannot be determined

137. What percentage of the total profit making of Pollaris Company in 2011 and 2012 is the total profit making of Contigent Company in 2007 and 2008?
(a) 113.3% (b) 95.3%
(c) 90.3% (d) 133.3%

138. If the income of Contigent Company in 2008 was ₹ 200 crores, what was its profit in 2009?
(a) ₹ 21.5 Crore (b) ₹ 46.15 Crore
(c) ₹ 153 Crore (d) Cannot be determined

139. What is the difference between the company with highest annual average profit percentage and that of the company with lowest annual average profit percentage?
(a) 5.17 (b) 8.33
(c) 9.17 (d) 4.33

140. What is the percentage increase in profit of Pollaris Company from year 2010 to 2011?
(a) 42.86 (b) 75
(c) 175 (d) Cannot be determined.

A newly formed state government wants to bring more development in the state. Therefore, the government proposed to launch various welfare programmes. Before bringing up any welfare programme, the state government intended to understand the population percentage of the state by age groups, so that the government could plan the welfare programmes accordingly. The state government found that the state's 30 per cent of the population were children between the age group of 0-15. Next to child population, 17.75 per cent of the population were adolescents between the age group of 16 and 25. The early adult population, i.e., the age groups 26 to 35 were 17.25 per cent, 36 to 45 were 14.50 per cent, respectively. The population who are between the age group of 46 to 55 constitute 14.25 per cent and the elderly population of the state, i.e., 56 to 65 (5.12%) and 66 above (1.13%) was comparatively less than the other age groups. To get a better clarity, the state government concerned is seeking the answers to following questions:

141. Out of every 5,600 persons, what is the number of persons below the age of 26 years?
(a) 2515 (b) 1746
(c) 1660 (d) 2674

142. There are 400 million people below 36 years. How many million (approx.) people are in the age group 56-65?
(a) 32.72 million (b) 25.75 million
(c) 31.50 million (d) 59.30 million

143. If there are 20 million people in the age group 56 to 65, what is the difference between the number of people in the age groups 16-25 and 46-55?
(a) 15.6 million (b) 12.18 million
(c) 28.4 million (d) 34.7 million

144. If the difference between the number of people in the age groups 46-55 and 26-35 is 15.75 million, then total population of the state is approximately?
(a) 360.23 million (b) 390 million
(c) 400 million (d) 525 million

145. Which age group accounts for the maximum population in the state?
(a) 16 to 25 (b) 26 to 35
(c) 36 to 45 (d) None of the above.

COVID-19 pandemic turned life upside-down for many families across the world. Mr. Abhishek was working as a sale executive in a famous Marketing Company. Due to COVID-19 pandemic lockdown and restrictions, Mr. Abhishek was not able to achieve his monthly targets which resulted in the reduction of his salary. So far, he spent his income lavishly without any planning and prior calculations. However, the prevailing situation compelled him to plan his expenditure to adjust his life to the present income. Therefore, he analysed his spendings of last year i.e., 2019, so that he can plan his present year 2020 spendings. Through his brief analysis, he found that in the year 2019, he spent 23 per cent of his income on food, 15 per cent on Housing, and 12 per cent on his child's education. For his transport, he spent 10 per cent, and for clothing of his family he spent 10 per cent. In the meanwhile, Mr. Abishek also saved 15 per cent of his income in the year 2019, and the remaining 20 per cent of expenditure he kept as other spendings. Answer the following questions to provide deeper insight to Mr. Abhishek.

146. If the total amount spent during the year 2019 was ₹56,000, what was the amount spent on food?
(a) ₹ 12,000 (b) ₹ 12,880
(c) ₹ 23,880 (d) ₹ 23,000

147. If the total amount spent was ₹ 56,000, how much money was spent on clothing and housing together?
(a) ₹ 11,500 (b) ₹ 12,500
(c) ₹ 14,000 (d) ₹ 15,000

148. What was the ratio of the total amount of money spent on housing to that spent on education?
(a) 5:2 (b) 2:5
(c) 4:5 (d) 5:4

149. If the total expenditure of the family for the year 2019 was ₹ 56,000, what was the amount saved by the family during the year?
(a) ₹ 8,400 (b) ₹ 5,600
(c) ₹ 6,900 (d) ₹ 3,067

150. If the total amount spent during the year 2019 was ₹ 56,000, the amount spent on other spendings and clothing together was higher than
(a) Housing and Child Education
(b) Food and Transport
(c) Food and Housing
(d) Housing and Saving

ANSWER KEY

English

1. (b)	**6.** (a)	**11.** (b)	**16.** (b)	**21.** (a)	**26.** (a)
2. (a)	**7.** (b)	**12.** (d)	**17.** (d)	**22.** (d)	**27.** (b)
3. (a)	**8.** (d)	**13.** (a)	**18.** (c)	**23.** (c)	**28.** (a)
4. (d)	**9.** (b)	**14.** (d)	**19.** (c)	**24.** (b)	**29.** (d)
5. (c)	**10.** (c)	**15.** (d)	**20.** (d)	**25.** (c)	**30.** (c)

Current Affairs and General Knowledge

31. (c)	**36.** (a)	**41.** (c)	**46.** (c)	**51.** (d)	**56.** (d)	**61.** (b)
32. (c)	**37.** (b)	**42.** (a)	**47.** (a)	**52.** (a)	**57.** (c)	**62.** (c)
33. (b)	**38.** (d)	**43.** (b)	**48.** (b)	**53.** (c)	**58.** (d)	**63.** (b)
34. (d)	**39.** (c)	**44.** (d)	**49.** (c)	**54.** (b)	**59.** (a)	**64.** (a)
35. (d)	**40.** (a)	**45.** (b)	**50.** (a)	**55.** (c)	**60.** (c)	**65.** (d)

Legal Reasoning

66. (b)	**72.** (c)	**78.** (a)	**84.** (d)	**90.** (b)	**96.** (c)	**102.** (c)
67. (a)	**73.** (b)	**79.** (c)	**85.** (b)	**91.** (d)	**97.** (a)	**103.** (d)
68. (a)	**74.** (d)	**80.** (b)	**86.** (d)	**92.** (a)	**98.** (b)	**104.** (b)
69. (d)	**75.** (d)	**81.** (a)	**87.** (c)	**93.** (b)	**99.** (b)	**105.** (c)
70. (c)	**76.** (b)	**82.** (d)	**88.** (d)	**94.** (d)	**100.** (d)	
71. (a)	**77.** (d)	**83.** (a)	**89.** (d)	**95.** (c)	**101.** (a)	

Logical Reasoning

106. (c)	**111.** (b)	**116.** (b)	**121.** (b)	**126.** (a)	**131.** (a)
107. (b)	**112.** (c)	**117.** (a)	**122.** (c)	**127.** (b)	**132.** (b)
108. (a)	**113.** (a)	**118.** (c)	**123.** (a)	**128.** (c)	**133.** (c)
109. (b)	**114.** (a)	**119.** (c)	**124.** (a)	**129.** (c)	**134.** (a)
110. (d)	**115.** (d)	**120.** (d)	**125.** (d)	**130.** (a)	**135.** (d)

Quantitative Techniques

136. (b)	**139.** (c)	**142.** (c)	**145.** (a)	**148.** (d)
137. (a)	**140.** (b)	**143.** (b)	**146.** (b)	**149.** (a)
138. (d)	**141.** (d)	**144.** (d)	**147.** (c)	**150.** (a)

CLAT 2020

ENGLISH

Climate change is considered to be one of the most serious threats to sustainable development, with adverse impact on the environment, human health, food security, economic activity, natural resources and physical infrastructure. According to the Intergovernmental Panel on Climate Change (IPCC), the effects of climate change have already been observed, and scientific findings indicate that precautionary and prompt action is necessary. Vulnerability to climate change is not just a function of geography or dependence on natural resources; it also has social, economic and political dimensions which influence how climate change affects different groups. Poor people rarely have insurance to cover loss of property due to natural calamities, i.e., drought, floods, super cyclones, etc. The poor communities are already struggling to cope with the existing challenges of poverty and climate variability and climate change could push many beyond their ability to cope or even survive. It is vital that these communities are helped to adapt to the changing dynamics of nature. Adaptation is a process through which societies make themselves better able to cope with an uncertain future. Adapting to climate change entails taking the right measures to reduce the negative effect of climate change (or exploit the positive ones) by making the appropriate adjustments and changes. These range from technological options such as increased sea defences or flood proof houses on stilts to behavioural change at the individual level, such as reducing water use in times of drought. Other strategies include early warning systems for extreme events, better water management, improved risk management, various insurance options and biodiversity conservation. Because of the speed at which climate change is happening due to global temperature rise, it is urgent that the vulnerability of developing countries to climate change is reduced and their capacity to adapt is increased and national adaptation plans are implemented. Communities must build their resilience, including adopting appropriate technologies while making the most of traditional knowledge, and diversifying their livelihoods to cope with current and future climate stress. Local coping strategies and knowledge need to be used in synergy with government and local interventions. The need of adaptation interventions depends on national circumstances. There is a large body of knowledge and experience within local communities on coping with climatic variability and extreme weather events. Local communities have always aimed to adapt to variations in their climate. Local coping strategies are an important element of planning for adaptation. Traditional knowledge can help to provide efficient, appropriate and time tested ways of advising and enabling adaptation to climate change in communities who are feeling the effects of climate changes due to global warming.

1. To address the challenge of Climate Change, Developing countries urgently require:
(a) Implementation of National Adaptation Plans
(b) Adoption of short term plans
(c) Adoption of technological solutions
(d) Imposition of Climate Change tax

2. Given below are the factors of vulnerability of poor people to climate changes. Select the option that contains the correct answer.
(a) Their dependence on natural resources
(b) Geographical attributes
(c) Lack of financial resources
(d) Lack of traditional knowledge

Codes:
(a) (2), (3) *and* (4)
(b) (1), (2), (3) *and* (4)
(c) (3) *only*
(d) (1), (2) *and* (3)

3. Which of the following is <u>against</u> the idea portrayed in the passage?
(a) Co-ordination between regional and national efforts is necessary.
(b) The process of adaptation to climate change does not take into account the factor of prevailing national circumstances.
(c) Social dimensions of climate change also need to be appreciated.
(d) Combining traditional knowledge with appropriate technology is the need of the hour.

4. The traditional knowledge should be used through
(a) Improvement in national circumstances
(b) Synergy between Government and local interventions
(c) Imposition of Climate Change Tax.
(d) Its dissemination

5. What is the meaning of the word 'Resilience' occurring in the passage?
(a) Toughness
(b) Fragility
(c) Flexibility
(d) Vulnerability

The uncovering of a private Instagram group styling itself 'Bois Locker Room' featuring students from some prominent South Delhi schools discussing their female classmates in disturbingly violent ways including plans of sexual assault is a wakeup call for parents and authorities. The group formed last month or so kicked up a social media storm when screenshots surfaced. Police have questioned a 15 year old boy to identify other members. Similar incidents involving minors discussing rape/gang rape of classmates have been reported on other digital platforms like WhatsApp too, across cities. The exchanges in the now deleted group require precise responses from police, parents and school authorities around whom the fates of the juveniles involved now revolve. It is important to recognize where a teenager spouting objectification of his female counterparts is coming from. People of all ages, not just children, are retreating deeper into the recesses of their online avatars during this lockdown. But the heavy technological investment in children's education, including flooding them with personal smartphones, has not been matched by serious conversations centred on responsible internet usage and equality. Young, impressionable minds absorb the normalisation of rape from the adults around them. When what they see, read and hear is toxic masculinity, that is what they perform. That's what peer pressure becomes about. But if this youthful role play of macho dominance receives timely counselling, it can prevent far graver adult offences. Schools and parents have a critical role to play in educating children on gender equality. Digital platforms which claim to have zero tolerance towards content that violates community standards must also explain why such abuses go undetected, despite boasts about Artificial Intelligence-driven technologies to stop them. They should play a more proactive role in stopping the sexual harassment of real people in the guise of virtual sport.

[*Editorial Published in Times of India, dated 6 May, 2020*]

6. What is the <u>Central Idea</u> being conveyed by the Author in the passage above?
(a) Modern Social Networking platforms must take the lead in regulating young people from using these platforms for sexual abuse.
(b) It is significant to educate children and youngsters about gender equality.
(c) Digital Platforms need to have a zero tolerance policy towards content leading to sexual abuse.
(d) None of the above.

7. As per author, why is this incident a wake-up call for parents?
(a) Because even the parents are indulged heavily in social networking platforms.
(b) Because parents have failed to stop their children from committing such blunders.
(c) Because it is the primary responsibility of parents to control their children.
(d) Because the parents have failed in educating their children regarding fair internet usage and have simply invested in the technology driven education of their children.

8. According to the author, in order to understand the root cause of such insensitive incidents, it is important to:

(a) Understand and examine the kind of socialisation process these children are exposed to.
(b) Adopt Artificial Intelligence driven technologies.
(c) Strengthen the environment of discipline in schools and colleges.
(d) All of the above.

9. On the basis of your reading of the passage, which of the following statements can be inferred?

(a) Sexual Offenses can be reduced by timely counselling from parental and quasi-parental authorities, i.e., parents and teachers, respectively.
(b) If digital platforms implement a Zero Tolerance Policy towards such a menace, sexual offences can be completely stopped.
(c) Investment in education of children is enough to curb the menace.
(d) All of the above.

10. Which of the following words are synonymous with the word 'Spouting'?

(a) Pouring
(b) Streaming
(c) Erupting
(d) All of the Above.

The snow was falling, and the Cat's fur was stiffly pointed with it, but he was imperturbable. He sat crouched, ready for the death-spring, as he had sat for hours. It was night but that made no difference, all times were as one to the Cat when he was in wait for prey. Then, too, he was under no constraint of human will, for he was living alone that winter. Nowhere in the world was any voice calling him; on no hearth was there a waiting dish. He was quite free except for his own desires, which tyrannized over him when unsatisfied as now. The Cat was very hungry. almost famished, in fact. For days, the weather had been very bitter... and the Cat's long hunt had availed him nothing. But he waited with the inconceivable patience and persistency of his race; besides, he was certain. The Cat was a creature of absolute convictions, and his faith in his deductions never wavered. The rabbit had gone in there between those low-hung pine boughs. The Cat had seen her enter...so he sat down and waited, and he waited still in the white night, listening angrily to the north wind starting in the upper heights of the mountains with distant screams, then swelling into an awful crescendo of rage, and swooping down with furious white wings of snow like a flock of fierce eagles into the valleys and ravines. The Cat was on the side of a mountain, on a wooded terrace. Above him, a few feet away towered the rock ascent as steep as the wall of a cathedral. He had often looked with wonder at the rock, and miauled bitterly and resentfully as man does in the face of a forbidding Providence. At his left was the sheer precipice. Behind him... was the frozen perpendicular wall of a mountain stream. Before him was the way to his home. When the rabbit came out she was trapped; her little cloven feet could not scale such unbroken steeps. So the Cat waited. The tangle of trees and bushes clinging to the mountain-side with a stern clutch of roots, the prostrate trunks and branches, the vines embracing everything with strong knots and coils of growth, had a curious effect, as of things which had whirled for ages in a current of raging water, only it was not water, but wind, which had disposed everything in circling lines of yielding to its fiercest points of onset. It was as if ice needles pricked his skin through his beautiful thick fur, but he never faltered and never once cried. He had nothing to gain from crying, and everything to lose; the rabbit would hear him cry and know he was waiting.

[*Excerpts from a Short story, 'The Cat' by Mary E. Wilkins Freeman*]

11. Which of the following suggests a synonymous meaning to the words 'Providence' and 'Crescendo', respectively?

(a) Nemesis, Apex
(b) Zenith, Nadir
(c) Laxity, Prudence
(d) Short-sightedness, Upsurge

12. The passage has been adorned with numerous figure of speeches. Which of the following combinations is correct?
(a) Irony and Sarcasm
(b) Alliteration and Pun
(c) Simile and Personification
(d) Metaphor and Onomatopoeia

13. The passage best demonstrates which one of the following motifs of Cat's Life?
(a) To satisfy the pangs of hunger
(b) To survive the harsh winters
(c) A never ending wait
(d) To hunt for Rabbit

14. The Author's description of "...he was under no constraint of human will, for he was living alone..." implies:
(a) Cat's absolute freedom from everything
(b) Cat's no association with human beings
(c) Cat's loneliness
(d) Cat's tyrannical demeanour

15. The lines, "...but he never faltered and never once cried. He had nothing to gain from crying, and everything to lose...", suggest that the Cat is:
(a) Reflective (b) Apologetic
(c) Resilient (d) Frustrated

I am losing my interest in human beings; in the significance of their lives and their actions. Someone has said it is better to study one man than ten books. I want neither books nor men; they make me suffer. Can one of them talk to me like the night – the Summer night? Like the stars or the caressing wind?

The night came slowly, softly, as I lay out there under the maple tree. It came creeping, creeping stealthily out of the valley, thinking I did not notice. And the outlines of trees and foliage nearby blended in one black mass and the night came stealing out from them, too, and from the east and west, until the only light was in the sky, filtering through the maple leaves and a star looking down through every cranny. The night is solemn and it means mystery.

Human shapes flitted by like intangible things. Some stole up like little mice to peep at me. I did not mind. My whole being was abandoned to the soothing and penetrating charm of the night. The katydids began their slumber song: they are at it yet. How wise they are. They do not chatter like people. They tell me only: "sleep, sleep, sleep." The wind rippled the maple leaves like little warm love thrills. Why do fools cumber the Earth! It was a man's voice that broke the necromancer's spell. A man came today with his "Bible Class." He is detestable with his red cheeks and bold eyes and coarse manner and speech. What does he know of Christ? Shall I ask a young fool who was born yesterday and will die tomorrow to tell me things of Christ? I would rather ask the stars: they have seen him.
[*Short Story by Kate Chopin*]

16. Why has the author lost interest in human beings?
(a) Because they make the author suffer.
(b) Because the human beings do not bring with them the warmth and the comfort which comes naturally with the night, starts and the wind.
(c) Because human beings are not mysterious.
(d) All of the above.

17. The author has compared the night with:
(a) The Katydids
(b) The Necromancer's spell
(c) Stars
(d) All of the above.

18. Why has the author called the 'katydids' wise?
(a) Because they sing a slumber song.
(b) Because they tell the author to only 'sleep'.
(c) Because they do not indulge in unnecessary and unimportant talks.
(d) Because they are not fools.

19. Which of the following can be inferred from the passage?
(a) Being close to nature can bring one closer to God.
(b) Nature is just a mystery.
(c) Books and Man are both detestable.
(d) None of these.

20. Which of the following words from the passage mean 'rough'?

(a) Solemn (b) Caressing
(c) Coarse (d) Slumber

It was the strangest murder trial I ever attended, where the old woman was found battered to death. He was a heavy stout man with bulging bloodshot eyes. All his muscles seemed to be in his thighs. The clock had just struck two in the morning. Mrs Salmon in 15 Northwood Street had been unable to sleep: she heard a door click shut and thought it was her own gate. So she went to the window and saw Adams (that was his name) on the steps of Mrs Parker's house. He had just come out and he was wearing gloves. He had a hammer in his hand and she saw him drop it into the laurel bushes by the front gate. But before he moved away, he had looked up at her window. The fatal instinct that tells a man when he is watched exposed him in the light of a streetlamp to her gaze-his eyes suffused with horrifying and brutal fear, like an animal's when you raise a whip.

Mrs Salmon was called in the Court.

'And do you see the man here in court?'

[She looked straight at the big man in the dock, who stared hard at her with his Pekingese eyes without emotion.]

'Yes,' she said, 'there he is.'

'You are quite certain?'

She said simply, 'I couldn't be mistaken, sir.'

'Thank you, Mrs Salmon.'

[Counsel for the defence rose to cross-examine.]

'Now, Mrs Salmon, you must remember that a man's life may depend on your evidence.'

'I do remember it, sir.'

'Is your eyesight good?'

'I have never had to wear spectacles, sir.'

'You are a woman of fifty-five?'

'Fifty-six, sir.'

'And the man you saw was on the other side of the road?'

'Yes, sir.'

'And it was two o'clock in the morning. You must have remarkable eyes, Mrs Salmon?'

'No, sir. There was moonlight, and when the man looked up, he had the lamplight on his face."

'And you have no doubt whatever that the man you saw is the prisoner?'

'None whatever, sir. It isn't a face one forgets.'

Then he said, 'Do you mind, Mrs Salmon, examining again the people in court?

No, not the prisoner. Stand up, please, Mr Adams! And there at the back of the court with thick stout body and muscular legs and a pair of bulging eyes, was the exact image of the man in the dock.

'Now think very carefully, Mrs Salmon. Can you still swear that the man you saw drop the hammer in Mrs Parker's garden was the prisoner and not this man, who is his twin brother?' Of course she couldn't.

[*Excerpts from The Case for the Defence' by Graham Greene*]

21. Why do you think, has the Author called the trial, 'strangest' murder trial he ever attended?

(a) Because the accused had a very strange personality.
(b) Because, despite having a potential witness and evidence against the accused, his wrong could not be proved.
(c) Because, Mrs. Salmon's evidence could not be proved before the Court.
(d) None of these.

22. "...his eyes suffused with horrifying and brutal fear, like an animal's when you raise a whip." can be called as:

(a) Personification
(b) Simile
(c) Onomatopoeia
(d) None of the above

23. The expression '*Pekingese eyes*' used in the passage refers to which of the following?

(a) Bulging eyes
(b) Red eyes
(c) Small eyes
(d) None of them

24. Why was Mrs. Salmon convinced that the man she saw had committed the crime?
(a) Because she saw the man on the steps of Mrs. Parker's House and he was wearing gloves.
(b) Because he had a hammer in his hand and she saw him drop it into the laurel bushes by the front gate.
(c) Because when he looked up at her window, his eyes were suffused with horrifying and brutal fear.
(d) Because she had seen him clearly in the light of street lamp.

25. Who was murdered in the scene described in the passage?
(a) Mrs. Wheeler
(b) Mrs. Parker
(c) Mrs. Salmon
(d) It cannot be inferred.

The world has very few devices left to fight COVID-19 with, but technology remains one of them. Whether it is employing the state-of-the-art technology in the discovery of cures or vaccines, or traditional technology services to enhance health care and consultations, or even tools that keep people at home occupied/productive, it is clear that technology will serve humanity at one of its darkest moments. The pandemic has contributed, in no small measure, to the understanding of the myriad ways in which available technologies have not been put to better use, and presented people with multiple opportunities to harness these devices, techniques and methods to get on with life in the time of lockdown. Among the primary uses is telemedicine, rendered inexorable now, by the temporary paralysis brought on by a freeze on movement. The Centre's recent guidelines allowing for widespread use of telemedicine services came as a shot in the arm for telehealth crusaders in the country, among them the Telemedicine Society of India that has long been battling to use the technology in its complete arc to reach remote areas in India. This move finds consonance with the rest of the world where several nations, also deeply impacted by the pandemic, have deployed telemedicine to reach people who have been unable to come to hospital, to reduce footfalls in hospitals, and to even provide medical and mental health counselling to countless people. It was way back in 2000 that telemedicine was first employed in India, but the progress has been excruciatingly slow, until the pandemic. However, it does seem as if the medical community was only held back by the lack of legislation to enable tele consultations. For no sooner was the policy announced, than hospitals and clinicians hurried to jump onto the bandwagon, advertising contact information for patients. The advantages are peculiar in the current context, when putting distance between people is paramount, as tele consultations are not barred even when health care professionals and patients may have to be quarantined. The advancement of telecommunication capabilities over the years has made the transmission of images and sound files (heart and lung sounds, coughs) faster and simpler. Pilot telemedicine experiments in ophthalmology and psychiatry have proven to be of immense benefit to the communities. Telemedicine's time is here, finally. While unleashing the full potential of telemedicine to help people, experts and government agencies must be mindful of the possible inadequacies of the medium, and securing sensitive medical information; such cognisance should guide the use of the technology.

[*From an Editorial published in 'The Hindu' on* April 17, 2020]

26. Which one of the following words from the passage means 'unavoidable'?
(a) Inexorable
(b) Myriad
(c) Excruciatingly
(d) Bandwagon

27. Which of the following best summarizes the <u>main idea</u> of the passage?
(a) It is time to unleash the full potential of Telemedicine.
(b) It is time to unleash the full potential of Telemedicine with cognisance of its possible flaws.

(c) Technology has not been utilised to its fullest to suit the current needs.
(d) People should not be skeptical about the advantages of telemedicine.

28. Which of the following is a significant factor contributing in slow employment of Telemedicine in India?
(a) Telemedicine was never employed in India.
(b) There was an absence of regulations regarding the use of telemedicine consultations and medication systems.
(c) Telemedicinal Society of India failed in its efforts to promote the importance of such a system in the country.
(d) All of the above.

29. Telecommunication based medication has the potential for an easy outreach because:
(a) Pilot experiments in telemedicine have been proved to be successful.
(b) It helps in easier communication of medical images from one place to another.
(c) It helps in securing sensitive medical information.
(d) All of the above.

30. What is the meaning of the expression 'Shot in the arm' used in the passage ?
(a) Hitting the nail on its head.
(b) Bull's Eye
(c) Positive Impact on something
(d) All of the above.

CURRENT AFFAIRS INCLUDING GK

Prime Minister Narendra Modi on Saturday said major global firms are looking at India as a major investment destination, which is reflected by a robust inflow of Foreign Direct Investment (FDI) last financial year, and through 'Atmanirbhar Bharat Abhiyan' (Self-Reliant India initiative) the country is shifting its focus from 'Make in India' to 'Make for world'. He said Independent India should be "vocal for local" and asked citizens to glorify Indian products to promote 'Atmanirbhar Bharat'. Unveiling his vision of a Self-Reliant India, the Prime Minister said that the government has unveiled over ₹110 lakh crore National Infrastructure Pipeline (NIP) to boost the economy and create jobs. "In order to rapidly modernise India, there is a need to give a new direction to overall infrastructure development," he said, adding that over 7,000 projects under NIP have been already identified. "This will be, in a way, a new revolution in the field of infrastructure. This is the time to end silos in infrastructure. There is a plan to connect the entire country with multi-model connectivity infrastructure," he said. NIP will play a crucial role in overcoming the adverse impact of Covid-19 on the economy and catapult the economy in a higher growth trajectory, he said. The government on December 31 last year unveiled the NIP with an aim to make India a $5 trillion economy by 2024-25. The focus of the infrastructure pipeline is to accelerate growth and create employment in both urban and rural areas.

Source: *Excerpt from Hindustan Times, written by Rajeev Jayaswal. (Dated 15th August, 2020)*

31. The Government announced a stimulus package under the Self Reliant India Scheme for the amount of.
(a) 2 trillion (b) 20 trillion
(c) 5 trillion (d) 100 trillion

32. Which of the following is not a goal of the stimulus package announced under the "Atmanirbhar" India?
(a) It will help in alleviating the distress of migrants when they return to their villages.
(b) It will help in achieving the goal of a self-sustainable rural economy.
(c) It would boost the One Nation One Market objective and help India to become the food factory of the world.
(d) It will help in elevating quality of life in urban areas.

33. Which of the following events can be seen as the stepping stone for the growth of the Foreign Direct Investment (FDI) in India?
(a) The launch of 'Make in India' initiative in 2014.
(b) The Economic liberalisation in the year 1991.

(c) The Amendment in the FDI policy to increase the upper cap from 26% to 49%.
(d) All of the above.

34. Which of the following is not related to the "Vocal for Local" initiative of the Indian Government?
(a) Rebooting the MSMEs especially the Khadi and village industries.
(b) Generating new opportunities of employment at the local level.
(c) Creating new economic hubs through disinvestment and FDIs.
(d) Promoting the indigenous manufacture and support through financial aid.

35. Under the National Infrastructure Pipeline, the Government plans to invest more than ₹ 102 lakh crore on infrastructure projects by 2024-25, with the Centre, States and the private sector to share the capital expenditure. What is the ratio of such expenditure by each of the stake holders?
(a) 50:25:25 (b) 40:40:20
(c) 39:39:22 (d) 34:33:33

The central bank doesn't disclose its foreign exchange management strategy, but it was evident in the last few years that the rupee was not allowed to appreciate despite healthy inflows, resulting in a rapid build-up of foreign exchange. From a low of $275 billion in September of 2013, when rupee came under severe pressure due to so-called 'taper tantrums' by the US Federal Reserve, India now has record foreign exchange reserves of [1] billion, as on 21 August — a 95 per cent rise over seven years. Despite the Covid-19 pandemic, the foreign exchange kitty swelled by $62 billion since March. In this seven-year period, rupee ended the year with an appreciation against the dollar only once — in 2017. This year, the rupee is so far down by 2.04 per cent against the dollar. The latest RBI statement suggested that it is not uncomfortable with the appreciation in rupee, confirming the speculation among currency analysts that a departure was made in the exchange management policy.

The Reserve Bank of India (RBI) said that it will conduct liquidity operations worth ₹ 20,000 crore in two tranches through sale and purchase of government securities (G-Secs). The two open market operations (OMOs) of ₹ 10,000 crore each will be conducted on September 10 and 17, the central bank said in an official release. This is now the second such announcement in as many weeks. Last week, RBI had announced sale and purchase of G-Secs worth ₹ 20,000 crore, in two tranches, slated to be conducted on August 27 and September 3. In another move, RBI announced the infusion of ₹ 1 lakh crore in mid-September through long-term repo operations (LTROs) at floating rates, or the prevailing repo rate. Moreover, the central bank also gave an option to lenders who have earlier availed funds through LTROs, to reverse their transactions before maturity.

Source: Excerpt taken from the Print.in, written by Manojit Saha. (Dated 2nd September, 2020.)

36. Which of the following has been replaced by [1] in the above passage?
(a) $ 537
(b) $ 498
(c) $ 502
(d) $ 756

37. Which of the following economic policies have been recently used by the RBI to boost the economy during the current Pandemic situation?
(a) FOREX SWAP
(b) LTROs (Long Term Repo Operations)
(c) OMOs (Open Market Operations)
(d) All of the above.

38. Which of the following statements relate to the Long Term Repo Operations as measure to support the economy in corona pandemic situations?
(a) It is a measure that is expected to bring down short-term rates and also boost investment in corporate bonds.
(b) It would encourage banks to undertake maturity transformation smoothly and seamlessly

so as to augment credit flows to productive sectors.
(c) It will enhance liquidity in the banking system by ₹ 1 trillion.
(d) All of the above.

39. Which of the following will be used as a platform for core banking solutions to implement the LTRO?
(a) E-cartel
(b) E-kuber
(c) E-CBS
(d) E-RBICBS

40. What is the notified amount of sum offered by the RBI under measures of the Foreign Exchange Swap?
(a) $ 5 billion
(b) $ 16.71 billion
(c) $ 16.21 billion
(d) $ 5.02 billion

The first batch of five Rafale jets flew out of France on July 25 and will arrive in India on Wednesday, July 29, when the fighter jets will officially be inducted and join the Indian Air Force fleet in Haryana's Ambala. The fighter jets, built by French aviation firm [1], took off from the Merignac airbase in southern France's Bordeaux today and landed safely at Al Dhafra airbase in the UAE after a sortie of more than seven hours. The five aircraft will be the first tranche of the 36 planes bought by India from France in a ₹ 59,000-crore intergovernmental deal in 2016. "Delivery of ten aircraft has been completed on schedule. Five will stay back in France for training Mission. The delivery of all thirty six aircraft will be completed on schedule by the end of 2021," the Indian embassy in France said in a statement.

The Rafale fighter jets are capable of carrying a range of highly effective weapons, including the Meteor air-to-air missile and Scalp cruise missile. The Rafale jets will come with various India-specific modifications, including Israeli helmet-mounted displays, radar warning receivers, low-band jammers, 10-hour flight data recording, infra-red search and tracking systems among others. The Air Force has readied the required infrastructure to welcome the jets in its line-up.

Source: Excerpt taken from the NDTV, *Reported by Vishnu Som, Edited by Shylaja Varma.* (Dated- 27th July, 2020)

41. The Rafale deal between India and France is seen to carry great strategic significance. Which of the following is directly impacted by this deal?
(a) The Joint Strategic Vision of India-France Cooperation in the Indian Ocean Region.
(b) The one belt one road mission of the China.
(c) The Chinese initiative to build a new Silk route.
(d) The trade route of the Middle East.

42. The Indian Air Force is also in the process of procuring a new generation medium-range modular air-to-ground weapon system Hammer to integrate with the Rafale jets. What does the term Hammer stands for?
(a) Highly Advanced Modular Mutation Extended Range.
(b) Highly Agile Modular Munition Extended Range.
(c) Highly Advanced Modular Mitigation Extended Rafale.
(d) Highly Agile Modular Munition Extended Rafale.

43. Which of the following has been replaced by [1] in the passage?
(a) LAMSCO
(b) LUAD Defence France
(c) DASSAULT
(d) BORESCOPE

44. Which of the following indigenous organisations is responsible for the design, assembly and fabrication of combat aircrafts in India?
(a) DRDO
(b) HAL
(c) DRAI
(d) ISRO

45. Which of the following organisations/institutions is a major offset partner of India in the Rafale Deal?
(a) Hindustan Aeronautics Limited
(b) Reliance Defence Limited
(c) Reliance Naval and Engineering Limited
(d) Pipavav Defence

On May 8, India's Defence Minister virtually inaugurated a new 80 km-long road in the Himalayas, connecting to the border with China, at the Lipulekh pass. The Nepali government protested immediately, contending that the road crosses territory that it claims and accusing India of changing the status quo without diplomatic consultations. Among the many escalatory moves since then, Nepal deployed police forces to the region, summoned the Indian ambassador in Kathmandu, and initiated a constitutional amendment to formalise and extend its territorial claims over approximately 400 sq km. India, on the other hand, has conveyed its openness to a dialogue but does not seem to share Nepal's sense of urgency: its initial statement agreed to a dialogue, but only after the COVID-19 crisis. India has been in effective possession of this territory for at least sixty years, although Nepal claims it conducted a census there in the early 1950s and refers to the 1815 Sugauli Treaty as legitimising its claims. But India's new road, up to the Lipulekh pass, is not an unprecedented change in the status quo. India has controlled this territory and built other infrastructure here before, besides conducting its administration and deploying military forces up to the border pass with China. The region is of strategic importance, and the new road is now one of the quickest links between Delhi and the Tibetan plateau. In a 2015 statement, China also recognised India's sovereignty by agreeing to expand trade through the Lipulekh pass.

Source: *Excerpt from the brookings.edu, written by* Dr. *Constantino Xavier.* (*Dated-* 11th *June*, 2020)

46. Which of the following incidents can be seen as the direct cause of the border dispute between India and Nepal?
(a) The Defence Minister inaugurated a motorable link road that connects India and China.
(b) The 2015 agreement between India and China for using the Lipulekh pass for trade.
(c) India published a new map which showed the region of Kalapani as part of the Indian Territory.
(d) All of the above.

47. The confusion between Nepal and India consists of a dispute over a trijunture of ________.
(a) Kali – Susta – Ganga.
(b) Kalapani – Saraswati – Ganga.
(c) Kalapani – Limpiyadhura – Lipulekh.
(d) Kalapani – Limpiyadhura – Kali.

48. The treaty of Sugauli was signed between which of the following pairs?
(a) India and Nepal
(b) United Kingdom, India and Nepal
(c) India, China and Nepal
(d) East India Company and Nepal

49. Recently Nepal has issued a map claiming Lipulekh pass as part of its territory included in the district of:
(a) Kailali (b) Darchula
(c) Dipayal (d) Doti

50. Which of the following rivers is called as Narayani River in Nepal?
(a) Bramhaputra
(b) Gandak
(c) Ganga
(d) Kali

One thing struck us as a major difference between the new National Education Policy (NEP) 2020 and its predecessor. The earlier national policies on education (NPE) from 1986 and 1992 presented themselves as attempts to consolidate and build on earlier efforts, particularly the NPE, 1968. The new NEP 2020 policy, on the other hand, is very keen to establish that it is different from everything in the past, including in its name. Nowhere does this attitude come across as starkly as it does in the section on higher education.

It comes across fairly clearly on how the higher education ecosystem will be by 2040. By this time — if the policy has its way — the Indian higher education ecosystem will be populated with higher education institutions (HEI). These will comprise Universities and Colleges and the public and private sectors, all of which will be 'multi-disciplinary', with each populated by more than 3,000 students, with at least one "in or near every district". Universities will conduct research and post-graduate and under-graduate teaching, some research-intensive and others teaching-intensive. Colleges will largely teach at the under-graduate level, with a number of them having their medium of instruction in either bilingual or local / Indian languages. The colleges can manifest in clusters around universities as constituent colleges or may be standalone autonomous ones. Ideally, all HEIs will eventually become "independent self-governing institutions" with considerable "faculty and institutional autonomy". They will have complied with a series of regulatory exercises that are "light-but-tight" and will be operated by a large number of private accreditors, overseen by a new set of regulatory institutions at the national level.

Source: *Excerpt taken from downtoearth.org.in, written by* Nitin *Mehta & Gagan Mehta*. (*Dated 14th August*, 2020)

51. Which of the following statements are not true in relation to the changes envisioned by the NEP 2020?

(a) The NEP 2020 aims at making India a global knowledge superpower.

(b) The renaming of the Ministry of Human Resource Development to the Ministry of Education.

(c) The development of National Course Curriculum to provide new curriculum by 2021.

(d) The New Education Policy aims to facilitate an inclusive, participatory and holistic approach

52. The NEP 2020 aims to provide a holistic change to the current education system in India. Which of the following is not related to the aim of NEP 2020?

(a) Universalization of education from preschool to secondary level with 100% Gross Enrolment Ratio.

(b) To bring 20 million out of school children back into the mainstream through an open schooling system.

(c) Vocational Education to start from Class 6 with Internships.

(d) To achieve 80% Gross Enrolment Ratio at the under graduate level.

53. Which of the following is proposed as a change in the structure of institutions responsible for affiliation and accreditation under the NEP 2020?

(a) Higher Education Commission of India (HECI) will be set up as a single umbrella body for the entire higher education.

(b) University Grant Commission to be renamed as AICTE.

(c) National Affiliation and Accreditation Council to be renamed as National Standard Council of India.

(d) National Council for Education Research and Teaching to be renamed as BCERT.

54. Which of the following is not a vertical under the Higher Education Commission of India (HECI)?

(a) National Higher Education Regulatory Council (NHERC)

(b) Higher Education Grants Council (HEGC)

(c) National Educational Council (NEC)

(d) National Accreditation Council (NAC)

55. What is the proposed percentage of expenditure for education out of GDP under the NEP 2020?

(a) 11 percent

(b) 6 percent

(c) 4.6 percent

(d) 9 percent

Days after India-Pakistan tensions spilled over into a meeting of the Shanghai Cooperation Organisation (SCO), External Affairs Minister S. Jaishankar and Pakistan Foreign Minister Shah Mehmood Qureshi are expected to meet via a video conference at the South Asian Association for Regional Cooperation (SAARC) meeting on September 24. "All member countries have confirmed participation in the meeting, to be chaired by Pradeep Kumar Gyawali, [1] of Nepal. The respective Foreign Ministers will take part," sources familiar with preparations for the meeting told The Hindu, referring to the eight members of SAARC, including [2], Bangladesh, [3], India, [4], Nepal, Pakistan and Sri Lanka. A senior Indian official also confirmed that Mr. Jaishankar will attend despite the incident at the SCO virtual meeting of National Security Advisors on Tuesday. During that meeting, National Security Advisor Ajit Doval stormed out after he saw that the Pakistan Special Advisor on National Security Moeed Yusuf had used a map of Pakistan that claimed Indian Territory.

"This was in blatant disregard to the advisory by the host [5] against it and in violation of the norms of the meeting. After consultation with the host, the Indian side left the meeting in protest at that juncture," the MEA had said about the incident. When asked, the sources said that no specific guidelines on background or maps have been issued by the SAARC Secretariat in Kathmandu that is also the Chair of the SAARC at present, but they hope it would go "smoothly". A meeting of SAARC Finance Ministers, where an Additional Secretary represented India instead of Finance Minister Nirmala Sitharaman, and Pakistan was represented by its Special Advisor on Finance, took place on Wednesday without incident.

Source: *Excerpt taken from The Hindu, written by Suhasini Haider. (Dated 17th September, 2020.)*

56. Which of the following has been replaced by [1] in the passage?
(a) Prime Minister
(b) Minister of Finance
(c) Minister of External Affairs
(d) Minister of Home Affairs

57. Which of the following Nations is part of the South Asian Association for Regional Cooperation?
(a) Indonesia
(b) Thailand
(c) Myanmar
(d) Maldives

58. Which of the following has been replaced by [5] in the passage?
(a) Russia
(b) China
(c) Japan
(d) Pakistan

59. India had not agreed to attend a summit hosted in Pakistan, but it remains an important promoter of the SAARC process. In which of the following years the SAARC leaders' summit was held lately?
(a) 2018
(b) 2014
(c) 2016
(d) 2019

60. The above passage mentions about Pakistan's Special Advisor on National Security Moeed Yusuf using a map of Pakistan claiming Indian Territory. Which of the following territory is in context here?
(a) Junagadh
(b) Aksai Chin
(c) Pangong Tso
(d) Limpiyadhura

In the middle of a pandemic, the geopolitics of the world's most troubled region took a historic turn this week, when the UAE and Israel, under the benevolent gaze of US President Donald Trump, signed an agreement to "normalise" relations. The deal opens up new opportunities for India to play a much larger role in the regional security and stability in the Gulf, where New Delhi enjoys special relations with both Abu Dhabi and Jerusalem. The barebones of the deal envisages establishing regular diplomatic relations between the UAE, the rising influential power in the Gulf, and Israel, the "Incredible Hulk" of the region, but a country officially not on speaking terms with most of its Arab neighbours. In his first tweet, Crown Prince Mohammed bin Zayed said: 'During a call with President Trump and Prime Minister Netanyahu, an agreement was reached to stop further Israeli annexation of Palestinian territories. The UAE and Israel also agreed to cooperation and setting a roadmap towards establishing a bilateral relationship." In return, Israel agreed to "suspend" its annexation plans for West Bank that would have been deeply destabilising. Benjamin Netanyahu gets a diplomatic victory, which may be short-lived, given the nature of Israeli politics. But Israel gets a diplomatic and economic opening with the big power in the Gulf that could open other doors, give its security interests legitimacy and, perhaps, open the door to Middle East peace.

Many of the other Arab powers, such as Oman, Bahrain, Egypt and Jordan, apart from the big global powers, and India, have welcomed the deal. Iran has slammed it, as have Turkey and Syria. Saudi Arabia has been very quiet. Given the close ties between Mohammed bin Zayed and Mohammed bin Salman, it is unthinkable that KSA was not consulted, particularly when the US is the third pole in this agreement. The deal gives UAE pole position as the premier Gulf Arab power, with diplomatic leverage with Israel and the US. "This deal is about positioning in Washington, DC," said James Dorsey, Gulf and Middle East expert.

Source: *Excerpt from the Economic Times, written by Indrani Bagchi.* (*Dated - 16th August*, 2020)

61. The US is seen as a major role player in the peace deal between Israel and UAE. Which of the following is not a reason for the involvement of US in the deal?

(a) The deal grants a diplomatic win to the US President Donald Trump ahead of the Presidential election.

(b) The efforts of the USA to bring the war in Afghanistan to an end have not been a success yet.

(c) The efforts of USA to bring peace between Israel and the Palestinians have not been successful yet.

(d) The deal gives a central strategic rule to USA in the Middle East.

62. Which of the following is true in relation to the stake of Palestine in the peace deal between UAE and Israel?

(a) Israel has recognised Palestine as an Independent Nation.

(b) This can be an opportunity for the Palestine to establish diplomatic relations with Israel.

(c) The deal marks both a win and setback to the Israel-Palestine relations.

(d) A peace treaty would also be signed between Israel and Palestine.

63. Which of the following is not a direct impact of the peace deal in the Middle East region?

(a) The deal smoothens the UAE's international campaign to be seen as a beacon of tolerance in the Middle East.

(b) It puts the UAE as leader in a regional power dynamics among neighbouring Gulf Arab states.

(c) The deal gives Netanyahu a domestic boost at a time when Israel's coalition government is in crisis due to coalition compulsions.

(d) The deal marks a historic day and a significant step towards peace in the Middle East.

64. The peace deal between Israel and UAE can also be seen as a great opportunity for India in the Middle East region. Which of the following is not related to strategic goals of India in the Middle East?

(a) India should revamp its defence and security relations with the UAE.

(b) India should move fast to capture the extended neighbourhood market before it comes under the influence of China.

(c) India should ensure space for Iran in any future security deal in the region.

(d) None of the above.

65. Which of the following is correct?
(a) Israel does not have a Constitution.
(b) Israeli Constitution is like ordinary law.
(c) There is no Constitution but a Basic Law of 1950.
(d) Israel has a Constitution of 1967.

66. Israel is a theocratic Jewish state but it follows legal pluralism. Accordingly it has:
(a) Jewish Courts to decide cases of all religious communities.
(b) Secular Courts will apply Uniform Civil Code in respect of all communities.
(c) Each religious community has its own Religious Court to deal with Personal law disputes.
(d) No distinction between Personal law and Public law.

LEGAL REASONING

The COVID-19 pandemic has taken the entire world hostage in less than four months, and the global economy has been hit the hardest with governments across the globe implementing stringent policies including lockdown to control the coronavirus outbreak. The pandemic today presents unprecedented challenges and impediments to businesses in conducting their normal operations. The lockdown across the world has caused delays in the performance of contracts and transactions. Now, the question that arises is whether the current situation can enable parties to a contract to alter their obligations with non-compliance of terms neither being regarded as a "default committed by any party" nor a "breach of contract"? There are certain well-accepted practices for dealing with such extraordinary situations in commercial transactions by the inclusion of force majeure & material adverse effect (MAE) clauses. Determination of the types of circumstances so covered by the force majeure clause contained in a contract is essential. Provisions of force majeure often cover natural disasters like hurricanes, floods, and earthquakes as "acts of God." Other covered events may include war, terrorism, civil disorder, fire, disease medical epidemics or by reasons of applicable laws or regulations. Broadly, the Courts have interpreted the term "Force Majeure" as an event that can neither be anticipated nor controlled by either of the contracting parties. A force majeure clause applies in the context of ongoing contractual arrangements, whereas, an MAE or material adverse change (MAC) clause applies to the allocation of risk in transactions before their closure or completion. Pandemic and related consequences such as government action is a type of event covered by a force majeure clause, however, its impact on the affected party's ability to perform its contractual obligations may vary depending upon contractual terms. It is common for force majeure clauses to specify the impact that the event or circumstances in question must have, in order for the clause to be triggered. References may be made, for example, to the event or circumstances having "prevented", "hindered" or "delayed" performance. These terms require different levels of impact on performance before a party can claim recourse to these clauses. In other words, the force majeure and MAC clauses act as an exception to what would otherwise be treated as a breach of contract. Certain contracts may state that, if a force majeure clause is applied, the contract may automatically be terminated. On the other hand, some contracts may even state that the duty to fulfil the contractual obligation may be suspended for a certain period of time and if the force majeure event is not curbed or treated even after such time, then eventually the contract may be terminated. Though there cannot be a one-size-fits-all solution to this question, and it depends upon how the force majeure clause is worded in a specific contract; and in the absence of the same, applicable laws related to the same will be required to be taken into consideration.

[*Excerpt from Business Today, by Ranjana Roy Gawai*, April 17, 2020]

67. Based on the Author's argument in passage above, which of the following is correct?
(a) Force Majeure Clauses, generally have a uniform impact on the performance of Contracts in all the cases.
(b) The Impact on the performance of Contracts by the usage of Force Majeure Clauses is

dependent upon the way such clauses have been constructed in a particular Contract.

(c) Both Force Majeure and Material Adverse Change Clauses have similar impact on the performance of Contracts.

(d) All of the above.

68. Imagine, there is a domestic commercial Contract for supply of certain goods for certain price between A and B. However, in pursuance of the same, both A and B forget to negotiate and agree on the terms of a Force Majeure event and the Contractual document does not contain the Force Majeure clause. In such a situation, what would be the fate of the Contract in the event like that of COVID 19?

(a) As the parties did not negotiate on the Force Majeure Clause, either of them cannot take an exception to the Breach of Contract.

(b) The parties can invoke the Material Adverse Change Clause.

(c) In absence of such clauses in the Contract, the Courts may resort to the applicable law, i.e., the Indian Contract Act, 1872 to give relief to the parties.

(d) None of the above.

69. In the same fact situation as mentioned above with a modification that there is a Force Majeure Clause in the Contract between A and B, let us suppose, that B, who was to supply goods to A on certain date and time, faced issues in relation to procurement of goods due to mill strike and also because of rise in prices of goods. In this case, can B claim the suspension of performance of Contract on the basis of the Force Majeure Clause?

(a) Yes, B can, depending upon the way, the Force Majeure Clause is worded.

(b) Such situation cannot be covered under Force Majeure as it is just a case of disappointed expectations and hence B cannot invoke the clause. It is merely a case of commercial hardship.

(c) B can invoke the Force Majeure clause as the clause is too broad to cover such situations.

(d) None of the above.

70. Typically, the MAE (Material Adverse Change) provision in an agreement contemplates events which if they occur, or are likely occur, would have a "materially adverse change or effect on the assets, business, property, liabilities, financial condition, results, operations of the target" or that "affects the ability of the transacting parties to consummate the transaction" or the "validity or enforceability of the transacting parties to its rights and remedies under the transaction documents". Which of the following sample clauses in a contract resembles an MAE clause?

(a) "In the event either party is unable to perform its obligations under the terms of this agreement because of Act of God, strikes, equipment of transmission failure or damage reasonably beyond its control, such party shall not be liable for damages to the other for any damages resulting from such failure to perform..."

(b) "Except with respect to payment obligations under this agreement, no party shall be liable for, nor such party shall be considered in breach of this agreement due to, any failure to perform its obligations under this agreement as a result of cause beyond its control, including any earthquake, labour problem, unavailability of supplies..."

(c) Both of the above.

(d) None of the above.

The issue of Obscenity has vexed the Courts in India and abroad for a long time now. The intriguing question has always been the same, i.e., what should be the standards to qualify something as obscene in the eyes of law? In the United Kingdom, way back in 1868, the Court laid down the Hicklin test in Regina v. Hicklin (1868 L.R. 2 Q.B. 360), and held that: "*The test of Obscenity is whether the tendency of the matter charged as Obscenity is to deprave and corrupt those whose minds are open to such immoral influences and into whose hands a publication of this sort may fall.*" Hicklin test postulated that a publication has to be judged for obscenity based on isolated passages of a work considered out of context and judged by their apparent influence on most susceptible readers, such as children or weak-minded adults. However, this test was later rejected by most of the jurisdictions. There were many judgments where it was stipulated by the Indian Courts that, Obscenity has to be judged in the context of contemporary social mores, current socio-moral attitude of the community and the prevalent norms of acceptability/ susceptibility of the community, in relation to matters in issue. [For example, in Ranjit D. Udeshi v. State of Maharashtra AIR 1965 SC 881; Chandrakant Kalyandas Kakodar v. State of Maharashtra 1969 (2) SCC 687 etc.] These judgements indicated that the concept of Obscenity would change with the passage of time and what might have been O"obscene" at one point of time would not be considered as obscene at a later period. This came to be known as "Community Standards Test". In Bobby Art International & Ors. v. Om Pal Singh Hoon (1996) 4 SCC 1, the Court, upholding the Community standards test held that, complete message and context of the objectionable scene/ firm/picture etc., needs to be examined in order to find out whether the alleged material is obscene or not.

71. A, daily local newspaper called 'Ramanand Bazar Patrika' having wide circulation in Anandnagar published, on 1st July, 2019, an article with a picture of Boris Becker, a world renowned Tennis player, posing nude with his dark-skinned fiancee by name Barbara Feltus, a film actress, which was photographed by none other than her father. The article states that, in an interview, both Boris Becker and Barbara Feltus spoke freely about their engagement, their lives and future plans and the message they wanted to convey to the people at large, for posing to such a photograph. Article picturises Boris Becker as a strident protester of the pernicious practice of "Apartheid". Further, it was stated that the purpose of the photograph was also to signify that love champions over hatred. Will the alleged picture classify as an Obscene Material in India?

(a) No, according to the Hicklin Test, it will not classify as Obscene.
(b) Yes, according to the Community Standards Test, the picture will classify as Obscene.
(c) No, according to the Community Standards Test, the picture will not classify as Obscene.
(d) Both (a) and (c).

72. The difference between Hicklin Test and Community Standards Test is:

(a) The former focuses on the susceptibility of the minds of individuals to get corrupted while the later hinges upon the context, intended meaning and contemporaneous socio-cultural environment of the society.
(b) As per Hicklin Test, a nude picture of a women *per se* can be obscene while as per the later, the picture should be suggestive of deprave mind and designed to excite sexual passion in persons who are likely to see it.
(c) The former considers Obscenity as a changing concept with changing times while the later does not.
(d) All of the above.

73. The issue of 'Obscenity' is fundamentally related with which of the following?

(a) Freedom of Religion of an individual.
(b) Freedom of Speech and Expression of an individual.
(c) Right to Privacy of an individual.
(d) All of the above.

74. Consider the following situations. Choose the correct option as per the Hicklin's Test.

1. A Movie scene where there are rows of Jewish naked men and women, shown frontally, being led into the Gas Chambers of Nazi Concentration Camp. Not only they are about to die but they are stripped off their basic dignity in the last moments of their life.
2. The controversial movie scene of Phoolan Devi, the Bandit queen where she is paraded naked and made to draw water from the well within the circle of a hundred men.

(a) 1 is Obscene but 2 is not.
(b) 2 is Obscene but 1 is not.
(c) Both 1 and 2 are Obscene.
(d) Neither 1 and 2 are Obscene.

75. An activist, while being semi-nude, allowed her body to be used as a canvas to paint on by her two minor children who were properly clothed. She uploaded this video of hers on an online platform with a message that she intended to normalise the female form for her children and not allow distorted ideas about sexuality to pervade their mind. An advocate who sees the video, registers a case of Obscenity against her. Is it a case of Obscenity as per the Community Standards Test?

(a) This is a pure case of Obscenity and she is spreading it.
(b) This is a pure case of Obscenity as well as Child Pornography as her children were exposed to her nudity.
(c) This is not a case of Obscenity because as per the Community Standards Test the video must not be seen in isolation but in the contextual set up of the message that the activist has put on normalisation of a female's sexuality.
(d) This is a case of Obscenity as per the Community Standards Test as the video was blatantly obscene.

On 7th May 2020, a major leakage of Styrene gas was reported from the plastics-manufacturing plant 'LG Polymers' located on the outskirts of the Visakhapatnam city. The accident took place when the cooling system of a polymers plant got clogged due to the mismanagement of factory workers and resulted in turning the city into a gas chamber. The gas which leaked was styrene gas, which is a 'hazardous chemical' under Rule 2(e) plus Entry 583 of Schedule I of the Manufacture, Storage and Import of Hazardous Chemical Rules 1989.

Principle 1: Polluter Pays Principle

The 'Doctrine of Polluter Pays' is a well-established principle of environmental law, which places an obligation of compensating the damage to the people who ought to reimburse it and also have the capacity to disburse it. The principle explicitly affirms that the person who damages or destructs the environment has the absolute obligation to bear the cost of ameliorating the environment. In *Enviro Legal Action v. Union of India* case, the Apex Court of India held that the polluter is legally responsible to reimburse the individual sufferers as well as pay for the revitalization of the damaged environment.

Principle 2: Principle of Strict Liability

The principle of Strict Liability was established in the year 1868 in the case of *Rylands v. Fletcher*, where the Court held that any person who uses his/her land in an 'unnatural manner' and who keeps any 'hazardous substance' on such premises would be held liable under the principle of strict liability for any 'damage' occurred on the 'escape' of such perilous substance. However, the person is liable only when there is non-natural use of land; the principle also restricts liability when the escape is due to an act of strangers, Act of God, for example a natural calamity; due to the person injured or when it happens with the consent of the person injured or with statutory authority.

Principle 3: Principle of Absolute Liability

The absolute liability is a stringent form of Strict Liability as it is devoid of any exceptions that were mentioned under the earlier principle. for the first time in the case of M.C. *Mehta v. Union of India*. This principle implies that whenever an enterprise is engaged in any dangerous or hazardous activity that threatens the people working in the enterprise and those living nearby, it owes an absolute and non-delegable duty to the community that no harm will be caused. If harm is indeed caused, the enterprise will have to compensate for damages, and can't use exceptions provided in the case of strict liability. The enterprise can't claim that the harm has not been caused due to negligence (absence of due care) or that it had taken all reasonable precautions.

76. Under which of the following principles, will the company LG Polymers be liable?
(a) Polluter Pays Principle
(b) Strict Liability
(c) Absolute Liability
(d) All of the above

77. As per the Polluter Pays Principle, LG Polymers will be liable to pay:
(a) Amount of Money for restoration of environment only.
(b) Amount of Money for restoration of environment and compensation to Individuals who suffered the loss.
(c) Compensation to the victims.
(d) None of the above.

78. A company ABC limited operates an industrial chemical plant in the city of Azadnagar. Due to an earthquake on July 22, 2020, the valves of the reactors in the plant got damaged due to which the operators could not properly transport the hazardous gas for chemical vaporisation, resulting in the gas leakage. The gas leakage resulted in the death of 12 workers of the plant and also some people living nearby the Plant. In this situation, in order to decipher the liability of ABC Limited, choose the best option:
(a) ABC Limited can be held liable under the principles of Strict and Absolute Liability and Polluter pays principle as well.
(b) ABC Limited can be held liable under the Polluter Pays Principle and the Principle of Absolute Liability, but can be exempted under the rule of Strict Liability.
(c) ABC Limited will not be held liable under any of the Principles.
(d) ABC Limited will be held liable under Strict and Absolute Liability principles but the Principle of "Polluter Pays" will not be applicable to this situation.

79. The argument of LG Polymers that, they did not know that the Styrene Gas could leak:
(a) is a strong argument and can reduce their liability under the Polluter Pays Principle.
(b) is a strong argument and can reduce their liability under the Strict Liability Principle.
(c) is a weak argument and will not help in reducing the liability of LG Polymers under any of the principles.
(d) is a weak argument but may help in reducing their liability under the Strict Liability Principle.

80. XYZ is a company operating a Pesticide Factory in the city of Rampur. On one day, due to the negligence of Factory staff, there is a leakage of the Pesticide gas as a result of which, many pests and insects which feed on the plantation crops in the nearby farm are killed. There is no harm caused to the people living nearby or the workers of the Pesticide Factory. However, the leakage was so humungous that it reduced the quality of air in the city causing breathing problems for the people living around in the area. In this case,
(a) XYZ will be absolutely liable but not strictly liable.
(b) XYZ will not be liable under the Strict and Absolute liability principles because the leakage only killed the pests and insects.
(c) XYZ's liability under the Strict and Absolute liability principles will depend upon the inquiry as to whether the leaked pesticide gas was a hazardous substance/activity or chemical or not and; XYZ will be liable under the Polluter Pays Principle.
(d) XYZ will not be liable under the Polluter Pays Principle.

Principle of Natural Justice is derived from the word '*Jus Natural*' of the Roman law and it is closely related to Common law and moral principles but is not codified. It is a law of nature which is not derived from any statute or constitution. The principle of Natural Justice is adhered to by all the citizens of civilised State with Supreme importance. Natural justice simply means to make a sensible and reasonable decision making procedure on a particular issue. Sometimes, it doesn't matter what is the reasonable decision but in the end, what matters is the procedure and who all are engaged in taking the reasonable decision. It is not restricted within the concept of 'fairness' it has different colours and shades which vary from the context. Basically, natural justice consists of 3 rules.

The first one is "*Hearing rule*" which states that the person or party who is affected by the decision made by the Panel of expert members should be given a fair opportunity to express his point of view to defend himself. Secondly, "*Bias rule*" generally expresses that Panel of expert should be free from bias while taking the decision. The decision should be given in a free and fair manner which can fulfil the rule of natural justice. And thirdly, "*Reasoned Decision*" which states that order, decision or judgement of the Court given by the Presiding authorities with a valid and reasonable ground. The principles of Natural Justice have been adopted and followed by the judiciary to protect public rights against the arbitrary decision by the administrative authority. One can easily see that the rule of natural justice include the concept of fairness: they stay alive and support to safeguard the fair dealing.

Source: Excerpt taken from blog.ipleaders.in (Dated - 12th June, 2019)

81. "*Nemo Judex in causa sua*" or the principle that '*No one can be a judge in his own case*", relates to which of the following rule of the Natural Justice?
(a) Bias rule
(b) Reasoned decision rule
(c) Hearing rule
(d) All of the above.

82. Mr. X is a Public Servant, employed in a PSU and Mrs Y who is the wife of Mr. X is also an employee of the same PSU. Ms A files a complaint against Mr. X for sexual harassment at workplace before the ICC (Internal Complaints Committee), which is headed by Mrs Y. After completing her inquiry she held that Mr. X is guilty and recommended disciplinary proceedings against him. Now, on what grounds Mr. X may challenge her findings?
(a) Mrs Y is an employee of the same institution and the inquiry should have been conducted by a person outside the institution.
(b) The complaint was filed by a female employee, so the inquiry must have been conducted by a male employee.
(c) Mrs Y is the wife of Mr. X and she holds a personal bias in the case, so the inquiry should not have been conducted by her.
(d) Mr. X being the accused should have conducted the inquiry himself.

83. Mr. A is a judge and he is also the landlord of Mr. B, who resides in an apartment owned by Mr. A. Due to non-payment of rent for 3 consecutive months, Mr. A served an eviction notice to Mr. B. Now, choose the most appropriate option amongst the following.
(a) Being a judge himself, Mr. A cannot issue such notice of eviction.
(b) Mr. A can issue such notice because it is his duty as a Judge, apart from being a landlord.
(c) Such notice is illegal as Mr. B was not given an opportunity to present his case.
(d) Mr. A issued such notice in his personal capacity as a landlord and not being a judge.

84. Which of the following is not in violation of the principles of Natural justice?
(a) Withholding of an increment of a public servant without giving him an opportunity to defend.
(b) Non-renewal of a contract of employment of an employee after the period of contract is over.
(c) Initiating a departmental inquiry against a public servant, without giving him an opportunity to submit representation during such inquiry.
(d) All of the above.

85. On the basis of your understanding about Natural Justice in the passage above, state which of the following is true:
(a) Adherence to the reasoned decision rule is not required if other two rules are complied with.
(b) Compliance of bias rule itself rejects the need of the hearing and the reasoned decision rule.

(c) Principle of Natural Justice is incomplete without the compliance of any of its rules.
(d) The Reasoned Decision rule is a substitute for the bias rule.

Tension prevailed in the Jawahar area in Palghar district after three Mumbai residents, travelling in a Ford Ecosport to Silvassa, were allegedly lynched late on Thursday night. The Kasa police said the incident occurred near Gadakchinchale village under their jurisdiction. "Information received by us indicates that the three occupants of the SUV hailed form Kandivali in Mumbai and were going to attend a funeral in Silvassa," Superintendent of Police Gaurav Singh, Palghar police said. A large mob of villagers surrounded the car within a matter of minutes and started attacking it with sticks, irons rods and their bare hands, leading to the death of all three occupants. "One of our patrolling vehicles later spotted the severely injured trio lying on the road and stopped to find out the matter. However, our team was also attacked by the mob and the vehicle pelted with stones. Our personnel had to flee and were unable to rescue to the victims," an officer with the Kasa police said. A wireless alert was sent out later apprising all police stations and units of the incident following which reinforcements were sent to the village and a combing operation was undertaken. "Prima facie information indicates that the trio were mistaken for thieves and attacked. The villagers were on edge due to the ongoing lockdown and unavailability of essential supplies. For the past few days, several rumours have been doing the rounds on social media about thieves and dacoits targetting villages on the highway. As a result, villagers have been patrolling the highway and stopping late night travellers on suspicion," the officer said.

Source: Excerpt from The Hindu, written by Alok Deshpande (22/04/2020)

86. Which of the following statements given below justifies criminalisation of Mob Lynching?
(a) In a democracy the actual power rests with the people and their actions cannot be penalised by the state.
(b) There is no law in India which specifically prohibits mob lynching and therefore it is a justified act of the people.
(c) It is impossible to punish the wrongdoer in case of Mob Lynching.
(d) Violence cannot be a tool to implement the will of the majority and such actions are failure of the state.

87. Which of the following statement justifies the criminalisation of mob lynching as a distinct offence apart from 'Murder'?
(a) The offence of Murder is committed by la single individual or a group but mob lynching involves a large group of individuals.
(b) When violence is committed by a mob it creates a situation of terror and anarchy having potential to disturb the public peace for a longer period.
(c) Mob lynching is an offence which supports the idea of 'might is right', and cannot be accepted in a democratic society.
(d) All of the above.

88. The above passage states about the existence of rumours in the area regarding the thieves and dacoits robbing the villagers or committing child lifting. In the light of this proposition which if the following statement is correct?
(a) The villagers should not be punished as there was a genuine mistake on their part.
(b) The villagers should be punished as they do not have any right to punish any person unless he is an offender.
(c) The villagers should be punished as no individual in the country is entitled to take law in his own hand and punish the wrongdoer.
(d) The villagers should not be punished as they have the right of private defence against such incidents under which they can even kill a person.

89. In the light of the above passage, which of the following incidents of mob violence would be justified?
(a) A group of people committing violence against people who are selling meat of an

animal considered to be sacred under their religious beliefs.

(b) The residents of a boy's hostel caught a drug paddler selling drugs in their hostel and killed him by beating.

(c) The villagers injured a woman by pelting stone on her considering her to be witch.

(d) None of the above.

90. Assertion (A): Mob Lynching can be justified only in circumstances where the religious sentiments or feelings of a large group of people is associated.

Reason (R): Religious sentiments and feelings are of paramount consideration for the state and should not be interfered with.

(a) Both (A) and (R) are correct

(b) (A) is correct but (R) is incorrect

(c) Both (A) and (R) are incorrect

(d) (A) is incorrect but (R) is correct.

The bench of Dr DY Chandrachud and MR Shah, JJ has refused to transfer to CBI the criminal cases lodged against Republic TV Editor in-Chief Arnab Goswami for alleged defamatory news show telecast on April 21 in connection with the Palghar mob-lynching case. It also quashed all FIRs against Arnab Goswami except one which was filed in Nagpur and which has been transferred to Mumbai via order dated 24.04.2020.

[*Excerpt from* SCC *Online Blog, May* 19, 2020]

Delivering the verdict, Justice Chandrachud said, "*Article 32 of the Constitution constitutes recognition of the constitutional duty entrusted to this Court to protect the fundamental rights of citizens. The exercise of journalistic freedom lies at the core of speech and expression protected by Article 19(1)(a). The petitioner is a media journalist. The airing of views on television shows which he hosts is in the exercise of his fundamental right to speech and expression under Article 19(1)(a). India's freedoms will rest safe as long as journalists can speak truth to power without being chilled by a threat of reprisal... Free citizens cannot exist when the news media is chained to adhere to one position. Yuval Noah Harari has put it succinctly in his recent book titled "21 Lessons for the 21st Century": "Questions you cannot answer are usually far better for you than answers you cannot question.* "

[*Excerpt from Arnab Ranjan Goswami vs Union Of India on 19 May*, 2020]

91. The above passage mentions about the Journalist's request to transfer the case to the CBI (Central Bureau of Investigation) for investigation. What could be the appropriate reason for such request?

(a) The CBI is a central investigating agency and conducts more scientific investigation.

(b) Where State government is an interested party, the investigation conducted by the state police, may be biased.

(c) The FIRs relate to an offence of defamation of the President of a national party, so the matter should be investigated by the CBI.

(d) None of the above.

92. The above passage quotes the observation of the Court in relation to freedom of speech and expression as, "Questions you cannot answer are better than questions you cannot question." Now, based on such observation, chose the most appropriate option which describes the scope of such questions.

(a) The term "questions" mentioned are not subject to limitations imposed upon the Freedom of Speech and Expression.

(b) Those question are limited to the information warranted by the person.

(c) The court is referring to the right to information through the above quote.

(d) The questions are also subject to limitations imposed upon the Freedom of Speech and Expression.

93. It is an established principle of law that the offence of defamation (harming the reputation) has many exceptions and the imputation of truth is one of those, but the accused must prove that such imputation was true and also for the public good. In the light of this statement which of the following questions/statements are not defamatory?

(a) An article published in a newspaper about the unaccounted property of a public servant in the form of a questionnaire.

(b) A question to a female actress about her sexual relationship with a married man.

(c) A question to a public servant about his extra-marital relationship with a colleague.
(d) An Article published in a magazine stating a female politician as 'B grade' actress.

94. In the above passage, the Court ordered for the merging of different FIRs into one and the investigation to be conducted at Mumbai. What is the reason behind such order?
(a) Multiple FIRs mean multiple investigations and the same might cause hardships to the accused.
(b) The first FIR was registered at Mumbai and the investigation should be conducted at Mumbai.
(c) The accused resides at Mumbai and the investigation should be conducted only at Mumbai.
(d) Multiple FIRs are frivolous and there is only one cause of action.

95. Defamation is punishable:
(a) Both as a Civil wrong as well as a Crime.
(b) Only as a Civil wrong.
(c) Only as a Criminal wrong.
(d) None of the above.

Common intention implies a pre-arranged plan and acting in concert pursuant to the plan. Common intention comes into being prior to the commission of the act, which need not be a long gap. To bring common intention into effect a pre-concert is not necessarily be proved, but it may well develop on the spot as between a number of persons and could be inferred from facts and circumstances of each case. For example A and B caught hold of C where only B stabbed C with a knife but A is also liable for murder as there was a pre-concerted action. In the case Pandurang v. State of Hyderabad, Supreme court emphasized on this point that prior concert need not be something always very much prior to the incident, but could well be something that may develop on the spot, on the spur of the moment.

Common Intention and Similar Intention

Common intention does not mean similar intention of several persons. To constitute common intention it is necessary that the intention of each one of them be known to the rest of them and shared by them. In the case of Dukhmochan Pandey v. State of Bihar, the Supreme Court, held that: "*Common intention which developed at the spur of the moment is different from the similar intention actuated a number of person at the same time....the distinction between a common intention and similar intention may be fine, but is nonetheless a real one and if overlooked, may lead to miscarriage of justice....*" The mere presence of accused together is not sufficient to hold that they shared the common intention to commit the offence in question. It is necessary that the intention of each one of 'several persons' be known to each other for constituting common intention.

96. A gang of six members went to a bank, armed with weapons to commit a heist. While five of the gang members went inside the bank, Mr. A (the sixth member) waited outside the bank to alert them on any threat. During the heist, one of the gang members fired a gun at the branch manager, as a result he died. All five escaped but Mr. A was caught and arrested. Now, choose the most appropriate option as per the principle stated in the above passage.
(a) Mr. A is not liable for murder as he was outside the bank and there was no common intention.
(b) Mr. A along with all other members of the gang are liable for murder as there was common intention.
(c) Only that person is liable for murder who actually fired the gun.
(d) Mr. A is liable only for the heist and no other offence.

97. Raman and Raghav were riding on a motorcycle on a busy street, suddenly Aman (another biker) bumped into their bike. A heated argument started between the three of them. While Raghav started abusing Aman, Raman hit Aman with an iron rod lying on the road and as a consequence he died. Now, chose the correct option.
(a) Both Raman and Raghav are liable for murder as there was a common intention developed on the spot.

(b) Raghav is not liable for murder as there was no common intention to kill Aman.
(c) No one is liable as Aman was a wrongdoer himself and he started the fight.
(d) Only Raghav is liable for murder as he started abusing Aman.

98. After reading the passage which of the following is not correct in relation to the difference between Common and Similar intention?
(a) Similar intention is developed prior to the commission of offence but the common intention is developed only at the time of commission of offence.
(b) Under Common intention each of the offender is equally liable for the offence but under similar intention each of the offender is differently liable.
(c) In order to determine the existence of Similar or Common intention, one must analyse the fact and circumstances of each case.
(d) The boundary between Similar and Common intention is very fine and it may sometime overlap.

99. Mr. X and Mr. Y entered into a house at night to commit theft, while committing theft Mr. Y committed sexual assault on a minor girl of aged 11 years. Identify for which of the following offences Mr. X is liable for.
(a) Both Theft and Sexual Assault as there was a Common intention.
(b) Only Theft as there was a Similar intention.
(c) Only Theft as Mr. X had a different intention from Y.
(d) He would not be liable for any offence.

100. Which of the following statements is correct in relation to the difference between common intention and similar intention?
(a) The intention of the accused and co-accused can be inferred from the facts and circumstances of each case.
(b) Under common intention, it is considered that all the accused have jointly committed the offence themselves and are jointly liable.
(c) Each accused is liable for the offence he has actually committed, if the common intention cannot be proved.
(d) All of the above.

Article 20(1) of the Indian Constitution prohibits Ex Post Facto laws. The expression Ex Post Facto Law means a law, which imposes penalties or convictions on the acts already done and increases the penalty for such acts. In other words, Ex Post Facto Law, imposes penalties retrospectively. For example, The Dowry Prohibition Act, 1961 came into force from 20.5.1961. A person guilty of accepting dowry is punishable under the Act after 20.5.1961 and not before 20.5.1961.

Ex post facto laws are of three kinds as follows:(a) A law which declared some act or omission as an offence for the first time after the completion of that act or omission. (b) A law which enhances the punishment or penalty for an offence subsequent to the commission of that offence. (c) A law which prescribes a new and different procedure for the prosecution of an offence subsequent to the commission of that offence.

Clause (1) of Art. 20 provides protection only in respect of the above first two categories of expost facto laws, i.e., laws which declare acts as offences subsequent to the commission to those acts and laws which enhance the penalty subsequently.

Article 20(1) provides: N*o person shall be convicted of any offence except for violation of a law in force at the time of the commission of the act charged as an offence, nor be subjected to a penalty greater than that which might have been inflicted under the law in force at the time of the commission of the offence.* The first part of clause (1) provides that no person shall be convicted of any offence except for violation of law in force at the time of the commission of the act charged as an offence. The second part of clause (1) protects a person form a penalty greater than that which he might have been subjected to at the time of the commission of the offence.

101. The Parliament of India legislated the Sexual Harassment at Workplace Act, in the year 2013 and simultaneously some new offences were also added to the Indian Penal Code, 1860. Mr. A is an employee of an institution, against whom departmental enquiry has been initiated for committing sexual harassment of a female colleague in the year 2012. Now, choose the correct option.
(a) Such inquiry is valid as per Article 20 (1) of the Constitution as the complaint was made after the act came into force.
(b) Article 20 (1) will not be applicable as the matter does not relate to an offence.
(c) As the Act was passed in the year 2013, any inquiry under such Act is invalid.
(d) Only inquiry may be conducted but no penal action can be taken against him after such inquiry.

102. Article 20 (1) would not affect which of the following acts of the legislature?
(a) Act of the legislature enhancing the term of imprisonment.
(b) Act of the legislature enhancing the amount of fine.
(c) Act of the legislature changing the punishment of death to life imprisonment.
(d) Act of legislature changing the nature of imprisonment from simple to rigorous.

103. Mr. A is a student of Law, aged 19 years. He is socially active and expresses his opinion on every social and political event of the nation through social media platforms. In one of his blog, he severely criticised the policy of a state government of changing names of cities and towns. He also stated that the government is biased towards a particular religion. The said blog was posted on 19th April, 2020 and subsequently, an amendment was made to Indian Penal Code whereby 'Hate Speech' was made a distinct offence and punishment was prescribed. An action was brought against him under the said provision for the blog. Now, choose the most appropriate option amongst the following
(a) Mr. A may be liable for the offence of Hate speech as the blog was not removed even after the amendment.
(b) Mr. A may be liable for the offence of Hate speech as Article 20 (1) does not cover such areas.
(c) Mr. A may not be liable for the offence because the act was done before the amendment.
(d) Mr. A may not be liable for the offence as his blog was innocent and a fair criticism.

104. Considering the fact situations given in the above question, the Parliament passes a legislation in September 2020, whereby an amendment is made to the Juvenile Act and now a person below the age of 20 would be a Juvenile and special procedure would be followed for his trial. Choose the most appropriate option amongst the following
(a) Mr. A would not be considered as juvenile as it is prohibited under the scheme of Article 20 (1).
(b) Mr. A would not be considered as juvenile because the amendment came after he committed the offence.
(c) Mr. A would be considered a Juvenile and tried under the new procedure.
(d) None of the above.

105. Considering the fact situation in the third question to this passage, the Parliament passes a legislation for the Probation of Offenders, under which any offender below the age of 21 will not serve the sentence of imprisonment in a prison, instead he will serve the sentence in a probation house. Now, choose the most appropriate option.
(a) Mr. A will get the benefit of Probation of Offenders Act.
(b) Mr. A will not get the benefit of Probation of Offenders act as it is prohibited by Article 20 (1) of the Constitution.
(c) It is discretion of Mr. A to decide whether he wants such benefit or not.
(d) None of the above.

LOGICAL REASONING

Some readers wondered whether my reading of the crisis in the news media is about journalism or about the news industry. Though the fortunes of the news industry have a bearing on journalism, there is, indeed, a difference between looking at issues that govern journalism and the factors that contribute to the financial stress of the media industry. Over the last few years, I have been discussing the impact of digitalisation on journalism. The pandemic has accelerated the process of digital transformation of the news media. Therefore, these issues need close scrutiny. One of the defining elements of analog journalism was the way two crucial functions of journalism — bearing witness and making sense — complemented each other and helped people make informed choices. When I talk about the strength of analog, I am neither romanticising the past nor am I a Luddite. Most importantly, I do not believe in nostalgia. Many scholars have established "how rose-coloured glasses always leads to an unfair distortion — looking back on the best of the past while comparing it to the worst of the present." Hence, when I talk about the digital information news environment, I am talking about how there needs to be a conducive atmosphere for credible information to resonate with the people. Literature on misinformation, disinformation and malinformation reveals a new distinction in the minds of the citizens. Editors and journalists have to contend with a new breed of sceptics. These are the people who trust social media forwards more than evidence-based, data-driven journalism. Their confirmation bias flows from encrypted social media platforms that are full of conspiracy theories.

[*Excerpt from an Article by* A.S. *Panneerselvan*, *The* Hindu, *dated* August 10, 2020]

106. Which of the following conveys the main idea expressed in the passage?
- (a) Those who subscribe to newspapers are sceptics.
- (b) Those who subscribe to newspapers and news channels often contribute in distortion of the truth.
- (c) Social media journalism distorts the truth.
- (d) All of the above.

107. In this line, "*Hence, when I talk about the digital information news environment, I am talking about how there needs to be a conducive atmosphere for credible information to resonate with the people*" the Author assumes that:
- (a) The Digital news is neither evidence based nor data driven.
- (b) The Digital journalism does not help people in making informed choices.
- (c) Both (a) and (b)
- (d) The impact of Digital journalism has created an informed platform of journalism.

108. Which of the following strengthens the Author's argument?
- (a) Conspiracy theories have become an alternative truth.
- (b) The Pandemic is the only reason behind the dependence of people on Social media journalism.
- (c) The News industry is witnessing a tremendous change.
- (d) None of the above.

109. What does the Author indicate when he quotes that "*Rose coloured glasses always lead to unfair distortion*"?
- (a) Digital Journalism is twisted.
- (b) Author means to say that he does not have any disproportionate bias for analog journalism.
- (c) Rosy picture of every news cannot be created.
- (d) All of the above.

110. The Author has severely targeted and criticized which one of the following factors of Digital Journalism?
- (a) Social Outreach
- (b) Credibility of Information
- (c) Lack of Information
- (d) None of the above.

In 1985, Mikhail Gorbachev, launched an ill-fated anti-alcohol campaign in the then Soviet Union. The anti-alcohol campaign had some beneficial public health consequences: Crime fell and life expectancy rose. But the campaign was a political and economic disaster. Gorbachev forgot that the addiction of the state to alcohol revenue was even more incurable than the addiction of some citizens to alcohol itself. The budgetary losses created an economic crisis. Historians suspect that more than the loss of the Soviet Empire, it was this campaign that delegitimised Gorbachev. An old Soviet joke went like this: A disaffected and angry citizen, fed up of standing in lines for vodka, decided to go assassinate Gorbachev. He soon came back and ruefully reported that the lines to assassinate Gorbachev were even longer than the lines for Vodka. As the lockdown eased in India, and social distancing went for a toss at alcohol outlets, we were reminded of how difficult an issue alcohol is to rationally discuss in India. The stampede was caused by the ineptness with which the opening was handled in most cities. Alcohol has also migrated from being a question of personal freedom and choice to an issue in broader cultural wars, an odd site on which we measure progressivism in India. It is also a window on how liberalism has been misunderstood. Liberals should, rightly, be suspicious of prohibition on moral and practical grounds. Government grossly exceeds its legitimate power when it interferes with the rights of individuals to lead their lives as they please, and fashion their selves after their own ideals, interests and preferences. And certainly, moralism or puritanism on alcohol cannot be the basis of state policy. That moralism has no basis, and it violates the dignity and freedom of individuals.

[*Excerpt from an Opinion by* Bhanu Pratap *Mehta*, The Indian Express, May 7, 2020]

111. In the above passage, the author uses a/an to strengthen his argument.

(a) Metaphor
(b) Analogy
(c) Personification
(d) None of the above

112. Which of the following can be inferred from the passage above?

(a) State must not interfere at all with the individual's right to drink.
(b) Liberalism has always been misunderstood.
(c) It is very difficult to discuss any issue relating to personal freedom of individuals with rationality in India.
(d) None of the above.

113. Which of the following statements weakens the argument that Moralism on Alcohol cannot be the basis of State Policy?

(a) The State should not interfere with people's right to drink; but there will be a backlash if drinking takes forms that inflict great social harms.
(b) Freedom should not be divorced from Moderation.
(c) The State should not interfere in matters of sexuality or intimacy. But norms of freedom will impose serious costs and will not survive if the expressions of sexuality are consistently degrading or violent, as we have seen in the locker room scandals.
(d) All of the above.

114. Which of the following is true as per the passage above?

(a) Liberals should not be concerned about prohibition on Alcohol at all.
(b) Moralism should be based on justified ideals.
(c) Moralism must not be the basis of any State action.
(d) All of the above.

115. According to the passage, which of the following could be part of State's policy to regulate Alcohol use in India?

I. Ban on Alcohol shops.
II. Education on Intelligent Drinking.
III. Regulating Outlet density of Alcohol shops
IV. Community Intervention Policy

(a) I, II and III
(b) II and IV
(c) II, III and IV
(d) I, II, III and IV.

Don't miss the cloud behind the silver lining. The Class XII CBSE pass result has soared to an all-time high of 88.8%. The number of students scoring 95% and above has more than doubled. If only these higher marks were a reflection of students getting more skilled and more competitive. Instead, the odds are they simply mirror an assessment scheme relaxed to compensate students for the many disruptions originating in the pandemic. The goal of reducing student stress levels during this turbulent time is excellent and laudable. But it is a fallacy that high marks can accomplish this by themselves. The real stressor, after all, is shortage of opportunities. When every bout of grade inflation raises cut-offs for higher education even higher, it is no succour. That India's Gross Enrolment Ratio is only 27% compared to Indonesia's 36%, Thailand's 49% and the US's 88% is just one measure of the toll taken by our failure to build adequate colleges and universities. Licence raj continues to suppress autonomy and expansion in this sector. For example, a new national education policy is reportedly mulling at least 20% of students being able to attend private higher educational institutions through freeships and another 30% through scholarships, besides fee caps. On top of the stasis already wreaked by reservations, this would be disastrous. Browbeating the private sector to make up for public sector deficiencies is counterproductive. As the pandemic has underlined the key role of good government services in healthcare, so too is raising the standard of publicly funded schools and universities essential. What the students need is an ecosystem where government institutions deliver quality education and private options are plentiful. It is better prospects alone that will best alleviate students' stress. Meanwhile, crudely chopping syllabi will only worsen their disorientation and should be reconsidered.

[TOI Edit, *Times of India Editorials, Dated July* 15, 2020].

116. What is the 'cloud behind the silver lining' in the passage above?

(a) The Pandemic which is impacting the current education system.

(b) That, the Governmental educational institutions are not able to deliver quality education.

(c) Scoring Higher marks or percentage in school education does not guarantee skilled and competitive candidature of the student.

(d) License Raj has negatively impacted Higher education.

117. Which of the following statements <u>weakens</u> the argument that chopping the syllabi in the times of Pandemic will only worsen a student's disorientation and hence should be reconsidered?

(a) It does not matter even if syllabi is chopped. The students who don't want to study will even not study in the minimal syllabi structure even during the pandemic.

(b) Students don't care about syllabi. They study only for marks and grades.

(c) Reduced syllabi will help in achieving the teaching-learning targets in due time and hence won't put pressure on students.

(d) All of the above.

118. The number of students scoring 95% and above in XII class board exams has more than doubled. Which of the following statements serves as a <u>plausible explanation</u> for the same?

(a) Students have started studying with sincerity and concentration.

(b) Evaluation of answer scripts has become liberal.

(c) Question papers these days are easier to solve.

(d) All of the above.

119. For developing a student friendly ecosystem of education, which of the following serve as need of the hour, as per the Author?

I. Increasing the Syllabi in School education.

II. Building adequate number of public colleges and universities.

III. Eliminating Reservation in admissions to Higher education system.

IV. Creating a quality based education system

(a) Only I and II.

(b) Only I, II and IV.

(c) Only III.
(d) Only II and IV.

120. Which of the following can be inferred from the passage above?
(a) Scoring High marks in XII class can help in reducing stress amongst students in the times of Pandemic.
(b) High Cut-off of marks also contribute in reducing opportunities for the students.
(c) Private institutions should not be regulated.
(d) License Raj should be done away with.

If anything, the novel coronavirus disease (COVID-19) pandemic has taught us to rethink our lifestyles and question our need to travel to work every day. After all, in the age of internet, zoom meetings and webinars can be virtually conducted and physical distancing is possible. A large nature of work in cities is of tertiary nature, a major part of which can be done from home. This can affect the way offices function and reduce the need for all employees to be physically present every day. Information Technology companies are already contemplating a move of making many of its employees work from home and make this a 'new normal'. If more firms follow suit, the need for huge office buildings and central business districts would change. Apartments cannot get bigger at the same rate, and people may not have the space or atmosphere to work from home. This would mean that more people would opt for co-working spaces close to their homes. This could be a game changer, for it would provide the cities to better distribute their activities throughout the spaces and rid themselves of the idea of zoning. Only a handful of professionals are allowed to function from residential zones, including doctors, lawyers, architects, etc. This needs serious rethinking. Many more professions of similar nature that do not disturb surrounding residence and have no requirements of special services should be added to the list. This new work culture would bring associated demand for food joints, cafes, stationary shops, etc.

[*Excerpt from 'Down to Earth' Magazine, Blog authored by Sugeet Grover, August 17, 2020*]

121. Which of the following is the main idea behind the passage?
(a) Work from home is the new normal.
(b) Work from home will result in shutting down of big buildings.
(c) Work from home culture will result in systematization of City planning and development.
(d) More professionals should be included in the 'work from home' list.

122. Which of the following can be inferred from the passage above?
(a) The 'work from home' culture is a no-chaos culture.
(b) There is lack of distribution of activities in the 'work from home' scenario.
(c) The routine culture as opposed to 'work from home' does not benefit the society in any way.
(d) All of the above.

123. Which of the following can be associated benefits of the new culture ?
(a) It will save commute time.
(b) The city's land can be used more efficiently
(c) Better distribution of activities would be associated with safer streets and public spaces as they would not go unused and hence have less likelihood of being used for unlawful activities.
(d) All of the above.

124. Consider the following statement: "Work from home culture is a sustainable method of business and should be extended to all professions."
Which of the following weakens the Author's argument?
(a) Not every type of profession fits in the 'work from home' culture as different professions have different requirements and need different environmental and work space settings.
(b) 'Work from home' impacts a person's mental health.
(c) Both (a) and (b)
(d) Neither (a) nor (b)

125. Which of the following weakens the author's argument that 'Work from home' culture will enable better city planning?
(a) Development of Co-working spaces will further create chaos in terms of land planning.
(b) City planning is not only about reducing spaces.
(c) Work from home will also reduce the flow of money in the economy.
(d) All of the above.

Following is an array of questions to test your reasoning ability in different situations. Answer each of them according to the question asked in each of them, respectively:

126. If highways were restricted to cars and only those trucks with capacity of less than 8 tons, most of the truck traffic would be forced to run outside highways. Such a reduction in the amount of truck traffic would reduce the risk of collisions on highways. The conclusion drawn in the first sentence depends on which of the following assumptions?
(a) The roads outside highway would be as convenient as highway for most drivers of trucks.
(b) Most of the roads outside highways are not ready to handle truck traffic.
(c) Most trucks that are currently running in highway have a capacity of more than 8 tons.
(d) Cars are at greater risk of being involved in collisions than are trucks.

127. Read the debate between Harry and Potter and identify the main issue: Harry: Within democracies, voters are entitled to know the down-side to a candidate and the other side is obviously well placed to voice it. To stifle one's ability to voice negative things about a candidate would be to obstruct democracy and limit free speech.

Potter: Negative advertisements produce the politics of the personal, since an easiest advert is an attack-advert which focuses on the personality or personal qualities of one's opponent. A negative advertisement is one that focuses upon a rival product, in this case, a rival election candidate or party in order to point its flaws and to persuade the public to not vote for it.
(a) Whether negative advertisement strengthens democratic governance?
(b) Whether the practice of negative advertisements is good for democracy and politics?
(c) Whether negative advertising needs to be banned?
(d) Whether negative advertising produces the politics of the personal?

128. Which alternative applies to the following Statement and Assumption?

Statement: Go by Aeroplane to reach Delhi from Chennai quickly.

Assumptions:
I. Chennai and Delhi are connected by Air service.
II. There is no other means to commute from Chennai to Delhi.
III. The Air distance between Delhi and Chennai is less.
(a) Only I is implicit.
(b) Only I and II are implicit.
(c) Only I and III are implicit.
(d) Only II is implicit.

129. Ananya and Krishna can speak and follow English. Bulbul can write and speak Hindi as Archana does. Archana talks with Ananya also in Bengali. Krishna cannot follow Bengali. Bulbul talks with Ananya in Hindi. Who can speak and follow English, Hindi and Bengali?
(a) Archana (b) Bulbul
(c) Krishna (d) Ananya

130. If '367' means 'I am happy'; '748' means 'you are sad' and '469' means 'happy and sad' in a given code, then which of the following represents 'and' in the code?
(a) 3 (b) 6
(c) 9 (d) 4

One of the biggest casualties of the Covid-19 pandemic and the resultant lockdown has been institutionalised education. Schools have been shut to prevent the spread of the virus and this has given way to online classrooms, a very new concept in

India even for the most sophisticated schools. It is commendable how easily some educational institutions have moved to virtual classrooms, all thanks to tools such as Zoom, Google Hangouts and Microsoft Teams. But there are some still struggling to get online. The online classes, whatever the enabling technology, is only as good as the teachers and the ability of the students to grasp the new teaching technique. One of the teachers felt students are actually more responsive and active in online classrooms, compared to when they are in physical ones. "*This could be because this is a new concept and they are excited to explore it with the teachers. They also don't get distracted by their classmates, which frequently happens in a regular class.*" Teachers do find the absence of a blackboard a disadvantage and network connectivity a constant problem. "*We miss the clarity that a blackboard gives us, we are kind of making do with the virtual whiteboard on Zoom*'" Shweta Kawatra, a parent who teaches in a New Delhi school, highlights that many students have not been able to take advantage of the virtual platform because they do not have a suitable device at home or lack a good internet connection. "*It has its own share of disadvantages too. Too much screen time can be perilous for health. Prolonged online sessions can be overwhelming and may lead to problems related to vision, body posture and sleep disorder,*" Kawatra adds.

[*Excerpt from an Article by Sneha Saha, The Indian Express, dated April 18, 2020*]

131. What is the Central Idea of the passage above?
(a) Institutionalised education was much better than the current online education system.
(b) Institutionalized education cannot be replaced by any other system of education.
(c) Virtual Classroom teaching is a sustainable approach to education in modern times.
(d) None of the above.

132. Which of the following statements cannot be inferred from the passage above?
(a) Virtual Classroom teaching is a sustainable approach to education.
(b) Virtual Classroom teaching causes health problems.
(c) Institutionalized education system has its advantages.
(d) All of the above.

133. Which of the following is an implicit assumption in the observation that students are more active and responsive in online classrooms as compared to that in physical ones?
I. Students are not serious while studying in physical classrooms.
II. Online classrooms inculcate more interest in students towards studies than the physical classrooms.
III. Students don't like physical classrooms at all.
IV. Students sleep in physical classrooms.
(a) Only I and II
(b) Only III and IV
(c) I and IV
(d) I, II, III and IV.

134. Which of the following can be inferred from the passage above?
(a) There is a divide in opinions of people on the merits and demerits of Online education.
(b) Online education system is going to replace the Institutionalized education system.
(c) The institutionalized education system is not at all perilous for health of students.
(d) All of the above.

135. Consider this statement: 'Virtual education provides for various online seminars, opportunities to interact with learned experts, pro-bono education classes etc., for students across India irrespective of their economic status and background.'
Which of the following statements weakens the statement?
I. Many students in remote areas do not have access to internet facilities.
II. Many students in rural areas do not have devices to take advantage of the Virtual classrooms.
III. Online Seminars and pro bono classes are not interesting and do not cater to the needs of students across India.

IV. The mobile phone data packages to access such heavy online contents are not enough and participation in such events involves costly data packages which is dependent upon the economic status of those students.

(a) Only I, II, III
(b) Only III and IV
(c) Only I, II and IV.
(d) Only I and II.

QUANTITATIVE TECHNIQUES

The following data presents the cases of Japanese Encephalitis in five states of India.

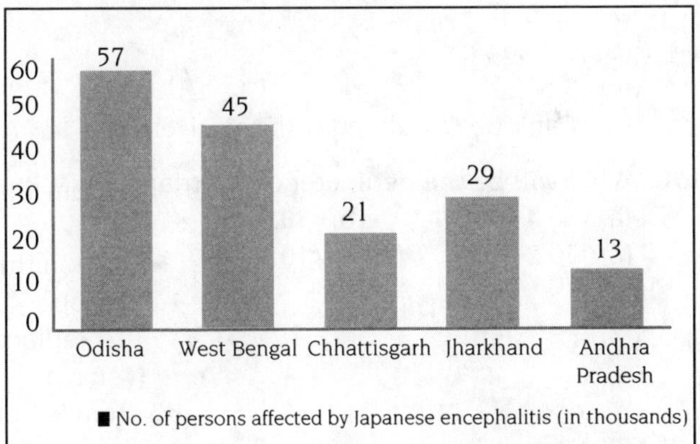

States	Ratio of males to females
	Male : Female
Odisha	12 : 7
West Bengal	6 : 3
Chhattisgarh	5 : 2
Jharkhand	15 : 14
Andhra Pradesh	7:6

136. Number of females affected by Japanese encephalitis in West Bengal are what percentage (up to 1 decimal) more or less than that of females affected in Odisha?
(a) 28.6 % less (b) 29.7 % more
(c) 26.8 % less (d) 25.8 % more

137. What is the average number of males affected by Japanese encephalitis in all the five states?
(a) 9,000 (b) 13,500
(c) 18,400 (d) 20,600

138. If the total number of males affected by Japanese Encephalitis in other states are 87 % more than the average number of males in Odisha, West Bengal, Chhattisgarh and Jharkhand, the total number of males affected in India is:
(a) 44,880 (b) 1,40,880
(c) 1,47,880 (d) 68,880

139. By what percentage is the average of males in Chhattisgarh, Jharkhand and Andhra Pradesh together more or less than the average of females in West Bengal, Jharkhand and Odisha together who are affected by Japanese encephalitis?
(a) 22 (b) 24
(c) 26 (d) 28

140. What is the percentage (up to 1 decimal) of females affected by 'Japanese encephalitis' of the total affected population across five states?
(a) 25.4 (b) 36.7
(c) 24.5 (d) 37.6

A room having the dimensions as mentioned in the chart below has a table, a bed and a chair. There are three books kept on the table (side by side) and also a lamp having radius, 3.5 inch. Now, on the basis of information given below answer the following?

Sr. No.	Object	Length	Breadth	Height
1.	Room	18 feet	12 feet	12 feet
2.	Bed	3.5 feet	6 feet	3 feet
3.	Table	3 feet	4 feet	4 feet
4.	Chair	2 feet	2.5 feet	4 feet
5.	Books	12 inch	6 inch	3 inch

141. What would be the area of the room which is not covered by any object as mentioned above?
(a) 176.5 sq. ft. (b) 178 sq. ft.
(c) 367 sq. ft. (d) 245.5 sq. ft.

142. What is the area of the table which is uncovered by any of the objects?
(a) 1656 sq. inch
(b) 1617.52 sq. inch
(c) 1473.52 sq. inch
(d) 1512 sq. inch

143. How many tables are required to cover the floor surface of the room completely?
(a) 18
(b) 11
(c) 21
(d) Data inadequate

144. If the entire room is to be filled by books having same dimensions as lying on the table, then how many books are required?
(a) 2,00,736 (b) 20,736
(c) 11,736 (d) 17,522

145. How many chairs can be put inside the room so as to cover the entire floor area of the room?
(a) 40 (b) 21
(c) 43 (d) 18

Direction: *In the figure given below, a goat is tied to a pole (at point O) which is the center of the semi-circular plot. The area of the plot is equal to its perimeter. BO is the length of the rope through which the goat is tied to the pole. Answer to the closest decimal.*

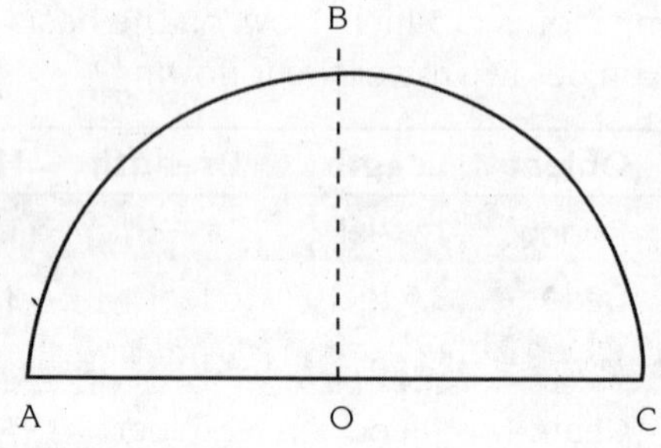

146.*The length of the rope is
(a) $2 + \pi$ (b) $2 + \pi/2$
(c) $2 + 2/\pi$ (d) 2

147.*The area of the plot is
(a) 18.13 (b) 21.83
(c) 28.13 (d) 11.83

148. If a triangle is created by joining points A, B, and C. What will be the length of AB?
(a) 3.73
(b) 7.33
(c) 1.86
(d) Can't be calculated with the given data

149. What will be the area of the triangle ABC?
(a) 6.96
(b) 9.66
(c) 3.66
(d) Can't be calculated with the given data

150.*What will be the perimeter of the triangle ABC?
(a) 40.4 (b) 30.3
(c) 20.2 (d) 10.1

* For the UG Programme: Q. 46, 47 and 50 were dropped by the consortium and the evaluation was done out of 147 Questions.

ANSWER KEY

English

1. (a)	6. (a)	11. (a)	16. (d)	21. (b)	26. (a)
2. (d)	7. (d)	12. (c)	17. (b)	22. (b)	27. (b)
3. (b)	8. (a)	13. (c)	18. (c)	23. (a)	28. (b)
4. (b)	9. (a)	14. (c)	19. (a)	24. (d)	29. (d)
5. (c)	10. (d)	15. (c)	20. (c)	25. (d)	30. (c)

Current Affairs Including GK

31. (b)	36. (a)	41. (a)	46. (d)	51. (c)	56 (c)	61. (d)
32. (d)	37. (d)	42. (b)	47. (c)	52. (d)	57. (d)	62. (c)
33. (b)	38. (d)	43. (c)	48. (d)	53. (a)	58. (a)	63. (d)
34. (c)	39. (b)	44. (b)	49. (b)	54. (c)	59. (b)	64. (c)
35. (c)	40. (a)	45. (b)	50. (b)	55. (b)	60. (a)	65. (c)

Legal Reasoning

67. (b)	73. (b)	79. (c)	85. (c)	91. (b)	97. (b)	103. (a)
68. (c)	74. (c)	80. (c)	86. (d)	92. (d)	98. (a)	104. (c)
69. (b)	75. (c)	81. (a)	87. (d)	93. (a)	99. (c)	105. (a)
70. (d)	76. (d)	82. (c)	88. (c)	94. (a)	100. (d)	
71. (c)	77. (b)	83. (d)	89. (d)	95. (a)	101. (d)	
72. (a)	78. (b)	84. (b)	90. (c)	96. (b)	102. (c)	

Logical reasoning

106. (c)	111. (b)	116. (c)	121. (c)	126. (c)	131. (d)
107. (c)	112. (d)	117. (d)	122. (a)	127. (b)	132. (a)
108. (a)	113. (d)	118. (d)	123. (d)	128. (c)	133. (a)
109. (b)	114. (b)	119. (d)	124. (c)	129. (d)	134. (a)
110. (b)	115. (c)	120. (b)	125. (d)	130. (c)	135. (c)

Quantitative techniques

136. (a)	139. (c)	142. (c)	145. (c)	148. (d)
137. (d)	140. (d)	143. (a)	146. (c)	149. (d)
138. (b)	141. (b)	144. (b)	147. (b)	150. (d)

CLAT 2019

ENGLISH

Directions: *From each set of sentences given below in question 1 to 10, choose the sentence that is grammatically correct.*

1. (a) A few judges have cut short their vacation to clear a long pending cases.
(b) A few judges have cut short vacation to clear the long pending cases.
(c) A few judges has cut short its vacation to clear the long pending cases.
(d) A few judges have cut short their vacation to clear the long pending cases.

2. (a) Where's Hari? Here is he, right in front of us!
(b) Where's Hari? Here he is, right in front of us!
(c) Wheres' Hari? He is here, right in front of us!
(d) Where's Hari? Is he here, right in front of us!

3. (a) Customs officer's do not allow passenger to carry banned items into or out of the country.
(b) Customs officers does not allow passengers to carry banned items into or out of country.
(c) Customs officers do not allows passengers to carry banned items into or out of country.
(d) Customs officers do not allow passengers to carry banned items into or out of the country.

4. (a) Neither this nor that machine is working.
(b) Neither this nor that machine are working.
(c) Neither this and that machine is working.
(d) Neither this but that machine is working.

5. (a) I shall be doing a MBA online, and continue with my present job.
(b) I shall do a MBA online, and continue with my present job.
(c) I shall do an MBA online, and continue with my present job.
(d) I shall do an MBA online, but continuing with my present job.

6. (a) As soon as I boarded the train, I realized that I left my wallet at home.
(b) As soon as I boarded the train, I realize that I had left wallet at home.
(c) As soon as I board the train, I realized that I leave my wallet at home.
(d) As soon as I boarded the train, I realized that I had left my wallet at home.

7. (a) We can take either the morning flight nor the one in the afternoon.
(b) We can take neither the morning flight or the one in the afternoon.
(c) We can take either morning flight or the one in afternoon.
(d) We can take either the morning flight or the one in the afternoon.

8. (a) The management have promised that it will consider my appeal.
(b) The management has promised that it will consider my appeal.
(c) The management has promise that they will consider my appeal.
(d) The management has promised that it will considered my appeal.

9. (a) Tourists must follow the norms set upon the country they visit.
(b) Tourists must follow norms set by country they visit.
(c) Tourists must follow the norms set by the country they visit.
(d) Tourists must follow the norms set by the country they visits.

10. (a) An important file, along with two uniforms, are missing from the police station.
(b) A important file, along with two uniforms, is missed from the police station.
(c) An important files, along with two uniforms, are missing from the police station.
(d) An important file, along with two uniforms, is missing from the police station.
(A) adbc (B) cbad
(C) bcad (D) bdac

Directions (questions 11–15): *In each of the questions given below in questions 11 to 15, each sentence is labelled with a letter. From the given choices, choose the most logical order of sentences that constructs a coherent paragraph.*

11. a. One of them copied and pasted large portions of the required text from a website.
b. Before assigning the project to his students, the guide gave a presentation on plagiarism.
c. The expulsion order that followed was not alarming.
d. A few students did not pay much heed to the consequences of the illegal act.
(A) cabd (B) dbca
(C) badc (D) bdac

12. (a) Goals are set, and relevant data is collected and analyzed.
(b) Strategies are made on the basis of the data and resources made available.
(c) There are various stages in framing a management-strategy, and its implementation.
(d) The strategies are implemented and monitored to ensure that the goals are achieved.
(A) abdc (B) acbd
(C) cabd (D) cbad

13. (a) Despite the awareness, some citizens fail to pay their taxes honestly.
(b) One of the factors that impacts our country's economy is income-tax.
(c) Awareness regarding this aspect of our economy is often made through the education system and media.
(d) Most of these defaulters not only get into trouble, but they also create additional work for the income-tax department.

14. (a) The responsible citizen helped to foil the plan of a hijack.
(b) The deep pockets of his leather jacket contained what had been feared!
(c) A person called up the airport and gave a message.
(d) All the passengers were carefully frisked, and one of them was asked to step aside.
(A) badc (B) cdba
(C) dacb (D) cdab

15. (a) In the following years, more layers of snow add up to the existing mass.
(b) Consequently, the weight of the snow compresses and turns into solid ice.
(c) Most glaciers are found near the Poles.
(d) They begin to form when snow remains in the same area all year round.
(A) acbd (B) cdba
(C) abdc (D) cdab

Directions (questions 16–20): *Choose the correct meaning for each of the foreign language words and phrases given below in questions 16 to 20.*

16. inter vivos
(a) a transaction made for obtaining a legacy
(b) an agreement to promote the welfare of one's country
(c) a transaction made between living people
(d) an agreement between warring nations

17. quantum ramifactus
(a) the amount of damages suffered
(b) the quality of goods supplied
(c) the amount of relief given for damages caused
(d) the weightage given to someone's suggestion

18. malus
(a) mass
(b) harmless
(c) harmful
(d) comforting

19. Volvo
(a) I roll (b) I run
(c) I leap (d) I jump

20. Charade
(a) series (b) charter
(c) pretense (d) spate

Directions (questions 21–25): *Choose the correctly spelled words in questions 21 to 25 to fill in the blanks.*

21. Malti Ahuja is making a sincere effort to pay off her ————.
(a) crediter (b) creditar
(c) credittor (d) creditor

22. It is our responsibility to leave a green and clean world for our ————.
(a) descendents (b) decendants
(c) descendants (d) descendantes

23. The patient's death was the result of sheer ———— on the part of the surgeon.
(a) negligience (b) negligence
(c) negligennce (d) neglegence

24. The scientist's biography is a blatant ———— of facts.
(a) misrepresentation
(b) misreprezentation
(c) misrepresentetion
(d) misreprisentation

25. It was a ———— to work with these scientists.
(a) previlege (b) priviledge
(c) privilige (d) privilege

Directions for Questions 26 to 30: *Fill in the blank with the correct options.*

26. Son, ————! Research the company before you apply for the job.
(a) build castles in the air
(b) hit the ceiling
(c) get off on the wrong foot
(d) hold your horses

27. Please, ————! This is not the time to get anxious.
(a) pull yourself together
(b) pass the buck
(c) bark up the wrong tree
(d) go on a wild goose chase

28. In our company, we don't accept such carelessly done work. ————
(A) So far so good.
(B) Get your act together.
(C) We'll cross the bridge when we come to it.
(D) Your guess is as good as mine.

29. I can't work on this assignment anymore! I think I have ————.
(A) broken the ice
(B) added insult to injury
(C) chewed cud
(D) bitten off more than I can chew

30. I'm a historian. I'm a ———— in this seminar on robots!
(A) drop in the bucket
(B) fish out of water
(C) fly in the ointment
(D) fly on the wall

Directions for Questions 31 to 40: *The questions in this section are based on what is stated or implied in the passage given below. For each question, choose the option that most accurately and completely answers the question.*

The words invention and Innovation are closely linked, but they are not interchangeable. The inventor is a genius who uses his intellect, imagination, time and resources to create something that does not exist. But this invention may or may not be of utility to the masses. It is the enterprising innovator who uses various resources, skills and time to make the invention available for use. The innovator might use the invention as it is, modify it or even blend two or more inventions to make one marketable product. A great example is that of the iPhone which is a combination of various inventions.

If an invention is the result of countless trials and errors, so can be the case with an innovation. Not every attempt to make an invention is successful. Not every innovation sees the light of the day. Benjamin Franklin had the belief that success doesn't come without challenge, mistake, and in a few cases failure.

One of the world's most famous innovators, Steve Jobs says, "Sometimes when you innovate, you make mistakes. It is best to admit them quickly and get on with improving your other your other innovations."

Thus, inventors and innovators have to be intrepid enough to take risks; consider failures as stepping stones and not stumbling blocks.

Some inventions are the result of a keen observation or a simple discovery. The inventor of Velcro, also called the zipless zipper, is the Swiss engineer George de Mestral. He was hiking in the woods when he found burrs clinging to his clothes and his dog's fur. Back at home, he studied the burrs. He discovered that each burr was a collection of tiny hooks which made it cling on to another object. A few years later, he made and patented the strips of fabric that came to us as Velcro.

The world of inventions and innovations is a competitive one. But the race does not end here; it is also prevalent in the case of getting intellectual property rights. There have been inventors who failed to get a single patent while there have been some who managed to amass numerous patents in their lifetime. Thomas Edison had 1,093 patents to his credit!

We relate the telephone with Alexander Graham Bell. It is believed that around the same time, Antonio Meucci had also designed the telephone, but due to lack of resources and various hardships, he could not proceed with the patent of his invention. It is also believed that Elisha Gray had made a design for the telephone and applied for the patent at the U.S. patent office on the same day as Graham Bell did. By sheer chance, Graham's lawyer's turn to file the papers came first. Hence, Graham was granted the first patent for the telephone.

It is not easy, and at times almost impossible, for an inventor to be an innovator too. There are very few like Thomas Edison who graduated from being an incredible inventor to a successful manufacturer and businessman with brilliant marketing skills.

While innovations that have helped to enhance the quality of life are laudable, equally laudable are the inventions that laid the foundation of these very innovations.

31. The text in the passage can be best termed as
(a) narrative
(b) descriptive
(c) persuasive
(d) expository

32. The main idea of the author is to
(a) highlight the difficulties faced by innovators.
(b) focus on the hardships of patent -seekers.
(c) compare innovators to inventors.
(d) reveal the importance of inventors.

33. The author believes that
(a) innovators enhance the utility of inventions.
(b) innovators face fewer challenges than inventors do.
(c) every inventor has a patent for the invention.
(d) invention is the same as innovation.

34. Benjamin Franklin and Steve Jobs, believe that
(a) there is no place for mistakes in the process of making an innovation.
(b) making a mistake before finding success is not unusual.
(c) failure is a permanent stumbling block.
(d) all innovators have to go through failure.

35. Velcro can be best described as
(a) a highly-planned and deeply researched invention
(b) the fruit of failure
(c) the need of the hour
(d) an accidental invention

36. It is believed that Graham Bell became the first patent holder of the telephone because of
(a) his ingenuity and good fortune.
(b) the carelessness of Elisha's lawyer.
(c) the clever trick played by his lawyer.
(d) the biased officials in the patent office.

37. Which of the following is Untrue?
(a) Inventors may not be innovators.
(b) Innovators are not expected to be enterprising.

(c) To get a patent, the applicant has to follow a legal process.
(d) Intellectual property rights are not always easy to get.

38. Which of the following texts from the passage clearly indicates failure?
(a) The world of inventions and innovations is a competitive one.
(b) Not every innovation sees the light of the day.
(c) Thus, inventors and innovators have to be intrepid enough to take risks;
(d) None of the above

39. Which of these words can replace the word intrepid?
(a) hasty (b) intellectual
(c) daring (d) rich

40. Which of these words is the antonym of laudable?
(a) praiseworthy (b) challenging
(c) tiring (d) disgraceful

GENERAL KNOWLEDGE AND CURRENT AFFAIRS

41. The Chief Central Information Commissioner at present is:
(a) Sudhir Bhargava
(b) R.K. Mathur
(c) Sridhar Acharyulu
(d) Handu

42. India has recently set up the latest ISRO's Satellite Tracking and Data Reception Centre in:
(a) Maldives (b) Sri Lanka
(c) Bhutan (d) Nepal

43. The number of complaints with the Banking Ombudsman registered during 2018 increased by:
(a) 10% (b) 15%
(c) 20% (d) 25%

44. Which of the following formally quit from UNESCO recently?
(a) U.S.A (b) China
(c) Sweden (d) India

45. The maximum punishment for a cyber-stalker imposed by an anti-terrorism court in Pakistan is:
(a) 5 years (b) 14 years
(c) 10 years (d) 24 years

46. In a major relief to micro, small and medium enterprises, the GST Council has recently increased the tax exemption limit per annum to:
(a) 20 lakhs (b) 30 lakhs
(c) 40 lakhs (d) 60 lakhs

47. Which of the following fruits got the Geographical Indication during October 2018?
(a) Shahi Litchi
(b) Laxman Bhog Mango
(c) Sirumalai Hill Banana
(d) Mahabaleshwar Strawberry

48. The richest person in the world as per the details revealed in March 2019 is:
(a) Bill Gates
(b) Jeff Bezos
(c) Amancio Ortega
(d) Bernard Arnault

49. The number of EB–5 visa applications, also known as 'Cash for Green Card' visa to the U.S has increased in the last two years by about:
(a) 100% (b) 200%
(c) 300% (d) 400%

50. India purchased surveillance aircrafts (AWACS) during 2016 from:
(a) USA (b) France
(c) Russia (d) Israel

51. The fastest train in India is:
(a) Gatiman Express
(b) Shatabdi Express
(c) Vande Bharat Express
(d) Rajdhani Express

52. The first humanoid police robot was introduced in the State of:
(a) Karnataka
(b) Delhi
(c) Gujarat
(d) Kerala

53. The world's first Diesel to Electric locomotive twin engine of 10,000 horse power was flagged off in:
(a) U.S.A. (b) China
(c) India (d) South Korea

54. The Headquarters of International Solar Alliance consisting of more than 121 countries is located in:
(a) India (b) South Africa
(c) Malaysia (d) China

55. The prestigious Seoul Peace Prize for 2018 was conferred on:
(a) Kofi Annan
(b) Angela Merkel
(c) Narendra Modi
(d) Putin

56. Which of the following countries during 2019 provided life time personal tax exemption to women with four children?
(a) India (b) Hungary
(c) Norway (d) Finland

57. In the 64th Film Fare Award, who won the best actress award?
(a) Katrina Kapoor
(b) Priyanka Chopra
(c) Deepika Padukone
(d) Alia Bhatt

58. Recently, the Government of India relaxed the Angel Tax Norms for Start-ups and enhanced the investment limit to:
(a) Rs. 25 Crore
(b) Rs. 20 Crore
(c) Rs. 15 Crore
(d) Rs. 30 Crore

59. India's first Chairperson of Lokpal is:
(a) Justice Dipak Mishra
(b) Justice Dilip Bhosale
(c) Justice P.C. Ghose
(d) Justice Thakur

60. In how many phases the 17th Lok Sabha elections were held in 2019?
(a) Six (b) Seven
(c) Five (d) Eight

61. How many States went to polls along with the 2019 Lok Sabha elections?
(a) Three (b) Four
(c) Five (d) Two

62. The National Common Mobility Card (NCMC), launched by the Central Government recently is also dubbed as:
(a) One Nation One Card
(b) Citizenship Card
(c) Aadhar Card
(d) Shopping Card

63. Which of the following cities bagged the Cleanest City Award for three consecutive years?
(a) Mysore
(b) Ahmedabad
(c) Chandigarh
(d) Indore

64. Who is known as the 'Father of Local Government in India'?
(a) Lord Curzon (b) Lord Mayo
(c) Lord Wellesley (d) Lord Ripon

65. Under which of the following missions, India has successfully tested its first-ever Anti-Satellite (A-SAT) Missile capability?
(a) Mission Shakti
(b) Mission Agni
(c) Mission Raftar
(d) Mission Sahas

66. Which Indian personality is the recipient of the Oxford University's Bodley Medal 2019?
(a) Raghuram Rajan
(b) Amartya Sen
(c) Manmohan Singh
(d) Shashi Tharoor

67. What is the name of the book containing English translation of the 100 year old classic Punjabi poem about Jallianwala Bagh massacre?
(a) Drummer Hodge
(b) Poems of the Jallianwala Bagh massacre
(c) Poems about war
(d) Khooni Vaisakhi

68. Which country has released a special stamp on Hindu epic Ramayana to commemorate the 70th anniversary of the diplomatic ties with India?
(a) Indonesia
(b) Bangladesh
(c) Sri Lanka
(d) India

69. Which day is observed as International Mother Earth Day?
(a) April 20
(b) April 21
(c) April 23
(d) April 22

70. Which state's Kandhamal Haldi (turmeric) received Geographical Indications (GI) tag recently?
(a) Odisha
(b) Karnataka
(c) Kerala
(d) Tamil Nadu

71. Which country's Navy department has signed first reliable communication link with the Indian Navy and Pacific Naval Commands under the COMCASA pact?
(a) Sri Lanka
(b) Japan
(c) Russia
(d) US

72. Name the script writer, who won the Deenanath Mangeshkar Lifetime Award 2019 recently.
(a) Javed Akhtar
(b) Vishal Bhardwaj
(c) Anurag Kashyap
(d) Salim Khan

73. Which space agency has recorded the first 'mars-quake,' quake on the mars due to volcanic eruptions or land tides?
(a) JAXA (Japan Aerospace Exploration Agency)
(b) NASA (National Aeronautics and Space Administration)
(c) ISRO (Indian Space Research Organisation)
(d) Chines Space Agency

74. Name the third edition of bilateral maritime exercise between Australia and India that was held in Visakhapatnam.
(a) Vajra Prahar (b) Cobra Gold
(c) Ausindex 19 (d) Ausind 19

75. Holkhomang Haokip, who passed away recently, was a ___________?
(a) Writer
(b) Producer
(c) Football player
(d) Politician

76. Name the Howitzers guns inducted into Indian Army recently.
(a) Dhanush
(b) Panter
(c) M102 howitzer
(d) BL 9.2-inch howitzer

77. Who was the first Indian President to visit Croatia?
(a) Abdul Kalam
(b) Pratibha Patil
(c) Pranab Mukherjee
(d) Ram Nath Kovind

78. Which Island was notified as Island Protection Zone (IPZ) 2019 by Union Ministry of Environment, Forest and Climate Change recently?
(a) Andaman and Nicobar Island
(b) Kurumgad Island
(c) Khanderi Island
(d) Worli Island

79. Name the organization, which released the report on food crises titled 'Global Report on Food Crises' annually.
(a) International Food Policy Research Institute (IFPRI)
(b) Food and Agriculture Organization (FAO)
(c) Food Corporation of India (FCI)
(d) Food Security Information Network (FSIN)

80. Which is the happiest country as per the 2019 World Happiness Index?
(a) Finland (b) Denmark
(c) Norway (d) Sweden

81. The Headquarters of Asian Development Bank is situated in
(a) Manila, Philippines
(b) Jakarta, Indonesia
(c) Colombo, Sri Lanka
(d) Honoi, Vietnam

82. The 'Golden Peacock' Award is given for excellence in
(a) Corporate Social Responsibility
(b) Energy Savings
(c) Literature
(d) Corporate Governance

83. Which planet is known as Red Planet?
(a) Venus
(b) Mercury
(c) Mars
(d) Neptune

84. What is Psephology?
(a) Statistical study of elections, voting, etc.
(b) Study of rainfall pattern
(c) Study of gene disorder
(d) Study of female prisoners

85. The Global Teacher Award, 2019 was awarded to a teacher in:
(a) South Korea
(b) Japan
(c) Canada
(d) Kenya

86. Which state in India is the first State to achieve 100 percent sanitation coverage?
(a) Andhra Pradesh
(b) Karnataka
(c) Sikkim
(d) Manipur

87. The book titled 'God Save the Honourable Supreme Court' was authored by:
(a) Soli Sorabjee
(b) Fali S. Nariman
(c) K.K. Venugopal
(d) Justice Katju

88. The book titled 'Anita Gets Bail' was authored by:
(a) Amitab Ghosh
(b) Kiran Bedi
(c) Indira Jaisingh
(d) Arun Shourie

89. The first Indian Athlete to qualify for Olympics 2020 is:
(a) K.T. Irfan
(b) Jinson Johnson
(c) Tintu Lukka
(d) Sunita Rani

90. The South Asian nation that has won the SAFF Women's Championship for five times successively is:
(a) Nepal
(b) India
(c) Sri Lanka
(d) Bhutan

MATHEMATICS

91. The Municipality of a town increases water tax by 20% and water consumption decreased by 20%. Then the percentage of increase or decrease in the monthly expenditure is:
(a) 4% increase
(b) 4% decrease
(c) 5% increase
(d) 5% decrease

92. A child was born on 13th January 1976 which was a Tuesday. What day of the week will be the child's birth day in the year 1986?
(a) Sunday
(b) Friday
(c) Saturday
(d) Monday

93. The perimeter of a rectangle is 60 cms. If its length is twice its breadth, then its area is:
(a) 200 cm2
(b) 180 cm2
(c) 1630 cm2
(d) 220 cm2

94. A tree grows at the rate of 1/5th of its height annually. By how much height will it grow after 2 years, if its present height is 75 cms?
(a) 108 cms (b) 90 cms
(c) 144 cms (d) 112 cms

95. A train 600 meters long is running at a speed of 90 kms/hr. If it crosses a tunnel in one minute, then the length of the tunnel is:
(a) 500 meters (b) 550 meters
(c) 600 meters (d) 900 meters

96. A book seller sold a box of 10 pencils for Rs. 80 and incurred a loss. Had he sold it for Rs. 98, his gain would have been twice the loss he incurred earlier. The cost price of the box of pencils is:
(a) Rs. 84 (b) Rs. 86
(c) Rs. 88 (d) Rs. 90

97. In a 100 meters race, A beats B by 20 meters B beats C by 5 meters. In the same race, A beats C by:
(a) 26 meters (b) 25 meters
(c) 24 meters (d) 22 meters

98. Beena got married 8 years ago. Today, her age is 11/4 times her age at the time of marriage. If her daughter's age is 1/10 times her age, then her daughter's age is:
(a) 3 years (b) 4 years
(c) 5 years (d) 2 years

99. A clock gains 2 minutes every hour. Then the angle traversed by the second hand in one minute is:
(a) 360° (b) 370°
(c) 390° (d) 372°

100. 80% of students of a class took Statistics and 45% took Mathematics. If each student took Statistics or Mathematics and 40 took both, the total number of students in the class was:
(a) 160 (b) 180
(c) 200 (d) 225

101. Kiran's brother is 5 years older to her. Her father was 30 years old when Kiran's sister was born, while her mother was 28 years old when Kiran was born. If Kiran's sister was 2 years old when her brother was born, what was the age of their father when Kiran's brother was born?
(a) 32 (b) 34
(c) 37 (d) 30

102. If Second Saturday and Sunday of every month is a holiday, then the total number of working days in a month of 31 days beginning with a Wednesday will be
(a) 23 (b) 24
(c) 25 (d) 26

103. A mess contractor can either serve 450 students with the meal that he prepares or can cater to 270 cops with the same meal. If 300 students have already eaten in the mess, how many cops can be fed with the remaining meal?
(a) 20 (b) 45
(c) 90 (d) 180

104. A car driver increases the average speed of his car by 3 km/hr every hour. The total distance travelled in 7 hours if the distance covered in first hour was 30 km, is
(a) 266 km (b) 273 km
(c) 280 km (d) 287 km

105. A grocer mixes coffee powder of 2 types, one of which is priced at Rs. 60 and the other at Rs. 90. What should be the ratio of combining the two, to sell the blended mix coffee powder of the two types at Rs. 80?
(a) 2:1 (b) 2:3
(c) 1:2 (d) 3:2

106. The smallest number that should be subtracted from 2085, so that the new number is completely divisible by 23 is
(a) 9 (b) 15
(c) 20 (d) 19

107. A tank is connected to three pipes – Pipe A, B and C. Pipe A can fill the tank in 6 hours, B can fill the tank in 8 hours and Pipe C can empty the full tank in 12 hours. How much time will it take to fill the tank completely if all three pipes are working together?
(a) 4 hours (b) 4 hours 48 minutes
(c) 5 hours (d) 5 hours 20 minutes

108. Naresh bought a bicycle each for his two sons, each bicycle priced at Rs. 3500. If the first bicycle is sold at a profit of 5%, the how much should the other bicycle be sold for, to gain a total of 20% on both?

(a) 15% (B) 10%
(c) 25% (d) 35%

109. An employee of an organization invests a total of Rs 25,400 in two different schemes X and Y at a simple interest rate of 18% per annum and 10% per annum respectively. If a total of Rs. 6460 has been earned as simple interest in 2 years, what amount was invested in Scheme Y?

(a) Rs. 8,625
(b) Rs. 16,775
(c) Rs. 12,240
(d) Rs. 10,930

110. The difference between Simple Interest and Compound Interest on Rs. 500 for 1 year at 10% per annum, reckoned half yearly is

(a) Rs. 1 (b) Rs. 1.25
(c) Rs. 1.5 (d) Rs. 2

LEGAL APTITUDE

This section consists of fifty (50) questions. Each question consists of legal principle(s) (hereinafter referred to as 'principle') and facts. Such proposition may or may not be true in the real and legal sense, yet you have to conclusively assume them to be true for the purposes of this section. Principles have to be applied to the given facts to arrive at the most reasonable conclusion. Only one of the alternatives, i.e., (A), (B), (C), or (D) is the most reasonable conclusion. In other words, in answering the following questions, you must not rely on any principle except the principles that are given herein below for every question. Further you must not assume any facts other than those stated in the question. The objective of this section is to test your ability in legal aptitude, study of law, research aptitude and problem solving ability even if the 'most reasonable conclusion' arrived at may be absurd or unacceptable for any other reason.

111. Principle: Acceptance of proposal must be the exact mirror image of the proposal.

Facts: 'A' made a proposal to 'B' to sell a chair for Rs. 500. 'B' is desirous of buying the said chair for Rs. 400.

(a) B has accepted the proposal of A.
(b) B has not accepted the proposal of A.
(c) It is not clear if B has accepted the proposal of A.
(d) It is not clear whether A made a proposal of B.

112. Principle: An agreement with a boy below the age of eighteen years is not enforceable by law.

Facts: A man entered into an agreement with a girl of seventeen years of age.

(a) The agreement is enforceable by law.
(b) The agreement is not enforceable by law.
(c) The agreement is enforceable by the girl.
(d) No inference can be drawn.

113. Principle: Sale of liquor is illegal. All agreements relating to prohibited items do not exist in the eyes of law.

Facts: 'A' entered into an agreement with 'B' for the sale of liquor. 'A' failed to supply the agreed quantity of liquor to B.

(a) B can bring a legal action against A.
(b) B cannot bring any legal action against A.
(c) A can bring a legal action against B.
(d) A and B can initiate appropriate legal proceeding against each other.

114. Principle: The communication of a proposal is complete when it comes to the knowledge of the person to whom it is made.

Facts: A' sent a letter making a proposal to 'B' to purchase the house of B.

(a) The communication of proposal is complete when A sent the letter.
(b) The communication of proposal is complete when B's wife received it.
(c) The communication of proposal is complete when B's wife haded over the letter to B.
(d) The communication of proposal is complete when B's reads the letter.

115. Principle: An agreement may be entered into orally, in writing, or by conduct.

Facts: 'A' went to the shop of 'B' and picked a tooth brush and gave a cheque of Rupees twenty to B and left the shop.

(a) A entered into an agreement with B.
(b) A did not enter into an agreement with B.
(c) Payment of tooth brush cannot be made through a cheque.
(d) A should have carried a currency note of Rupees twenty to make the payment.

116. Principle: Property consists of right to posses, right to use, right to alienate and right to exclude others. Sale is complete when property gets transferred from the seller to the buyer.

Facts: 'A' sold his car to 'B' B requested A to keep the car in his care on behalf B for one month. A agreed.

(a) Sale of car is complete.
(b) Sale of car is not complete.
(c) Sale will be completed when B keeps the car in his own care.
(d) Sale will be automatically completed after the expiry of one month.

117. Principle: A person, who is usually mad, but occasionally not mad, may make a contract when he is not mad.

Facts: 'A' generally remains in the state of madness and rarely becomes capable of understanding anything.

(a) A can make a contract.
(b) A can never make a contract.
(c) A can make a contract at any time whenever he pleases.
(d) A can make a contract only for his own benefit.

118. Principle: An agreement without free consent can be enforced only at the option of the party whose consent was not free.

Facts: A obtains the consent of B to enter into an agreement by putting a gun on the head of B's girl friend.

(a) B can enforce the agreement.
(b) B cannot enforce the agreement.
(c) A can enforce the agreement.
(d) Neither A nor B can enforce the agreement.

119. Principle: Where one of the parties to a contract was in position to dominate the decision of the other party, the contract is enforceable only at the option of the party who was in a position to dominate decision of the other party.

Facts: A doctor asked his patient to make a payment of Rs. 10,00,000/-(Ten Lac Only) for treatment of his fever. The patient paid an amount of Rs. 5,00,000/-(Five Lac Only) and promised to pay the remaining amount after the treatment. After treatment the patient recovered from fever. The doctor demanded the remaining amount from the patient. The patient refused to pay.

(a) The contract is enforceable against the doctor.
(b) The contract is enforceable against the patient.
(c) The contract is not enforceable.
(d) The contract is not enforceable against the patient.

120. Principle: When, at the desire one person, any other person has done or abstained from doing something, such act or abstinence or promise is called a consideration for the promise.

Facts: X, the uncle of Y, made a promise to pay him an amount of Rs. 1,00,000/-as reward if Y quits smoking and drinking within one year. Y quit smoking and drinking within six months.

(a) Consideration has moved from the side of X.
(b) Consideration has moved from the side of Y.
(c) No consideration has moved from the side of Y.
(d) Quitting smoking and drinking cannot be a consideration.

121. Principle: Law never enforces an impossible promise.

Facts: 'A' made a promise to 'B' to discover treasure by magic.

(a) Law will enforce the promise.
(b) Law will not enforce the promise.
(c) Law will enforce the promise only at the option of A.
(d) Law will enforce the promise only at the option of B.

122. Principle: When a person who has made a promise to another person to do something does not fulfill his promise, another person becomes entitled to receive, from the person who did not fulfill his promise, compensation in the form of money.

Facts: X made a promise to Y to repair his car engine. Y made the payment for repair. After the repair, Y went for a drive in the same car. While driving the car, Y met with an accident due to bursting of the tyre.

(a) X will be entitled to receive compensation from Y in the form of money
(b) Y will be entitled to receive compensation from X in the form of money
(c) X will not be entitled to receive compensation
(d) Y will not be entitled to receive compensation from X

123. Principle: Whoever takes away any moveable thing from the land of any person without that person's consent is said to commit theft.

Facts: During his visit to the home of C, A asks B, the son of C, to accompany A to a

(a) A has committed theft
(b) A has not committed theft
(c) A has committed theft as soon as he entered the home of C.
(d) A has not committed theft till B did not accompany him.

124. Principle: Nothing is an offence if it is done in good faith for the purpose of preventing or avoiding greater harm or damage to person or property.

Facts: A jumps into a swimming pool to save a boy from drowning. While pulling the boy from water A was hit by C. A left the boy in the water and attacked C. The boy died in the water.

(a) A has not committed the offence of killing the boy.
(b) A has committed the offence of killing the boy.
(c) The boy has committed the offence of suicide.
(d) The boy has committed the offence of drowning.

125. Principle: Causing of an effect partly by an act and partly by an omission is an offence.

Facts: A did not provide any food to his daughter D. He also confined D in a room. Consequently, D died.

(a) A committed the offence of not providing food to D.
(b) A committed the offence of confining D.
(c) A committed the offence of killing D.
(d) A committed no offence.

126. Principle: Nothing is an offence which is done in the exercise of the right of private defence. Nothing is an offence which is done in madness.

Facts: A, under the influence of madness, attempts to kill B. B to save his life kills A.

(a) A has committed the offence of attempt to murder
(b) A has committed an offence of being mad
(c) B has committed an offence
(d) B has not committed an offence

127. Principle: A man is guilty of not only for what he actually does but also for the consequences of his doing.

Facts: A wanted to kill the animal of B. He saw B standing with his animal and fired a gun shot at the animal. The gun shot killed B.

(a) A is guilty of killing B.
(b) A is not guilty of killing B.
(c) B is guilty of standing with the animal.
(d) A did not know that the gun shot will kill B.

128. Principle: Mere silence as to facts likely to affect the decision of a person to enter into a contract is not fraud.

Facts: A sells to B (A's daughter who is a minor) a horse which A knows to be unsound. A says nothing to B about the unsoundness of the horse.

(a) A has committed fraud
(b) A has committed no fraud
(c) There cannot be a contract between a father and daughter
(d) The daughter did not ask therefore the father did not tell, hence no fraud

129. Principle: Whoever attempts to commit the offence of cheating, commits an offence.

Facts: A with an intention to defraud B, obtains from him an amount of Rs. 500.

(a) A has committed no offence
(b) A has committed the offence of cheating
(c) A has attempted to commit the offence of cheating
(d) A has attempted to commit and has committed the offence of cheating

130. Principle: Whoever by words publishes any imputation concerning any person is said to defame that person.

Facts: During a marriage ceremony, A circulated a pamphlet saying sister of the bride 'S' is a thief, she has stolen the shoes of the bridegroom.

(a) A defamed S
(b) A did not defame S
(c) A defamed the bridegroom
(d) A defamed the bride

131. Principle: An employer is liable for an injury caused to an employee in the course of the employment.

Facts: 'A' and 'B' were working in a factory as unskilled laborers. A was carrying a basket of stones on his head. B was sitting on the ground. When A crossed B, all of a sudden a stone fell down from the basket and hit B on his head. B died instantaneously.

(a) The employer will be liable
(b) The employer will not be liable
(c) A will be liable
(d) Both employer and A will be liable

132. Principle: Damages the money recompense, as far as money can do, for the loss suffered by a person.

Facts: A, an Indian citizen, having a right to vote, was not allowed to cast his vote on the polling booth, by the returning officer. Name of A was mentioned in the voter's list. A has also reported at the polling booth in time. However, the candidate in whose favor A would have cast his vote won the election. A filed a suit claiming damages.

(a) A will be entitled to damages
(b) A will not be entitled to damages
(c) A will be entitled to only nominal damages
(d) A will be entitled to exemplary damages

133. Principle: When a party to a contract has refused to perform, or disabled himself from performing, his promise in its entirety, the other party shall not put an end to the contract.

Facts: A engaged B on April 12 to enter his service on June 1, but on May 11, A wrote to B that his services would not be needed. On May 22, B joined C for employment.

(a) B cannot put the contract to an end.
(b) B can put the contract to an end.
(c) C can put his contract with B to an end.
(d) A must pay damages to B.

134. Principle: Everyone shall be permitted to take advantage of his own wrong.

Facts: A legatee was heavily drunk and driving his car at a speed of 100 Km/per hour in a crowded market. All of a sudden his testator came on the road. There were other people on the road at that time. The car driven by legatee hit the testator and four other persons. All the five persons hit by the car died.

(a) The legatee can take the benefit under the will
(b) The legatee cannot take the benefit under the will
(c) The legatee will be punished
(d) The property of the testator will go to his heirs

135. Principle: Property can be transferred only by a living person to another living person.

Facts: 'A' transfers property of which he is the owner in favor of the unborn child of B.

(a) Property has been transferred to the unborn child
(b) Property has been transferred to B
(c) Property has not been transferred to the unborn child
(d) Property will be transferred to the unborn child after his birth

136. Principle: An interest created, dependent upon a condition fails, if the fulfillment of the condition is impossible.

Facts: A promises to pay Rs. Ten Lakh to B on condition that he shall marry A's

(a) B's interest fails
(b) B's interest fail because of immorality
(c) B's interest fail because of prohibition by law.
(d) B's interest does not fail

137. Principle: A condition must be complied with after the happening of the event to which such a condition is attached.

Facts: A promises to pay Rs. 5,000 to B on the condition that he shall marry with the consent of C, D and E. B marries without the consent of C, D and E, but obtains their consent after the marriage.

(a) B has fulfilled the condition
(b) B has not fulfilled the condition
(c) The condition is illegal
(d) B must divorce his wife

138. Principle: A condition must be complied in order to claim the benefit of an agreement.

Facts: A agrees to transfer a farm to B, if B shall not go to England within three years after the date of the agreement, his interest in the farm shall cease. B does not go to England within the term prescribed.

(a) B's interest in the farm continues
(b) B's interest in the farm does not continue
(c) B has a fundamental right to go to England or not to go to England and hence the condition is illegal
(d) The agreement between A and B is void

139. Principle: Existence of all the alleged facts is relevant whether they occurred at the same time and place or at different times and places.

Facts: A, a citizen of England, is accused of committing murder of B in India by taking part in a conspiracy hatched in England.

(a) The facts that A accused of commission of murder and of conspiracy are relevant facts
(b) Only the fact that A is accused of committing murder of B is relevant
(c) Only the fact that A is accused of conspiracy hatched in England is relevant
(d) A citizen of England cannot be tried in India

140. Principle: One who asserts must prove.

Facts: A desires a Court to give judgment that B, C and D shall be punished for a crime which A says B, C and D have committed.

(a) A must prove that B, C and D were present at the place of crime
(b) A must prove that B, C and D have committed the crime
(c) B, C and D must prove that they have not committed the crime
(d) Police must prove that B, C and D have committed the crime

141. Principle: Foreign judgment binds the parties and is conclusive unless it is obtained by fraud.

Facts: A obtains judgment from US court by producing fake documents.

(a) New Suit can be filed in India on the same facts
(b) Judgment can be enforced in US
(c) Judgment can be enforced in India
(d) New suit can not be filed in India on same facts

142. Principle: Decision of Court is Null and Void, if it is given by court which does not have jurisdiction over the subject matter.

Facts: A obtains decision from a court which did not have jurisdiction to deal with the subject matter.

(a) Decision can be enforced because both the parties were present
(b) Decision cannot be enforced because decision is null and void
(c) Decision can be enforced because it is given a court
(d) Decision can be enforced

143. Principle: Civil Suit can be filed where defendant resides or carries on business or where cause of action arises.

Facts: 'A' carries on business in Gurgaon, 'B' carries on Business in Mumbai. 'B' through his agent in Gurgaon purchases goods in Gurgaon and takes delivery through agent in Gurgaon. Where Civil Suit for payment of price can be filed by 'A'?

(a) Gurgaon only where cause of action arises
(b) At Mumbai where B carries on Business
(c) At either of the places i.e. Mumbai or Gurgaon
(d) Anywhere in India

144. Principle: Civil Suit can be filed where defendant resides or carries on business or where cause of action arises.

Facts: An agreement is signed and executed in New Delhi between A and B for supply of goods wherein B is to supply goods to be delivered at New Dehli to client of A. A carries on business at Haryana and B carries on Business in UP. Civil suit by 'B' for payment of consideration can be filed against 'A' at

(a) Only at New Delhi, where cause of action arises
(b) Only at Haryana where 'A' carries on business
(c) Only at UP where 'B' carries on business
(d) At Haryana or at New Delhi

145. Principle: No court can execute the decisions unless it is having territorial jurisdiction over the property or the person against whom decision is to be executed. The Court which gave the decision can transfer the matter to the court which has the territorial jurisdiction over the person or property.

Facts: A decision is given by court at New Delhi on a contractual matter against X in a suit between X and Y. X is resident of Maharashtra and he has properties in Maharasthra and Gujarat.

(a) New Delhi court can transfer the proceedings to Court at Maharashtra only
(b) New Delhi court can execute the decision because it had the jurisdiction to decide the matter so it can execute also
(c) New Delhi court can transfer the proceedings to court at Gujarat only
(d) New Delhi court can transfer the proceedings to either of the courts i.e. Maharasthra or Gujarat

146. Principle: Nothing is an offence by reason of any harm it may cause to another person, if it is done in good faith and for the benefit of that person even without that person's consent.

Facts: A is attacked by a Lion and Lion drags him while he is crying for help. B, a passer by picks up A's gun in good faith and fires at Lion which injures A. B has never used the gun before.

(a) B is liable for the injury because he knew that he can injure A as he has never used any gun before
(b) B is not liable as he has done the act in good faith
(c) B is liable because he has not taken A's consent before firing
(d) B is liable because he has used A's gun without his consent

147. Principle: Nothing is an offence if it is done under intoxication and the person commiting the offence was incapable to understand the nature of the Act. Intoxication should be without knowledge or against the will of the person.

Facts: A, B and C were having a party in Bar where A pursuaded B and C to take alcoholic drinks. On the persistent pursuation B and C also consumed alcohol along with A. B and C had never consumed

alcohol before. After intoxiation, there was some argument between B and C where C pushed B with full force causing serious injury to B.
(a) C is liable
(b) C is not liable because he was intoxicated
(c) A is liable because A pursuaded them to consume alcohol whereas they had never consumed alcohol
(d) A and C both are liable

148. Principle: Everyone has the right of private defence to defend his body and property by use of reasonable force unless that person had time to have recourse to protection of public authorities.

Facts: X receives information at 5.00 pm that Y along with few friends is planning to burn his crop at midnight which is ready to be harvested. He does not inform the village Police Station which was just one kilometer away. He gathers his family members and directs them to collect some weapons in the form of swords and lathis to protect his field/crop. At around 11.00 pm Y and his aides attack the crop and a severe fight ensues wherein Y is seriously injured.
(a) X is not liable as he was exercising his right of private defence
(b) X and his family are not liable for the injuries caused as they were exercising the right of private defence
(c) X is liable
(d) X and his family is liable as they have not informed the police

149. Principle: Anyone who induces or attempts to induce a voter to vote in a particular manner on the ground that the voter will face divine displeasure, shall be guilty of offence of interfering with free exercise of right to vote.

Facts: During election campaign period one candidate X told the voters that if they do not vote for her, voters will be cursed because the election candidate is the God's own child and those who do not vote for her, they will not be liked by God.
(a) X has committed an offence
(b) X has not committed an offence because she only narrated what she felt
(c) X has not committed an offence because she has freedom of speech and expression
(d) X has not committed an offence because she did not compel anyone to vote for her

150. Principle: Doing of an act which causes common injury, danger or annoyance to public or which is likely to cause such injury or annoyance is Public nuisance. A common nuisance is not excused because it causes some nuisance or advantage.

Facts:'A' a farmer having large farmlands burns crop residue (stubble) on his fields after harvesting the crop to make the field ready for next crop as this is the easy, fast and convenient method of making the field ready for next crop. His farmlands are adjoining a densely inhabited residential area and people pass through the smoke while travelling on the road adjoining his farmlands. The smoke caused by fire also enters the houses in the colony
(a) A has not committed any offence since he does not cause any specific injury to any specific person
(b) A has not committed any offence because he does not gain any advantage from persons living in the vicinity
(c) A has committed public nuisance
(d) A has not committed any offence because the alleged acts are done on the fields owned and used by him and acts are done without any intention to cause harm.

151. Principle: Death caused by rash or negligent act of a person is an offence.

Facts: X was driving his SUV car in a lonely road leading to a forest at 160 km per hour. Suddenly, someone appears from the forest on the road and in the resultant accident, the car hits the commuter causing his death.
(a) X is not guilty of an offence as the accident has occurred on a lonely road
(b) X is not guilty because there was no intention to kill the deceased

(c) X is guilty of an offence death by rash or negligent act
(d) X is not guilty because he was also injured in the accident

152. Principle: Whoever causes death by rash or negligent act commits an offence.

Facts: X is having a house on the roadside which is also having a street on the back of the house. He has a lawn on the back of his house where he has built a toilet. To prevent the intruders from entering his house, he got the fence charged with a high voltage live electric wire. Z was passing through the street at the backyard of the house of X and sat down to take rest near the fence. While getting up, his hands came in contact with the fence which was connected to high voltage electric wire causing his death.

(a) X has not committed any offence because he has right to prevent trespass
(b) X has committed an offence of causing death by rash and negligent act
(c) X has committed no offence because he does not have any enmity with X
(d) X has committed an offence of Murder

153. Principle: Killing is not murder, if it is committed in a sudden fight without pre-meditation in a heat of passion upon a sudden quarrel.

Facts: X and Y were buying liquor from a liquor shop at 7 pm. Y abused X and there was quarrel between them. X told Y that he will not spare him and Y shouted that his house is adjoining the shop only and if X had the guts, he can come anytime. X went back to his shop which was nearby, procured a knife and went to Y's residence at 9 pm and stabbed him to death.

(a) X has committed murder
(b) X has not committed an offence of murder since it was committed in sudden fight in a heat of passion
(c) X has not committed murder of Y because he had no enimity with Y
(d) X has committed no offence

154. Principle: Use of criminal force intentionally knowing that it would cause or is likely to cause injury or annoyance to the person against whom force is used, is an offence.

Facts: X, a renowned social worker who had launched a movement for liberation of women, pulls up a Muslim women's veil in public in good faith without her consent causing annoyance to her.

(a) X is a renowned social worker and he has committed no offence because his motive was good
(b) X acted in good faith to liberate her from clutches of tradition and has hence has committed no offence
(c) X has done the act in public and not in secrecy therefore had not committed any offence
(d) X has committed an offence by use of criminal force

155. Principle: Inducing any animal to move or to change its motion and thereby intentionally causing fear of injury or annoyance to others by such act, is an offence of use of criminal force.

Facts: X incites his dog to chase and run after his neighbour Y, to teach Y to stay away from him. The act is done without neighbour' consent and against his will

(a) X has committed no offence
(b) X has committed no offence because no harm is caused to Y
(c) X has committed no offence because he intention only to put fear in the mind of Y
(d) X has committed an offence of use of criminal force

156. Principle: A spouse is not permitted to put in evidence in any court, any communication during marriage between the spouses without the consent of the person who made the communication.

Facts: X who is the wife of Y saw her husband (Y) coming out of the neighbour's house at 6.00 am in the morning. Y told his wife X that he has murdered the neighbour and handed over the jewellery of that neighbour to his wife.

(a) X is allowed to appear as a witness in court to depose that her husband has told her that he committed a murder
(b) X is not allowed to appear as a witness at all in any court
(c) X is not allowed to appear as a witness to depose what was told by the husband to her, however, she can depose what she saw
(d) X is an independent woman and she can do whatever she wants

157. Principle: Oral evidence must always be direct i.e. of the person who says he saw the event and hearsay evidence is no evidence.

Facts: X was told by Y (whom X trusts) that Z has murdered A
(a) Statement of X is admissible
(b) Statement of X is not admissible because he has not seen Z murdering A
(c) Statement of X is admissible because he trusts Y and Y never tells a lie
(d) Statement of X is admissible because he is a renowned social activist and has a huge reputation to fight for the truth

158. Principle: Terms of any written contract can be proved by producing the written contract only and oral evidence is excluded.

Facts: A gives B receipt for money paid by B. Oral evidence is offered to prove payment.
(a) Oral evidence to prove payment is allowed
(b) Oral evidence to prove payment is not allowed
(c) Oral evidence is always allowed to prove all facts
(d) Oral evidence is generally disallowed

159. Principle: Employer is liable for the injury caused to the employee in the course of his employment.

Facts: X organized a party and hired a caterer. During the party, generator set went out of order and he requested one employee of caterer i.e. Y to bring the mechanic on his vehicle and promised to pay 1000 for the same to Y. Y met with an accident while going to fetch the mechanic and he seeks compensation.
(a) X is liable as Y was working in the course of employment offered by X
(b) X is not liable as Y is not his employee
(c) X is liable because party was organized by him
(d) Caterer is liable as Y is his employee

160. Principle: Master is liable for the acts of his servant done in the course of his duties.

Facts: X hired an employee Y in his construction business. Y was the property in-charge who received construction material and gave receipts for the material received by him. Z claimed payment for cement supplied to X which was duly received by Y. X denied the payment on the ground that he has only received half of the material and the balance was misutilized by the employee Y.
(a) X is liable for the entire amount
(b) X is liable for the part amount only i.e. for payment of the cost of half of the material
(c) X is not liable for the misconduct/embezzlement of his employee
(d) Z can claim the balance payment only from Y

LOGICAL REASONING

161. If in English Alphabet 'e' and every alternate letter from 'e' onwards is written in Capitals, then how will sixth month from March will be coded
(a) SEPTEmbER
(b) SEptEMbEr
(c) SepTeMber
(d) SEPtEmbER

162. If in a certain code, 'Clever; is written as 'XOVEVI', then 'Smart' would written as
(A) HZNGI
(B) HNZIG
(C) GHNGI
(D) GIHZN

163. Fill in the blank : Q4RT, __________, QRT6, QR7T, Q8RT
(a) QTR7 (b) QR5T
(c) RQ9T (d) TRQ6

164. Fill in the blank : 257, 291, ________, 365, 405
(a) 313 (b) 322
(c) 327 (d) 343

165. Manoj walks a distance of 5 meters towards North, then he turns to east and walks a distance of 10 meters. Then he turns to his right and covers a distance of 15 meters. He then turns to his left and covers a distance of 15 meters. Which direction is he facing now?
(a) North (b) East
(c) West (d) South

166. A man introduces a girl as the daughter of the sister of his father. How the girl is related to the man
(a) Daughter
(b) Niece
(c) Grand daughter
(d) Cousin

Directions (questions 167–170): *Read the following information for questions 167 to 170 and chose the most appropriate option*:
P and Q are good in driving Motor cycle and Jeep. R and P are good in driving Jeep and Lorry. R, S and T are good in driving Motor Cycle and Lorry. T and R are good in driving Bus and Tempo. S and Q are good in driving Bus and Jeep.

167. Who is good in driving motorcycle, lorry and tempo?
(a) P (b) Q
(c) T (d) S

168. Who is good in driving motor Cycle, Jeep and Lorry but not bus?
(a) R (b) S
(c) P (d) T

169. Who is good in driving Tempo, Motor Cycle, Lorry but not Jeep?
(a) S (b) T
(c) R (d) Q

170. Who is good in driving all the vehicles?
(a) R (b) P
(c) S (d) T

171. In a bag there are some gold coins. In another bag there are 1/3rd extra gold coins as compared to first bag. If the difference in the number of gold coins in first and second bag is 5, then how many coins are there in the first bag?
(a) 7 (b) 9
(c) 13 (d) 15

Directions: *Examine the following numbers and identify the next number*:

172. 53, 50, 45, 38, 29, _____
(a) 11 (b) 17
(c) 18 (d) 21

173. 20, 30, 42, 56, 72, _____
(a) 82 (b) 90
(c) 92 (d) 94

174 The words in the bottom row are related in the same way as the words in the top row. Fill in the blank. Rose, Flower, Plant Flat, House, ____________
(a) City (b) Tent
(c) Building (d) Village

175. If Ocean: Waves, then Desert : ____________
(a) Water
(b) Sand
(c) Brave
(d) Sand dunes

176. If $1\times 7 = 8$, $2 \times 7 = 16$, $3 \times 7 = 24$, $4 \times 7 = 32$, then what is value of 9×7?
(a) 63 (b) 72
(c) 81 (d) 90

177. Find the odd one out :
Onlookers, Theatre goers, Queue, Spectators
(a) Onlookers
(b) Theatre goers
(c) Queue
(d) Spectators

178. Find the odd one out :
Heart, Lungs, Kidney, Liver
(a) Skin (b) Lungs
(c) Heart (d) Kidney

179. Find the odd - man out :
(a) http://www.scholar.gogle.com
(b) http://www.manupatra.com
(c) http://www.lexisnexis.com
(d) http://www.westlawindia.com

180. Find the odd one out :
Symphony, Orchestra, Guitar, Mob
(a) Guitar (b) Orchestra
(c) Mob (d) Symphony

Directions (questions 181–185):: *read the information given below to answer the Question*

(i) Mohan's reading schedule consists of reading only subject on a given day of week.
(ii) The subject are Physics, Chemistry, Mathematics, Biology, and Social Science.
(iii) Monday to Saturday are reading days including one day only for play. Sunday is a complete holiday for Mohan.
(iv) Mathematic day is neither on the first day on the last day but earlier than the chemistry day.
(v) Biology day is ob the immediate next day of chemistry day
(vi) Physics day is on the immediate next previous day of the play day.
(vii) Biology day and Social Science day have a gap of two days between them.
(viii) Social Science day on the immediate next say of the play day.

181. Which of the following day is the play day ?
(a) Monday (b) Tuesday
(c) Wednesday (d) Thursday

182. Which of the following day is the play day ?
(a) One (b) Two
(c) Three (d) Four

183. Which day is Social Science day ?
(a) Monday (b) Tuesday
(c) Wednesday (d) Thursday

185. Which of the following is the correct statement?
(a) Biology day is after Chemistry day
(b) Physics day is on Wednesday
(c) Play day is on Monday
(d) Chemistry day is earlier than Physics day

Directions (questions 186–190): *Read the information given below to answer the questions.*

A, B, C, D, E, F, G and H want to have a dinner on a round table and they have worked out the following seating arrangements.
(a) A will sit beside C.
(b) H will sit beside A.
(c) C will sit beside E.
(d) F will sit beside H.
(e) E will sit beside G.
(f) D will sit beside F.
(g) G will sit beside B.
(h) B will sit beside D.

186. Which of the following is wrong?
(a) A will be to the immediate right of C
(b) D will be to the immediate left of B
(c) E will be to the immediate right of A
(d) F will be to the immediate left of D

187. Which of the following is correct?
(a) B will be to the immediate left of D
(b) H will be to the immediate right of A
(c) C will be to the immediate right of F
(d) B will be to the immediate left of H

188. A and F will become neighbours if:
(a) B agrees to change her sitting position
(b) C agrees to change her sitting position
(c) G agrees to change her sitting position
(d) H agrees to change her sitting position

189. During sitting:
(a) A will be directly facing C
(b) B will be directly facing C
(c) A will be directly facing B
(d) B will be directly facing D

190. H will be sitting between:
(a) Cand B (b) Aand F
(c) Dand C (d) Eand G

Directions (questions 191–193): *Choose the set of three statements where the third statement can be logically derived from the preceding two.*

191. Statements:

1. Some students love reading.
2. Some adults do not love reading.
3. Some students are not adult.
4. Some students are adult.
5. No reading lover is an adult.
6. Some men do not love reading.

The set of statements is:

(a) 1, 3,4 (b) 1, 5,3
(c) 1, 2,4 (d) 6, 2,4

192. Statements:

1. All boys need books.
2. All girls need books.
3. Punjabis are girls.
4. Some Punjabis need book.
5. All boys are girls.
6. Some boys are Punjabis. The set of statements is:

(a) 5, 4,1 (b) 2, 5,3
(c) 6, 5,3 (D) 5, 2,1

193. Statements:

1. All human beings need education.
2. All teachers need training.
3. Education is provided by the teachers.
4. X is a teacher.
5. X needs training.
6. Students are future of a nation. The set of statements is:

(a) 1, 2,5 (b) 2, 3,4
(c) 2, 4,5 (d) 4, 5,6

Directions (questions 194–196): *Each of the following questions has a main statement followed by four statements: 1, 2, 3, 4. Choose the ordered pair of statements where the first statement implies the second, and the two statements are logically consistent with the main statement.*

194. Main statement: Only if the teaching standard is destroyed, will examination result be poor.

1. Examination result is poor.
2. Teaching standard is not destroyed.
3. Examination result is not poor.
4. Teaching standard is destroyed. The ordered pair of statements is:

(a) 2, 3 (b) 2, 4
(c) 1, 3 (d) 1, 2

195. Main statement: The computer will not work if operating system fails.

1. Operating system fails.
2. Operating system does not fail.
3. The computer does not work.
4. The computer works. The ordered pair of statements is:

(a) 2, 1 (b) 2, 3
(c) 1, 4 (d) 4, 2

196. Main statement: Either X or Y will take the only computer in the room.

1. X took the computer.
2. Y did not take the computer.
3. X did not take the computer.
4. Y took the computer. The ordered pair of statements is:

(a) 3, 1 (b) 1, 3
(c) 4, 3 (d) 1, 2

197. 'All men are mortal and Victoria is a woman and hence Victoria is mortal'. This statement is:

(a) Logically Valid
(b) Logically Invalid
(c) Logically True
(d) Logically False

198. All men are chairs. John Doe is a man. In logical language, therefore:

(a) John Doe is a chair
(b) John Doe is a human being and therefore he cannot be a chair
(c) A man cannot be a chair in any case
(d) Chairs can be men

199. Identify the missing number:

1 and 3,4 and 6,7 and 9, ...and 12

(a) 10 (b) 11
(c) 12 (d) 13

200. Cobra: Snake :: Greyhound : ___________

(a) Eagle (b) Black Mamba
(c) Python (d) Dog

ANSWER KEY

English

1. (d)	7. (d)	13. (c)	19. (a)	25. (d)	31. (d)	37. (b)
2. (b)	8. (b)	14. (b)	20. (c)	26. (d)	32. (c)	38. (b)
3. (d)	9. (c)	15. (d)	21. (d)	27. (a)	33. (a)	39. (c)
4. (a)	10. (d)	16. (c)	22. (c)	28. (b)	34. (b)	40. (d)
5. (c)	11. (d)	17. (a)	23. (b)	29. (d)	35. (d)	
6. (d)	12. (c)	18. (c)	24. (a)	30. (b)	36. (a)	

General Knowledge

41. (a)	49. (c)	57. (d)	65. (a)	73. (b)	81. (a)	89. (a)
42. (c)	50. (d)	58. (a)	66. (b)	74. (c)	82. (d)	90. (b)
43. (d)	51. (c)	59. (c)	67. (d)	75. (d)	83. (c)	
44. (a)	52. (d)	60. (b)	68. (a)	76. (a)	84. (a)	
45. (d)	53. (c)	61. (b)	69. (d)	77. (d)	85. (d)	
46. (c)	54. (a)	62. (a)	70. (a)	78. (a)	86. (c)	
47. (a)	55. (c)	63. (d)	71. (d)	79. (d)	87. (b)	
48. (b)	56. (b)	64. (d)	72. (d)	80. (a)	88. (d)	

Mathematics

91. (b)	94. (a)	97. (c)	100. (a)	103. (c)	106. (b)	109. (b)
92. (d)	95. (d)	98. (b)	101. (a)	104. (b)	107. (b)	110. (b)
93. (a)	96. (b)	99. (d)	102. (d)	105. (c)	108. (d)	

Legal Aptitude

111. (b)	119. (b)	127. (a)	135. (c)	143. (c)	151. (c)	159. (a)
112. (d)	120. (b)	128. (b)	136. (a)	144. (d)	152. (b)	160. (a)
113. (b)	121. (b)	129. (b)	137. (a)	145. (d)	153. (a)	
114. (d)	122. (d)	130. (a)	138. (b)	146. (b)	154. (d)	
115. (a)	123. (b)	131. (a)	139. (a)	147. (a)	155. (d)	
116. (a)	124. (a)	132. (b)	140. (b)	148. (d)	156. (c)	
117. (a)	125. (c)	133. (a)	141. (a)	149. (a)	157. (b)	
118. (a)	126. (d)	134. (a)	142. (b)	150. (c)	158. (a)	

Logical Reasoning

161. (b)	167. (c)	173. (b)	179. (a)	185. (a)	191. (b)	197. (b)
162. (b)	168. (c)	174. (c)	180. (c)	186. (c)	192. (d)	198. (a)
163. (b)	169. (b)	175. (d)	181. (b)	187. (b)	193. (c)	199. (a)
164. (c)	170. (a)	176. (b)	182. (d)	188. (d)	194. (a)	200. (d)
165. (d)	171. (d)	177. (c)	183. (c)	189. (c)	195. (d)	
166. (d)	172. (c)	178. (a)	184. (d)	190. (b)	196. (d)	

All India Law Entrance Test (2026-2019)

AILET 2026

SECTION A: ENGLISH

I. Read the given passage and answer the following questions by choosing the most appropriate response.

The advent of social media has dramatically transformed the way individuals consume and share information. In earlier times, people largely depended on newspapers, radio, or television as their primary sources of knowledge about the world. These were institutions that followed established editorial practices and fact-checking processes. With the rise of digital platforms, however, the traditional 'gatekeepers' of information have been bypassed. Today, anyone with internet access can create content, express an opinion, or broadcast an idea to a global audience within seconds. This shift has certainly democratized access and given voice to communities and individuals who were often ignored by mainstream media. Yet, this democratization comes with challenges. Alongside genuine voices, social media has also amplified misinformation, rumours, and half-truths. Unlike traditional journalism, where accountability and verification are built into the system, social media thrives on speed, virality, and emotion. A misleading headline, a misinterpreted statistic, or even a doctored image can travel across the world before fact-checkers have the chance to intervene. The consequences of such unchecked information can be serious, ranging from the spread of fear and panic to the manipulation of public opinion. The impact of this transformation extends beyond individual users to institutions and democracies. Political campaigns, corporate branding, and even social movements are now shaped by algorithms that decide what people see and when they see it. These algorithms prioritize engagement, often promoting content that provokes stronger emotional reactions rather than balanced analysis. As a result, echo chambers form, online spaces where people are repeatedly exposed to opinions that mirror their own, reinforcing biases and reducing openness to differing perspectives. This has contributed to increasing polarization in societies across the world. Moreover, the competition for attention has blurred the line between information and entertainment, leading to the rise of sensationalism even in serious public discourse. The credibility of expertise, too, has been undermined, as opinions from unverified sources are often placed on the same footing as evidence-based knowledge. In response, several governments and technology companies are exploring ways to promote digital literacy, enhance transparency in algorithms, and strengthen fact-checking collaborations. Ultimately, the challenge lies in balancing the openness of digital spaces with mechanisms that ensure responsibility and trustworthiness in public communication.

1. According to the passage, what is a key difference between traditional media and social media?
   (a) Traditional media is more entertaining than social media.
   (b) Social media is more regulated by governments than traditional media.
   (c) Traditional media is based on facts; social media is driven by emotion.
   (d) Social media cannot reach a global audience as traditional media can.

2. Which of the following is NOT mentioned as a consequence of the spread of unchecked information via social media?
(a) Spread of fear and panic
(b) Improvement in media literacy
(c) Manipulation of public opinion
(d) Amplification of misinformation

3. What is implied by the phrase 'traditional gatekeepers of information have been bypassed'?
(a) Traditional media is more widely used than ever
(b) Social media companies have begun hiring editors
(c) Traditional media is no longer the sole source of information
(d) Fact-checking has become more robust in the digital era

4. Which of the following best captures the central idea of the passage?
(a) Traditional journalism has become obsolete due to the rise of social media.
(b) Social media has made it easier to spread government propaganda.
(c) Social media has democratized information sharing but introduced challenges such as misinformation.
(d) People no longer rely on newspapers and television for any information.

5. In the context of the above passage, consider the following Assertion (A) and Reason (R), and select the appropriate option:

Assertion (A): Social media allows anyone with internet access to broadcast ideas to a global audience.

Reason (R): Traditional media platforms were exclusively available to trained journalists and editors.

(a) Both (A) and (R) are true, and (R) is the correct explanation of (A).
(b) Both (A) and (R) are true, but (R) is not the correct explanation of (A).
(c) (A) is true, but (R) is false.
(d) (A) is false, but (R) is true.

6. Which of the following approaches is identified in the passage as a constructive response to the challenges created by social media's algorithm-driven information environment?
(a) Integrating digital literacy and promoting greater transparency in platform algorithms
(b) Encouraging governments to regulate all online content before publication
(c) Relying on users to self-regulate misinformation without institutional support
(d) Expanding algorithmic reach to ensure content receives maximum engagement

7. Which of the following best illustrates the functioning of an 'echo chamber' on social media, as described in the passage?
(a) A user joins multiple discussion groups with differing viewpoints to better understand opposing perspectives on current issues.
(b) A fact-checking organization collaborates with social media companies to label misleading or false information online.
(c) A user frequently encounters posts that align with their political opinions because the platform's algorithm prioritizes content similar to what they have previously liked.
(d) A digital news outlet curates trending stories from diverse sources to ensure balanced coverage of global events.

II. Read the given passage and answer the following questions by choosing the most appropriate response.

I have still to be brother to a Prince, though I once came near to kinship with what might have been a veritable King, and was promised the reversion of a Kingdom, army, law-courts, revenue and policy, all complete. But today, I greatly fear that my King is dead, and if I want a crown, I must go and hunt it for myself. The beginning of everything was in a railway train upon the road to Mhow from Ajmir. There had been a deficit in the Budget, which necessitated travelling, not Second class, which is only half as dear as First class, but by Intermediate, which is very awful indeed.

There are no cushions in the Intermediate class, and the population is either Intermediate, which is Eurasian, or native, which, for a long night journey, is nasty; or Loafer, which is amusing though intoxicated. Intermediates do not patronize refreshment rooms. They carry their food in bundles and pots, and buy sweets from the native sweet meat sellers, and drink the roadside water. That is why in the hot weather, Intermediates are taken out of the carriages dead, and in all weathers are most properly looked down upon. My particular Intermediate happened to be empty till I reached Nasirabad, when a huge gentleman in shirt sleeves entered, and, following the custom of Intermediates, passed the time of day. He was a wanderer and a vagabond like myself, but with an educated taste for alcohol. He told daring tales of things he had seen and done, of out-of-the-way corners of the Empire into which he had penetrated, and of adventures in which he risked his life for a few days' food. 'If India were filled with men like you and me, not knowing more than the crows where they'd get their next day's rations, it isn't seventy millions of revenue the land would be paying, it's seven hundred million,' said he; and as I looked at his mouth and chin, I was disposed to agree with him. We talked politics, the politics of Loaferdom that sees things from the underside where the lath and plaster is not smoothed off, and we talked postal arrangements because my friend wanted to send a telegram back from the next station to Ajmir, which is the turning off place from the Bombay to the Mhow line as you travel westward. He had the air of one who had seen strange countries and stranger men, yet bore himself without vanity. There was a restless light in his eyes, the sort that belongs to men who have lived too long without a fixed purpose. When he spoke of the Empire, it was not with loyalty nor with bitterness, but with the detached amusement of one who has played his part and lost interest in the game. His laughter came easily, though it seemed to echo from some remembered hardship. It struck me then that his stories were less of adventure than of survival.

8. In the context of the passage, what does the word 'vagabond' mean?
(a) A respected officer
(b) Criminal on the run
(c) Homeless wanderer
(d) Spiritual Monk

9. The narrator implies that the Intermediate class is unpleasant because it lacks ________________
(a) ventilation and windows
(b) cushions and respectable company
(c) hygiene and privacy
(d) food and friendly passengers

10. What can we infer about the narrator's attitude toward the man he meets?
(a) He sees him as arrogant and unpleasant
(b) He envies his wealth and contacts
(c) He respects his courage and past life
(d) He doubts the truth of his stories

11. What does the narrator mean when he refers to 'politics of Loaferdom'?
(a) High-level political negotiations
(b) Corrupt behind-the-scenes dealings
(c) Policies crafted by beggars and thieves
(d) Observations from society's lowest ranks

12. What does the phrase 'looked at his mouth and chin' suggest in context?
(a) He was assessing his character for trustworthiness.
(b) He was noticing his facial features.
(c) He was judging the man's cleanliness.
(d) He found him good-looking and decent.

13. The narrator perceives the stranger as a:
(a) Cynic disillusioned with authority yet unbroken in spirit
(b) Sentimental dreamer longing for recognition
(c) Patriot hiding disappointment under forced laughter
(d) Contented traveller who found peace in detachment

14. When the narrator observes that the man's stories were 'less of adventure than of survival', he most likely implies that:

(a) The man exaggerated his experiences for dramatic effect
(b) His life excitement masked hardship and endurance
(c) He sought sympathy rather than admiration from his listener
(d) The narrator had grown weary of hearing tall tales of danger

III. Read the given passage and answer the following questions by choosing the most appropriate response.

Democracy, often hailed as the most equitable form of governance, is a system where power ultimately rests in the hands of the people. The word itself derives from the Greek words 'demos', meaning 'people' and 'kratos', meaning 'power' or 'rule'. Democracy aims to provide equal political participation and protect the individual freedoms of all citizens. However, while the ideal of democracy is simple, its practice is frequently complex and fraught with challenges. At its core, democracy functions on the principle of majority rule, yet it simultaneously guarantees the protection of minority rights.

This balance ensures that while the majority has the power to make decisions through voting, the fundamental rights of minorities are not trampled upon. Such a system requires consistent vigilance and respect for the rule of law. Without these, democracies can devolve into majoritarian tyranny or authoritarianism. The practice of democracy is not merely limited to voting in elections. It encompasses freedom of speech, an independent judiciary, a free press, and the protection of individual rights. These elements together create a political environment where citizens can express dissent, hold leaders accountable, and participate actively in decision-making. When any one component is weakened, the democratic process becomes vulnerable. In recent times, democracies worldwide have grappled with new challenges. The rise of misinformation and 'fake news' has eroded public trust in institutions and polarized societies. Social media platforms, meant to facilitate communication, have sometimes amplified divisive narratives and falsehoods. This has resulted in voter manipulation and a growing skepticism towards democratic processes. Literacy in media and critical thinking is increasingly vital to safeguard democracy from such threats. Economic inequality poses another significant challenge. While democracies promise equal rights politically, vast disparities in wealth and opportunity undermine this ideal. Economic power often translates into political influence, skewing representation and policy-making. This phenomenon raises questions about whether true democracy is achievable without addressing socioeconomic inequalities. Furthermore, the involvement of citizens is crucial. Democracy thrives when people are informed, engaged, and willing to participate beyond just casting votes. Civic education and awareness campaigns play an essential role in nurturing responsible citizenship. Apathetic or disengaged electorates weaken the democratic fabric, opening avenues for corruption and authoritarian tendencies. In conclusion, democracy is a dynamic and evolving system that requires constant effort to sustain. It is a system built on ideals of equality, freedom, and justice but challenged by human complexities and contemporary issues. The survival of democracy depends on the collective responsibility of governments and citizens to protect its pillars and ensure inclusive, fair governance.

15. The word 'democracy' originally means
(a) Rule by kings
(b) Power of the people
(c) Freedom from laws
(d) Majority rule only

16. What does 'inclusive' mean in the phrase 'inclusive, fair governance'?
(a) Exclusive (b) Accepting
(c) Limited to a few (d) Chaotic

17. In the context of the above passage, consider the following statements, and select the appropriate option:

Statement 1: Voting is the only element of democracy.

Statement 2: Freedom of speech and an independent judiciary are essential for democracy.

(a) Both statements are true and 2 is the correct explanation of 1.
(b) Both statements are true and 2 is not the correct explanation of 1.
(c) Statement 1 is false, but statement 2 is true.
(d) Statement 1 is true, but statement 2 is false.

18. What does 'vulnerable' as used in 'the democratic process becomes vulnerable' mean?
(a) Robust and well-protected
(b) Weak or exposed to harm
(c) Balanced and autonomous
(d) Completely undone and destroyed

19. Which of the following is NOT listed as a challenge faced by democracy?
(a) Shortage of essential natural resources impacting governance
(b) The spread of false information through social platforms
(c) Vast disparities in wealth affecting political influence
(d) Low levels of citizen participation and awareness

20. What role does economic inequality play in weakening democracy?
(a) It promotes a more equal distribution of power among citizens.
(b) It encourages policies that lessen disparities in economic opportunities.
(c) It permits the rich to exert undue influence over political decisions.
(d) It results in increased political engagement from all socioeconomic classes.

21. Identify the sentence in the passage that contains a participial phrase.
(a) Democracy aims to provide equal political participation and protect the individual freedoms of all citizens.
(b) Social media platforms, meant to facilitate communication, have sometimes amplified divisive narratives and falsehoods.
(c) This has resulted in voter manipulation and a growing skepticism towards democratic processes.
(d) Civic education and awareness campaigns play an essential role in nurturing responsible citizenship.

22. Which of the following best illustrates the paradox presented in the discussion of majority rule in a democracy?
(a) The majority rules but must respect minority rights.
(b) Democracies rely on citizens to choose leaders fairly.
(c) Economic inequality can lead to political inequality.
(d) Civic education helps citizens make better voting decisions.

23. Based on the passage, which statement best captures the author's perspective on the link between democracy and inequality?
(a) Democracies often tolerate economic inequality to preserve individual freedom.
(b) Socioeconomic inequality is a consequence, not a cause, of weakened democracies.
(c) Democratic systems are capable of functioning fairly despite economic gaps.
(d) Political equality cannot be fully realized without addressing economic disparities.

IV. Read the given passage and answer the following questions by choosing the most appropriate response.

In recent years, urban gardening has emerged as a widespread movement in cities across the globe. Prompted by increasing concerns surrounding food security, sustainability, and mental well-being, urban dwellers are reimagining their limited spaces, including balconies, rooftops, alleyways, and windowsills, as viable sites for food cultivation. At the heart of this shift lies the desire for fresh, organic produce, especially in cities where access to pesticide-free food remains both costly and inconsistent. By growing their own fruits, vegetables, and herbs, individuals can reduce their dependence on commercial supply chains, which often entail extensive transportation, energy consumption, and synthetic chemical use. This not only empowers consumers to take control of their dietary choices but also enhances awareness about nutrition, food origins, and environmental impact. Urban gardening is also lauded for its ecological contributions. Plants in urban environments combat the urban heat island effect, a condition where metropolitan areas are significantly warmer than their rural counterparts due to concentrated human activity and infrastructure. Vegetation improves air quality by absorbing carbon dioxide and releasing oxygen, while also managing rainwater runoff and reducing pressure on often-overburdened drainage systems. Yet, the advantages of urban gardening extend beyond the tangible. On a psychological level, cultivating plants offers therapeutic benefits, including reduced stress, improved mood, and greater mindfulness. In the high-speed urban landscape, tending to a plant provides a rare opportunity to engage with nature, fostering patience and a sense of achievement. For many, these small pockets of greenery represent not just a practical solution but an emotional and symbolic reclamation of space and agency. However, urban gardening is not without its limitations. Scarcity of space, inadequate sunlight, and poor soil quality pose significant hurdles. In response, gardeners have turned to innovative methods such as vertical farming, hydroponics, and compost enrichment. Moreover, community gardens in shared spaces have flourished, enabling collective effort, resource sharing, and social cohesion. While urban gardening may not supplant industrial agriculture, it marks a meaningful shift toward more localized, responsible, and connected living, an act as much philosophical as it is practical.

24. What is the 'urban heat island effect' mentioned in the passage?
(a) The rise in temperature commonly observed in tropical urban locations
(b) The condition where urban areas become warmer than rural ones due to human activity
(c) The method of using retained heat energy for rooftop gardening in cities
(d) The process through which cities generate and utilize renewable heat energy

25. Which innovative method mentioned in the passage directly addresses poor soil quality?
(a) Collecting rainwater through harvesting systems for irrigation
(b) Installing rooftop gardens with specially designed green covers
(c) Using compost enrichment to improve the fertility of the soil
(d) Growing herbs and vegetables in small boxes on window ledges

26. Why might urban residents be motivated to cultivate their own food rather than rely solely on commercial sources?
(a) To decrease expenses related to gardening equipment
(b) To eliminate the need for home meal preparation
(c) To obtain fresher produce free from synthetic chemicals
(d) To outperform grocery retailers in food production

27. Which of the following best captures the combined ecological significance of urban gardening?
(a) It lowers city temperatures, filters polluted air, and manages rainwater.
(b) It reduces transport costs while expanding industrial farm production.
(c) It prevents further growth of infrastructure and building construction.
(d) It substitutes completely for natural forests in urban environments.

28. Which of the following is NOT identified in the passage as a practical challenge faced by urban gardeners?
(a) The lack of organized communal support for local gardening efforts
(b) Inadequate access to direct sunlight in densely built environments
(c) Spatial constraints that limit the scale of cultivation in cities

(d) Soil conditions that are unsuitable for traditional planting methods

29. The phrase 'symbolic reclamation of space and agency' most appropriately refers to:
(a) Transforming unused industrial spaces into productive garden plots
(b) Using gardening practices as a subtle or direct form of civil protest
(c) Requesting access to public land from authorities for food cultivation
(d) Gaining emotional and psychological well-being through small-scale gardening

30. What assumption underlies the author's argument in favour of community gardens?
(a) Individuals are incapable of gardening alone.
(b) Social cooperation enhances the benefits of gardening.
(c) Community gardens are more cost-effective than private ones.
(d) Governments support all communal gardening efforts.

31. According to the passage, what deeper motivation underlies urban gardening beyond access to fresh food?
(a) Competing financially with existing industrial agricultural systems
(b) Seeking more autonomy over personal food and environmental choices
(c) Avoiding all types of reliance on common community food networks
(d) Replacing all large-scale commercial farming with individual gardens

32. Why is urban gardening described as 'an act as much philosophical as it is practical?
(a) Because it reflects cultural traditions rather than food requirements.
(b) Because it is mainly a contest with large-scale commercial farming.
(c) Because it provides a complete substitute for rural food production.
(d) Because it expresses values of sustainability, choice, and connection.

33. Which of the following best describes the role of 'innovation' in the success of urban gardening?
(a) It reduces the reliance on large public spaces for carrying out cultivation.
(b) It introduces creative methods to overcome space, soil, and sunlight limits.
(c) It eliminates the need for people to collaborate in shared gardening projects.
(d) It guarantees government funding to replace industrial farming completely.

V. Read the given passage and answer the following questions by choosing the most appropriate response.

The integration of Artificial Intelligence (AI) into law enforcement practices has sparked a global debate on ethics, privacy, and accountability. From facial recognition systems in public spaces to predictive policing algorithms, AI is transforming how crimes are detected and prevented. However, the benefits of efficiency and data-driven decision-making are accompanied by concerns about fairness, bias, and the potential erosion of civil liberties. One of the most controversial applications is predictive policing, which uses historical crime data to forecast where crimes are likely to occur or who might commit them. Proponents argue that this allows police to allocate resources more efficiently and reduce crime rates. However, critics warn that such systems may reinforce existing societal biases. If past data reflect biased policing practices, such as over-policing in marginalized communities, then the algorithm may perpetuate these injustices by disproportionately targeting the same areas or groups. Facial Recognition Technology (FRT) is another AI-driven tool that has gained traction. While it has proven useful in identifying suspects, it raises serious concerns regarding surveillance and individual privacy. Studies have also shown that FRT is less accurate in identifying people of colour and women, increasing the risk of false accusations and wrongful detentions. The lack of transparency in how these systems operate further complicates the ethical landscape. Many AI tools used in law enforcement are developed by private companies that treat their algorithms as proprietary, meaning that even law enforcement officers may not fully understand how decisions are made by these AI tools. This is often referred to as the 'Black Box' problem. This opaqueness undermines accountability, making it difficult to challenge wrongful predictions or decisions in a court of law. As AI continues to evolve, lawmakers and civil rights advocates are calling for stronger regulations to ensure that these technologies are used responsibly. Proposals include mandatory auditing of algorithms, public disclosure of data sources, and legal safeguards to protect against discrimination. Without such measures, the unchecked use of AI could lead to a justice system that prioritizes efficiency over equity, ultimately compromising democratic values and the rule of law. While AI holds the promise of revolutionizing law enforcement, its application must be guided by ethical frameworks that prioritize human rights, transparency, and fairness. Otherwise, technology intended to protect society may end up harming the very individuals it seeks to serve.

34. What is the central concern raised in the passage regarding AI in law enforcement?
(a) Replacing human officers
(b) High operational costs
(c) Reinforcing bias and reducing fairness
(d) Inability to analyze real-time data

35. Which of the following would best justify the use of predictive policing, despite the ethical concerns discussed in the passage?
(a) It will allow law enforcement to increase arrest quotas.
(b) It helps deploy police more efficiently in high-risk areas.
(c) It can eliminate the need for community engagement.
(d) It will replace the need for police training programs.

36. Based on the passage, how does facial recognition technology potentially lead to injustice?
(a) By exhibiting higher error rates for specific demographic groups
(b) By decreasing reliance on human judgment in policing
(c) By increasing costs and limiting deployment in critical areas
(d) By generating occasional misidentifications across all populations equally

37. Why does the lack of transparency in AI algorithms pose a challenge within judicial proceedings?
(a) It complicates efforts to scrutinize and contest algorithm-driven outcomes.
(b) It leads to greater reliance on community surveillance.
(c) It restricts the professional development of law enforcement personnel.
(d) It discourages investment in emerging AI technologies for policing.

38. The word 'opaqueness' in the paragraph refers to:
(a) Clear and understandable legal processes
(b) Lack of visibility or understanding
(c) Openness and transparency in systems
(d) Restricted access due to security levels

39. What measure is most essential to prevent AI systems from reinforcing existing social biases?
(a) Training AI systems on large datasets without reviewing for fairness
(b) Allowing AI tools to evolve independently without human oversight
(c) Reviewing training data for historical bias and ensuring algorithmic accountability
(d) Prioritizing efficiency and rapid deployment over fairness and oversight

40. A government proposes a new AI-driven sentencing tool that assigns prison terms based on statistical models trained on past sentencing data. The tool is designed to ensure consistency and eliminate human error. Civil liberties groups oppose the tool, arguing it may encode past judicial biases. Which of the following objections is most consistent with the concerns raised in the passage?

(a) AI systems should not be used in criminal justice unless they are cheaper than traditional methods.
(b) Sentencing tools can never make mistakes if trained on real court data.
(c) Without transparency and bias audits, AI may reinforce systemic injustices embedded in the data.
(d) Automated sentencing ensures faster trials and should replace human judges entirely.

41. Which of the following assumptions, if true, would undermine concerns raised in the paragraph?

(a) AI models incorporate bias-correction mechanisms that adjust for historical disparities in sentencing patterns.
(b) The training data used by the AI model reflects systemic inequalities and disproportionate sentencing against certain communities.
(c) The AI system operates as a closed algorithm, with no transparency regarding how sentencing decisions are derived.
(d) Studies from other jurisdictions show that similar AI systems have not amplified racial and gender biases in sentencing outcomes.

VI. Read the given book descriptions and answer the following questions by choosing the most appropriate response.

The Rule of Law by Tom Bingham	**Justice: What's the Right Thing to Do? by Michael J. Sandel**	**Letters to a Law Student by Nicholas J. McBride**
In *The Rule of Law*, former Lord Chief Justice Tom Bingham explores how the principle of legality underpins modern democratic life. He defines the rule of law as more than just adherence to formal rules, it is the assurance that power is exercised within clear, fair, and publicly known boundaries. Bingham distils the concept into eight principles, including equality before the law, access to justice, and respect for fundamental human rights. Drawing on cases and historical examples, he warns that national security and administrative efficiency must never override the rights of individuals. The book bridges legal philosophy and practice, arguing that law must be both predictable and humane. For Bingham, the rule of law represents a moral ideal, one that sustains public trust in justice and curbs arbitrary governance.	Michael Sandel's *Justice: What's the Right Thing to Do?* examines moral reasoning in law and politics. Through examples like price gouging, affirmative action, and taxation, Sandel invites readers to explore competing notions of fairness. He engages with philosophical traditions, utilitarianism, libertarianism, and Rawlsian egalitarianism, to show that questions of justice cannot be separated from questions of virtue and the common good. Sandel rejects the idea of a morally 'neutral' legal system, arguing that public deliberation about values is essential to democracy. His conversational style makes complex ideas accessible, while his conclusions challenge readers to evaluate how legal principles reflect collective moral choices. Ultimately, Sandel argues that a just society is one that cultivates civic responsibility, not merely individual rights.	Nicholas McBride's *Letters to a Law Student* is a practical and reflective guide for aspiring lawyers. Written as a series of letters to a student beginning law school, it explores what legal study truly involves: mastering case analysis, understanding precedents, and developing critical reasoning. McBride distinguishes between knowing the law and thinking like a lawyer, the latter requiring analytical discipline and ethical awareness. He emphasizes that good lawyers combine intellectual rigour with moral judgment and clarity of expression. Beyond academic success, McBride's letters urge students to reflect on the law's purpose, to balance order, justice, and compassion in human affairs. The book thus offers both pragmatic advice and a deeper meditation on the vocation of law in shaping a fair society.

42. According to Tom Bingham, the rule of law primarily serves to:
(a) Guarantee the enforcement of criminal sanctions and civil penalties in equal measure.
(b) Ensure that the exercise of public power remains fair, transparent, and subject to moral constraint.
(c) Promote the swift execution of governmental decisions for administrative convenience.
(d) Establish the authority of the judiciary over all branches of governance in perpetuity.

43. From Sandel's argument, one may reasonably infer that he would most likely:
(a) Support limiting ethical debates in law to preserve neutrality in governance.
(b) Oppose moral discussion in legal reasoning as a source of subjective bias.
(c) Encourage public reasoning about moral values as essential to a democratic legal order.
(d) Suggest that moral philosophy and legal practice should remain entirely independent disciplines.

44. The phrase 'arbitrary governance' in Bingham's description most nearly means:
(a) Government based on fixed and universally accepted principles.
(b) Authority exercised without consistency, justification, or accountability.
(c) Decision-making guided by collective moral judgment and civic consensus.
(d) Administrative action founded on transparent, legal, and rational reasoning.

45. In the context of the above passage, consider the following Assertion (A) and Reason (R), and select the appropriate option:

Assertion (A): McBride believes that studying law is not merely about acquiring knowledge of legal rules.

Reason (R): He argues that true legal understanding requires both analytical
skill and ethical reflection.

(a) Both (A) and (R) are true, and (R) is the correct explanation of (A).
(b) Both (A) and (R) are true, but (R) is not the correct explanation of (A).
(c) (A) is true, but (R) is false.
(d) (A) is false, but (R) is true.

46. Which of the following conclusions can be logically deduced as a point of agreement among the perspectives of the three authors?
(a) Justice is attainable only when laws remain morally neutral and socially detached.
(b) Legal education and moral philosophy are unrelated domains of study.
(c) Legal authority should rest solely on codified statutes and administrative precedents.
(d) Law must integrate both technical precision and moral purpose to maintain legitimacy.

47. If McBride were to respond to Bingham's conception of the rule of law, he would most likely argue that:
(a) Moral ideals should not interfere with the practical application and interpretation of legal principles.
(b) The cultivation of ethical reasoning in lawyers strengthens, rather than weakens, the rule of law.
(c) Legal predictability and procedural certainty must always prevail over questions of moral reflection.
(d) The ethical dimension of law remains largely irrelevant to the duties and functions of legal practitioners.

48. Which of the following can be reasonably inferred from the combined viewpoints of Bingham, Sandel, and McBride?
(a) Law must balance procedural clarity with the ethical responsibilities of those who interpret it.
(b) Legal education should remain separate from broader moral and civic discussions in society.
(c) The authority of law depends primarily on its technical accuracy and institutional hierarchy.
(d) The legitimacy of justice systems is secured when personal morality is excluded from legal reasoning.

49. According to the passage, which thinker most directly connects the study of law to practical skill and ethical reflection for future practitioners?

(a) Tom Bingham, by emphasizing moral ideals and public trust in justice.

(b) Michael Sandel, by analyzing competing philosophical theories of fairness and civic virtue.

(c) Nicholas McBride, by guiding students on case analysis, critical reasoning, and ethical judgment.

(d) All three equally focus on legal practice rather than theory or moral reasoning.

50. Which of the following statements best represents the philosophical core common to all three books?

(a) The integrity of law depends upon the harmonious integration of justice, morality, and human reason.

(b) The moral relevance of law diminishes when interpreted through abstract ethical theories.

(c) Legal philosophy and professional ethics must function independently to preserve objectivity.

(d) The practice of law attains legitimacy only when it excludes moral and civic considerations.

SECTION B: CURRENT AFFAIRS AND GENERAL KNOWLEDGE

51. Iga Swiatek won the Women's Singles title at the 2025 Wimbledon Championships. Who did she defeat in the finals?

(a) Marketa Vondrousova

(b) Amanda Anisimova

(c) Barbora Krejcikova

(d) Jasmine Paolini

52. Madhubani painting is a famous art form of which Indian state?

(a) Rajasthan (b) Bihar

(c) Gujarat (d) West Bengal

53. The Ministry of Defence has decided to observe 2025 as the ' Year of Reforms' with the aim of:

(a) enhancing defence manufacturing capabilities to achieve full self-reliance and global competitiveness

(b) strengthening inter-services collaboration for improved operational synergy and resource use

(c) enhancing welfare measures for ex-servicemen and their families through comprehensive support systems, improved resettlement schemes, and better healthcare access

(d) transforming the Armed Forces into a technologically-advanced, combat-ready force capable of multi-domain integrated operations

54. 'Chu-faat' is a dance form associated most prominently with the state of

(a) Tripura

(b) Sikkim

(c) Jharkhand

(d) Chhattisgarh

55. The 2025 Nobel Peace Prize was awarded to Maria Corina Machado. She received the prize for:

(a) promoting democratic rights for the people of Venezuela and the struggle to achieve a just and peaceful transition from dictatorship to democracy.

(b) efforts to mediate peace negotiations between the State of Israel and Hamas, and for the protection of children orphaned due to the conflict.

(c) advocacy for women's education and leadership in post-conflict communities affected by drug cartel violence in Columbia.

(d) championing various on-ground initiatives supporting refugee rights and humane asylum policies and practices in Hungary.

56. India's first woman Chief Minister was:

(a) Nandini Satpathy

(c) Janaki Ramachandran

(b) Sucheta Kripalani

(d) Sheila Dikshit

57. Match the following:

	Tribe		State
I	Damor	A	Rajasthan
II	Reang	B	Tripura
III	Gaddi	C	Himachal Pradesh
IV	Sora	D	Orissa

Select the most appropriate option:
(a) A-I, B-III, C-II, D-IV
(b) A-I, B-II, C-III, D-IV
(c) A-IV, B-III, C-I, D-II
(d) A-II, B-I, C-IV, D-III

58. Which of the following is India's first indigenously discovered antibiotic noted for its effectiveness against resistant respiratory infections?
(a) Biofungicin
(b) Cephalexin-M
(c) Polymyxin-N
(d) Nafithromycin

59. Which of the following countries has NOT formally recognised Palestine as a state?
(a) France (b) Canada
(c) Australia (d) Japan

60. The India-AI Impact Summit 2026 will be the first-ever global AI summit to be hosted in a Global South nation. Deliberations at the Summit will be organized around seven interconnected Chakras, i.e., areas of multilateral cooperation designed to channel collective energy towards holistic societal transformation. Which of the following is NOT specifically noted as a chakra?
(a) Resilience, Innovation and Efficiency
(b) AI Governance and Regulation
(c) Inclusion for Social Empowerment
(d) Science

61. Recently, India announced its vision of MAHASAGAR, expanding its maritime engagement from a regional to a global outlook, with particular focus on the Global South. This initiative seeks to promote security and growth through cooperative partnerships with maritime and island states, strengthening defence, economic, and developmental collaboration, and advancing humanitarian and capacity-building efforts. What does it stand for?
(a) MegaRegional Alliance for Holistic Advancement of Security Across Geopolitical Areas
(b) Mutual and Holistic Advancement for Security and Growth Across Regions
(c) Maritime Alliance for Security and Growth Across the Regions
(d) Mutual Advancement for Humanitarian Aid and Security Across Geopolitical Areas

62. There is a rich diversity of regional music in India. Match the following:

	Music		State
A	Sohar	I	Manipur
B	Sana Lamok	II	Uttar Pradesh
C	Laman	III	Maharashtra
D	Powada	IV	Himachal Pradesh

Select the most appropriate option:
(a) A-I, B-III, C-II, D-IV (b) A-I, B-II, C-III, D-IV
(c) A-IV, B-III, C-I, D-II (d) A-II, B-I, C-IV, D-III

63. Which 1971 study conducted at a major US University by Philip Zimbardo, often cited in discussions on abuse of power and institutional accountability, did college students, randomly assigned contrasting social roles within a simulated correctional environment, begin exhibiting extreme behaviours that revealed the powerful influence of situational factors on human conduct and authority?
(a) The Milgram Obedience Experiment
(b) The Stanford Prison Experiment
(c) The Robbers Cave Experiment
(d) The Bobo Doll Experiment

64. Who among the following is NOT a Bharat Ratna Awardee?
(a) PV Narasimha Rao
(b) LK Advani

(c) Bhupendra Kumar Hazarika
(d) Ratan Naval Tata

65. International Women's Day is celebrated on
(a) 8th March (b) 8th May
(c) 8th July (d) 8th December

66. In addition to the National Literary Awards, many states also confer Literary Awards. Match the following awards with the state that presents them:

State		Literary Award	
A	Gujarat	I	Sur Samman
B	Haryana	II	Ezhuthachan Puraskaram
C	Kerala	III	Thiruvalluvar Award
D	Tamil Nadu	IV	Sahitya Gaurav Puraskar

Select the most appropriate option:
(a) A-I, B-III, C-II, D-IV
(b) A-IV, B-I, C-II, D-III
(c) A-IV, B-III, C-I, D-II
(d) A-II, B-I, C-IV, D-III

67. Which country instituted proceedings against Israel before the International Court of Justice, alleging that Israeli military action in Gaza violated the Genocide Convention?
(a) India (b) Belgium
(c) France (d) South Africa

68. Who were the officers who conducted the press briefings on Operation Sindoor?
(a) Wing Commander Vyomika Singh and Colonel Sofiya Qureshi
(b) Wing Commander Bhumika Sharma and Colonel Zainab Iqbal
(c) Wing Commander Niharika Vyas and Colonel Fatima Ahmed
(d) Wing Commander Vandana Chhatwal and Colonel Amina Khurshid

69. Who recently took charge as the first Woman Prime Minister of Japan?
(a) Yuriko Koike (b) Sanae Takaichi
(c) Seiko Noda (d) Renho Murata

70. India recently achieved a major breakthrough in gene therapy, marking the first successful indigenous clinical trial for haemophilia treatment. The trial was supported by the Department of Biotechnology, Government of India and was done in which major hospital?
(a) Christian Medical College, Vellore
(b) AIIMS, New Delhi
(c) Tata Memorial Hospital, Mumbai
(d) King George Medical College, Lucknow

71. Which franchise won the 2025 edition of the Indian Premier League (IPL)?
(a) Mumbai Indians
(b) Royal Challengers Bengaluru
(c) Gujarat Titans
(d) Chennai Super Kings

72. The GRAP framework was introduced as an emergency response mechanism to combat the extreme air quality and pollution conditions in Delhi-NCR. What does GRAP stand for?
(a) Generalised Response Assessment Protocol
(b) Graded Response against Air Pollution
(c) Graded Response Action Plan
(d) Ground-level Restoration and Action Policy

73. Organic fisheries cluster focuses on an ecologically healthy fish farming system, avoiding the use of harmful chemicals, antibiotics and pesticides. This also ensures minimal environmental pollution and prevents damage to aquatic ecosystems, contributing to sustainable fish production practices. A first-of-its-kind organic fisheries cluster in India was launched in:
(a) Jangoan, Telangana
(b) Soreng, Sikkim
(c) Nanded, Maharashtra
(d) Birbhum, West Bengal

74. The nPROUD initiative, aimed at the collection and safe disposal of unused and expired medicines in a scientific manner, was recently launched by which State?
(a) Uttar Pradesh (b) Telangana
(c) Bihar (d) Kerala

75. During the Republic Day parade, states showcase their culture, heritage, and achievements through vibrant tableaux. Which state won the Best State Tableau prize for its creative and thematic presentation in 2025?
(a) Gujarat (b) Rajasthan
(c) Uttar Pradesh (d) Madhya Pradesh

76. The National Quantum Mission (NQM), launched in 2023, aims to seed, nurture, and scale up scientific and industrial R&D, and create a vibrant ecosystem in Quantum Technology (QT) in India. Four Thematic Hubs (T-Hubs) were established under NQM to strengthen India's position as a global leader in quantum technology. These hubs are located in:
(a) IISC Bengaluru; IIT Madras; IIT Bombay; IIT Delhi
(b) National Innovation Foundation, Ahmedabad; IIT Kharagpur; IIT Delhi; SN Bose National Centre for Basic Science, Kolkata
(c) Institute of Nano Science and Technology, Mohali; IIT Roorkee; JNU Delhi; North East Centre for Technology Application and Reach Meghalaya
(d) IIT Madras; National Academy of Sciences Allahabad; IISc Bengaluru; Tata Institute of Fundamental Research

77. Which of the following series was awarded the Best Series 2025 at the International India Film Awards (IIFA) Digital Awards 2025, held in Jaipur?
(a) Patal Lok (b) Bandish Bandits
(c) Panchayat(d) Kota Factory

78. In late 2024, Google announced the development of a state-of-the-art quantum chip, which is considered to be a big step towards developing a large-scale, error-corrected quantum computer. The chip is named:
(a) Sentinel (b) Willow
(c) Polaris (d) Orion

79. Indian Railways has introduced a number of initiatives to improve passenger services. Match the following initiatives with their focus areas:

	Initiative		Focus areas
A	Amanat	I	Regular drives are conducted by RPF against touts and action is taken against persons found involved
B	Matrishakti	II	Acting against the menace of unauthorized hawking and vending in Railway premises and in trains
C	Uplabdh	III	Cases of left behind passengers' luggage are secured and handed over them to the right person
D	Dusra	IV	Ladies RPF personnel assist pregnant women who go into labour during train journeys

Select the most appropriate option:
(a) A-I, B-III, C-II, D-IV
(b) A-III, B-IV, C-I, D-II
(c) A-IV, B-III, C-I, D-II
(d) A-II, B-I, C-IV, D-III

80. NITI Aayog, in collaboration with DP World, recently announced the *'We Rise'* initiative. The initiative aims to:
(a) promote rural women's participation in local self-governance through leadership and digital literacy training.
(b) encourage women in STEM fields through scholarships and industry–academia collaborations.
(c) provide microfinance support to women-led self-help groups in aspirational districts.
(d) help women entrepreneurs in India to scale their businesses globally through trade facilitation, mentorship, and strategic partnerships.

SECTION C: LOGICAL REASONING

81. Complete the series: A1B, D4E, H9I, M16N, ___
(a) S25T (b) R25S
(c) R24S (d) S25R

82. All Birds can Fly. All Penguins are Birds. Some Birds Migrate. Some who Migrate Swim. Which of the following conclusions necessarily follows?
(a) Penguins can fly.
(b) All who migrate are birds.
(c) Penguins migrate long distances.
(d) No birds can swim.

83. In a certain code, LIGHT is written as NKKFR. How is CLOUD written in that code?
(a) ENSSA (b) FNRRA
(c) ENSSB (d) DORRB

84. Complete the following series: B2, E4, I8, N16, ________
(a) T30 (b) S32
(c) T32 (d) U34

85. Doctor : Hospital = ?
(a) Chef : Recipe (b) Driver : Engine
(c) Soldier : Parade (d) Teacher : Classroom

86. Online grocery stores in Delhi have reported a 50% increase in sales over the past year. Analysts attribute this to the convenience of home delivery and competitive pricing. Which of the following must be assumed for the analysts' conclusion to hold?
(a) Customers in Delhi value convenience over in-store shopping.
(b) Grocery store employees prefer working in delivery services.
(c) Online grocery stores are more profitable than physical stores.
(d) All customers in Delhi have access to the internet.

87. Some Birds are Flightless. All Sparrows are Birds. All Birds have Beaks. Which of the following conclusions necessarily follow?
I. All Sparrows have Beaks.
II. Some Flightless are Sparrows.
III. Some Beaked are Flightless. Select the most appropriate option
(a) Only I follows
(b) Both I and III follow
(c) Both II and III follow
(d) Only III follows

88. All Contracts are Agreements. Some Agreements are Void. No Void is Enforceable. Which of the following conclusions necessarily follow? I. Some Contracts are not Enforceable.
II. No Enforceable is Void.
III. Some Agreements are not Enforceable. Select the most appropriate option:
(a) Both II and III follow
(b) Only II follows
(c) Only I follows
(d) Only III follows

89. All Scripts are Code. Some Code is Optimized. No Optimized code is Verbose. Which of the following conclusions necessarily follow?
I. Some Scripts are Verbose.
II. Some Code is not Verbose.
III. All Scripts are Optimized.
Select the most appropriate options:
(a) Only II follows
(b) Only I follows
(c) Both I and II follow
(d) Only III follows

90. A study shows that students in schools with longer library hours read more books. Policymakers conclude that extending hours will increase reading everywhere. Which assumption underlies this conclusion?
(a) Students will utilize the extended hours to read books.
(b) Students in those schools are more intelligent.
(c) Infrastructure costs are irrelevant.
(d) Reading depends only on hours, not on resources or programmes.

91. A company switches to a 4-day workweek and observes no productivity drop. Leaders claim the schedule is efficient. Which assumption is needed to support the leaders' claim?

(a) Productivity was measured accurately and comparably before and after the change.
(b) Employees prefer longer weekends due to a higher tendency to burnout in longer weeks.
(c) Office rent decreased after the switch since people were only coming in for four days.
(d) Competitors already use a 4-day workweek.

92. Recruiters prefer candidates from top-tier colleges, believing they perform better. Which assumption underpins this practice?
(a) Top-tier graduates always outperform others.
(b) Interviewers dislike screening many applicants.
(c) Reputation matters more than skill.
(d) College brand is a reliable proxy for a candidate's likely performance.

93. A survey finds that most employees prefer flexible hours over a higher salary.
Which inference is most reasonable?
(a) Work-life balance is highly valued.
(b) Salary is unimportant to everyone.
(c) Only young workers were surveyed.
(d) Employees don't want promotions.

94. 4, 9, 19, 34, 54, ?
(a) 69 (b) 74
(c) 79 (d) 84

95. 3, 5, 9, 17, 33, ?
(a) 49 (b) 57
(c) 63 (d) 65

96. Oxygen : Lungs = Fuel : ?
(a) Car (b) Engine
(c) Road (d) Energy

97. Author : Book = Composer : ?
(a) Piano (b) Symphony
(c) Stage (d) Scorecard

98. 4, 10, 18, 28, ?
(a) 46 (b) 42
(c) 40 (d) 48

99. Shopkeepers are Big. Some Big persons violate night curfew. All who violate night curfew are fined. Anil is Big. Examine the following statements:
I. Anil is a Shopkeeper
II. Anil may violate a night curfew
III. Anil will definitely violate night curfew IV. If Anil is a shopkeeper, he will get fined V. Anil will definitely get fined
Select the correct option:
(a) Only I, III and IV (b) Only II
(c) Only I and III (d) Only I and V

100. Some Cyclists are Marathoners. All Marathoners train rigorously. Some Trainees are Amateurs. Which of the following conclusions necessarily follows?
(a) Some cyclists train rigorously
(b) All cyclists are amateurs
(c) No trainee is a marathoner
(d) Some amateurs are marathoners

101. All Poets write Poems. Some Poets are Critics. No Critic ignores Structure.
Which of the following conclusions necessarily follows?
(a) Some poets do not ignore structure
(b) All critics write poems
(c) No poet is a critic
(d) Some critics do not write poems

102. The University examination department is attempting to devise a schedule for the end-of-term examination. The subjects are Constitutional Law, Taxation, Regulatory Governance, Sociology and Criminal Law. The following considerations must be kept in mind.
I. Regulatory Governance must follow Criminal Law.
II. Sociology and Criminal Law cannot immediately precede or follow each other.
III. Regulatory Governance must immediately precede Taxation.
IV. Constitutional Law cannot be the first or the last exam.
V. Examinations for all subjects are held once. Which of the following schedules is a valid schedule?
(a) Sociology, Criminal Law, Constitutional Law, Regulatory Governance, Taxation

(b) Constitutional Law, Criminal Law, Regulatory Governance, Taxation, Sociology
(c) Sociology, Constitutional Law, Criminal Law, Regulatory Governance, Taxation
(d) Criminal Law, Constitutional Law, Taxation, Regulatory Governance, Sociology

103. Some Apps are Free. All Free Apps have Ads. Some Ad-supported Apps are highly rated. Which of the following conclusions necessarily follows?
(a) Some free apps are highly rated.
(b) All highly rated apps have ads
(c) No free app is highly rated
(d) All ad-supported apps are free

104. Recycling bins are placed in a mall, and trash volume falls. Which assumption is necessary to claim recycling caused the drop?
(a) People are driven towards recycling, given the opportunity
(b) The aesthetics of the recycling infrastructure drives usage
(c) Mall footfall remained stable during the observation period
(d) Mall introduced fees for usage of bins

105. Introducing cycling lanes reduces minor collisions in a district. Which of the following more strongly supports the causal link between these events?
(a) A decline in collisions was largely confined to stretches of road where the new cycling lanes were introduced, with little change elsewhere in the district.
(b) After the introduction of the cycling lanes, the local government also launched a citywide awareness campaign promoting road safety for all commuters.
(c) Data from the same period show that average vehicular traffic volumes declined due to fuel price increases and the expansion of public transport routes.
(d) Several nearby districts, which did not introduce cycling lanes, reported similar reductions in minor collisions during that year.

106. Free school meals increased attendance. Which assumption is needed to claim that free meals caused attendance to rise?
(a) Meal distribution was the main change during the period.
(b) Teachers were more vigilant about taking attendance.
(c) School built new classrooms that could accommodate more students.
(d) Local incomes doubled, leading to a flux of new admissions.

107. All Architects are Visionary. Some Visionary people are Designers. No Designer is a Lawyer. Which of the following conclusions necessarily follows?
I. Some Visionary people are not Lawyers.
II. Some Architects are Designers.
III. All Designers are Visionary. Select the most appropriate option:
(a) I and III follow (b) Only I follows
(c) Only III follows (d) I and II follow

108. All Astronauts are Smokers. All Drivers Ski. Some Astronauts are Drivers. Kamlesh is an Astronaut.
I. Kamlesh Skis.
II. Kamlesh does not Ski.
III. Kamlesh is a Smoker.
IV. Kamlesh is not a Smoker.
V. Kamlesh is a Driver.
VI. Kamlesh is not a Driver.
Select the most appropriate response:
(a) Only III and VI (b) Only III
(c) Only I and V (d) Only V

109. Complete the following series: C, FGH, MNOPQ,
(a) XZBDFHI (b) YZBCEFG
(c) XYZABCD (d) YZABCDF

110. All renewable energy plants are environment friendly. Some solar plants are renewable energy plants. No coal plant is environment friendly.

Which of the following conclusions necessarily follows?
I. Some solar plants are environment friendly.
II. No coal plant is a renewable energy plant.
III. Some coal plants are solar plants.

Select the most appropriate option:
(a) I and II follow (b) Only I follows
(c) II and III follow (d) All follow

111. All scientists hold Ph.D. Some engineers are scientists. No scientist works without access to the laboratory. Which of the following are the most appropriate conclusions?
I. All scientists work in the laboratory.
II. Some engineers have a Ph.D.
III. All engineers are scientists. Select the most appropriate option:
(a) I and II follow
(b) I and III follow
(c) Only I follows
(d) All follow

For Questions 112-113

The phenomenon of urbanization has led to significant changes in social structures and community interactions. As people migrate from rural areas to cities, they often face challenges such as increased cost of living, social isolation, and a disconnection from their traditional support networks. Studies indicate that urban residents tend to form new types of relationships, often relying on informal networks and community groups to adapt to their new environments. While urban living can foster innovation and economic opportunities, it can also contribute to feelings of loneliness and a decline in mental health if social connections are not established.

112. If the above is true, which of the following conclusions is most contradicted by it?
(a) Urbanization creates both opportunities and challenges for individuals transitioning from rural to urban living.
(b) Social isolation in urban areas can negatively impact individuals' mental health and well-being.
(c) People who migrate to cities typically maintain their traditional support networks from their rural communities.
(d) Informal networks and community groups are essential for urban residents to establish new social connections.

113. If the above is true, which of the following can be most readily inferred from the passage?
(a) The economic benefits of urbanisation outweigh its social and psychological costs for most urban residents.
(b) Migration to urban areas invariably leads to social isolation and deteriorating mental health among new residents.
(c) Urban living inherently discourages the formation of meaningful interpersonal relationships.
(d) Urbanisation transforms traditional social ties but compels individuals to seek alternative forms of community to sustain social well-being.

114. All teachers are creative people. All creative people are sensitive. No insensitive person is a teacher. Which of the following conclusions necessarily follows?
I. Some sensitive people are teachers.
II. All sensitive people are teachers.
III. No teacher is insensitive.
Select the correct option:
(a) Only I (b) Only II and III
(c) Only I and III (d) I, II and III

115. Anamika complains that in her debate club, she is always assigned to the less-preferred side of the argument, while another member consistently gets the more popular choice. Which of the following, if true, supports Anamika's complaint?
(a) Assignments are rotated randomly, and Anamika's side often ends up unpopular by chance.
(b) The club president privately admits giving the popular side to the other member due to personal friendship.
(c) Both members are equally skilled in debating.
(d) Anamika has only recently joined the club.

116. Principle: A driver is responsible for controlling their vehicle and avoiding harm to pedestrians, unless the pedestrian acted recklessly or unlawfully.

Facts: A driver hits a pedestrian who suddenly runs across the road outside a crosswalk without looking. The driver was obeying all traffic rules. Which of the following is correct?
(a) The driver is liable for the pedestrian's injuries.
(b) The pedestrian's reckless action absolves the driver of liability.
(c) Both the driver and pedestrian share liability equally.
(d) The driver is always liable in pedestrian accidents.

117. Justice : Law = ?
(a) Medicine : Doctor
(b) Governance : Policy
(c) Teacher : School
(d) Engineer : Bridge

118. Keyboard : Typist = Paintbrush : ?
(a) Artist (b) Canvas
(c) Painting (d) Colour

119. Roots : Tree = Foundation : ?
(a) House (b) Wall
(c) Architecture (d) Floor

120. **Principle:** A public official must avoid conflicts of interest that could undermine public trust, even if no actual wrongdoing occurs.

Facts: A city mayor awards a major construction contract to a company owned by her cousin. She discloses the relationship publicly and follows all procurement procedures.

Apply the principle and select the most appropriate option:
(a) contract should proceed since procedures were followed.
(b) contract should be avoided to maintain public trust.
(c) cousin should sell the company before bidding.
(d) mayor should resign.

121. The numbers in the series 3, 9, 27, , 243, follow a pattern. What is the missing number?
(a) 30 (b) 60
(c) 81 (d) 90

122. Every Mathematician is a Statistician. Some Statisticians are also Computer Scientists. No Computer Scientist is a Mathematician. Which of the following conclusions necessarily follows?
I. Some Statisticians are not Mathematicians.
II. All Statisticians are Computer Scientists.
III. Some Mathematicians are Computer Scientists.
Select the most appropriate option:
(a) Only I (b) Only II and III
(c) Only I and III (d) I, II and III

For Questions 123-124

Research indicates that regular physical activity is crucial for maintaining overall health and preventing severe diseases. Engaging in moderate exercise can improve overall health, enhance mood, and boost immune function. Despite these benefits, many individuals remain sedentary due to a lack of motivation or resources. Studies have shown that community programmes aimed at increasing physical activity, such as group fitness classes and public parks, significantly enhance participation levels and improve community health.

123. Which of the following, if true, would most strengthen the argument presented above?
(a) Individuals who engage in regular physical activity are more likely to have access to health care services.
(b) Communities that have implemented fitness programs report higher levels of overall satisfaction with their health on a long-term basis.
(c) Many people cite a lack of time as the primary reason for not participating in physical activity.
(d) Group fitness classes are often less expensive than personal training sessions.

124. Which of the following, if true, would most seriously weaken the argument above?
(a) Participants of community exercise programs tend to revert to sedentary habits once the programs conclude, leading to no lasting improvement in health outcomes.
(b) Some individuals prefer exercising alone rather than in group-based or community fitness programs.

(c) Communities with greater access to public parks often report higher levels of general well-being and lower stress.
(d) Local governments that invest in community health programs typically experience reduced long-term healthcare costs.

125. In a family,
I. A is the father of B.
II. C is the son of A.
III. D is the brother of E.
IV. E is the daughter of B.
How is C related to D?
(a) Brother (b) Uncle
(c) Cousin (d) Nephew

126. All renewable energy sources reduce carbon emissions. Some renewable energy sources are expensive to install. Solar energy is a renewable energy resource. Consider the following conclusions:
I. Solar energy reduces carbon emissions.
II. All expensive energy sources are renewable.
III. Some renewable energy resources are not expensive. Select the most appropriate option:
(a) Only I follows.
(b) Both I and III follow.
(c) Only III follows.
(d) Both II and III follow.

127. Artist : Painting = ?
(a) Author : Novel
(b) Teacher : Student
(c) Doctor : Prescription
(d) Athlete : Coach

128. All Parathas are Sustainable. Some Sustainable are Cost-Effective. All Cost-Effective are Popular. Consider the following conclusions that necessarily follows:
I. Some Popular are Parathas.
II. All Parathas are Popular.
III. Some sustainable are Popular. Select the most appropriate option:
(a) Only I follows.
(b) Only III follows.
(c) Both I and III follow.
(d) Both II and III follow.

129. Roorkee City plans to replace all diesel buses with electric buses within five years to reduce air pollution. Officials claim this will significantly improve air quality and reduce respiratory illnesses. Which of the following is an assumption made by the officials?
(a) Electric buses are affordable for the city to maintain.
(b) Air pollution in Roorkee City is primarily caused by diesel buses.
(c) Residents will support the transition to electric buses.
(d) Other sources of pollution will also be reduced during this period.

130. Many schools have introduced digital textbooks, arguing that they are more cost-effective and environmentally friendly than printed books. Which of the following, if true, would most weaken this argument?
(a) Digital textbooks require devices that many students cannot afford.
(b) Printed books are more fragile than electronic devices.
(c) Some teachers prefer using printed books.
(d) Students find digital textbooks more engaging.

131. The city's new bike-sharing programme has been widely adopted, reducing traffic congestion and promoting healthy lifestyles. Which of the following is a necessary assumption?
(a) The bike-sharing programme has improved air quality.
(b) Many residents prefer biking to driving.
(c) There has been a quantifiable increase in the usage of bikes by city residents
(d) The city will expand the programme to all neighbourhoods.

132. Researchers claim that planting trees in urban areas can significantly reduce summer temperatures. Which of the following, if true, most strengthens this claim?

(a) Trees provide shade and release water vapour through transpiration.
(b) Planting trees is more expensive than other cooling measures.
(c) Urban residents enjoy spending time in green spaces.
(d) Trees improve air quality by absorbing pollutants.

133. Principle: A person who keeps or engages with hazardous or inherently dangerous substances or activities is liable for any or all harm resulting from their escape or impact, regardless of the precautions taken, unless the harm was caused by an act of God, an act of a third party, or the consent of the victim.

Fact: Seema owns a perfume factory that lawfully stores large quantities of chemicals used in fragrance production. One night, a sudden lightning strike causes a fire, leading to the release of toxic fumes that harm nearby residents. Seema had complied with all safety requirements and had fireproof storage facilities in place.

Applying only the given principle to the fact, is Seema liable? Select the most appropriate option:

(a) No, because the harm resulted from an act of God, not from her negligence.
(b) Yes, because the chemicals were hazardous, and she owns the factory.
(c) No, because she had taken all reasonable precautions to prevent such an accident.
(d) Yes, because she failed to anticipate natural disasters while storing dangerous substances.

134. All Samosas are Delicious. Some Delicious is Spicy. No Spicy is Steamed.
Which of the following conclusions necessarily follows? I. Some Samosas are Spicy.
II. Some Delicious are not Steamed. III. No Samosa is Steamed.
Select the most appropriate option:

(a) Only I follows (b) Both I and II follow
(c) Only III follows (d) Only II follows

135. All Engineers know Mathematics. Some Coders are Engineers. No Artist is an Engineer. Which of the following conclusions necessarily follows?

I. Some Coders know Mathematics.
II. Some Mathematicians can also Code.
III. Some Artists know Mathematics. Select the most appropriate option:

(a) Only II follows
(b) Only I follows
(c) Both I and II follow
(d) Only III follows

136. All Emails are Messages. Some Messages are Urgent. No Urgent Messages are Casual. Which of the following conclusions necessarily follows?

I. Some Emails are Casual.
II. Some Messages are not Casual.
III. All Urgent Messages are Emails. Select the most appropriate option:

(a) Only II follows
(b) Only III follows
(c) Both I and II follow
(d) Both I and III follow

137. Principle: Negligence may be inferred when the incident causing harm is of a kind that ordinarily does not occur without someone's negligence, the instrumentality or control that caused the harm was under the defendant's management, and the plaintiff did not contribute to the harm.

Fact - Anita visits a hospital for a routine check-up. While waiting in the lobby, a large ceiling fan suddenly detaches and falls, injuring her shoulder. The hospital authorities claim that the fan had been regularly serviced and no defect was known before the accident.

Applying only the given principle to the fact, is the hospital liable? Select the most appropriate option:

(a) No, because Anita cannot prove which employee was responsible for the fan.
(b) Yes, because a ceiling fan does not ordinarily fall without some negligence in its maintenance.

(c) No, because the hospital claims regular maintenance was carried out.
(d) Yes, but only if Anita can prove that the fan was installed more than five years ago.

138. A city plans to replace cash bus fares with a QR-only system to reduce revenue leakage. Critics argue ridership among the elderly will drop. Which assumption best supports the critics?
(a) A large proportion of elderly commuters lack smartphones or find QR payments difficult.
(b) Younger commuters prefer QR payment due to higher smartphone use.
(c) Conductors are not trained to handle QR codes.
(d) A study found that QR systems reduce revenue leakage in other cities with similar public transport systems.

139. Excessive sugar-sweetened beverage intake correlates with higher cavity rates. A claim is made that such beverages cause cavities. Which, if true, most weakens the causal claim?
(a) Participants with high sugar-sweetened beverage consumption were also found to have poorer oral hygiene and less frequent dental check-ups compared to low-consumption participants.
(b) The study's large sample size included diverse populations, which may have introduced uncontrolled variability affecting the observed correlation.
(c) Surveys indicate that many dental professionals believe sugar contributes to cavities, regardless of other lifestyle factors.
(d) Evidence shows that cavity formation depends on multiple factors, including genetics, diet, and oral microbiome, and sugar alone may not be sufficient to cause cavities.

140. Congestion pricing approach reduces peak-hour car trips in several cities.

Which assumption supports using it in a new city?
(a) Drivers will respond to price signals by shifting time or mode of travel.
(b) Public transport would be able to fulfil the demand.
(c) Drivers dislike road taxes and would therefore stop using cars to avoid them.
(d) Fuel prices will fall due to lower consumption.

141. B2, D4, G7, K11, ?
(a) O14 (b) N15
(c) P16 (d) Q17

142. If WORD = GVDI, then QUEEN = ?
(a) BCRKC (b) ABQJB
(c) ABRKB (d) ACQJD

143. An econometric study using the difference-in-differences technique finds no significant employment effect from a minimum-wage hike. Which evidence most strengthens this finding?
(a) Some firms in the treated region reported difficulty in hiring, even though aggregate employment did not change significantly.
(b) Overall labour costs increased slightly in the treated region, but wages for most workers remained unchanged.
(c) Employment trends in similar regions without a minimum wage hike were nearly identical to the trends in regions with the hike before and after the policy change.
(d) Workers' hours declined in certain industries, despite stable employment levels.

For Questions 144-145

Diversity may bring people to the same room, but inclusion ensures that every voice is heard, valued, and allowed to shape the conversation. It demands that institutions go beyond representation to transformation, to question who holds the power, who defines norms, and whose stories remain unheard. It is the process of turning the promise of democracy into practice, one case, one reform, and one act of courage at a time.

144. Based on the passage above, which of the following can be most logically inferred?
(a) Inclusion requires active structural and cultural change within institutions, not merely diverse representation.

(b) Diversity and inclusion are interchangeable concepts referring to the representation of different groups.
(c) Democracy automatically ensures inclusion without further institutional effort.
(d) Increasing the number of under-represented individuals in decision-making spaces is adequate to secure inclusion.

145. Which of the following, if true, would most strengthen the author's argument in the passage above?
(a) Institutions that create deliberate mechanisms for inclusive participation tend to make more equitable and widely supported policy decisions.
(b) Employees value visible diversity in workplaces as a sign of progressive leadership.
(c) Efforts to improve inclusion sometimes face resistance from individuals who feel existing structures are already fair.
(d) In some organizations, diverse representation has increased, but decision-making continues to be dominated by a small core group.

146. In a study on workplace productivity, employees with flexible schedules reported higher job satisfaction. However, productivity levels between flexible and fixed schedule employees were almost the same. Which of the following conclusions can be logically drawn?
(a) Job satisfaction always leads to higher productivity.
(b) Productivity is influenced by factors other than work schedules.
(c) Flexible schedules harm team coordination.
(d) Most employees prefer fixed schedules.

147. Public health officials warn that air pollution increases the risk of respiratory disease. A recent drop in pollution levels coincided with a fall in new respiratory disease cases. Which of the following, if true, most strengthens the officials' warning?
(a) Respiratory disease cases usually peak in winter.
(b) The cities with the largest drop in pollution saw the largest fall in cases.
(c) The decline in cases was higher in rural areas than in urban areas.
(d) There was a major health awareness campaign during the period.

148. The government announced subsidies for electric vehicles (EVs) to encourage consumers to buy more EVs. However, sales of EVs remained stagnant. Which of the following, if true, would best explain the outcome?
(a) Charging infrastructure for EVs remains inadequate.
(b) EV manufacturers released new affordable models.
(c) Petrol prices fell marginally during the period.
(d) Public awareness about EVs increased significantly.

149. A vaccine trial reports a 60% reduction in disease incidence in the trial population. Which is the safest inference?
(a) The vaccine is effective in similar populations under similar conditions.
(b) The vaccine eliminates the disease everywhere.
(c) No further studies are needed.
(d) Effectiveness is identical across all age groups.

150. Series: A2, C6, F12, J20, ____________?
(a) O30 (b) N32
(c) P32 (d) M34

ANSWER KEY

Section A: English

1. (c)	**9.** (b)	**17.** (c)	**25.** (c)	**33.** (b)	**41.** (a)	**49.** (c)
2. (b)	**10.** (c)	**18.** (b)	**26.** (c)	**34.** (c)	**42.** (b)	**50.** (a)
3. (c)	**11.** (d)	**19.** (a)	**27.** (a)	**35.** (b)	**43.** (c)	
4. (c)	**12.** (a)	**20.** (c)	**28.** (a)	**36.** (a)	**44.** (b)	
5. (b)	**13.** (a)	**21.** (b)	**29.** (d)	**37.** (a)	**45.** (a)	
6. (a)	**14.** (b)	**22.** (a)	**30.** (b)	**38.** (b)	**46.** (d)	
7. (c)	**15.** (b)	**23.** (d)	**31.** (b)	**39.** (c)	**47.** (b)	
8. (c)	**16.** (b)	**24.** (b)	**32.** (d)	**40.** (c)	**48.** (a)	

Section B: Current Affairs and General Knowledge

51. (b)	**56.** (b)	**61.** (b)	**66.** (b)	**71.** (b)	**76.** (a)
52. (b)	**57.** (b)	**62.** (d)	**67.** (d)	**72.** (c)	**77.** (c)
53. (d)	**58.** (d)	**63.** (b)	**68.** (a)	**73.** (b)	**78.** (b)
54. (b)	**59.** (d)	**64.** (d)	**69.** (b)	**74.** (d)	**79.** (b)
55. (a)	**60.** (b)	**65.** (a)	**70.** (a)	**75.** (c)	**80.** (d)

Section C: Logical Reasoning

81. (a)	**91.** (a)	**101.** (a)	**111.** (a)	**121.** (c)	**131.** (c)	**141.** (c)
82. (a)	**92.** (d)	**102.** (c)	**112.** (c)	**122.** (a)	**132.** (a)	**142.** (b)
83. (c)	**93.** (a)	**103.** (a)	**113.** (d)	**123.** (b)	**133.** (a)	**143.** (c)
84. (c)	**94.** (c)	**104.** (c)	**114.** (c)	**124.** (a)	**134.** (d)	**144.** (a)
85. (d)	**95.** (d)	**105.** (a)	**115.** (b)	**125.** (b)	**135.** (c)	**145.** (a)
86. (a)	**96.** (b)	**106.** (a)	**116.** (b)	**126.** (b)	**136.** (a)	**146.** (b)
87. (b)	**97.** (b)	**107.** (b)	**117.** (b)	**127.** (a)	**137.** (b)	**147.** (b)
88. (a)	**98.** (c)	**108.** (b)	**118.** (a)	**128.** (b)	**138.** (a)	**148.** (a)
89. (a)	**99.** (b)	**109.** (c)	**119.** (a)	**129.** (b)	**139.** (a)	**149.** (a)
90. (a)	**100.** (a)	**110.** (a)	**120.** (b)	**130.** (a)	**140.** (a)	**150.** (a)

AILET 2025

SECTION A: ENGLISH

I. Read the given extract and answer the following questions by choosing the most appropriate answer.

The rise of renewable energy sources has become a crucial topic in the global fight against climate change. Solar and wind power, in particular, have gained traction due to their ability to provide clean energy while reducing dependence on fossil fuels. Governments worldwide are investing in technology to enhance energy efficiency and storage solutions, aiming to create a more sustainable energy landscape. As the costs of renewable technologies continue to decrease, the transition from traditional energy sources is becoming not only environmentally necessary but also economically viable. However, this transition faces several challenges. The intermittent nature of renewable energy sources, such as solar and wind, requires advancements in energy storage to ensure a reliable supply. Additionally, existing infrastructure often relies heavily on fossil fuels, necessitating significant investment to upgrade or replace systems. Policymakers must navigate these complexities, balancing environmental goals with economic realities. The future of energy will likely depend on collaboration between governments, industries, and consumers to foster innovation and implement sustainable practices.

1. What is one of the major challenges faced in the transition to renewable energy?
   (a) The decreasing costs of fossil fuels
   (b) The need for advancements in energy storage
   (c) The complete lack of government interest
   (d) The sheer abundance of fossil fuel resources

2. According to the passage, what is essential for a successful transition to renewable energy?
   (a) Collaboration among various stakeholders
   (b) Increased fossil fuel production
   (c) Over reliance on the existing infrastructure
   (d) Eliminating all government regulations

3. Why is the transition to renewable energy described as becoming economically viable?
   (a) Because fossil fuels are becoming more expensive
   (b) Due to the decrease in costs of renewable technologies
   (c) Due to government subsidies for fossil fuels
   (d) Renewable energy sources are less reliable

4. What does the term 'intermittent nature' refer to in the context of renewable energy sources?
   (a) Their ability to provide consistent energy supply.
   (b) Their integration into existing infrastructure for production.
   (c) Their complete dependence on fossil fuels for energy.
   (d) Variability in energy production due to weather conditions.

5. Which of the following best describes the tone of the paragraph?
   (a) Skeptical (b) Dismissive
   (c) Balanced (d) Indifferent

II. Read the given extract and answer the following questions by choosing the most appropriate answer.

The levels of dissolved oxygen in the world's ocean waters are declining precipitously. Just like humans, fish need oxygen to survive, and so in ocean areas experiencing significant levels of oxygen scarcity, or hypoxia, fish populations are plummeting. Although some hypoxic areas, called 'dead zones,' occur naturally, hypoxia in coastal areas and inland waters is caused mainly by agricultural run-off and by discharge of industrial wastewater. More than one hundred permanent dead zones, many covering thousands of square miles, exist worldwide today. Since reproductive success is the most critical factor in the sustainability of any species, the extent of this threat to marine life and genetic diversity can hardly be overstated. After several months in hypoxic waters, female fish produce fewer eggs. Moreover, hypoxic conditions serve to alter the normal ratio between two particular hormones manufactured during the embryonic stage when a fish's gender is determined. During gestation and under these conditions, the mother produces more testosterone (and less estradiol), which inhibits the development of female reproductive organs and other female characteristics in the embryo, while promoting the development of male traits. The implications of declining oxygen levels extend beyond individual species to entire ecosystems. Marine biodiversity is at risk as species that cannot adapt to hypoxic conditions may face extinction, leading to a cascade of effects throughout the food web. Predators may struggle to find adequate prey, while other marine organisms, such as coral reefs, which rely on healthy fish populations for symbiotic relationships, may also deteriorate. The loss of biodiversity can disrupt ecosystem services that are essential for human communities, including fisheries, tourism, and coastal protection.

6. How does hypoxia affect female fish reproduction?
(a) It increases egg production.
(b) It has no effect on reproduction.
(c) It decreases egg production.
(d) It improves the survival rate of embryos.

7. What term is used in the passage to describe areas with significantly low levels of oxygen?
(a) Oxygen-rich zones
(b) Dead zones
(c) Marine reserves
(d) Hypoxic waters

8. What effect do altered hormone levels during gestation have on fish embryos in hypoxic conditions?
(a) They promote the development of female traits.
(b) They cause all embryos to become hermaphrodites.
(c) They have no impact on gender determination.
(d) They inhibit female traits and promote male traits.

9. What broader ecological impact does declining oxygen levels have, as mentioned in the passage?
(a) Increase in hypoxic fish populations
(b) Enrichment of coral reefs
(c) Disruption of entire ecosystems
(d) Degradation of marine biodiversity

10. Why is reproductive success critical for any species, according to the passage?
(a) It ensures the continuation of genetic diversity.
(b) It determines the physical traits of the species.
(c) It affects the feeding habits of the species.
(d) It influences the increase in habitat size.

11. Which of the following implications of hypoxia is not mentioned in the passage?
(a) Permanent loss of fish populations in affected areas
(b) Changes in the gender ratio of fish populations
(c) Increased competition among fish species
(d) Decline in ecosystem services such as fisheries and tourism

12. In the context of the passage, which of the following best characterizes the term '*sustainability*'?
(a) Maintaining current fish populations at all costs including government initiatives
(b) Ensuring the reproductive success of marine species for future generations
(c) Focusing solely on economic benefits derived from marine resources
(d) Prioritizing industrial growth over environmental health

III. Read the book descriptions for three different books and answer the questions by choosing the most appropriate options.

The Politics of Change	The Change in Politics	Politics and Change: A Global Perspective
In 'The Politics of Change,' political analyst Dr Emily Harper examines the dynamics of social movements and their impact on policy reform. Through detailed case studies, she explores how grassroots organizations, protests, and advocacy campaigns shape public opinion and influence lawmakers. Dr Harper provides insights into the strategies that successful movements employ and discusses the challenges they face in a complex political landscape. She discusses key strategies, such as coalition-building, media engagement, and the use of digital platforms to amplify voices.	This book by a veteran journalist Mark Stevens investigates the shifting political landscape in the 21st century. Focusing on major elections, emerging political parties, and the role of social media, Stevens analyzes how technology and demographics are transforming political engagement and voter behaviour. Through interviews with political leaders, campaign strategists, and everyday voters, Stevens uncovers how demographic shifts and technological advancements are reshaping political discourse in urban areas. He analyzes the implications of these changes for traditional political institutions and explores how movements like #MeToo and Black Lives Matter have disrupted conventional narratives.	In this insightful work, international relations scholar Dr Anika Patel presents a global analysis of political change across various regions. She explores the factors that drive political transitions, including economic shifts, cultural movements, and international influences. Dr Patel emphasizes the interconnectedness of global politics and how local changes can have far-reaching implications. She analyzes various factors driving political transitions, including economic upheaval, cultural shifts, and the impact of globalization. She provides case studies from diverse regions, such as the Arab Spring, democratic movements in Latin America, and shifts in power in Asia. The book serves as a vital resource for understanding the complexities of political evolution in a rapidly changing world.

13. In 'The Politics of Change,' Dr Emily Harper analyzes various grassroots movements. Which of the following factors does she most likely attribute to the success of these movements?
(a) The use of traditional media over social media.
(b) The historical context of each movement's emergence.
(c) The ability to engage a broad coalition of stakeholders.
(d) The lack of governmental opposition.

14. What major factors does Mark Stevens discuss in 'The Change in Politics' regarding the evolution of political engagement?
(a) Historical events and their consequences
(b) The role of technology and demographic changes
(c) Economic theories and their application
(d) Environmental issues affecting policy

15. In 'Politics and Change: A Global Perspective,' what does Dr Anika Patel emphasize about the influence of local political changes?
(a) They have no impact on global politics.
(b) The broad implications for international relations.
(c) They only affect neighbouring countries.
(d) They are primarily driven by economic factors.

16. Which of the following strategies does Dr Emily Harper argue is essential for social movements to effectively influence policy reform in 'The Politics of Change'?
(a) Sole reliance on traditional media
(b) Engaging in public apathy
(c) Utilizing digital platforms for outreach
(d) Focusing exclusively on local issues

17. Dr Anika Patel's 'Politics and Change: A Global Perspective' explores the effects of globalization on local politics. Which of the following concepts is most likely a focus of her analysis?
(a) The isolation of national policies
(b) The role of international organizations in local governance
(c) The historical significance of colonialism on current political structures
(d) The effectiveness of local movements in a globalized world

18. In 'The Change in Politics,' Mark Stevens highlights demographic shifts as a transformative factor in politics. Which demographic change might, he argues, has the most significant influence on recent electoral outcomes?
(a) The ageing population's impact on social security policy
(b) The increasing diversity of voters in urban areas
(c) The declining trend of rural populations
(d) The rise in youth voter participation in mid-term elections

19. In 'Politics and Change: A Global Perspective,' Dr Anika Patel emphasizes the interconnectedness of political systems. According to the passage, which approach would Dr Anika Patel be most likely to use to assess the impact of local changes on global politics?
(a) A purely economic lens focusing on trade relations.
(b) A cultural approach examining regional identities.
(c) A systemic analysis of international relations theories.
(d) A narrative approach emphasizing personal stories of political figures.

20. In 'The Change in Politics,' Mark Stevens highlights the role of digital platforms in political engagement. Which of the following outcomes would he most likely argue is a direct consequence of increased digital engagement?
(a) A decrease in overall voter turnout due to information overload.
(b) Enhanced polarization among voters as a result of targeted content.
(c) A uniform political discourse across different demographics.
(d) An increase in apathy as digital engagement replaces real-world activism.

21. Dr Anika Patel's 'Politics and Change: A Global Perspective' posits that local political movements are interconnected with global trends. Which of the following would best illustrate this relationship?
(a) Local protests against environmental policies influencing international climate agreements.
(b) National elections occurring independently of global economic conditions.
(c) Cultural differences leading to isolated local movements without global relevance.
(d) The presence of international influence in local governance decisions.

22. Considering Dr Anika Patel's arguments in 'Politics and Change: A Global Perspective,' which of the following statements would best summarize her perspective on the role of local leaders in a globalized world?

(a) Local leaders are primarily responsible for maintaining national sovereignty
(b) They have limited influence on global issues and should focus on local governance
(c) Their actions can create a ripple effect that influences international policy
(d) They are often overlooked in favour of national leaders in global discussions

IV. Read the following passage and answer the following questions by choosing the most appropriate answer.

The intricate world of modern manufacturing is a web of precision and innovation, where even the tiniest components play a pivotal role. One such element, often overlooked but crucial, is the sub-subpart. Whether it's a carpenter fashioning a bespoke piece of furniture or an automobile engineer designing the next generation of vehicles, the creation of sub-subparts is a fundamental process that demands meticulous craftsmanship and cutting-edge technology. In the realm of woodworking, carpenters frequently work with sub-subparts like dowels, screws, and hinges. These minute components may appear insignificant, yet they determine the structural integrity and functionality of the final product. Crafting a dowel, for instance, begins with selecting the appropriate wood species, followed by precision cutting and shaping. The result is a perfectly cylindrical, sturdy sub-subpart that seamlessly joins two larger pieces of wood. The advent of computer-aided design (CAD) and computer numerical control (CNC) machines has revolutionized this process, enabling carpenters to create sub-subparts with unparalleled precision. Similarly, in the automobile industry, sub-subparts are the unsung heroes of vehicle construction. Take, for instance, the ball bearing—a minuscule but essential component in the wheels and transmission system. Manufacturing these precision-engineered spheres involves intricate processes like forging, heat treatment, and precision machining. Modern techniques such as laser cutting and 3D printing have streamlined production, ensuring that these sub-subparts meet the demanding standards of the automotive sector. The manufacturing of sub-subparts is a testament to the convergence of traditional craftsmanship and cutting-edge technology. Whether it's a carpenter's workshop or a high-tech automotive assembly line, the quest for perfection in sub-subpart creation remains unwavering. The attention to detail and precision required in these processes is a testament to the dedication of craftsmen and engineers alike. To conclude, while sub-subparts may be small in size, their significance in various industries cannot be overstated. Whether it's a carpenter working on a timeless piece of furniture or an automotive engineer striving for superior performance, the manufacturing of sub-subparts is a crucial step towards achieving excellence in craftsmanship and technology. This fusion of tradition and innovation accentuates the essence of modern manufacturing.

23. In the intricate world of modern manufacturing, the sub-subpart can be compared to:
(a) The foundation of a building
(b) The finishing touches on a masterpiece painting
(c) The ingredients of a gourmet dish
(d) The alphabet in a language

24. According to the passage, what is the primary reason modern carpenters use computer-aided design (CAD)?
(a) To select the most expensive wood species
(b) To replace traditional woodworking tools
(c) To revolutionize precision and enhance craftsmanship
(d) To create unique, one-of-a-kind furniture designs

25. What is the overarching message conveyed by the passage regarding the significance of sub-subparts in carpentry?
(a) Sub-subparts are an outdated concept in modern carpentry.

(b) Sub-subparts are primarily aesthetic and don't affect functionality.
(c) Sub-subparts play a pivotal role in ensuring the quality and functionality of woodworking projects.
(d) Sub-subparts are exclusively used in the automotive industry.

26. Which term best characterises the fusion of traditional craftsmanship and cutting-edge technology in the context of creating sub-subparts, as discussed in the passage?
(a) Dichotomy (b) Outmodedness
(c) Paradox (d) Synergy

27. **Assertion (A):** Sub-subparts like dowels and screws are often overlooked in woodworking.

Reasoning (R): Sub-subparts play a crucial role in determining the structural integrity and functionality of the final product.

Select the option that applies correctly to the assertion and reasoning.
(a) Both (A) and (R) are true, and (R) is the correct explanation of (A).
(b) Both (A) and (R) are true, but (R) is not the correct explanation of (A).
(c) (A) is true, but (R) is false.
(d) (A) is false, but (R) is true.

28. The author would probably agree with which of the following statements?
(a) Sub-subparts are irrelevant in modern carpentry.
(b) Modern techniques like laser cutting have improved precision in sub-subpart creation.
(c) Traditional craftsmanship has no place in woodworking today.
(d) Sub-subparts are only used for aesthetic purposes in carpentry.

29. Which of the following might the author cite as an example of the fusion of traditional craftsmanship and cutting-edge technology, as described in the passage?
(a) The decline of traditional woodworking methods.
(b) The exclusive use of 3D printing in carpentry.
(c) The abandonment of sub-subparts in modern carpentry.
(d) The use of CAD for designing of wood pieces.

30. Given the author's position on the importance of sub-subparts in carpentry, what stand would the author probably take on the issue of using alternative materials in woodworking?
(a) The author would likely advocate for alternative materials.
(b) The author would likely reject alternative materials in favour of traditional ones.
(c) The author's stance on alternative materials is unclear.
(d) The author would likely argue for a balanced approach, incorporating both traditional and modern materials.

31. Which of the following lines best summarizes the essence of the conclusion regarding the significance of sub-subparts in modern manufacturing?
(a) Traditional craftsmanship is no longer relevant in today's industries.
(b) Sub-subparts are insignificant in modern manufacturing compared to larger components.
(c) The fusion of tradition and innovation stresses the importance of sub-subparts in modern manufacturing.
(d) Manufacturers should prioritise speed and quantity over craftsmanship.

V. Read the following passage and answer the following questions by choosing the most appropriate answer.

The Story of Coffee

Coffee, a beloved beverage enjoyed by millions around the globe, has a rich and captivating history that spans centuries. The story of coffee begins in the ancient highlands of Ethiopia, where, according to legend, a goat herder named Kaldi discovered the stimulating effects of coffee beans. One day, Kaldi noticed his goats frolicking with unusual energy after eating red berries from a certain tree. Curious, he tried the berries himself and experienced a newfound alertness. This discovery soon spread to monasteries, where monks used it to stay awake during long hours of prayer. From Ethiopia, coffee cultivation and consumption spread to the Arabian Peninsula, particularly in Yemen, where the practice of roasting coffee beans and brewing the drink began to take shape. By the 15th century, coffee had become a popular beverage in the Islamic world, with coffee houses known as *'qahveh khaneh'* emerging as social hubs for conversation, music, and intellectual exchange. These coffee houses became centers of culture and commerce, influencing the spread of coffee to Turkey and beyond, eventually reaching Europe. In Europe, coffee initially faced resistance from religious authorities who considered it a 'Muslim drink' and tried to ban it. However, its popularity persisted, and by the 17th century, coffee houses had sprung up in major European cities, becoming important gathering places for artists, writers, and thinkers. The stimulating effects of coffee were embraced during the Age of Enlightenment, where it was seen as a catalyst for intellectual discussion and innovation. The journey of coffee continued with the establishment of colonial plantations in tropical regions such as the Caribbean, Central and South America, and Southeast Asia. These plantations fuelled the global demand for coffee, transforming it from a regional speciality to a major commodity. The Industrial Revolution further accelerated coffee production and consumption, leading to innovations in coffee brewing methods and the development of instant coffee. In the modern era, coffee has evolved into a deeply ingrained part of daily life for people worldwide. Its cultural significance spans from the bustling cafes of Paris to the quiet coffee farms of Colombia. Today, coffee remains not only a popular beverage but also a symbol of social interaction, productivity, and enjoyment. Whether sipped slowly over a conversation with friends or grabbed hastily on the way to work, the story of coffee continues to unfold, intertwining with the histories and cultures of countless societies across the globe.

32. What did Kaldi observe that led to the discovery of coffee?
(a) Monks brewing coffee in a monastery
(b) Goats eating red berries and becoming energetic
(c) Coffee beans being roasted in a coffee house
(d) Coffee plantations being established

33. How did the Industrial Revolution impact coffee consumption?
(a) It led to the decline of coffee popularity
(b) It resulted in the establishment of coffee plantations in Europe
(c) It accelerated coffee production and introduced new brewing methods
(d) It made coffee an exclusive drink for the wealthy

34. Consider the following statement - *Coffee originated in Ethiopia and quickly spread to the Arabian Peninsula and beyond, where it became popular.* Which of the following best supports the statement?
(a) Coffee houses transformed into vital centers of cultural exchange and economic activity within the Islamic world.
(b) Monastic communities utilized coffee as a means to enhance concentration during extended periods of prayer.
(c) The invigorating properties of coffee gained significant appreciation among intellectuals during the Age of Enlightenment.
(d) The dissemination of coffee from Ethiopia catalyzed its cultivation across various regions, including Turkey and Europe.

35. **Statement 1:** The introduction of coffee to the European market was met with immediate acceptance and no resistance from religious authorities.

Statement 2: The cultural significance of coffee houses in Europe during the Age of Enlightenment extended beyond mere beverage consumption to become venues for political and philosophical discourse.

Choose the correct option:
(a) Both Statement 1 and Statement 2 are true.
(b) Statement 1 is true, but Statement 2 is false.
(c) Statement 1 is false, but Statement 2 is true.
(d) Both Statement 1 and Statement 2 are false.

36. What does the phrase 'emerging as social hubs' mean in the context of the passage?
(a) Gradually becoming popular locations for individual study and reflection.
(b) Gradually becoming isolated areas with limited social activity and interaction.
(c) Transforming into commercial businesses with some community involvement.
(d) Developing into centers for community interaction and cultural exchange.

37. Which of the following words is a synonym for 'cultivation' as used in the context of the passage?
(a) Development (b) Tending
(c) Growth (d) Destruction

38. Which among the following sentences uses the word 'frolicking' in the same sense as used in the passage?
(a) The athletes were frolicking about their training regimen before the competition.
(b) The children were frolicking along the beach, their joy palpable in the cool evening air.
(c) She found the frolicking music to be very relaxing during her study session.
(d) The artist spent the afternoon frolicking with her paintbrushes on the canvas.

39. **Statement 1:** The spread of coffee cultivation in tropical regions was solely driven by domestic consumption in Ethiopia.

Statement 2: The global demand for coffee prompted the establishment of plantations in various parts of the world, significantly influencing trade patterns.

Choose the correct option:
(a) Both Statement 1 and Statement 2 are true.
(b) Statement 1 is true, but Statement 2 is false.
(c) Statement 1 is false, but Statement 2 is true.
(d) Both Statement 1 and Statement 2 are false.

40. What factors contributed to the transformation of coffee from a regional speciality to a major global commodity?
(a) The establishment of colonial plantations and the growing global demand for coffee.
(b) The initial rejection of coffee by European consumers and its subsequent revival.
(c) The decrease in the prominence of coffee houses and a transition to home brewing.
(d) The popularity of instant coffee and a growing preference for tea instead of coffee.

41. In what ways has coffee maintained its cultural significance in modern society?
(a) Coffee is only enjoyed in traditional ceremonies and has lost its daily appeal.
(b) Coffee is now primarily consumed in fast food chains, diminishing its cultural role.
(c) Coffee has become a luxury item, only accessible to wealthy consumers.
(d) Coffee remains a popular beverage and symbolizes social interaction.

VI. Read the excerpt from a Handicrafts Manual: 'Advanced Knitting Techniques' and answer the following questions by choosing the most appropriate answer.

THE FAIR ISLE METHOD: Fair Isle knitting is a traditional technique that involves using two or more colours of yarn in a single row to create intricate patterns and designs. This method requires careful tension management to ensure even stitches and prevent puckering. To begin, select your colours and cast on the desired number of stitches. As you knit, alternate between colours every few stitches, carrying the unused yarn along the back of the work. Mastering the Fair Isle technique allows you to create stunning visual effects in garments, accessories, and home textiles.

THE CONTINENTAL STYLE: The Continental knitting style, often referred to as 'picking,' involves holding the yarn in the left hand while the right hand manipulates the needles. This method allows for greater speed and efficiency, particularly when working with complex patterns or multiple colours. To practice this style, start by casting on your stitches and using your left hand to tension the yarn. With each stitch, simply 'pick' the yarn with your right needle, forming a quick and fluid motion. As you become comfortable with this technique, you may find that your overall knitting speed and comfort improve significantly.

THE SHORT-ROW TECHNIQUE: Short-row knitting is an advanced technique that allows for the creation of shaped garments, such as sleeves and shoulders, without the need for complex shaping. To make a sleeve using this technique, begin by casting on the required number of stitches. Work a portion of the row, then turn your work and return without completing the full row to create the 'short rows' that shape the curves of the sleeve. To prevent holes at the turn, wrap the stitch before you turn your work. Repeat this process as needed to achieve the desired shaping and dimension of the sleeve. Once you have shaped the sleeve, you can then sew the side seams to connect the pieces of your garment and finally, complete the edges to ensure a clean finish. This method not only helps shape curves but also adds dimension to your piece, allowing you to enhance fit and style.

42. Ensuring 'even stitches and prevent puckering' refers to the
(a) Tension management
(b) Colour selection
(c) Yarn thickness
(d) Stitch pattern

43. What is the correct order of stitching steps to make a sleeve using the short-row technique?
(a) Cast on stitches, create short rows, sew side seams, finish edges
(b) Create short rows, cast on stitches, sew side seams, finish edges
(c) Sew side seams, cast on stitches, create short rows, finish edges
(d) Cast on stitches, sew side seams, finish edges, create short rows

44. What is the primary focus of the Fair Isle method?
(a) Creating seamless garments
(b) Using multiple colours for intricate patterns
(c) Speed and dexterity in knitting
(d) Shaping complex garments using coloured yarns

45. What does the emphasis on wrapping the stitch before turning to suggest about the short-row technique?
(a) It is a complicated method that requires extensive practice.
(b) It is only relevant for advanced knitters.
(c) Proper execution is crucial to ensure a polished finish.
(d) It is optional and can be skipped for faster results.

46. Based on the description of the Continental style, which of the following can be inferred about its efficiency?
(a) It is slower than other knitting methods.
(b) It is best suited for complex patterns only.
(c) It requires more yarn than traditional methods.
(d) It enables quicker advancement in design.

47. Considering the techniques discussed, what might be inferred about the overall skill level required for mastering Fair Isle and Continental knitting?
(a) Both techniques can be mastered without any prior experience.
(b) Advanced techniques require a strong foundation in basic knitting skills.
(c) They are accessible only to expert knitters with years of experience.
(d) No specific skills are necessary for these techniques.

48. Which option includes the most appropriate meaning of the underlined phrase in the given sentence? '*With each stitch, simply pick the yarn with your right needle, forming a quick and fluid motion.*'
(a) Grasp the yarn firmly
(b) Lift the yarn easily
(c) Catch the yarn smoothly
(d) Pull the yarn tightly

49. What can be inferred about the relationship between mastering advanced knitting techniques and a knitter's design capabilities?
(a) Mastering advanced techniques limits a knitter's creativity to specific patterns.
(b) Advanced techniques enhance a knitter's ability to create innovative and varied designs.
(c) Mastery of these techniques is irrelevant to design capabilities.
(d) A knitter can achieve the same results using only basic techniques.

50. How might the integration of both the Fair Isle method and the short-row technique influence a knitter's approach to garment construction?
(a) It streamlines the process, making it easier for all skill levels to create garments.
(b) It fosters creativity through intricate designs, needing advanced skills to execute.
(c) It restricts the knitter to simple patterns, limiting creative possibilities.
(d) It minimizes the need for precision, allowing for a more relaxed approach to knitting.

SECTION B: CURRENT AFFAIRS AND GENERAL KNOWLEDGE

51. Which nation became the first country to adopt Bitcoin as a legal tender?
(a) Nigeria
(b) El Salvador
(c) Republic of Turkey
(d) Central African Republic

52. Which among the following is considered as the world's largest stateless population?
(a) Chakmas (b) Feyli Kurd
(c) Rohingyas (d) Tibetan Refugees

53. Which athlete achieved the distinction of becoming the first Indian athlete from independent India to win two medals in a single edition of the Summer Olympics?
(a) Neeraj Chopra (b) Harmanpreet Singh
(c) Lakshya Sen (d) Manu Bhakar

54. Who is credited with being the first oncologist in India to have successfully performed a bone marrow transplant?
(a) Dr K. K. Agarwal (b) Dr Suresh H. Advani
(c) Dr Mansoor Hasan (d) Dr Indira Hinduja

55. Which of the following is considered to be the closest equivalent of a 'Nobel Prize' in the field of Mathematics?
(a) Hess-Leffler Medal
(b) Gording-Harmander Award
(c) Fields Medal
(d) Shaw-Wolf Prize

56. The 2024 International Booker Prize was awarded to the book 'Kairos' by Jenny Erpenbeck. Which of the following makes this win notable?
(a) First book translated from German to win the prize
(b) First book written by a stateless person to win the prize
(c) First book to win both the Booker Prize and Pulitzer Prize in the same year
(d) First autobiography to win the prize

57. M.S. Dhoni is considered to be one of the most successful captain and player in the popular Indian Premier League(IPL). Which other franchise in addition to the Chennai Super Kings, has Dhoni played for?
(a) Rising Pune Supergiants
(b) Gujarat Titans
(c) Rajasthan Royals
(d) Sunrisers Hyderabad

58. Which Indian football sporting club won the inaugural ASEAN Football Championship hosted by Indonesia in 2003?
(a) Mohan Bagan AC
(b) Salgaocar FC
(c) NorthEast United FC
(d) East Bengal FC

59. Perseverance Rover, launched by NASA, is famous for its mission to explore the surface of which celestial body, particularly to seek signs of ancient life and collect samples for future return to Earth.

(a) Mercury (b) Mars
(c) Juno (d) Titan

60. The Nobel Peace Prize for 2024 was awarded to
(a) Organization for the Prohibition of Chemical Weapons
(b) Amnesty International
(c) Nihon Hidankyo
(d) UN Peacekeeping Force

61. Which of the following is not member of the United Nations?
(a) Taiwan (b) United States of America
(c) Honduras (d) Brazil

62. The third Japan-India 2+2 Ministerial Meeting was held in New Delhi in 2024. Which is a core focus area for these meetings?
(a) joint space exploration programme
(b) bilateral security and defence cooperation
(c) regional migration framework
(d) joint climate change action plan

63. The following listed items are joint military exercises conducted by India, with another foreign nation. Match the following:

S.No	Item	S.No.	Item
A	Veer Guardian	I	Mongolia
B	Nomadic Elephant	II	United States of America
C	Vajra Prahar	III	Japan
D	Exercise Maitree	IV	Thailand

Select the correct option:
(a) A-I, B-IV, C-II, D-III
(b) A-III, B-I, C-IV, D-II
(c) A-III, B-I, C-II, D-IV
(d) A-IV, B-II, C-I, D-III

64. *Nupi Lan*, also known, as the 'Women War' was a significant revolt against the British and is often credited as one of the earliest uprisings in India to be led entirely by women. In which present-day state did the uprising take place?
(a) Manipur (b) Arunachal Pradesh
(c) Chhattisgarh (d) Tripura

65. Who is the current Secretary General of the United Nations?
(a) Ban-Ki Moon
(b) Kofi Annan
(c) Ursula von der Leyen
(d) Antonio Guterres

66. What is the international significance of 21st June?
(a) Human Rights Day
(b) Women's Day
(c) International Day of Yoga
(d) World Day Against Child Labour

67. According to the Swachh Survekshan 2023 rankings, which of the following city was ranked as the cleanest in India?
(a) Pune (b) Indore
(c) Bhopal (d) Tirupati

68. The following are various dance forms found in different parts of India. While a certain dance form may be associated with more than one state, select the most appropriate response to the noted options below:

S.No	Dance form	S.No.	State
A	Bharatanatyam	I	Assam
B	Sattriya	II	Andhra Pradesh
C	Kathakali	III	Tamil Nadu
D	Kuchipudi	IV	Kerala

Select the correct option:
(a) A-III, B-I, C-IV, D-II
(b) A-III, B-IV, C-II, D-I
(c) A-II, B-I, C-IV, D-III
(d) A-IV, B-II, C-I, D-III

69. Vinesh Phogat was disqualified from the wrestling competition at the 2024 Paris Olympics after exceeding the weight limit by 100 grams during the weigh-in for her 50 kg final. Her disqualification was upheld on appeal. To which international

body did Vinesh Phogat and the Indian Olympic Association appeal?
(a) Court of Arbitration for Sports
(b) International Sports Arbitration Tribunal
(c) International Athletic Arbitration Authority
(d) Tribunal Internacional de Arbitraje

70. In September 2024, a new scheme, Bio-RIDE, was approved in the area of biotechnology. Identify the components of the scheme.
I. Biotechnology Research and Development
II. Industrial & Entrepreneurship Development
III. Biomanufacturing and Biofoundry
IV. Biotechnology parks and International Collaborations

Select the correct option:
(a) I, II, III (b) I, II, IV
(c) I, III, IV (d) II, III, IV

71. The quality of drinking water is regularly measured in terms of TDS. Higher the TDS poorer the quality of drinking water. What does TDS stand for?
(a) Total Dilution Solubility
(b) Total Dissolved Solids
(c) Total De-Salination
(d) Total Density Solution

72. In 2004, the Government of India decided to create a new category of languages known as 'Classical Languages'. What are the latest criteria, announced in 2024, for inclusion of languages within this category?
I. High antiquity of its early texts/recorded history over a period of 1500- 2000 years.
II. A body of ancient literature/texts, which is considered a heritage by generations of speakers.
III. Knowledge texts, especially prose texts in addition to poetry, epigraphical and inscriptional evidence.
IV. The classical languages and literature could be distinct from its current form or could be discontinuous with later forms of its offshoots.
V. The literary tradition be original and not borrowed from another speech community.

Select the correct option:
(a) Only I, II, III & V (b) Only II III & IV
(c) Only I, II & III (d) Only I, II, III & IV

73. The movie 'The Man Who Knew Infinity' depicts the life story of
(a) Apurba Ramchandran
(b) Ramanbhai Patel
(c) Srinivasa Ramanujan
(d) Venki Ramakrishna

74. Who was known as the 'Bard of Brahmaputra'?
(a) Tarali Sarma (b) Bhupen Hazarika
(c) Bishakh Jyoti (d) Niranjan Rout

75. In 2024, the Government of India introduced the Rashtriya Vigyan Puraskar, recognising key contributions in the field of Science and Technology in India. In the first edition awards were presented in the following four categories:
I. Vigyan Ratna
II. Vigyan Shri
III. Vigyan Yuva
IV. Vigyan Team
V. Vigyan Aavishkar

Select the correct option:
(a) Only I, II, III, IV (b) Only II, III, IV, V
(c) Only I, III, IV, V (d) Only I, II, IV, V

76. As part of its NTMHP initiative, the Government of India recently introduced the TELE-MANAS, a 24/7 toll-free helpline (14416). What does TELE-MANAS stand for?
(a) Tele Mental Health Assistance and Networking Across States
(b) Tele Medicine Assistance and National Support
(c) Tele Mental Assistance and National Aid Service
(d) Tele Medical Aid and Networking Across States

77. Festivals in India are a vibrant reflection of its diverse culture, heritage and traditions. Match the following festivals with the State with which it is most frequently associated. While a festival may be celebrated in many states, select the most appropriate response from the noted options below.

S.No	Festival	S.no	State
I	Kadalekayi Parishe	A	Gujarat
II	Bohag Bihu	B	Orissa
III	Uttarayan	C	Assam
IV	Nuakhai	D	Karnataka

Select the correct option:

(a) I-C, II-D, III-A, IV- B
(b) I-D, II-C, III-A, IV-B
(c) I-B, II-C, III-D, IV-A
(d) I-A, II-C, III-B, IV-D

78. In the ongoing Israeli- Palestinian conflict frequent references have been made to the 'Iron Dome'. What does it refer to?

(a) ancient architectural buildings particularly religious buildings featuring a dome.
(b) an advanced cyber shield ensuring multilayer protection against invasive cyberattacks.
(c) a continuous remote sensing surveillance technology to detect deep underground tunnels.
(d) multipurpose missile defense system designed to protect against a wide range of indirect and aerial threats.

79. The Indian Air Force recently inaugurated a new training establishment, the Weapon Systems School (WSS), with the aim of recalibrating and transforming the Indian Air Force as a future-oriented force. In which city was the WSS located?

(a) Gorakhpur, UP
(b) Begumpet, Hyderabad
(c) Tezpur, Assam
(d) Jodhpur, Rajasthan

80. Which of the following statements best describes the nature of the National Automated Clearing House (NACH) implemented by the National Payment Corporation of India (NPCI)?

(a) It is a web-based solution to facilitate inter-bank, high volume, electronic transactions which are repetitive and periodic in nature.
(b) It is utilized to modify in real time individual transactions between bank accounts.
(c) It facilitates direct government disbursements to beneficiaries under various schemes.
(d) It is an RBI mobile app to facilitate international wire transfers and foreign remittances.

SECTION C: LOGICAL REASONING

81. Some Hyenas are Lions. All Lions are Cats. Some Cats are Wolves. Examine the following statements:

I. Some Cats are Lions.
II. Some Wolves are Lions.
III. Some Cats are Hyenas.

Select the correct option:

(a) Both I & II follow
(b) Both II & III follow
(c) Both I & III follow
(d) Only III follows

82. All Squirrels are Herbivores. Some Herbivores are Elephants. All Elephants are Mammals. Some Mammals are Carnivores. Examine the following statements:

I. Some Mammals are Herbivores.
II. All Elephants are Squirrels.
III. Some Carnivores are Herbivores.

Select the correct option:

(a) Only I follows
(b) Both II & III follow
(c) Both I & III follow
(d) Only II follows

83. All Engineers are Mathematicians. Some Mathematicians are Authors. No Author is a Scientist. Some Engineers are Scientists. Examine the following statements:

I. No Author is an Engineer.
II. Some Scientists are Engineers.
III. Some Mathematicians are not Scientists.

Select the correct option:
(a) Only II follows
(b) Both I & III follow
(c) Both II & III follow
(d) Only I follows

84. All gadgets are machines. Some gadgets are tools. All machines are useful. Examine the following statements:
I. Some tools are useful.
II. All that is useful are machines.
III. All tools are gadgets.

Select the correct option:
(a) Only I follows
(b) Only II follows
(c) Both I & III follow
(d) Both II & III follow

85. All International Court of Justice (ICJ) judgments are binding on parties involved in the case. Some ICJ judgments have persuasive value in domestic courts. Judgments of domestic courts can be referenced by the ICJ, but they are not binding. Examine the following statements:
I. Some ICJ judgments are binding on domestic courts.
II. Some domestic court judgments are binding on the ICJ.
III. ICJ judgments can be used to strengthen arguments in domestic courts.

Select the correct option:
(a) Only I follows
(b) Both I & II follow
(c) Both I & III follow
(d) Only III follows

86. All drivers are Tall. Some Tall persons violate traffic lights. All who violate traffic lights are fined. B is Tall. Examine the following statements:
I. B is a driver.
II. B may violate a traffic light.
III. B will definitely violate traffic light.
IV. If B is a driver, he will get fined.
V. B will definitely get fined.

Select the correct option:
(a) Only I, III and V
(b) Only II
(c) Only I and III
(d) Only I and V

87. A consumer advocacy group published a report accusing Alpha Electronics Company of producing faulty products, misleading advertising, and failing to provide adequate customer service. The report presented various customer testimonials and product reviews as evidence of these issues.

Which of the following assumptions, if true, most strengthens the advocacy group's claims?
(a) Alpha's competitors made larger profits than Alpha in the immediately previous year.
(b) Alpha had recently changed its advertising strategy to highlight customer satisfaction more prominently.
(c) Alpha was recently fined by a regulatory body for not complying with consumer protection standards.
(d) Alpha recently appointed a new CEO.

88. In scientific inquiry, the hypothesis is a testable statement that predicts the relationship between variables. According to the scientific method, the validity of a hypothesis is determined by its ability to withstand empirical testing and produce consistent results. Critics of this approach argue that relying solely on empirical data can lead to the neglect of theoretical frameworks that provide context for understanding phenomena.

Which of the following assumptions would allow the above statements to be properly made?
(a) Empirical data alone can be sufficient to explain complex scientific phenomena.
(b) Theoretical frameworks often provide critical insights that cannot be derived from empirical testing alone.
(c) Many scientific theories are based on assumptions that cannot be empirically tested.
(d) Both b) and c) above.

89. Recent studies indicate that the implementation of remote work policies has led to an increase in employee productivity in many companies. Factors contributing to this trend include reduced commuting time, greater flexibility in work hours, and the ability for employees to create personalized work environments. However, the studies also note that employees who work remotely may experience feelings of isolation and disconnection from their colleagues, which could impact team cohesion and communication. Companies that have adopted remote work policies are now considering whether to continue, modify, or return to traditional in-office work arrangements.

Which of the following conclusion can be most accurately drawn from the above?

(a) Remote work policies are universally beneficial for all companies and employees.

(b) The increase in productivity from remote work is solely due to employees' ability to create personalized work environments.

(c) Companies that implement remote work policies may need to address potential feelings of isolation among employees to maintain team cohesion.

(d) Traditional in-office work arrangements are more effective in promoting team communication and collaboration than remote work.

90. In education policy, the concept of inclusive education advocates for integrating students with disabilities into mainstream classrooms to promote diversity and equal opportunities. However, critics claim that focusing too much on inclusion can strain resources and may lead to a decline in educational quality for students both with and without disabilities.

Which of the following arguments would most strengthen the critics position?

(a) Many parents prefer traditional classrooms for their children over inclusive settings.

(b) Schools often lack the resources needed to effectively implement inclusive education practices.

(c) The academic performance of students without disabilities is negatively impacted by inclusive classrooms.

(d) The academic performance of students with disabilities is negatively impacted by inclusive classrooms.

91. In business strategy, the concept of diversification involves expanding a company's operations into new markets or product lines to reduce risk and enhance growth potential. Though diversification can lead to increased revenue streams and a more resilient business model, critics contend that diversification can dilute a company's core competencies and result in inefficiencies, ultimately harming overall performance.

Which of the following assumptions would allow the above statements to be properly drawn?

(a) Companies often face significant challenges when trying to manage multiple product lines effectively.

(b) Diversification strategies usually require little investment and resources.

(c) A strong focus on core competencies is essential for maintaining optimal output.

(d) Both (a) and (c) above.

92. A recent survey of smartphone users revealed that 70% of respondents believe that data privacy is important. However, only 30% actively use privacy settings on their devices. The survey indicates that a major reason for this is that many users find privacy settings confusing and difficult to navigate.

Which of the following assumptions would allow the above statements to be properly drawn?

(a) The majority of smartphone users are not concerned about data privacy at all

(b) Users who care about data privacy often do not have the technical skills to manage privacy settings

(c) Most smartphone manufacturers do not provide sufficient information on privacy settings

(d) Many users believe that their data is safe without needing to adjust privacy settings

93. Statement: Urban gardening has gained traction in recent years as a way for city dwellers to grow their own food and improve their mental well-being. This movement was partly fuelled by growing concerns about food deserts, environmental sustainability, and the desire for a connection to nature. However, critics argue that urban gardening often does not address the systemic issues of access to fresh food and can sometimes lead to gentrification, where original community members are displaced as property values rise. Despite these criticisms, many individuals find personal fulfilment and community among fellow urban gardeners.

Conclusion:

I. Urban gardening can heighten food insecurity in cities.

II. Many individuals benefit emotionally and socially from participating in urban gardening.

III. Urban gardening can unintentionally contribute to the gentrification of neighbourhoods, harming long-term residents.

Based on the above statement, which conclusion necessarily follows?

(a) Only I follows (b) Only II follows
(c) Only III follows (d) Both II and III follow

94. Statement: A fundamental principle of artificial intelligence (AI) development is to ensure that AI systems are designed with fairness and inclusivity in mind. Developers are expected to implement algorithms that do not discriminate against any demographic group, as bias in AI can lead to significant societal harm. Furthermore, transparency in how AI models make decisions is essential to building trust among users and stakeholders.

Conclusion:

I. It is inappropriate to criticize AI developers for biased outcomes if they have made efforts to promote fairness and transparency in their models.

II. AI developers must prioritize eliminating biases in their algorithms as a key objective.

Based on the above statement, which conclusion necessarily follows?

(a) Only I follows
(b) Only II follows
(c) Both I and II follow
(d) Neither I nor II follows

95. Statement: The discovery of electricity centuries ago led to profound changes in communication, transportation, and industry, significantly altering daily life and economic structures. It is also important to note that the rapid industrialization that followed was accompanied by notable environmental degradation, giving rise to early conservation movements that sought to protect natural resources. Some modern political movements propagate a narrative that portrays technological progress as inherently beneficial, often overlooking the environmental costs associated with it.

Conclusion:

I. Many political movements today ignore the environmental impacts of technological advancements.

II. It is not possible to have industrial progress without environmental degradation.

III. The discovery of electricity has had both positive and negative effects on society. Based on the above statement, which conclusion necessarily follows?

(a) Only I follows (b) Only II follows
(c) Only III follows (d) Both I and III follow

96. Statement: The invention of antibiotics in the early 20th century revolutionized healthcare by drastically reducing mortality rates from infectious diseases and enabling more complex surgeries. However, the overuse of antibiotics in recent decades has contributed to the rise of drug-resistant bacteria, posing new health risks. Simultaneously, public health policies have had to balance the benefits of antibiotic use with the dangers of resistance. Some modern pharmaceutical practices focus primarily on maximizing profits, often sidelining the long-term risks of resistance.

Conclusion:

I. Profit-driven motives always undermine public health priorities.

II. Overuse of antibiotics has resulted in significant health challenges.

III. Advances in healthcare can introduce unintended risks over time.

Based on the above statement, which conclusion necessarily follows?

(a) Only I follows
(b) Only II follows
(c) Both I and II follow
(d) Both II and III follow

97. Statement: The widespread adoption of social media services in the 21st century has transformed how people communicate, enabling instant global connections. However, this shift has also contributed to the spread of misinformation, impacting public trust and social cohesion. In response, some governments have introduced stricter regulations, but these efforts raise concerns about potential censorship and freedom of expression. Some activists argue that controlling misinformation through regulation is necessary, even at the expense of individual freedoms.

Conclusion:

I. The rise of social media services has both benefits and drawbacks for society.

II. Governments should prioritize freedom of expression over controlling misinformation.

III. Efforts to regulate misinformation come with complex trade-offs.

Based on the above statement, which conclusion necessarily follows?

(a) Only I follows
(b) Only III follows
(c) Both I and III follow
(d) Both II and III follow

98. Statement: Sports competitions foster teamwork and discipline, providing athletes with opportunities to develop skills and achieve personal goals. However, the rampant commercialization of sports has shifted the focus toward profit, sometimes leading to unethical practices such as match-fixing and doping. While some argue that strict regulations are needed to preserve the integrity of sports, others believe that over-regulation may hinder athletic performance and creativity. Striking the right balance between commercial interests and ethical standards remains a challenge.

Conclusion:

I. The commercialization of sports has led to unethical practices.

II. Stricter regulations are always beneficial for sports integrity.

III. There is a need for balance between commercial interests and ethical practices in sports.

Based on the above statement, which conclusion necessarily follows?

(a) Only I follows
(b) Both I and III follow
(c) Only III follows
(d) Both II and III follow

99. Statement: Culinary arts have evolved significantly over the years, with chefs increasingly focusing on sustainable and locally sourced ingredients. This shift has allowed for a resurgence of interest in traditional cooking techniques alongside modern innovations. However, some culinary purists argue that these trends threaten the authenticity of classic recipes, while others believe that the focus on sustainability enhances the overall dining experience. The debate about preserving culinary heritage versus embracing new practices continues among food enthusiasts.

Conclusion:

I. The emphasis on sustainability has both benefits and challenges in the culinary world.

II. Traditional recipes will eventually become obsolete due to modern trends.

III. The culinary arts are enriched by the combination of tradition and innovation.

Based on the above statement, which conclusion necessarily follows?
(a) Only I follows
(b) Only III follows
(c) Both II and III follow
(d) Both I and III follow

100. Statement: The rise of independent bookstores in recent years has sparked a renewed interest in reading and community engagement, offering curated selections that reflect local tastes and values. These bookstores often host events, such as author readings and book clubs, creating spaces for meaningful conversations and connections among readers. However, some critics argue that the increasing popularity of online retailers poses a significant threat to the survival of these independent stores, potentially leading to a homogenisation of literary culture. Others believe that the unique experiences and personal touch offered by independent bookstores can sustain their relevance in a digital age.

Conclusion:
I. Independent bookstores play a crucial role in fostering community and promoting local culture.
II. The unique experiences provided by independent bookstores can help them thrive despite digital competition.
III. Online retailers will inevitably lead to the decline of independent bookstores.

Based on the above statement, which conclusion necessarily follows?
(a) Only I follows
(b) Only III follows
(c) Both I and II follow
(d) Both II and III follow

101. Statement: The rise of global tourism has significantly impacted local economies by providing job opportunities and boosting income for many communities. However, it has also led to challenges such as environmental degradation and cultural dilution, as traditional practices and lifestyles are altered to cater to tourists. As a result, many experts advocate for sustainable tourism practices that balance economic benefits with the preservation of local culture and the environment.

Conclusion:
I. All communities benefit equally from the economic opportunities presented by global tourism.
II. Sustainable tourism practices are essential to minimize the negative impacts of tourism on local cultures and environments.
III. The rise of tourism has no significant negative effects on local communities.

Based on the above statement, which conclusion necessarily follows?
(a) Only I follows (b) Only II follows
(c) Only III follows (d) Both I and II follow

102. BCXHADBT is written as 23681422 in a certain code. How is KTLVPTBA written in that code?
(a) 22347221 (b) 68563427
(c) 22893221 (d) 92675221

103. Complete the following series: B, DEF, HIJKLMN, ________?
(a) PQRSTUVWXYZABCDEF
(b) PQRSTUVWXYZAB
(c) QRSTUVWXYZABC
(d) PQRSTUVWXYZABCD

104. Complete the following series: X2A, V6C, T12E, R20G, ________?
(a) O42H (b) P30I
(c) P24J (d) P40I

105. Complete the following series: A3B, C5E, G9H, M15K, ________?
(a) Q21N (b) P23N
(c) U23N (d) U19L

106. Complete the following series: 2A, 4C, 8F, 16J, ________?
(a) 32O (b) 30N
(c) 30P (d) 32P

107. Complete the following series: 1A, 2B, 4D, 8H, ________?

(a) 10H (b) 16P
(c) 16I (d) 14K

108. Complete the following series: Z2, X5, U10, Q17, __________?

(a) L26 (b) M25
(c) L25 (d) N23

109. Complete the following series: 9, 19, 39, 79, __________?

(a) 149 (b) 159
(c) 169 (d) 153

110. All buildings constructed with EarthTech materials are energy efficient. Buildings that are energy efficient qualify for government tax rebates. None of the buildings constructed by Cloudline Developers are energy efficient.

What necessarily follows if the above is true?

(a) Some buildings constructed by Cloudline Developers may qualify for government tax rebates.
(b) All buildings that qualify for government tax rebates use EarthTech materials.
(c) None of the buildings constructed by Cloudline Developers use EarthTech materials.
(d) Some buildings constructed with EarthTech materials do not qualify for government tax rebates.

111. In recent years, research in nutrition and health has highlighted the importance of dietary habits in influencing physical well-being and preventing long-term diseases. Studies indicate that a balanced diet rich in fruits, vegetables, whole grains, and lean proteins is associated with lower rates of obesity, diabetes, and heart disease. Moreover, food choices are often shaped by factors such as socioeconomic status, availability of healthy food options, and cultural preferences, suggesting that environmental influences play a critical role in dietary habits.

If the paragraph above is true, which of the following statements is most contradicted by the paragraph?

(a) Cultural influences can significantly impact the types of foods that people choose to eat.
(b) Genetic predispositions play a significant role in determining an individual's dietary preferences.
(c) Individuals from lower socioeconomic backgrounds may have limited access to healthy food options.
(d) Regular consumption of processed foods can lead to negative health outcomes.

112. The field of psychology has increasingly recognized the role of emotional intelligence (EI) in personal and professional success. Research indicates that individuals with high EI are better equipped to manage stress, communicate effectively, and resolve conflicts. Furthermore, EI has been linked to improved leadership qualities and team dynamics. While cognitive intelligence (IQ) remains important, many experts argue that EI may be a better predictor of success in the workplace. However, the measurement of emotional intelligence can be subjective and varies across different cultural contexts.

Which of the following statements is the most inconsistent with the information provided in the paragraph above?

(a) The influence of cognitive intelligence is diminishing in workplace success assessments.
(b) High emotional intelligence enhances skills in managing stress and resolving conflicts.
(c) Many experts believe emotional intelligence surpasses cognitive intelligence as a success predictor.
(d) The evaluation of emotional intelligence may vary significantly across different cultural environments.

113. Many students find that their study habits significantly impact their academic performance. Those who establish a consistent study schedule often report better retention of information and higher grades. Additionally, the use of active learning techniques, such as summarizing material and teaching concepts to peers, enhances understanding. However, some students struggle to find the right balance between studying and leisure activities, which can lead to stress and decreased productivity.

Based on the paragraph, which of the following statements would most reasonably complete the sentence below?

The variation in student performance suggests that ________

(a) Some students prioritize leisure over studying, which negatively affects their grades.
(b) Consistent study routines are not always sufficient to guarantee academic success.
(c) Active learning techniques are universally effective for all students.
(d) A lack of balance between studying and leisure can create unnecessary stress for students.

114. Effective teamwork is crucial for project success in any organization. Research indicates that diverse teams, which include members with different backgrounds and skill sets, often produce more innovative solutions than homogeneous teams. However, team dynamics can be affected by conflict if not managed properly. Studies show that teams with effective conflict resolution strategies tend to achieve their goals faster and with higher satisfaction levels among team members. In organizations, it is essential to implement training programs that teach conflict resolution techniques to enhance team performance.

Which of the following can be inferred from the above passage?

(a) Organizations should avoid forming diverse teams to reduce conflict.
(b) Homogeneous teams are always more effective than diverse teams.
(c) Conflict within teams is always detrimental to project outcomes.
(d) Training programs on conflict resolution can improve team dynamics.

115. All mobile phones with advanced camera features are popular among social media influencers. Mobile phones that are popular among social media influencers often have high storage capacity. None of the mobile phones manufactured by Brand B have advanced camera features.

Which of the following necessarily follows if the above is true?

(a) All mobile phones that are popular among social media influencers have high storage capacity.
(b) Mobile phones manufactured by Brand B are popular among social media influencers.
(c) None of the mobile phones manufactured by Brand B are popular among social media influencers.
(d) All mobile phones with high storage capacity also have advanced camera features.

116. The study of ancient civilisations reveals much about human history and cultural development. Archaeological findings indicate that societies that engaged in trade and cultural exchange often experienced advancements in art, architecture, and technology. For instance, the exchange of ideas and goods between the Egyptians and Mesopotamians led to significant innovations in farming and engineering. However, some civilisations that isolated themselves from others faced stagnation in cultural and technological progress.

Which of the following can be inferred from the above passage?

(a) Isolation leads to greater cultural advancements than interaction with others.
(b) All ancient civilisations experienced the same level of development regardless of their interactions.
(c) Trade and cultural exchange can be key drivers of societal progress.
(d) Art and architecture have no relationship to the progress of technology in ancient societies.

117. The exploration of space has captivated humanity for decades, sparking advancements in various scientific fields. Astronomers have discovered numerous celestial bodies, expanding our understanding of the universe and our place within it. Additionally, space missions have led to significant developments in technology, such as satellite communications and materials science. While the costs of space exploration can be high, the potential benefits, including inspiring future generations and fostering international collaboration, are profound.

Which of the following can be inferred from the above passage?

(a) The financial costs of space exploration can sometimes outweigh its benefits.
(b) Space exploration primarily serves scientific communities more than society in general.
(c) Technological advancements resulting from space missions are limited to astronomy.
(d) The potential benefits of space exploration include inspiring future generations and promoting global cooperation.

118. Art has long served as a powerful means of expression and communication. Throughout history, artists have utilized various mediums—such as painting, sculpture, and music—to convey their thoughts, emotions, and critiques of society. Many art movements have emerged in response to cultural and political changes, highlighting the dynamic relationship between art and the world around it. Additionally, exposure to diverse forms of art can enhance creativity and foster empathy among individuals, making it a vital aspect of the human experience.

Which of the following can be inferred from the above passage?

(a) Art only serves to reflect societal norms and values
(b) Exposure to diverse art forms can enhance creativity and promote empathy
(c) Engaging with different art forms has limited impact on individual creativity
(d) The relationship between art and societal changes is static and unchanging

119. Select the correct option:

If Tree : forest then ____________

(a) Bee : honey (b) Star : galaxy
(c) Door : cabinet (d) Book : knowledge

120. Select the correct option:

If Lotus : water then ____________

(a) Toe : feet
(b) Tea : beverage
(c) Grasshopper : insect
(d) Lice : hair

121. Select the correct option:

If Cheese : milk then ____________

(a) Omelette : eggs
(b) Coffee : sugar
(c) Bread : rice
(d) Rice : farm

122. Select the correct option:

If Cement : buildings then ____________

(a) Wood : fire (b) Clay : pots
(c) Gas : food (d) Soil : crops

123. Select the correct option:

If Photographer : camera then ____________

(a) Carpenter : sofa
(b) Chef : food
(c) Painter : brush
(d) Doctor : hospital

124. Select the correct option:

If Familiar : strange then ____________

(a) Warm : hot
(b) Careful : careless
(c) Sturdy : muscular
(d) Intelligent : emotional

125. A company, GreenFuel, argues that its new biofuel product is entirely eco-friendly because it is made from renewable resources. GreenFuel claims that since the product is derived from organic matter, it has zero negative impact on the environment.

Which of the following, if true, most weakens GreenFuel's argument above?

(a) The process of producing the biofuel emits significant greenhouse gases due to the energy required for extraction and processing.
(b) Although biofuel is renewable, its widespread cultivation leads to deforestation and the destruction of natural habitats.
(c) Production of biofuel is significantly more costly than extraction of fuel from non renewable sources.
(d) Both (a) and (b) above.

126. Advocates for early coding education argue that teaching programming skills to children from a young age will enhance their problem-solving abilities and prepare them for a technology-driven future. Therefore, coding should be introduced as a mandatory subject in elementary schools.

Which of the following, if true, most strengthens the argument above?
(a) Coding languages evolve slowly, and therefore what is taught today is likely to remain relevant in future as well.
(b) Many successful programmers learned coding only in their adulthood and excelled without early exposure.
(c) Children are fast learners and likely understand coding languages easily.
(d) Early exposure to problem-solving techniques enhances cognitive development in children.

127. Recent research indicates that excessive consumption of processed foods is linked to an increased risk of obesity. A five-year study tracked two groups: one that regularly consumed processed foods and another that followed a whole-foods- based diet. The study found that the processed-food group had a 25% higher rate of obesity by the end of the study. Therefore, the study concluded that processed food consumption directly causes obesity.

Which of the following, if true, most strengthens the argument above?
(a) Some participants in the whole-foods group occasionally consumed small amounts of processed foods.
(b) Both groups were matched for physical activity levels, age, and overall caloric intake during the study period.
(c) Other studies have shown that regular exercise reduces the risk of obesity, regardless of diet.
(d) Processed foods are often high in sugars and unhealthy fats, which contribute to weight gain.

128. Prakash has been working as a software engineer at Company A for 10 years. Recently, he discovered that a new hire, who has less experience and fewer qualifications, is being paid more than him. Prakash approached his manager with this concern and was told that the new hire's pay is based on market demand for talent in that particular programming language. Prakash believes he is being treated unfairly based on his seniority and qualifications.

Which of the following, if true, most strengthens Prakash's claim of unfair treatment?
(a) The new hire was offered a higher salary to meet the industry standard for that particular programming language.
(b) Prakash has consistently taken on high-responsibility projects and delivered strong results throughout his tenure at Company A.
(c) Prakash and the new hire obtained their basic and advanced degrees from the same institution.
(d) Both (a) and (b) above.

129. Sarab and her brother Sateesh have been sharing household chores for several years. Recently, Sarab noticed that Sateesh consistently gets lighter tasks, such as taking out the trash, while she is assigned more time-consuming duties, like cooking and cleaning the entire house. When Sarab brought this up to their parents, they explained that Sateesh is assigned tasks based on his school workload and extracurricular activities, which are more demanding than Sarab's. Sarab believes she is being treated unfairly and that the division of chores is biased.

Which of the following, if true, most strengthens Sarab's claim of unfair treatment?

(a) Sarab is involved in several extracurricular activities and has an equally demanding schedule as Sateesh.
(b) Sateesh volunteered to help Sarab with her chores on several occasions but has rarely been assigned the more time-consuming tasks himself.
(c) Sateesh voluntarily took on additional extracurricular activities, which were not mandatory part of the school work.
(d) Sarab's parents often help her in completion of household chores.

130. An enterprise has the responsibility to ensure the safety of its products before selling them to the public. While no product can be entirely risk-free, if an enterprise knows that a product has significant defects that could harm consumers, it is their duty to either fix those defects or provide clear warnings. Unfortunately, some enterprises prioritize profits over safety and release products that may pose serious risks to the public.

Which of the statements below is most consistent with the paragraph above?

(a) Consumers are solely responsible for assessing the risks of the products they buy.
(b) It is acceptable for enterprises to release potentially harmful products if the risk of harm is low.
(c) Enterprises should always prioritize consumer safety over profit, even if it affects their financial performance.
(d) Enterprises have no obligation to warn consumers about every possible risk, only significant defects.

131. A wildfire has broken out in a large national park, spreading quickly due to dry conditions and strong winds. The forest officers only have a limited amount of firefighting resources, including helicopters, water trucks, and personnel. They must decide where to allocate these resources to save as much of the park as possible. To maximize their efforts, they prioritize the areas of the park that are home to endangered species and ecosystems that would be the hardest to recover if destroyed by the fire.

Which of the following most mirrors the principle in the passage above?

I. A university offers a limited number of scholarships each year. To ensure the best use of its funds, it prioritizes applicants from underprivileged backgrounds and those with academic potential, believing this will have the most significant long-term impact on the community.
II. A charitable foundation receives an influx of donations for disaster relief. In distributing the funds, it focuses on the hardest-hit communities where homes were completely destroyed, providing them with emergency shelter and rebuilding services before addressing other needs.
III. A large grocery store faces a major food supply shortage due to transportation issues. To minimize the impact on customers, the store decides to limit the sale of high-demand items like milk, bread, and meat, allowing each shopper to purchase only a small amount to ensure everyone can get basic supplies.

Select the correct option:

(a) Only I
(b) Only I & II
(c) Only II & III
(d) I, II & III

132. Where public safety or the protection of human life is at stake, it is justified to limit personal freedoms and privacy in order to ensure the well-being of the broader public. Based on the above principle, which of the following actions would be justified?

(a) Pinto, a public health official, enforced a temporary closure of all schools during a severe flu outbreak to prevent the spread of the virus among students, despite protests from parents.

(b) Laila, a private company CEO, ordered the installation of surveillance cameras inside employee restrooms to prevent theft in the workplace, arguing it would protect company assets.
(c) Sanju, a police officer, initiated random searches of people's homes without a warrant, arguing that it was necessary to prevent potential burglaries in the neighbourhood.
(d) Sarita, a local politician, proposed limiting internet access in her town to prevent residents from accessing certain websites, claiming it would improve public morality and safety.

133. The rapid advancement of technology has significantly changed the way people interact with one another. While technology facilitates communication and connects people across distances, it can also lead to feelings of isolation and disconnection in face-to-face relationships. Many individuals find that they are more comfortable sharing their thoughts and feelings online rather than in person, which can diminish the quality of their real-world interactions.

Based on the above passage, which conclusion necessarily follows?
(a) Technology has completely replaced the need for in-person communication.
(b) People prefer online interactions over face-to-face conversations.
(c) While technology can enhance connections, it may also hinder personal relationships.
(d) All of the above.

134. Principle: The impact of leadership styles on historical events can shape the course of nations and influence the outcomes of conflicts.

Facts: During the late 20th century, two prominent leaders emerged during a territorial dispute: X advocated for peaceful negotiations and diplomacy, while Y supported aggressive military action to assert dominance. After a series of failed internal talks, Y's approach led to a major conflict, resulting in significant casualties and territorial loss for both sides. In contrast, X's proposed solution, although initially rejected, eventually gained support and led to de-escalation of the conflict.

Based on the above, which of the following statements is most accurate?
(a) Y's aggressive strategy ultimately resulted in a favourable outcome for his side.
(b) X's diplomatic approach was ineffective since it did not prevent the conflict from escalating.
(c) The historical context suggests that both X and Y acted correctly based on the circumstances they faced.
(d) The eventual support for X's solution highlights the importance of diplomacy in conflict resolution.

135. Principle: A property owner is responsible for maintaining the safety of their premises and is liable for any injuries that occur due to hazardous conditions in the premises, unless the injured party was trespassing.

Facts: Tara owns a retail store, and a heavy rainstorm caused a leak in the ceiling of the store. Tara was aware of the leak but did not have time to fix it before customers arrived the next morning. She placed a sign warning customers of the wet floor. However, Aman, who entered the store to browse, slipped on the wet floor and injured his leg. Aman did not see the warning sign.

Based on the above which of the following statements is most accurate?
(a) Tara is liable for Aman's injury since the wet floor was a hazardous condition.
(b) Tara is not liable because she placed a warning sign, informing customers of the hazard.
(c) Aman is not entitled to compensation because he failed to notice the sign.
(d) Tara is not liable since the injury occurred due to a natural event beyond her control.

136. Principle: A party to a contract is responsible for fulfilling their obligations under the agreement and is liable for damages if they fail to do so.

Facts: Richa enters into a contract with a catering company, Big Bites, to provide catering services for her wedding reception. The contract specifies that Big Bites will provide food for 125 guests on a specific date. On the day of the event, Big Bites only delivers food for 75 guests due to road closure on account of VIP movement. Richa is forced to make last-minute alternate arrangements to feed the additional guests, incurring extra costs.

Select the most appropriate option:

(a) Richa can recover costs incurred to make alternate arrangements from Big Bites.
(b) Richa is not required to pay any amount to Big Bites since the contract was not fulfilled.
(c) Richa is entitled to recover damages since Big Bites failed to deliver the agreed-upon amount of food.
(d) There is insufficient information to decide.

137. Principle: A party who receives a benefit at the expense of another party is required to make restitution to prevent unjust enrichment.

Facts: Anita hires a construction company, Best Builders, to renovate her swimming pool. The contract states that Best Builders will install new water purifiers for a total cost of INR 10,000. During the renovation, Best Builders installs high-end purifiers worth INR 15,000 instead of the standard ones specified in the contract. When the project is completed, Anita enjoys the upgraded purifiers but only pays the agreed-upon amount of INR 10,000.

Select the most appropriate option:

(a) Best Builders is entitled to receive the full value of the purifiers INR 15,000 since Anita is using the purifier.
(b) Anita can keep the purifiers and is entitled to a refund of INR 10,000, since the purifiers installed by Best Builders are not as agreed under the original contract.
(c) Anita can keep the purifiers without paying any additional amount since they were not part of the original contract.
(d) None of the above.

138. Principle: The opportunity cost of a decision is the value of the next best alternative that is forgone when a choice is made.

Facts: Shyam is an aspiring artist who has a chance to exhibit his paintings at a local gallery for two months. He can either take this opportunity, which would allow him to showcase his work and potentially sell pieces for a total profit of INR 50,000, or he can accept a temporary job offer for the same duration of two months, that would earn him INR 30,000 in total. After careful consideration, Shyam decides to exhibit his paintings at the gallery.

Which of the following statements is true regarding Shyam's decision?

(a) Shyam's opportunity cost for choosing to exhibit his paintings is INR 50,000, as that was the profit he could have earned from the gallery.
(b) By choosing to exhibit his paintings, Shyam has no opportunity cost since he is pursuing his passion.
(c) Shyam's decision to exhibit his paintings resulted in a net gain of INR 20,000 in opportunity cost.
(d) Shyam's opportunity cost for choosing to exhibit his paintings is INR 30,000, as that was the amount he could have earned from the temporary job.

139. Principle: Confirmation bias is the tendency to search for, interpret, and remember information in a way that confirms one's pre-existing beliefs.

Facts: Mala is an avid believer in the benefits of a plant-based diet and often shares articles and studies that support her view on social media. When she comes across a scientific study that suggests a balanced omnivorous diet can also provide significant health benefits, she dismisses it without reading, focusing instead on the findings of studies that align with her beliefs.

Which of the following statements is true regarding Mala's behaviour?

(a) Mala is exhibiting confirmation bias by ignoring evidence that contradicts her views.
(b) Mala is making a rational decision by focusing on information that supports her beliefs.
(c) Mala should only trust information that aligns with her beliefs to ensure consistency in her opinions.
(d) Mala's behaviour is beneficial because it strengthens her knowledge of plant-based diets.

140. Principle: The Dunning-Kruger effect is a cognitive bias wherein individuals with low ability at a task overestimate their ability, while those with high ability may underestimate their competence.

Facts: Tutu, a new employee at a tech company, recently completed a basic coding course. Feeling confident, she frequently shares her opinions about software development with her colleagues, often dismissing their suggestions as unnecessary. Meanwhile, Saba, a senior developer with years of experience, is careful about her own ideas and often second-guesses her suggestions during team meetings.

Which of the following statements is true regarding Tutu and Saba's behaviours?
(a) Tutu alone is exhibiting Dunning-Kruger effect.
(b) Saba alone is exhibiting Dunning-Kruger effect.
(c) Both Tutu and Saba are demonstrating Dunning-Kruger effect.
(d) Neither Tutu nor Saba are demonstrating Dunning-Kruger effect.

141. Principle: Any person who publishes false statements that result in significant financial losses to a business shall be guilty of an offence.

Facts: Jatin publishes a news article claiming that a popular restaurant has been serving unsafe food. Jatin sincerely believes this to be true. The restaurant suffers significant financial losses as a result. However, it is later revealed that the statements in Jatin's article were false.

Has Jatin committed an offence?
(a) Yes, because he published false statements that caused financial losses, and his intention or knowledge is immaterial.
(b) No, because he was unaware of the consequences.
(c) Yes, if it can be proven that his false statements directly led to financial losses.
(d) There is insufficient information to decide.

142. A ban on cell phones in schools is necessary as it distracts students from their academics, it is unnecessary as in an emergency the school landlines can be used. A break from social media during the school day would remove the stress and help students build their concentration and enhance their learning.

What is the assumption being made about cell phones?
(a) That cell phones are harmful to students and their ability to focus and remain stress free.
(b) That cell phones can be replaced by landlines in an emergency.
(c) A break from cell phones is necessary to build concentration.
(d) Cell phones are necessary for learning.

143. Caroline Hoxby has produced a large body of research looking at college applications by low-income students. In 'The Missing One-Offs,' she and Christopher Avery showed that students with high grades and low economic standing often refrain from applying to more prestigious schools, despite those schools' better financial support. Their research suggests that students who avoid selective schools are usually choosing to apply to the same schools their friends and economic peers do. Hoxby and Avery conclude that this is either a consequence of their being underinformed about their options (a fault of recruitment) or believing that the culture and atmosphere of prestigious colleges wouldn't be very inviting to them (a fault of the schools and their PR).

Which of the following can be properly inferred from the passage?

(a) Low Income Students refrain from applying to prestigious schools, because they are under-informed or they are intimidated by the culture of prestigious colleges
(b) Low Income Students refrain from applying to prestigious schools, because they are more influenced by peer pressure to conform to certain choices
(c) Low Income Students refrain from applying to prestigious schools, because they are influenced by the public relations
(d) Low Income Students refrain from applying to prestigious schools, because they are repelled by the culture of prestigious colleges

144. University Academic Department is finalizing class schedules for the incoming batch. The subjects are Criminal Law, Property Law, Economics, Legal Methods and English. The following considerations are kept in mind:

I. All subjects must be held once
II. Legal Methods and English cannot immediately precede or follow each other
III. Economics must immediately precede Property Law
IV. Economics must immediately follow English
V. Criminal Law cannot be the second or the last subject

Which of the following schedules is valid?

(a) Legal Methods, Criminal Law, English, Economics, Property Law
(b) Property Law, Economics, English, Criminal Law, Legal Methods
(c) Economics, Property Law, Legal Methods, English, Criminal Law
(d) Criminal Law, English, Economics, Property Law, Legal Methods

145. Vinay is trying to decide the sequence in which to watch the following movies – Sholay (SH), RRR, Slumdog Millionaire (SM), PK and Dangal (DL). The sequence must adhere to the following conditions:

I. SH and DL must not immediately precede or follow each other.
II. RRR must go after SM.
III. PK cannot be the first or the last movie.
IV. DL must necessarily be one removed from SM.

Which of the following is a valid sequence?

(a) SH, RRR, PK, DL, SM
(b) PK, DL, RRR, SM, SH
(c) DL, SM, PK, RRR, SH
(d) DL, PK, SM, RRR, SH

146. Sanjana is attempting to create an exercise plan for a 5-day week. She has decided on the following exercises – A, X, B, Y, C, in accordance with the following conditions.

I. A and Y cannot be on the consecutive days
II. C must always be followed by B
III. B and A cannot be done on alternate days
IV. X cannot be done on the first day of the week
V. No exercise can be repeated in the week

Which of the following is a valid plan?

(a) A, Y, B, C, X
(b) Y, C, B, X, A
(c) Y, C, B, A, X
(d) X, C, B, A, Y

147. All Rabbits are Sleepers. All Tortoise paints. Some Rabbits are Tortoise. Siri is a Rabbit. Examine the following statements:

I. Siri paints
II. Siri does not paint
III. Siri is a Sleeper
IV. Siri is not a Sleeper
V. Siri is a Tortoise
VI. Siri is not a Tortoise

Choose the most appropriate answer:

(a) Only III
(b) Only V
(c) Only I, IV, VI
(d) Only II, III, VI

148. All Cherry are Pink. Some Pink are made into cake. All cake is eaten. Banana is Pink. Examine the following statements:

I. Banana is a Cherry
II. Banana is not a Cherry
III. Banana may be made into cake
IV. Banana will definitely be made into a cake
V. If Banana is Cherry, then it will be eaten

Choose the most appropriate answer:

(a) Only III (b) Only II and III
(c) Only IV and V (d) Only V

149. Assertion: The rise of OTT platforms is challenging the traditional movie theatre business.

Argument 1: OTT platforms and traditional movie theatre present completely different experience and therefore are unlikely to affect each other.

Argument 2: OTT platforms ensure instant availability of diverse content, which a traditional movie theatre cannot emulate.

Choose the most appropriate answer:

(a) Only Argument 1 is strong
(b) Only Argument 2 is strong
(c) Both Arguments are strong
(d) Neither Argument is strong

150. Issue: Is football the most popular sport in the world?

Argument 1: Yes, Football World Cup (FIFA) have over five times global viewership as compared to Formula 1 Grand Prix (Car racing) or the Wimbledon Championships (Tennis).

Argument 2: Yes, Lionel Messi is the most followed footballer across social media platforms.

Argument 3: No, the Cricket World Cup has been the most profitable sports event worldwide for the last three decades.

Choose the most appropriate answer:

(a) Only Argument 1 is strong
(b) Only Argument 2 is strong
(c) Only Argument 3 is strong
(d) Both Arguments 1 and 3 are strong

ANSWER KEY

Section A: English

1. (b)	9. (c)	17. (b)	25. (c)	33. (c)	41. (d)	49. (b)
2. (a)	10. (a)	18. (b)	26. (d)	34. (d)	42. (a)	50. (b)
3. (b)	11. (c)	19. (c)	27. (b)	35. (c)	43. (a)	
4. (d)	12. (b)	20. (b)	28. (b)	36. (d)	44. (b)	
5. (c)	13. (c)	21. (a)	29. (d)	37. (a)	45. (c)	
6. (c)	14. (b)	22. (c)	30. (d)	38. (b)	46. (d)	
7. (b)	15. (b)	23. (a)	31. (c)	39. (c)	47. (b)	
8. (d)	16. (c)	24. (c)	32. (b)	40. (a)	48. (c)	

Section B: Current Affairs and General Knowledge

51. (b)	56. (a)	61. (a)	66. (c)	71. (b)	76. (a)
52. (c)	57. (a)	62. (b)	67. (b)	72. (d)	77. (b)
53. (d)	58. (d)	63. (c)	68. (a)	73. (c)	78. (d)
54. (b)	59. (b)	64. (a)	69. (a)	74. (b)	79. (b)
55. (c)	60. (c)	65. (d)	70. (a)	75. (a)	80. (a)

Section C: Logical Reasoning

81. (c)	91. (d)	101. (b)	111. (b)	121. (a)	131. (a)	141. (a)
82. (a)	92. (b)	102. (a)	112. (a)	122. (b)	132. (d)	142. (a)
83. (c)	93. (d)	103. (d)	113. (b)	123. (c)	133. (b)	143. (d)
84. (a)	94. (b)	104. (b)	114. (d)	124. (b)	134. (a)	144. (d)
85. (d)	95. (d)	105. (c)	115. (c)	125. (d)	135. (c)	145. (c)
86. (b)	96. (d)	106. (a)	116. (c)	126. (d)	136. (c)	146. (a)
87. (c)	97. (c)	107. (b)	117. (d)	127. (b)	137. (a)	147. (a)
88. (d)	98. (c)	108. (a)	118. (b)	128. (b)	138. (d)	148. (c)
89. (c)	99. (d)	109. (b)	119. (b)	129. (a)	139. (a)	149. (d)
90. (b)	100. (c)	110. (c)	120. (d)	130. (d)	140. (a)	150. (a)

AILET 2024

SECTION A: ENGLISH

I. Read the given extract and answer the following questions by choosing the most appropriate answer.

The past century has drastically changed the concept of community, no matter if you live in a rural area, a suburban neighbourhood, or an urban metropolis. Families no longer co-habitat as intergenerationally as they once did, especially as the appeal of the nuclear family began to increase. The move from rural living to urban lifestyles to suburbia and then back to citylife has meant that extended families often fracture and live further and further apart. We are often caught up in the reality of constant "busy-ness" that we don't take the time to get to know our neighbours. And social media has redefined "connection" and "friendship," leaving us staring at screens more than engaging with the people around us.

The impact of this is apparent on parents and children. The adage "it takes a village to raise a child" is absolutely still true. But somewhere along the way, we've lost the "village" we need to raise kids in nurturing, creative, and safe ways. And as a result, families are missing out on crucial learning experiences and much needed support systems. in the end. Many parents feel isolated and alone in their struggles, and kids don't have the opportunity to engage with a diverse group of people and personalities.

1. The primary reason for breaking up of the traditional community set up is
   (a) preference for expanding suburban neighbourhoods.
   (b) attraction of the small family unit.
   (c) changing concept of cohabiting in the modern world.
   (d) the lack of desire to live with the oldest family members.

2. The reason people do not know their neighbour very well is because
   (a) they are always in transit.
   (b) their lifestyle is self-destructive.
   (c) they are constantly preoccupied with their own affairs.
   (d) their self-centredness keeps them from interacting with the neighbour.

3. The writer's attitude towards the 'connections' formed via social media is
   (a) disparaging (b) concurrence
   (c) apathetic (d) elusive

4. Which of the following statements is incorrect with respect to the passage?
   (a) The community provides a safe and healthy environment for positive interaction with the children.
   (b) Crucial learning experiences and much needed support systems at home clash with the values of the community.
   (c) The collective effort of the community raises children in nurturing, creative, and safe ways.
   (d) Modern communities lack meaningful interactions, leaving the parents feeling isolated and alone in their struggles.

5. **Statement 1:** People are available to raise other people's children.
   Statement 2: The nature of communities has undergone tremendous transformation regardless of their location.
   Choose the most appropriate answer.

(a) Both statements are true and 2 is the correct explanation of 1.
(b) Both statements are true but 2 is not the correct explanation of 1.
(c) Statement 1 is true but statement 2 is false.
(d) Statement 1 is false but statement 2 is true.

II. Read the given extract and answer the following questions by choosing the most appropriate answer.

I used to be the person that would strive for perfection from the beginning of a creative process. With more time given at the beginning an obvious decline of quality is seen and it has become a pattern all throughout my other works. Here's why, I had to change my system of production.

Being stuck at the beginning of a creative process (i.e., writing, designing, painting) due to overthinking will have a ripple effect on the entire output. In art school, I have had many classmates taking their time planning on how to produce a material and half of the time given for production was wasted. They then had more pressure to finish their works just to meet the deadline and sacrifice the quality of output all together.

Being a working student to help support myself in school, I never had the luxury of time that my classmates had when we were in college; when we were given a project, I started immediately. I call my process "Finished, Not Perfect Method" (FNPM).

FNPM allows me to be efficient. I divide the amount of time I have by the number of parts my project has - Beginning, Middle, End, improvements. Each part is given focus and time for potential improvements or changes. A friend or two could tell you what their opinion is and you may add the necessary changes based on their input. However, keep the maximum number of people you consult for opinion to two. Anything more than that will create more opinions that will paralyse you from progressing later on.

When your work can give what's needed and you've finished your work on time (if not earlier), then the next step is to stop and find a way to be happy about it. Contentment is important in this stage for people always feel regret for not doing their best in a work they've laboured so hard for.

6. Although the writer described herself as being a perfectionist, the eventual quality of her work was ______? Choose the most appropriate answer.
(a) dilapidated (b) disappointing
(c) devastating (d) distorted

7. 'Overthinking' posed a big hurdle for the narrator as
(a) she would be coerced into being dull.
(b) she would sulk over her spoiled assignments.
(c) it would not allow her to start her work.
(d) it would make her anxious about her submission.

8. Identify the sequence of events that ultimately led to art school students submitting subpar work.
(1) Quality of work compromised to meet the deadline
(2) Large amount of time invested on planning
(3) Mounting pressure to complete the task
(4) Wasted half of the time in production
Choose the appropriate option:
(a) (2), (3), (4), (1) (b) (2), (3), (1), (4)
(c) (2), (4), (3), (1) (d) (2), (4), (1), (3)

9. 'Ripple effect' means
(a) the continuing and spreading results of an event or action.
(b) the cumulative effect produced when one event sets off a chain of similar or other events.
(c) anything that can go wrong will go wrong.
(d) moving in a circular path towards the centre of the circle.

10. 'Time' is referred to as a 'luxury' because
(a) she had to work after classes and thus, could not spare any time.
(b) she had a lot of time on her hands to get things done slowly.
(c) time was a valuable commodity she paid a heavy price for.
(d) she was mostly running out of time because of overthinking.

11. The writer had to innovate her "Finished, Not Perfect Method" (FNPM) since:
- (a) she had to get better grades than her privileged classmates.
- (b) her overthinking pattern was a dismal failure.
- (c) she had very little time to spare.
- (d) chasing perfection never got her work done.

12. Segregating the various parts of the project helps
- (a) while consulting friends for their opinion.
- (b) to work on each part separately and improve it.
- (c) to reduce production time at the beginning.
- (d) reduces stress that is usually accompanied by missed deadlines.

III. Read the given extract and answer the following questions by choosing the most appropriate answer.

In recent years, medical schools and institutions have increasingly integrated VR (Virtual Reality) into their curriculum, offering near real experiences for training future healthcare professionals. While VR offers numerous advantages in medical training, it also presents significant challenges that must be addressed.

One of the primary benefits of VR in medical education is its ability to provide realistic and immersive simulations of medical procedures. Medical students can use VR to practice surgeries, diagnose illnesses, and engage in patient interactions in a controlled and risk-free environment. These simulations allow students to gain valuable hands-on experience before they encounter real patients, thereby increasing their confidence and competence.

Furthermore, VR can enhance the understanding of complex anatomical structures. By immersing students in 3D models of the human body, they can explore organs, tissues, and systems from various angles, improving their spatial awareness and comprehension. This interactive learning experience fosters a deeper understanding of human anatomy, a crucial foundation for medical practice.

However, the integration of VR into medical education is not without its challenges. Firstly, the cost of implementing VR technology in medical schools can be substantial. High-quality VR equipment and software require a significant financial investment, which may strain the budgets of educational institutions. Additionally, ongoing maintenance and updates are necessary to ensure the technology remains effective.

Another challenge lies in the development of accurate and comprehensive VR medical simulations. Creating realistic virtual patients and medical scenarios that mimic real-world complexities demands extensive research and development efforts. Ensuring the accuracy of simulations is crucial to the educational value of VR training.

Moreover, VR raises concerns about potential over-reliance on technology. Medical students must strike a balance between virtual training and hands-on clinical experience. While VR offers a safe and controlled environment for learning, it cannot replace the valuable lessons learned through direct patient interaction.

To sum up, Virtual Reality has the potential to transform medical education but it also presents financial and developmental challenges, as well as concerns about balancing virtual and real-world experiences. Addressing these challenges will be crucial in harnessing the full potential of VR for medical education.

13. This passage most likely appeared as part of a ______. Complete the sentence with an appropriate option.
- (a) Technology magazine feature
- (b) Medical school's informational brochure
- (c) Government report on education
- (d) Debate on the future of medical training

14. The author's primary purpose in this passage is ______
- (a) To advocate for the complete replacement of traditional medical training with VR.
- (b) To provide a balanced discussion of the advantages and challenges of using VR in medical education.

(c) To persuade readers to invest in VR technology for medical schools.
(d) To critique the high cost of VR equipment in medical education.

15. The passage mentions *"immersive experiences"* to emphasise ______
(a) The potential for escapism in VR.
(b) The intensity and realism of VR training.
(c) The need for virtual tours of medical facilities.
(d) The limited scope of VR simulations.

16. Identify the sentence in the passage that contains a participial phrase.
(a) 'Virtual reality technology has been steadily advancing.'
(b) 'This immersive experience can significantly enhance their learning.'
(c) 'It allows them to practice complex surgical procedures.'
(d) 'The medical students, wearing VR headsets, feel as if they are in an operating room.'

17. According to the passage, why is the cost of implementing VR in medical schools a challenge?
(a) VR technology is difficult to maintain.
(b) VR equipment is currently unavailable.
(c) VR requires a significant financial investment.
(d) VR simulations are not realistic enough.

18. What does the passage suggest about the balance between VR training and hands-on clinical experience?
(a) VR training can entirely replace hands-on clinical experience.
(b) VR training should be the sole focus of medical education.
(c) Clinical experience is no longer relevant in medical education.
(d) A balance between VR training and real-world experience is essential.

19. The author's discussion of the challenges of VR in medical education is primarily intended to ______
(a) present a well-rounded view of the topic.
(b) convince readers that VR is not suitable for medical training.
(c) discourage investment in VR technology.
(d) highlight the need for more research and development in VR.

20. Which word from paragraphs 4-5, in the passage could be substituted with *'financially burden'*, without changing the meaning?
(a) Integration (b) Accuracy
(c) Mimic (d) Strain

21. In the passage, the phrase 'fosters a deeper understanding', is best defined as
(a) Promotes a more profound insight.
(b) Creates a stronger resistance.
(c) Reduces the complexity of.
(d) Develops a superficial grasp of.

22. Which of the following, if true, would most weaken the conclusion that addressing the challenges is crucial for harnessing the full potential of VR in medical education?
(a) Medical schools are rapidly adopting VR without considering the costs.
(b) Traditional medical training methods are becoming less effective.
(c) VR technology is becoming more affordable and accessible.
(d) VR simulations can replace all aspects of clinical experience.

IV. Read the given extract and answer the following questions by choosing the most appropriate answer.

Why do we relentlessly pursue these gleaming awards and coveted certificates? These tokens of recognition, ranging from simple course completion certificates to the grandeur of global trophies, what drives us? Do we not have an innate sense of our own value? The human pursuit of accolades and certificates, an intricate interplay of self-worth, external validation, and societal pressures.

At the heart of our chase for these honours lies an unquenchable thirst for acknowledgment and validation. No matter how confident or self-assured one may be, the allure of external validation is irresistible. it's not about doubting our capabilities; it's about the affirmation that our dedication and hard work have been seen, recognized, and applauded. In this light, awards and certificates stand not just as tokens but as symbols of our relentless pursuit of excellence.

Our relentless pursuit of accolades is deeply woven into the fabric of our society. From an early age, we are indoctrinated to compete, to shine in academics, sports, or our careers. Society's measure of success often hinges on these tangible milestones, which illustrate our ability not just to meet but to exceed expectations.

Moreover, these recognitions bestow an unparalleled sense of accomplishment and pride. They are emblematic of the tireless hours, the unwavering dedication, and the indomitable spirit invested in chasing our dreams. This recognition is transformative, elevating an individual's self-esteem, inspiring them to reach for the stars, and to redefine their self-worth. The satisfaction gleaned from these acknowledgments extends beyond the realm of external validation; it is an ode to personal growth.

However, as we embark on this relentless journey, we must tread with caution. A relentless pursuit of external validation can lead to a superficial sense of self-worth. A person's true worth cannot be distilled from the certificates adorning their walls or the trophies glittering on their shelves. Intrinsic motivation and personal fulfilment must hold equal sway.

To conclude, our burning desire for awards and certificates mirrors our unyielding quest for recognition, validation, and the unquenchable sense of accomplishment they bring. These accolades undeniably hold great significance, but we must not forget that our self-worth should not be tethered solely to the whims of external validation. Our achievements are undeniably important, but they represent just one facet of our intricate, multidimensional identities.

23. What is the tone of the passage?
(a) Informative (b) Reflective
(c) Persuasive (d) Ironic

24. What is the cause-and-effect relationship presented in the passage?
(a) Cause: Pursuit of awards and certificates, Effect: Increased self-worth
(b) Cause: Intrinsic motivation, Effect: Pursuit of awards
(c) Cause: Unquenchable sense of accomplishment, Effect: Extrinsic validation
(d) Cause: Ironic tone, Effect: Entertainment of readers

25. What is the purpose of the word "relentless" in the passage?
(a) To describe the journey as short-lived.
(b) To emphasise the continuous and persistent nature of the pursuit.
(c) To indicate a sudden change in direction.
(d) To convey a sense of calm and tranquillity.

26. Which of the following, if true, would most weaken the conclusion that external validation is superficial in determining self-worth?
(a) Individuals who possess numerous awards tend to have high self-esteem.
(b) The pursuit of awards and certificates is often driven by personal goals and intrinsic motivation.
(c) People who lack external validation through awards still maintain high levels of self-worth.
(d) Studies show that individuals with more certificates are perceived as more competent by employers.

27. The author would probably agree with which of the following statements?
(a) "Awards and certificates are the sole determinants of self-worth."
(b) "Intrinsic motivation plays no role in the pursuit of external validation."
(c) "The pursuit of awards and certificates is driven by societal pressures."
(d) "Personal growth is solely influenced by external validation."

28. The author implies that pursuing awards and certificates would be ______ to personal growth. Choose the most appropriate answer.

(a) detrimental (b) irrelevant
(c) integral (d) insignificant

29. Given the author's position on the pursuit of awards and certificates, what stand would the author probably take on the issue of external recognition in academia?
(a) The author would argue for stricter external recognition criteria in academia.
(b) The author would likely advocate for a reduced emphasis on external recognition in academia.
(c) The author would insist on increasing the number of awards available in academia.
(d) The author would emphasise the importance of formal dress codes in academic institutions.

30. In the passage, which sentence correctly uses the past perfect tense?
(a) "Our relentless pursuit of accolades is deeply woven into the fabric of our society."
(b) "No matter how confident or self-assured one may be, the allure of external validation is irresistible."
(c) "The human pursuit of accolades and certificates, an intricate interplay of self-worth, external validation, and societal pressures."
(d) "These recognitions had been elusive until recently, but now they have become more attainable."

31. Which of the following substitutions for 'emblematic of' in the given sentence would NOT change the meaning of the quoted sentence?"

They are emblematic of the tireless hours, the unwavering dedication, and the indomitable spirit invested in chasing our dreams.

(a) Similar to (b) Representative of
(c) Proof of (d) Conducive to

32. What is the writer's aim in referring to people as "multi-dimensional identities"?
(a) To emphasise that individuals possess numerous facets that contribute to their complexity.
(b) To suggest that people are hard to understand and often contradictory.
(c) To indicate that individuals should focus on their external accomplishments.
(d) To convey that people have only one defining trait that leads them to success.

V. Read the following passage and answer the following questions by choosing the most appropriate answer.

In recent years, Electric Vehicles (EVs) have emerged as a catalyst for change, not only in terms of sustainable transportation but also in empowering individuals to become micro-entrepreneurs. Particularly in Tier 2 markets, where access to traditional job opportunities may be limited, EVs have opened up new avenues for women to assert their economic independence and contribute significantly to household income. According to our data, an inspiring 25% of women in these markets have embraced the EV platform as a means to earn their livelihoods. Electric vehicles, be it e-rickshaws, e-carts, or e-bikes, offer an affordable and eco-friendly mode of transportation that can be easily adopted by individuals. This has allowed women to enter various service sectors like last-mile delivery, transportation, and local commuting, empowering them to generate income and uplift their communities.

33. The popularity of EVs can be ascribed to it being
(1) the latest technology.
(2) a sustainable mode of transportation.
(3) a means of empowerment.
(4) easily available.

Choose the most appropriate answer.

(a) (1) and (2)
(b) (1) and (4)
(c) (2) and (3)
(d) (2) and (4)

34. A significant limitation in Tier 2 cities is
(a) the lack of enough EVs.
(b) the dearth of sufficient number of jobs.
(c) the slow pace of development.
(d) the absence of adequate number of entrepreneurs.

35. The use of the word "catalyst" conveys that it is something
(a) that initiates a sudden and important change.
(b) that becomes the end to justify the means.
(c) that contributes to sustainable growth.
(d) surfaces at regular intervals of time.

36. Statement 1: EVs are extremely versatile and have a wider range to offer.
Statement 2: More women than men have bought EVs. Choose the most appropriate answer.
(a) Both statements are true and 2 is the correct explanation of 1.
(b) Both statements are true but 2 is not the correct explanation of 1.
(c) Statement 1 is true but statement 2 is false.
(d) Statement 1 is false but statement 2 is true.

37. "Last-mile delivery" refers to the journey of the product
(a) reaching the customer's doorstep.
(b) in the back of a delivery truck.
(c) from the warehouse shelf.
(d) at the manufacturing plant.

38. In which of the following sentences is the word 'avenue' used in the same sense as given in the passage?
(a) As you go through the entrance, you are surrounded by an avenue of golden trees.
(b) The authors suggest several further avenues of research in which their findings could prove useful.
(c) In spite of the late hour, the lights at 22 Canning Avenue were still ablaze.
(d) One of these improvements consists of a central avenue cut across the old city to the water-front.

39. In which sectors have electric vehicles (EVs) enabled women to generate income and empower their communities in Tier 2 markets?
(a) Healthcare and education
(b) Agriculture and farming
(c) Last-mile delivery, transportation, and local commuting
(d) Manufacturing and heavy industries

VI. Read the following passage and answer the following questions by choosing the most appropriate answer.

It is not surprising that students are experiencing a wide range of mental health challenges, such as paralyzing stress, anxiety and depression. In 2021–22, the National Health Survey found that college students' anxiety and depression were at historic levels, with 37 percent reporting some anxiety and 44 percent experiencing some depression in the two weeks prior to the survey. Moreover, approximately 83 percent reported that emotional or mental difficulties had impaired their academic performance at some time during the month prior to taking the survey. Although some observers might try to dismiss these statistics as just a result of the pandemic, national data suggest that mental health issues were on the rise before the virus arrived. It is vital that institutions pay more attention and take more responsibility for their part in causing these trends.

Research in this area suggests that cultivating caring, affirming and connected communities on college campuses is critical when it comes to mental health. Networks of professors, staff and fellow students who care can become lifelines when college stressors become all consuming. And if colleges affirm student cultures, values and identities, they can boost students' self-esteem and sense of empowerment, help them feel less isolated and promote a greater sense of belonging. Prioritizing caring, connected and affirming communities helps more students thrive. A curriculum that allows students to simultaneously deepen their connections to their community's cultural values and their learning environment can help them feel like they belong to both. Research also shows that culturally relevant learning experiences improve academic success. Campuses therefore should provide mental health services that are culturally responsive, via professionals who understand diverse student backgrounds and experiences. Offering counselling services, support groups and outreach programs designed for diverse communities can help students feel understood and supported.

40. Based on the data from the National Health Survey, what could be a potential consequence for educational institutions if they don't address the mental health challenges of their students?
(a) Improved student performance
(b) No impact on the institution
(c) Decreased student enrolment
(d) Decreased academic success and retention rates

41. In what ways might educational institutions contribute to the rising trend in student mental health challenges, as mentioned in the paragraph?
(a) Higher educational institutions have no role in this trend
(b) By appointing dedicated mentors for all students
(c) Through insufficient awareness and support for student mental health
(d) By increasing the academic rigor

42. What broader implications can be drawn from the statistics in the paragraph for the overall well-being of society?
(a) An indication of the need for more stringent admission standards in educational institutions to address mental health concerns.
(b) A potential decline in workforce productivity and innovation due to mental health issues.
(c) An increased emphasis on academic rigor and competitiveness in the job market.
(d) A call for re-evaluation of social support systems to address mental health challenges, as these issues extend beyond educational institutions.

43. According to research, what is the relationship between culturally relevant learning experiences and academic success?
(a) They have no correlation.
(b) Culturally relevant learning experiences primarily hinder academic success.
(c) Culturally relevant learning experiences can improve academic success.
(d) They are only relevant for certain student populations.

44. What is the significance of a curriculum that allows students to deepen their connections to both their community's cultural values and their learning environment?
(a) It hinders academic success.
(b) It has no impact on the sense of belonging.
(c) It helps students feel like they belong to both the institution and their culture.
(d) It emphasizes academic rigidity.

VII. Read the following passage and answer the following questions by choosing the most appropriate answer.

Linguistics, an intricate and ever-evolving academic discipline, has undergone a remarkable transformation in recent decades, transcending its origins as a mere study of language to become a profound exploration of the complexities of human cognition and communication. The expanding purview of linguistics is a testament to its growing significance in understanding our world and enhancing our technological prowess.

One of the most fundamental paradigm shifts within linguistics has been its transition from a prescriptive to a descriptive approach. Early linguistic studies, embodied by the structuralist principles of Ferdinand de Saussure, predominantly focused on normative rules and language structures. However, the advent of modern linguistics, spearheaded by Noam Chomsky's groundbreaking generative grammar theory, has heralded a new era of linguistic inquiry—one that seeks to understand not how languages should be used but how they are used in practice. This transformation has enabled linguists to uncover the underlying universals that govern human language, revealing its intricate tapestry.

The synergy between linguistics and computer science has been instrumental in shaping our digital age. The birth of computational linguistics has given rise to transformative technologies, such as machine translation, speech recognition, and sentiment analysis. These applications, weaving the intricacies of human language with cutting-edge technology, have revolutionised fields as diverse as e-commerce, healthcare, and social media. The confluence of linguistics and computer science continues to chart new frontiers, shedding light on the symbiotic relationship between humans and machines.

Moreover, interdisciplinary collaborations have propelled linguistics into uncharted territories. Cognitive linguistics marries linguistic theory with insights from psychology, neuroscience, and anthropology, unravelling the profound interplay between language and human cognition. Sociolinguistics and anthropological linguistics delve into the social and cultural dimensions of language, elucidating linguistic variations and their socio-cultural implications. This interdisciplinary nexus enriches our understanding of how language permeates all facets of human life.

45. What does the term 'ever-evolving' imply in the first paragraph?
(a) Linguistics is becoming stagnant and unchanging.
(b) Linguistics is a dynamic field that continuously develops and changes.
(c) Linguistics has reached its peak and will not change further.
(d) Linguistics is regressing and losing its significance.

46. Which option does NOT correctly infer the meaning based on the following sentence from the first paragraph?

"The expanding purview of linguistics is a testament to its growing significance in understanding our world and enhancing our technological prowess."

(a) Linguistics plays a significant role in our comprehension of the world and technological advancements.
(b) The scope of linguistics has grown, reflecting its increasing importance in understanding our world and advancing our technological capabilities.
(c) Linguistics has a declining influence on our understanding of the world and technological advancements.
(d) Expanding the field of linguistics has led to a greater focus on understanding the world and enhancing our technological capabilities.

47. Why has the writer used the word "tapestry" in the phrase "revealing its intricate tapestry"?
(a) To emphasise the colourful and decorative nature of linguistic studies.
(b) To suggest that linguistics involves the crafting of physical artworks.
(c) To indicate the presence of hidden and mysterious aspects in linguistics.
(d) To imply that linguistics is like a woven fabric of interconnected elements.

48. Select the option that correctly analyses the impact of the writer's use of words like "synergy" and "confluence".
(a) To highlight the tension and conflicts between linguistics and computer science.
(b) To illustrate the collision of linguistic theories with computer science, creating chaos in both fields.
(c) To describe the harmonious collaboration between linguistics and computer science, resulting in transformative technologies.
(d) To depict the isolation of linguistics from other academic disciplines and its struggle to adapt.

49. How can the relationship between humans and machines be described as 'symbiotic'? (paragraph 3)
(a) Because machines fully depend on humans for their functionality.
(b) As humans and machines work together, benefiting from each other's capabilities.
(c) Because machines have replaced humans in various linguistic tasks.
(d) As humans have become overly reliant on machines for linguistic analysis.

50. What is an example of an interdisciplinary collaboration mentioned in the passage? (Paragraph 4)
(a) Collaboration between linguistics and art history to study language's visual representation.

(b) Collaboration between linguistics and chemistry to analyse language composition.
(c) Collaboration between linguistics and psychology, neuroscience, and anthropology to understand the interplay between language and human cognition.
(d) Collaboration between linguistics and astronomy to explore the influence of celestial bodies on human languages.

SECTION B: CURRENT AFFAIRS AND GENERAL KNOWLEDGE

51. The 'COP26' conference has been a significant global event. What is its primary focus?
(a) An annual event celebrating cinematic achievements
(b) A global summit addressing climate change and environmental sustainability
(c) A technology conference for the gaming industry
(d) A forum for discussions on international trade agreements

52. A key thrust area for the Supreme Court of India has been towards securing diversity and inclusion in its ranks. Who was the first woman judge of the Supreme Court of india?
(a) Justice Ranjana Prakash Desai
(b) Justice BV Nagarathna
(c) Justice M Fathima Beevi
(d) Justice Sujata V Manohar

53. What does the Gross Domestic Product (GDP) measure?
(a) Total government revenue collection and expenditure incurred during a financial year.
(b) Total money in circulation in the economy at any given point of time.
(c) Measure of income distribution and inequality within a country.
(d) Broadly understood as the final value of the goods and services produced within the geographic boundaries of a country during a specified period of time.

54. The Sustainable Development Goals (SDGs) were adopted by the United Nations in 2015 as a universal call for peace and prosperity. Which of the following statements about SDGs is NOT true?
(a) Plan of action for people, plant and prosperity
(b) Development must balance social, economic and environmental sustainability
(c) Creativity, knowhow, technology and financial resources from all of society is necessary to achieve the goals in every context
(d) Rank countries according to their economic growth and GDP per capita

55. In 1960, a Standford Professor, Walter Mischel, conducted an interesting experiment called the 'Marshmallow Experiment' to test the connection between delayed gratification and better success later in various facets of life. The outcome of the experiment can also be referred to as
(a) Present Bias
(b) G.I.Joe Fallacy
(c) Cognitive Dissonance
(d) Confirmation Bias

56. Which international agreements remain central in efforts to enable a permanent solution to the geopolitical tensions between Russia and Ukraine?
(a) Minsk Agreements
(b) Geneva Conventions
(c) Baku Accords
(d) Moscow Peace Treaty

57. The world's tallest statue, an ode to Sardar Vallabhbhai Patel, situated in Kevadia, Gujarat is also referred to as
(a) Statue of Equality
(b) Statue of Independence
(c) Statue of Unity
(d) Statue of Belief

58. In 2022, India introduced the KAVACH system, which is.
(a) indigenously developed Automatic Train Protection (ATP) System
(b) software network developed by DRDO and used by intelligence agencies to intercept and analyse internet traffic.

(c) constellation of remote sensing satellites to monitor weather patterns and early warning of natural disaster.
(d) indigenously developed counter drone systems most recently deployed during the G20 summit.

59. The 'Five Eyes Alliance' is a global intelligence network, pooling resources and sharing sensitive information to collectively secure peace and combat global threat. The following countries make up the alliance:
(a) US, UK, France, Germany, Japan
(b) US, UK, Australia, Japan, india
(c) US, UK, Germany, Australia, New Zealand
(d) US, UK, Canada, Australia, New Zealand

60. The G20 Summit in india brought together leaders from the World's major economies to address pressing global issues. India used this platform to underscore its commitment to fostering global growth and stability. Which of the following areas was NOT a focus of the summit?
(a) Managing Global Debt Vulnerabilities
(b) Eliminating Hunger and Malnutrition
(c) Bridging the Gender Digital Divide
(d) Making space exploration more equitable

61. The Indian Premier League is a professional T20 cricket league. It was established in 2008, and has since become one of the most popular cricketing leagues in the world. Which of the following player has played for the same team (franchise) since the inaugural edition?
(a) David Warner (b) Virat Kohli
(c) Ben Stokes (d) Hardik Pandya

62. The NASA OSiRiS-REx mission (Origins, Spectral interpretation, Resource Identification and Security – Regolith Explorer) recently brought back a capsule of rocks and dust collected from
(a) Asteroid Bennu
(b) Mars
(c) Saturn's rings
(d) Halley's comet

63. Which is the longest river in india?
(a) Godavari (b) Ganga
(c) Narmada (d) Mahanadi

64. A key indian foreign policy initiative is the 'Act East Policy'. Which statement correctly captures its objective?
(a) Is to promote economic cooperation, cultural ties and develop strategic relationship with countries in the Indo-Pacific region.
(b) Securing an active intelligence sharing network between india, Sri-Lanka and Bangladesh.
(c) Promotes a key partnership to combat human and drug trafficking through South East Asian nations.
(d) Promotes India as a hub of scientific education by attracting best minds from various South East Asian nations.

65. The Jnanpith Award recognizes the most outstanding contributions in the field of
(a) Medicine
(b) Literature
(c) Science and Engineering
(d) Public Affairs

66. Which of the following global companies is NOT led by a CEO of indian origin?
(a) Starbucks (b) Microsoft
(c) Chanel (d) RedBull GmBH

67. The Reserve Bank of India having regard to the needs of securing the monetary stability in the country, prescribes the CRR (Cash Reserve Ratio). Which of the following most closely explains this ratio?
(a) Percentage of bank's total deposits that is required to be maintained either in cash or as deposits with the Reserve Bank of India
(b) Minimum rate at which Reserve Bank of india lends funds to commercial bank
(c) Minimum percentage of net profit to cash flow over that banks require to maintain over a financial year
(d) Maximum percentage of deposits that can be extended as loans by a bank at any given point of time

68. Which Author made history by being the first Indian (non-expatriate) to win the Booker Prize?

(a) Arundhati Roy – God of Small Things
(b) Kiran Desai – The inheritance of Loss
(c) Arvind Adiga – White Tiger
(d) Chetan Bhagat – Five Point Someone

69. Who among the following is NOT a recipient of a Nobel Prize?

(a) Mother Teresa
(b) Kailash Satyarthi
(c) Amartya Sen
(d) Mahatma Gandhi

70. Pick the INCORRECT combination.

(a) New Horizons – Pluto
(b) Cassini Huygens – Saturn
(c) Juno – Jupiter
(d) Ignis – Sun

71. Which of the following countries is NOT a member of SAARC?

(a) Afghanistan
(b) Bhutan
(c) Cambodia
(d) Bangladesh

72. Dr. APJ Abdul Kalam, known as the Missile Man of india, was instrumental in the creation of which of these offices? He was also the first person to hold this office.

(a) Principal Scientific Advisor to the Government of India
(b) Director of the Indian Space Research Organisation
(c) Director of the Defence Research and Development Organisation
(d) Secretary to the Department of Atomic Energy

73. Which of the following countries have neither signed nor ratified the Rome Statute?

i. India
ii. United States of America
iii. Russian Federation
iv. Azerbaijan

Choose the most appropriate answer.

(a) i, ii, iv
(b) Only i
(c) Only i and iv
(d) All of the above

74. Omar al-Bashir was the first Head of State to be indicted by the International Criminal Court. He was indicted by the Court in relation to which of the following incidents?

(a) Alleged war crimes committed under his Presidency during the Sudanese Civil War.
(b) Alleged war crimes and crimes against humanity committed at Darfur between at least 2003 to 2008.
(c) Alleged crimes against humanity of murder and rape committed in the Central African Republic in between 2002 to 2003.
(d) Alleged crimes against humanity resulting from waging war against South Sudan.

75. A big roadblock towards concluding Brexit was the failure of the UK and the EU to agree on transport of goods to Ireland (a member of the EU) through Northern ireland (one of the constituent countries of the UK). This problem was resolved with the conclusion of the Windsor framework, effectively the final step in the Brexit process. Which of the following statements about the Windsor Framework are accurate?

i. It is a tripartite agreement between England, Northern Ireland, and the United Kingdom.
ii. The agreement proposes to establish red and green lanes for goods moving into Northern Ireland to reduce checks and paperwork related hurdles on such goods.
iii. The agreement does not provide for separation of goods entering Northern ireland from those entering Ireland.
iV. The agreement is concluded between the United Kingdom and the European Union.

Choose the most appropriate answer.

(a) i, ii and iii. (b) ii and iv.
(c) Only ii. (d) ii, iii, iv.

76. Which of the following statements about BRICS is NOT incorrect?
   i. South Africa is not an original member of the BRICS coalition.
   ii. The bloc was started as an attempt to strategically assist the United States of America as allies.
   iii. The BRICS member countries represent at least 40% of the world's population.
   iV. The acronym for the bloc was coined in 2001 by then Goldman Sachs chief economist Jim O'Neill in a research paper that underlined the growth potential of Brazil, Russia, India and China.

   Choose the most appropriate answer.
   (a) i and ii. (b) Only ii.
   (c) i, iii and iv. (d) All of the above.

77. India recently hosted the G20 Conference in New Delhi as it served as the President for the coalition. Which of the following is the only country to have permanent guest invitee status at the G20?
   (a) Spain (b) Ireland
   (c) South Africa (d) Portugal

78. A change in exchange rate leads to a change in supply and demand of foreign goods in the domestic market and domestic goods in the foreign market. This also leads to an imbalance in the balance of payments. What is Balance of Payments?
   (a) Balance of payments is the statement of a country's trade with other nations.
   (b) Balance of payments is the money a country owes other nations.
   (c) Balance of payments is the money owed to a country from another nation.
   (d) None of the above.

79. The gaming industry witnessed its largest acquisition in recent history involving the following major entities:
   (a) Microsoft – Activision
   (b) Sony - Nintendo
   (c) Apple – Tencent
   (d) Google – Electronic Arts

80. ISRO's PSLV has been the workhorse for Indian space programme, launching many critical payloads including the recent Chandrayaan mission. What does PSLV stand for?
   (a) Plasma Synthesis Launch Vehicle
   (b) Planetary Surface Lander Vehicle
   (c) Polar Satellite Launch Vehicle
   (d) Planetary Survey and Lander Vehicle

SECTION C: LOGICAL REASONING

81. All Supreme Court judgements are binding on all High Courts. All High Court judgements have persuasive value in other High Courts. Some High Court judgements also have persuasive value in the Supreme Court.

   Examine the following statements:
   i. Some High Court judgments are binding on the Supreme Court.
   ii. Some judgements with persuasive value are binding on High Courts.
   iii. Some High Court judgements are persuasive in both the Supreme Court and the High Courts.

   Choose the most appropriate answer.
   (a) Only i follows
   (b) Both i and ii follow
   (c) Only iii follows
   (d) Both ii and iii follow

82. All ducks are birds. Some birds fly, and no reptiles are birds. A snake is a reptile. If the given are true, which of the following would also be true?
   (a) Snakes do not fly.
   (b) No snakes are ducks.
   (c) All ducks fly.
   (d) Some birds are snakes.

83. All cats are singers. All birds dance. Some cats are birds. Albert Einstein is a Singer. Examine the following statements:
   i. Albert Einstein does not dance.
   ii. Albert Einstein dances.
   iii. Albert Einstein is a bird.

iV. Albert Einstein is not a bird.
V. Albert Einstein is not a cat.
Vi. Albert Einstein is a cat.

Which of the following conclusion(s) is necessarily correct? Choose the most appropriate answer.
(a) Only iii and vi
(b) Only ii, iii and v
(c) Only iii
(d) None of the above

84. All watches are chronographs. Some chronographs are antiques. All antiques are expensive. D is a Chronograph. Which of the following statements necessarily follows?
(a) D is a watch.
(b) If 'D' is antique, it must be a watch.
(c) D must be expensive.
(d) None of the above.

85. All philosophers are logicians. Some logicians are critical thinkers. All Critical thinkers are rationalist. Z is a rationalist. Examine the following statements:
i. Z is a logician.
ii. Z may be a logician.
iii. Z is a philosopher.
iv. Z is a critical thinker.

Choose the most appropriate answer.
(a) Only iv
(b) Only iii and iv
(c) Only ii
(d) None of the above

86. Some rivers are ponds. All ponds are oceans. No ocean is sea.
Examine the conclusions:
(i) Some ponds are sea
(ii) All rivers are oceans
(iii) Some seas may be a river.

Which of the conclusions necessarily follows? Choose the most appropriate answer:
(a) Only i
(b) Only ii
(c) Only iii
(d) None of the above

87. Some ships are boats. All Boats are submarines. Some submarines are yachts. Examine the following statements:
(i) Some yachts are boats.
(ii) Some submarines are ships.
(iii) Some yachts are ships.

Choose the most appropriate answer:
(a) Only i
(b) Only ii
(c) Only iii
(d) None of the above

88. All states are countries. Only some countries are states. Some states are democratic. Given that X is democratic, examine the following conclusions:
i. X is a state.
ii. X is a country.
iii. X is not a state.
iV. X is not a country.

Choose the most appropriate answer:
(a) Only i follows.
(b) i and ii follow.
(c) iii and iv follow.
(d) None of the four conclusions necessarily follow.

89. **Statement I:** All books are valuables.
Statement II: Some souvenirs are books.
Statement III: Some books are souvenirs.
Statement IV: No valuables are souvenirs.
Choose the most appropriate answer:
(a) Statements I, II and III are consistent with each other.
(b) Statements II, III and IV are consistent with each other.
(c) Both 'a' and 'b' are correct.
(d) None of the above.

90. All lions are animals. No animal is a zombie. All zombies are rainbows. All rainbows are zombies.
Given this information, which of the options necessarily follows?
(a) No lions are rainbows.
(b) Some lions are rainbows.

(c) All lions are rainbows.
(d) None of the above.

91. 'Frankly, technology is often baffling to me, too. Luckily, I have kids who delight in parenting me – advising, explaining and guiding me, on all things digital. But studies suggest that this helpfulness might not be as beneficial as we think. Grappling with new and baffling things forces the ageing brain to work in novel ways. A recent study from the University of Texas involving more than 200 elderly adults found that those who engaged with technology had better cognition and memory than their non-engaging peers.'

Which of the following assumptions is made in the above passage?

(a) Elderly adults are technology averse.
(b) All elderly adults are incapable of understanding technology without significant help.
(c) At present technology is designed in a manner that most elderly adults find difficult to work with.
(d) Elderly adults must engage with technology as it improves their health.

92. Depression among the elderly is on the rise and often goes unnoticed. Most Gerontologists now believe that it is an extremely common psychiatric disorders among the elderly – with half of all cases going undiagnosed. When elderly parents become depressed (many of them come from a generation not accustomed to talking about their mental health), it can be difficult to know how to respond.

Which of the following assumptions is made in the above passage?

(a) Gerontologists unanimously agree on the prevalence of depression in the elderly.
(b) Depression is increasingly prevalent among the elderly.
(c) If the elderly talk more often, it is easy to detect if they have depression.
(d) While they may not talk about mental health, the elderly are very aware about the condition.

93. Players have long been able to buy virtual items with real money in video games, such as special weapons and features. But Nintendo raised the ire of parents and Regulators in 2018 when it added so-called loot boxes—a virtual lottery for in-game items—to its kid-friendly game 'Animal Crossing: Pocket Camp.' That same year, the US Federal Trade Commission said it would investigate loot boxes, which critics liken to a slot machine or a scratch ticket that is more accessible to children. The video game industry pushed back hard, arguing that loot boxes are an integral part of the strategy and skills players use to compete.

The passage assumes which of the following?

(a) Video games industry's sole purpose is to maximise profit via active exploitation of players through any means possible without consideration as to the age of the player.
(b) There are no limitations in US as to who can make an in-game purchase, since children have access to loot boxes.
(c) The highest utilisation of loot boxes happens in Nintendo's games.
(d) By choosing to investigate the matter, the US FTC has expressed its displeasure at presence of loot boxes in video games.

94. Any attempt at fighting the camp's psychopathological influence on the prisoner by psychotherapeutic or psychogenic methods has to aim at giving inner strength by pointing out to him a future goal to which he could look forward. Instinctively some of the prisoners attempted to find one on their own. It is a peculiarity of man that he can only live by looking to the future. And this is his salvation in the most difficult moments of his existence, although he sometimes has to force his mind to the task.

Which one of the following conclusions can be properly inferred from the passage?

i. Each individual has the ability to preserve their sanity by remaining focussed on the future.
ii. Looking to the future is difficult for many, as they get caught up in the present.

iii. Those going through a tough time must rely on their past experiences for inner strength.

Choose the most appropriate answer.

(a) Only i (b) Only ii
(c) i and ii (d) i and iii

95. The problem with eugenics and genetic engineering is that they represent the one-sided triumph of wilfulness over giftedness, of dominance over reverence, of moulding over beholding. But why, we may wonder, should we worry about this triumph? Why not shake off our unease with enhancement as so much superstition? What would be lost if biotechnology dissolved our sense of giftedness?

Which of the following conclusions can be properly inferred from the passage?

i. Genetically engineered kids would be ungifted.
ii. Genetic engineering might make people more focussed on controlling things and less respectful of natural abilities.
iii. Controlling and dominating abilities through genetic engineering should be seen as natural part of human progress.

Choose the most appropriate answer.

(a) Only i (b) Only ii
(c) Only ii and iii (d) Only i and iii

96. Statements: Young adults spend most of their time on social media. Young adults should spend more time making connections in the real world.

Conclusions

i. Young Adults should avoid social media.
ii. Young adults cannot make real life connections because they spend most of their time on social media.

Which of the following conclusions can be properly inferred? Choose the most appropriate answer.

(a) Only i follows.
(b) Only ii follows.
(c) Both i and ii follows.
(d) Neither i nor ii follows.

97. While television and print media are still bound by regulations that require a modicum of truthful content, social media is a battleground of facts, lies, and deception, where governments, journalists, law enforcement, and activists are on an uneven playing field. Lack of stringent regulation or periodic verification, enable unbridled access to social media, resulting in unchecked dissemination of information with elusive credibility.

Which of the following conclusions can be properly inferred from the passage?

i. Anyone can post anything on the social media.
ii. It is generally difficult to ascertain the accuracy of content posted on social media.
iii. People are easily influenced by what they read on social media.

Choose the most appropriate answer.

(a) Only iii (b) Only ii
(c) Both i and ii (d) i, ii and iii

98. Fitness tracking devices often recommend we take 10,000 steps a day.

But the goal of taking 10,000 steps, which many of us believe is rooted in science, in fact rests on coincidence and sticky history rather than research. Research suggests use of time, not steps, and suggests we exercise for at least 150 minutes a week, or half an hour most days, in addition to any moving around we do as part of our normal daily lives.

Which of the following conclusions can be properly inferred from the passage?

(a) Most people walk 10,000 steps but become frustrated when no apparent benefits are noticeable.
(b) It is better to measure effort through time rather than number of steps, being a more scientific measure.
(c) Most people find it difficult to complete 10,000 steps daily.
(d) None of the above.

99. Human beings are entitled to dignity and rights while non-human animals are not, because human beings are autonomous while animals are heteronomous. In other words, animals are not in control of their actions and are guided entirely by pleasure and pain, while human beings are capable of acting, for moral reasons, even contrary to pleasure and consonant with pain.

Which of the following assumptions is made in the above passage?

(a) Entitlement to dignity and rights flows from the ability to act, for moral reasons, contrary to pleasure and consonant with pain.
(b) Human beings are worthy of asserting superiority over animals.
(c) Both (a) and (b)
(d) Neither (a) nor (b)

100. The negative psychological effects of pornography, including addiction and emotional distress, are well-documented. We have a moral obligation to protect our society from these potential harms. Banning pornography is a responsible step to safeguard the mental well-being of individuals, especially our youth.

Which of the following assumptions is made in the above passage?

(a) The negative psychological effects of pornography are significant and concerning enough to warrant a ban on pornography.
(b) There are no substantial positive or beneficial aspects to pornography consumption that might counterbalance the negative effects.
(c) Both (a) and (b)
(d) Neither (a) nor (b)

101. Excessive use of mobile phones has been associated with a range of health issues. Prolonged screen time and constant connectivity can lead to physical problems like eye strain, neck and back pain, and disrupted sleep patterns. Additionally, excessive use of mobile phones raises concerns about the potential long-term health effects of exposure to electromagnetic radiation. Therefore, one should not use mobile phones.

Which of the following assumptions is made in the above passage?

(a) One should not use anything the excessive use of which can cause health problems.
(b) One should not use anything associated with electromagnetic radiation.
(c) Both (a) and (b)
(d) Neither (a) nor (b)

102. Dark comedy should be banned. Dark comedy often relies on humour that is edgy and insensitive, making light of serious or sensitive topics such as death, mental illness, or tragedy. It can normalize insensitivity and desensitize people to the gravity of these issues. Over time, individuals may become less empathetic or more willing to dismiss the real-life pain and suffering of others as mere punchlines.

Which of the following assumptions is made in the above passage?

(a) Insensitive things should be banned.
(b) It is not acceptable to dismiss the real-life pain and suffering of others.
(c) Both (a) and (b)
(d) Neither (a) nor (b)

103. An environmental organization claims that replacing traditional light bulbs with LED bulbs in households will significantly reduce electricity consumption.

Which of the following, if true, would most support this claim?

(a) LED bulbs are more expensive than traditional light bulbs.
(b) LED bulbs have a longer lifespan than traditional light bulbs.
(c) LED bulbs emit less heat than traditional light bulbs.
(d) LED bulbs are available in a variety of colours.

104. A research study concluded that regular exercise leads to better mental health. The study found that individuals who exercised on an average for 30 minutes every day reported lower levels of stress and anxiety.

Which of the following, if true, would undermine the study's conclusion?

(a) The study included participants from a wide range of age groups.
(b) Individuals who exercised for longer durations reported did not report marked decrease in stress and anxiety.

(c) The study was limited in its geographic scope.
(d) Participants who exercised experienced physical injuries.

105. Gun violence in schools is a significant and concerning issue, and discussing ways to prevent it and ensure the safety of students and faculty is crucial. An important way of limiting it is by implementing background checks and waiting periods for gun purchases. This can prevent individuals with mental health issues from obtaining firearms. Which of the following is the most appropriate assumption required by the above passage?

(a) Gun violence in school is primarily committed by individuals with mental health issues.
(b) Individuals with mental health issues are more likely to purchase guns to commit a crime.
(c) Both (a) and (b)
(d) Neither (a) nor (b)

106. The question of whether colonialism was 'good' is a complex and debated topic. Some argue that colonialism led to advancements in technology, infrastructure, and education in some regions. However, it also brought about immense suffering, exploitation, and the loss of sovereignty for many indigenous populations. The negative consequences, including cultural erosion, displacement, and violence, often outweigh any potential benefits. In contemporary discourse, it is generally recognized that the harms of colonialism far outweigh any perceived 'good,' and its legacy continues to shape global inequalities and injustices.

Which of the following is/are most appropriate conclusion(s) of the above passage?

i. It is important to see both the 'good' and 'bad' of colonialism to understand its true impact.
ii. Irrespective of the 'good' that colonialism brought, it can never justify the 'bad' it perpetrated.
iii. It was necessary to do 'bad' to attain the good in colonialism.
iv. Discussions on effects of colonialism must end with attainment of independence, otherwise it tends to become a continuing excuse.

Choose the most appropriate answer.

(a) Only i (b) Only ii
(c) Both i and ii (d) None of the above

107. The Examination Department at prominent National Law School is considering setting its class schedules for the incoming batch. The subjects are Sociology, Contracts, Political Science, Constitutional Law and Administrative Law. The following considerations are kept in mind:

i. All classes must be held every day.
ii. Political Science must immediately follow Contracts on any day.
iii. Sociology cannot be the first or the last subject on any day.
iv. Constitutional Law and Administrative law cannot immediately precede or follow each other.

If Administrative Law is the third class of the day, what does the class schedule for that day looks like?

(a) Constitutional Law, Sociology, Administrative Law, Contracts, Political Science
(b) Contracts, Political Science, Administrative Law, Constitutional Law, Sociology
(c) Contracts, Constitutional Law, Administrative Law, Sociology, Political Science
(d) Sociology, Contracts, Administrative Law, Political Science, Constitutional Law

108. Before announcing its policy of Non-Performing Assets (NPA), the Finance Ministry has decided to consult heads of six of the largest banks in the country (A,B,C,D,E,F). It is a well-known fact that not all heads get along very well with each other and prefer not to sit next to each other in any meeting. During the meeting, they all will sit in a line facing the finance minister. You have been tasked to devise a seating plan keeping in mind the following conditions.

i. A cannot be on the immediate left or right of B.
ii. D cannot be at either end.

iii. E and F would ideally like to sit next to each other.

iv. C would prefer to sit one seat removed from E.

Which of the following is a possible seating arrangement?

(a) D, A, F, E, B, C (b) E, F, A, B, D, C
(c) A, D, E, F, C, B (d) F, E, C, A, D, B

109. Cities are the engines of a nation's progress. However, many cities are poorly managed and struggle to provide a basic standard of living to many residents. At the core of the problem is the question of autonomy of cities that are almost always dependent on central or state governments for even basic needs. A new report suggests that this can be remedied through constitutional amendments to provide more autonomy, means of revenue- generation and discretion in spending to cities.

Which of the below facts, if true, most weakens the above argument?

(a) Cities which are self-governing have historically not been able to provide a good standard of living to its residents.
(b) Constitutional amendments may take some time to be passed.
(c) It is easier for the central or state governments to administer cities.
(d) None of the above.

110. A town was faced with the problem of an excessive number of rats. To solve this, the town started offering a financial reward for every rat killed, which was to be proved by showing the severed tail of the rat.

Which of the following facts, if true, would be an argument in favour of the town's policy?

(a) Merely cutting off the tail of a rat does not stop that rat from surviving and producing more rats.
(b) Once the tail of a rat is cut off, the rat cannot survive.
(c) Cutting off tails is an inhumane way to solve the problem.
(d) None of the above

111. Not wearing a seatbelt in a moving vehicle is illegal and punishable. However, X argues that since not wearing a seatbelt can at most only harm the person who has chosen not to wear a seatbelt, and does not harm any other person, it should not be illegal or punishable.

Which of the following facts, if true, would weaken X's argument?

(a) People who don't wear a seatbelt are likely to suffer severe injuries in the event of an accident, and consequently make use of public health resources such as government hospitals.
(b) In the event of an accident, people who are not wearing a seatbelt may also be thrown about and cause harm to other people or property.
(c) Both (a) and (b)
(d) Neither (a) nor (b)

112. Certain tennis tournaments have started a policy for equal pay for men and women players. Supporters of the policy argue that lack of equal pay would violate the principle of equal pay for equal work. Which of the following arguments most weakens the supporters' argument?

(a) Men's matches generate more revenue than women's matches.
(b) Men usually play 5-set matches while women play 3-set matches, i.e. men usually play longer matches.
(c) The principle of equal pay for equal work did not originate in sports.
(d) None of the above.

113. Certain tennis tournaments have started a policy for equal pay for men and women players. Critics of the policy argue that because men's matches generate more revenue than women's matches, this policy is ill-conceived. Which of the following most weakens the critics' argument?

(a) Revenue generation should result in equal pay.
(b) Organisers of tennis tournaments have more than enough money and can afford to pay all players high amounts.
(c) Both (a) and (b)
(d) Neither (a) nor (b)

114. Statement: "Nudge theory" is the theory that by shaping the environment, also known as the choice architecture, one can influence the likelihood that one option is chosen over another by individuals, without adding any significant incentives or disincentives for any option. For example, a retail store may place its more expensive items at eye-level, and cheaper items at a lower shelf. Perhaps the most frequently mentioned example of nudge theory is the setting of defaults, which are pre-set courses of action that take effect if nothing is specified by the decision-maker.

Which of the following facts, if true, best supports the above statements?

i. If a default option is provided, decision-makers are likely to choose that option.
ii. Consumers in a retail store are likely to choose items that are placed at eye level rather than items which are placed on a lower shelf.

Choose the most appropriate answer.

(a) Only i (b) Only ii
(c) Both i and ii (d) None of the above

115. Some children's books which were published in the 1950s contain racist and sexist language that would be unacceptable today. These books should be re-published with the racist and sexist language omitted.

Which of the following most strengthens the above argument?

(a) Children who are exposed to racist or sexist language will think that such language is acceptable.
b) Racist or sexist language should never be permitted to be published for any reason.
(c) Both (a) and (b)
(d) Neither (a) nor (b)

116. Darshan is attempting to build a 5-day meal-plan from 6 dishes - U, V, W, X, Y, and Z - in accordance with the following conditions:

i. No dish may be repeated unless two other dishes are cooked before the repetition.
ii. W and V must not be made on consecutive days.
iii. U and Z must not be made on alternate days.
iv. Y must always be followed by X.

Which of the following is a valid meal-plan if V must be included?

(a) X, U, V, X, Y
(b) X, U, Y, W, V
(c) Z, V, U, W, X
(d) None of the above

117. Joseph must decide which songs - A, B, C, D, and E - to sing in a 5-day performance schedule, with each song being performed only on one day, in accordance with the given conditions:

i. C and D must not be scheduled on adjacent days.
ii. B may immediately follow E, but not *vice-versa*.
iii. The first day must either be A or C.
iv. The last day cannot be D.

If B is the mid-point of the performance schedule, which of the following is a valid 5-day schedule?

(a) A, E, B, C, D
(b) A, D, B, E, C
(c) C, A, B, D, E
(d) None of the above

118. Anisha must decide how to seat her friends - V, W, X, Y, Z - at a circular wedding table in accordance with the following conditions:

i. Z and W must sit next to each other.
ii. Y may only sit with V if Y is also sitting with Z.
iii. X is happy to sit with anyone.

If Y and X arrive early and take seats 1 and 3, which of the following is a valid arrangement?

(a) Y, V, X, Z, W
(b) Y, Z, X, W, V
(c) Y, W, X, Z, V
(d) None of the above

119. Arjun is prioritizing his set of tasks for the day - V, W, X, Y, and Z - in accordance with the following conditions:

i. X must not be the last task.
ii. If Z is the first task, then it must be followed by either V or Y.

iii. X and W cannot be prioritized sequentially.
iv. V must be followed by either W or Y.

If Arjun assigns Y to position 3, which of these is a possible ordering for the tasks?

(a) Z, W, Y, X, V
(b) V, X, Y, W, Z
(c) X, Z, Y, V, W
(d) None of the above

120. Principle 1: Whoever enters into another person's property with intent to intimidate, insult or annoy that person, commits "criminal trespass".

Principle 2: An act which causes harm which is so slight that no person of ordinary sense and temper would complain of such harm, is deemed not to amount to intimidation, insult or annoyance.

Facts: X enters into Y's property at midnight, uninvited, and points a gun at Y. A few minutes later, he reveals that the gun is a toy gun.

Choose the most appropriate answer:

(a) X has committed criminal trespass, because Y finds X annoying.
(b) X has not committed criminal trespass, because the gun was a toy gun and could not possibly have caused any harm to Y.
(c) X has committed criminal trespass because entering uninvited into a property at midnight and pointing a gun at a person would intimidate any person of ordinary sense and temper.
(d) None of the above

121. Principle: Any person who knowingly disseminates false information with the intent to defraud shall be guilty of an offence.

Facts: Dravid shares a news article containing false information about a popular cryptocurrency investment scheme. He claims it is a ground-breaking opportunity. Many people invest and later lose money.

Is Dravid guilty of an offence?

(a) Yes, because he knowingly disseminated false information.
(b) No, because he did not have the intent to defraud.
(c) Yes, if investors can prove substantial financial harm.
(d) There is insufficient information to decide.

122. Principle: Any individual who recklessly operates a motor vehicle, causing injury to another person, shall be guilty of an offense.

Facts: Salman, while driving, becomes momentarily distracted and accidentally hits a pedestrian, causing minor injuries. Salman argues that it was a genuine accident and not reckless behaviour.

Is Salman guilty of an offense?

(a) Yes, because he caused injury to another person.
(b) No, because momentary distractions don't amount to recklessness.
(c) Yes, because he acted recklessly.
(d) There is insufficient information to decide.

Consider the following principles and respond to the Q.123–126.

i. **Principle 1:** Vicarious liability is a doctrine holding one person strictly liable for the wrong of another, without regard to fault.
ii. **Principle 2:** An employer may be vicariously liable for the employee's action if the employee's act was an outgrowth of his employment, inherent in the working environment, typical of or broadly incidental to the employer's business, or, in a general way, foreseeable from his duties.
iii. **Principle 3:** No vicarious liability on employers for the intentional wrongs by employees unless the employee's actions were done, at least in part, to serve the interest of the employer.

123. Which of the following will NOT result in vicarious liability?

(a) A, working as delivery driver for Flipkart, runs over Mr. X's foot while on a personal errand on a weekend in his own car.
(b) A, working as delivery driver for Flipkart, runs over Mr. X's foot on his way to stop at the local coffee shop between deliveries, needing a caffeine boost to make it through the day.

(c) A, working as delivery driver for Flipkart, runs over Mr. X's foot on his way home from work in his truck, which the company allows drivers to take home each work night.

(d) All the above

124. Which of the following may result in vicarious liability?

(a) A collision when the driver using the employer's vehicle for the purpose of visiting family for the holidays.

(b) The driver causes injury when he is driving his truck between deliveries and intentionally runs over a man, he believes to be his wife's lover.

(c) The driver causes injury when he intentionally hits a car in front of him, as the car in front of him was moving too slowly while the driver was trying to make deliveries on time.

(d) All the above.

125. An unknown person knocks down a few hundred jars of baby food in the supermarket. Many of the jars shattered, making a big, slippery mess on the floor. Laila, the supermarket manager, closes down the aisle with bright orange cones and orders all available stock personnel to clean the mess. Arun, who is not paying attention while shopping in the supermarket, wanders past the orange cones, slips, and breaks his arm. Is the supermarket vicariously liable?

(a) Yes, as Laila is an employee of the supermarket.

(b) Yes, as Arun sustained injuries at the supermarket.

(c) No, as Arun was also at fault.

(d) No, as Laila did no wrong.

126. Phogat works as a bouncer at the Hot Spot, a local nightclub. One night Dash arrives outside the Hot Spot with a group of his friends. Dash is intoxicated and acting obnoxiously, hooting at the women going in and out of the club. Dash's behaviour annoys Phogat, who asked Dash twice to stop acting in this way, but Dash ignored him on both occasions. Phogat then punches Dash in the face, breaking his nose. Dash sues the Hot Spot and Phogat, claiming that the Hot Spot is vicariously liable. Is the Hot Spot vicariously liable for the actions of Phogat?

(a) No, because Phogat committed an intentional wrong.

(b) No, because there is no evidence the Hot Spot was negligent in supervising Phogat.

(c) Yes, because employers are always liable for the torts of their employees.

(d) Yes, because such action by a bouncer may at times use force to prevent patrons from misbehaving.

Consider the following scenario and respond to the Q.127–130.

Imagine that society can be divided into Xs and Ys, and X and Y refer to people with different physical characteristics or other characteristics that can easily be observed or discovered, such as race, ethnicity, immigrant status, or religious practices. Within each group, there are good and bad types. Assume that the Xs are wealthier and more politically powerful than the Ys perhaps because they are more numerous, or because they are descended from a politically powerful group. Under such conditions, it is possible that members of X will signal their cooperative propensity by discriminating against the Ys. Discrimination functions as a signal because it is costly (one gives up the opportunity to do business or socialize with Ys who are good types), and because conspiracy theories based on traditional fears of people with physical or cultural differences, or people who are recent arrivals, provide a focal point: Given these beliefs, those who discriminate against outsiders will appear to be loyal to the insiders. in equilibrium all or most Xs will avoid Ys (and those who do not will be ostracized by the Xs and may seek refuge with the Ys), and almost all Y's will avoid the Xs, falling back on each other when it is desirable to enter cooperative ventures. Finally, we assume that because of their political and economic dominance, members of X control the government, including the criminal justice system.

127. Which of the following observations is incorrect?
- (a) If X is a numerically large group, Y comprises of small ethnic groups.
- (b) If X is a tiny minority of people with aristocratic lineage, Y consists of the masses.
- (c) Numerical strength of X is always higher than that of Y.
- (d) X may or may not be a numerically larger group.

128. Which of the following observations is incorrect, if the Xs operate the criminal justice system to the disadvantage of the Ys?
- (a) Ys must rely heavily on each other for protection against criminals.
- (b) Ys may form a solidary group and signal their loyalty to the group.
- (c) Ys may express loyalty to Ys by engaging in activities that the Xs disapprove of and even punish.
- (d) Y who engages in activities disapproved by Xs can never be trusted in comparison with other Ys.

129. Assume that criminal punishments will have different effects on Xs and Ys.

Which of the following is incorrect?
- (a) Ys obtain more respect from other Ys when they become subject to criminal punishments.
- (b) A criminal punishment will deter a Y less than it will deter a similarly situated X, who obtains no enhanced respect.
- (c) Criminal punishments impact Xs and Ys in the same manner so long as the very nature of the punishment is the same.
- (d) A 'Y' who has a criminal record will not be trusted by Xs.

130. Assume that semi-voluntary punishment is a reliable signal of a Ys loyalty to the other Ys. Which of the following is an incorrect observation?
- (a) Y has an incentive to get himself punished by the Xs.
- (b) Y may commit a crime even if Y does not have a particular desire to commit a crime.
- (c) Y will commit a crime only if X provokes Y to commit a crime.
- (d) A criminal punishment that was kept hidden from the public would deter a Y from crime more effectively than a criminal punishment that broadcasts his offense.

131. Consider the following principle.

In a dispute between Anil and Sunil, Sunil can sue Anil in:
- i. the city where the dispute arose, OR
- ii. in the city of Anil's place of business

Facts: Anil and Sunil enter into a contract for delivery of specialised machinery. Anil was to deliver the machinery to Sunil's warehouse within a stipulated period of time. Anil's residence is in Delhi, but his place of business is Bengaluru, whereas Sunil is a resident of Mumbai. Anil fails to deliver the machinery during the agreed time.

Where can Sunil sue Anil?
- (a) In Delhi
- (b) In Bengaluru
- (c) In Mumbai
- (d) Both in Bengaluru and Mumbai provided the dispute arose in Mumbai

132. "*All paintings jump. Some paintings are plants. All basketballs are plants.*"

Football is a basketball. Which of the following is true?
- (a) Football is a plant and it jumps.
- (b) Football is a plant and a painting.
- (c) Football is a plant but neither jumps nor is a painting.
- (d) Football is a plant. As to whether it is painting, and as to whether it jumps, there is not sufficient information.

133. "*All paintings jump. Some paintings are plants. All basketballs are plants.*"

Mona Lisa jumps. Which of the following is true?
- (a) Mona Lisa is a painting.
- (b) Mona Lisa is not a plant.
- (c) Mona Lisa is not a basketball.

(d) As to whether Mona Lisa is a painting, a plant or a basketball, there is not sufficient information.

134. "*All paintings jump. Some paintings are plants. All basketballs are plants.*"

Dragon is a plant that jumps. Which of the following is true?

(a) Dragon is a painting.
(b) Dragon is not a painting.
(c) Dragon is a basketball.
(d) As to whether Dragon is a painting or a basketball, there is not sufficient information.

135. "*All paintings jump. Some paintings are plants. All basketballs are plants.*"

Aloe Vera is a basketball and a painting. Which of the following is true?

(a) Aloe Vera is a plant and it jumps.
(b) Aloe Vera is a plant but does not jump.
(c) Aloe Vera is not a plant but it jumps.
(d) Aloe Vera jumps. As to whether it is a plant, there is not sufficient information.

136. "It is well known that the world isn't the same anymore — politically, economically or, for that matter, financially. Macroeconomic settings have turned adverse — from ultra-low to higher-for-longer interest rates — and raised the levels of debt, especially public debt, uncertainties, and volatility. It follows that these conditions will bear upon future growth. The breaking up of trade supply chains and their reshaping, for example, will be costly for the world in general, according to calculations, and costlier for the emerging and the developing countries."

Which of the following assumptions is made in the above passage?

(a) Economic events in one part of the world always shape other parts of the world.
(b) When macroeconomic settings turn adverse, future growth gets impacted.
(c) Both (a) and (b)
(d) Neither (a) nor (b)

137. "Travelling in a bus can be an enjoyable experience if you have your own seat, the vehicle is not crowded, and there is a nice breeze. But if the bus is packed with people, you can get irritable. Something similar happens to atoms: If they are contained in a vessel at a low density, they behave in a certain way, but if they are packed densely together, with little moving space, something new happens."

Which of the following assumptions is made in the above passage?

(a) Less crowd is essential to an enjoyable bus ride.
(b) Atomic behaviour can always be understood by drawing analogies to real-world events.
(c) Both (a) and (b)
(d) Neither (a) nor (b)

138. "The issue of "tamperability" of EVMs has been doing the rounds ever since they were first introduced. Every time a political party loses an election, it blames the machine. However, none of them has been able to prove their allegations against the credibility of EVMs, and neither do they apologise when they win the elections where the same EVMs have been used. All that this manages to do, however, is shake the trust of people in the system. Many critics, giving the example of Germany, say that EVMs have been declared illegal by the German Supreme Court."

Which of the following assumptions is made in the above passage?

(a) EVMs are tamper proof.
(b) Criticism of any system shakes people's trust in it.
(c) Both (a) and (b)
(d) Neither (a) nor (b)

139. "The art of war is of vital importance to the State. it is a matter of life and death, a road either to safety or to ruin. Hence it is a subject of inquiry which can on no account be neglected."

Which of the following assumptions is made in the above passage?

(a) Matters of life and death should not be neglected.

(b) Matters of life and death are of vital importance to the State.
(c) Both (a) and (b)
(d) Neither (a) nor (b)

140. In a survey of IT professionals in Bangalore, those who regularly practiced yoga reported fewer instances of work-related stress than those who did not. Priyanka, an iT professional from Bangalore, rarely feels work-related stress. Which of the following can be inferred?

(a) Priyanka practices yoga daily.
(b) Priyanka never practices yoga.
(c) Priyanka might be practising yoga.
(d) None of the above.

141. In English tort law, the principle of 'strict liability' is applied to hold a person legally responsible for the consequences flowing from an activity, even in the absence of fault or criminal intent on the person's part. In 1987, the Supreme Court of india introduced a new principle- 'absolute liability', a far more stringent rule of liability without any exceptions, particularly to deal with industrial accidents. This principle imposed a liability on individuals who engaged in an inherently dangerous or hazardous activity for any harm done to any person while carrying out the activity.

Which one of the following assumptions is necessary to ensure the above argument logically follows?

(a) English legal principles are not compatible with the indian court system.
(b) Post-independence, the Supreme Court opted to create new names for colonial-era legal principles.
(c) The principle of strict liability was inadequate to protect citizens' rights due to the entry of foreign companies in Indian markets.
(d) The principle of strict liability was inadequate to protect citizens' rights in the light of the rapid industrialisation in the 20th century.

142. A study conducted on a group of students found a strong correlation between the number of hours spent studying and their exam scores. However, one student who studied significantly less than the others achieved a top score. Which of the following, if true, would weaken the general applicability of the study's findings?

(a) The top-scoring student had a photographic memory.
(b) The study included a wide range of students from various backgrounds.
(c) The top-scoring student had prior knowledge of the exam questions.
(d) The study was conducted in a controlled environment.

143. Company A announced record-breaking profits this year, attributing its success to a new marketing strategy. However, Company B, a competitor in the same market segment, also reported significant profits without changing its marketing approach. What conclusion can most likely be drawn about the effectiveness of respective marketing strategies?

(a) Company A's previous marketing strategy was flawed in its conception.
(b) Company B's marketing strategy was significantly more effective than Company A's revised strategy.
(c) Company A's profits were solely influenced by its marketing strategy.
(d) Company B's profits were solely due to its marketing strategy.

144. The recent surge in demand for electric vehicles has led to increased lithium-ion battery production.

Which of the following can be inferred?

(a) The increase in lithium-ion battery production is solely driven by the demand for electric vehicles.
(b) Lithium-ion batteries are the only type of batteries used in electric vehicles.
(c) Increased production of lithium-ion batteries will lead to a decrease in their cost.
(d) None of the above.

145. The education system needs comprehensive reform to address the diverse learning needs of students.

Which of the following can be inferred?

(a) Comprehensive reform will guarantee equal educational outcomes for all students.

(b) The current education system is not equipped to cater to diverse learning needs.

(c) Comprehensive reform is easy to implement and will not face resistance.

(d) Diverse learning needs can be met without changing the education system.

146. The education system must prioritize critical thinking skills to prepare students for the challenges of the modern world.

Which of the following can be inferred?

(a) Critical thinking skills are currently not emphasized in the education system.

(b) Prioritizing critical thinking skills is the only way to prepare students for the modern world.

(c) Critical thinking skills are not relevant to the challenges of the modern world.

(d) Students do not need other skills besides critical thinking to succeed.

147. If in a certain code LiGHT is NFLAE, then TABLE would be ________

(a) VXGEP (b) WUHiG

(c) WiJKL (d) VYTAB

148. If in a certain code TALK is YUPC, then LiSTEN would be ________

(a) QCZLND (b) PNZCRC

(c) QNYBND (d) PMYCQC

149. TALE : XGTO :: LONG : ?

(a) OTUX (b) PUVQ

(c) QVWC (d) RWXT

150. BELL : DATV :: MATE : ?

(a) OWBO (b) PXCQ

(c) QYDS (d) SABX

ANSWER KEY

Section A: English

1. (b) 2. (c) 3. (a) 4. (b) 5. (d) 6. (b) 7. (c) 8. (c)
9. (a) 10. (a) 11. (d) 12. (b) 13. (b) 14. (b) 15. (b) 16. (d)
17. (c) 18. (d) 19. (a) 20. (d) 21. (a) 22. (c) 23. (c) 24. (a)
25. (b) 26. (a) 27. (c) 28. (b) 29. (b) 30. (d) 31. (b) 32. (a)
33. (c) 34. (b) 35. (a) 36. (c) 37. (a) 38. (b) 39. (c) 40. (d)
41. (c) 42. (d) 43. (c) 44. (c) 45. (b) 46. (c) 47. (d) 48. (c)
49. (b) 50. (c)

Section B: Current Affairs and General Knowledge

51. (b) 52. (c) 53. (d) 54. (d) 55. (a)
56. (a) 57. (c) 58. (a) 59. (d) 60. (d)
61. (b) 62. (a) 63. (b) 64. (a) 65. (b)
66. (d) 67. (a) 68. (a) 69. (d) 70. (d)
71. (c) 72. (a) 73. (d) 74. (b) 75. (b)
76. (c) 77. (a) 78. (a) 79. (a) 80. (c)

Section C: Logical Reasoning

81. (c) 82. (b) 83. (d) 84. (d) 85. (c) 86. (d) 87. (b) 88. (d) 89. (c) 90. (a) 91. (c) 92. (b)
93. (b) 94. (c) 95. (b) 96. (d) 97. (c) 98. (b) 99. (a) 100. (c) 101. (a) 102. (b) 103. (c) 104. (b)
105. (d) 106. (c) 107. (a) 108. (c) 109. (a) 110. (b) 111. (c) 112. (b) 113. (d) 114. (c) 115. (a) 116. (d)
117. (c) 118. (d) 119. (c) 120. (c) 121. (d) 122. (b) 123. (a) 124. (c) 125. (d) 126. (d) 127. (c) 128. (d)
129. (c) 130. (c) 131. (d) 132. (d) 133. (d) 134. (a) 135. (a) 136. (b) 137. (d) 138. (d) 139. (c) 140. (c)
141. (d) 142. (c) 143. (a) 144. (a) 145. (b) 146. (a) 147. (a) 148. (a) 149. (b) 150. (a)

AILET 2023

Directions: I to X: Each set of questions in this section are based on the passage. The questions are to be answered on the basis of what is stated or implied in the passage. Choose the most appropriate response that accurately and completely answer the question.

PART-1

SECTION–A: ENGLISH

I. Aristotle, an ancient philosopher, was one of the first to discuss syllogisms. In *Prior Analytics*, published around 350 BCE, Aristotle outlined the basic form of syllogism which represented the earliest branch of formal logic. For Aristotle, logic revolved around deduction: *"speech in which certain things having been supposed something different from those supposed results of necessity because of their being so."*

If that sounds confusing – that's ancient philosophy for you! Let's break it down. "The things that have been supposed" are what we now call "premises". "What results necessarily" from those premises being true is a conclusion.

To Aristotle, if an argument was valid, it would be impossible for premises X and Y to be true and for conclusion Z to be false. Aristotle named this method of proving validity "reductio ad impossibile": a syllogism is valid when the denial of the conclusion but acceptance of the premises would lead to a contradiction.

Aristotle divided syllogistic propositions into four different categories: universal affirmative, particular affirmative, universal negative and particular negative.

A universal affirmative syllogistic sentence: All humans need food.

A particular affirmative syllogistic sentence: Some birds can fly.

A universal negative syllogistic sentence: No dogs are cats.

A particular negative syllogistic sentence: Not all cars have four doors.

During the rise of modern formal logic, German philosopher Gottlob Frege refined Aristotle's syllogistic theory through the addition of non-categorical syllogisms. These are syllogisms that rely on premises and can be hypothetical, or which include disjunctions like 'or'. The hypothetical form of syllogisms can be traced back to Stoic philosophy, but modern philosophers tend to attribute the theory to Frege. In the 19th century, British philosopher and economist John Neville Keynes also helped make non-categorical syllogisms popular.

Here's an example of a hypothetical syllogism:

1. If it is sunny tomorrow, I can go running.
2. It is sunny.
3. Therefore, I can go running.

Here's an example of a disjunctive syllogism:

1. Patrick studies English or Linguistics.
2. Patrick is not studying Linguistics.
3. Therefore, he is studying English.

In the *Begriffsschrift* (German for "Concept-Script"), he refined Aristotle's system by developing a logical system that explained how quantifiers (words like "all" and "some") work. His system also became the basis for modern computer science.

1. Select the appropriate option to fill the blank.
In the line, 'Aristotle outlined the basic form of syllogism…' in paragraph 1, the writer means that Aristotle ______________ the topic.

(a) shared an introductory insight on
(b) paraphrased features of
(c) wrote a detailed discussion on
(d) presented the main aspects of

2. The writer's use of an exclamation mark in the line '... that's ancient philosophy for you!', from paragraph 2. What is the most likely tone this indicates?
(a) derogatory (b) humorous
(c) sarcastic (d) provocative

3. Select the option that is true for both (1) and (2) below, according to paragraph 3.
(1) A conclusion is the main feature of a premise.
(2) Premises need to be proven true for a conclusion to occur.
(a) (1) is true but (2) is false.
(b) Both (1) and (2) are true.
(c) (2) is true but (1) cannot be inferred from the text.
(d) (1) is true but (2) cannot be inferred from the text.

4. Select the option that substitutes the underlined word correctly in the given line. 'These are syllogisms that rely on premises being hypothetical...'
(a) conjectural (b) climatic
(c) conciliatory (d) corroborative

5. Select the option that uses a 'quantifier', as mentioned in the last paragraph.
(a) We saw a lot of birds at the sanctuary.
(b) The sanctuary is located beyond the city walls.
(c) The birds migrate to the sanctuary in March.
(d) We planned the trips to the bird sanctuary.

II. During her grandfather's reign, Elizabeth was third in the line of succession to the British throne, behind her uncle Edward and her father. Her younger and only sister Margaret was next in the line of succession. When her grandfather died in 1936 and her uncle succeeded as Edward VIII, she became second in line to the throne, after her father. Later that year, Edward abdicated without any issue (i.e., child), after his proposed marriage to divorced socialite Wallis Simpson provoked a constitutional crisis. Consequently, Elizabeth's father became king, taking the regnal name George VI. Since Elizabeth had no brothers, she became heir presumptive. If her parents had subsequently had a son, he would have been heir apparent and above her in the line of succession, which was determined by the male-preference primogeniture (as against female-preference primogeniture or primogeniture *simpliciter*) in effect at the time.

George VI's health declined during 1951, and Elizabeth frequently stood in for him at public events. When she toured Canada and visited President Harry S. Truman in Washington, D.C., in October 1951, her private secretary, Martin Charteris, carried a draft accession declaration in case of the King's death while she was on tour. In early 1952, Elizabeth and Philip set out for a tour of Australia and New Zealand by way of the British colony of Kenya. On 6 February 1952, they had just returned to their Kenyan home, Sagana Lodge, after a night spent at Treetops Hotel, when word arrived of the death of George VI and Elizabeth's consequent accession to the throne with immediate effect. Philip broke the news to the new queen. She chose to retain Elizabeth as her regnal name; thus she was called Elizabeth II, which offended many Scots, as she was the first Elizabeth to rule in Scotland. She was proclaimed queen throughout her realms and the royal party hastily returned to the United Kingdom. Elizabeth and Philip moved into Buckingham Palace.

6. Elizabeth's father had to ascend the throne because Edward had to step down. Select the correct reason he had to step down.
(a) Edward was a king without an heir.
(b) Edward was involved in a controversy.
(c) Edward objected to the line of succession.
(d) Edward wished to marry the same year as his father's death.

7. The word 'provoked' in the line 'provoked a constitutional crisis', refers to ________.
(a) deliberately rousing anger
(b) giving rise to a reaction
(c) pressuring for a response
(d) denying responsibility

8. What can be inferred as common between the understanding of *heir apparent* and *heir presumptive*?
(a) brothers (b) parental support
(c) age (d) birth of another

9. The phrasal verb 'stood in' is used in the line, '...stood in for him at public events.' Select the option that DOES NOT display a phrasal verb.
(a) get by (b) break down
(c) double minded (d) fall apart

10. Select the option that negates the given opinion, based on the textual information.
The Scots objected to Elizabeth's accession.
(a) No, Elizabeth became the undisputed monarch as the heir of George VI.
(b) No, the Scottish people embraced Elizabeth because of her Scottish lineage.
(c) No, Elizabeth was hastily crowned Queen at Buckingham Palace.
(d) No, Philip only shared the news of the death of George VI with Elizabeth.

III. What is phishing?

Phishing is one of the easiest forms of cyberattack for criminals to carry out, and one of the easiest to fall for. It's also one that can provide everything hackers need to ransack their targets' personal and work accounts.

Usually carried out over email – although the phishing scam has now spread beyond suspicious emails to phone calls (so-called 'vishing') social media, messaging services (aka 'smishing') and apps – a basic phishing attack attempts to trick the target into doing what the scammer wants. That might be handing over passwords to make it easier to hack a company, or altering bank details so that payments go to fraudsters instead of the correct account.

Phishing is also a popular method for cyber attackers to deliver malware, by encouraging victims to download a document or visit a link that will secretly install the malicious payload in attacks that could be distributing trojan malware, ransomware or all manner of damaging and disruptive attacks. The aim and the precise mechanics of the scams vary: for example, victims might be tricked into clicking a link through to a fake web page with the aim of persuading the user to enter personal information – it's estimated that an average of 1.4 million of these websites are created every month.

More complex phishing schemes can involve a long game, with hackers using fake social media profiles, emails and more to build up a rapport with the victim over months or even years in cases where specific individuals are targeted for data that they would only ever hand over to people they trust.

That data can range from personal or corporate email address and password, to financial data such as credit card details or online banking credentials or even personal data such as date of birth, address and a social security number.

How does a phishing attack work?

A basic phishing attack attempts to trick a user into entering personal details or other confidential information, and email is the most common method of performing these attacks.

The sheer number of emails sent every single day means that it's an obvious attack vector for cyber criminals. It's estimated that 3.7 billion people send around 269 billion emails every single day.

Researchers at Symantec suggest that almost one in every 2,000 of these emails is a phishing email, meaning around 135 million phishing attacks are attempted every day.

Most people simply don't have the time to carefully analyse every message that lands in their inbox – and it's this that phishers look to exploit in a number of ways.

Scams vary in their targets – some are aiming at unwary consumers. Here, their email subject line will be designed to catch the victim's eye – common phishing campaign techniques include offers of prizes won in fake competitions such as lotteries or contests by retailers offering a 'winning voucher'.

In this example, in order to 'win' the prize, the victims are asked to enter their details such as name, date of birth, address and bank details in order to claim. Obviously, there's no prize and all they've done is put their personal details into the hands of hackers.

11. Select the option that correctly completes the following.
Doctors : cardiologist:: ____________.
(a) lotteries : victims (b) malware : victims
(c) social media : scam (d) criminals : hackers

12. Select the appropriate option to complete the sentence. This text is most likely to be published as a
(a) news item (b) personal narrative
(c) speech draft (d) magazine article

13. Select the appropriate option to complete the sentence.
The purpose of the prolonged phishing game is to ____________.
(a) develop believable profiles
(b) research the victims
(c) gain in-depth information
(d) establish faith

14. What about the victims often works favourably for phishers using emails?
(a) They face language issues
(b) They remain very busy
(c) They lack tech savviness
(d) They have delayed access

15. Replace the underlined word with its correct meaning from the given options. 'Phishers scam people.'
(a) loot (b) dupe
(c) harm (d) betray

IV. Great Pacific Garbage Patch, a zone in the Pacific Ocean between Hawaii and California that has a high concentration of plastic waste. The extent of the patch has been compared to the U.S. State of Texas or Alaska or even to the country of Afghanistan.

Garbage that reaches the ocean from the west coast of the United States and from the east coast of Japan is carried by currents – including the California Current, the North Equatorial Current, the North Pacific Current, and the Kuroshio – into the North Pacific subtropical gyre, the clockwise rotation of which draws in and traps solid matter such as plastics. Some 80 percent of the plastics in the garbage patch come from the land. It takes years for debris to travel from the coasts to the gyre, and as it is carried along, photodegradation causes the plastics to break down into tiny, nearly invisible bits. While there are some larger objects that come from ships and offshore oil rigs, the garbage patch could more accurately be described as a soup of microplastics. The dimensions and depth of the patch are continuously changing.

Scientists had been aware of the growing problem of plastic debris in the world's oceans since the late 1980s. However, the Great Pacific Garbage Patch came to public attention only after 1997, when yachtsman Charles Moore, returning home after participating in the biennial Transpacific Race, chose a route that took him through the North Pacific subtropical gyre. He found himself traversing a sea of plastics. When he returned to the area the following year, he discovered that the patch had grown in both extent and density. Moore began making speeches and writing articles – notably a 2003 essay in *Natural History* magazine – and he changed the mission of the Algalita Research Foundation, which he had founded in 1994 to improve water quality along California's coast. The organization now focuses on studying and publicizing the problem of plastics in oceans, in particular in the Great Pacific Garbage Patch. A 2006 series of articles in the *Los Angeles Times* about the garbage patch won a Pulitzer Prize and raised general awareness of the problem.

In 2015 and 2016, the Dutch-based organization Ocean Cleanup found that the density of the debris in the garbage patch was much greater than expected and that the plastics absorbed pollutants, making them poisonous to marine life. The Great Pacific Garbage Patch is the best known of several such zones, others of which exist in the Atlantic and Indian oceans.

16. Select the appropriate option to complete the sentence.
The word 'Great' in the name 'Great Pacific Garbage Patch' alludes to the ____________.

(a) vastness of the ocean
(b) magnitude of the issue
(c) uniqueness of the location of the garbage patch
(d) extent of the garbage patch

17. Which is the contextual clue that best helps us understand the meaning of 'gyre'?
(a) continuously changing
(b) carried along
(c) clockwise rotation
(d) invisible bits

18. Select the appropriate option to fill the blank.
The 'photo' in *photodegradation* points to the role of in the degradation of the plastic.
(a) water
(b) sun
(c) type of plastic
(d) duration of plastic at coast

19. Which of the given literary devices does the writer use in the line, 'He found himself traversing a sea of plastics.'?
(a) pun (b) symbolism
(c) irony (d) imagery

20. Select the option that displays a title likely to belong to an article of the 2006 series.
(a) Marine Life Conservation
(b) Trash to Infiltrate the Food Chain
(c) Marine Debris and Trash
(d) Ocean Cleanups Around the World

V. Primogeniture

All titles are inherited by the oldest eligible child. Note that a dead child's progeny takes precedence over younger siblings. If no eligible descendants exist, the ruler's oldest eligible sibling is preferred. If lateral branches provide no candidate, the line of succession moves up to the primary parent* and repeats the aforementioned steps.
*the father if patrilineal marriage, the mother if matrilineal marriage.

Ultimogeniture

All titles are inherited by the youngest eligible child. Note that a dead child's progeny takes precedence over older siblings. If no eligible descendants exist, the ruler's youngest eligible sibling is preferred. If lateral branches provide no candidate, the line of succession moves up to the primary parent* and repeats the aforementioned steps.
*the father if patrilineal marriage, the mother if matrilineal marriage.

House seniority

All titles are inherited by the oldest eligible house member.
Note: The above rules of inheritance can take the following forms: gender-neutral; male preference, where younger men take precedence over older women; and vice versa for female preference.

Disowning

If a person is validly disowned, his/ her position in the line of succession ceases to exist. Only a person who has become a ruler in accordance with any of the rules of succession mentioned above can disown a person in the line of succession. A person in the line of succession may also choose to adopt monkhood, which automatically results in his/her permanent removal from the line of succession.

21. Select the option that completes the following correctly. Precedence : priority:: ______________ .
(a) progeny : offspring
(b) lateral : vertical
(c) eligible : privileged
(d) primary : secondary

22. Select the option that can be the most suitable introductory line to this text.
(a) Inheritance laws served as important means of preserving both the size of the property and the power and prestige.
(b) What distinguishes the Western Property System from the systems of most is that its category of private property is a default category.
(c) Public regulation of land use has increased drastically in the 20th century.
(d) A will is valid if it meets the formalities of the law, which usually, but not always requires that it be witnessed.

23. Select the option that correctly reflects in the given part of the line. "If lateral branches provide no candidates..."
(a) interrogation (b) consequence
(c) condition (d) reason

24. Select the option that substitutes the underlined words in the given sentence without changing its meaning.
'If a person is validly (1) disowned, his/her position in the line of succession ceases (2) to exist.'
(a) (1) technically; (2) begins
(b) (1) unanimously; (2) tries
(c) (1) justifiably; (2) desists
(d) (1) functionally; (2) struggles

25. Monkhood results in a permanent removal from the line of succession because of its feature of.
(a) recognising a higher power
(b) renouncing the material world
(c) embracing a new home
(d) establishing new relationships

VI. If you have ever watched a Grand Prix, you may have asked yourself, 'how do Formula One cars generate downforce?'

Motorsports is all about speed. Being the fastest around will mean victory. But there is a limit to how fast one can travel on the ground without the car taking off. For attaining great speeds a car needs to remain firmly on the ground and have a good grip on the racing track. This means that all cars need to generate a downward force sufficient enough to keep them firmly on the ground for the speed that they intend to attain.

One way to remain on the ground at great speeds is to increase the weight of the car. But an increased weight will need more power to drive the car and make the handling of the car difficult. The alternative to this is to create the required force to stay grounded. Downforce can be generated from the air flowing around the car and will increase as the speed of the car increases.

The wings of an aeroplane help it to take off in the air at a specified speed. The same wing, if installed inverted on a car can make the car stay firmly on the ground. Just like in an aeroplane, as the speed of the car increases, the wings will press the car more firmly on the ground, thereby making handling of the car through twists and turns easier at high speed. This force that presses the car to the ground is called downforce.

Aerodynamic downforce plays an important role in the performance of Formula One cars, DTM, Indy cars and touring cars. Good grip on the racing track is equally important as the power generated by a racing car engine. Good ground adhesion gives the car stability and better cornering ability. Hence a racing car must generate a ground force equal to several times its weight.

Modern Formula One cars can generate as much as 5G downforce. That means, at full speed, the effective weight pressing down on the track will be 5 times the weight of the car. Almost all the surfaces of a Formula One car are engineered to produce downforce. The downforce by the front portion of the car has to be balanced by the downforce produced by the rear portion.

While the downforce on either side of the car can be balanced by symmetry, the downforce between the front and the rear cannot. This downforce has to be balanced by design. Most of the downforce in Formula One cars is produced by the wings and by diffusers. The downforce required by the car for ultimate performance will vary from track to track and on the conditions of the track.

While too much front downforce could lead to understeer, too much downforce generated by the rear portion could lead to oversteer. The balancing of the downforce between the front and the rear can be done by careful designing of the body parts of the car. The balancing act of the downforce also comes with an increased drag on the car.

26. Select the option that correctly sorts facts (F) and opinions (O).
i. Grand Prix is worth watching.
ii. Formula One cars are beautifully designed unlike other types of cars.

iii. Symmetry is unable to address the downforce between the front and rear of a racing car.
iv. The weight of a racing car has to be far less than the ground force generated.
(a) F- (iii) & (iv); O- (i) & (ii)
(b) F- (i), (ii) & (iii); O- (iv)
(c) F- (ii) & (iii); O- (i) & (iv)
(d) F- (iv); O- (i), (ii) & (iii)

27. Select the idiomatic expression that addresses the given text, most appropriately.
(a) A vicious cycle
(b) Two can play at the game
(c) Dot the i's and cross the t's
(d) The tip of the iceberg

28. What type of text could the given piece, best be categorised under?
(a) analytical
(b) expository
(c) descriptive
(d) inspirational

29. In the line, 'The alternative to this is to create the required force to stay grounded.', what is the nature of meaning for 'staying grounded', that the writer DOES NOT refer to?
(a) metaphorical (b) exact
(c) non-figurative (d) literal

30. Select the most appropriate option as a concluding remark for the given text.
(a) Racing regulations make it hard to gain an advantage over competitors.
(b) The total aerodynamic package of the race car is emphasized now more than ever before.
(c) We can understand the downforce concept both mathematically and logically.
(d) Downforce ensures that cars are firmly planted on the road at speed.

VII. Mining cryptocurrency was a great way to use your best graphics card to make a little money on the side. Being able to use an idle GPU to crunch numbers when not playing games allows you to make the most of the performance available. Unfortunately, since we originally created this guide, the crypto markets have crashed and Ethereum has moved to a proof of stake.

While it's not as easy to make a tidy earning with your GPU mining cryptocurrencies as before, there may be some other coins that may be worth it if you're mindful of energy use and initial cost. The absolute best gaming graphics card does not equal the best value and returns for mining using your PC. We've got a recommendation for everyone here.

What is the best GPU for crypto mining?

Choosing the best graphics card for crypto mining isn't as simple as picking the absolute most expensive card you can locate and calling it a day. There are various factors to consider when shopping around for a new GPU to (hopefully) make some money with. The most important factor of any GPU for crypto mining is efficiency — you want a high hash rate for as little electricity as possible.

Take our highest recommendation here, for example. It's the NVIDIA GeForce 3060 Ti, an incredible GPU for gaming, but it's also excellent for crypto mining. It won't win awards for the highest hash rate, but for the more affordable price, it'll get you up and running without issue. If you wanted something a little cheaper without sacrificing too much in performance, the NVIDIA GeForce RTX 2070 is your guy.

But there are countless other GPUs that are worth considering and not only from NVIDIA. The AMD Radeon RX 5700 XT is our favorite GPU for value, offering an impressive hash rate for the asking price. Then there's the AMD Radeon RX 580, which is perfect for those on a tight budget who wish to save a few Bitcoins or Ethereum to weather a financial storm.

You don't have to spend much at all to make money mining cryptocurrency. So long as the hash rate will pull in coins for you to sell and make enough to cover electricity costs, you're already in the green. Once you factor in a few months to pay off the GPU, you're in profit — and that's not taking into account the resale value of the card itself.

When deciding on a GPU for crypto mining, you need to bear in mind a few factors. Do you want to pay more upfront now and potentially earn higher returns? Or do you feel as though the mining scene will dissipate slightly with lower returns and wish to spend only a small amount on a GPU to make a little extra on the side?

The cryptocurrency market is a financial one, and that means it's extremely susceptible to media coverage and human emotion. Take the damning environmental reports about Bitcoin that coincided with the Chinese crackdown to send the price spiraling. If you're about to spend $2,000 on a GPU to mine cryptocurrencies, you best be sure you can at least recuperate the initial purchase cost.

This is why we're not recommending only the most powerful (and expensive) GPUs available today. That doesn't make sense in the current climate, but it's also outright bad advice for those new to the wonderful world of mining digital currency. Unlike gaming, where only the best GPU you can afford will do, choosing one for crypto mining is a little more challenging.

What about all other GPUs for crypto mining?

There are plenty of GPUs out there, and many of them offer considerably high hashrates, making them ideal for cryptocurrency mining. We couldn't include every graphics card here, and so this collection only includes handpicked recommendations that cover multiple price ranges.

So long as the GPU you consider buying will make more money than the electrical cost to run the PC, you're good to go. Leave it running for a few months, and you'll have accumulated enough to pay off the card. You could stop here and sell the card to recuperate some of the initial cost or continue with passive income.

31. Select the appropriate option to complete the sentence.
The writer uses the word 'crunch numbers' in the first paragraph to communicate that it involves ________.
(a) generating unique algorithms to develop recreation products
(b) solving algorithms that help solve money-matters
(c) large-scale processing of numerical data
(d) gathering numerical data for financial research

32. Select the option that correctly reflects what the idiom in the given sentence means. 'Choosing the best graphics card isn't as simple as picking the absolute most expensive card, you can locate and calling it a day.'
(a) not compromising on quality
(b) making informed choices
(c) getting confused
(d) ceasing work

33. Select the option that displays what aspect the text titled 'What is best GPU for crypto mining' DOES NOT present.
i. information ii. prediction
iii. suggestion iv. precaution
v. introduction
(a) i, ii and iv (b) ii and v
(c) Only iii (d) i and iii

34. What is the writer's most likely intent of using question headings in this text?
(a) retain a certain measure of deniability
(b) compel the reader to agree with explanation that follows
(c) create an atmosphere of uncertainty and suspense
(d) present information in a systematic chronology

35. Select the option that displays words similar in meaning to 'recuperate', from the last line of the text.
(a) represent, remove, regain
(b) renew, return, represent
(c) remove, retain, reinstall
(d) regain, recover, retrieve

VIII. Who are your first cousins?

Family members who are considered first cousins share grandparents with you. If your mom or dad have siblings, and those siblings have children, the kids are your first cousins! To your mom and dad, they're nephews and nieces, but to you, they're first cousins. Often these are the relatives people mean when they say, "she's my cousin." If they're not adopted, you share about 1/8 of your DNA with your first cousins!

So what are second cousins?

Second cousins have the same great-grandparents as you. Think of it this way: your mom's first cousin's child is your second cousin. Or, your grandpa's brother's grandchild (your dad's aunt's grandchild) is your second cousin. You're in the same generation, they're just not as closely related.

What about a second cousin once removed?

A cousin once removed means they're from the generation immediately above or below you. So your first cousin once removed would be your first cousin's child or your parent's first cousin. Your second cousin once removed is your second cousin's child or your parent's second cousin.

So a cousin twice removed is...?

"Twice removed" means that there's a two generation gap: this cousin is from either your grandparents' generation, or your grandchild's generation. So your first cousin twice removed would be your grandparent's first cousin or your first cousin's grandchild. Your second cousin twice removed is your second cousin's grandchild or your grandparents' second cousin.

And what about third cousins?

Third cousins share the same great-great-grandparents! Your third cousin is your mom's great aunt's great-grandkid. OK, that's a little confusing. How about this: your great-great-uncle's great-grandchild is your third cousin. You might need another look at the chart. Or you can just call them "cousin."

There's a knack to remember which cousin is which. First, second, and third cousins (and so on unto infinity cousins) are an equal number of generations removed from the common ancestor. First cousins are both the second generation removed from their shared grandparents. Second cousins are the third generation removed from shared great-grandparents. So: cousin plus one is the number of generations back.

So "grand" doesn't mean cousins?

The word "grand" means that there's a two-generation gap between the people: your brother's grandchild is your grand-niece, and your mom's father is your grandfather. There is an exception: Your parents' sibling is your aunt or uncle, but your parents' aunt or uncle is usually referred to as a great-aunt or -uncle, despite the two-generation gap rule. Grand-aunt just sounds a bit weird.

But "great" usually goes with "grand"?

The use of "great" is usually paired with grand, and it means that there is a three-generation gap between you and your relative. Your niece's grandchild is your great-grandniece or -nephew, and your grandkid's kid is your great-grandchild! Of course, there's another exception for aunts and uncles: Your mom's uncle is your great-uncle, but your mom's great-uncle is your great-great-uncle.

36. What does the writer convey via the use of exclamation marks in the first paragraph of the text?
(a) dramatic effect (b) ambiguity
(c) astonishment (d) conviction

37. Which aspect of the text indicates that the writer is engaging with the reader?
(a) The paragraphing (b) The punctuations
(c) The conclusion (d) The headlines

38. In the text titled, 'And what about third cousins?', what does the word 'chart' allude to?
(a) pictures or photographs
(b) anecdotes
(c) pedigree
(d) family communication

39. The confusing relationships in the text can be best applied to ______________ .
(a) ted talk (b) stand up show
(c) debate (d) awareness rally

40. Select the appropriate option to fill the blank. When the writer offers a 'knack' to remember which cousin in which, she recognises the fact that the information can be ____________ will be welcome.

(a) dense and a method to paraphrase it
(b) mind-boggling and a tip to simplify it
(c) irrelevant and a reminder suggesting otherwise
(d) mundane and a digression

IX. Wesley Hohfeld, a Harvard law professor in the early part of the 20th Century, developed an analytical framework for understanding interests in property. Hohfeld's eight terms are arranged in two tables of 'correlatives' and 'opposites' that structure the internal relationships among the different fundamental legal rights.

Jural Opposites:

Right	Privilege	Power	Immunity
No-right	Duty	Disability	Liability

A privilege is the opposite of a duty ; a no-right is the opposite of a right. A disability is the opposite of a power; an immunity is the opposite of a liability.

Jural Correlatives:

Right	Privilege	Power	Immunity
Duty	No-right	Liability	Disability

"Correlatives" signifies that these interests exist on opposing sides of a pair of persons involved in a legal relationship. If someone has a right, it exists with respect to someone else who has a duty. If someone has a privilege, it exists with respect to someone else who has no-right. If someone has a power, it exists with respect to someone else who has a liability. If someone has an immunity, it exists with respect to someone else who has a disability.

A right can be enforced by a lawsuit against the person who has the correlative duty. A privilege negates that right and duty, and typically would be asserted as an affirmative defense in the lawsuit. A power is the capacity to create or change a legal relationship. For example, when someone makes an offer of a contract, that gives the offeree the power to create a contract by accepting the offer (or not). If the power to create the contract is exercised, then both parties have rights and duties with respect to each other. Courts have power, only if plaintiffs or prosecutors exercise their power to commence a lawsuit. Sovereign states are immune because courts lack power over them, in which case courts are said to have a disability with respect to sovereigns.

If I "own" property, it means that I have various rights with respect to the thing constituting my property--the "bundle" of sticks or rights. I probably have the right to exclude and everyone else in the world has a correlative duty not to use my property. Some people may have a privilege, however, as to fly over it. I also have power with respect to my property because I can create rights in others, as by transfering some or all of the property to them, as by creating an easement, which gives the grantee certain rights *vis-a-vis* others and certain rights and privileges *vis-a-vis* me.

41. The text is an example of a passage that is
(a) literary (b) descriptive
(c) argumentative (d) informative

42. Select the words from the text that correctly substitutes the underlined words in the following sentence:
She gained <u>exemption</u> from the <u>accountability</u> of paying excessive maintenance, when the apartment owner changed.
(a) power, defence (b) privilege, offeree
(c) respect, contract (d) immunity, liability

43. Which option includes a foreign word used in the English language from the text?
(a) correlative (b) plaintiff
(c) *vis-a-vis* (d) grantee

44. Select the option that can be used as a title from the text.
(a) All Rights Reserved (b) Fine Print
(c) Letter of the Law (d) Burden of Proof

45. Select the option that includes information that is an appropriate fit into the passage.
(a) Hegel, Kant, Hume and others say that 'right' refers to the power of self-expression. However, Duguit opposes this vehemently.

Another theorist of Rights is Ihering, a great German jurist.

(b) Human rights are those which considering their rationality, faith, age, race is intrinsic to all human beings. One of the great achievements of the U.N. is the creation of a comprehensive body of human rights law.

(c) A legal right is an interest accepted and protected by law. If these rights get violated then the person has the right to move the Court for enforcing rights.

(d) Any debasement of any legal right is punishable by law. Employment and discrimination laws provide the legal framework defining an employee's rights to freedom from being discriminated against by the employer.

X. The compass is one of the oldest navigational tools we have. Since mankind began to understand more about navigation, compasses have been crucial to the achievement of major feats such as the first transoceanic voyages and the circumnavigation of the globe. None of this would have been possible without the aid of the compass in performing navigation calculations over long distances.

Early explorers had to use local landmarks and the stars to navigate. This made it very difficult to travel to far or unknown destinations. Compasses were one of the key breakthroughs that made such voyages possible. So how exactly does a compass work?

A compass works by detecting and responding to the Earth's natural magnetic fields. The Earth has an iron core that is part liquid and part solid crystal, due to gravitational pressure. It is believed that movement in the liquid outer core is what produces the Earth's magnetic field. Like all such fields, the Earth's magnetic field has two poles - North and South. These magnetic poles are slightly off from the Earth's axis of rotation, which is used as the basis of the geographic poles - however the magnetic and geographic poles are close enough to allow a compass to serve as a valuable navigation tool, especially when adjustments are made for the polar differences - such adjustments being referred to as declination.

In September 2019, for the first time in over 360 years, compasses at Greenwich pointed true north. Most of the time, however, compasses don't actually point precisely towards the North Pole.

True north is the direction that points directly towards the geographic North Pole. This is a fixed point on the Earth's globe. Magnetic north is quite different: it is the direction that a compass needle points to as it aligns with the Earth's magnetic field.

The magnetic North Pole shifts and changes over time in response to changes in the Earth's magnetic core: it isn't a fixed point.

This difference between true North and the North heading on a compass forms an angle, referred to as declination. Declination varies from place to place because the Earth's magnetic field is not uniform - it dips and undulates.

46. Select the option that corresponds to a 'feat'.
(a) The diversion of traffic
(b) A student's tribute to the mentor
(c) An acrobatic performance
(d) The cancellation of a flight booking

47. The writer refers to the compass as a "key" breakthrough, to highlight its ______________.
(a) importance (b) scientific nature
(c) ease of use (d) novelty

48. Select the option that can be used, both as a noun as well as a verb, in the given form.
(a) uniform, magnetic, point
(b) Only uniform
(c) uniform and core
(d) point, iron and core

49. Identify the meaning of the adjective in the given line from the text. '..... compasses at Greenwich pointed true north.'
(a) aimed (b) precise
(c) topmost (d) sharp

50. Which action suitably corresponds with 'undulates'?
(a) praying
(b) walking a dog
(c) sharing a secret
(d) dancing

SECTION – B: LOGICAL REASONING

51. Let the following premises be true: "If it is sunny on any given day, I can go running.", and "It is not sunny today." Which of the following must be true?
(a) I cannot go running today.
(b) I can go running today.
(c) I can go walking today.
(d) None of the above

52. If a majority of spoons are forks, then which of the following *could be true*?
(a) A majority of forks are spoons
(b) A minority of forks are spoons
(c) All forks are spoons
(d) All the above

53. Assume that (a) a majority of blankets are sheets, (b) a majority of blankets are tablecloths, and (c) no non-blanket sheet (i.e., a sheet that is not a blanket) is a non-blanket tablecloth (i.e., a tablecloth that is not a blanket). Which of the following is true?
(a) No sheets are tablecloths
(b) Some sheets are tablecloths
(c) All sheets are tablecloths
(d) Cannot be determined

54. A minority of wallets are purses. A majority of wallets are perfumes. Which of the following could be true?
(a) No purses are perfumes
(b) All purses are perfumes
(c) Both (a) and (b)
(d) Neither (a) nor b)

55. A majority of Formula 1 cars are race-cars. All race-cars drive on four wheels. All four-wheeled cars are twenty times as fast as cars that drive on any other number of wheels. Speed is the only determining factor for winning a race that involves cars. Which of the following is/are correct?
(a) In a Formula 1 race, a non-four-wheeled car (i.e., a car that does not drive on four wheels) will never be able to win.
(b) In a Formula 1 race, the winner of a race among 20 cars can be predicted using only the number of wheels that a car drives on.
(c) In an Indy500 race, where all participating cars are race-cars, the winner of a race among 50 cars can be predicted.
(d) Both (a) and b).

56. A minority of folders are documents. Which of the following is not true?
(a) If there are folders, there are documents.
(b) If there are documents, there are at least 2 folders.
(c) If there are no documents, there are no folders.
(d) All of the above are true.

57. All moons are asteroids. All planets are celestial bodies. Some planets are moons. Therefore,
(a) All asteroids are celestial bodies.
(b) All asteroids are planets.
(c) Some asteroids are planets.
(d) None of the above

58. Which of the following is true for Queen Elizabeth in the period described in the first sentence of the passage, "During her grandfather's reign, Elizabeth was third in the line of succession to the British throne, behind her uncle Edward and her father."?
(a) Her uncle Edward had a child.
(b) She was not the oldest child of her father.
(c) Her uncle Edward was younger than her father.
(d) Her father was younger than her uncle Edward.

59. If, during the reign of George VI, George VI and his queen-consort had given birth to a boy, then: [for the purpose of this question, assume that heir presumptive and heir apparent are conceptually the same]
(a) The boy would have been third in line of succession – behind Elizabeth and Margaret (Elizabeth's younger sister)
(b) The boy would have been the heir presumptive.

(c) Elizabeth would have been the heir presumptive since she was the oldest among the George VI's children and the succession was determined by primogeniture, i.e., the eldest child is the heir presumptive.
(d) Both (a) and c)

60. X was the reigning monarch of a country, which followed the rule of primogeniture for determining succession. The law of succession also holds that children born out of wedlock cannot be in the line of succession. Looking at a picture of the heir presumptive, he, i.e. X, said, "He is the son of my mother's daughter." Which of the following is correct? [for the purpose of this question, assume that heir presumptive and heir apparent are conceptually the same]
(a) X is married to his sister.
(b) X does not have any children.
(c) X does not have any siblings.
(d) Both (b) and (c)

61. Which of the following can be deduced from the passage?
(a) Elizabeth II ruled over Scotland.
(b) Elizabeth I did not rule over Scotland.
(c) Both (a) and (b)
(d) Neither (a) nor b)

62. X and Y were married. They had three children: P, Q and R (in increasing order of ages). P had three children with her husband Q: A, B and C (in increasing order of ages). R had one child with her husband W: J. A, B, C and J do not have any children of their own. Which of the following is the correct line of succession after the death of X (the current monarch) assuming that the law regulating succession follows the rule of primogeniture?
(a) R, J, Q, A, B, C, P
(b) R, J, Q, C, B, A, P
(c) P, A, B, C, Q, R, J
(d) Q, A, B, C, P, R, J

63. Viserys is the current monarch of a country that follows the law of primogeniture. The laws of the country also prevent children born out of wedlock from being in the line of succession. Viserys' family is as follows: his brother Daemon, his daughter Rhaenyra from his marriage with Aemma (who died while giving birth to a stillborn child, Baelon), his sons Aegon and Aemond, and his daughter Halaena (the three of them being born from his marriage with Alicent, who is currently the queen- consort). Rhaenyra, Aegon, Aemond and Halaena are unmarried and do not have any children. Alicent wants to make her eldest son, Aegon, the heir presumptive. Which of the following options would help her succeed in her plan? [for the purpose of this question, assume that heir presumptive and heir apparent are conceptually the same]
(a) Kill Rhaenyra
(b) Kill Viserys
(c) Both (a) and (b)
(d) Neither (a) nor (b)

64. In the facts of the question above, assume that Rhaenyra had the following children out of wedlock: Jacaerys, Lucerys and Joffrey (in decreasing order of ages). None of them have any children of their own. What would be the place of Daemon in the line of succession during Viserys' lifetime?
(a) Fourth (b) Fifth
(c) Eighth (d) Ninth

65. Which of the following logical relations is/are correct?
(a) Scamming is a superset of which phishing, vishing and smishing are mutually-exclusive subsets.
(b) Scamming and phishing are mutually exclusive sets; vishing and smishing are subsets of phishing.
(c) Vishing and smishing are subsets of scamming.
(d) None of the above.

For Questions 31 – 36: A company has designed a bot to filter scam emails. The method used by the filter is to convert emails to a code using a proprietary software, and then to check the code to see if it meets the following conditions. If the converted code meets each of the said conditions, then it is filtered out as scam.

i. The code should not contain special characters (i.e. non-alphanumeric characters)
ii. The code should not contain any character appearing twice consecutively
iii. The code should not contain any character appearing thrice consecutively
iv. The code should not contain any string that contains a numeric character followed by an alphabetical character

66. Which of the following emails (converted to code) is scam according to the filter?
(a) 55923423 (b) ersfjtncjlx
(c) 243434p123 (d) 3454xxx`

67. Which of the following emails (converted to code) is scam according to the filter?
(a) Thisemailisscam
(b) Thisemailisnotscam
(c) Thisemaillikelyisscam
(d None of the above

68. Which of the following statements is correct about the conditions used in the filter?
(a) Condition (ii) is redundant in light of Condition (iii)
(b) Condition (iii) is redundant in light of Condition (ii)
(c) Condition (i) is redundant because no codes have special characters in them in any event
(d) Both (a) and b)

69. Can this bot be used to filter phishing emails?
(a) This bot will necessarily filter some (but not all) phishing emails.
(b) This bot may filter only some (but not all) phishing emails.
(c) This bot will not filter any phishing emails.
(d) This bot will filter all phishing emails.

70. A scammer has figured out a way to manipulate the working of the bot. However, he has not yet figured out the manner in which the bot categorizes email as scam or not-scam. The loophole works by using a certain "macro" in an email. The "macro" transforms the code of the email into a new code using the following sequential steps: first, letters t – z are transformed into numbers 1 – 7, respectively; second, numbers 1 – 9 are transformed into letters a – i, respectively; and third, number 0 is transformed into the letter j. Which of the following can be codes generated by the "macro"?
(a) Abcgiijg2s (b) Abcgiijgzs
(c) Abc0iijgs (d) Abcoiijgs

71. The company that created the bot reverse-engineered the scheme of the scammer. The company wants to use the following steps to transform the "macro"-generated code into the original code.
i. Transform numbers 1 – 7 to letters t – z, respectively
ii. Transform letters a – i to numbers 1 – 9, respectively
iii. Transform letter j to number 0

What is the order in which these steps should be undertaken to fulfil the company's aim?
(a) (i) followed by (ii) followed by (iii)
(b) (iii) followed by (ii) followed by (i)
(c) (ii) followed by (i) followed by (iii)
(d) These steps, in whichever order, cannot achieve the company's aim

72. Which of the following assumptions is/are necessary to conclude that plastic waste emerging from land would be the smallest in size as it accumulates in the Great Pacific Garbage Patch?
(a) Extent of photodegradation is inversely related to time spent by plastic in oceanic water.
(b) Plastic waste emerging from land and other sources are of somewhat equivalent sizes at the source of origin.
(c) Both (a) and (b)
(d) Neither (a) nor (b)

73. A researcher showed that for every thousand kilometres a piece of plastic travels through oceanic water, it breaks down into 100 pieces. Each of those pieces would then also break down into 100 more pieces upon traveling a thousand kilometres.

This phenomenon is analogically equivalent to ____________.

(a) Reproduction of amoeba – each amoeba splits into two in a certain period of time; which then again split into two in the same period of time.
(b) A train locomotive accumulating two coaches at each station it crosses.
(c) Case-load of a Court increasing as a result of more fresh cases being filed every day compared to cases being disposed in the same day.
(d) All the above

74. It was found that between two pieces of plastic, the lighter one travels at twice the speed of the heavier one. If there are ten pieces of plastic (each with a different weight) that start from the same geographical location, the speed of the fastest piece would X times the speed of the slowest piece. X is
(a) 10
(b) $2 \times 10 = 20$
(c) $2 \times 9 = 18$
(d) $2^9 = 512$

75. Theoretically, filtering out all plastics from water bodies flowing into the sea and preventing direct disposal of any plastic from land into sea would
(a) Eliminate the Great Pacific Garbage Patch over a sufficiently long time period.
(b) Stop the growth of the size and depth of the Great Pacific Garbage Patch over a sufficiently long time period.
(c) Stop the speed of growth of the size and depth of the Great Pacific Garbage Patch over a sufficiently long time period.
(d) All the above

76. A teacher wants to demonstrate the futility of Ocean Cleanup. She believes that unless plastic-removal is faster than plastic-accrual, the overall size and depth of the Great Pacific Garbage Patch would stay stagnant or may even increase. Which of the following analogies can she draw to drive home her argument?
(a) A filled bucket eventually empties as a result of an open outlet at the bottom of the bucket.
(b) Water level in a partially filled bucket with an outlet at its bottom rises if the amount of water coming through the inlet is faster than the amount of water that goes out through the outlet.
(c) Water level in a partially filled bucket with an outlet at its bottom goes down if the amount of water coming through the inlet is slower than the amount of water that goes out through the outlet.
(d) Both (b) and (c)

77. From the passage, it is clear that both plastic accumulation and oceanic pollution are negatively affecting marine life. As a scientist, you conduct a series of experiments to determine the extent (if any) of their contribution to degradation of marine life. The details of the experiments and their results are below:
i. Check if plastic accumulation in sterile, non-polluting conditions affects marine life. It turns out that marine life is negatively affected. The measurement of the effect is X units.
ii. Separately, check if any kind of pollution in some non-plastic environment affects marine life. It turns out that marine life is not affected at all.
iii. Separately, check if pollution absorbed by accumulated plastic affects marine life. It turns out that marine life is negatively affected. The measurement of the effect is 2X units.

What, if anything, can be concluded from the experiment?
(a) Pollution is always dangerous to marine life.
(b) Pollution is dangerous for marine life only if it takes place in an environment where plastic has accumulated.
(c) Plastic accumulation poses no threat in a non-polluted environment.
(d) None of the above conclusions can be drawn.

78. It is found in a series of experiments that big pieces of plastic (defined as being larger than $100cm^2$ in size) take T amount of time to break into halves due to photodegradation, and smaller pieces of plastic (defined as being smaller than

$10 cm^2$ in size) take T/3 amount of time to break into halves due to photodegradation, which of the following is correct?

(a) Rate of photodegradation is inversely related to size of original piece of plastic.
(b) Rate of photodegradation is directly related to size of original piece of plastic.
(c) Rate of photodegradation is independent of size of original piece of plastic.
(d) Rate of photodegradation is not dependent on any factor other than size of original piece of plastic.

79. A ruler's first-born son, at the moment of his birth, is first in the line of succession.
This statement is ____________
(a) Always correct with respect to the rule of primogeniture.
(b) Always correct with respect to the rule of house seniority.
(c) Capable of being correct in case of ultimogeniture.
(d) All the above

80. A ruler's last-born son, at the moment of his birth, is first in the line of succession.
This statement is ____________
(a) Always correct with respect to the rule of ultimogeniture.
(b) Never correct with respect to the rule of house seniority.
(c) Capable of being correct in cases of primogeniture.
(d) All the above

81. Different rules of inheritance can never create situations where the same person is first in the line of succession. This statement is ____________
(a) Correct if seen only in context of the rules of primogeniture and ultimogeniture.
(b) Not correct even if it is seen only in context of the rules of primogeniture and ultimogeniture.
(c) Correct if seen only in context of the rules of primogeniture and house-seniority.
(d) Both (a) and (c)

82. Y is the youngest child of X, the current ruler, who has 5 other children (each of them older than Y). Y is first in the line of succession. Which of the following inferences can be drawn for certain about their realm from the above two statements?
(a) If the rule of primogeniture is followed, then Y's elder siblings have all been disowned.
(b) Even if one or more of Y's elder siblings were not disowned, it is possible that the rule of primogeniture is followed.
(c) The only possible rule governing their realm is the rule of ultimogeniture.
(d) All the above

83. Which of the following scenarios is/are possible?
(a) A realm follows the rule of house-seniority. The ruler's eldest brother.
(b) Even if one or more of Y's elder siblings were not disowned, it is possible that the rule of primogeniture is followed.
(c) The only possible rule governing their realm is the rule of ultimogeniture.
(d) All the above

84. X is the ruler of a realm. X has three younger sisters: W, Y and Z (in increasing order of ages). X is married to A, with whom he has three sons (B, C and D (in increasing order of ages)) and two daughters (E and F (in increasing order of ages)). F is younger than B. W is older than D. E is married to P and has two children: Q and R (in increasing order of ages). E dies. Stricken by grief after E's death, X dies. Assuming the realm follows gender-neutral ultimogeniture, the throne passes to ____________
(a) W (b) F
(c) B (d) Q

85. In the facts of the question above, if the realm followed the rule of house seniority, the throne would pass to ____________
(a) Z (b) D
(c) F (d) R

86. If the orientation of the wings in a Formula One car were reversed (and all other things remain equal), the effective weight pressing down on the track would be X times the weight of the car. X is

(a) = 1 (b) > 1

(c) < 1 (d) Cannot be determined

87. A super car has a greater acceleration and top-speed compared to a Formula One car, but does not have wings that generate even half the down-force as compared to a Formula One car. The super car would still handily lose a race against a Formula one car. Which among the following statements is correct the race track?

(a) The race track is straight.
(b) The race track has at least a few turns.
(c) The race track is made of soft, rubber-y surface.
(d) The race track is made of asphalt.

88. Without downforce-generating apparatus in a Formula One car, the drivers would ___________.

(a) A Formula One car without any apparatus affecting aerodynamics would act like an aeroplane.
(b) Need to slow their car down to make turns.
(c) Need to gain a lot of weight (or add weight to the car) to keep the car on the ground.
(d) All the above

89. Assume that an object enters into free-fall if the force attracting it towards the earth is less than the force pushing it away from the earth. Further assume that all objects on earth are pushed away from it with a force equal to 1G. A Formula One car, therefore, ___________ ?

(a) Is in free-fall at all times during a race.
(b) Is not in free-fall at any time during a race.
(c) Is in free-fall at some (but not all) times during a race.
(d) Cannot be determined.

90. Downforce generated by the wings of a Formula One car creates force towards the floor of the car thereby keeping the floor of the car closer to the surface it is being driven on. As mentioned in the passage, this downforce can be around 5 times the gravitational force exerted by the earth on the car. This implies that ___________

(a) A Formula One car, if driven at a high enough speed, can drive upside-down in a tunnel (i.e., on the roof of the tunnel) without falling down.
(b) A Formula One car cannot drive upside-down in a tunnel (i.e., on the roof of the tunnel) at all.
(c) Gravity and downforce always act in the same direction.
(d) Both (b) and (c)

91. In a race among ten drivers (A, B, C, D, E, F, G, H, I and J, who started in this order, i.e. A started 1st and J started 10th), D, E and F made 2, 2, and 5 overtakes, respectively. No one else made any overtakes. What are the new respective positions of D, E and F ___________?

(a) 2nd, 3rd and 1st
(b) 3rd, 2nd and 1st
(c) 1st, 2nd and 3rd
(d) Cannot be determined

92. How many overtakes does a person starting 10th in a race need to make to get to 1st position, assuming no other person makes any overtakes?

(a) 9 (b) 10

(c) 11 (d) 8

93. On the basis of this article, a rational person decided that X was a better GPU for crypto mining than Y. He found that the initial cost of X was much lower than Y. It therefore follows that:

(a) X's hashrates were higher than Y's
(b) X's hashrates were lower than Y's
(c) X's hashrates were the same as Y's
(d) Cannot be determined

94. If total cost of mining N bitcoins using GPU X was lower than the total cost of mining the same number of bitcoins using GPU Y, then it follows that:

(a) X's per-unit-time electricity consumption is lower than Y's per-unit-time electricity consumption
(b) X's per-unit-time electricity consumption is more than Y's per-unit-time electricity consumption
(c) X's cost price is lower than Y's cost price
(d) Cannot be determined

95. What is the relationship between profits made using crypto-mining and hashrates?
(a) High hashrates necessarily lead to high profits
(b) High hashrates necessarily lead to some profits
(c) Low hashrates cannot lead to profits
(d) None of the above

96. Assuming that the cost price and hashrates of two GPUs are identical, which of the following statements is true?
(a) The profits made by crypto-mining using the GPUs in different time-periods and thereafter selling the GPUs would be identical.
(b) The profits made by crypto-mining using the GPUs in the same time-period and thereafter selling the GPUs would be identical.
(c) The profits made by crypto-mining using the GPUs in the same time-period and thereafter selling the GPUs could be different.
(d) None of the above

97. GPUs are made of infinitesimally small chips made out of semiconductors. Due to the pandemic, companies manufacturing these chips had to shut down. Assuming that the prices of cryptocurrencies and electricity remained constant, this would lead to
i. Higher cost prices of GPUs
ii. Lower profits made by people mining cryptocurrency
iii. Lesser hashrates of GPUs
iv. Losses for people mining cryptocurrency
(a) i, iii, iv (b) i, ii
(c) i, iv (d) i only

98. A certain extremely expensive GPU has the best hashrates among all GPUs. This GPU would
(a) Have high resale value
(b) Have high electricity consumption
(c) Give less profit in crypto-mining
(d) None of the above

99. A goes to a shop. At the shop are two salesmen – X and Y. X always says the truth. Y always speaks falsehoods. X and Y are aware of each other's tendencies. A does not know which salesman is X and which salesman is Y. Both salesmen say to A, "If you asked the other salesman, he would tell you that GPU G1 is better than GPU G2." What can be said about G1 and G2?
(a) G2 is better than G1
(b) G1 is better than G2
(c) G1 is the same as G2
(d) Cannot be determined

100. Talking about the woman in a picture, X says, "Oh, I do miss my great-aunt! Doesn't she look awesome in this picture? You know, her daughter and my mother taught me how to play cricket." Which of the following assumptions would need to be made to determine that the woman in the picture was X's great-aunt on the maternal side?
(a) The woman in the picture was X's mother's aunt
(b) The woman in the picture was X's grandmother's aunt
(c) X's great-aunt's daughter and X's mother were siblings
(d) None of the above

101. X's grandson's paternal grandson's sister's father's father's father is X's
(a) Son (b) Daughter
(c) One of (a) or (b) (d) Grandson

102. X and Y are sisters. A is X's grandson's niece. Y is A's
(a) Great-grand-aunt (b) Great-great-aunt
(c) Great-great-niece (d) Great-grand-niece

103. Who among the following would be X's second cousin, once removed?
(a) X's father's father's brother's grandchild
(b) X's father's father's brother's son
(c) X's father's father's sister's granddaughter
(d) None of the above

104. X is A's first cousin. Y is X's first cousin. Z is Y's first cousin. What is the closest relationship possible between X and Z?
(a) Sibling (b) First cousin
(c) Second cousin (d) Third cousin

105. Who is the common ancestor between X and Y, who is X's first cousin twice removed?

(a) X's grandparent's grandparent and Y's grandparent
(b) X's grandparent and Y's grandparent's grandparent
(c) Either (a) or (b)
(d) Neither (a) nor (b)

106. X's father's aunt is X's
(a) Great-aunt
(b) Grand-aunt
(c) Great-great-aunt
(d) None of the above

107. If X has a right *vis-à-vis* everyone else, and Y has a privilege *vis-à-vis* X, then X has a ______________ *vis-à-vis* Y.
(a) No-right (b) Duty
(c) No-duty (d) None of the above

108. X and Y enter into a contract that provides as follows: "The quantum and time of payment, if any, shall be determined by A on the basis of the parties' performance of their obligations under this contract." Here, A has ______________ *vis-à-vis* X and Y.
(a) Immunity (b) Right
(c) Power (d) Disability

109. Every person can travel on any road, unless it is blocked by a person who owns that road. Every person has ______________ *vis-à-vis* the owner of the road.
(a) A right (b) A privilege
(c) An immunity (d) None of the above

110. In the facts of the question above, the owner of the road has ______________ *vis-à-vis* everyone else.
(a) A right (b) A privilege
(c) An immunity (d) None of the above

111. If A has a right to claim damages from B, then B has ______________ to pay damages to A.
(a) Duty (b) Liability
(c) Immunity (d) Disability

112. The owner of land can lease the property to any other person. Under that lease, the owner can allow sub-leasing. The owner of the land has ______________ *vis-à-vis* the property.
(a) Right (b) Power
(c) Immunity (d) Liability

113. If X infringes Y's copyright, Y can sue X. Y has ______________ *vis-à-vis* X.
(a) Right (b) Power
(c) No-duty (d) Immunity

For Questions 114 – 117: 5 towers made by civilisation X were declared to be protected heritage building. Uniquely, four of them are placed geographically such that they are the vertices of a square. The fifth is placed at the point of intersection of the two diagonals of the square. Let the towers be named A, B, C, D and E. The following information is given to you about the five towers:

i. C, A and B are in a straight line (in no particular order) that runs from south-east to north-west.
ii. If one looks directly east from B, no tower is visible. This is not true for A and D.
iii. If one looks directly north from D, a tower is visible.

114. Based on the above information, which tower is in the centre?
(a) A (b) B
(c) C (d) Insufficient information

115. If one seeks to travel to D from A, one has to go
(a) East (b) South-east
(c) West (d) South

116. If one seeks to travel to B from A, one has to go
(a) East (b) South-east
(c) West (d) Cannot be determined

117. At sunset, A's shadow points ______________ .
(a) Towards B (b) Towards C
(c) Towards D (d) Towards E

118. A compass (circular in shape) consists of two parts: a magnetic needle that points towards the magnetic north, and a circular piece of paper with directions written on it. If, somehow, the piece of paper rotates a quarter-circle counter-clockwise, which geographic direction does needle point towards?
(a) Approximately east (b) Exactly east
(c) Approximately west (d) Exactly west

119. A is holding a compass at the time of sunrise. He points it towards the direction of the sunrise and sees that it reads "SW". This means that the compass has rotated ______
(a) 135 degrees counter-clockwise or 225 degrees clockwise
(b) 135 degrees clockwise or 225 degrees counter-clockwise
(c) 45 degrees clockwise or 315 degrees counter-clockwise
(d) 45 degrees counter-clockwise or 315 degrees clockwise

120. In the facts of the question above, what actual direction is "NW" on the compass pointing towards?
(a) North (b) South
(c) East (d) West

PART-2

GENERAL KNOWLEDGE AND CURRENT AFFAIRS

121. Who won the Nobel Peace Prize, 2022?
(a) Ales Bialiatski (b) Annie Ernaux
(c) Svantee Paabo (d) John Clauser

122. In order to reduce plastic waste in India, the Indian government in July, 2022 banned ______.
(a) All plastic bags
(b) Single-use plastic
(c) Only polyethene bags
(d) Only toothbrushes

123. There is a fear that certain nanoplastics would become a part of human food, thereby causing severe harm to the human body. What is the size of one nanometre?
(a) 10^{-9} m (b) 10^{-6} m
(c) 10^{-12} m (d) 10^{-3} m

124. X water body connects the Pacific Ocean to the Atlantic Ocean. Identify X.
(a) Panama Canal
(b) Strait of Magellan
(c) Both (a) and (b)
(d) Neither (a) nor (b)

125. The following Indian driver is currently participating in Formula Two series:
(a) Narain Karthikeyan (b) Jehan Daruvala
(c) Jack Doohan (d) Karun Chandhok

126. Before adopting Riyal as its currency, Qatar's currency was equivalent to which foreign (to Qatar) currency?
(a) US Dollars (b) Canadian Dollars
(c) Indian Rupee (d) UAE Dirham

127. As a result of air pollution and nearby sewage, the ______ is reported to be turning yellow. Built in the 17th century, it is one of the seven wonders of the world.
(a) Taj Mahal
(b) Statue of Liberty
(c) Christ the Redeemer (statue)
(d) The White House

128. Who among the following rely on medicines to cure mental illnesses?
(a) Psychologists (b) Psychiatrists
(c) Both (a) and (b) (d) Neither (a) nor (b)

129. Twitter, a social media platform, was recently acquired by Elon Musk. Which of the following entities is not owned/ controlled by Elon Musk?
(a) Solar City (b) Neuralink
(c) Waymo (d) The Boring Company

130. Which of the following statements is correct about Fundamental Duties in the Constitution of India?
(a) Fundamental Duties were part of the original Constitution
(b) A person can be sued merely for failure to abide by Fundamental Duties
(c) Both (a) and (b)
(d) Neither (a) nor (b)

131. Human Rights Day is celebrated on
(a) 26 January (b) 10 December
(c) 1 March (d) None of the above

132. How many Youth World Titles in Chess have been won by Grand Master Praggnanandhaa?
(a) None (b) One
(c) Two (d) Three

133. The first Indian to have won a Medal in Asian Cup Table Tennis is
(a) Sreeja Akula
(b) Archana Kamat
(c) Manika Batra
(d) S. Gnanasekaran

134. After winning Gold Medal in Olympics, Neeraj Chopra has also won the Javelin throw in
(a) Commonwealth
(b) Diamond League
(c) Both (a) and (b)
(d) None

135. The first Indian to win a Medal in Olympics Badminton is
(a) P. V. Sindhu
(b) Prakash Padukone
(c) Saina Nehwal
(d) Gopichand Pullela

136. The first Indian to have won the All England Badminton Championship is
(a) Gopichand Pullela
(b) Prakash Padukone
(c) P. V. Sindhu
(d) Saina Nehwal

137. The Prime Minister of which country was in news for dancing in a 'wild party'?
(a) Finland (b) New Zealand
(c) Canada (d) None

138. The present Chairman of the National Human Rights Commission is
(a) Justice Arun Kumar Mishra
(b) Justice H. L. Dattu
(c) Justice Pinaki Chandra Ghose
(d) Justice P. C. Pant

139. How many Amendments have been made to the Indian Constitution so far?
(a) 103 (b) 104
(c) 105 (d) 106

140. The Supreme Court in ______________ upheld the constitutional validity of the EWS reservation.
(a) State of Tamil Nadu v. Union of India
(b) EWS Association v. Union of India
(c) Janhit Abiyan v. Union of India
(d) State of Maharashtra v. Union of India

141. The new Election Commissioner who joined in November 2022 is
(a) Rajiv Kumar
(b) Arun Goel
(c) Sushil Chandra
(d) Justice Kuldeep Singh

142. How many World Heritage sites are there in India?
(a) 12 (b) 28
(c) 40 (d) 52

143. India's rank in the Global Hunger Index out of 121 countries is
(a) 89 (b) 107
(c) 98 (d) 112

144. The 2022 G20 Meeting was held in November 2022 in
(a) Bali (b) Rome
(c) Beijing (d) New Delhi

145. The National Education Policy, 2020, excluded the following disciplines from its ambit
(a) Law (b) Medicine
(c) Technical (d) Both (a) and (b)

146. Which among the following states admitted more foreign tourists in 2021?
(a) Goa (b) Karnataka
(c) Maharashtra (d) Kerala

147. Recently the IMF approved a loan of US$ 2.9 billion to
(a) Myanmar (b) Sri Lanka
(c) India (d) Nepal

148. The Foreign Universities can set up their institutions in
(a) GIFT city
(b) Metropolitan Cities
(c) District Headquarters
(d) Municipal Towns

149. The name of the privately built rocket that was launched from Sriharikota in November 2022 is
(a) Skyroot (b) Vikram – S
(c) Arya – B (d) Chand – I

150. The Voters Day in India is celebrated on
(a) 26th January (b) 26th November
(c) 25th January (d) 25th November

ANSWER KEY

Part-1

Section–A: English

1. (d)	**9.** (c)	**17.** (c)	**25.** (b)	**33.** (b)	**41.** (d)	**49.** (b)
2. (b)	**10.** (a)	**18.** (b)	**26.** (a)	**34.** (a)	**42.** (d)	**50.** (d)
3. (c)	**11.** (d)	**19.** (d)	**27.** (c)	**35.** (d)	**43.** (c)	
4. (a)	**12.** (d)	**20.** (b)	**28.** (b)	**36.** (c)	**44.** (c)	
5. (a)	**13.** (d)	**21.** (a)	**29.** (a)	**37.** (d)	**45.** (c)	
6. (b)	**14.** (b)	**22.** (a)	**30.** (b)	**38.** (c)	**46.** (c)	
7. (b)	**15.** (b)	**23.** (c)	**31.** (c)	**39.** (b)	**47.** (a)	
8. (d)	**16.** (d)	**24.** (c)	**32.** (d)	**40.** (b)	**48.** (d)	

Section–B: Logical Reasoning

51. (d)	**61.** (c)	**71.** (d)	**81.** (b)	**91.** (d)	**101.** (a)	**111.** (a)
52. (d)	**62.** (b)	**72.** (d)	**82.** (b)	**92.** (a)	**102.** (b)	**112.** (b)
53. (b)	**63.** (c)	**73.** (a)	**83.** (b)	**93.** (d)	**103.** (d)	**113.** (a)
54. (c)	**64.** (b)	**74.** (d)	**84.** (d)	**94.** (d)	**104.** (a)	**114.** (d)
55. (a)	**65.** (c)	**75.** (c)	**85.** (a)	**95.** (d)	**105.** (c)	**115.** (d)
56. (a)	**66.** (b)	**76.** (d)	**86.** (c)	**96.** (c)	**106.** (a)	**116.** (b)
57. (c)	**67.** (d)	**77.** (d)	**87.** (b)	**97.** (d)	**107.** (a)	**117.** (d)
58. (d)	**68.** (b)	**78.** (a)	**88.** (d)	**98.** (d)	**108.** (c)	**118.** (a)
59. (b)	**69.** (d)	**79.** (c)	**89.** (a)	**99.** (a)	**109.** (d)	**119.** (b)
60. (a)	**70.** (d)	**80.** (c)	**90.** (a)	**100.** (a)	**110.** (a)	**120.** (b)

Part-2

Current Affairs and General Knowledge

121. (a)	**126.** (c)	**131.** (b)	**136.** (b)	**141.** (b)	**146.** (c)
122. (b)	**127.** (a)	**132.** (d)	**137.** (a)	**142.** (c)	**147.** (b)
123. (a)	**128.** (b)	**133.** (c)	**138.** (a)	**143.** (b)	**148.** (a)
124. (c)	**129.** (c)	**134.** (b)	**139.** (c)	**144.** (a)	**149.** (b)
125. (b)	**130.** (d)	**135.** (c)	**140.** (c)	**145.** (d)	**150.** (c)

AILET 2022

SECTION–A: ENGLISH

I. Read the excerpt from a ruling of the Court (Civil Action: American Library Association v. U.S.A.) and answer the following questions by choosing the most appropriate answer.

Under strict scrutiny, a public library's use of filtering software is permissible only if it is narrowly tailored to further a compelling government interest and no less restrictive alternative would serve that interest. We acknowledge that use of filtering software furthers public libraries' legitimate interests in preventing patrons from accessing visual depictions of obscenity, or in the case of minors, material harmful to minors. Moreover, use of filters also helps to prevent patrons from being unwillingly exposed to patently offensive, content on the Internet.

1. Select which of the following assumptions is the ruling of the Court is based on.
   (a) Filtering software is the preferred alternative by the patrons of public libraries.
   (b) Filtering software is the most restrictive of all the alternatives used in public libraries.
   (c) Filtering software is the only tool that can be scrutinised by the public libraries.
   (d) Filtering software safeguards the interests of the patrons of public libraries.

2. What, according to the passage, is the primary purpose of filtering software within a public library?
   (a) Permit the use of classified materials.
   (b) Check the use of all visual content of a library.
   (c) Record the number of searches made by patrons.
   (d) Prevent the access to inappropriate content.

3. Which of the following words is an antonym to the word "compelling" used in the text?
   (a) singular
   (b) strange
   (c) weak
   (d) popular

II. Read the following news post and answer the questions by choosing the most appropriate answer.

INDIA'S MARINE EXPORTS REACH ALL TIME HIGH OF $ 7,740 MILLION

Vijayawada: Exports of marine products from India have reached an all-time high of US $ 7,740 million in 2021-22 against the targeted US $ 7,809 million fixed by the centre.

Marine Products Exports Development Authority joint director A. Jeyabal in a statement here on Friday said India's exports of marine products grew 30 percent compared to 2020-21 in value terms. The compound annual growth rate of sea-food exports during the past decade has been 8.23 percent, he pointed out.

Jeyabal explained that India exported marine products to 121 countries during 2021-22, the US being the top destination with exports worth US $ 3,315 million in 2021-22 against the target of $ 3,021 million.

China and Japan stood at number two and three positions respectively. All three top destinations of Indian marine exports constitute 63 percent of India's exports in value terms.

4. The phrase "an all-time high" indicates that India's marine

(a) export rate has never been so high.
(b) exports have grown less expensive.
(c) export rate increases with each month.
(d) exports have reached their highest limit.

5. Substitute the underlined phrase with the option closest in meaning.
"The compound annual growth rate of seafood exports during the past decade has been 8.23 per-cent, he pointed out."
(a) calculated
(b) announced
(c) specified
(d) shared

6. Which of the following statements are true for the given text?
(i) 2022 is fast becoming the most successful year for Indian exports, in terms of marine products.
(ii) The director of "Marine Products Exports Development Authority" is Mr. A. Jeyabal.
(iii) Mr. A. Jeyabal is sure that India will grow as an exporter of marine products.
(iv) There is most demand for India's marine products in the US.
(a) (i), (ii) and (iii)
(b) (i) and (iv)
(c) (ii), (iii) and (iv)
(d) (i) and (ii)

7. The most appropriate by-line for the article would be
(a) Glowing Prospects
(b) A Legacy
(c) A Befitting Tribute
(d) Profiting from Sustainability

8. It can be inferred from the text that
(a) All of India's marine exports to Japan and China are done from Vijayawada.
(b) More than half of India's marine exports go to the US, China and Japan, in value terms.
(c) India is the leading exporter of marine goods to 121 countries.
(d) India reached the proposed sales target determined by the centre in the year 2021–22.

9. Select the sentence that is the most appropriate conclusion for the given text.
(a) Several exports promotion schemes for Fisheries have been implemented by the Marine Products Export Development Authority (MPEDA), a statutory body set up in 1972.
(b) The twin Godavari districts contributed to 50 per cent exports of the Vannamei shrimp.
(c) Despite the heavy odds faced by the sector, India's marine products exports reached a record high.
(d) With a budget of ₹20,050 crores, this is the biggest ever investment to bring about a Blue Revolution through sustainable and respon-sible development of the fisheries sector in India.

III. Read the book descriptions for three different books up for sale online and answer the ques-tions by choosing the correct options.

The *On Being a Veterinarian* Series gives pre-vet and veterinary students a glimpse into what it's really like to be a small animal veterinarian. Each book in the series provides insight on a different aspect of small animal veterinary medicine to help future veterinary doctors better prepare for the challenges of this career. Book puts the reader in the doctor's shoes for a day to illustrate the importance of emotional resilience. Tools for building resilience are provided, as are scientific explanations for how and why they work.	*So, You Want to be a Veterinarian* is suggested reading for aspiring veterinarians, their parents, and their mentors. It succinctly describes colleges of veterinary medicine and their admission requirements, application procedures, curriculums, faculties, and facilities, and provides information that increases the odds of success in the admission process. It goes on to describe the veterinary profession and its multiple practice types, species and disciplinary specialties, and employment opportunities in industry, government, academy, and the military.	I Want to be a Veterinarian is part of a new I Can Read series that introduces young readers to important community helpers. This Level One I Can Read is perfect for children learning to sound out words and sentences. Whether shared at home or in a classroom, the short sentences, familiar words, and simple concepts of Level One books support success for children eager to start reading on their own. For anyone looking for books about community helpers for kids, this book is a great choice as it is bright and upbeat and feature characters who are diverse in terms of gender, race, age, and body type.

10. By using the phrase "gives a glimpse into", the text suggests that *On Being a Veterinarian* Series
(a) imparts extensive knowledge about the personal and professional aspects of a veterinarian's life.
(b) gives detailed descriptions about the veterinary profession and its multiple practice types.
(c) offers comprehensive health advice to small animal veterinary doctors.
(d) provides salient features of small animal veterinary medicine to help prepare future doctors for the difficulties of their profession.

11. A 'small animal veterinarian' involves dealing with
(a) farm animals
(b) companion animals
(c) zoo animals
(d) endangered animals

12. Which underlined phrase is similar in meaning to "increases the odds of success"? (*So, You Want to be a Veterinarian*)
(a) The estimates for chances in achieving the goal are maximum when you plan ahead.
(b) The increases in bets to gain victory, are not just common in academic circles.
(c) When a business studies the competition, it improves its chances of surging ahead.
(d) A lesser-known fact is that focussing on yourself ensures long-term gains.

13. Select the option that correctly displays the meaning of 'succinctly' as used in the given line, from the text about *So, You Want to be a Veterinarian*.

'It succinctly describes colleges of veterinary medicine...'

(a) polite, short and sweet, brief, relevant
(b) compact, discursive, concise, polite
(c) condensed, compact, brief, to the point
(d) short and sweet, condensed, discursive, systematic

14. Which book/s of the three mentioned in the text is/are like to include the following line?

How long it takes to become a vet can vary, but if you really love animals and think caring for them is up your alley, then becoming a veterinarian may be the right choice for you.

(a) Both, *On Being a Veterinarian and So, You Want to be a Veterinarian*
(b) Only *So, You Want to be a Veterinarian*

(c) All three—I *Want to be a Veterinarian*, *On Being a Veterinarian* and *So, You Want to be a Veterinarian*
(d) Only *On Being a Veterinarian*

15. Which topic would be a part of 'disciplinary specialities' in *So, You Want to be a Veterinarian*?
(a) Remount and Veterinary Corps
(b) Internship allowance
(c) International Institute of Veterinary Education & Research
(d) Sports medicine and rehabilitation

16. Upon reading the passage, which of the following is likely to be inferred about the main aim of I *Want to be a Veterinarian*?
(a) Learn about characteristics of veterinarians.
(b) Learn about inclusion and diversity.
(c) Learn about various community helpers.
(d) Learn how to read by oneself.

17. Select the option that matches the books to the most likely readerships, according to the text. Choose three appropriate options from out of four options given.

Name of the book	Type of readers
A. I *Want to be a Veterinarian*	(i) school students/ graduates
B. *So, You Want to be a Veterinarian*	(ii) children
C. *On Being a Veterinarian Series*	(iii) pre-vet and veterinary students
	(iv) academics and practicing veterinarians

(a) A-(i), B-(ii), C-(iv) (b) A-(i), B-(iii), C-(ii)
(c) A-(ii), B-(i), C-(iii) (d) A-(ii), B-(iv), C-(i)

IV. Read the excerpt from a handicrafts' manual titled 'Woodwork Joints' and answer the following questions by choosing the most appropriate answer.

THE SCARF JOINT

The method known as "scarfing" is used for the joining of timber in the direction of its length, enabling the workman to produce a joint with a smooth or flush appearance on all its faces. One of the simplest forms of scarfed joint is known as the half lap, in which a portion is cut out at the end of each beam or joist, equal in depth to half the full depth of the beam, and of equal length to the required scarf. The two pieces, before they are placed together, form a joint with the projecting part fitting into the recessed portion and the two pieces being secured in their respective positions by screws.

A tabled scarf joint is very easy to make and fit, and is not materially affected by shrinkage. Rectangular wrought iron straps are knocked up over the joint after the two pieces engage. A lapped scarf joint is secured with nuts and bolts and effectively resists compressional stress in vertical posts.

THE PUZZLE JOINTS

These are not only interesting in themselves, but are often excellent studies in craftsmanship. The majority of them, if to be satisfactory as puzzles, call for very careful setting out and cutting, entailing the same degree of skill that is demanded for high-class cabinet work. For this reason, several illustrations of examples may well find a place in a volume dealing with woodwork joints. As a rule, these puzzles should be made in hardwood, such as dark walnut or beech, as in whitewood the joints are soon liable to wear.

18. Ensuring the 'flush appearance on all its faces' refers to the
(a) finishing
(b) strength
(c) stability
(d) variation

19. Which option includes the correct meaning of the underlined phrase in the given sentence?
Rectangular wrought iron straps are <u>knocked up</u> over the joint after the two pieces engage.
(a) carved
(b) assembled
(c) removed
(d) created

20. Select the reason why several illustrations of puzzle joint examples are often showcased in a volume dealing with woodwork joints.
(a) To contrast characteristics of puzzle joints with other types of joints.
(b) To address the growing demand for wooden cabinets.
(c) To cater to the popular and extensive usage among carpenters.
(d) To foster a better understanding of the required precision and skill.

21. Choose the correct order of the following statements in the passage.
(i) The workman cuts out a portion at the end of each beam or joist.
(ii) The two pieces are placed together to form a joint.
(iii) The two pieces are secured in their respective positions by screws.
(iv) The workman measures out a portion in the beam that is equal in depth to half the full depth of the beam, and of equal length to the required scarf.
(a) (i), (iv), (iii), (ii) (b) (ii), (iv), (i), (iii)
(c) (iv), (i), (ii), (iii) (b) (iv), (ii), (i), (iii)

22. Which quality makes hardwood the choice for puzzle joints?
(a) high moisture content
(b) colour and shine
(c) sturdiness or density
(d) shrinkage and swelling

V. Read the excerpt of a published interview by Lawrence Rubin where he speaks to Jessica Stone on Play Therapy in the Digital Age. Answer the following questions by choosing the most appropriate answer.

LAWRENCE RUBIN: *Hi, Jessica. Thanks for **joining** me today. How did you become interested in **digital play** therapy, which really is cutting-edge and somewhat **controversial** with children?*

JESSICA STONE: I am a licensed psychologist with a specialty in play therapy. Within it, digital play therapy has become one of those areas of interest over the last 20 years, stemming from experiences with my own kids, who had this whole portion of their world that I didn't really understand, know about, or enter into. It struck me as a little bit ironic and maybe even hypocritical that here I spend my time at work and my energy in learning and doing play therapy with children and entering their world, while my own kids have this whole portion of theirs that I was putting no effort into understanding. And so, I kind of had to smack myself upside the head and say, all right, I need to learn more about this. Why is this important to them? Why are they interested in it?

Long story short, I ended up entering an online game that my oldest two (of four children) were both playing at the time. I am no digital native by any means, and I was not very good at these games, but the point was that I was taking interest. I was listening to them. I was asking them questions. We were having conversations about what happened in the game, what quest they were working on; things that were important to them that prior to my entering their world, I couldn't participate in or even understand. I began to see that because this co-play was so impactful with my own children, I needed to incorporate it into my work, which really opened the door to what I have been doing for all these years.

LAWRENCE RUBIN: *So, you recognized that <u>technology</u> was so important and present in your kids' life that you would be almost doing a disservice to your young clients if you didn't cross that bridge into their digital world. Tell me, what exactly is digital play therapy?*

JESSICA STONE: Digital play therapy is a modality that is based in speaking the client's language through what I call the four C's, which are competency, culture, comfort, and capability. These are basic elements of therapy in general, but digital play therapy in particular is couched within the broader context of prescriptive play therapy, which taps into what Charles Schaefer calls the therapeutic powers of play. So, the point is that there is a foundation for it. It's not just, oh, let's just jump on this bandwagon and start throwing these digital things into what we're doing. We as clinicians need to have a very firm and solid foundation in what it is we're doing and why we're doing it regardless of our theoretical foundation, therapeutic modality, and interventions, or whether the platform is virtual or face-to-face. And as in all therapies, we must ground our interventions in solid case conceptualization and treatment planning.

23. What is the primary purpose of this passage?
(a) To highlight the necessity of "digital play therapy" in terms of its foundational benefits and theoretical advantages.
(b) To showcase the debate regarding the pros and cons of "digital play therapy" with opinions of an expert.
(c) To alert the readers to the inevitability of a shift from conventional therapeutic methods to modern ones like "digital play therapy".
(d) To explore the mindset of an expert with regards to the fallibilities of the new "digital play therapy".

24. What is the tone conveyed by the speaker when she states— "... I kind of had to smack myself upside the head..."?
(a) reflective
(b) discouraged
(c) confident
(d) hypocritical

25. In the line, "*... you would be almost doing a disservice to your young clients ...*", the word 'disservice' refers to being
(a) prejudiced
(b) unfair and unhelpful
(c) misled
(d) stubborn and inflexible

26. How was Jessica Stone impacted by an online game?
(a) She could finally understand her children's behaviour.
(b) She began to productively communicate with her children.
(c) She noticed a degression in her professional life.
(d) She grew to love online games herself.

27. What does the interviewee mean when she says "I am no digital native"?
(a) She wasn't born into a family with digital skills.
(b) She was averse to all technology, especially online games.
(c) She was an amateur in using technology or playing digital games.
(d) She lacked the technical training required to operate digital technology.

28. Which skill does the interviewee display with the usage of the phrase, "Long story short"?
(a) rephrasing (b) circumvention
(c) discussion (d) brevity

29. Which of these options best describes the expression "jump on this bandwagon"?
(a) To get to the conclusion too hastily
(b) To adopt an opinion because it is fashionable
(c) To re-think previously made decisions
(d) To jump into action before thinking it through

30. Which of the following is the least likely inference to be drawn from the given passage?
(a) "digital play therapy" shares the basic elements with any general type of therapy.
(b) "digital play therapy" became an point of interest for Jessica Stone because of her experiences at home.
(c) "digital play therapy" still lacks a proper foundation to make it worthwhile for use.
(d) "digital play therapy" allowed Jessica Stone to find a new way of conversing with children.

31. What does the phrase 'speaking the client's language' refer to, in the text?
(Digital play therapy is a modality that is based in <u>speaking the client's language</u>...)
(a) Highlighting the pros
(b) Providing lucrative offers
(c) Making the services popular
(d) Addressing their needs

32. What is Jessica Stone's opinion on "digital play therapy" as per the text?
(a) It has to be accepted as the new form of therapy as the world is growing increasingly digitalised.
(b) It has replaced "prescriptive play therapy" because it has more therapeutic powers.
(c) It has to be regarded as an important part of "play therapy" because allows for communication through its mode of co-play.
(d) It can be practiced by everyone who wishes to engage in co-play with their children.

Direction for Questions from VI to IX Passages: Read the given passage and answer the questions by choosing the most appropriate answer.

VI. Down in rain-swept Wiltshire last week, I was able to enjoy a Christmas tree, Christmas crackers, mistletoe, etc. I was able to sing carols and wish everyone I met a happy Christmas. In America, it seems, I'd have been outlawed if I'd attempted any such thing. According to Andrew Stephen in the New Statesman, Americans have become so desperate not to offend religious minorities that Christmas in America is now most definitely not politically correct and, in some cases, literally illegal.

In Kentucky, for example, school bus drivers were warned on no account to say "Merry Christmas" to children getting on or off their buses. In Philadelphia, you are breaking the law, says Stephen, "if you have a Christmas tree in your home – you may be subject to a $300 fine". A nursery school teacher in Washington, he goes on, has temporarily removed the "t" from the letters of the alphabet that she has strung around the classroom: "It looked a bit too much like a cross for comfort". Oh, and schools in Scarsdale, New York "have banned the American tradition of "candy canes", striped mint sweets in the shape of walking sticks; they could be construed as shepherds' crooks, you see, and we all know what that means at the time of the year".

My Christmas in Wiltshire may have been wet but at least it felt like a real Christmas and not like this kind of anodyne travesty, disinfected of all reference to what the holiday is about.

33. Which of the statements do you think does not support the author's idea in the passage?
(a) A nursery school teacher's extreme attempt not to offend authorities during holiday time.
(b) The visible signs of festivities were not inconspicuous in America.
(c) Prohibition of candy canes since they were obvious holiday shapes.
(d) The conventional etiquette of the season was discouraged in public.

34. The last sentence in the passage conveys that the writer:
(a) tacitly approves of the way Christmas is approached in America.
(b) disagrees with the views and opinions of Andrew Stephen.
(c) is content to have had his share of the season's revelry in Wiltshire.
(d) sympathizes with the religious minorities.

35. Which of the following words from the passage, most closely resemble the meaning "anodyne" and "construed"?
(a) pernicious, blatant
(b) jilted, misinterpreted
(c) unobjectionable, interpreted
(d) menacing, unequivocal

36. What parts of speech do the words 'religious', 'travesty' and 'temporarily' belong to?
(a) adjective, noun, adverb
(b) noun, adjective, adjective
(c) adverb, verb, adverb
(d) noun, noun, adjective

37. Which of the following is the most appropriate title for the passage?
(a) Abolishing Christmas
(b) Christmas past and present
(c) The everchanging tradition of Christmas
(d) Transcending beliefs

VII. Economic historians have argued that the Industrial Revolution in Britain could not have occurred without the capital that became available from the plunder of India. The sudden acceleration of the revolution in Britain, R. P. Dutt points out, coincides with the establishment of British rule in India. He writes, "In 1757 came the Battle of Plassey and the wealth of India began to flood the country in an ever-growing stream... in 1764 came the spinning jenny of Hargreaves; in 1765 came Watt's steam engine, patented in 1769; in 1769 came the water frame of Arkwright followed by his patents in 1775 for carding, drawing and spinning machines; in 1779 the mule of Crompton and 1785 the power loom of Cartwright; and in 1788 the steam engine was applied to blast furnaces." These inventions, Dutt argues, did not result from some "special and unaccountable burst of inventive genius," but from the accumulation of enough capital to make possible the largescale outlay needed to turn the inventions into functional fortunes.

Contemporary accounts attest to the devastation that followed in India. "This fine country," one of the East India's own residents reported, "which flourished under the most despotic and arbitrary government is verging towards ruin." Francis Buchanan, who surveyed the country in the early 1800s, wrote: "The natives allege that, although they were often squeezed by the Mogul officers, and on all occasions were treated with utmost contempt, they preferred suffering these evils to the mode that has been adopted of selling their lands when they fall in arrears, which is a practice they cannot endure. Besides, bribery went a great way on most occasions, and they allege that, bribes included, they did not actually pay one half of what they do now."

Both agricultural self-sufficiency and what by many accounts was a growing industrial economy were broken down. For the peasant, insecurity, impoverishment, and indebtedness followed. The shadow of famine stalked the next century. The new system of land taxes introduced with the Permanent Settlement of 1793 turned the zamindars, who were originally tax collectors, into landowners with new rights to evict the peasants who cultivated the lands for not paying the revenues.

38. According to the passage, which of the options accelerated the burst of inventive genius in Britain?
(a) The plethora of inventions in the spinning industry
(b) The prevalent custom of bribery in the bureaucracy
(c) The funds from its colony that fell into the coffers of the British Raj
(d) Inventions that turned the country into functional fortunes.

39. Which could be the prime attributing factor responsible for the disintegration of the Indian economy?
(a) The growing indebtedness among the farmer fraternity
(b) Widespread penury among the masses
(c) The plight of those who were still reeling under the Mogul atrocities
(d) All of the above

40. The first paragraph is a fine example of
(a) oral histories
(b) review writing
(c) chronological data
(d) journal jottings

41. After the Permanent Settlement of 1793, the turn of events led to
(a) Tax collectors monopolising the levy on peasants' lands
(b) Zamindars proclaiming themselves to be legal land owners
(c) Mogul officers donning the garb of tax collectors and harassing farmers
(d) Peasants were forced to become victims of the widespread famine in the country

42. The passage could probably be an excerpt from
(a) an economic report
(b) the national movement
(c) a memoir
(d) a scientific abstract

VIII. The news made me very happy indeed. I would be married. There would be music, I would hear the women ululating. How exciting that would be! Yet I felt scared at the same time. I cannot express the apprehensions that came to my mind. Meanwhile, the various things necessary for the ceremony began to arrive. Relatives and guests began pouring in. I was scared to death by all this. I did not talk to anyone but spent most of the time weeping. Everybody did their best to reassure me. They embraced me, but the unspoken agony in my mind did not lift.

Later on, I was cheered up by the ornaments, the red wedding sari and the wedding music. I forgot my earlier worries and went about laughing and watching the elaborate preparations. My happiness knew no bounds. When everything was over the next day, I heard people asking my mother, "Are they leaving today?" I thought they were referring to the guests. Then the music started. There was an air of festivity. The guests must be leaving now, I thought. It made me happy and I went about following my mother. Presently everybody assembled in the house. Some looked happy, but others were in tears. They made me really frightened. Then my brothers, aunts, uncles, and my mother all took me in their arms by turn as they burst into tears. Their tears made me so sad that I began to cry too. I knew my mother was going to hand me to the other family. I tightened my hold on her and pleaded, "Don't give me over to them, Mother!" that made everybody present even more upset. They broke down and tried to say nice words to console me. My mother took me in her arms and said, "You are a good girl, you understand everything, don't you?" God is with us; you needn't be afraid. You are going to come back to us in a few days' time. Every girl has to go to her in-laws' house. Nobody else cries like this. There is no reason to be upset. Please calm down and talk to me." But I was trembling with fear. I was quite unable to speak. Somehow, I managed to say through my tears: "are you sure that God will go with me?" Mother promptly reassured me that he most certainly would. "He will be with you all the time, so stop crying now." But in spite of her soothing words my apprehensions kept growing and I could not check my tears.

43. In the passage, the people ask the narrator's mother, "Are they leaving today?"

Who are 'they' according to the narrator and the passage?

(a) the narrator's relatives ... the groom's people
(b) the groom's party ... the bride, the groom, and his folks
(c) the wedding guests ... the groom's family
(d) the narrator and her people ... wedding guests

44. The women 'ululating' in the passage refers to them

(a) shedding tears of joy
(b) wailing high and low
(c) loud sounds expressing mirth
(d) vocalising blessings for the couple

45. The tone and mood of the passage is

(a) Depressing and emotional
(b) Satirical and depressed
(c) Introspective and empathetic
(d) Vitriolic and reassuring

46. Give the appropriate antonyms for : elaborate, agony and apprehension.

(a) basic, assuagement, solicitude
(b) embellished, anguish, dismay
(c) plain, solace, repose
(d) baroque, distress, inapprehension

47. Identify the type of sentence: "You are a good girl, you understand everything, don't you?"

(a) Tag question
(b) Interrogative statement
(c) Imperative negative statement
(d) Echo question

IX. What colors can animals see? Is the world more brightly colored or duller to animals than it is to us? To find out the answers to these questions scientists have used a method of training the animals to come to different colors, which is similar in principle to the method used in studying the sense of hearing in animals.

Let us take bees first of all, partly because more exact scientific research has been done on the color-sense of bees than of almost any other animal. It is especially interesting to know what colors bees see because these insects visit flowers to get sweet nectar from them to make honey, and in doing so the bees incidentally carry pollen from flower to flower. On the face of it, it would seem very likely that bees are attracted to flowers by their bright colors. But possibly it is the scents that attract the bees, or perhaps it is both color and scent. So, among other things, we want to know whether bees can really see the colors of flowers, and if so, what colors they can see. Exactly how is this found out?

A table is put in a garden, and on the table a piece of blue cardboard is placed, on which there is a watch-glass containing a drop of syrup. After a short while bees come to the syrup and suck some of it. The bees then fly to their hive and give the syrup to other bees in the hive to make honey. Then they return to the feeding place which they have discovered. We let the bees go on doing this for a while, after which we take away the blue cardboard with the syrup on it. Instead of this card we now put on the table a blue card on the left side of the first feeding-place, and a red card to the right of the first feeding-place. These new cards have no syrup on them but only an empty watch-glass lying on each. Thus, the blue card is on the left, the red card on the right, and there is nothing where the first blue feeding-card used to be. After we have arranged these new cards, we have not long to wait. Very soon bees arrive again, and it can be seen that they fly straight on to the blue card; none go to the red card.

48. What two things can be indicated from the behaviour of the bees?
(a) Bees remember that blue means syrup and they fly to the blue.
(b) Bees can distinguish blue from red.
(c) Bees have a keen sense of scent and sight.
(d) Both (a) and (b)

49. Which of the following statements is valid enough to make this experiment on bees' incomplete?
(a) Perhaps the bees had really been trained to identify colors.
(b) What if the bees, like human beings, suffer from colour-blindness?
(c) Both (a) and (b)
(d) None of the above

50. According to the passage, which of the following is not true in the case of the subjects mentioned in the study?
(a) More exact scientific research has been done on the color-sense of bees than of almost any other animal.
(b) Bees are attracted to flowers by their bright colors.
(c) Possibly it may be either color or scent that attract the bees.
(d) None go to the red card.

Section–B: Current Affairs And General Knowledge

51. Why did the United States Food and Drug Administration (FDA) restrict Johnson & Johnson's COVID-19 Vaccine?
(a) Due to its inefficacy towards new variants
(b) Due to its extremely high price
(c) Due to a risk of rare but serious blood clots
(d) None of the above

52. The board of the Pulitzer Prizes has recently honored Ukrainian journalists for their "courage, endurance and commitment to truthful reporting" on the war between Russia and Ukraine. Which of the following is not true?
(a) The Pulitzer Prize is awarded in music
(b) The Pulitzer Prize is not awarded in fiction
(c) The Pulitzer will designated Washington as its seat of administration of prizes
(d) All of the above

53. Who was the first woman judge of the Supreme Court of the United States?
(a) Sandra D. Connor (b) Ketanji Jackson
(c) Ruth Ginsberg (d) Amy Barrett

54. What is the system of 'six raised dots' relevant for?
(a) Cryptocurrency
(b) Block-chain
(c) Braille
(d) Baking

55. Why was UK-Iranian dual citizen Nazanin Zaghari-Radcliffe detained and jailed in Iran from 2016 to 2022?
(a) On charges of driving in western clothing
(b) On charges of obscenity in public
(c) On charges of inciting Iranian women to violence
(d) On charges of espionage

56. Desmond Tutu is credited with establishing and heading the Truth and Reconciliation processes in South Africa. Which of the following statements about him is not true?
(a) His activism was deeply rooted in Christian ethos of forgiveness.
(b) He advocated for victims to forgive the perpetrators of apartheid.
(c) He saw religious prayer and social action as being intrinsically linked.
(d) He justified discrimination against homosexuals and sought to differentiate that from apartheid.

57. May 10th marks the anniversary of the 1857 revolt against the British. Who among the following did not play a role in the revolt?
(a) Maulavi Liyaqat Ali
(b) Veer Kunwar Singh
(c) Nana Saheb
(d) Chiranjit Lal

58. The 'Buddha and His Dhamma', originally titled 'Buddha and his Gospel' is a manuscript written by
(a) M. R. Masani
(b) Daisaku Ikeda
(c) B. R. Ambedkar
(d) Pema Chodron

59. Nicknamed 'Daughter of Palestine', Shireen Abu Alekh was among the Arab world's first female field reporters and was allegedly shot dead by Israeli forces while reporting for Al Jazeera from the occupied West Bank. Which of these countries partly owns Al Jazeera?
(a) Sultanate of Oman
(b) United Arab Emirates
(c) Kingdom of Saudi Arabia
(d) State of Qatar

60. India recently won the Thomas Cup in Badminton for the very first time. Which of these nations have won the Thomas Cup for the maximum number of times?
(a) China
(b) Malaysia
(c) Denmark
(d) Indonesia

61. Dressed in red and blue, 'Spidey' ('Spider-man') is a fixture at protests against the military regime. In which country has 'Spidey' become a popular symbol of resistance?
(a) Bangladesh
(b) Sri Lanka
(c) Sudan
(d) Chile

62. After 396 years, Barbados replaced the Queen of England as head of State. Which of the following is true?
(a) Barbados became a republic but will remain part of the Commonwealth
(b) Barbados became a republic and will no longer be part of the Commonwealth
(c) Barbados became independent in 2021
(d) None of the above

63. Which of the following is not a member of the QUAD that met in the United States in 2021 just after the withdrawal of troops from Afghanistan?
(a) Japan (b) Australia
(c) India (d) Canada

64. What is the name of the world's first cryptocurrency cruise ship?
(a) Makoshi
(b) Satoshi
(c) Bloomer
(d) Rikishi

65. Why did Canada recently decide to ban Huawei and ZTE from 5G network?
(a) Pressure from the Five Eyes network
(b) Pressure from the Government of India
(c) Pressure from Canadian University students
(d) Pressure from the Government of the United States

66. Timor-Leste recently celebrated 20 years of independence. On 20 May 2002, the United Nations formally handed power to the new Timorese government. Who did they gain independence from?
(a) Indonesian occupation
(b) British occupation
(c) Portuguese colonisation
(d) Dutch colonisation

67. Savita Halappanavar was a dentist from Karnataka. In 2012, her death in Ireland resulted in a huge furore. What did Amnesty International term her death to be a consequence of?
(a) Stringent immigration detention conditions in Ireland
(b) Stringent anti-abortion laws of Ireland
(c) Prison violence in Ireland
(d) Discriminatory hospital care for foreign nationals in Ireland

68. Nilgiri Biosphere Reserve is found at the intersection of which of the following States/ Union Territories?
(a) Tamil Nadu, Puducherry, Andhra Pradesh, Telangana
(b) Tamil Nadu, Andhra Pradesh, Karnataka
(c) Kerala, Karnataka, Telangana
(d) Tamil Nadu, Kerala, Karnataka

69. Which of the following is not a Satyajit Ray film?
(a) Devi
(b) The Music Room
(c) Charulata
(d) Pyasa

70. In 2018, Chintamani Shivdikar wrote "*Papletwali*" which became viral on YouTube. The song is adopted from a Koli folk tune. Who are the Koli people?
(a) They are said to be the first inhabitants of Bombay.
(b) They are said to be the upper castes of particular regions of Bombay.
(c) They are said to belong to the fishing communities of Sri Lanka.
(d) They are said to belong to the carpenter community of Dharwad.

71. The Supreme Court of India declared the Act providing 10.5% internal reservations to the Vanniyar community in Tamil Nadu to be 'unconstitutional' because
(a) The State Government lacked competence to enact this statute.
(b) Only the President can determine those who are most backward.
(c) Reservations are against the basic structure of the Constitution of India.
(d) The Vanniyars do not constitute a class apart from other OBC categories and hence this goes against Articles 14, 15 and 16 of the Constitution of India.

72. Which country won the Uber Cup Badminton International Championship held in 2022?
(a) India
(b) Denmark
(c) Indonesia
(d) South Korea

73. Who was the first Indian to win an Olympic gold in athletics?
(a) Abhinav Bindra
(b) Neeraj Chopra
(c) Sindhu
(d) P. T. Usha

74. Which country got its name changed in the United Nations in June 2022?
(a) Turkey (b) Cuba
(c) Morocco (d) Benin

75. According to Germanwatch's Climate Change Performance Index (CCPI), 2022, what is the rank of India?
(a) 7th (b) 8th
(c) 9th (b) 10th

76. The National Commission for Backward Classes was accorded the constitutional status by
(a) The Constitution (One Hundred and First Amendment) Act, 2016
(b) The Constitution (One Hundred and Second Amendment) Act, 2018
(c) The Constitution (One Hundred and Third Amendment) Act, 2019
(d) The Constitution (One Hundred and Fourth Amendment) Act, 2019

77. The Durand Line is the line demarcating the boundaries between
(a) India and Afghanistan
(b) India and China
(c) India and Pakistan
(d) None

78. The 2021 AI Readiness Index, published by Oxford Insights, ranks 160 countries as to how prepared their governments are in the use of AI in public services. India is ranked at
(a) 36th (b) 48th
(c) 51st (b) 67th

79. The first Artificial Intelligence ship to study marine pollution, avoid collisions and detect marine animals is named as
(a) Poseidon 400 (b) Mayflower 400
(c) AIS 400 (d) Titanic 400

80. In which of the following States, the first Emergency Landing Facility on a National Highway was inaugurated?
(a) Karnataka (b) Gujarat
(c) Goa (d) Rajasthan

Section–C : Logical Reasoning

81. All whales are mammals. All creatures breathe. Some whales are creatures.

Mickey Mouse is a whale.

Examine the following statements:

I. Mickey Mouse breathes.
II. Mickey Mouse does not breathe.
III. Mickey Mouse is a creature.
IV. Mickey Mouse is not a creature.
V. Mickey Mouse is a mammal.
VI. Mickey Mouse is not a mammal.

Choose the most appropriate answer.
(a) Only II, IV and V follow
(b) Only V follows
(c) I, III and V follow
(d) Only VI follows

82. All whales are mammals. All creatures breathe. Some whales are creatures.

Eiffel Tower is a mammal.

Examine the following statements:

I. Eiffel Tower breathes.
II. Eiffel Tower does not breathe.
III. Eiffel Tower is a creature.
IV. Eiffel Tower is not a creature.
V. Eiffel Tower is a whale.
VI. Eiffel Tower is not a whale.

Choose the most appropriate answer.
(a) Only I and III follow
(b) Only II, IV and VI follow
(c) Only V follows
(d) None of the above

83. All whales are mammals. All creatures breathe. Some whales are creatures.

Internet is a creature.

Examine the following statements:

I. Internet breathes.
II. Internet does not breathe.
III. Internet is a whale.
IV. Internet is not a whale.
V. Internet is a mammal.
VI. Internet is not a mammal.

Choose the most appropriate answer.
(a) Only I follows
(b) Only I, II and V follow
(c) Only I, IV and VI follow
(d) Only III follows

84. All whales are mammals. All creatures breathe. Some whales are creatures. Further, anything that breathes is a mammal.

Mickey Mouse is a whale. Eiffel Tower is a mammal. Internet is a creature.

Examine the following statements:

I. Only one out of Mickey Mouse and Internet breathes.
II. At least one out of Mickey Mouse, Internet and Eiffel Tower does not breathe.
III. It is possible that all of Mickey Mouse, Internet and Eiffel Tower breathe.
IV. All of Mickey Mouse, Internet and Eiffel Tower are mammals.
V. If it is true that Mickey Mouse breathes, then it is also true that Mickey Mouse is a creature.

Choose the most appropriate answer.

(a) Only IV follows
(b) Only III and IV follow
(c) Only I, II, and IV follow
(d) Only V follows

85. Capitalism is a philosophy. All ideas are fictional objects. Only fictional objects are philosophy.

Examine the following statements:

I. Capitalism is an idea.
II. Capitalism is a fictional object.
III. Capitalism is not an idea.

Choose the most appropriate answer.

(a) Only I and II follow
(b) Only II and III follow
(c) Only II follows
(d) None follows

86. All khaps are fair institutions. No fair institutions are democratic. Only courts are democratic.

Examine the following statements:

I. Some courts are fair institutions.
II. No courts are fair institutions.
III. It is possible that all courts are fair institutions.

Choose the most appropriate answer.

(a) Only I follows
(b) Only II follows
(c) Only III follows
(d) None follows

87. All thieves are persons. Some persons are dishonest. All dishonest persons go to jail.

'X' is a person.

Examine the following statements:

I. X is a thief.
II. X may be dishonest.
III. X is necessarily dishonest.
IV. If X is a thief, he will go to jail.

Choose the most appropriate answer.

(a) I and IV follow
(b) Only IV follows
(c) Only II follows
(d) Only III follows

88. All black money funds terrorist activities. All terrorist activities are financed solely by corrupt politicians. If the Lokpal Bill is passed, all assets and financial sources of all corrupt politicians will be frozen. If demonetisation is declared, all black money will disappear.

If the above statements are true, which of the following follow(s)?

I. If demonetisation is declared, funding of terrorist activities will completely stop.
II. If the Lokpal Bill is passed, funding of terrorist activities will completely stop.
III. If demonetisation is declared and the Lokpal Bill is passed, funding of terrorist activities will completely stop.

Choose the most appropriate answer.

(a) Only I follows
(b) Only II follows
(c) Only III follows
(d) Both II and III follow

89. All laptops are computers. Some computers are useful. Everything that is useful is precious.

X is a computer.

Which of the following statements necessarily follows?

(a) All precious objects are useful.
(b) If 'X' is useful, it must be a laptop.
(c) X must be precious.
(d) If 'X' is a useful laptop, it must be precious.

90. All democratic governments are elected. Some elected governments are fair. No dictatorships are elected.

'X' is a dictatorship.

Which of the following statements necessarily follows?

(a) X may be a democratic government.
(b) X cannot be fair.
(c) X cannot be a democratic government.
(d) None of the above

91. Some apples are fruits. All fruits are ducks. Some ducks are books.

Which of the following statements necessary follows?

(a) Some books are apples
(b) At least some books are ducks
(c) No ducks are apples
(d) All ducks are fruits

92. Some White are Blue. Some Blue are Green. Some Green are Red. Some Red are Yellow. Some Red are Blue. Some Red are White. Some Yellow are White. Some Yellow are Blue. All Green are White. All Blue are Red.

If the above statements are true, which of the following follow(s)?

I. No Yellow is Green.
II. Of the Red which are White, some are also Yellow.
III. Of the Red that are Green, some are also Blue.
IV. Some White are Green.

Choose the most appropriate answer.

(a) Only II and III follow
(b) Only III and IV follow
(c) Only I and IV follow
(d) All follow

93. Only Tigers are Fish. Only Rabbits are Fish. Only Rabbits are Tigers. Some Deer are Tigers.

If the above statements are true, which of the following follow(s)?

I. If A is a Rabbit, A is also a Deer.
II. If B is a Deer, B is also a Rabbit.
III. Some Deer are Fish.
IV. Some Deer are Rabbits.

Choose the most appropriate answer.

(a) Only IV
(b) Only II
(c) Only I and II
(d) None follows

94. Most persons are individuals. Some companies are State. Most State are individuals.

If the above statements are true, which of the following follow(s)?

I. Some persons are State.
II. Some State are companies.
III. Some companies are persons.
IV. Some companies are individuals.

Choose the most appropriate answer.

(a) Only II and III
(b) Only I and II
(c) Only II
(d) None follows

95. Statement: "We are short on time so we better send these documents via speed post."

Assumption made:

(a) Sending documents via speed post will take less time than some other means of sending documents.
(b) Documents must always be sent via speed post.
(c) Sending documents via speed post will take less time than all other means of communication.
(d) None of the above

96. "The best telecom services in the world are to be found in South Korea and Japan, and neither country allocates spectrum on the basis of auctions. Spectrum is assigned on the basis of discretion, the focus being on ensuring the availability of cutting-edge telecom services and the revenue the super-enabled industry would generate, rather than on generating revenue from spectrum auctions. Neither the Japanese nor the Koreans are squeamish about eating almost anything that creeps, crawls, swims, flies or runs. But when it comes to geese that lay golden eggs, they apparently lay off."

Which of the following assumptions is made in the above passage?

(a) Geese are not consumed as food in Japanese and South Korean cultures
(b) Auctioning telecom spectrum would generate a great deal of revenue for the Japanese and South Korean Governments
(c) Governments that wish to provide good telecom service should not auction telecom spectrum
(d) Governments that wish to provide good telecom service should auction telecom spectrum

97. Even before the coronavirus, lack of sleep was a simmering public-health crisis associated with a suite of maladies. Roughly 10 to 15 percent of people worldwide were suffering from chronic insomnia, the struggle to fall or stay asleep at least three nights a week for three months or longer. Crises such as natural disasters or terrorist attacks are known to trigger short-term sleeplessness. But experts say the pandemic's unprecedented global impact and protracted nature threaten to expand the rate of chronic insomnia, which is much harder to treat.

Which one of the following is an assumption required by the argument?

(a) Increasing levels of obesity in the world population have exacerbated chronic insomnia.
(b) There has been an uptick in natural disasters and terrorist attacks in recent times.
(c) Heightened levels of stress contribute to short-term as well as long-term sleeplessness.
(d) The treatment of chronic insomnia is costly for public health systems across the world.

98. Scientists say they have completed the first full and seamless catalogue of genetic instructions of humans. Until now, about 8% of the human genome code was missing from the blueprint. The quest to decipher and complete a gapless DNA sequence has taken decades. The resource helps explain how to create every human cell in the body, which could shed light on how to treat, prevent and cure disease. Now, just 10 million bases or letters of human DNA out of roughly 3 billion, are unknown.

The conclusion drawn above follows logically if which one of the following is assumed?

(a) Until the discovery it had been impossible to explain how any human cell in the body is created.
(b) It has been possible to complete the full seamless catalogue of human genetic instructions using 2.99 billion letters of human DNA.
(c) Scientists will be able to explain how to treat and prevent cellular diseases only once the remaining 10 million letters of human DNA are known.
(d) The 8% of missing human genome code has taken the longest time to be deciphered.

99. Read the Statement given below and decide which of the Assumptions listed thereafter are implicit in the Statement.

Statement: India should generate solar energy to meet its unmet energy requirements.

Assumptions:

I. Solar energy is cheaper than other forms of energy.
II. India is capable of generating solar energy.
III. India is unable to meet its energy requirements using non-solar sources of energy.

Choose the most appropriate answer.

(a) Only I is implicit.
(b) Only II is implicit.
(c) Only III is implicit.
(d) Both II and III are implicit.

100. Read the Statement given below and decide which of the Assumptions listed thereafter are implicit in the Statement.

Statement: To catch the rats running around in the house, you should use a rat trap.

Assumptions:

I. Rats are likely to step into rat traps.
II. Food will be kept inside the rat trap.
III. Rat traps are small in size.

Choose the most appropriate answer.

(a) Both I and II are implicit
(b) All are implicit
(c) Only I is implicit
(d) Only II is implicit

101. Carmakers are taking the middle path in their electrification journey in India, with powerful hybrids flagging off the 'green race' for three leading Japanese car manufacturers. Japanese carmakers believe introducing hybrids will eventually lead to higher localization of parts for electric vehicles, making them more accessible to a larger customer base. These manufacturers have no plans of launching an electric car in India before 2025 and are currently working on localisation of hybrid vehicle parts.

The passage assumes which one of the following?

(a) Carmakers in Japan have been successful in scaling up production of electric vehicles in the past.
(b) Indian customers are unable to afford electric vehicles.
(c) Manufacturing processes for electric and hybrid vehicles are similar to the extent that production of the latter shall ease future production of the former.
(d) There will be no electric car production in India until 2025.

102. Read the Statement given below and decide which of the Assumptions listed thereafter are implicit in the Statement.

Statement: Employers must offer flexible working schedules or risk resignations by talented employees.

Assumptions:

I. Employers should offer flexible working schedules.
II. Some employees want flexible working schedules.
III. Some employees value flexible working schedules so much that they would resign if these are not offered.

Choose the most appropriate answer.

(a) Both II and III are implicit
(b) All are implicit
(c) Only I is implicit
(d) Only II is implicit

103. Even though switching to veganism may be costly and sometimes inconvenient, it is a good change if one wishes to improve their chances of leading a healthy life, while benefitting the environment.

Which of the following is an assumption necessarily taken for granted in the above statement?

(a) The costs involved and inconvenience of making a change act as deterrents for most people.
(b) It is possible to undertake practices that may impact how healthy a life one lives.
(c) Non-vegetarianism impacts the environment most adversely.
(d) Costly and inconvenient choices must always be made to effect positive change.

104. 'X' and 'Y', enter into a contract (i.e. X and Y are parties to the contract) for supply of goods by X to Y in exchange for payment from Y to X. Consider the following Clause in the contract:

(Sub-Clause 1) Neither party shall be held liable for failure to comply with its obligations under this contract if such failure is due to any kind of natural disaster or human event beyond its control.

(Sub-Clause 2) The successful invocation of this Clause by either party shall protect that party from liability for non-fulfilment of its obligations under the contract only until the natural disaster or human event in Sub-Clause 1 continues to affect that party."

The contract requires X to deliver goods from his house to Y's house latest by 30th May. Both X and Y live in the same city. On the morning of 30th May, there is a big earthquake near X's house which causes all roads in the area to be blocked. The blockage remains present until 31st May.

Can X claim that this situation falls under Sub-Clause 1?

(a) Yes, because the earthquake is a natural disaster beyond X's control.
(b) Yes, because X's failure to deliver the goods to Y by 30th May was due to the earthquake.
(c) No, because X could have delivered the goods to Y before 30th May and his failure to deliver the goods to Y is due to his laziness and not only due to the earthquake.
(d) Combination of options 'a' and 'b'.

105. Consider the following principle:

In a dispute between X and Y, Y can sue X:

(i) In the city of X's residence, OR
(ii) In the city where the dispute arose

X and Y enter into a contract which requires X to deliver goods from his house to Y's house latest by 30th May. X lives in Delhi and Y lives in Calcutta. X fails to deliver the goods by 30th May due to an earthquake in Delhi. Y wants to sue X for breach of the contract.

Y can sue X:

(a) In Delhi only
(b) In Calcutta only, assuming that the dispute arose in Calcutta
(c) In either one of Delhi and Calcutta, assuming that the dispute arose in Calcutta
(d) None of the above

106. Consider the following principle:

In a dispute between X and Y, Y can sue X:

(i) In the city of Y's residence, OR
(ii) In the city of X's residence, OR
(iii) In the city where the dispute arose

Y lives in Calcutta and is the owner of the restaurant 'Y's Yummilicious Restaurant', located in Calcutta. X lives in Delhi and starts a restaurant named 'Yummilicious Restaurant' in Delhi. Y wants to sue X for infringement of the name 'Yummilicious Restaurant'.

Y can sue X:

(a) In Delhi only
(b) In Calcutta, but only if the dispute arose in Calcutta
(c) In either one of Delhi and Calcutta, regardless of where the dispute arose
(d) None of the above

107. All contracts are agreements. Only agreements enforceable by law are contracts.

Y is a government official tasked with issuing driving licenses to applicants who meet the criteria. X has applied for a driving license but does not meet the criteria. X and Y enter into an oral agreement that X will pay Y ₹5000 to issue a driving license to X. With reference to the facts given above, X says "I have entered into a contract with Y."

(a) X is wrong because the agreement is not in writing.
(b) X is wrong because an agreement not enforceable by law is not a contract.
(c) X is right.
(d) There is insufficient information to reach the conclusions in Options a, b and c

108. Anyone who pleads on behalf of another in a Court is a pleader. All lawyers are pleaders.

X, a lawyer, pleads his own case in Court.

(a) X is a pleader in this case.
(b) X is not a pleader in this case as he is not pleading on behalf of another.
(c) As long as he is a lawyer, X is a pleader in all cases.
(d) None of the above

109. All offences are punishable. Not everything that is punishable is an offence. Only that which is punishable is an offence.

X, a school student, does not submit her homework on time and is punished by being given extra homework.

(a) X has certainly committed an offence
(b) X has certainly not committed an offence
(c) We do not have sufficient information to determine whether X has committed an offence
(d) None of the above

110. Only registered trademarks can be infringed. Copying a registered trademark is sufficient to constitute infringement.

X owns the trademark 'Yummilicious Restaurant'. Y copies this trademark. X sues

Y for infringement.

(a) If X's trademark was registered, Y has necessarily infringed X's trademark
(b) Y has necessarily infringed X's trademark only if X's trademark was registered and Y was aware of X's trademark
(c) Y has definitely not infringed X's trademark
(d) None of the above

111. Limitation Principle: A suit for recovery of money can be filed only within 3 years from the date the money becomes due to be recovered. Suits filed after this period are not maintainable. Suits filed within this period are necessarily maintainable.

Money became due from Y to X on March 17, 2017. X filed a suit for recovery of money on March 1, 2022.

(a) X's suit is not maintainable
(b) X's suit is maintainable
(c) There is insufficient information to determine if X's suit is maintainable
(d) None of the above

112. Issue: Is Lebron James the best professional basketball player of all time?

Argument 1: Yes. Lebron James has had the largest fan base among all professional basketball players in the history of the sport.

Argument 2: No. Lebron James has changed his team too many times.

Argument 3: Yes. No other player has scored more points in their professional career than Lebron James has.

Choose the most appropriate answer.

(a) Only Argument 1 is strong
(b) Only Argument 2 is strong
(c) Only Argument 3 is strong
(d) Both Arguments 1 and 3 are strong

113. Person 1: Children should not read novels that contain instances of racism.

Person 2 in response to Person 1: Parents and teachers of children can use such novels to educate children against racism.

Which of the following is correct?

(a) Person 1 and Person 2 agree that some novels contain instances of racism.
(b) Person 2 supports racism.
(c) Both 'a' and 'b'
(d) Neither 'a' nor 'b'

114. Cocoa is rich in plant chemicals called flavanols that may help to protect the heart. Dark chocolate contains up to 2-3 times more flavanol-rich cocoa solids than milk chocolate. Flavanols have been shown to support the production of Nitric Oxide (NO) in the endolethium (the inner cell lining of blood vessels) that helps to relax the blood vessels and improve blood flow, thereby lowering blood pressure. Flavanols in chocolate can increase insulin sensitivity in short term studies; in the long run this could reduce risk of diabetes.

Which of the following, if true, strengthens the explanation above?

(a) Communities with high levels of dietary intake of dark chocolate exhibit low rates of death from hypertension (high blood pressure).
(b) Individuals with low levels of nitric oxide in the endolethium exhibited relaxed blood vessels and robust blood flow.
(c) There is no peer-reviewed study which proves the link between intake of cocoa flavanols and reduction in risk of diabetes.
(d) None of the above

115. AI often elicits a sense of amazement, of wonder, of possibility for the future. But just as AI offers advancements, there is also the potential for a bleak future – machines are prone to bias and racism. These machines learn by running training data through algorithms, each crafted by human handlers. Therefore, if the data inputted into the system is biased, the result will be biased too. This is dangerous and the threat needs to be addressed before biased AI systems become ubiquitous. Ultimately, AI systems have the potential to deepen existing systemic inequalities, particularly in industries like healthcare, employment, and criminal justice.

Which one of the following is an assumption required by the argument?

(a) Existing data sets can incorporate the biases of human handlers which reflects in AI output.
(b) Large-scale deployment of AI systems has been hindered by the likelihood of biased results.
(c) Human handlers have tried to manipulate AI systems through the use of biased data.
(d) Industries like healthcare, employment, and criminal justice are in urgent need of AI systems.

116. Fake news and sophisticated disinformation campaigns are especially problematic in democratic systems, and there is growing debate on how to address these issues without undermining the benefits of digital media. In order to maintain an open, democratic system, it is important that government, business, and consumers work together to solve these problems.

Which one of the following explanations, if valid, most helps to justify the above reasoning?

(a) An effective means of countering fake news and disinformation campaigns is to revert to print media for critical information.
(b) Only governments have the power to counter fake news and sophisticated disinformation campaigns.
(c) Autocratic systems of government ensure that only verified and accurate information is disseminated.
(d) Democratic societies are underpinned by freedom of speech and expression.

117. **Legislator:** We recently evaluated the impact that an amendment to a particular national legislation would have on the population, by undertaking a survey in the most populous state of the country as well as a nation-wide survey. We were unable to get any information from the national survey results. However, we found that the response to the amendment was highly promising in the state-wide survey. We concluded that the national population's response would be promising as well.

The Legislator's reasoning does which of the following?

(a) infers a statistical generalisation by deploying statistical tools to different data sets.
(b) bases the prediction about the impact of a phenomenon on the impact of the phenomenon's cause.
(c) makes a prediction about future events on facts from multiple recent comparable events.
(d) uses evidence from a case where direct evidence is available to make a conclusion about a dissimilar case where direct evidence is not available.

118. **Statement:** The Criminal Procedure (Identification) Bill, 2022 ("Bill") seeks to authorise the taking of measurements (such as finger-impressions) of convicts and other persons for the purposes of identification and investigation in criminal matters.

Person 1: The Bill should not become a law because it allows for collection of measurements without any provisions for data protection.

Person 2: I disagree. Data protection measures can be developed. But the Bill will help law enforcement agencies to utilise the latest technology to identify criminals.

Which of the following is correct?

(a) Person 1 and Person 2 agree that the Bill should not become a law under any circumstances.
(b) Person 1 and Person 2 agree that data protection is a valid concern with respect to the Bill.
(c) According to Person 2, concerns about data protection are sufficient to reject the Bill.
(d) None of the above

119. **Issue:** As of April 2022, a few cases of the COVID XE variant have been found in India, which may be more transmissible than previous variants.

Person 1: (in April 2022): The government should institute a national lockdown pre-emptively to prevent a potential new wave of COVID XE. Although lockdowns cause great difficulty for people, there is no other way to prevent a potential new wave.

Person 2: (in April 2022): A national lockdown is a drastic measure that severely harms businesses and people. The risk posed by the new COVID XE variant does not justify a national lockdown, at least at this stage.

Which of the following is correct?

(a) Person 1 and Person 2 agree that a lockdown will definitely be needed in future.
(b) Person 2 thinks that a national lockdown is never justified.
(c) Person 1 and Person 2 agree that a lockdown has negative consequences.
(d) None of the above

120. Children who enjoy reading books usually do so indoors. Children should spend time playing outdoors.

Conclusions:

I. Children should not read books.
II. Children who enjoy reading books never play outdoors.

Choose the most appropriate answer.

(a) Only I follows
(b) Only II follows
(c) Both I and II follow
(d) Neither I nor II follows

121. The quickest way to decarbonise in the near term is scaling up renewable energies to replace coal and gas. This will be even more important as transport and home heating become electrified. While electrification and the deployment of renewables can go a long way, for some sectors this will not be enough. Cement and steel manufacture, for instance, cannot be simply electrified and powered by renewables. Similarly, heavy duty transport — such as air travel, shipping and long-haul trucking — presents a challenge.

Which one of the following statements can be properly inferred from the passage?

(a) Transport and home heating cannot be powered using coal and gas.
(b) Air travel and shipping can be decarbonised over the long-term using current renewable energy technologies.
(c) Existing modes of generating renewable energy are insufficient for decarbonising cement manufacturing.
(d) Long-haul trucking can only be powered using coal and gas.

122. The cloud-burst caused extensive damage to roadways around the town, making them unsuitable for heavy vehicles such as trucks and buses carrying more than 20 people. As a result, the villagers are being extracted via air. The roadways cannot be mended until everyone is extracted safely.

Based on the information above, which conclusion necessarily follows?

(a) Materials for mending the roadways will have to be transported via air.
(b) No person or vehicle is entering the town via roadways.
(c) The villagers would have used trucks to leave the town if the roads weren't damaged.
(d) None of the above

123. Ayurveda is a traditional branch of medical science in India. Ayurveda techniques have great capabilities, and complex procedures including surgeries can be performed effectively using the principles of Ayurveda.

Based on the information above, which conclusion necessarily follows?

I. Ayurveda is a better form of medicine than allopathy.
II. Ayurveda is a neglected science.

Choose the most appropriate answer.

(a) Only I follows
(b) Only II follows
(c) Both I and II follow
(d) Neither I nor II follows

124. There are many ways to be successful in life. One way is to work hard and be good at your job. Another way is to be street smart and develop a great emotional quotient. Yet another way is to always follow the advice of your elders.

Based on the information above, which conclusion necessarily follows?

I. All three are equally easy ways of being successful in life.

II. It is possible to be successful without working hard.

Choose the most appropriate answer.

(a) Only I follows
(b) Only II follows
(c) Both I and II follow
(d) Neither I nor II follows

125. The freedom of speech is not absolute. Certain categories of speech, such as hate speech, sedition, defamation, etc., are not protected by the Constitution.

Based on the information above, which conclusion necessarily follows?

I. Obscene speech is protected by the Constitution.
II. Defamation is a criminal offence.

Choose the most appropriate answer.

(a) Only I follows
(b) Only II follows
(c) Both I and II follow
(d) Neither I nor II follows

126. It is statistically proven that those who play sports suffer from less stress than those who do not play sports. In fact, regularly playing sports is associated with an overall higher level of mental health. Further, outdoor sports are associated with better mental health than indoor sports.

Based on the information above, which conclusion necessarily follows?

I. Sports are essential to maintain good mental health.

II. People who regularly play sports never face mental health issues.

Choose the most appropriate answer.

(a) Only I follows
(b) Only II follows
(c) Both I and II follow
(d) Neither I nor II follows

127. Since their inception in the 1970s, video games have often been criticized by some for violent content. Politicians, parents, and other activists have claimed that violence in video games can be tied to violent behavior, particularly in children, and have sought ways to regulate the sale of video games. However, numerous studies have failed to find any connection between video games and violent behavior.

Based on the information above, which conclusion necessarily follows?

I. Video games have no relationship with violence.
II. Better studies need to be conducted to find a link between video games and violence.

Choose the most appropriate answer.

(a) Only I follows
(b) Only II follows
(c) Both I and II follow
(d) Neither I nor II follows

128. In 2008, the Bar Council of India framed a rule stipulating that an advocate is prohibited from advertising or soliciting his work either directly or indirectly, through circulars, advertisements, interviews, touts, and personal communications. The idea of the prohibition of advertising practices in the legal profession has been taken from the law in the UK, where the legal profession is considered noble, and it is believed that its commercialization will cause dishonor to the profession and will lead to unfair practices.

Based on the information above, which conclusion necessarily follows?

I. The Bar Council of India has copied the law in the UK without applying its own mind as to whether such a restriction on advertising would be conducive in the Indian context.

II. Lawyers in India are not allowed to commend themselves to persons looking for legal assistance.

Choose the most appropriate answer.

(a) Only I follows
(b) Only II follows
(c) Both I and II follow
(d) Neither I nor II follows

129. The Government of Kerala has reserved 75% seats in all public educational institutions for persons having 'domicile' status in the State of Kerala. The reason cited by the Government is that other States in the country have taken similar measures with respect to their residents. The approach adopted by the State of Kerala is improper because every State authority is required to independently apply its own mind before arriving at a decision.

Based on the information above, which conclusion necessarily follows?

I. 75% seats in all public institutions are in fact occupied by persons holding 'domicile' status in the State of Kerala.

II. The reason behind the introduction of 'domicile' reservations by the State of Kerala is not an assessment of backwardness of certain parts of the State.

Choose the most appropriate answer.

(a) Only I follows
(b) Only II follows
(c) Both I and II follow
(d) Neither I nor II follows

130. The April 1986 disaster at the Chernobyl nuclear power plant in Ukraine was a direct consequence of Cold War isolation and the resulting lack of any safety culture. While no-one in the West was under any illusion about the safety of early Soviet nuclear reactor designs, some lessons learned have also been applicable to Western plants. Since then, the safety of all Soviet-designed reactors has improved vastly. This is due largely to the development of a culture of safety encouraged by collaboration between East and West, and substantial investment in improving the reactors.

Which one of the following statements can be inferred from the passage?

(a) Financial investment in nuclear reactor-safety was not a priority for governments prior to the Chernobyl disaster.
(b) In the period preceding the Chernobyl disaster, Western nuclear scientists believed their nuclear reactors are superior than Soviet reactor designs.
(c) The level of collaboration between Western and Eastern nations in the pre-Chernobyl era/before 1986, in relation to safe nuclear reactor designs, was lower compared to the post-Chernobyl era.
(d) Both (b) and (c)

131. Black people are about twice as likely to develop Alzheimer's disease as White people, but for years the pharmaceutical industry has mostly left them out of trials intended to prove new drugs are safe and effective. Two trials organized by a leading pharmaceutical company for its drug 'X', the first Alzheimer's drug approved in almost two decades, were among those with the lowest Black representation. Only 19 people, or 0.6%, of 3,285 participants in its two final-stage trials identified themselves as Black. There are good reasons to study Alzheimer's in broader populations: The disease is still poorly understood, and the brain pathology and disease genetics may be different in groups with different ancestry.

Which one of the following statements can be inferred from the passage?

(a) Drug companies find it economical to enroll non-black participants in clinical trials.
(b) Black people are reluctant to enroll in clinical trials.
(c) The approval of Drug X will enable pharmaceutical companies to better understand Alzheimer's disease.
(d) The approved Drug 'X' may not be as safe and efficacious among Black patients as it would be among White patients.

132. Geeta is buying three ice-cream bars and must distribute them amongst five of her friends - V, W, X, Y and Z - in accordance with the following conditions:

(i) If V gets an ice-cream bar, W and Y must also get an ice-cream bar.
(ii) If Z gets an ice-cream bar, X cannot get an ice-cream bar.
(iii) At least one of W or X must get an ice-cream bar.
(iv) Each ice-cream bar can only go to one person.

If X gets an ice-cream bar, the other two ice-cream bars can go to:

(a) Only V and W
(b) Only W and Y
(c) Only W and Z
(d) None of the above

133. A school principal must schedule classes for five subjects – English, Maths, Science, Social Studies, and Music – in accordance with the following conditions:

(i) All subjects except Music must be scheduled at least once a day.
(ii) Science must be scheduled immediately after Maths on any day.
(iii) English cannot be the first or last subject scheduled on any day.
(iv) Social Studies cannot be immediately followed by Music. Music cannot be immediately followed by Social Studies.

If English is the second subject scheduled on a given day, which of these is a possible order of subjects for that day?

(a) Music, English, Maths, Social Studies
(b) Science, English, Music, Social Studies
(c) Social Studies, English, Maths, Science
(d) Maths, English, Science, Social Studies

134. An athlete who enjoys playing football, tennis, badminton, cricket and basketball must somehow play all five of these sports during a given 7-day week (starting on Monday and ending on Sunday) in accordance with the following conditions:

(i) Football cannot be played on Monday or Sunday.
(ii) Badminton cannot be played on the day immediately before or immediately after the day on which tennis is played.
(iii) Basketball cannot be played on Thursday.
(iv) At least two of the five sports must be played twice during the week.
(v) Only one sport can be played each day.
(vi) No sport can be played for two consecutive days.

If Badminton is played on Monday and Basketball is played on Saturday, which of the following is a possible order of sports for the week?

(a) Badminton (Monday), Tennis (Tuesday), Cricket (Wednesday), Football (Thursday), Cricket (Friday), Basketball (Saturday), Badminton (Sunday)
(b) Badminton (Monday), Football (Tuesday), Tennis (Wednesday), Football (Thursday), Cricket (Friday), Basketball (Saturday), Basketball (Sunday)
(c) Badminton (Monday), Football (Tuesday), Tennis (Wednesday), Football (Thursday), Cricket (Friday), Basketball (Saturday), Cricket (Sunday)
(d) None of the above

135. Seven locations (Classroom, Hostel, Library, Auditorium, Dining Hall, Meeting Room, and Common Room) within an unusual college campus are to be assigned floor numbers from 1 (lowest) to 7 (highest). Each location can only have one floor number, and each floor number can only be assigned to one location. The numbering is to be done in accordance with the following conditions:

(i) The Classroom is on a lower floor than the Auditorium.
(ii) The Meeting Room is exactly one floor lower than the Hostel.
(iii) The Library is either on Floor 1 or on Floor 7.
(iv) The Common Room is on Floor 4.

Which of the following is a possible arrangement of the seven locations, going from Floor 1 to Floor 7?

(a) Classroom, Auditorium, Dining Hall, Common Room, Library, Meeting Room, Hostel
(b) Classroom, Dining Hall, Auditorium, Common Room, Meeting Room, Hostel, Library

(c) Classroom, Meeting Room, Dining Hall, Common Room, Hostel, Auditorium, Library
(d) Library, Dining Hall, Common Room, Meeting Room, Hostel, Classroom, Auditorium

136. Some laptops are chocolates. All toffees are chocolates.

Examine the following statements:

I. Some laptops are toffees.
II. No toffees are laptops.
III. All toffees are laptops.
IV. All laptops are toffees.

Choose the most appropriate answer.

(a) Either I or II follows.
(b) Either III or IV follows.
(c) Both I and III follow.
(d) Both I and IV follow.

137. All boxes are plugs. All plugs are bottles.

Examine the following statements:

I. All plugs are boxes.
II. All bottles are boxes.
III. No bottles are boxes.

Choose the most appropriate answer.

(a) Only Statement I is certainly false.
(b) Both Statements II and III are certainly false.
(c) Both Statements I and III are certainly false.
(d) Only Statement III is certainly false.

138. Only fruits are pasta. All noodles are pasta.

Examine the following statements:

I. No fruits are noodles.
II. All pasta are noodles.
III. All fruits are noodles.

Choose the most appropriate answer.

(a) Only Statement I is certainly false.
(b) Both Statements II and III are certainly false.
(c) Both Statements I and III are certainly false.
(d) Only Statement III is certainly false.

139. People are always blaming circumstances for their difficulties. Most who succeed in this world are people who get up and look for the circumstances they want, and if they cannot find them, they make them.

Which of the following is an assumption necessarily taken for granted in the above statement?

(a) Failure is always a consequence of not trying hard enough.
(b) Those who do not complain about their circumstances are successful in life.
(c) There is some correlation between desired circumstances and success.
(d) Both (b) and (c)

140. Online retailers do not have to pay for overheads such as shop rent and sales staff salaries, owing to which they can charge lower prices for products than brick-and- mortar stores which have to incur such costs.

The conclusion drawn above follows logically if which of the following is assumed?

(a) Online retailers pay lesser salaries than brick-and-mortar stores.
(b) Consumers prefer to pay less prices.
(c) Shop rent and sales staff salaries add to the price consumers have to pay for products.
(d) Both (b) and (c)

141. The world sees tech companies as giants with trillion-dollar market values and global networks. Cue renewed regulatory efforts to undermine their dominance. Shortly after the EU agreed stringent legislation to regulate Big Tech, the UK this week set out details of its plan. Such moves are a response to Big Tech's competition-stifling scale. Amazon will account for an estimated 39.5 per cent of the US e-commerce market this year, according to research. Meta has 3.6bn users around the world and is the world's largest social media company. Google has 92 per cent of the search engine market, according to data.

Which of the following is the most appropriate assumption required by the above passage?

(a) Tech companies with small market shares will go bankrupt not survive in the absence of regulatory intervention.
(b) The regulatory efforts will help bolster the market shares of the competitors of Amazon, Meta and Google.

(c) Regulators have been struggling to rein in Big Tech.
(d) Tech companies with large market shares merit regulatory intervention in order to maintain competitive markets.

142. Ethanol can be blended into petrol to reduce the quantity of petrol required to run a vehicle, thus reducing dependency on imported, costly and polluting petroleum. For India to meet its target of 20% ethanol blended in petrol by the year 2025 (commonly known as the E20 target), it will have to bring in more land under cultivation of feedstock – agricultural products that can be converted into ethanol—area that can be better utilised for the generation of renewable energy and for furthering the electric vehicles adoption programme in the country, according to a new report. Besides, the ethanol target will not reduce earth-warming emissions drastically, it may be detrimental to India's food security, and will only help us inch towards energy security, experts say.

The conclusion drawn above follows logically if which of the following is assumed?

(a) India's food security is already under threat.
(b) Dearth of renewable energy is hindering the adoption of electric vehicles in the country.
(c) India is lagging behind in achieving its E20 target.
(d) Land to be used for feedstock cultivation has conditions suited for renewable energy generation.

143. The Constitution of India is a vital document. It lays out our rights and duties and places meaningful restrictions on our elected representatives. It is imperative on our part to educate ourselves about the Constitution. Therefore, every person must endeavour to place a copy of the Constitution in their home.

Which of the following is an assumption required by the above passage?

(a) Our elected representatives cannot be trusted.
(b) People are more likely to read a text if it is placed inside their home.
(c) The Constitution Framers were great visionaries.
(d) None of the above

144. Rather than adopt conventional ways of water consumption, we should all start storing our water in copper containers so that we can get the benefits of copper intake. It is now well-proven that storing water in a container for 24-48 hours is very effective in transmitting some copper content into the water.

Which of the following is an assumption required by the above passage?

(a) It is safe to drink water out of a copper container.
(b) We should drink adequate amounts of water every day.
(c) Storing water in copper containers is one of the best ways to ensure that the requisite copper content reaches your body.
(d) None of the above

145. "Mental-health issues and stress or high anxiety often go together. Finding an emotional release like painting allows a person's mind to relax and let go of all the problems that contribute to a high-stress level. When people create something beautiful through painting, they stimulate the creative mind while relieving mental strain. A low-stress level leads to a happier, healthier lifestyle and helps improve overall mental health." Which of the following is an assumption required by the above passage?

(a) People can have a creative mind.
(b) The act of painting involves expressing emotions.
(c) Stress reduces the quality of life.
(d) All of the above

146. Principle: An advocate is bound to accept any brief in the Courts or Tribunals or before any other authorities in or before which he proposes to practise at a fee consistent with his standing at the Bar and the nature of the case.

Facts: You are an advocate practising in the Supreme Court of India and specialising in criminal law. You are approached by a Pakistani national who has been convicted of serious terrorism and murder charges by the Delhi High Court. He wants you to represent him before the Supreme Court. He is willing to pay any fee you may quote. However, you have a serious moral objection to taking up this case since it concerns the security of the country.

Choose the most appropriate answer.

(a) You can refuse to represent the terrorist on account of your strong moral objection.

It is unfair to force a lawyer to argue a case against his moral beliefs.

(b) You can refuse to represent the terrorist on account of your strong moral objection. It would be unfair to the client if his lawyer does not believe in his case strongly.

(c) You are under an obligation to accept the case because the principle makes no exceptions for advocates having moral objections.

(d) None of the above

147. Principle: No person accused of an offence involving commercial quantity of narcotic drugs shall be released on bail or on his own bond unless the court is satisfied that there are reasonable grounds for believing that he is not guilty of such offence and that he is not likely to commit any offence while on bail.

Facts: Michael is accused of possessing commercial quantities of cocaine (a narcotic drug), which is an offence. However, he has not yet been arrested by the police. He moves the relevant court for anticipatory bail, praying that he should not be arrested for the alleged offences. The Court finds a good case for grant of anticipatory bail; however, the Court is not ready to state that "there are reasonable grounds for believing that he is not guilty of such offence".

Choose the most appropriate answer.

(a) The Court is not bound by the given principle, because the principle speaks of "release" of a person on bail, thus implying that it does not apply to cases of anticipatory bail.

(b) The Court is still bound by the given principle because it would be absurd to suggest that persons in custody and those not yet arrested are governed by different rules.

(c) The Court is not bound by the given principle because its language is only in the form of a recommendation. The Court is free to grant bail based on its own sense of fairness and justice.

(d) None of the above

148. Principle: The appeal by a candidate or his agent or by any other person with the consent of a candidate or his election agent to vote or refrain from voting for any person on the ground of his religion, race, caste, community or language, shall be a "corrupt practice".

Facts: Ms. Tickoo, a candidate from the Krantikari Party, says to her voters: *"Vote for me because you are all Christians and your interests will be protected by me."*

Choose the most appropriate answer.

(a) Ms. Tickoo is guilty of a corrupt practice because she has appealed to religion.

(b) Ms. Tickoo is not guilty of corrupt practice because she has appealed neither to her own religion nor to another candidate's.

(c) Ms. Tickoo is not guilty of corrupt practice because the principle only applies to male candidates.

(d) None of the above.

149. There must be mandatory vaccination against communicable diseases.

Argument 1: Yes, the collective wellbeing of the population must override individual choice.

Argument 2: No, individuals must have agency over what they inject into their bodies.

Argument 3: No, this would lead to profiteering by vaccine manufacturers.

Choose the most appropriate answer.

(a) Only arguments 1 and 2 are strong.

(b) All arguments are strong.

(c) Only arguments 2 and 3 are strong.

(d) Only arguments 1 and 3 are strong.

150. Should there be a limit on the number of times an individual may be elected as a head of a state?

Argument 1: Yes, it prevents concentration of power in a single individual for a prolonged time and reduces the possibility of misuse of power.

Argument 2: No, an incumbent individual will know how to best run the country, given their experience.

Argument 3: No, the population must be free to give the democratic mandate to the person of their choosing, even if they win multiple times.

Choose the most appropriate answer.

(a) Only argument 1 is strong.
(b) Only argument 1 and 3 are strong.
(c) Only argument 3 is strong.
(d) Only arguments 2 and 3 are strong.

ANSWER KEY

Section–A: English

1. b	**7.** a	**13.** c	**19.** b	**25.** b	**31.** d	**37.** a	**43.** b	**49.** d
2. d	**8.** b	**14.** a	**20.** d	**26.** b	**32.** c	**38.** c	**44.** c	**50.** c
3. c	**9.** d	**15.** d	**21.** c	**27.** c	**33.** b	**39.** d	**45.** a	
4. a	**10.** d	**16.** d	**22.** c	**28.** d	**34.** c	**40.** c	**46.** c	
5. c	**11.** b	**17.** c	**23.** a	**29.** b	**35.** c	**41.** b	**47.** a	
6. b	**12.** c	**18.** a	**24.** a	**30.** c	**36.** a	**42.** b	**48.** d	

Section–B: Current Affairs and General Knowledge

51. c	**55.** d	**59.** d	**63.** d	**67.** b	**71.** d	**75.** d	**79.** b
52. a	**56.** d	**60.** d	**64.** b	**68.** d	**72.** d	**76.** b	**80.** d
53. a	**57.** d	**61.** c	**65.** a	**69.** d	**73.** b	**77.** a	
54. c	**58.** c	**62.** a	**66.** a	**70.** a	**74.** a	**78.** c	

Section–C: Logical Reasoning

81. b	**90.** c	**99.** d	**108.** c	**117.** d	**126.** d	**135.** b	**144.** a
82. d	**91.** b	**100.** a	**109.** c	**118.** b	**127.** d	**136.** a	**145.** d
83. a	**92.** b	**101.** c	**110.** a	**119.** c	**128.** b	**137.** d	**146.** c
84. b	**93.** a	**102.** a	**111.** a	**120.** d	**129.** b	**138.** a	**147.** a
85. c	**94.** c	**103.** b	**112.** c	**121.** c	**130.** c	**139.** c	**148.** b
86. d	**95.** a	**104.** d	**113.** a	**122.** d	**131.** d	**140.** b	**149.** a
87. c	**96.** b	**105.** c	**114.** a	**123.** d	**132.** b	**141.** d	**150.** b
88. d	**97.** c	**106.** c	**115.** a	**124.** b	**133.** c	**142.** d	
89. d	**98.** b	**107.** b	**116.** d	**125.** d	**134.** c	**143.** b	

AILET 2021

ENGLISH

Directions questions 1–5: *Read the given passage and answer the questions that follow.*

'The night I arrived in Delhi on a visit in January 1996, the elevator at the Maurya Sheraton took us up to the twelfth floor in a breath-taking six or seven seconds. 'Remarkable,' I commented admiringly to the friendly hotel employee in a maroon sari and business-like pageboy haircut, who had draped a three-kilogram marigold garland around my neck as I stepped across the threshold. 'We couldn't have ascended faster in the U. S. of A.'

She took my praise in stride, as well she should have. Jet-lagged after an eighteen-hour journey from New York, I had failed to notice that this was not some superfast new elevator technology that the Maurya had brought to Delhi, but rather some highly creative labelling. When I finally woke up and looked out my window, I realized that what the elevator buttons had called the twelfth floor was in fact the second. The gleaming Maurya elevator had merely taken me for a ride – and a shorter ride I'd imagined.

I couldn't help the accusatory tone out of my voice the next time I ran into the maroon sari. 'Twelfth floor, huh?' I said pointedly. 'I didn't think liberalization meant being liberal with the facts.'

She was surprised that I had taken offense. 'Our foreign visitors much prefer to think of themselves as being on eleventh and twelfth floors than the first or second,' she replied with wide-eyed innocence. 'And they don't look out of the windows that much.'

Welcome, I thought, to the new India. An India I was discovering for the first time: an India of five-star hotels, welcoming garlands, and smooth-talking hotel staff, where nothing is quite what it seems (not even the elevator buttons), where windows are not meant to be opened and appearances are the only reality. [Shashi Tharoor, India : *From Midnight to the Millennium and Beyond* (Arcade Publishing, 1997) 275-276]

1. After reading the last line of the first paragraph, 'We couldn't have ascended faster in the U. S. of A.', which of the options do you think the author is most likely to agree with?
(a) India never fails to surprise.
(b) Indians have been great innovators.
(c) Foreigners are turning to India's technical advancement.
(d) It's a fact that India hasn't made significant progress.

2. As used in the third paragraph, the underlined word 'accusatory' most nearly means all options, except
(a) denunciative (b) criminate
(c) eulogistic (d) censuring

3. It can be inferred from the passage that the author's impression
(a) transgresses from being proud to being even prouder.
(b) plummets from a sense of pride to a sense of disillusionment.
(c) trends from a level of disappointment to a level of condemnation.
(d) remains steadfast on the thought of being an Indian.

4. In the line, '...taken me for a ride–and a shorter ride I'd imagined'. means
(a) the elevator had taken them very swiftly.
(b) the hotel was treating its guests like royalties.
(c) technology had advanced in third world countries.
(d) people were being hoodwinked.

5. The tone of the passage could be summed up to be
(a) pensive and remorseful.
(b) matter of fact and sombre.
(c) humorous and reflective.
(d) fiery and critical.

Directions questions (6–11): *Choose an appropriate word to fill in each blank space.*

__________(6) are increasingly awarding large__________(7) to plaintiffs who have experienced__________(8) comments and harassment or been denied promotions and __________(9) because of their family responsibilities. These__________(10) are more likely to prevail than other employment-related cases.__________(11) suits on behalf of caregivers are on the rise as well.

6. (a) Judge (b) Juries
(c) Prosecutors (d) Defendants

7. (a) personal injuries (b) kickbacks
(c) rewards (d) settlements

8. (a) derogatory (b) directive
(c) abusive (d) adulatory

9. (a) perks (b) raises
(c) rises (d) reimbursements

10. (a) suits (b) complains
(c) accusations (d) remarks

11. (a) Torts (b) Act of Law
(c) Class Action (d) Procedural Law

Directions For questions (12–14): *Find the correct meaning of the highlighted word in each of the sentences from the choices given below.*

12. Ravi was an ***impecunious*** student noted for his academic excellence.
(a) brilliant and studious
(b) rude and arrogant
(c) shrewd and manipulative
(d) having little or no money

13. The lady looked rather ***lugubrious.***
(a) sad and sorrowful
(b) eager and anxious
(c) happy and cheerful
(d) high and energetic

14. She displayed a ***recalcitrant*** attitude.
(a) enthusiastic
(b) resisting authority or discipline
(c) weak and frightened
(d) hollow and insincere

Directions questions 15 and 16: *Choose the most appropriate option that completes the given sentences.*

15. To be successful, managers must see themselves more as catalysts for problem solving than as problem solvers__________.
(a) *Per se* (b) *A priori*
(c) *Pro rata* (d) *Faux pas*

16. The art of speaking or writing effectively is__________.
(a) rhetoric (b) brevity
(c) garrulousness (d) verbosity

17. What do we call someone who tries to 'put something across', good or bad and who does not want scrutiny or criticism, but a specific action?
(a) Enthusiast (b) Sloganeer
(c) Propagandist (d) Zealot

18. Choose the most appropriate option that best explains the figure of speech in this line:
In rivers the water that you touch is the last of what passed and the first of that which comes: so, with time present. (*Leonardo Da Vinci*)
(a) Personification of the tangible and the intangible
(b) Simile that compares water and time
(c) Hyperbole that reveals elements of similarities
(d) Metaphysical analogy that divides time past from time future

19. Choose the most appropriate option that most nearly means the same as the expression, 'the kiss of Judas' in the English language :
(a) A friend at court
(b) A snake in the grass
(c) A fair-weather friend
(d) A match made in heaven

20. Choose the most appropriate option that best expresses the statement:
Since I was planning on a Euro tour, I decided to incuess my French.
(a) try my hand at
(b) make up for
(c) brush up on
(d) master the art of

21. Choose the most appropriate option that could be the best analogy for the given pair of words : tree : lea ::?
(a) tiger : cubs
(b) bows : arrows
(c) plants : sunlight
(d) flower : petal

Directions questions (22–25): *Do as Directed*:

22. Choose the most appropriate option that is grammatically incorrect.
(a) A growing bodies of evidence shows that simple rules match or beat more complicated analysis across a wide range of decision.
(b) Rules may be developed using sophisticated statistical models or through analysis, but they shouldn't be difficult to grasp.
(c) Because they are easy to put into practice, simple rules can induce action without unnecessarily limiting oppositions.
(d) All firms must balance two conflicting but equally important demands: efficiency and flexibility.

23. Choose the most appropriate option that has a grammatically incorrect interrogative statement.
(a) What information and language should the problem statement include?
(b) How we will ensure that a solution is being implementing from its inception?
(c) Do we have the necessary support for soliciting and evaluating possible solutions?
(d) Are complex organisations far more difficult to manage than merely complicated ones?

24. Choose the most appropriate option that best connects the sentence.
Companies that correctly match their strategy-making processes to their competitive circumstances perform__________:
(a) better than those that don't
(b) well as those who aren't
(c) as good as those that don't
(d) best to the ones that doesn't

25. Choose the most appropriate option that punctuates the sentence well.
(a) The professor demanded, 'What makes you think that 'discredited' or 'repudiated' are synonymous with defeated?'
(b) The professor demanded, 'What makes you think that 'discredited' or 'repudiated' are synonymous with 'defeated'?
(c) The professor demanded, 'What makes you think that, 'discredited' or repudiated are synonymous with 'defeated'?'
(d) The professor demanded, 'What makes you think that 'discredited' or 'repudiated' are synonymous with 'defeated'?'

Directions questions (26–30): *In each sentence a word or phrase is underlined. Below each sentence are four other words or phrases. Choose the one word or phrase which would best keep the meaning of the original sentence if it were substituted for the underlined word.*

26. The old age of the equipment is a definite liability to the factory.
(a) cost (b) disadvantage
(c) aid (d) capacity

27. Having lived in a ghetto most of her life, she despaired of ever living 'the good life'.
(a) segregated slum
(b) visitor's quarters
(c) public house
(d) high-rise apartment

28. The president considered the vote on his tax bill to be crucial.
(a) extremely important
(b) unimportant
(c) hard fought
(d) far off

29. The panorama from their porch encompassed a large part of the Rocky Mountains.
(a) cooking utensil
(b) unbroken view over a large area
(c) TV screen
(d) small patch of land

30. The candidate felt that his academic credentials were sufficient to win him the job.
(a) important (b) educational
(c) costly (d) experience

***Directions* questions (31–35):** Read the following sets of words and find the odd one out from the group of four words.

31. (a) Tadpole (b) Fledgling
(c) Cub (d) Kitten

32. (a) Skin (b) Nails
(c) Eyes (d) Nose

33. (a) Progression (b) Headway
(c) Forge ahead (d) Deviant

34. (a) Abatement (b) Declination
(c) Elevation (d) Subsidence

35. (a) Mare (b) Gazelle
(c) Antelope (d) Stag

GENERAL KNOWLEDGE

36. Who was appointed as Election Commissioner to the Election Commission of India during June 2021?
(a) Rajiv Kumar
(b) Anup Chandra Pandey
(c) Sushil Chandra
(d) Sunil Arora

37. India's foreign exchange reserve in June 2021 touched
(a) US $ 900 billion
(b) US $ 700 billion
(c) US $ 500 billion
(d) US $ 600 billion

38. Who is the newly elected President of the United Nations General Assembly in 2021?
(a) Volkan Bozkir
(b) Peter Thomson
(c) Abdulla Shahid
(d) Matian Fernanda

39. The U. S. Vice President had to use the casting vote to get the Senate's confirmation for the appointment of
(a) Neera Tandon
(b) Kiran Ahuja
(c) Aruna Khilanani
(d) P. Rupa Ranga

40. Who is the most philanthropic person in the world in the past 100 years?
(a) Bill and Melinda Gates
(b) Warren Buffett
(c) Jamsetji Tata
(d) Azim Premji

41. Who was top seeded in 53 kg category in wrestling for the Tokyo Olympics 2021?
(a) Venesh Phogat (b) Mayu Mukaida
(c) Qianyu Pang (d) Ravi Dahiya

42. Joe Biden is the ____________ President of the United States of America.
(a) 45th (b) 46th
(c) 47th (d) 44th

43. Which country sent 9 satellites into space from the first sea-based commercial launches?
(a) India (b) China
(c) France (d) U. S. A.

44. One among the major economies / country to phase out both coal based and atomic energy based power generation is
(a) Germany (b) France
(c) U. S. A. (d) Canada

45. Which of the following recently released the 'closest ever breath taking' pictures of the Sun?
(a) ISRO (b) SPACE-X
(c) NASA (d) ROSCOSMOS

46. According to Public Affairs Index, 2020, which are the two best governed States in India?
(a) Kerala and Goa
(b) Kerala and T. N.
(c) Goa and Chhattisgarh
(d) Goa and Telangana

47. Which of the following is the fastest growing 'Tech-Hub'?
(a) San Francisco (b) Bengaluru
(c) London (d) Mumbai

48. India was elected a Member of U.N. Commission on Status of Women during September 2020 defeating
(a) Afghanistan (b) Sri Lanka
(c) China (d) Pakistan

49. India signed an agreement on 15-7-2020 to expand cooperation in cyber security with
(a) U. S. A. (b) Germany
(c) France (d) Israel

50. The quadilateral security dialogue also known as QUAD is and informal strategic forum to check the economic and military power of China consists of
(a) U. S. A., France, Australia and India
(b) U. S. A., Japan, Australia and India
(c) France, Australia, Japan and India
(d) Australia, Japan, Germany and France

51. Nobel prize for Economics, 2020 was awarded jointly to two Economists based in the
(a) University of Oxford (b) Harvard University
(c) Stanford University (d) Yale University

52. The present Chairperson of the National Human Rights Commission is
(a) Justice Dattu (b) Justice Verma
(c) Justice Bobde (d) Justice Arun Mishra

53. National Voters' Day in India is observed on
(a) 26th January (b) 25th January
(c) 15th August (d) 16th August

54. Which of the following cannot cast their votes remotely through the postal ballot system in India?
(a) Members of the armed forces (Army, Air Force and Navy)
(b) Government employees posted outside India
(c) Government employees serving outside their state
(d) Voters under preventive detention

55. Which of the following recently became the first to successfully provide 100% functional household tap connections in rural areas?
(a) Sikkim (b) Ladakh
(c) Kerala (d) Goa

56. The Government of India decided to celebrate the birth anniversary of which freedom fighter as 'Parakram Diwas'/'Day of Valour' on January 23rd every year?
(a) Maulana Abdul Kalam Azad
(b) Syama Prasad Mookherjee
(c) Subhash Chandra Bose
(d) Bhagat Singh

57. Which of the following bodies is neither a constitutional body nor a statutory body?
(a) Law Commission of India
(b) Central Consumer Protection Authority
(c) National Anti-Profiteering Authority
(d) National Disaster Management Authority

58. In September 2020, the Parliament of India passed three 'Farm Bills', i.e., the Farmers' Produce Trade and Commerce (Promotion and Facilitation) Act, 2020, the Farmers (Empowerment and Protection) Agreement on Price Assurance and Farm Services Act, 2020 and the Essential Commodities (Amendment) Act, 2020. Which of these subjects are NOT dealt with in any of the three legislations?
(a) Selling of produce outside Agriculture Produce Market Committees
(b) Contract farming
(c) Removal of income tax exemption granted to agricultural income
(d) Restriction of situations in which supply of foodstuffs can be regulated

59. Which internet giant committed to investing $10 billion over the next 5-7 years towards digitising the Indian economy, as part of its 'India Digitisation Fund' - that will focus on enabling affordable access to the Internet for Indians in their own languages apart from building new products and services?
(a) Facebook (b) Apple
(c) Paytm (d) Google

60. The Government of India recently signed a pact for a $500 million project to build safe and green national highway corridors in Rajasthan, Himachal Pradesh, Uttar Pradesh and Andhra Pradesh, with which of these organisations?
(a) Asian Development Bank
(b) G20
(c) World Bank
(d) International Monetary Fund

61. What is a diplomatic mission between two commonwealth nations called?
(a) Embassy (b) Consulate
(c) High Commission (d) Permanent Mission

62. A joint session of the Parliament is presided over by
(a) Speaker of the Lok Sabha
(b) President of India
(c) Vice President of India
(d) Chief Justice of India

63. Cyclone Tauktae was recently in the news in May 2021. 'Tauktae' means gecko/ highly vocal lizard in its language of origin. From which of these languages was the word taken?
(a) Bahasa Melayu
(b) Vietnamese
(c) Burmese
(d) Khmer

64. On January 16, 2021, a team of ten climbers from Nepal made history by achieving which of these feats?
(a) Summiting Mount K2 in winter
(b) Being the largest team to climb Mount Everest
(c) Being the fastest team to climb Mount Everest
(d) Summiting Kanchenjunga in winter

65. What is the name of the 2020 Tokyo Olympics mascot?
(a) Hodori (b) Fuwa
(c) Waldi (d) Miraitowa

66. On 29 July, 2020, the Ministry of Human Resource Development (since renamed the Ministry of Education) unveiled the National Education Policy 2020 (NEP 2020), which recommends sweeping changes to the Education System in India. Which of the following is not a feature of the NEP 2020?
(a) Change in academic structure from 10+2 to 5+3+3+4
(b) No hard separations between 'arts' and 'sciences'
(c) Complete removal of B.Ed. (Bachelor of Education) degrees, and focus on subject specialisation instead
(d) Multiple exit options during undergraduate degree programs

67. Where is the headquarters of the International Solar Alliance with over 120 member countries situated?
(a) Paris (b) Baku
(c) Gurugram (d) Sochi

68. By scoring half centuries in each of the innings in her test debut against England at Bristol in June 2021, which Indian cricketer became the youngest woman to achieve this feat?
(a) Smriti Mandhana (b) Mithali Raj
(c) Sneh Rana (d) Shafali Varma

69. In the history of tennis in the Open Era, who among the following has the highest number of Grand Slam Singles' titles?
(a) Rafael Nadal (b) Steffi Graf
(c) Serena Williams (d) Roger Federer

70. What is the 'Belt and Road Initiative'?
(a) An initiative in NCT of Delhi to reduce traffic congestion
(b) An initiative to increase Government spending on infrastructure in India
(c) A multi-country infrastructure project by the Chinese Government
(d) A multi-country infrastructure project by the Asian Development Bank

LEGAL APTITUDE

***For questions* 71 *to* 96:** Apply the given legal principles to the facts provided in each of the questions and select the most appropriate answer.

71. PRINCIPLE 1: A misrepresentation arises when a person makes a false statement of fact to another which induces the other party to enter into a contract, resulting in loss to that other party.

PRINCIPLE 2: When consent to an agreement is caused by misrepresentation, the agreement is a contract voidable at the option of the party whose consent was so caused.

FACTS: It was Kritika's mother's 50th birthday on 9th February 2021. Kritika decided to organise a lavish celebration to celebrate the event. Kritika's mother used to play the piano before her marriage. However, after Kritika was born, she was unable to take out any time to pursue her interest in playing the instrument. Kritika learnt about this from her maternal grandmother a few days before her mother's birthday. She decided to give her mother a piano on her 50th birthday.

She visited Himanshu's piano store for this purpose. Himanshu showed Kritika all the pianos available at his store and explained the features of each model. Kritika had no prior knowledge of pianos and hence relied upon Himanshu's opinion. She saw a vintage piano and was immediately drawn to it. Being a shrewd businessman, Himanshu saw an opportunity to sell the piano and said 'They don't make them like this anymore. It's got a fine tone and it's really cheap at ₹50,000'. Kritika purchased the piano and gifted the same to her mother. However, when her mother started playing it, she immediately realized that the piano was of an inferior quality and that the tone was not proper. Kritika and her mother approached Himanshu and asked him to either replace the piano or refund the money. Himanshu refused to do either. What would be the strongest argument that Himanshu could make?

(a) Himanshu is not liable to do either because it is only Kritika's mother's subjective opinion that the piano was 'inferior' and that the tone was not 'proper'.

(b) Himanshu is not liable to do either because there is nothing to suggest that Kritika's decision was based purely on Himanshu's statement.

(c) Himanshu is not liable to do either the piano since Kritika should have done her due diligence and should have been more careful in selecting the piano.

(d) Himanshu is not liable to do either because he only gave Kritika his opinion and did not make any false statement of fact.

72. PRINCIPLE: No confession made to a Police Officer, shall be proved as against a person accused of any offence.

FACTS: Ritu was accused of having murdered Akash over a property dispute. After arrest, Ritu made a confession to the Inspector that she had in fact murdered Akash. The confessional statement of Ritu was written on a paper and Ritu signed the same. The police carried on further investigation but were not able to find any other evidence to produce before the court. Can the confessional statement signed by Ritu be proved in court?

(a) No, such a confessional statement cannot be proved since the confession was made to a police officer.

(b) Yes, such a confessional statement can be proved since it is not an oral confession. It has been duly signed by Ritu and hence there is no doubt that she made the confession herself.

(c) Yes, since there is no other evidence, it is necessary to rely on this statement or else a serious offender will escape the clutches of criminal law.

(d) Both (b) and (c).

73. PRINCIPLE: No tenant of immovable property shall, during the continuance of the tenancy, be permitted to deny that the landlord of such tenant had, at the beginning of the tenancy, a title to such immovable property.

FACTS: Aishwarya rented a flat from Nidhi for 2 years. She signed a rent agreement and regularly paid the monthly rent to Nidhi for 6 months. In the seventh month, Ashish approached Aishwarya and told her that he is the real owner of the property and that Nidhi is defrauding Aishwarya as well as Ashish. Ashish showed Aishwarya the original property papers which showed him to be the real owner. Satisfied that the papers were genuine and that Ashish is the actual owner, Aishwarya stopped paying the rent to Nidhi and started paying the same to Ashish. Nidhi filed a suit against Aishwarya for the recovery of rent arrears. Aishwarya took the defence that Nidhi was never the real owner of the flat and that she will pay the rent to the real owner, i.e., Ashish. Decide.

(a) Aishwarya should pay the rent to Nidhi since she took the property on rent from Nidhi and now she cannot deny Nidhi's title over the property.
(b) Aishwarya has checked the property papers herself and it is clear to her that Ashish is the actual owner. Thus, she can deny Nidhi's title and should pay the rent to Ashish.
(c) Aishwarya should deposit the money in court and let the court decide who to give the money to.
(d) A disputed property should never be given on rent until the dispute is resolved.

74. PRINCIPLE: A person who suffers an injury caused as a result of a risk to which they consented, cannot complain of the consequent damage. The defendant must have the capacity to give consent to risks involved, have complete knowledge of the extent as well as nature of risks and agree to the risk voluntarily.

FACTS: Q urged his older brother Z to allow him to ride Z's motorbike. Q had recently obtained a motorbike driving license and was eager to ride Z's motorbike. The motorbike had a complex operation mechanism, which Q did not understand. Z did not bother to explain this to Q and let him ride the bike. Q met with an accident and is suing Z for the injuries caused. Z contends that Q consented to the risk. Decide.

(a) Q did not consent to the risk because he did not have capacity to consent to the risk.
(b) Q did not consent to the risk because his consent was not voluntary.
(c) Q consented to the risk because he urged Z to let him ride the motorbike.
(d) Q did not consent to the risk because he did not have knowledge of the extent and nature of risk.

Questions 75 and 76 Have Same Principles.

75. PRINCIPLE: An employer is liable for the acts of their employee if a tort is committed by the employee in the course of employment.

To determine whether an act falls within the course of employment, one must look at the functions/work that the employee was tasked with and then evaluate if there was a close connection between the employee's job function and the wrongful act in question.

FACTS: G was employed as a security guard by a restaurant. He was tasked with maintaining security around the restaurant and escorting guests inside. One night after G's shift, a group of unruly passers-by initiated an altercation with G near the restaurant. Greatly upset by the altercation, G went home and got into an inebriated state. In this state, he negligently caused a fire in his home. G's family members wish to make the restaurant liable.

(a) The restaurant is liable for G's actions because G would not have had the altercation but for being present in that location due to his job.
(b) The restaurant is liable for G's actions because a security guard is likely to have altercations with people in the course of employment.
(c) The restaurant is not liable for G's actions because his acts were outside the course of employment.
(d) None of the above.

76. PRINCIPLE: Same As Q. 75

FACTS: G was employed as a security guard by a restaurant. He was tasked with maintaining security in and around the restaurant as well as escorting guests inside. One night a group of unruly guests got into a verbal altercation with G in the restaurant. G, being short-tempered, got irritated and ended up hitting one of the guests. The guests wish to make the restaurant liable.

(a) The restaurant is liable for G's actions because his acts were within the course of employment.
(b) The restaurant is not liable for G's actions because the guests had started the fight.
(c) The restaurant is not liable for G's actions because his acts were outside the course of employment.
(d) None of the above.

77. PRINCIPLE: Whoever, takes any movable property out of the possession of any person without that person's consent, moves that property in order to such taking, is said to commit theft.

FACTS: W visits her friend B's house for a party. She noticed that B possessed a rare gold ornament. Fearing search and detection if she took the ornament, W hid it in an air duct in the ceiling, where it was unlikely to be discovered by B. W intended on returning to B's house at a future date to take the ornament. Has W committed theft?

(a) No, because she did not take the ring with her.
(b) Yes, W committed theft when she moved the ring.
(c) No, because she did not take the ring out of the possession of B.
(d) None of the above.

78. PRINCIPLE: Whoever, intending to dishonestly take any movable property out of the possession of any person without that person's consent, moves that property in order to such taking, is said to commit theft.

FACTS: R owns an antique watch but is unsure of its value. She took it to a jeweller Y for a free valuation that was offered by Y. Y took the watch home instead of valuing it and does not provide any explanation. R enters Y's home, pushes Y to one side, and retrieves her watch by force. Has R committed theft?

(a) Yes, because R took the watch out of Y's possession.
(b) Yes, because R unlawfully entered Y's home.
(c) Yes, because R assaulted Y.
(d) None of the above.

79. PRINCIPLE: Whoever enters into or upon property in the possession of another with intent to commit an offence in relation to that property or to intimidate, insult or annoy any person in possession of such property is said to commit criminal trespass.

FACTS: H entered his friend L's property because it was adjoining C's home. From L's garden, H shouted insults and tried to intimidate C. C seeks to sue for criminal trespass.

(a) H committed criminal trespass.
(b) L committed criminal trespass.
(c) H did not commit criminal trespass.
(d) None of the above

80. PRINCIPLE: Whoever gives a gratification to any person with the object of inducing him or any other person to exercise any electoral right or of rewarding any person for having exercised any such right commits the offence of bribery.

FACTS: Mr. T, a candidate for elections, decided to visit rural households as part of an election campaign. He visited a household where an elderly man 'A' required an immediate but extremely expensive life-saving medical procedure. Mr. T gave money to the family for the operation. While leaving, he drew the family's attention towards his party's symbol in light of the upcoming elections. Has Mr. T committed the offence of bribery?

(a) Yes, he has committed the offence of bribery.
(b) No, he has not committed the offence of bribery. His intentions were noble.
(c) No, as doing public good outweighs criminal intentions.
(d) None of the above.

81. PRINCIPLE: Whoever causes death by doing an act with the intention of causing death, or with the intention of causing such bodily injury as is likely to cause death, or with the knowledge that he is likely by such act to cause death, commits the offence of culpable homicide.

FACTS: P was hunting in a small forested area which he knew to be inhabited by villagers and frequented by other hunters in large numbers. His friends did not know that other persons were likely to be present in the area. P wagered with his friends that he could hunt without using his visual senses. P put on a blindfold and on hearing some rustling leaves, shot multiple times, killing three people in the process. Has P committed culpable homicide?

(a) P has committed culpable homicide.
(b) P has not committed culpable homicide.
(c) P has committed battery.
(d) None of the above.

82. PRINCIPLE: Fraud includes the suggestion, as a fact, of that which is not true, by one who does not believe it to be true or the active concealment of a fact by one having knowledge or belief of the fact, with intent to deceive another party or her agent to enter into the contract.

FACTS: Wind-on Ltd. is a leading manufacturer of wind turbines to harness wind energy to produce electricity. It is based out of Nagaland in India and has been manufacturing wind turbines since the early 1990s with national and international fame. Z Infrastructures Ltd. is a leading infrastructure firm with a proven track record in building energy installations and highways across India. Z Infrastructures wanted to expand its portfolio and operate a wind energy park to supply clean electricity. Representatives from Wind-on and Z Infrastructures carried out extensive negotiations, advised by leading law firms and commercial advisory firms on both sides, for the latter to establish a wind park in Odisha. Z Infrastructure wanted Wind-on to guarantee that the turbines will generate 54 lakhs Kwh of energy per turbine annually. Wind-on's stated position was that generation of energy is dependent on availability of wind and they could not guarantee it. However, they provided an 'estimate' in the contract for supply of turbines that the turbines will be able to generate around 50 lakhs Kwh per turbine annually. The turbines were supplied by Wind-on and operated by Z Infrastructure in Odisha for over 2 years. During this period, Z Infrastructure found that the average energy generation of each turbine came to around 35 lakhs Kwh annually. They were frustrated as the actual generation of each turbine was significantly lower than the generation estimate provided by Wind-on. They reached out to Lal & Co., a leading dispute resolution law firm to understand if they could initiate action against Wind-on for fraudulently representing the generation estimate of each turbine.

You are a lawyer at Lal & Co., and were asked if Wind-on had committed fraud by providing an inflated energy generation estimate. What will be your opinion?

(a) Yes, as Wind-on was an expert in the wind turbine business and Z infrastructure relied on its expertise as a new entrant in the field.
(b) No, as Wind-on clearly specified that the energy generation figure was merely an estimate and it could not provide a guarantee.
(c) Yes, as Wind-on should have predicted a figure that was closer to the actual generation figure of 35 lakhs Kwh per turbine per annum.
(d) Yes, as Wind-on should not have provided any estimate at all.

83. PRINCIPLE 1: A 'bailment' is the delivery of goods by one person to another for some purpose, upon a contract that they shall, when the purpose is accomplished, be returned. The person delivering the goods is called the 'bailor'. The person to whom they are delivered is called the 'bailee'.

PRINCIPLE 2: In all cases of bailment the bailee is bound to take as much care of the goods bailed to him/her as a person of ordinary prudence would, under similar circumstances, take of his/her own goods of the same bulk, quantity and value as the goods bailed.

FACTS: Aparna entered into a contract with Gagan to keep her goods in his warehouse until she was able to find a suitable buyer for them. Gagan kept his own goods also at the same warehouse. One night, certain thieves entered the warehouse and stole the goods of both Gagan and Aparna. It was discovered that even though Gagan had locked the main door, he had carelessly left the windows open and that the thieves had entered through the open windows. Aparna sued Gagan for damages as Gagan had failed to take due care of her goods. Decide.

(a) Gagan is liable since he left the windows open which shows that he did not take as much care as a person of ordinary prudence.
(b) Gagan is not liable since he took as much care of Aparna's goods as he took of his own goods.
(c) Gagan is not liable since he locked the door and a person of ordinary prudence cannot be expected to check the windows as well.
(d) None of the above.

84. PRINCIPLE 1: There are four stages of commission of any offence- formation of intention, preparation, attempt and commission of offence. The first two stages are not punishable but the last two stages are punishable. The attempt to commit an offence is an offence in itself.

PRINCIPLE 2: In order to be designated as an attempt to commit an offence, the act or series of acts done must be sufficiently proximate to the accomplishment of the intended offence.

FACTS: Sachin bought a matchbox and lit a match near a haystack. He was about to light the haystack on fire and commit the offence of arson. However, before he could do the same, he realized that someone was secretly recording a video of him. Fearing that he would be easily caught, he extinguished the match. Sachin is prosecuted for the attempt to commit arson. Decide.

(a) Sachin is not guilty of having committed attempt to arson as his act of lighting the match was not the penultimate act before the commission of the intended offence.
(b) Sachin is guilty of having committed attempt to arson as lighting the match was the penultimate act before the commission of the intended offence.
(c) Sachin is not guilty since the match was extinguished by him on his own.
(d) Sachin is guilty of having committed attempt to arson since there is sufficient proximity between the act of lighting the match and the intended offence of arson.

85. PRINCIPLE: Double jeopardy: No person shall be prosecuted and punished for the same offence more than once.

FACTS: Arun was a Government Employee working in the examination and admissions department of Indian Institute of Science and Technology (IIST), the best engineering college in India. Arun was accused of having leaked the entrance examination paper to Kamlesh for a hefty bribe. Disciplinary proceedings were initiated against Kamlesh by IIST wherein he was found guilty and as a penalty, he was removed from employment. Thereafter, a criminal case was registered against him for having committed the offence of cheating by leaking the entrance paper. Arun takes the defence that the criminal prosecution is not permitted by the principle of double jeopardy. Decide.

(a) The principle of double jeopardy will not apply as the disciplinary proceedings by IIST cannot be termed as prosecution since they were mere departmental proceedings and not criminal prosecution.
(b) The principle of double jeopardy will apply as Arun has already been found guilty and punished by IIST.
(c) The principle of double jeopardy will not apply as Arun is accused of a serious offence of cheating the public at large.
(d) Both (a) and (c).

86. PRINCIPLE: Nuisance shall be defined as use of land in a manner that causes unreasonable interference with another's enjoyment of their land.

It is no defence to a claim of nuisance to say that the plaintiff(s) knew of the interference that would be caused.

FACTS: The village of Xandiapur has a centuries old cricket ground which is owned by Xandiapur Cricket Club and hosts matches between local teams every week. It is the only sports ground in the village and serves as a critical source of recreation for the villagers. Mr. and Mrs. XYZ purchased a home right on the edge of the cricket ground's boundary. Balls from cricket matches frequently fall into their residence's garden and have caused severe damage to their windows. They have unsuccessfully tried to request the Cricket Club to install nets around the part of the boundary that is adjacent to their home. They seek to claim nuisance against the Xandiapur Cricket Club.

(a) Mr. and Mrs. XYZ will be unsuccessful because it is their fault—they purchased a home on the edge of a cricket ground. Further, the cricket ground is important for recreation.
(b) Mr. and Mrs. XYZ will be successful because use of the cricket ground is causing unreasonable interference with their enjoyment of their home. Further, the Cricket Club cannot claim that Mr. and Mrs. XYZ brought trouble on their head.
(c) Mr. and Mrs. XYZ will be unsuccessful because even though the ground is a source of interference, it is not unreasonable interference.
(d) Mr. and Mrs. XYZ will be successful because they are old and have a right to live peacefully.

87. PRINCIPLE: Any invasion of private property, howsoever minor, is a trespass unless it is expressly authorised by the law.

Police personnel may enter and/or search private property only on express authorisation from a Judicial Officer.

FACTS: Ms. A, a vocal critic of certain policies of the Queen of Asgardia, was due to lead a protest against prevailing government policies. Solely on the instructions of the Queen, a Police Officer secretly entered Ms. A residence to search through her computer and discover her plan for the protest. However, Ms. A's laptop was at the repair shop and the Police Officer was forced to exit Ms. A's house after a few seconds. Ms. A seeks to sue for trespass.

(a) Ms. A will be successful since the Queen was planning on quelling dissent through illegal means.
(b) Ms. A will be unsuccessful since the search was authorised by the Queen.
(c) Ms. A will be successful since the entry of the Police Officer constituted an invasion of personal property without authorisation from a Judicial Officer.
(d) Ms. A will be unsuccessful since the Police Officer was at her residence for only a few seconds and was unable to access her computer. There was no invasion of personal property.

88. PRINCIPLE: The doctrine of privity mandates that only a party to a contract can claim upon it.

FACTS: P started the business of manufacturing table lamps which he sold to a distributor ('Q') who in turn sold the lamps to a store owner ('R') in the city. P entered into an agreement with Q which mandated that Q can only sell the lamps to store owners at a minimum retail price of ₹50, failing which Q would have to pay P ₹5 for each lamp sold below ₹50. Q entered into an identical contract with R, mandating that R can only sell the lamps to customers for ₹50, failing which R would have to pay Q ₹5 for each lamp sold below ₹50. R sold a lamp to a customer for ₹40 and P seeks to claim against R.

(a) P will not be successful since there is no privity of contract between P and R.
(b) P will not be successful since R is free to sell the product at the price of their choosing.
(c) P will not be successful since Q has not been made a party to the proceedings.
(d) P will not be successful since there is no privity of contract between P and Q.

89. PRINCIPLE: Competence to contract is essential for an agreement to be considered a contract.

'Competence to contract': Any person who is of the age of majority according to the applicable law and is of sound mind and is not disqualified from contracting by any applicable law.
'Age of majority': Every person shall attain the age of majority on their completing 18 years of age and not before.

FACTS: Z sought to purchase a property belonging to K (a minor) two days before K completed 18 years of age. K really liked Z's offer and six months later they entered into a contract for sale of the property to Z. Was K competent to contract?

(a) K was not competent to contract because he was influenced by Z when K was a minor.
(b) K is competent to contract because he entered into the contract after completing 18 years of age.
(c) K was not competent to contract because Z had approached him before he completed 18 years of age.
(d) None of the above.

90. PRINCIPLE: Acceptance must be communicated to the offeror to constitute a binding contract. Mere intention to accept, without communication does not lead to a contract.

FACTS: J wanted to purchase her uncle T's television. J wrote a letter to T indicating that she wished to purchase his television for ₹5,000. T was pleased with J's offer and decided to call J to accept the offer. T called J twice, but J did not pick up her phone. The next day, T found a buyer for the television for ₹6,000 and sold the television to this buyer. J is alleging breach of contract.

(a) J will be unsuccessful because even though the contract was binding, T found a buyer who offered a higher price for the television.
(b) J will be successful because T's action of calling J is equivalent to communication of acceptance.
(c) J will be successful because T was happy with J's offer and had intended to accept.
(d) J will be unsuccessful since T's acceptance had not been communicated to constitute a binding contract.

91. PRINCIPLE: In relation to the law of contracts, in instances where both parties to an agreement are under a mistake about a matter of fact essential to the agreement, the agreement is void.

FACTS: L agrees to sell to M a consignment of food grains which was supposed to be on a ship on its way from Africa to Mumbai. However, two days before the agreement was reached, the ship carrying the grains met with an accident and all the goods were lost. L's agent had informed L about this on the day the accident happened. Is the agreement void because of a mistake as to a matter of fact?

(a) Yes, since both parties committed a mistake by entering into the contract.
(b) No, since L had dishonest intentions.
(c) No, since L was aware that the goods were lost.
(d) None of the above.

92. PRINCIPLE: Both parties to a contract are discharged from their respective outstanding obligations in situations where a supervening event significantly changes the nature of contractual rights and/or obligations from what the parties could have reasonably contemplated at the time of executing the contract.
The supervening event must not be a result of default by either party, nor should the contract make a provision for it.

FACTS: In the city of Vortoria which is highly susceptible to public health crises, S (a supplier of raw food products) entered into a contract with H (a restaurant owner) for 2 years, whereby S would supply certain raw products to H at predetermined prices. Their agreement also provided that - 'In case of interruption of operations of H on account of epidemics, pandemics or any other public health crisis, the contract will be suspended until the crisis is declared to be over by the government and thereafter pending contractual obligations shall resume.'
Three months were left on the contract when there was a highly contagious virus outbreak in the city,

which caused restaurant owners (including H) to suspend operations. Once the outbreak was declared to be over six months later, H refused to purchase raw materials from S arguing that he was discharged from obligations under the contract.

(a) H is discharged from his obligations because the virus outbreak was a supervening event which changed the nature of contractual rights and obligations.
(b) H is not discharged from his obligations because the contract contained a provision dealing with outbreaks. Further the parties could have reasonably contemplated the occurrence of an outbreak.
(c) H is not discharged from his obligations because the contract had ended by the time the virus was declared to be over.
(d) H is discharged from his obligations because the outbreak is likely to have affected his business badly.

93. PRINCIPLE: When a defendant brings onto their land anything that is likely to do mischief in case it escapes, they must do so at their own peril. If such a thing does escape and causes foreseeable harm, then the defendant is liable for damage caused provided that the land from which escape occurs had been changed such that it would be considered a non-natural use of the land.

The defendant can avoid liability if they can show that the situation that caused damage was a result of an unforeseeable act of a stranger, which could not be controlled by the defendant.

FACTS: M decided to keep a tiger as a pet and to that end, he brought a caged tiger to his house. Jealous of M's pet, M's neighbour S (whom M had never met) decided to break into M's heavily guarded house while M was away and open the tiger's cage. The tiger escaped and mauled pedestrians near the house. The pedestrians wish to sue M for damages. Decide.

(a) The pedestrians will be successful because it is illegal to keep a tiger as a pet.
(b) The pedestrians can claim against M because he brought a dangerous thing onto his land (amounting to non-natural use) and it escaped, causing foreseeable damage. The escape should have been foreseen by M.
(c) M can escape liability because the escape was caused by the unforeseeable act of a stranger, which could not have been controlled by M.
(d) None of the above.

94. PRINCIPLE: Agreements, the meaning of which is not certain, or capable of being made certain, are void.

FACTS: Ila Nayak wants to buy a motorbike to reduce her waiting time for her daily commute to work. She can pay up to ₹35,000 for a second hand motorbike. Dev Patnaik agrees to sell his recently purchased Honda motorbike to Ila for ₹31,000 or ₹30,000. Decide.

(a) This is a valid agreement since Ila can pay up to thirty five thousand rupees for Dev's motorbike.
(b) This agreement is void for uncertainty since there is nothing to show which of the two prices was finally agreed.
(c) This agreement is voidable at the option of Ila.
(d) This agreement is valid as there is an offer from Dev and acceptance from Ila.

95. PRINCIPLE: Agreements, the meaning of which is not certain, or capable of being made certain, are void.

FACTS: Ila Nayak wants to buy a motorbike to reduce her waiting time for her daily commute to work. She can pay up to ₹35,000 for a second hand motorbike. Dev and Ila agree that Ila will initially pay a sum of ₹31,000 for the motorbike and if the mileage given by the motorbike exceeds 60 km per litre on an average for five months following the sale - then Ila will pay an additional sum of ₹3,000. Is this a valid agreement?

(a) This is an invalid agreement since Ila is not paying the entire price of the motorbike at once.
(b) This is a valid agreement as the price of the motorbike is capable of being made certain.

(c) This is a valid agreement as Ila has already paid thirty one thousand rupees which was accepted by Dev.
(d) This is an invalid agreement since Dev and Ila can disagree if the motorbike was actually able to give a mileage of 60 km per litre for five months.

96. PRINCIPLE: Damages consequent to a breach of contract seek to compensate the innocent party for the loss suffered by it so that the innocent party is put in the same situation, with respect to damages so far as money can do it, as if the contract had been performed.

FACTS: A agrees to sell 30 kgs of strawberries to B knowing that B uses the strawberries to run his juice center. B's juice center is located off St. John's College of Delhi University, and is very popular with the students. A supplies sub-standard quality of strawberries to B. However, B is able to use all the strawberries for his juice centre. None of the customers of B are able to make out the difference or complain about the juice or for that matter face any issues after drinking the juice. Can B recover damages from A?
(a) A is liable to compensate B for supplying sub-standard quality of strawberries.
(b) A is not liable to compensate B since B suffers no monetary loss.
(c) A is not liable to compensate B because the contract did not prevent A from supplying sub-standard quality of strawberries.
(d) A is not liable to compensate B since none of the customers of B have proceeded against A for supplying bad quality strawberry juice.

97. Name the only erstwhile princely State in India that was allowed to have its own separate Constitution on its accession to India.
(a) Hyderabad
(b) Jammu & Kashmir
(c) Baroda
(d) Gwalior

98. Which of the following statements accurately captures India's position on torture?
(a) India is a not a signatory to the UN Convention Against Torture.
(b) India has signed the UN Convention Against Torture but has not ratified it.
(c) The Supreme Court has asked the Union of India to introduce a domestic legislation against torture.
(d) Torture is defined as a crime in the Indian Penal Code.

99. 'Basmati' rice is an example of what type of intellectual property?
(a) Geographical indication
(b) Copyright
(c) Trade secret
(d) Domain name

100. In Part VIII of the Constitution of India, the Parliament is empowered to create local legislature and council of ministers for certain Union Territories. Name the Union Territory or Territories in India that have a legislative assembly and council of ministers.
(a) NCT of Delhi only
(b) Chandigarh only
(c) NCT of Delhi, Puducherry and Jammu & Kashmir
(d) NCT of Delhi and Puducherry

101. Who is the only Judge of the Supreme Court of India to also have been the Vice President of India?
(a) Justice A. N. Ray
(b) Justice Mohammad Hidayatullah
(c) Justice Patanjali Sastri
(d) Justice P. N. Bhagwati

102. Who replaced Justice Ruth Bader Ginsburg on the Supreme Court of the United States?
(a) Neil Gorsuch
(b) Brett Kavanaugh
(c) Amy Coney Barrett
(d) Sonia Sotomayor

103. Which of the following positions is not provided for in the Constitution of India?
(a) Attorney General for India
(b) Solicitor General of India
(c) Advocate General of the State
(d) Chairperson of the Union Public Service Commission

104. In Kulbhushan Jadhav's case between India and Pakistan before the International Court of Justice, the 15-1 majority found Pakistan to be in violation of obligations under which international law instrument?
(a) Vienna Convention on Consular Relations
(b) International Convention on Civil and Political Rights
(c) United Nations Standard Minimum Rules for the Treatment of Prisoners
(d) United Nations Convention Against Torture

105. Who among the following was not a judge of the Supreme Court of India?
(a) Justice R. Banumathi
(b) Justice Gyan Sudha Mishra
(c) Justice Manjula Chellur
(d) Justice Ranjana Prakash Desai

REASONING

Read the following passage and answer questions 106–108 that follow:

A tennis coach is trying to put together a team of four players for the forthcoming tournament. For this, 7 players are available : males A, B and C and females W, X, Y and Z. All players have equal capability and at least 2 males will have to be there in the team. For a team of four, all players must be able to play with each other. But, B cannot play with W, C cannot play with Z and W cannot play with Y.

106. If Y is selected and B is rejected, then the team will consist of which one of the following groups?
(a) A, C, W and Y
(b) A, C, X and Y
(c) A, C, Y and Z
(d) A, W, Y and Z

107. If B is selected and Y is rejected, then the team will consist of which of the following groups?
(a) A, B, C and W
(b) A, B, C and Y
(c) A, B, C and X
(d) A, W, Y and Z

108. If all the three males are selected, then how many combinations of four-member teams are possible?
(a) 1 (b) 2
(c) 3 (d) 4

In each of the following questions (109 to 115), a statement followed by some assumptions are given. An assumption is something supposed or taken for granted. You have to consider the statement and decide which of the assumptions is implicit in the statement?

Choose the most appropriate answer/
(a) If only assumption I is implicit.
(b) If only assumption II is implicit.
(c) If neither assumption I nor II is implicit.
(d) If both assumptions I and II are implicit.

109. **Statement:** Be humble even after gaining victory.
Assumptions:
1. Many people are humble after gaining victory.
2. Generally, people are not humble.

110. **Statement:** The target of a fiscal deficit of 5% of GDP could not be met, because of a major shortfall in revenue collections.
Assumptions:
1. Shortfall in revenue collections lead to an increase in fiscal deficit.
2. Shortfall in revenue collections lead to a decrease in fiscal deficit.

111. **Statement:** The Government has decided to run all commercial vehicles only on biofuels in order to save the depleting fossil fuel reserves.
Assumptions:
1. It is possible to switch over from fossil fuel to biofuels for vehicles.
2. Sufficient amount of biofuel can be produced in the country to run all commercial vehicles.

112. Statement: COVID-19 is a pandemic issue now.
Assumptions:
1. Government should work towards complete eradication of diseases like COVID-19.
2. COVID-19 is not a serious disease and treatment is available.

113. Statement: Drastic increase in pollution is now a global phenomenon.
Assumptions:
1. All countries have realized it and are working towards control.
2. Growing population, industries, highways and constructions are beyond control.

114. Statement: Minute traces of nitrate sometimes present in cattle fodder B may be responsible for the poor health of the cattle. Therefore, use fodder G to ensure that your cattle remain healthy.
Assumptions:
1. Cattle fodder G does not contain nitrate.
2. Nitrate is toxic to all living beings.

115. Statement: The impact of economic sanctions on an economy that is already so weak could be devastating.
Assumptions :
1. Economic sanctions impact only a weak economy.
2. The impact of economic sanctions varies from economy to economy.

116. Consider the following statements.
I. All machines consume energy.
II. Electricity provides energy.
III. Electric machines are cheap to maintain.
IV. Electric machines do not cause pollution.

Which one of the following inferences can be drawn from the above statements?
(a) All machines are run by electric energy.
(b) There is no form of energy other than electricity.
(c) Most machines are operated on electric energy.
(d) Electrically operated machines are preferable to use.

117. India's neighbouring countries have seen a surge in their imports of the metal. This gold is then being carried across into India by smugglers. Which of the following inferences can best be drawn from the above statements?
(a) There is a duty differential between India and its neighbouring countries.
(b) The tough restriction on the metal's imports could be eased.
(c) India has a high current account deficit.
(d) There has been a sharp depreciation of the rupee.

118. A new apparel store has been opened by a telecom company XYZ, from which customers have very high expectations.
Which of the following statements can be inferred from the above statement?
(a) Apparel stores were previously operated in telecom industry only.
(b) Expansion is the best strategy to have competitive edge in the market.
(c) To be successful in an expansion, one needs to be a leader in telecom industry.
(d) XYZ has already established brand name in the market through its telecom business.

In the following questions (119 to 123), a statement is given followed by some arguments. Study the statement carefully and mark the correct alternative.

119. Statement: Should the government impose restrictions on access to sensitive information to journalists to avoid media hype?
Arguments:
I. Yes, the media creates hype and publishes distorted information at times.
II. No, journalists should have access to all the information as media is the best source to expose the malfunctions in the society.
III. Yes, at times it leads to harassment of those who are affected and alleged to be involved in the crisis.
(a) Arguments I and II are strong.
(b) Arguments II and III are strong.
(c) Arguments I, II and III are strong.
(d) None of the above.

120. Statement: Should the Government introduce a system of obtaining bonds from students for working in India before sanctioning education loans for higher studies?

Arguments:

I. No, this is not a workable solution and will obstruct the development of young talent in the country.

II. Yes, this is the only way to ensure use of the talent of our country for the development of the country and not only an individual.

III. No, this step will be too harsh.

(a) Only argument I is strong.
(b) Only argument II is strong.
(c) Arguments I and II are strong.
(d) None is strong.

121. Statement: Should people with educational qualification higher than the optimum requirements be debarred from seeking jobs?

Arguments:

I. No, it will further aggravate the problem of educated unemployment.

II. Yes, it creates insecurities among employees and affects the work adversely.

III. No, this goes against the basic rights of the individuals.

IV. Yes, this will increase productivity.

(a) Argument I is strong.
(b) Argument II is strong.
(c) Argument III is strong.
(d) All arguments are strong.

122. Statement: Should all the youngsters below the age of 21 years be disallowed from going to a pub?

Arguments:

I. No, it is not correct to prevent matured youngsters above 18 years of age, who can vote, from having fun.

II. Yes, the entry fee to such pubs should also be hiked.

III. No, there is no such curb in Western countries.

IV. Yes, this will help in preventing youngsters from imbibing unhealthy habits.

(a) Only argument I is strong.
(b) Arguments I and III are strong.
(c) Arguments III and IV are strong.
(d) Arguments I and IV are strong.

123. Statement: Should all the school teachers be debarred from giving private tuitions?

Arguments :

I. No, the needy students will be deprived of the expertise of these teachers.

II. Yes, this is an injustice to the unemployed educated people, who can earn their living by giving tuitions.

III. Yes, only then the quality of teaching in schools will improve.

IV. Yes, now salary of these teachers is reasonable.

(a) Arguments I and III are strong.
(b) Arguments III and IV are strong.
(c) Arguments I, II and III are strong.
(d) None of the above.

124. Statement: In a one-day cricket match, the total runs made by a team were 200. Out of these 160 runs were made by spinners.

Conclusions:

I. 80% of the team consists of spinners.

II. The opening batsmen were spinners.

(a) Only conclusion I follows.
(b) Only conclusion II follows.
(c) Either I or II follows.
(d) Neither I nor II follows.

125. Statement: The old order changed yielding place to new. **Conclusions:**

I. Change is the law of nature.

II. Discard old ideas because they are old.

(a) Only conclusion I follows.
(b) Only conclusion II follows.
(c) Either I or II follows.
(d) Neither I nor II follows.

126. Statement: Prime age school-going children in urban India have now become avid as well as more regular viewers of television, even in households without a TV. As a result, there has been an alarming decline in the extent of readership of newspapers.

Conclusions:

I. Method of increasing the readership of newspapers should be devised.

II. A team of experts should be sent to other countries to study the impact of TV on the readership of newspapers.
   (a) Only conclusion I follows.
   (b) Only conclusion II follows.
   (c) Either I or II follows.
   (d) Neither I nor II follows.

127. Statement: The standard of education in private schools is much better than Municipal and Zilla Parishad-run schools.

Conclusions:

I. The Municipal and Zilla Parishad should make serious efforts to improve standard of their schools.

II. All Municipal and Zill a Parishad schools should be closed immediately.
   (a) Only conclusion I follows.
   (b) Only conclusion II follows.
   (c) Either I or II follows.
   (d) Neither I nor II follows.

128. Statement: Domestic demand has been increasing faster than the production of indigenous crude oil.

Conclusions:

I. Crude oil must be imported.

II. Domestic demand should be reduced.
   (a) Only conclusion I follows.
   (b) Only conclusion II follows.
   (c) Either I or II follows.
   (d) Neither I nor II follows.

***Direction* to Solve questions (129–131):** *Each of the following questions contains a small paragraph followed by a question on it. Read each paragraph carefully and answer the question given below it.*

129. The attainment of individual and organisational goals is mutually interdependent and linked by a common denominator - employee work motivation. Organisational members are motivated to satisfy their personal goals, and they contribute their efforts to the attainment of organisational objectives as means of achieving these personal goals.

The passage best supports the statement that motivation:
   (a) encourages an individual to give priority to personal goals over organisational goals.
   (b) is crucial for the survival of an individual and organisation.
   (c) is the product of an individual's physical and mental energy.
   (d) is the external force which induces an individual to contribute his efforts.

130. Due to enormous profits involved in smuggling, hundreds of persons have been attracted towards this anti-national activity. Some of them became millionaires overnight. India has a vast coastline both on the Eastern and Western Coast. It has been a heaven for smugglers who have been carrying on their activities with great impunity. There is no doubt, that from time to time certain seizures were made by the enforcement authorities, during raids and ambush but even allowing these losses the smugglers made huge profits.

The passage best supports the statement that :
   (a) smuggling hampers the economic development of a nation.
   (b) smuggling ought to be curbed.
   (c) authorities are taking strict measures to curb smuggling.
   (d) smuggling is fast increasing in our country owing to the quick profit it entails.

131. Exports and imports, a swelling favourable balance of trade, investments and bank-balances, are not an index or a balance sheet of national prosperity. Till the beginning of the Second World War, English exports were noticeably greater than what they are today. And yet England has greater national prosperity today than it ever had. Because the income of average Englishmen, working as field and factory labourers, clerks, policemen, petty shopkeepers and shop assistants, domestic workers and other low-paid workers, has gone up.

The passage best supports the statement that :

(a) a country's balance of trade is the main criteria of determining its economic prosperity.
(b) a country's economic standard can be best adjudged by per capita income.
(c) a nation's economy strengthens with the increase in exports.
(d) english trade has continually increased since the Second World War.

Direction questions (132–134): *Understand the relation between the set of words and choose the correct options:*

132. FISH: SCHOOL
(a) wolf : pack (b) cow : farm
(c) herd : peacock (d) elephant : jungle

133. PASTORAL: RURAL
(a) harvest : autumn
(b) sleepy : nocturnal
(c) metropolitan : urban
(d) agrarian : benevolent

134. SOUND : CACOPHONY
(a) speech : oration (b) touch : massage
(c) smell : stench (d) taste : style

Direction questions 135 and 136: *Identify the missing letters in the sets of Letter Series given below:*

135. QPO, NML, KJI,__________, EDC.
(a) HGF (b) CAB
(c) JKM (d) GHD

136. ATNHG, DKCMB, CVPJI, GNFPE, EXRLK, JQISH, GZTNM,_
(a) QMTH (b) TLVK
(c) RIJTU (d) HSKUJ

137. Ramesh travelled from a point and straight to Y at a distance of 90 m. He turned right and walked 40 m, then again turned right and walked 70 m. Finally, he turned right and walked 40 m. How far he is from the starting point?
(a) 70 m (b) 10 m
(c) 20 m (d) 30 m

138. Ram and Sunil start from a fixed point. Ram moves 4 km to the South, then turns left and moves 3 km. Sunil moves 3 km towards West, then turns right and moves 4 km further. How far apart are they now?
(a) 7 km (b) 13 km
(c) 10 km (d) 14 km

139. Rashmi travels 10 km towards the north, turns left and travels 4 km and then again turns right and covers another 5 km and then turns right and travels another 4 km. How far is she from the starting point?
(a) 5 km (b) 10 km
(c) 19 km (d) 15 km

140. Man : Biography : : Nation:?
(a) Geography (b) History
(c) People (d) Leader

MATHEMATICS

141. 500 students are taking one or more courses out of Chemistry, Physics and Mathematics. Registration records indicate course enrolment as follows : Chemistry (329), Physics (186), Mathematics (295), Chemistry and Physics (83), Chemistry and Mathematics (217) and Physics and Mathematics (63). How many students are taking all 3 subjects?
(a) 37 (b) 53
(c) 47 (d) 43

142. X bullocks and Y tractors take 8 days to plough a field. If we halve the number of bullocks and double the number of tractors, it takes 5 days to plough the same field. How many days will it take for X bullocks alone to plough the field?
(a) 30 (b) 35
(c) 40 (d) 45

143. If the radius of a right circular cone is increased by 50%, its volume increases by
(a) 75% (b) 100%
(c) 125% (d) 237.5%

144. It takes 30 minutes to empty a half-full tank by draining it at a constant rate. It is decided to simultaneously pump water into the half-full tank while draining it. What is the rate at which water has to be pumped in so that it gets filled in 10 minutes?
(a) 4 times the draining rate
(b) 3 times the draining rate
(c) 2.5 times the draining rate
(d) 2 times the draining rate

145. In the summer of 2012, in New Delhi, the mean temperature of Monday to Wednesday was 41°C and of Tuesday to Thursday was 43°C If the temperature on Thursday was 15% higher than that of Monday, then the temperature in °C on Thursday was
(a) 40 (b) 43
(c) 46 (d) 49

146. Taxi charges in a city consists of fixed charges and remaining depending upon the distance travelled in kilometers. If a person travels 70 kms, he pays ₹1,130 and for travelling 100 kms, he pays ₹1,550. Find the charges for travelling 140 kms.
(a) 2000 (b) 2260
(c) 2170 (d) 2110

147. Amit started a shop by investing ₹5,00,000. In the first year he incurred a loss of 5%. However, during the second year he earned a profit of 10% which in the third year rose to 12%. Calculate his % Profit.
(a) 12% (b) 17%
(c) 19% (d) 15%

148. A sum invested at compound interest amounts to ₹8,800 in 1 year and to ₹10,648 in 3 years. Calculate the rate percent and the sum.
(a) 10 and ₹8,000
(b) 12 and ₹5,000
(c) 10 and ₹6,000
(d) 12 and ₹8,000

149. If the price of sugar increased by 25%, by how much percent a housewife should reduce the consumption so as not to increase the expenditure.
(a) 25% (b) 20%
(c) 22.5% (d) 27.5%

150. A, B and C can finish a piece of work in 12, 15 and 20 days respectively. If all the three work at it together andtheyarepaid₹9,600forthewholework,whatisB's share?
(a) 4,000 (b) 3,200
(c) 2,400 (d) 2,700

ANSWER KEY

English

1. (a) **2.** (c) **3.** (b) **4.** (d) **5.** (c) **6.** (b) **7.** (d) **8.** (a) **9.** (b) **10.** (a) **11.** (c) **12.** (d) **13.** (a) **14.** (b) **15.** (a) **16.** (a) **17.** (c) **18.** (d) **19.** (b) **20.** (c) **21.** (d) **22.** (a) **23.** (b) **24.** (a) **25.** (d) **26.** (b) **27.** (a) **28.** (a) **29.** (b) **30.** (b) **31.** (b) **32.** (b) **33.** (d) **34.** (c) **35.** (a)

General Knowledge

36. (b) **37.** (d) **38.** (c) **39.** (b) **40.** (c) **41.** (a) **42.** (b) **43.** (b) **44.** (a) **45.** (c) **46.** (a) **47.** (b) **48.** (c) **49.** (d) **50.** (b) **51.** (c) **52.** (d) **53.** (b) **54.** (c) **55.** (d) **56.** (c) **57.** (a) **58.** (c) **59.** (d) **60.** (c) **61.** (c) **62.** (a) **63.** (c) **64.** (a) **65.** (d) **66.** (c) **67.** (c) **68.** (d) **69.** (c) **70.** (c)

Legal Aptitude

71. (d) **72.** (a) **73.** (a) **74.** (d) **75.** (c) **76.** (a) **77.** (b) **78.** (d) **79.** (c) **80.** (a) **81.** (a) **82.** (b) **83.** (a) **84.** (d) **85.** (a) **86.** (b) **87.** (c) **88.** (a) **89.** (b) **90.** (d) **91.** (c) **92.** (b) **93.** (c) **94.** (b) **95.** (b) **96.** (b) **97.** (b) **98.** (b) **99.** (a) **100.** (c) **101.** (b) **102.** (c) **103.** (b) **104.** (a) **105.** (c)

Reasoning

106. (b) **107.** (c) **108.** (b) **109.** (c) **110.** (a) **111.** (d) **112.** (c) **113.** (c) **114.** (a) **115.** (b) **116.** (d) **117.** (a) **118.** (d) **119.** (c) **120.** (a) **121.** (c) **122.** (a) **123.** (d) **124.** (d) **125.** (a) **126.** (d) **127.** (a) **128.** (c) **129.** (a) **130.** (d) **131.** (b) **132.** (a) **133.** (c) **134.** (c) **135.** (a) **136.** (b) **137.** (c) **138.** (c) **139.** (d) **140.** (b)

Mathematics

141. (b) **142.** (a) **143.** (c) **144.** (a) **145.** (c) **146.** (d) **147.** (b) **148.** (a) **149.** (b) **150.** (b)

AILET 2020

Directions (questions 1–5): *Each set of questions in this section is based on the passage. The questions are to be answered on the basis of what is stated or implied in the passage. For some of the questions, more than one of the choices could conceivably answer the question. However, you are to choose the best answer; that is, the response that most accurately and completely answers the questions.*

In order to understand the development of Gangetic Valley plains, scholars have traditionally relied primarily on evidence from historical documents. However, such documentary sources provide a fragmentary record at best. Reliable accounts are very scarce for many parts of Northern India prior to the fifteenth century, and many of the relevant documents from the fourteenth and fifteenth centuries focus selectively on matters relating to cultural or commercial interests.

Studies of fossilized pollens preserved in peats and lake muds provide an additional means of investigating vegetative landscape change. Details of changes in vegetation resulting from both human activities and natural events are reflected in the kinds and quantities of minute pollens that become trapped in sediments. Analysis of samples can identify which kinds of plants produced the preserved pollens and when they were deposited, and in many cases the findings can serve to supplement or correct the documentary record.

For example, analysis of samples from a bay in Jammu has revealed significant patterns of cereal-grain pollens beginning about fourth century. The substantial clay content of the soil in this part of Jammu makes cultivation by primitive tools difficult.

Historians thought that such soils were not tilled to any significant extent until the introduction of the wooden plough to India in the seventh century. Because cereal cultivation would have required tiling of the soil, the pollens evidence indicates that these soils must indeed have been successfully tilled before the introduction of the new plough.

Another example concerns flax cultivation in Jammu, one of the great linen-producing areas of India during the sixteenth century. Some aspects of linen production in Jammu are well documented, but the documentary record tells little about the cultivation of flax, the plant from which linen is made, in that area. The record of sixteenth century linen production in Jammu, together with the knowledge that flax cultivation had been established in India centuries before that time, led some historians to surmise that this plant was being cultivated in Jammu before the sixteenth century. But pollens' analyses indicate that this is not the case; flax pollens were found only in deposits laid down since the sixteenth century.

It must be stressed, though, that there are limits to the ability of the pollen record to reflect the vegetative history of the landscape. For example, pollen analysis cannot identify the species, but only the genus or family, of some plants. Among these is turmeric, a cultivated plant of medicinal importance in India. Turmeric belongs to a plant family that also comprises various native weeds, including Brahma Thandu. If Turmeric pollen were present in a deposit, it would be indistinguishable from that of uncultivated native species.

1. The phrase 'documentary record' (para 2 and 4) primarily refers to

(a) articles, books, and other documents by current historians listing and analyzing all the available evidence regarding a particular historical period.

(b) government and commercial records, maps, and similar documents produced in the past that recoded conditions and events of that time.

(c) documented results of analyses of fossilized pollen.
(d) the kinds and qualities of fossilized pollen grains preserved in peats and lake muds.

2. The passage indicates that pollen analyses have provided evidence against which one of the following views?
(a) In certain parts of Jammu, cereal grains were not cultivated to any significant extent before the seventh century.
(b) Cereal grain cultivation began in Jammu around fourth century.
(c) In certain parts of India, cereal grains have been cultivated continuously since the introduction of the wooden plough.
(d) Cereal grain cultivation requires successful tilling of the soil.

3. The passage indicates that prior to the use of pollen analysis in the study of the history of the Gangetic Valley plains, at least some historians believed which one of the following?
(a) Turmeric was not used as a medicinal plant in India until after the sixteenth century.
(b) Cereal grain was not cultivated anywhere in India until at least the seventh century.
(c) The history of the Gangetic Valley plains during the fourteenth and fifteenth centuries was well documented.
(d) The beginning of flax cultivation in Jammu may well have occurred before the sixteenth century.

4. Which of the following most accurately describes the relationship between the second paragraph and the final paragraph?
(a) The second paragraph describes a view against which the author intends to argue, and the final paragraph states the author's argument against that view.
(b) The second paragraph proposes a hypothesis for which the final paragraph offers a supporting example.
(c) The final paragraph qualifies the claim made in the second paragraph.
(d) The final paragraph describes a problem that must be solved before the method advocated in the second paragraph can be considered viable.

5. Which one of the following most accurately expresses the main point of the passage?
(a) While pollen evidence can sometimes supplement other sources of historical information, its applicability is severely limited, since it cannot be used to identify plant species.
(b) Analysis of fossilized pollen is a useful means of supplementing and in some cases correcting other sources of information regarding changes in the Gangetic Valley plains.
(c) Analysis of fossilized pollen has provided new evidence that the cultivation of such crops as cereal grains, flax, and turmeric had a significant impact on the Gangetic Valley plains.
(d) Analysis of fossilized pollen has proven to be a valuable tool in the identification of ancient plant species.

Directions (questions 6–8): *In each of the following questions, a word is highlighted. Choose the word which is a synonym of the highlighted word.*

6. The systematic vilification of facts and expertise, the violent **abnegation** of diverse thought, the constant blasts of paranoia-stoking crime reports and patriotic sound bites on an inescapable news network—could this be more now?
(a) indulgence (b) denial
(c) acceptance (d) adoption

7. Her 2014 autobiography, A *Fighting Chance*, and recent stump speeches are festooned in pep club spirit and folksy **blandishments**, cloying bits of business that have attached themselves to her life story.
(a) Cajolery (b) roughness
(c) Criticism (d) bully

8. Were other international trade negotiations to be put back because of the virus — for example, those being conducted between London and

Washington — Britain's government could start to look **obdurate** about the Brexit talks.
(a) sensitive (b) illusive
(c) flexible (d) callous

Directions (questions 9–11): *Complete the following sentences with an appropriate irregular verb and one of these phases.*

(i)		(ii)	
I.	Make	a.	From the jeweler
II.	Choose	b.	on the label
III.	Carry	c.	To the players
IV.	Give	d.	To represent India
V.	Print	e.	At today's meeting
VI.	Damage	f.	On the boulevard
VII.	Take	g.	In the storm

9. The road repairs _________ might delay traffic.
(a) I – b (b) VII – c
(c) VI – g (d) III – f

10. All the bijouterie _________ have now been recovered.
(a) VII – a (b) III – f
(c) VI – a (d) III – a

11. The admonition _________ about their behaviour on the pitch was ignored.
(a) I – a (b) VII – b
(c) VI – g (d) IV – c

Directions (questions 12–13): *Following are the questions based on the same words used as different parts of speech. Choose the correct matches.*

12. Back

1.	Noun	a.	The back portion of the house is in dilapidated condition.
2.	Adverb	b.	In a coalition government a number of parties back the single largest party to form the government.
3.	Adjective	c.	There is a road at the back of this theater.
4.	Verb	d.	She has come back from America.

(a) 1-a, 2-b, 3-c, 4-d
(b) 1-d, 2-c, 3-b, 4-a
(c) 1-c, 2-d, 3-a, 4-b
(d) 1-b, 2-a, 3-d, 4-c

13. Near

1.	Adjective	a.	Draw near while I speak to you.
2.	Verb	b.	There is a mango tree near our house.
3.	Adverb	c.	Lajwanti is a near relative of mine.
4.	Preposition	d.	I am nearing the end of the given work.

(a) 1-c, 2-d, 3-a, 4-b (b) 1-d, 2-c, 3-b, 4-a
(c) 4-c, 1-b, 2-d, 3-a (d) 3-c, 2-b, 1-a, 4-d

Directions (questions 14–16): *Observe the following sentences where some changes are made in the sentence but keeping the sense of the sentence same. In the following questions, the sentences have some element of similarity. You have to find out the similarity and choose the option which is odd one out.*

14. (a) His behaviour displeased his officers.
His officers were displeased at his behaviour.
(b) One must respect one's elders.
One's elders must be respected.
(c) I said, 'Do not speak of the past.'
I advised him not to speak of the past.
(d) A crash radio message was handed over to me.
They handed over a crash radio message to me.

15. (a) I don't expect to see him back here.
I don't expect that I will see him back here.
(b) In spite of his poverty, he is satisfied.
He is poor but he is satisfied.
(c) He gave them not only food but some money also.
Besides food, he gave him some money also.
(b) Escaping arrest, he ran away.
He ran away in order to escape arrest.

16. (a) The teacher was strict but always loving.
Though the teacher was strict, she was always loving.
(b) He is very rich and can buy a car.
He is so rich that he can buy a car.
(c) He ran hard but missed the bus.
Although he ran, he missed the bus.
(d) You know what my errand is.
You know my errand.

Direction (questions 17–22): *Choose the sentence which is correct grammatically.*

17. (a) 'Mr. Sharma has conveyed his heart-felt thanks to the Principal of the school and its management for their support to the cause of children with special needs.'
(b) 'The government was adviced to take immediate steps'.
(c) This colt will make a good mare.
(d) Is your mother the executrix of this deed?

18. (a) You have fallen in bad company.
(b) Please run through the book.
(c) He set every thing to naught.
(d) He is calling you a bad name.

19. (a) All of the reptiles lay eggs.
(b) Waiting in the queue for half an hour, Jay suddenly realized that he had left his wallet at home.
(c) 'Do you think Meena will remember your birthday?' 'I suspect not.'
(d) The coffee in this coffee shop is the best one in town.

20. (a) He has a shave every morning, but you wouldn't think he had.
(b) Supposing you don't get the job – what will you do then?
(c) The strikes were mainly concerned about working conditions.
(d) She is quite younger than me.

21. (a) Because I'd lost my watch, so I was late for the meeting.
(b) She lives in 38 Middle Street.
(c) He'd left his papers all across the room.
(d) There have been many problems with the new bridge.

22. (a) I had to go into work even though I was feeling terrible.
(b) Competition entries must be received until 12.00 on 10 August.
(c) Why on earth were you waving that knife around? What were you thinking about?
(d) Do you care if I smoke a cigar?

Direction (questions 23–26): *Choose the alternative which best expresses the meaning of the idiom/ phrase in the question.*

23. Purple Patch
(a) a dark period
(b) a period of success
(c) safe way to royalty
(d) mending old ties

24. French Leave
(a) an insulting defeat
(b) a time of revelry
(c) leave without permission
(d) a great deception

25. Hang out to dry
(a) to desert one in troubling situation
(b) to ridicule
(c) a time of truce
(d) be critical of

26. Down to the wire
(a) digging deep
(b) no chance of error
(c) in great details
(d) until the last moment

Directions (questions 27–29): *Replace the underlined word/words with one of these two- or three-word verbs in an appropriate form.*

27. If I <u>**tell**</u> you the secret, you must promise not to tell anyone else.
(a) let in on (b) bring in
(c) put down to (d) shoot down

28. They're going to **suffer** a lot of criticism for increasing bus fares by so much.
(a) put down to (b) gather up
(c) come in for (d) put up with

29. It's best to **attribute** his bad mood to tiredness and just forget it.
(a) flick through (b) put down to
(c) take on (d) see through

Direction (questions 30–35): *Choose the best word to fill in the blanks*

30. Owing to the combination of its proximity and __________ atmosphere, Mars is the only planet in our solar system whose surface details can be discerned from the Earth.
(a) viscous (b) ossified
(c) rarefied (d) copious

31. Using the hardships of the Ganguli family as a model, Jhumpa Lahiri's *The Namesake* effectively demonstrated how one clan's struggles epitomized the __________ experienced by an entire community.
(a) reticence (b) quiescence
(c) verisimilitude (d) tribulation

32. The Pyramid of Giza is more than just __________ edifice; this imposing structure was built to create a chirping echo whenever people clap their hands on the staircase.
(a) a venerable (b) a specious
(c) a prosaic (d) a humble

33. Some wealthy city-dwellers become enchanted with the prospect of trading their hectic schedules for a bucolic life in the countryside, and they buy property with a pleasant view of farmland – only to find the stench of the livestock so __________ that they move back to the city.
(a) bovine (b) atavistic
(c) olfactory (d) noisome

34. When Sheena brought home the irascible puppy, her more quiescent dogs were rattled by their new __________ housemate.
(a) languid (b) bellicose
(c) diminutive (d) phlegmatic

35. Despite the vast amount of time Tarun dedicated to learning six different languages, he was __________ communicator; his mastery of vocabulary and grammar failed to redress his inability to redress his inability to construct cogent prose.
(a) an astute (b) a prolific
(c) a maladroit (d) a florid

GENERAL KNOWLEDGE

36. Bru Settlement is regarding Bru refugee crisis and it was entered between
(a) Central Government, Tripura, Mizoram and Reang Tribe
(b) Central Govt. and Indian Coffee Trade Association
(c) Tripura, Mizoram and Reang Tribe
(d) Central Government, Indian Coffee Trade Association and Reang Tribe

37. Which Movie won the Best Picture in 92nd Academy Awards 2020?
(a) Joker
(b) Parasite
(c) Jojo Rabbit
(d) Once Upon a Time in Hollywood

38. Which State in India tops the Sustainable Development Goal (SDG) India Index 2019?
(a) Kerala
(b) Gujarat
(c) Andhra Pradesh
(d) Himachal

39. Which of the following statements is not correct about the Blue Dot Network (**BDN**)?
(a) Blue Dot network is an initiative to grade the infrastructure projects in terms of debt, environment safety, labour standards, etc.
(b) The Blue Dot Network project is being led by USA, Japan, and Australia.
(c) BDN offer public funds or loans for the project.
(d) It is expected to serve as a globally recognized evaluation and certification system with a focus on the Indo-Pacific region.

40. Who among the following is not a recipient of Padma Vibhushan Award 2020?
(a) Sushma Swaraj (b) George Fernandez
(c) Arun Jaitley (d) Teejan Bai

41. Which of the following from India is included in the SCO list of eight wonders of the world?
(a) Soho House
(b) Statue of Unity
(c) Signature Bridge
(d) Ajanta Caves

42. Which of the following statements on Bond Yields is /are true?
I. Yield from Government Bond is always lower than yields from corporate bonds.
II. When the economy is in recession, the Bond Yields usually tends to decrease.
III. Government Bonds are known as Treasury Bills in India.
IV. When the Bond price increases then Bond Yield decreases.
(a) II, IV (b) I, III
(c) I, II, III (d) I, II, III, IV

43. Which of the following first-ever talked about the concept of 'Sustainable Development'?
(a) Earth Summit 1992
(b) Kyoto Protocol
(c) Paris Summit
(d) Brundtland Report

44. In Global Democracy Index 2019, which of the following criteria is the main reason for India's sliding ranking?
(a) Electoral process and pluralism
(b) Civil liberties
(c) Functioning of government
(d) Political participation

45. From which of the following sites, the female skeleton 16614 is recovered whose DNA sequencing has revealed that the people in the Indus Valley Civilization have an independent origin?
(a) Ganveriwala
(b) Mohenjo-Daro
(c) Dholavira
(d) Rakhigarhi

46. Tishreen Revolution of 2019 is regarding:
I. Corruption
II. unemployment
III. inefficient public services
V. to stop Iranian intervention in Iraq
(a) I, II (b) II, III
(c) I, IV (d) I, II, III, IV

47. The term Cytokine Storm is related to which of the following?
(a) Earth's Weather
(b) Human body's Immune system
(c) Atomic energy
(d) Space Exploration

48. What is the main reason of people's protest in Hong Kong in 2019-20?
(a) Unemployment
(b) Economic slow down
(c) Extradition law
(d) labour laws

49. Which of the following is/are not true about the Organization of Islamic Cooperation (OIC)?
I. India is an observer to OIC.
II. Only Muslim majority states are members to the body.
III. It is the second largest inter-governmental organization after the United Nation.
IV. The recent summit of the OIC was held in Mecca, Saudi Arabia.
(a) I, II, III, IV (b) I, II, III
(c) I, II (d) III, IV

50. Who won the Ramon Magsaysay Award 2019 for Journalism?
(a) Ravish Kumar
(b) Dibang
(c) Sudhir Chaudhary
(d) Rahul Kanwal

51. Who is the writer of the patriotic song Saare Jahan Se Accha?
(a) Allama Mohd. Iqbal
(b) Rabindra Nath Tagore
(c) Bankim Chandra Chatterjee
(d) Kavi Pradeep

52. Apple has started a credit card named 'Apple Card' in collaboration with which of the following companies?
(a) MasterCard
(b) CitiBank
(c) American Express
(d) Goldman Sachs

53. India has signed the Singapore Convention on Mediation in 2019. It is regarding –
(a) Cross-border river disputes
(b) Cross-border commercial disputes
(c) Terrorism
(d) War crimes

54. Consider the following statements:
I. The Administer, appointed by the President, is the constitutional head of the Union Territory.
II. The relationship of the Union Territories with the Central Government is a part of the federal structure.

Which of the abovementioned statements is/are correct?
(a) I only (b) II only
(c) I, II (d) None

55. Where is the Nine Dash Line located?
(a) South China Sea
(b) North Atlantic Ocean
(c) Arctic Ocean
(d) East Philippine Sea

56. What is the duration of Solar Cycle?
(a) 100 years (b) 6 months
(c) 11 years (d) 12 months

57. Which city in the World is declared the Most Liveable City in 2019?
(a) Melbourne (b) Vienna
(c) Sydney (d) Osaka

58. The Central Board of Secondary Education has collaborated with which of the following companies for developing Artificial Intelligence (AI)-based tools for learning in schools?
(a) IBM (b) Google
(c) Intel (d) Wipro

59. Who has said 'How dare you? You have stolen my dreams, my childhood with your empty word.'?
(a) Malala Yousafzai
(b) Greta Thunberg
(c) Jaden Anthony
(d) Martinez

60. Sound cannot travel through-
(a) Gas (b) Liquid
(c) Metal (d) Vacuum

61. The chemical component which is found in most of the virus is -
(a) Protein (b) Lipids
(c) DNA (d) RNA

62. Ajanta Caves depicts paintings and sculptures from which of the following?
(a) Panchtantra Tales
(b) Animals
(c) Jataka Tales
(d) dance forms

63. In which of the following countries, a law to criminalize fake news came into effect in October 2019?
(a) Singapore (b) Finland
(c) China (d) India

64. 'Singularity' has been in the news in the context of the Black Hole image. It refers to which of the following?
(a) Gravitational waves generated by the merger of Black Holes.
(b) The boundary around a Black Hole, beyond which no light or other radiation can escape.
(c) It is a stage in the life-cycle of a star.
(d) It is the centre of the Black Hole, which contains a huge mass in an infinitely small space, where density and gravity become infinite.

65. Who has been elected as the Speaker of the 17th Lok Sabha?
(a) Rajiv Gaba
(b) Om Birla
(c) Adhir Ranjan Chowdhary
(d) Sumitra Mahajan

66. Who among the following became youngest ever elected Member of Parliament in India?
(a) Dushyant Chautala
(b) Tejasvi Surya
(c) Chandrani Murmu
(d) Raksha Khadse

67. Who has been appointed India's first Lokpal?
(a) Justice (retd.) Pinaki Chandra Ghose
(b) Shri. Suresh Mathur
(c) Justice (retd.) A. D. Koshal
(d) Justice (retd.) A.K. Sikri

68. Who has been declared the winner of the Nobel Peace Prize, 2019?
(a) Abhijit Banerjee
(b) Abdel Fattah el-Sisi, President of Egypt
(c) Greta Thunberg, Climate Activist
(d) Abiy Ahmed Ali, the Prime Minister of Ethiopia

69. The Neelakurinji flower, which grows after a period of 12 years, grows in which of the following areas?
(a) The Andaman and Nicobar Islands
(b) Lakshadweep
(c) The Western Ghats
(d) Arunachal Pradesh

70. Which of the following Statements correctly relates to 'Pink Tax'?
(a) It is a tax legally imposed on women in some countries.
(b) It is a tax imposed legally, the proceeds of which go for the development of women.
(c) It is the name of the phenomenon wherein women pay more for women-specific goods and services.
(d) It is a kind of tax relief given for women-specific products.

LEGAL APTITUDE

Directions: *Given below is a statement of legal principle followed by a factual situation. Apply the principle to the facts given below and select the most appropriate answer.*

Directions (questions 71–74): *Apply the legal principles to the facts given below and select the most appropriate answer.*

Legal Principles:

1. Negligence is a legal wrong that is suffered by someone at the hands of another who has a duty to take care but fails to take proper care to avoid what a reasonable person would regard as a foreseeable risk.
2. The test of liability requires that the harm must be a reasonably foreseeable result of the defendant's conduct, a relationship of proximity must exist and it must be fair, just, and reasonable to impose liability.
3. The claimant must prove that harm would not have occurred 'but for' the negligence of the defendant.
4. Duty of care is a legal obligation which is imposed on an individual requiring adherence to a standard of reasonable care while performing any acts that could foreseeably harm others.
5. Conversations between a doctor and patient are generally confidential but there are few exceptions.

71. A company called KLM, manufacturers of electrical equipment, was the target of a takeover by ABS Industries. KLM was not doing well. In March 2019, KLM had issued a profit warning, which had halved its share price. In May 2019, KLM's directors made a preliminary announcement in its annual profits for the year up to March. This confirmed that the position was bad. The share price fell again. At this point, ABS had begun buying up shares in large numbers. In June 2019, the annual accounts, which were done with the help of the accountant Dinesh, were issued to the shareholders, which now included ABS. ABS reached a shareholding of 29.9% of the company, at which point it made a general offer for the remaining shares, as the City Code's rules on takeovers required. But once it had control, ABS found that KLM's accounts were in an even worse state than had been revealed by the directors or the auditors.

It sued Dinesh for negligence in preparing the accounts and sought to recover its losses. This was the difference in value between the company as it had and what it would have had if the accounts had been accurate. Which of the following answers in incorrect?

(a) No duty of care had arisen in relation to existing or potential shareholders. The only duty of care the auditor's owed was to the governance of the firm.
(b) Dinesh is not liable as it is a case of pure economic loss in the absence of contractual agreements between parties.
(c) There are circumstances where an auditor will owe a duty of care in respect of reports produced. These are conditional that at the time the report is prepared it is known by the auditors that the results are for a specific class and for a specific purpose.
(d) An ability to foresee indirect or economic loss to another person as the result of a defendant's conduct automatically impose on the defendant a duty to take care to avoid that loss.

72. In 2005, the local council of Delhi approved building plans for the erection of a block of apartments. The approved plans showed the base wall and concrete foundations of the block to be three feet or deeper to the approval of local authority. The notice of approval said that the bylaws of the council required that notice should be given to the council both at the commencement of the work and when the foundations were ready to be covered by the rest of the building work. The council had the power to inspect the foundations and require any corrections necessary to bring the work into conformity with the bylaws, but was not under an obligation to do so. The block of apartments was finished in 2006. The builder (who was also the owner) granted 99-year leases for the apartments, the last conveyance taking place in 2010. In 2017, structural movements occurred resulting in failure of the building comprising cracks in the wall, sloping of the floors, and other defects. In 2019, the plaintiffs who were lessees of the apartments filed cases for negligence against the builder and the council. The plaintiffs claimed that the damage was a consequence of the block having been built on inadequate foundations, there being a depth of two feet six inches only as against the three feet or deeper shown on the plans and required under the bylaws. The plaintiffs claimed damages in negligence against the council for approving the foundations and/or in failing to inspect the foundations. Decide whether the council owed a duty of care to the claimants in respect of the incorrect depth of the foundations laid by the third-party builder?

(a) The Council is not liable for damages to the plaintiff as failing to inspect would not render the council liable unless it was considered that it had failed to properly exercise its discretion to inspect and that they had failed to ensure proper compliance with building regulations.
(b) The Council is liable for negligence as they failed to inspect the foundation.
(c) There is no negligence in building the apartments as there is minor difference between a foundation which is three feet deep and a foundation which is two feet six inches deep.
(d) The tenets have a duty to inspect the property properly before entering into such a long lease agreement.

73. Soman was the student of PRQ University. He met Pamela in a youth festival and fell in love with her. However, Pamela was not interested in having any serious relationship with Soman. Due to this, Soman went into emotional crisis and started consulting a psychologist in the PRQ Memorial Hospital. In October 2018, Soman murdered Pamela. Pamela's parents contended that only a short time prior, Soman had expressed his intention to murder their daughter to his therapist, Dr. Surana, a psychologist employed by the

University. They further alleged that Dr. Surana had warned campus police of Soman's intentions, and that the police had briefly detained him, but then released him. Pamela's parents filed a case of negligence against the Police Department and the University officials on two grounds: the failure to confine Soman, in spite of his expressed intentions to kill Pamela, and failure to warn Pamela or her parents. Defendants maintained that they owed no duty of care to the victim, and were immune from suit. Which of the following is incorrect?

(a) The police did not have the requisite proximity or special relationship with family of Pamela, sufficient to impose a duty to warn her of Soman's intention.

(b) The public policy favoring protection of the confidential character of patient-psychotherapist communications must yield to the extent to which disclosure is essential to avert danger to others. The protective privilege ends where the public peril begins.

(c) The therapists and Regents of University are liable for breach of duty to exercise reasonable care.

(d) Soman only once expressed the desire to kill Pamela. Such kinds of feelings are normal in any mentally ill patient. Moreover, information received during a counselling session is confidential in nature and so therapists cannot reveal it to the parents of Pamela.

74. R, T, and U were watchmen in Skypark Society. They were on night shift and began vomiting after drinking tea. They went to the SEM Hospital and complained to the nurse about it. The nurse thought they were vomiting because of alcohol they had been drinking earlier in the evening. However, the nurse reported it to the medical officer who refused to examine them and said that they needed to go home and contact their own doctors. They returned to their workplace, where U's condition deteriorated. U died of arsenic poisoning five hours later on way to hospital. U's wife brought a claim of negligence against the Hospital administration. She argued that the hospital was negligent in not identifying that U had been poisoned, and the doctor should therefore have seen to him when they first approached the hospital. The hospital denied they were negligent, and in any event said they did not cause his death. Decide.

(a) The hospital is not liable for negligence because even if the patient was examined five hours earlier to the death he would have died anyways. The test of causation was not satisfied. The Hospital did not cause U's death – But for the defendant's negligence, U would have died anyways.

(b) It was highly possible that the doctor would have identified U's condition as arsenical poisoning, and therefore U would have received the treatment he needed to survive.

(c) Where there are a number of possible causes, the claimant must still prove the defendant's breach of duty caused the harm or was a material contribution.

(d) Both (a) & (c)

75. Legal Principle: Generally, the owner of the property has a duty to maintain his property so as to make it reasonably safe for use. However, the occupier also owes a duty to take such care as is reasonable to see that the visitor is reasonably safe in using the premises for the purposes for which he is invited or permitted by the occupier to be therein.

Facts: Sheila is a painter. She went to her friend Ruchi's house for meeting her. Sheila requested to use the bathroom and injured her right hand on a broken water faucet handle. Sheila filed a personal injury action for hand injuries suffered alleging that Ruchi failed to warn her that her bathroom fixtures were cracked and dangerous. Ruchi says she had complained to the landlord about the broken handle so the landlord is liable. Decide whether the Sheila's injury the proximate cause of Ruchi's negligence?

(a) A licensee or social guest was obliged to take the premises as he or she found them, and the possessor of the premises owed a duty only to refrain from wanton or wilful injury.
(b) The landlord is liable as Ruchi had complained to the landlord about the broken handle and it is the duty of the landlord to get the repair work done.
(c) Ruchi is not liable as the use of toilet is not the purposes for which Sheila was invited or permitted by the occupier to be therein.
(d) Ruchi owes a duty to warn of a dangerous condition so the guest can take special precautions, like the host would, when they come in contact with it.

76. Legal Principle: Intimidation involves a threat to do something unlawful or 'illegitimate'; it must be intended to coerce the claimant to take or not take certain action.

Facts: Hari, a skilled draughtsman and employee of the Overseas Airways Corporation (OAC), resigned his membership of the Association of Engineering and Shipbuilding Draughtsmen (AESD), a registered trade union. It was agreed between OAC and AESD (among others) that no strike or lockout should take place and disputes should be handled by arbitration. He resigned from his union, the Association of Engineering and Shipbuilding Draftsman (AESD), after a disagreement. The Corporation and AESD had a contract that stipulates that the employer will only hire workers from a specific union and those workers can only remain with that employer while they are a part of the union so AESD threatened a strike unless Hari resigned also from his job or was fired. Corporation suspended Hari and, after some months, dismissed him with one week's salary in lieu of notice. Hari brought an action for damages alleging that he was the victim of a tortious intimidation. Decide.

(a) The union was guilty of the tort of intimidation. It was unlawful intimidation to use a threat to break their contracts with their employer as a weapon to make him do something which he was legally entitled to do but which they knew would cause loss to Hari.
(b) The Union was not guilty of intimidation as no unlawful means were used to induce Corporation to terminate his contract of service.
(c) There was a contract between Union and Corporation that stipulates that the employer will only hire workers from a specific union and those workers can only remain with that employer while they are a part of the union so the Union is not liable.
(d) Hari cannot claim damages as he was paid one week's salary in lieu of notice.

77. Legal Principles:

1. A deceit occurs when a misrepresentation is made with the express intention of defrauding a party, subsequently causing loss to that party.
2. 'Misrepresentation' means and includes—the positive assertion, in a manner not warranted by the information of the person making it, of that which is not true, though he believes it to be true; any breach of duty which, without an intent to deceive, gains an advantage of the person committing it, or any one claiming under him, by misleading another to his prejudice, or to the prejudice of any one claiming under him; causing, however innocently, a party to an agreement, to make a mistake as to the substance of the thing which is the subject of the agreement.

Fact: XY Company in its prospectus stated that the company was permitted to make engines that were powered by electricity, rather than by fuel. In reality, the company did not possess such a right as this had to be approved by the Government Board. Gaining the approval for such a claim from the Board was considered a formality in such circumstances and the claim was put forward in the prospectus with this information in mind. However, the claim of the company for this right was later refused by the Board. The individuals who had purchased a stake in the business, upon reliance on the statement, brought a claim for deceit against the defendant's business. Decide.

(a) The company is liable for false representation as their claims were eventually turned out to be false.

(b) The company is liable as their false statements has resulted in causing loss to the shareholders.

(c) The company is not liable as the statement in its prospectus was simply incorrect and not fraudulent.

(d) The shareholders should have collected as much information regarding the company as possible before purchasing a stake in it.

78. Legal Principles:

1. Private nuisance is a continuous, unlawful, and indirect interference with the use or enjoyment of land, or of some right over or in connection with it.
2. Generally, nuisances cannot be justified on the ground of necessity, pecuniary interest, convenience, or economic advantage to a defendant.
3. A person is liable if he can reasonably foresee that his acts would be likely to injure his neighbour.
4. In cases of nuisance, the court may grant an injunction restricting the nuisance from occurring in the future when the loss could not adequately compensated.

Facts: Tina purchased a house in an estate which was adjacent to a functioning, in use, cricket field. The members of Super Eleven Cricket Club used to play Cricket in that field for over 70 years. After Tina moved into the property, cricket balls began to fly over the field's protective barrier and into the Tina's property. Tina complained, which caused Super Eleven Cricket Club to erect a chain link fence. This improved matters as less balls were now flying onto the Tina's property but it did not fully solve the issue as some still got through. The club offered Tina to pay for any damage done or injuries received as a result of the balls landing onto her land, including fixing any broken windows and similar. Tina, however, refused all of the club's offers and filed a case against the members of the Club alleging nuisance and negligence and requested court to grant an injunction to prevent the club from playing cricket on their ground. Tina argued that even though the club offered to make good any damage and that there had been no injuries, she was not able to use her garden when matches were being played for fear of being struck by a cricket ball. Decide.

(a) The members of Club are not liable as Tina was aware about the activities of the Cricket Club and had willingly purchased the property.

(b) The members of the Club are liable for nuisance and court should pass an order of compensation as the injury is small and could be compensated in terms of money. Also, public interest considerations outweighed the private rights of the plaintiff and therefore a remedy of damages was sufficient in the circumstances.

(c) The members of the Club are liable for nuisance and court should pass an order of injunction. The plaintiff's right to enjoyment of her property outweighs the right of the members of the Club to play cricket.

(d) The Club is not liable as they have already taken sufficient measures to mitigate the effects of their act and are ready and willing to do so in future too.

79. Legal Principles:

1. According to rule of strict liability, any person who for his own purposes brings on his lands and collects and keeps there anything likely to do mischief if it escapes, must keep it in at his peril, and, if he does not do so, is prima facie answerable for all the damage, irrespective of fault, which is the natural consequence of its escape in respect of the non-natural use of land.
2. A person is liable if he can reasonably foresee that his acts would be likely to injure his neighbour.

Facts: PN was the owner of a gas pipe which passed under the surface of an old railway between Ramnagar and Kotpur. XY was the local council which was responsible for a water pipe which supplied water to a block of flats in the nearby Shining Apartment Complex. A leak developed which was undetected for some time. The water collected at an embankment which housed PN's high pressure gas main. The water caused the embankment to collapse and left the gas main exposed and unsupported. This was a serious and immediate risk and PN took action to avoid the potential danger. They then sought to recover the cost of the remedial works. PN argued that the XY Council was liable for negligence under strict liability.

(a) The Council is liable under strict liability rule as the damage is not remote as it was possible for the Council to reasonably foresee a leakage which would eventually lead to collapse of the gas main.

(b) The escape of water as a result of leak is sufficient to make the Council liable.

(c) The Council is not liable as PN should have been careful in detecting the leak earlier. They cannot shift the blame on the Council.

(d) The Council is not liable under rule of strict liability for the damage as the Council's use was neither a non- natural nor dangerous use of the land.

80. Legal Principles:

1. When the negligent act of two or more person results in the same damage, it is called composite negligence. The liability in such a case is joint and several of the tort-feasers.
2. A person is liable if he can reasonably foresee that his acts would be likely to injure someone.
3. The foreseeability of the type of damage is a pre-requisite of liability.
4. The claimant must prove that harm would not have occurred 'but for' the negligence of the defendant.

Facts: Zara filed a civil suit against five drug manufacturing companies. Zara's mother took synthetic estrogen while pregnant with her. As a result of receiving the drug in-utero, Zara developed cancer as an adult. The drug was manufactured by the Defendants, five major drug companies and by about 195 other companies not named in the suit. The Defendants together produced 90% of the drug. Zara is unable to identify which company produced the actual drug her mother took. Decide whether the Defendants only can be held liable for Zara's cancer.

(a) No, as the industry responsible for the production of this drug is large, so holding only the defendants responsible is not correct.

(b) Yes, as defendants joins a substantial share of the manufactures into the lawsuit, the chances of the actual tort-feasor escaping liability is greatly reduced.

(c) No, as defendants can be made liable if he can reasonably foresee that his acts would be likely to injure someone.

(d) No, Zara is not entitled to any damages as the drugs her mother was administered were needed at that time and her mother had taken the medicines voluntarily. Zara developed cancer after so many years and she must prove that harm would not have occurred 'but for' the negligence of the defendants.

81. Legal Principles:

1. Any intentional false communication, either written or spoken, that harms a person's reputation; decreases the respect, regard, or confidence in which a person is held; or induces disparaging, hostile, or disagreeable opinions or feelings against a person.
2. The statement must tend to lower the claimant in the estimation of right- thinking members of society.
3. A mere vulgar abuse is not defamation.
4. Defamation encompasses both written statements, known as libel, and spoken statements, called slander.
5. A public official or public figure can recover damages for defamation on a matter of public

concern only if he proves that the speaker acted with actual malice.

Facts: In 2018, a police officer, Suresh Singh, shot and killed Dayal. After the officer was convicted of culpable homicide not amounting to murder, Dayal's family retained a lawyer, Kaushal, to represent them in civil litigation against the officer. In a magazine called *Indian Opinion*, the Anti-Communist Society accused Kaushal of being a 'Naxalite' and a 'Communist-fronter' because he chose to represent clients who were suing a law enforcement officer. Because the statements contained serious inaccuracies, Kaushal filed a libel action against the editors of the magazine. Decide whether he will succeed.

(a) No, as it is mere vulgar abuse.

(b) The statement may be defamatory but the editors of the magazine are not liable unless Kaushal is able to establish actual malice in making the statement.

(c) No, as the statement does not tend to lower Kaushal in the estimation of right-thinking members of society and print media is known for such type of journalism.

(d) Yes, as statement is defamatory and Kaushal is not required to establish actual malice to successfully bring a claim of defamation.

82. Legal Principle: A contract may, in some circumstances, be discharged by a breach of contract. Where there exists a breach of condition this will enable the innocent party the right to repudiate the contract (bring the contract to an end) in addition to claiming damages.

Facts: In April, Sagar Tour &Travels agreed to employ Hiten as his courier for three months from 1 June 2020, to go on a trip around the European continent. On 11 May, Sagar Tour & Travels wrote to say that Hiten was no longer needed. On 22 May, Hiten sued Sagar Tour & Travels for breach of contract. Sagar Tour & Travels argued that Hiten was still under an obligation to stay ready and willing to perform till the day when performance was due, and therefore could commence no action before June 1, 2020.

(a) A breach of contract by renouncing the duty to perform the future obligation does not render the party liable immediately to a suit of action for damages by the injured party.

(b) The renunciation of a contract of future conduct by one party immediately dissolves the obligation of the other party to perform the contract.

(c) Hiten has suffered no harm and the offer can be revoked anytime before June 1, 2020 so he cannot claim any damages.

(d) A contract for future conduct do not constitutes an implied promise that, in the meantime, neither party will prejudice the performance of that promise.

83. Legal Principle: An agreement between two private parties that creates mutual legal obligations. A contract can be either oral or written.

Facts: Mr. Ram and Mr. Rahim were work colleagues who had an arrangement regarding shared lifts to work. Rahim would drive his motorbike and Ram would ride pillion in return for a weekly sum of money. Unfortunately, both were killed in a road traffic accident and the wife of Mr. Ram made a claim for damages against the estate of Mr. Rahim. However Rahim's insurance policy did not cover pillion passengers and as his estate had no assets or money to satisfy the judgment, Mrs. Ram pursued the Motor Insurance Bureau (MIB). The MIB have an agreement whereby accidents and consequential claims would be satisfied by the Government in circumstances where the driver has no relevant policy of insurance. However, the rules covering this situation require Mr. Ram was carried for 'hire or reward'. Mrs. Ram argues that there was a contract in place between Ram and Rahim for the lifts to work. Decide whether there was a contract so as to make Mrs. Ram eligible for claim from MIB.

(a) Notwithstanding the regular payment of money in return for the lift, it was not a legal obligation as to create a contract. There were no terms as to how long this was to last, what would happen in default of payment or the availability of transport, or anything written down so as to at least make their intention clear.

(b) Yes, there was clearly an offer of transport and this was accepted. In addition, the consideration exchanged by the parties was the service of transport and the money paid by Ram.

(c) Yes, the practice of agreements between colleagues sharing a lift to work (or 'car-pooling') is an accepted and wide spread practice. Parties will usually agree that one will take their car and in return the others will make a contribution towards the petrol costs.

(d) No, unless the wife of Ram can show that the accident happened due to rash and negligent driving of Rahim.

84. Legal Principles:

1. Offer is a proposal made by one person to another to do an act or abstain from doing it. The person who makes the offer is known as the promisor or offeror and the person to whom an offer is made is known as the promisee or the offeree.
2. A contract comes into being by the acceptance of an offer. When the person to whom the offer is made signifies his consent thereto, the proposal is said to be accepted and the parties are at *consensus ad idem* regarding the terms of the agreement.

Facts: Mr. Kumar visited the Holiday Bliss Hotel. He had not made an in advance booking and upon arrival requested a room for the night. He signed the register and there was no mention at that stage of any other terms or conditions that might impact upon his stay at the hotel. During the course of his stay Mr. Kumar discovered that someone had broken into his room and stolen certain property including a coat. Kumar filed a case of negligence on the Hotel administration. Nevertheless, the Hotel sought to rely upon an exclusion clause that was placed in the bedroom the claimant stayed in. This stated that the hotel would not accept liability for lost or stolen items belonging to customers. Decide whether the exclusion clause that was displayed in the bedroom constituted a valid term of the contract.

(a) The contract was made when Kumar signed the register at the reception and so the acceptance of the offer mean acceptance of all the terms of the offer.

(b) There is a valid contract between Kumar and Hotel and the Hotel has taken reasonable steps to bring exclusion clause to Kumar's attention in the room.

(c) Terms must be brought to the attention of the customer, consumer, or party against whom they are trying to be enforced at the moment the contract was entered into. Kumar was not given notice of this exclusion clause until he had already entered into the contract and therefore it was unenforceable against him.

(d) Though the terms must be brought to the attention of the customer, consumer, or party against whom they are trying to be enforced at the moment the contract was entered into. But, such type of clauses are generally part of all contracts and customers should be aware of such exclusion of liability clauses.

85. Legal Principles:

1. When one person signifies to another person his willingness to do or not do something (abstain) with a view to obtain the assent of such person to such an act or abstinence, he is said to make a proposal or an offer.
2. The communication of the offer is complete when it comes to the knowledge of the person to whom it is made.
3. Communication of acceptance is complete when it is put in the course of transmission to him as to be out of the power of the acceptor to withdraw the same and when it comes to the knowledge of the proposer.

4. In case of the proposer, the communication of the acceptance is complete when he puts such acceptance in the course of transmission.
5. The communication in case of the acceptor is complete when the proposer acquires knowledge of such acceptance.
6. An offer may be revoked at any time before the communication of its acceptance is complete as against the proposer, but not afterwards.

Facts: G offered to sell the L fleeces of wool for a certain price. G requested that the response be made by post. This letter was misdirected by G so that it was not received for 3 days after it was sent. L decided to accept the offer and responded on the same day. This was posted on the 5th July but not received until the 9th July. However, G decided on the 8th July that as he had not received a response so decided to sell the wool to someone else. But L argued that a contract had been created as he had accepted their offer. Decide.

(a) No contract was formed as L accepted the offer even before he received the offer by post. Contract will be entered upon when L had received the offer and then written to him saying that the terms were agreed.
(b) The contract was entered on the 9th September when the acceptance was received by G.
(c) G is free to withdraw his offer before 9th September.
(d) The contract was entered on the 5th September when the acceptance was posted, not when it was received.

86. Legal Principles:

1. In order to convert a proposal into a promise the acceptance must be absolute and unqualified.
2. Acceptance must be expressed in some usual and reasonable manner, unless the proposal prescribes the manner in which it is to be accepted. If the proposal prescribes a manner in which it is to be accepted, and the acceptance is not made in such manner, the proposer may, within a reasonable time after the acceptance is communicated to him, insist that his proposal shall be accepted in the prescribed manner, and not otherwise; but, if he fails to do so, he accepts the acceptance.

Facts: TUV's employee performing installation on Motorola's premises was injured due to the negligence of Motorola employees. TUV had executed a purchase order that contained an indemnity form. First purchase order contained indemnity provision which narrowly applied to damages caused by the negligence of TUV's employees. It attached a broader indemnity form page which would make TUV also responsible for the negligence of Motorola employees in connection with the work. This page was marked VOID. Amendment 2 to Purchase order contained same provision and attached same additional indemnity form which this time was not marked VOID. But also contained the additional language that 'acceptance should be executed on acknowledgement copy which should be returned to the buyer.' Employee was injured several months before the acknowledgement copy of the second purchase order was executed, but was in the course of performing work related to the second purchase order. Decide whether TUV liable under the broader indemnity provision.

(a) TUV is liable as workers have sustained injury during the course of their employment even though TUV has not accepted the amended purchase order as it did not execute the acknowledgement.
(b) Motorola's amendment gave a suggested mode of acceptance which did not preclude TUV's acceptance by another method. TUV accepted when TUV undertook performance of the work called for by the amendment with the 'consent and acquiescence' of Motorola.
(c) TUV is not liable under the broader indemnity provision as it did not execute the acknowledgement copy until several months after the employee sustained his injury.

(d) TUV is not liable as commencement of work was acceptance to the first purchase order in which the broader indemnity provision was marked as void.

87. Legal Principles:

1. A contract can become void when: It is unfairly one-sided; it goes against public policy; its subject matter is illegal; it is impossible to perform; it unfairly restricts one side's actions (such as the right to work); one of the parties is not legally competent to enter into a binding contract.
2. A contract is void as against public policy if: (1) it is a contract by the defendant to pay the plaintiff for inducing a public official to act in a certain manner; (2) it is a contract to do an illegal act; or (3) it is a contract that contemplates collusive bidding on a public contract.

Facts: BR Industries, a company manufacturing drills, machine parts and components thereof and a purchaser of subcontract work from other suppliers, won the bid from the HLK Company to supply certain parts to it at a specified price. BR industries then contracted with SU Co. to supply the parts under the contract for a much lower price. BR Industries then intended to keep the difference between the amount it billed the HLK Company and the amount SU Co. charged for the parts. BR Industries initiated an action for breach of contract when SU Co. failed to complete the order. In its defense, SU Co. asserts that the contract is void as against public policy because Defendant turned a profit of 84.09% on anvils, 39.13% on holder primers and 68.33% on plunger supports. Did plaintiff receive too much compensation deeming it unconscionable and against public policy?

(a) The contract is void as against public policy as it is a contract that contemplates collusive bidding on a public contract.

(b) The Contract is void as it unfairly one sided.

(c) Relative values of the consideration in a contract between business men at 'arms-length' without fraud will not affect the validity of the contract.

(d) Relative values of the consideration in a contract between business men will affect the validity of the contract as it amounts to abuse of dominance and unconscionable.

88. Legal Principles:

1. Offer is a proposal made by one person to another to do an act or abstain from doing it. The person who makes the offer is known as the promisor or offeror and the person to whom an offer is made is known as the promisee or the offeree.
2. A contract comes into being by the acceptance of an offer. When the person to whom the offer is made signifies his consent thereto, the proposal is said to be accepted and the parties are at ***consensus ad idem*** regarding the terms of the agreement.

Facts: In Dec. 2019, a convicted murderer who was sentenced to death escaped from the custody of Ramesh, a prison official. Ramesh later offered a reward of INR 50,000 to anyone who captured the fugitive and returned him to the authorities. In Jan. 2020, without knowledge or notice of the reward, Sunil captured the fugitive and took him to Ramesh's jail house. Ramesh refused Sunil's demands for the reward money. Sunil filed a case against Ramesh to recover the reward. Ramesh alleges that there is no contract between Ramesh and Sunil.

(a) A mere offer or promise to pay did not give rise to a contract. Rather, the assent or meeting of two minds gave rise to a contract, and therefore it was not complete until the offer was accepted. Having notice or knowledge of the existence of the reward when he captured the fugitive is essential to his right to recover the reward offered by Ramesh.

(b) The act of capturing the fugitive was acceptance of the offer of reward through conduct and so a valid contract is entered upon.

(c) There was an offer by Ramesh and acceptance by Sunil and it is immaterial whether Sunil had notice or knowledge of the existence of the reward when he captured the fugitive.

(d) Such an offer, like the reward here, could be accepted by anyone who performs the service called for, when the acceptor knows that it has been made and acts in performance of it.

89. Which of the following States have passed a Bill providing for life imprisonment and fine up to INR 5 Lakhs against accused in case of mob lynching leading to death of the victim?

(a) Madhya Pradesh
(b) Rajasthan
(c) Uttar Pradesh
(d) Haryana

90. The strength of Judges in Supreme Court of India has been increased from 31 to __________.

(a) 34 (b) 38
(c) 33 (d) 35

91. In September 2019, High Court of __________ has held that the right to have access to the internet is part of fundamental right to education and right to privacy under Article 21 of the Constitution of India.

(a) Delhi (b) Madhya Pradesh
(c) Kerala (d) Mumbai

92. Which of the following statements is/are correct regarding Delimitation Commission?

I. It determines the number and boundaries of constituencies to make population of all constituencies nearly equal.
II. The orders of Delimitation Commission have the force of law and can be challenged in a court of law.
III. Constitution of India has put a freeze on fresh delimitation until 2025.
IV. The constitution has also capped the number of Lok Shaba & Rajya Sabha seats to a maximum of 550 & 250 respectively

(a) I, II, III, IV (b) I, II, III
(c) II, III (d) I, IV

93. The Enemy Property Act applies to the property of which of the following?

(a) people who took citizenship of China & Pakistan
(b) people who took citizenship of Bangladesh, China, & Pakistan
(c) people who took citizenship of Bangladesh & China
(d) people who took citizenship of China & Myanmar

94. Epidemic Diseases Act, 1897 provides for which of the following powers to prevent the spread of an epidemic disease?

I. Inspection of person
II. detention of persons
III. penalties for disobeying provisions of the Act under Section 188, 269 & 271 Indian Penal Code
IV. legal protection of implementing officers

(a) I, II, III, IV (b) I, II, III
(c) I, II, IV (d) I, III, IV

95. Jammu and Kashmir Reorganisation (Adaptation of State Laws) Second Order 2020 under J&K Civil Services (Decentralization and Recruitment) Act provides for which of the following:

I. Anyone who has lived in the Union Territory of J&K for at least 10 years is a domicile.
II. Anyone who has studied there for at least seven years and appeared in Class X or Class XII examinations in any school in the region is a domicile.
III. Anyone who is registered as a migrant by the Relief and Rehabilitation Commissioner (Migrants) in the Union territory of Jammu and Kashmir is a domicile.
IV. A domicile of the UT shall be eligible for appointment to any post with a pay scale of not more than Level-4 under the UT or any local authority within the territory.

(a) II, III (b) I, II, III
(c) I, IV (d) II, III, IV

96. Which of the following statements regarding Anti-defection Law is/are incorrect?

I. Grounds of disqualification on ground of defection are provided in the 10th Schedule to the Constitution.

II. If 1/3rd of the members of the political party defect from it than it is not defection.

III. Decision of the Speaker regarding disqualification of a member under Anti-Defection Law cannot be challenged in a court of law.

IV. A legislator is deemed to have defected if he disobeys the directives of the party leadership on a vote.

(a) I, II, (b) I, II, IV
(c) II, III (d) I, II, III, IV

97. Which of the following statements is/are correct regarding the Essential Commodities (Amendment) Ordinance, 2020?

I. The Ordinance seeks to increase competition in the agriculture sector and enhance farmers' income.

II. The Ordinance requires that imposition of any stock limit on certain specified items must be based on price rise.

III. The provisions of the Ordinance regarding the regulation of food items and the imposition of stock limits will apply to any government order relating to the Public Distribution System or the Targeted Public Distribution System.

IV. Recently, sanitizers, masks and oxygen cylinders are included under the Act till June 30, 2020.

(a) I, II, III (b) I, II
(c) III, IV (d) only I

98. Recently, the Supreme Court of India has held that women officers are also entitled to Permanent Commission in __________.

(a) Indian Navy (b) Indian Army
(c) Indian Air Force (d) all of these

99. In February 2020, the Supreme Court has held that reservations in promotion, in government jobs, is not a fundamental right and refused to give directions to provide reservations to the government of which of the following States?

(a) Uttarakhand (b) Jharkhand
(c) Kerala (d) Delhi

100. Which of the following statements is incorrect regarding SC and ST (Prevention of Atrocities) Amendments Act?

(a) No arrest can be made without prior permission.
(b) No anticipatory bail can be granted to the accused under the Act.
(c) The Police must file an FIR and arrest the accused on receiving the complaint.
(d) The offences under the Act are cognizable.

101. Which of the following statements is/are correct regarding the Citizenship (Amendment) Act 2019?

I. The Act does not apply to tribal areas of Tripura, Mizoram, Assam and Meghalaya but apply to all other states and UTs in India.

II. The Act provides that that no order of cancellation of registration shall be passed unless the Overseas Citizen of India Cardholder has been given a reasonable opportunity of being heard.

III. The Act increases the period of naturalisation for such group of persons from six years to eight years.

IV. The Act applies to those who were 'forced or compelled to seek shelter in India due to persecution on the ground of religion'. It aims to protect such people from proceedings of illegal migration.

(a) I, IV (b) II, III, IV
(c) I, III, IV (d) II, IV

102. Which of the following statements is/are correct regarding preventive detention?

I. National Security Act as well as Article 22, Constitution of India provide for preventive detention in certain cases

II. Maximum duration in case of preventive detention can be till 12 months

III. In case of preventive detention, accused has the right to be informed about the grounds of arrest at the time of arrest.

IV. In case of preventive detention, accused has no right to be represented by a lawyer.

(a) I, II (b) III, IV
(c) I, III, IV (d) I, II, IV

103. Which of the following countries joined the International Criminal Court (ICC) in 2019?

(a) Turkey (b) Malaysia
(c) Myanmar (d) India

104. The Citizenship (Amendment) Act grants citizenship to the Hindus, Christians, Sikhs, Buddhist, Jains and Parsis — from __________ who had arrived in India before __________

(a) Afghanistan, Pakistan, and Bangladesh; 31 December 2014
(b) Afghanistan, Sri Lanka, and Bangladesh; 31 December 2014
(c) Myanmar, Pakistan, and Tibet; 31 December 2011
(d) Afghanistan, Pakistan, and Myanmar; 31 December 2011

105. Which of the following countries have abolished flogging as a form of punishment in April 2020?

(a) Indonesia (b) Maldives
(c) Saudi Arabia (d) Singapore

REASONING

Direction (questions 106–112): *Read the following information carefully and answer the questions given below.*

Sonu has to deliver seven parcels containing different items– Medicine, Book, Stationery, Grocery, Cosmetics, Clothes, and Chocolate – to houses on different floors of a building, one parcel each to a house. The seven floors of the building are numbered consecutively 1 through 7. Delivery of parcels to houses must meet the following conditions:

I. Medicine is delivered on a lower numbered floor than Grocery.
II. Clothes are delivered at one level below the floor at which Book is delivered.
III. Stationery is delivered at first floor or else seventh floor.
IV. Chocolate is delivered at fourth floor.

106. There can be at most how many floors between the floor at which Medicine is delivered and the floor at which Grocery is delivered?

(a) Two (b) Three (c) Four (d) Five

107. If Clothes are delivered at floor 1, which of the following could be true?

(a) Book is delivered at a floor one below than the floor at which Grocery is delivered.
(b) Book is delivered at a floor one below than the floor at which Cosmetics is delivered.
(c) Medicine is delivered at a floor one below than the floor at which Stationery is delivered.
(d) Cosmetics is delivered at a floor one below than the floor at which Book is delivered.

108. Which one of the following is an acceptable assignment of parcels to the floors in the building, in order from floor 1 through 7?

(a) Medicine, Clothes, Cosmetics, Chocolate, Book, Grocery, Stationery
(b) Stationery, Cosmetics, Chocolate, Clothes, Book, Medicine, Grocery
(c) Stationery, Clothes, Book, Chocolate, Grocery, Medicine, Cosmetics
(d) Medicine, Cosmetics, Grocery, Chocolate, Clothes, Book, Stationery

109. If Cosmetics is delivered at floor 2, which one of the following must be true?

(a) Medicine is delivered at a lower numbered floor than Chocolate.
(b) Chocolate is delivered at a lower numbered floor than Grocery.
(c) Grocery is delivered at a lower numbered floor than Stationery.
(d) Clothes are delivered at a lower numbered floor than Grocery.

110. If Cosmetics is delivered on floor 5, which one of the following is a pair of parcels that could be delivered, not necessarily in the order given, at floors whose numbers are consecutive to each other?

(a) Book, Grocery
(b) Clothes, Chocolate

(c) Stationery, Grocery
(d) Book, Stationery

111. If Book is delivered at one floor below the floor at which Medicine is delivered, then which one of the following must be true?
(a) Cosmetics is delivered on fifth floor.
(b) Medicine is delivered on third floor.
(c) Stationery is delivered on first floor.
(d) Clothes are delivered on fifth floor.

112. It must be true that the lowest numbered floor on which
(a) Book can be delivered on third floor.
(b) Medicine can be delivered on second floor.
(c) Cosmetics can be delivered on third floor.
(d) Grocery can be delivered on second floor.

Directions (questions 113–116): *Read the following information carefully to answer the following questions.*
I. 'X + Y' means that 'X is the mother of Y'.
II. 'X – Y' means that 'X is the sister of Y'.
III. 'X × Y' means that 'X is the father of Y'.
IV. 'X ÷ Y' means that 'X is the brother of Y'.

113. If it is given 'B + D × M ÷ N', then how is M related to B?
(a) grand-daughter (b) son
(c) grand-son (d) daughter

114. Which of the following represent 'J is the son of F'?
(a) J ÷ R – T × F
(b) J + R – T × F
(c) J ÷ R – N × F
(d) none of these

115. Which of the following represent 'R is the niece of M'?
(a) M ÷ K × T – R
(b) M – J + R – N
(c) R – M × T ÷ W
(d) M + T × K ÷ R

116. If it is given 'B × D – M', then which of the following is true?
(a) B is the brother of M
(b) B is the sister of M
(c) B is the uncle of M
(d) B is the father of M

Direction (questions 117–121): *Read the given information carefully and answer the* following questions.

Vidya, Umesh, and Tanu are sitting around a circular table. Arun, Bina and Chetan are sitting around the same table but two of them are not facing centre (they are facing the direction opposite to centre). Vidya is second to the left of Chetan. Umesh is second to the right of Arun. Bina is third to the left of Tanu. Chetan is second to the right of Tanu. Arun and Chetan are not sitting together.

117. Which of the following is not facing centre?
(a) Bina & Arun
(b) Chetan & Vidya
(c) Bina & Chetan
(d) Arun & Umesh

118. Which of the following is the position of Tanu in respect of Bina?
(a) third to the right
(b) second to the right
(c) third to the left
(d) third to the left & right, both

119. What is the position of Vidya in respect of Chetan?
(a) second to the right
(b) third to the left
(c) fourth to the right
(d) fourth to the left

120. Which of the following statement is correct?
(a) Arun, Bina, and Chetan are sitting together
(b) Vidya, Umesh, and Tanu are sitting together
(c) Only two people are sitting between Vidya and Tanu
(d) Those who are not facing centre are sitting together

121. What is the position of Arun in respect of Umesh?
(a) second to the left
(b) second to the right
(c) third to the right
(d) none of these

Directions (questions 122–123): *In each of the following questions is given a statement followed by two conclusions. You have to assume everything in the statement to be true, then consider the two conclusions together and decide which of these logically follows beyond reasonable doubt from the given information.* Give answer

(a) if only Conclusion I follows
(b) if only Conclusion II follows
(c) if both Conclusions I and II follow
(d) if neither Conclusion I nor II follows

122. Statement: The use of non-conventional sources of energy will eliminate the energy crisis in the world.

Conclusion I: Modern technology is gradually replacing the conventional source of energy.

Conclusion II: The excessive exploitation of environment has led to the depletion of conventional source of energy.

123. Statement: Computer advertisements now fill magazine pages but the real computer revolution in India is taking place quietly and is a likely organisation of Government.

Conclusion I: Both the Central and State Government are computerizing rapidly.

Conclusion II: The Government does not fill the magazine pages with its computer advertisements.

Direction (questions 124–125): *Each of these questions consists of a pair of words bearing a certian relationship. From among the options, find out the one that best illustrates a similar relationship.*

124. LOM : NMK : : PKI : ?
(a) RIG (b) RIH
(c) SHG (d) RHG

125. ABCD : OPQR : : WXYZ : ?
(a) EFGH (b) STUV
(c) KLMN (d) QRST

Direction (questions 126–127): *Find the one that does not belong to the group.*

126. (a) GMS (b) EKQ
(c) JOU (d) LRX

127. (a) RARCOT (b) NIATCRU
(c) BACGEBA (d) ILBJARN

128. If in a certain code language 'TEMPERATURE' is written as 'BZQDYXVBNXZ', then how will 'RAMP' be written in that language?
(a) XVQD (b) XVDQ
(c) XQVD (d) XDVQ

129. In a certain coding system, 'JUNE' is written as 'PQRS' and 'AUGUST' is written as 'WQFQMN'. How will 'GUEST' be written in that coding language?
(a) FQTMN (b) FPSMN
(c) FQSMN (d) FQSNM

130. A clock is set right at 5 am. The clock loses 16 minutes in 24 hours. What will be the right time when the clock indicates 10 pm on the 3rd day?
(a) 11:15 pm (b) 11 pm
(c) 12 pm (d) 12:30 pm

131. The minute hand of a clock overtakes the hour hand at intervals of 65 minutes of the correct time. How much does a clock gain or lose in a day?

(a) $10\frac{10}{143}$ minutes (gain)

(b) $10\frac{10}{143}$ minutes (loss)

(c) $9\frac{10}{143}$ minutes (gain)

(d) $9\frac{10}{143}$ minutes (loss)

132. If a day before yesterday was Tuesday, then what day of the week will it be on a day after tomorrow?
(a) Monday (b) Wednesday
(c) Friday (d) Saturday

133. If 15th August, 2017 was Tuesday, then what day of the week was it on 17th September, 2017?
(a) Sunday (b) Saturday
(c) Friday (d) Thursday

134. Tia and Renu both are walking away from point 'X'. Tia walked 3 m and

Renu walked 4 m from it, then Tia walked 4 m North of X and Renu walked 5 m South of Tia. What is the distance between them now? (a) 9.5 m (b) 9 m
(c) 16 m (d) 11.40 m

135. Tanaya travelled 4 km straight towards South. He turned left and travelled 6 km straight, then turned right and travelled 4 km straight. How far is he from the starting point?
(a) 8 km (b) 10 km
(c) 12 km (d) 18 km

Directions (questions 136–140): *Read the following short passages and choose the best answers to the questions that follow each passage.*

136. Therapists have just completed an extensive study of recently delinquent juveniles in order to determine which factors contributed most to the delinquency. The researchers found that in a great majority of the cases of delinquency, the parents met, on average, fewer than 4 times per week with their children. From this data, the therapists have determined that a failure to spend time together with the children is a major factor leading to delinquency.
Which one of the following, if true, would cast the most doubt on the researcher's hypothesis?
(a) Parents and children in the study who reported that they met each other more than four times per week also indicated that they tended to perceive their relationships as healthy.
(b) In many cases, people in unhappy family tend to express their displeasure by avoiding contact with each other when possible.
(c) Most of the families in the study who were unable to meet often with each other worked outside of the home.
(d) Many families who have a long and strong family bonding met each other fewer than four times per week.

137. Several coaching centres have recently switched at least partially from study material written by hand on printer paper from study material written on a computer and sent electronically with no use of paper at all. Therefore, less printer paper will be used as a result of these changes than would have been used if these coaching centres had continued to use handwritten study materials.
Which of the following, if true, most strengthens the argument above?
(a) The amount of printer paper needed to explain the electronic study material is less than the amount that would have been used for handwritten material.
(b) Coaching centres that used more printer paper were more likely to switch to electronic materials than centres that used less printer paper.
(c) Some of the Institutes that have switched at least partially to electronic study material still primarily used printer paper for other operations.
(d) More printer paper was used to create manuals for the use of electronic study materials than was used to write handwritten materials.

138. In visual media, it's possible to induce viewers to project their feelings onto characters on the screen. In one study, a camera shot of a girl's face was preceded by images of a still river. The audience thought the girl's face registered contentment. When the same girl's face was preceded by images of a mighty and violent tsunami wave, the audience thought the girl's face registered fear. Media news teams must be careful to avoid such manipulation of their viewers.
Which of the following is best supported by the information in the passage?
(a) The technique for manipulating audiences described in the passage would also work in an audio program that played dramatic music.
(b) Audiences should strive to be less gullible.
(c) Images of a still river engendered feelings of happiness in the audiences.
(d) The expression on the woman's face was, in actuality, blank.

139. Although measuring the productivity of outsourced workers is a complex endeavor. Company X, which relies heavily on outsourced workers, must find ways to assess the performance of these workers. The risks to a company that does not review the productivity of its human resources are simply too great. Last year, Company Y was forced into receivership after its productivity declined for three consecutive quarters.

The clauses in the italics in the above paragraph, play which of the following roles in the argument above?

(a) The first clause in italics express a position, and the second warns against the adoption of that position.

(b) The first clause in italics represents the author's conclusion, and the second supports the conclusion with an analogy.

(c) The first clause in italics states the author's premises, and the second states the author's conclusion.

(d) The first clause in italics provides background information, and the second offers evidence to contradict that information.

140. A telephonic poll conducted in two states asked respondents whether they get adequate water during summers. Ninety-nine percent of respondents said their houses were having running water through-out the day. The pollsters published their findings, concluding that ninety-nine percent of all homes in India have adequate water for use.

Which of the following most accurately describes a questionable technique employed by the pollsters in drawing their conclusions?

(a) The pollsters conducted the poll by telephone, thereby relying on the veracity of respondents.

(b) The pollsters never defined the term 'adequate' in terms of a specific quantity of water.

(c) The pollsters didn't visit respondent's houses in person, so no measure of adequacy of water during summers in a subject's house was actually made.

(d) The poll assumes conditions in the two states are representative of the entire country.

MATHEMATICS

141. If the third and the tenth term of an arithmetic progression are 14 and 56, respectively, then the arithmetic mean of the first 15 terms of the arithmetic progression is

(a) 40 (b) 44

(c) 80 (d) 34

142. Ronnie has a bag containing 7 red and 9 green balls. From it, he draws out 6 balls simultaneously at random. The probability that 4 of them are red and the rest are green is

(a) $\frac{24}{143}$ (b) $\frac{45}{286}$

(c) $\frac{155}{2001}$ (d) $\frac{302}{1005}$

143. City A is connected to City B by four highways and City B is connected to City C by three highways. Kesari wants to travel from City A to City C via City B. In how many ways, Kesari can do it?

(a) 4 (b) 7

(c) 10 (d) 12

144. The number of integral values of x satisfying the inequation $|x| < 4$ is

(a) 7 (b) 8

(c) 9 (d) 10

145. If the price of each book goes up by ₹5, then Asha can buy 20 books less for ₹1200.

Find the original price and the number of books Asha could buy at the original price.

(a) ₹25, 50 (b) ₹20, 60

(c) ₹15, 80 (d) ₹10, 90

146. If $2x = 7y = 14z$, then find the value of z in terms of x and y.

(a) $x + y/x - y$

(b) $xy/x + y$

(c) $x + y + xy$

(d) $xy - (x + y)$

147. Bhiku borrowed some money from Dhanraj to admit his daughter in a reputed Law School. He agreed to pay the interest-free loan of ₹60,000 in a monthly installments which increased by a constant amount. After the 20th installment, he found that he has paid ¾ of the loan. If the entire loan was cleared this way in 25 installments, find out the value of the first installment.

(a) ₹1560 (b) ₹1067
(c) ₹1680 (d) ₹1987

148. A vessel contains an 80% alcohol solution. 20% of the solution was removed and replaced with water. If this process is repeated, find the percentage of alcohol which remains in the solution.

(a) 64% (b) 51.2%
(c) 50.6% (d) 45%

149. Arsh takes up a job, wherein each working day he is given a target. For each day, he meets the target he is paid ₹105 and for each day he does not meet the target he is paid ₹18 less. If by the end of a month, he is paid total of ₹2988, then how many days does he meets the target?

(a) 21 (b) 12
(c) 10 (d) 14

150. A fruit vendor purchases two varieties of oranges at the rates of 12 oranges for ₹18 and 18 oranges for ₹12. He mixes the two varieties in the ratio of 2 : 3 and sells the mixed stock at a price of ₹144 for 10 dozens. What percentage of profit or loss does he make?

(a) 26 ¾% (b) 34¼%
(c) 20% (d) 28%

ANSWER KEY

English

1. (b)	5. (b)	9. (d)	13. (a)	17. (d)	21. (d)	25. (a)	29. (b)	33. (d)
2. (a)	6. (b)	10. (a)	14. (c)	18. (b)	22. (a)	26. (d)	30. (c)	34. (b)
3. (d)	7. (a)	11. (d)	15. (a)	19. (c)	23. (b)	27. (a)	31. (d)	35. (c)
4. (c)	8. (d)	12. (c)	16. (d)	20. (b)	24. (c)	28. (c)	32. (a)	

General Knowledge

36. (a)	40. (d)	44. (b)	48. (c)	52. (d)	56. (c)	60. (d)	64. (d)	68. (d)
37. (b)	41. (b)	45. (d)	49. (c)	53. (b)	57. (b)	61. (a)	65. (b)	69. (c)
38. (a)	42. (a)	46. (d)	50. (a)	54. (d)	58. (c)	62. (c)	66. (c)	70. (c)
39. (c)	43. (d)	47. (b)	51. (a)	55. (a)	59. (b)	63. (a)	67. (a)	

Legal Aptitude

71. (d)	75. (d)	79. (d)	83. (a)	87. (c)	91. (c)	95. (a)	99. (a)	103. (b)
72. (a)	76. (a)	80. (b)	84. (c)	88. (a)	92. (d)	96. (c)	100. (a)	104. (a)
73. (d)	77. (c)	81. (d)	85. (d)	89. (b)	93. (a)	97. (b)	101. (d)	105. (c)
74. (d)	78. (b)	82. (b)	86. (b)	90. (a)	94. (c)	98. (b)	102. (d)	

Reasoning

106. (c)	110. (c)	114. (d)	118. (d)	122. (d)	126. (c)	130. (b)	134. (d)	138. (c)
107. (b)	111. (b)	115. (b)	119. (c)	123. (a)	127. (b)	131. (a)	135. (b)	139. (b)
108. (d)	112. (d)	116. (d)	120. (d)	124. (a)	128. (a)	132. (d)	136. (b)	140. (d)
109. (a)	113. (c)	117. (c)	121. (a)	125. (c)	129. (c)	133. (a)	137. (a)	

Mathematics

141. (b)	143. (d)	145. (c)	147. (c)	149. (a)
142. (b)	144. (a)	146. (b)	148. (b)	150. (c)

AILET 2019

ENGLISH

Directions (questions 1–8): *Read the following passage carefully and then answer the questions that follow*

Surajendu Kumar's study on the effect of the modernization of a Government printing Press on Press maintenance work and workers is a solid contribution to debate that encompasses two lively issues in the history and sociology of technology: technological determinism and social constructivism.

Kumar makes the point that the characteristics of a technology have a decisive influence on job skill and work organization. Put more strongly, technology can be a primary determinant of social and managerial organization. Kumar believes the this possibility has been obscured by the recent sociological fashion, exemplified by Cravman, the analysis, that emphasizes the way machinery reflects social choices. For Carvman, the shape of a technological system is subordinate to the manager's desire to wrest control of the labour process from the workers. Technological change is construed as the outcome of negotiations among interested parties who seek to incorporate their own interests into the design and configuration of the machinery. This position represents the new mainstream called the social constructivism.

The constructivists gain acceptance by misrepresenting technological determinism technological determinists **are supposed to** believe, for example, that machinery imposes appropriate forms of order society. The alternative to constructivism, in other words, is to view technology as existing outside society, capable of directly influencing skills and work organization.

Kumar refutes the extremes of the constructivists by both theoretical and empirical arguments. Theoretically he define 'technology' in terms of relationship between social and technical variables. Attempts to reduce the meaning of technology to could, hard metal are bound to fail, for machinery is just scrap unless it is organized functionally and supported by appropriate system of operation and maintenance. At the empirical level, Kumar shows how a change at the Printing Press from maitenance-intensive electromechanical devices to semi-altered work tasks, skills, training opportunities, administration, and organization of workers. Some changes Kumar attributes to the particular way management and labor union negotiated the introduction of the technology, whereas other are seen as arising from the capabilities and nature of the technology itself. Thus, Kumar helps answer the question: 'When is social choice decisive and when are concrete characteristics of technology more important?'

1. The primary purpose of the passage is to

(a) challenge the position of advocates of technological determinism.

(b) consider a successful challenge to the constructivist view of technological change.

(c) suggest that the social causes of the technological change should be studied in real situation.

(d) advocated a more positive attitude towards technological change.

2. Which of the following statements about the modernization of the Printing Press is supported by the information provide in the passage?

(a) Some of the maintenance worker felt victimized by the new technology.

(b) The modernization was implemented without the consent of the employees directly affected by it.

(c) The new technology reduced the role of managers in labour negotiations.
(d) The modernization had an impact that went significantly beyond maintenance routines.

3. Which of the following most accurately describes Kumar's opinion of Cravman's position?
(a) He is sympathetic to its concern about the impact of modern technology of workers.
(b) He is concerned about its potential to impede the implementation of new technologies.
(c) He disapproves if its misplaced emphasis on the influence of managers.
(d) He admires the consideration it gives to the attitude of workers affected.

4. Which of the following statements from the passage suggests that the hypothetical sociological studies of change in industry most clearly exemplifies the social constructivists' version of technological determinism?
(a) It is the available technology that determines worker's skills, rather than workers skill influencing the application of technology.
(b) Some industrial technology eliminates jobs, but educated workers can create whole new skills areas by the adaptation of the technology.
(c) Most major technological advances in industry have been generated through research and development.
(d) All progress in industrial technology grows out of a continuing negotiation between technological possibility and human need.

5. According to the passage, Kumar believes if social constructivism had not gained widespread acceptance, then which of the following would be true?
(a) Modernization would have occurred at a slower rate.
(b) Businesses would be more likely to modernize without considering the social consequences of their actions.
(c) There would be greater understanding of the role played by technology in producing social change.
(d) Businesses would be less likely to understand the attitudes of employees affected by modernization.

6. According to the passage, constructivists employed which of the following to promote their argument?
(a) Construction of hypothetical situations that support their view.
(b) Empirical studies of business situations involving technological change.
(c) Descriptions of the breadth of impact of technological change.
(d) Contrasts of their view with a misstatement of an opposing view.

7. The author of the passage uses the expression 'are supposed to' in third para (highlighted) primarily on order to–
(a) Define the generally accepted position of determinists regarding the implementation of technology.
(b) Engage in speculation about the motivation of determinists
(c) Suggest that a contention made by constructivists regarding determinists is inaccurate.
(d) Lend support to a comment critical of the position of determinists

8. Which the following statements about Kumar's study of the Printing Press can be inferred from information in the passage?
(a) Kumar's study suggests that the implementation of technology should be discusses in the context of conflict between labor and management.
(b) Kumar examined the impact of change in the technology at the printing Press in terms of overall operations and organization.
(c) Kumar concluded that the implementation of new technology was equally beneficial to management and labor.
(d) Kumar's reason for undertaking the study was to undermine Cravman's analysis of the function of technology.

Directions (questions 9–11): *In each of the following questions, a word is highlighted. Choose the word which id a synonym of the highlighted word.*

9. The flaw of the genre is not in betraying the **loquacious** John williams and the chatty Father Foucquet, but in failing to schedule an interview with the reticent Eunice Williams and the tongue-tied john Hu.

(a) Talkative (b) Laconic
(c) Taciturn (d) Reserved

10. The above data suggest that common mechanisms underpin attachment organization in caregiver and infant, and the **precocious** emergence of mentalizing in the child?

(a) typical (b) late
(c) advance (d) Sudden

11. But there remains the **ineluctable** sense that something is badly, mysteriously wrong—if nothing else, because neither Kawhi nor the Spurs organization seems to need, or want, to clear thing up.

(a) unnecessary (b) illusive
(c) evitable (d) unavoidable

Directions (questions 12–13): *Following are the questions based on the same words used as different parts of speech. Choose the correct matches.*

12. Down

1. Adverb — A. He has seen the ups and downs of life.

2. Preposition — B. The porter was killed by the sown train.

3. Adjective — C. The fire engine came crashing down the hill.

4. Noun — D. Down went the 'Royal George.'

(a) 1-A, 2-B, 3-C, 4-D (b) 1 -D, 2-C, 3-B, 4-A
(c) 1-C, 2-D, 3-A, 4-B (d) 1-B, 2-A, 3-C, 4-D

13. Why

1. Interrogative adverb — A. Why did you do it?
2. Relative Adverb — B. I know the reason why he did it.
3. Interjection — C. Why, it is surely Nanak!
4. Noun — D. This is not the time to go into the why and the wherefore of it.

(a) 1-B, 2-D, 3-A, 4-C (b) 1 -D, 2-C, 3-B, 4-A
(c) 1-C, 2-D, 3-A, 4-B (d) 1-A, 2-B, 3-C, 4-D

Directions (questions 14–23): *Each of the following questions has sentence, part or all of which is underlined. Four sentences are given in the option. Choose the sentence Which is correct grammatically. Make sure in the sentence is clear, exact and free from redundancy. ambiguity and awkwardness.*

14. <u>Although she was considered among her contemporaries to be the better poet than her husband, later Kassia was overshadowed by his success.</u>

(a) Although she was considered among her contemporaries to be the better poet than her husband, later Kassia was overshadowed by his success.
(b) Later overshadowed by the success of her husband, kassia's poetry had been considered among her contemporaries to be better than that of her husband.
(c) Although Kassia 's success was later overshadowed by that of her husband, among her contemporaries she was considered the better poet.
(d) Kassia's poetry was considered among her contemporaries as better than her husband, but her success was later overshadowed by his.

15. <u>A ruined structure found at Aizawl, India, was probably a church, as indicated in its eastward orientation and by its overall plan, as well as artifacts, such as glass-oil lamp fragments, found at the site.</u>

(a) A ruined structure found at Aizawl, India, was probably a church, as indicated in its eastward orientation and by its overall plan, as well plan, as well as.

(b) A ruined structure found at Aizawl, India, once probably being a church, was indicated by its eastward orientation, overall plan, and
(c) A ruined structure found at Aizawl, India was probably a church, as indicates its eastward orientation and overall plan, as well as the.
(d) That a ruined structure found at Aizawl, India, was probably a church is indicated by its eastward orientation and overall plan,, as well as by the.

16. Octopus, with anywhere from five to eight arms, have a strong regenerative ability, and if one arm is lost it quickly replaces it, sometimes by the animal overcompensating and growing an extra one or two.
(a) One arm is lost it quickly replaces it, sometimes by the animals overcompensating and
(b) One arm is lost it is quickly replaced, with the animal sometimes overcompensating and.
(c) They lose one arm they quickly replaced it, sometimes by the animals overcompensating,
(d) They lose one arm it is quickly replaced, sometimes with the animal overcompensating,

17. The eyes of the catfish adapt to darkness more quickly than any other animal yet tested, thus allowing it to hunt efficiently under the gloomy conditions at its feeding depths of between 500 and 800 meters.
(a) The eyes of the catfish adapt to darkness more quickly than any other animal yet tested, thus allowing it
(b) The eyes of the catfish adapt to darkness more quickly than does any other animal yet tested, thus allowing them.
(c) The eyes of the catfish adapt to darkness more quickly than do those of any other animal yet tested, thus allowing it
(d) Because the eyes of the catfish adapt to darkness more quickly than do those of any other animal yet tested, thus allow them.

18. The first trenches that were cut into a 1000 acre site at Haji Piyada, Afghanistan, have yielded strong evidence for centrally administered complex societies in northern regions of Asia that were arising simultaneously with but independently of the more celebrated city- states of Indus Valley Civilization, in what is now northern India.
(a) that were cut into a 1000 acre site at Haji Piyada, Afghanistan, yieldes strong evidence that centrally administered complex societies in northern regions of Asia that were arising simultaneously with but also.
(b) Having been cut into a 1000 acre site at Haji Piyada, Afghanistan, have yielded strong evidence for centrally administered complex societies in northern regions of Asia that were arising simultaneously but.
(c) cut into a 1000 acre site at Haji Piyada, Afghanistan, yieldes strong evidence for centrally administered complex societies in northern regions of Asia arising simultaneously but also.
(d) cut into a 1000 acre site at Haji Piyada, Afghanistan, have yielded strong evidence for centrally administered complex societies in northern regions of Asia arose simultaneously with but.

19. While it costs about the same to run atomic power plants as other types of power plants, it is the fixed costs that stem from building atomic power plants that makes it more expensive for them to generate electricity.
(a) While it costs about the same to run atomic power plants as other types of power plants, it is the fixed costs that stem from building atomic power plants that makes it more expensive for them to generate electricity.
(b) While the costs of running atomic power plants is about the same as for other types of power plants, the fixed costs that stem from building atomic power plants that makes the electricity they generate more electricity.
(c) Even though it costs about the same to run atomic power plants as other types of power plants, it is the fixed costs that stem from building atomic power plants that makes the electricity they generate more expensive.

(d) It costs about the same to run atomic power plants as for other types of power plants, whereas the electricity they generate is more expensive, stemming from the fixed costs of building atomic power plants.

20. About 8 million acres in the British Isles have been invaded by leafy spurge, a herbaceous plant from Russia with milky sap that gives mouth sores to cattle displacing grasses and other cattle food and rendering grasslands worthless.

(a) Isles have been invaded by leafy spurge, a herbaceous plant from Russia with milky sap that gives mouth sores to cattle displacing grasses and other cattle food and rendering

(b) Isles have been invaded by leafy spurge, a herbaceous plant from Russia with milky sap that gives mouth sores to cattle and displaced grasses and other cattle food rendering

(c) Isles have been invaded by leafy spurge, a herbaceous plant from Russia having milky sap that gives mouth sores to cattle displacing grasses and other cattle food and rendering.

(d) Isles, have been invaded by leafy spurge, ***a herbaceous plant from* Russia** that has milky sap that giving mouth sores to cattle displacing grasses and other cattle food, rendering.

21. In Xonia, a lack of genetic variation in the Rodian ant has allowed the species to spread widely; due to their being so genetically similar to one another, the ants consider all their fellows to be a close relative and thus do not engage in the kind of fierce inter-colony struggles that limits the spread of this species in its native Rodia.

(a) Due to their being so genetically similar to one another, the ants consider all their fellows to be a close relative and thus do not engage in the kind of fierce inter-colony struggles that limits.

(b) Due to its being so genetically similar the ant considers all its fellows to a close relative and thus do not engage in the kind of fierce inter - colony struggles that limits.

(c) Because they are so genetically similar to one another, the ants consider all their fellows to be a close relative and thus do not engage in the kind of fierce inter-colony struggles that limits.

(d) Because of being so genetically similar to one another, the ants consider all their fellows to be a close relative and thus do not engage in the kind of fierce inter - colony struggles that limits.

22. Rivaling the Roman Colosseum or even the ancient of the Harappa and mohenjo-Daro as an achievement, the army of bronze warriors created to protects juan ming, indonesia's King, during his lifetime is more than 3,000 years old and took 900,000 artisans more than 40 years to complete.

(a) The army of bronze warriors created to protects Juan Ming, indonesia' s King, during his lifetime is more than 3,000 years old and took 900,000 artisans more than 40 years to complete.

(b) It took 900,000 artisans more than 40 years to create an army of bronze warriors more than 30,000 years ago that would protect Juan Ming, Indonesia's King, during his lifetime.

(c) More than 30,000 years ago 900,000 artisans worked than 40 years to create an army of bronze warriors to protest Juan Ming Indonesia's king during his lifetime.

(d) More than 40 years were needed to complete the army of bronze warriors that 900,000 artisans created 3,000 years ago to protect Juan Ming, Indonesia's King, during his lifetime.

23. Tides typically range from four to seven feet, but while some places show no tides at all, some other, such as the Bay of Bengal, have tides of at least twenty feet and more.

(a) The other, such as the Bay of Bengal, have tides of at least twenty feet.

(b) Other, such as the Bay of Bengal, have tides of at least twenty feet and more.

(c) Those as the Bay of Bengal,which has tides of more than twenty feet.

(d) The ones at the Bay of Bengal, have tides of at least twenty feet and more.

Directions (questions 24–29): *Following question are based on the various Figures of Speech.*

24. Which of the following statements is not an example of epigram?
(a) So innocent arch, so cunningly simple.
(b) A man cannot be too careful in the choice of his enemies.
(c) Fools rush in where angles fear to tread.
(d) Art lies in concealing art.

25. Which of the following statement is an example of litotes?
(a) I am a citizen of no mean city.
(b) Is life worth living?–It depends upon the liver.
(c) Why, man, if the river were dry, I am able to fill it with tears.
(d) He had his jest, and they had his estate.

26. Which of the following statement is an example of metaphor?
(a) The righteous shall flourish as the palm tree.
(b) The Assyrian came down came down like a wolf on the fold.
(c) As the hart panteth after the water-brooks, so panteth my soul after Thee, O God.
(d) Revenge is a kind of wild justice.

27. Which of the following statement is an example of Metonymy?
(a) Uneasy lies the head that wears the Crown.
(b) He was playing to the gallery.
(c) He has many mouths to feed.
(d) England won the first test match against Australia.

28. Which of the following statements is an example of Oxymoron?
(a) Not that I loved Caesar less, but that I loved Rome more.
(b) Speech is silvern, bur silence is golden.
(c) She accepted it as the kind cruelty of the surgeon' s knife.
(d) Give every man thy ear, but few thy voice.

29. Which of the following statements is an example of pun?
(a) No doubt but ye are the people, and wisdom shall die with you.
(b) An ambassador id an honest man who lies aboard for the good of his country.
(c) I must be taught my duty, and by you !
(d) One truth is clear: whatever is ,right.

Directions (questions 30–35): *Choose the best word to fill in the blanks*

Roshan acknowledges that late payment of rent will cause Ram, his landlord to (30)____________ costs not contemplated by their Lease, the exact amount of which will be extremely difficult to (31) ____________. These costs include, cut are not (32)____________ to, processing and accounting charges, and accounting charges, and late charges which may be (33)____________on Landlord by the terms of any Superior Leases and Mortgages. Accordingly, if any installment of Monthly Rent or payment of additional rent id not received by Ram or Landlord 's assignee within fifteen days after the amount is (34)____________., Roshan shall pay to Ram a late charge equal to ten per cent of said amount. Acceptance of late charges by Ram shall not constitute a waiver of Roshan 's default with respect to said amount, nor prevent Ran from (35)____________any of the other rights and remedies granted hereunder or at law or inequity.

30 (a) derive (b) acquire
(c) collect (d) incur

31 (a) affirm (b) classify
(c) ascertain (d) locate

32. (a) contained (b) limited
(c) held (d) bound

33. (a) imposed (b) dictated
(c) obliged (d) required

34. (a) owing (b) scheduled
(c) due (d) unpaid

35. (a) practising (b) exercising
(c) commanding (d) undertaking

GENERAL KNOWLEDGE

36. Why north-western India gets rainfall in winter season of January and February?
(a) Due to western disturbance in Mediterranean Sea
(b) Due to eastern disturbance in the Mediterranean Sea
(c) Due to western disturbance in the pacific Ocean.
(d) Due to eastern disturbance in Pacific Ocean.

37. Which of the following is/are true about Methanol Economy?

1. Future economy in which dimethyl ether replace fossil fuels as a means of energy storage.
2. It offers an alternative to the proposed hydrogen economy or ethanol economy.
3. China is the world's largest producer of methanol.
4. Menthol cannot bo made by chemical recycling of carbon-dioxide.

(a) I, II (b) II, III
(c) III, IV (d) I, II, III

38. Which airport is known as the 'World's Emptiest Airport'?
(a) Sigiriya Airptrt, Dambulla
(b) Ellinikon international Airport, Athens
(c) Mattala international Airport, Hambantota
(d) Berlin Tempelhof Airport, Germany

39. Who has prepared Global Risk Report 2019?
(a) United nation
(b) world Economic Forum
(c) Greenpeace international
(d) None of these

40. India's first Vertical-lift Bridge will connect ____________?
(a) Rameswaram to mainland India
(b) Ahmedabad to Mumbai
(c) Daman and Diu to Gujarat
(d) Kavaratti to mainland India

41. What was the cause of extreme cold in USA in January and February 2019?
(a) Strengthening of Polar Vortex
(b) Weakening of Polar Votes
(c) Extreme could in Antarctica
(d) Depletion of Ozone layer

42. Which of the following are the Administrative/Revenue unit of jammu and kashmir?
(a) Jammu and Kashmir
(b) Jammu, kashmir, Kargil
(c) Jammu, Kashmir, Leh
(d) Jammu, Kashmir, Ladakh

43. Which of the following is/are true about the Earth's Magnetic Field?
I. Earth Magnetic Field is shifting from Canada and moving towards Siberia.
II. The Magnetic Pole is moving fast because of turbulence in Earth's liquid outer core.
III. The constant shift is a problem for compasses in smartphones and some consumer electronics.
IV. GPS will also be affected by fast moving of Magnetic Pole.

(a) I, II, III, IV, (b) I, II, III
(c) I, II (d) III, IV

44. Which of the following is/are true about concept of Most Favored Nation (MFN)?
I. It establishes the sovereign equality of states with respect to trading policy
II. There are two forms of MFN treatment : conditional and unconditional.
III. Such treatment has always applied primarily to the duties charged on imports.
IV. Custom unions and free trade areas are exceptions to MFN principle.

(a) I, II, III (b) II, III, IV
(c) I, II, III, IV, (d) I, III, IV

45. Who has become highest wicket taker in International Cricket in 2018?
(a) Mohamed Shami
(b) Jaspreet Bumrah
(c) Billy Stanelcake
(d) Marcus Stoinis

46. Who is appointed as the New Chief minister of Madhaya Pradesh in 2018?
(a) Kamal Nath
(b) Shivraj Singh Chouhan
(c) Jyotiraditya Scindia
(d) Ashok Gehlot

47. Who is appointed as the New Chief Information Commission of India?
(a) R. K. Mathur (b) Vandan N. Sarna
(c) Sudhir Bhargava (d) Suresh Chandra

48. Which of the following countries have quit the membership of UNESCO?
(a) USA and China
(b) USA and Iran
(c) Israel and Iran
(d) Israel and USA

49. USA has ceased to be member of which of the following organizations?
(a) NAFTA (b) COP21
(c) UNHRC (d) All of the above

50. Which country has introduced GAFA tax on Global Internet Technology firms?
(a) Germany (b) Spain
(c) Belgium (d) France

51. The Yellow Vest protest of France is in respect of
(a) Greek Tax on fuel
(b) Labour policy
(c) Unemployment
(d) Economic Policy

52. The Cabinet has approved merger of Vijaya Bank and Dena Bank with?
(a) SBI
(b) Indian Bank
(c) Bank of Baroda
(d) Indian Overseas Bank

53. Which of the following countries recently assumed the seat of non-permanent member of UN security Council?
(a) South Africa (b) Netherlands
(c) Sweden (d) India

54. Which of the following country's Spacecraft has spacecraft has landed for the first time on the far side of the Moon?
(a) USA
(b) Russia
(c) China
(d) Japan

55. India's fastest train, Vande Bharat Express, will run from ______________ to ______________
(a) Delhi, Varanasi
(b) Delhi, Agra
(c) Delhi, Mumbai
(d) Mumbai, Bengaluru

56. The HQ of international Olympic committee is located in
(a) USA
(b) France
(c) Switzerland
(d) Germany

57. Which of the following statement is/are true?
I. According to Indus Water Treaty, India got the full right for Utilization of waters of three eastern river Ravi, Beas and Satluj.
II. Shahpur Kandi dam is planned to be built across the river Satluj.
III. Implementation of the Shahpurkandi Dam project would minimize wastage of water to Pakistan.
(a) I, II, III, (b) I, II,
(c) II, III (d) I, III

58. Hayabusa 2 was in news recently, Which of the following statement regarding it is correct?
(a) It is Japan's first Mars Mission, Funded by NASA.
(b) Asteroid sample-return mission operated by the Japanese Space Agency, JAXA,
(c) It is a military satellite by JAXA.
(d) It is Japan's first mission to Jupiter.

59. World's first privately funded mission to moon is launched by ______________
(a) USA (b) Russia
(c) Japan (d) Israel

60. Which of the following railway stations in India is NOT to be redeveloped in a PPP mode?
(a) Bhubaneshwar
(b) Habibganj
(c) Delhi Sarai Rohilla
(d) Jammu Tawi

61. ________ was one of the first countries in the world to propose a ban the sale of petrol and diesel cars by making the switch to electronic-powered Vehicles.
(a) France (b) UK
(c) Norway (d) Scotland

62. Which of the following statements is/are not true regarding Credit Rating Agencies (CRA) in India?
I. The Securities and Exchange Board of India (CRA) Regulations, 1999 empower SEBI to regulate CRAS operating in India.
II. All the credit agencies need to be registered with SEBI in order to operate in India.
III. There are several India Credit Rating Agencies viz. CRISIL, ICRA, CARE, India Rating and Research, SME RA, Information and Brickworks, Moody, Fitch,
IV. CRAs help strengthening of primary market by increasing borrower pool.
(a) I, II,III, IV (b) III, IV
(c) I,III (d) II, IV

63. Which of the following companies has designed gates and reader for the National Common Mobility Card in India?
(a) Bharat Electronics Limited
(b) Hindustan Electronic Limited
(c) Reliance
(d) Tata

64. Why Ratnagiri, Which will be Asia's largest oil Refinery, was in news recently?
I. Protest over acquisition of land by government
II. Protest over harm on eco-sensitive zone
III. Protest against impact on mango and cashew crops
IV. Protest over acquisition of land under State Law and not under Central law on acquisition of land.
(a) I,II, III, (b) II, III, IV
(c) I, II, IV (d) I,II, III,IV

65 World's largest Solar Park is Inaugurated in
(a) Karnataka, India
(b) Tengger Desert, China
(c) Gobi Desert, China
(d) Rajasthan, India

66. Which of the following movies got the 91st Academy Award for Best Picture?
(a) Black Panther
(b) Green Book
(c) Bohemian Rhapsody
(d) Roma

67. Bharat Ratna 2019 will be conferred to
I. Bhupen Hazarika
II. Pranab Mukherjee
III. Nanji Deshmuks
IV. Atal Bihari Bajpai
(a) I, II, III,IV (b) I, II
(c) I, II, III (d) II, III

68 Sunderban Reserve Forest was accorded the status of 'Wetland of International Importance' under which of the following International Instruments?
(a) Ramsar Convention
(b) Convention on Biological Diversity
(c) United Nations Framework Convention on Climate Change
(d) Kyoto Protocol

69 In March 2019, RBI has allowed White level ATM Operators to buy wholesale case above a threshold of ____________ pieces of any denomination, directly from the Reserve Bank and Currency Chests against full payment.
(a) 5 lakh (b) 3 lakh
(c) 2 lakh (d) 1 lakh

70. In March 2019, Which of the following countries Government Resigned after failure of flagship health and social care reform?
(a) Sweden (b) Finland
(c) Poland (d) Norway

LEGAL APTITUDE

Directions (questions 71–73): *Apply the legal principle to the facts gives below and select the most appropriate answer.*

Legal Principles:

1. An attempt os an act committed in part execution of a criminal design or intent, more than mere preparation, but failing short of actual commission.
2. Whoever, by deceiving any property fraudulently or dishonestly induces the person so deceived to deliver any property to any person or to consent that any parson shall ratain any property, or intentionally induces the person do deceived to do or omit to do anything which he would not do/omit if he were not so deceived, and which act or omission cause or is likely to cause damage or harm to that person in body, mind, reputation or property, is said to 'cheat'.
3 Preparation is the second stage in the commission of a crime. It means to arrange the necessary measure for the commission of the intended criminal act.
4. Whoever cause death by doing an act with the intention of causing such bodily injury as is likely to cause death, or with the knowledge that his act is likely to cause death, commits the offence of murder.
5. Whoever cause the death of any person by doing any rash or negligent act shall be guilty of negligence.

71. In which of the following cases, X is guilty of attempting to commit the offence?
    (a) X, in order to forge a document purporting to be executed by Y, send his servant to buy a stamp paper in the name of Y. As the servant reaches shop, he is arrested.
    (b) X shoots at Y whose back is to towards him. Y is not hurt as he is beyond the range of the gun.
    (c) X pours half a pint of subsiance from a bottle marked 'poison' into the drink of Y,Y is not aware of it. Later, it turns out that the bottle did not contain any poison
    (d) X administers some noxious substance to Ria so that an abortion result. The Woman was not pregnant.

72. **Facts:** Amar applied for the post of P. G. Teacher in a government school and submitted his application along with his degrees. He was called for the interview on 10 June 2018. But the school authorities on 10 May 2018 discovered that the copy of the degrees attached with Amar's application are forged and so the interview was cancelled.

    Is any offence committed by Amar?
    (a) Amar is guilty of cheating
    (b) Amar is guilty of preparation to cheat.
    (c) Amar is guilty of attempt to cheat.
    (d) Amar is not guilty of any offence as he is not called for the interview.

73. **Facts:** X tries to pickpocket Z, Z has a loaded pistol in his pocket, X's hand touches the pistol and triggers it, resulting in he death of Z.

    Which of the following offence is committed by X?
    (a) X is guilty of causing Z's murder.
    (b) X is guilty of culpable homicide by negligence
    (c) X is guilty of causing grievous hurt.
    (d) X is guilty of pickpocketing

Directions (questions 74–76): *Apply the legal principles to the facts given below and select the most appropriate answer.*

Legal Principal:

1. The Tort of Negligence is a legal wrong that is suffered by someone at the hands of another who fails to take proper care to avoid what a reasonable person would regard as a foreseeable risk.
2. The test of liability requires that harm must be a reasonably foreseeable result of the defendant's conduct, a relationship of proximity must exist and it must be fair, Just and reasonable to impose liability.
3. *Volenti non-fit injuria* is defence to action in negligence

74. **Facts:** In a sad incident,95 fans of a Football club died in a stampede in the Nehru Staduim. The

court has decided that the accident was caused due to the negligence of the Police in permitting to many supporters to crowd in one part of the stadium. Now, a suit is filed by Harman and several other people against the Commissioner of State Police. Harman and the other claimants had relatives who were caught up in the Nehru stadium disaster. The disaster was Broadcast on live television, where several claimants alleged, they had witnessed friends and relatives die, Other were present in the stadium of had heard about the events in other ways. All claimed damages for the psychiatric harm they suffered as a results. Determine whether, for the purposes of establishing in negligence, those who suffer purely psychiatric harm from witnessing an event at which they are not physically present are sufficiently proximate for a duty to be owed, and thus can be said to be reasonably within the contemplation of the tortfeasor?

(a) Police is liable for all of the consequences of their consequences of their negligence because they could reasonable foresee the injury. The liability towards victims who are not physically present is also there in all circumstances.

(b) Police is not liable because the duty of care to words Harman and others will be Breached if they were present at the event and the harm caused was being foreseeable. The liability towards victims who are not physically present in only in certain exceptional circumstances.

(c) Police is not liable because the incident was an accident and supporters were there by their own free will.

(d) Police is liable for only for the death of 95 fans burns and not for the psychiatric harm to relatives of deceased fans which happened due to their own delicate mental condition.

75. Facts: X Purchased a disused cinema with the intention of turning into a Multiplex. Six weeks after, X entered the building for the first time, it was set on fire by intruders and destroyed. As a result, the adjacent building were also affected and damaged The cinema building was a target to vandals and childrens who often played there, but X had no knowledge of previous attempts to start fire at the cinema buildings. The owners of the adjacent building brought an action for negligence against X on grounds that X failed to take reasonable care for the safety of the buildings by not keeping the cinema locked, making regular inspections and employing a caretaker. Decide whether the occupier of a property owe a duty of care to the adjoining occupier in respect of acts of trespass on his property resulting in damage to the adjoining properties?

(a) An occupier of a property owes a duty of care to the adjoining occupiers in respect of acts of trespass on his property resulting in damage to the adjoining properties under all circumstances.

(b) X was not aware of previous attempts of vandals to start fire and as such, the building did not present an abvious fire risk, so X was not under any duty to anticipate the possibility of fire and take measures to prevent the entry of vandals. So, no duty of care existed towards the adjoining properties in this case.

(c) Though X were not aware of previous attempts of vandals to start fire and as such and building did not present an obvious fore risk but he failed to take reasonable care, so X is liable.

(d) X is not liable as the adjoining occupiers are also negligent by not being careful in safeguarding their properties against fire.

76. Facts: A team of scientists imported a virus for the purpose of research. They carried out research on their premises into foot and mouth disease in cattle, and they were apparently responsible for the escape of some virus. As a result of an outbreak of foot and mouth disease in the area, and the Minister of Agriculture ordered two market to be closed. This caused the some of the traders, who were two firms of auctioneers, to suffer a loss of profits on a total of six market days for which they sought to recover, Decided whether the scientist owed a duty of care towards the traders?

(a) An ability to foresee indirect of economic loss to another person as the result as the result of a defendant's conduct automatically impose on the defendant a duty to take care to avoid that loss.

(b) The loss to traders was pecuniary. The suffered no physical harm to themselves or to any of their property. An ability to foresee indirect of economic loss to another person as the result of a defendant's conduct did not automatically impose in the defendant a duty to take care to avoid that loss.

(c) It is not proved that there was negligence on the part of the scientists which resulted in an escape of the virus so they are not liable.

(d) Though the scientists are negligent in handling the virus but they are not liable as take leakage of virus was by accident.

77. Legal Principles:

1. Private nuisance is a continuous, unlawful and indirect interference with the use or enjoyment of land, or of some right over or in connection with it.
2. A person liable if he can reasonable foresee that his acts would be likely to injure his neighbour.
3. The foreseeability of the type of damage is a prerequisite of liability in actions of nuisance.

Facts: Bharat Sugar Ltd. operated a sugar refinery on the bank of the river Ravi. They had a jetty from which raw sugar would be offloaded from barges and refined sugar would be taken. The sugar would be take by large vessels and then transferred to smaller barges to enable them to get through the shallow waters. As part of development Bharat Sugar Ltd. wished to construct a new jetty and dredge the water to accommodate the large vessels. At the same time the State was constructing new ferry terminals. The design of the ferry terminals was such that it caused siltation of the channels. After using the channels for a short while. Bharat Sugar's large vessels were no longer able use them. Further dredging at the cost of ₹ 7,50,000 was required to make the channel and usable by the vessels. Bharat Sugar Ltd. brought an action in nuisance to recover the cost of the extra dredging. Is the State liable?

(a) The loss caused by the construction of new ferry terminals could not amount to a private nuisance at law since at law since they did not possess any private right which enabled then to insist on any particular depth of water.

(b) The loss caused by the construction of new ferry terminals amount to a private nuisance at law since they did possess right to use the water at a particular depth.

(c) No, it cannot constitute private nuisance but the claimants can claim damages for loss suffered by them.

(d) Yes, the State's conduct was unreasonable in building the new terminals without thinking of all the consequences it will have on the rights of other parties.

78. Legal Principal: The tort of negligent misstatement is defined as an inaccurate statement made honestly but carelessly usually in the form of advice given by a party with special skill/ knowledge to a party that doesn't posses this skill or knowledge.

Facts: X and Y Co. were advertising agents placing contracts on behalf of a client on credit terms, X and Y Co. would be personally liable should the client default. To protect themselves, the X and Y asked their bankers to obtain a credit reference from K and L, the client's bankers. The reference (given both orally and then in writing)was given gratis and was favourable, but also contained an exclusion clause to the effect that information was given 'without responsibility on the part of this Bank or its officials'. X and Y relied upon this reference and subsequently suffered financial loss when the client went into liquidation. X and Y sued K and L Co. for negligence, claiming that the information was given negligently and was misleading. K and L argued there was no duty of care owed regarding the statements. Decide.

(a) The K and L's disclaimer was not valid to protect them from liability and X and Y's claim will not fail.

(b) The X and Y has a duty to obtain the necessary information themselves without relying upon the other party.

(c) It was reasonable for K and L to have known that the information that they had given would likely have been relied upon tor entering into a contract of same sort. That would give rise to a special relationship of trust, in which K and L would have to take sufficient care in giving advice to avoid negligence liability. However, on the facts, the disclaimer is sufficient to discharge any duty created by K and L's actions.

(d) It was reasonable for K and L to have known that the information that they had given would likely have been relied upon for entering into a contract of some sort. That would give rise to a special relation of trust, in which K and L would gave to take sufficient care in giving advice to avoid liability. Hence, liable for negligent misstatement.

Directions (questions 79–81): Apply the legal principles to the facts to the facts given below and select the most appropriate answer.

Legal Principles:

1. A contract comes into being from the acceptance of an offer. When the person to whom the offer is made signifies his assent thereto, the proposal is said to be accepted and the parties are at *consensus ad idem regarding* the terms of the agreement.
2. Consideration is something that moves from the promise to the promisor, at the implied or express request of the latter, in return for his promise. The item that moves can be a right, interest, profit, loss, responsibility given of suffered, forbearance of a benefit which is of some value in the eyes of law.
3. Contractual rights and liabilities are exclusive to the parties to contract.
4. There are few exceptions to the doctrine to privity of contract like agency, trust, assignment and third-party beneficiary.
5. A quasi contracts is a contract that is created by the court when no such official contract exists between the parties to prevent a party from being unjustly enriched, or from benefitting from the situation when he does not deserve to do so.

79. Facts: Goodtyre is a tyre manufacturer who agreed with their dealer to not sell the tyres below a recommended retail price (RRP). As part of the agreement, Goodtyre also required their dealers to gain the same agreement with their retailers, who in this instance was Bestmotors. The agreement held that if tyres were sold below the RRP. they would be required to pay ₹ 500 per tyre in damage to Goodtyre. This was agreed between the dealer and Bestmotors, which effectively made Goodtyre a third-party to that agreement. Something after this Bestmotor sold the tyres below the agreed price and Goodtyre sued for damages and an injunction to prevent them from continuing as this activity. Bestmotor is arguing that Goodtyre could not enforce the contract as it was not part of the contract between the dealer and the Bestmotor. The court decided that Goodtyre had no right to access damages. Which of the following are correct reasons?

I. Goodtyre could not claim for damages as only a party to a contract can claim damages under it.

II. Goodtyre had not given any consideration to Bestmotors and therefore there could be no binding contract between the parties.

III. Goodtyre was not listed as an agent within the contract and could therefore not be included as a valid third-party who had right to claim on the contract.

(a) I only (b) II only
(c) I and II (d) I, II, III

80 **Facts :** Nandini, by deed of gift, made over certain landed property to Reena, her daughter. By the terms of the deed, which was registered, it was stipulated that an annuity of Rs. 3,000 should be paid every year to the Subhashini, sister of Nandini, Rena executed in Subhashini's favour an agreement promising to give effect to the

stipulation. The annuity was, however, not paid and the subhashini sued to recover it. Reena id defending herself by claiming that there is no valid contract with Subhashini. Which of the following can be ground/s for court's decision?

I. A promise is enforceable if there is some consideration for it and it is quite immaterial whether in moves from the promise or any other person

II. Only a person who is a party to a contract may demand the execution of that contract from other party. But if there is third party beneficiary to contract then It is enforced to the extent of his/her benefit.

III. The agreement is valid as both Reena and Subhashini agreed to on the same thing in the same sense.

IV. There is no privity of contract a Subhashini has furnished no consideration. Reena had promised to subhashini but consideration was furnished by Nandini.

(a) I, II (b) III, IV
(c) I only (d) II only

81. Facts: Tanu's brother, Ishan, tries to talk her into building a greenhouse in her large back-yard. She declines, but Ishan is convinced that, if she were surprised by a lovely greenhouse, she would love it. Knowing that Tanu makes good money and could easily afford the greenhouse, Ishan contacts greenhouse builder Aditya and arranges to have him erect the structure while his sister is at work one day.

Tanu is not happy by her brother's initiation, but the deed is done. Ishan has directed Aditya to bill his sister for the greenhouse, and that turns out to be the biggest surprise for her, She declines to pay, and Ishan tells Aditya he cannot afford it. Aditya is now out, not only for payment for his many hours of hard work, but cash for the materials he used. He files a civil suit to claim against both with Tanu and Ishan Decide.

(a) Ishan is liable to pay as he has entered into contract with Aditya for hid services.
(b) Tanu is not liable to pay as there is no contract between Aditya and Tanu.
(c) Tanu is liable to pay Aditya the costs involved in building the greenhouse as she has being unjustly enriched by this deal.
(d) Tanu is liable as Ishan is her brother and was acting on her behalf under her implied consent as she liked greenhouse.

82. Legal Principles:

1. Vicarious liability is when employers are held liable for the torts of their employees that are committed during the course of employment.
2. A servant is a person subject to the command of his master as to the manner in which he shall do his work. The question of whether a person is an employee depends upon the degree of control which the employer exercises over the worker.

Facts: Raja is a travel agent and possesses certain house, which had an internal communication throughout, and which were used for the purposes of his business Ramesh looked after the houses, and lived in them for this purpose, but he was also a clerk in the Raja's pay at a set annual salary. He lived in the houses with his wife a child, and a servant. The case concerned the payment of inhabited house duty, There was statutory exemption for premises which were occupied by a "servant" or person occupying the premises "for the protection thereof". Raja was claiming the exemption from tax liability by claiming that Ramesh was the servant. Decide whether Ramesh was a servant or an independent contractor?

(a) Ramesh is not a servant as the premises was held purely for trade purposes, and as Ramesh's position was simply that of a caretaker.
(b) Ramesh earned a salary per annum in his separate role a clerk and merely enjoyed residence of the building with his family members. Thus, is an employee of the building owner for tax purposes.
(c) Ramesh is a servant as servant is a person subject to the command of his master as to the manner which he shall do his work.
(d) Ramesh is a servant as Raja can control his work of caretaker of the building as well as his job of clerk.

83. Legal Principles:

1. Private nuisance is a continuous, unlawful and indirect interference with the use or enjoyment of land, or of some right over or in connection with it.
2. The person who for his own purposes brings on his lands and collects and keeps there anything likely to do mischief if it escapes, must keep it in at his peril, and if he does not do so, os rima facie answerable for all the damage which is the natural consequence of its escape.
3. Generally, nuisance cannot be justified on the ground of necessity, pecuniary interest, convenience, or economic advantage to a defendant.

Facts: Dr. Hemant had for 18 years operated a clinic and hospital for the treatment of ENT. Dr Karan operated a renal clinic in which patients receive heamo-dialysis on the floor above the Dr. Hemant's clinic. The Karan was found liable for emitting from their clinic obnoxious fumes which escaped downwards into Hemant's clinic. Hemant his staff and patients were found to have suffered substantial damage ranging from skin diseases, ted and swollen eyes, headaches, lethargy and breathing difficulties Decide whether Karan is liable?

(a) Karan is not liable as the work is a public walfare requires, a nuisance may be permitted for special purposes.
(b) Hemant cannot claim damages as is voluntarily operating his clinic since a decade.
(c) Karan is not liable as his running the clinic for 18 years and Hemant has not raised any issues earlier.
(d) Karan is liable for the damages caused to Hemant and his staff and patients.

Directions (questions 84–85): *The following question consist of two statement, one labelled as 'Assertion' and the other as 'Reason'. Read both statement carefully and answer using the codes given below.*

(a) Both A and R are true and R is the correct explanation of A
(b) Both A and R are true and R is not true explanation of A
(c) A is true but R is false
(d) A is false but R is True

84. Assertion (A): The rule making power of the Supreme Court is not subject to any law made by the Parliament of India.

Reason (R): Only an impartial and independent judiciary can protect he right of the individual without fear or favour.

85. Assertion (A): The entries in the three legislative lists are not always set out with scientific precision.

Reason (R): The entries are not powers but only field of legislation.

86. Which of the following amendments are sought to be introduced in the Representation of the People Act through Amendment Bill, 2018?

I. Proxy voting
II. Gender neutral Provisions
III. Allocation of seats
IV. Delimitation of constituencies

(a) I, II, III, IV (b) III, IV
(c) I, II (d) I, II, IV

87. Which of the following offences can be prosecuted under the newly enacted Fugitive Economic Offenders Act, 2018?

I. Economic offences involving Rs. 100 crore and more
II. Dishonouring of cheques
III. Money laundering
IV. Benami transactions

(a) III, IV (b) I, II, III, IV
(c) II, IV (d) I, III, IV

88. The Constitution One Hundred and Third Amendment) Bill, 2019 seeks to amend __________ to include __________

(a) Article 15 and 29; Other Backward Class
(b) Article 15 and 30; Other Backward Class
(c) Article 29 and 30; Economically weaker sections
(d) Article 15 and 16; Economically weaker sections

89. Which of the following are the salient features of the Aadhaar and other laws (Amendment) Ordinance 2019?

I. The maximum penalty proposed is Rs. one crore.

II. The cognizance of an offence under the law can be taken only a complaint by UIDAI.

III. It changes definition of 'aadhaar number' to include 'virtual ID', in addition to the 12- digit number.

IV. The authority who can issue orders to disclose Aadhaar information is proposed to changed as'High Court Judge' from 'District Judge.

(a) I, II (b) II, III, IV
(c) I, III, IV (d) III, IV

90. Recently, Ram Janmabhoomi and Babri Masjid land dispute is referred to mediation by a panel, Which of the following is the correct constitution of the panel?

(a) Retd. Justice Kalifullah, Sadhguru
(b) Retd. Justice Altmas Kbir, Sadhguru, Sadhna Ramachandran
(c) Retd. Justice Altmas Kbir, Sri Sri Ravi Shanker
(d) Retd. Justice, Kalifullah, Sri Sri Ravi Shanker, Sriram Panchu

91. Who is heading the five-member committee set up to examine the issues related to framing of a proper, Structured scheme for providing of insurance cover to the advocates and also suggest modalities for the implementation of such scheme?

(a) Ravi Shankar Prasad
(b) Anand Patel
(c) Alok Srivastava
(d) Amrinder Khuller

92. What is the punishment under the Official Secrets Act, 1923 for the offence of spaying in relation to any work of defence establishment of in relation to any secret official code?

(a) Sentence of Death
(b) Imprisonment for 14 years
(c) Imprisonment for 10 years
(d) Imprisonment for life

93. Citizenship (Amendment) Bill 2019, seeks to grant citizenship on the basis of __________ to the people from __________

(a) Religion; Bangladesh. Pakistan, Afghanistan
(b) Religion; Bangladesh. Pakistan
(c) Birth; Bangladesh
(d) Descent; Bangladesh Afghanistan

94. Delhi High Court has allowed the transgenders to register complaints of sexual harassment under which provision of India Penal Code?

(a) Section 265
(b) Section 355 B
(c) Section 365
(d) Section 354 A

95. Who is the executive Chairperson of NALSA?

(a) Justice A K. Sikri
(b) Justice Madan B. Lokur
(c) Justice N F. Nariman
(d) Justice D. Y. Chandrachud

96. Who is the First Chief Justice of Telangana High Court?

(a) B.N. Srikrishna
(b) T.B.N. Radhakrishna
(c) K.R. Lakshmanan
(d) Hrishikesh Roy

97. A human wall was made up by women in Kerala as part of the State Sponsored initiative to uphold gender equality from __________ to __________

(a) Thrissur, Kollam
(b) Kasaragod, Thiruvananthapuram
(c) Kollan, Maradu
(d) Varkala, Thiruvananthapuram

98. Trade Unoin Act (Amendment) Bill 2019 will provide for which of the following benefits?

I. Recognition of Trade Unions at Central and State Level;

II. Ensure true representation of workers in the tripartite Bodies;

III. Check on the arbitrary nomination of workers' representatives by the Government and

IV. Reduce litigation and industrial unrest.

(a) I, II, III, IV (b) I, II, III
(c) II, III (d) I, II

99. Under the Forest Right Act, 2006, Other Traditional Forest Dwellers has to give proof that they have been living in the Forest areas for ______________ years.

(a) 50 years (b) 99 years
(c) 75 years (d) 100 years

100. Article 35 A, Constitution of India is regarding

(a) Special status of Delhi
(b) Special status of 99 years
(c) Empower the Jammu and Kashmir State's legislature to define "permanent resident 'of the State
(d) Empower State of Jammu and Kashmir to have its own separate laws

101 Which of the following statements, are true regarding the jurisdiction of the High Court?

I. High Court can punish for its contempt.
II. High Court tender advice on the legal question referred to it by the Governor of the State.
III. High Court confirms the depth sentences passed by lower judiciary.
IV. High Court can issue writs for enforcement of Fundamental rights.

(a) I, IV (b) I, II, III
(c) I, II, IV (d) I, III, IV

102. If the tax rate increases with the higher level of income, it is called

(a) Progressive Tax
(b) Proportional Tax
(c) Lumpsum Tax
(d) Regressive Tax

103. In February, 2019 a Public Interest Litigation has been lodged with the High Court of ______________, wherein a 11-year-old boy has sought ban on the PUBG game in all the schools in the State.

(a) Delhi (b) Karnataka
(c) Allahabad (d) Bombay

104. As per the Insolvency and Bankruptcy Code (Amendment) Ordinance, 2018 which of true?

I. Home Buyers Recognized as Financial creditors.
II. Extension of the application of the Code to personal Guarantors of Corporate Debtors and Proprietorship firms
III. A person shall be eligible to submit a resolution plan, if such person is an undischarged insolvent.
IV. A resolution applicant cannot withdraw a resolution application, From The National Company Law Tribunal (NCLT), After such process has initiated.

(a) I and II (b) I, III and IV
(c) I, II and IV (d) All of the above

105. The Supreme Court has said that FIR in respect heinous and serious offences cannot be quashed solely on the ground that the dispute was settles amicable between the parties. Which of the following were included in the list of "heinous and serious offences"?

I. Offences under Prevention of Corruption Act
II. Some Offences under Arms Act
III. Rape
IV. Offences by public servants in their official capacity.

(a) I, II (b) II, III
(c) I, II, III (d) I, II, III, IV

Directions (questions 106–112): *Read the following information carefully and answer the question given below.*

Shopper's Stop offers exactly 10 types of perfumes – both domestic and export varieties of Woods, Proposal, Rose, Neesh and Hydra. Shopper's Stop is having a sale on some of these types of perfumes. The following conditional must apply;

I. Export Rose is on sale; Domestic Proposal is not.
II. If both types of Rose are on sale, then Hydra is
III. If both types of Woods are on sale, then no Neesh is
IV. If neither types of Woods is on sale, then domestic Rose is
V. If either type of Neesh is on sale, then no Hydra is.

REASONING

106. Which one of the following could be a complete and accurate lost of the types of perfume that are on sale?
(a) export Proposal, export Rose, domestic Neesh export Neesh
(b) domestic Woods, export Rose, export Neesh domestic Hydra.
(c) domestic Woods, export Woods, export proposal, export Rose, domestic Neesh
(d) export Woods, export Rose, domestic export Hydra

107. If domestic Hydra is not on sale then which one of the following must be true?
(a) At least one type of Woods is not on sale.
(b) Domestic Neesh is not on sale.
(c) At least one type of Rose is not on sale
(d) Domestic Neesh is on sale

108. If both types of Woods are on sale, then which one of the following is the minimum number of types of domestic that could be included in the sale?
(a) One (b) two
(c) three (d) four

109. Which one of the following CANNOT be true?
(a) Neither type of Woods and neither type of Proposal is on sale.
(b) Neither type of Woods and neither type of Hydra is on sale.
(c) Neither type of Proposal and neither type of Neesh is on sale.
(d) Neither type of Proposal and neither type of Hydra is on sale.

110. If neither type of Woods is on sale, then each of the following must be true EXCEPT?
(a) Domestic Hydra is on sale.
(b) Export Hydra is on sale.
(c) Domestic Neesh is not on sale.
(d) Export Proposal is on sale.

111. If domestic Hydra is the only type of domestic perfume on sale, then which one of the following CANNOT be true?
(a) Export Hydra is not on sale.
(b) Export Neesh is not on sale.
(c) Export Woods is not on sale.
(d) Export Proposal is not on sale.

112. If exactly four of the five types of export perfume are the only on sale, then which one of the following could be true?
(a) Export Neesh is not on sale.
(b) Neither type of Woods is on sale.
(c) Neither type of Neesh and neither type of Hydra is on sale.
(d) Export Proposal is not on sale.

Directions (questions 113–115): *In each question is given a statement followed by two courses of action. On the basis of the information given in the statement you have to suggest course of action.*
(a) If only I follows
(b) If only II follows
(c) If both I and II follows
(d) If neither I nor II follows

113. Statement:
LightUp company has rejected first lot of switches supplied by company ABC and has cancelled its huge order quoting use of inferior-quality material and poor craftmanship.

Courses of Action:
I. The company ABC needs to investigate functioning of purchase, production and quality Control Departments.
II. The company ABC should inspect all the valves rejection by LightUp company.

114. Statement :
The State Government is expecting bumper crop of wheat this years under its 'Wheat Purchase Guarantee Scheme'.

Curse of Action :
I. Other farmers should start cultivation of wheat from the next year.
II. The price of wheat will increase in the open market.

115. Statement:
The eligibility for appearing in Common Admission Test (CAT) for law in the State of X is now raised to 70% from earlier 60% in the Higher Secondary Examination.

Courses of Action:

I. Many candidates from the State of X may not appear for CAT this year and may appear from other states.

II. At pre-examination screening candidates obtaining less than 70% at the Higher Secondary Examination will have to be eliminated.

Directions (questions 116–117): *In each question, there are statements followed by conclusions. Find out the most appropriate response on the basis of the given statements.*

116. Statement 1 - Some parrots are pigeons.

Statement 2 - All pigeons are crows.

Conclusions -
I. Some parrots are crows.
II. All parrots are crows.
III. Some crows are parrots.
IV. All pigeons are parrots.

(a) I, III (b) II, IV
(c) I, II, III (d) I, II, III, IV

117. Statement 1 - All singer are danders.

Statement 2 - Some dancer are actors.

Conclusions -
I. Some actors are singers.
II. No actors is singer.
III. All dancers are singers.
IV. All singers are actor s.

(a) IV (b) I, III
(c) either I or II (d) either II or III

Directions (questions 118–120): *In each of the following question there is a related pair of words followed by four pairs of words. Select that pair which expresses the relationship that is most similar to that the capitalized pair.*

118. Appeal : Refusal
(a) Obesity : over-eating
(b) Try : Failure
(c) Struggle : Victory
(d) Examination : Passing

119. Zephyr : Gale
(a) Decay : Age
(b) Death : Sickness
(c) Trickle : Torrent
(d) Imprint : Emboss

119. Zephyr : Gale
(a) Decay : Age
(b) Death : Sickness
(c) Trickle : Torrent
(d) Imprint : Emboss

120. Implicate : Incrimination
(a) Perjury Fraud
(b) Involve : Crime
(c) Embezzlement : Charging
(d) Exonerate : Acquittal

Directions (questions 121–122): *In each of the following questions, two Statements I and II are Provided. These may have a cause and effect relationship or may have independent causes.*

Give Answer
(a) If the Statement I is the cause and Statement II is its effect
(b) If the Statement II is the cause and Statement I is its effect
(c) If both the Statements are effects of Independent cause.
(d) If both the Statement are effects of some common cause.

121. **Statement 1 –** The price of Bronze has gone up from ₹ 30,000 per kg to ₹ 60,000 per kg in almost a year's time.

Statement 2 – India sculptors are receiving a lot of demand for bronze statues from English and Russian art collectors.

122. **Statement 1 –** Hallmark of gold jewelry has been made compulsory.

Statement 2 – Many persons do not prefer to buy hall marked jewelry.

Directions (questions 123–127): *Given below is a passage followed by several inferences you have to examine each inference separately in the context of the passage and decide upon its degree of truth or falsity. Mark your answer as*

(a) If the inference is 'definitely true'.
(b) If the inference is 'definitely true'.
(c) If the 'data provided is inadequate'.
(d) If the inference is 'probably false'.

In a proposal to Government of Xovia, Association of xovia Industry(AXI) has suggested a series of short and long-term initiatives to help the states to cope up with the specter of drought in the country particularly in the North, it has come out with a pater on 'How to tackle drought' and recommended the cultivation of selected crops such as short duration paddy and irrigated dry crops in the focus areas besides subsidization of their seeds by 50% Other short-term measures include a food-for-work program with the investment of relevant departments and rural bodies, the setting up of a task force headed by to government officials to moniter the drought relief program, the scrapping of schemes that facilitates subsidized power supply to irrigation pump set connection in water-scare blocks to ensure power supply for drinking water schemes and ban on export of fodder, In fact, fodder should be mobilized from all sources and cattle sheds should be opened wherever needed, Employment affirmation program should be lunched with central assistance. If possible, interest on-loans taken by farmers should by waived besides converting the short-term loans into long-term ones. It is necessary to work out a way to take over the loans taken from primitive money lenders or reschedule them. Coming to long-term steps, the AXI paper says new water resources be explored besides building water supply projects and creating rainwater storage facility, Dryland cultivation ought to be promoted apart from popularizing water-saving irrigation-technologies.

123. To cope up with the specter of draught, we should devise both short-term and long term policies.

124. During the draught, a bailout package should be given to the farmers.

125. Draughts are more devastating than floods.

126. We should work out a long-term and permanent strategy to tackle the frequent draught situations.

127. In case of draught situation, we should channelize all the meters to the field.

128. In a card party, six friends are playing a game of card. Lela is facing Leena who is sitting to the left of Shreya and to the right of Ritu. Shreya is sitting to the left of Arya. Megha is sitting to the lift of Ritu. If Arya exchanges her seat with Megha and Ritu exchanges with Leena, who will be sitting to the left of Arya?

(a) Shreya (b) Lela
(c) Megha (d) Leena

129. In the Diwali dinner, four men and four women are invited. They are sitting around a square table facing the center. One person is sitting at each corner and at the mid-point of each side of the table. Kiran is sitting diagonally opposite to Mona who is to the right side of Piya. Kishan who is to the left side of Piya is diagonally opposite to Chander who is to the left of Deepak. Ravi is not sitting to the right of Kiran but in front of Sheela. Who is sitting oppsoite to Deepak?

(a) Chander (b) Sheela
(c) Ravi (d) Piya

130. Sana has organized birthday party for Roma. Roma took her car to reach the venue of the party. She drove 30 km towards North and then 40 km towards West. She then turned to South and covered 8 km. Further she turned to East and moved 26 km. Finally, She turned right and drove 10 km and then turned left to travel 19 km. How far and in which direction is she from the starting point?

(a) South-East of the starting point, 5 km
(b) North-East of the starting point, 13 km
(c) North-East of the starting point, 6 km
(d) South-East of the starting point, 13 km

130. The houses of Asma and Seema face each other on a road going North-South. Asma's house is on the western side, she comes out of her house and turns left, travels for 5 km. She then turns right, travel 5 km and reaches the front of Geeta's house. Seema does exactly the same and reaches in front of Shobha's house In this context, which of the following statement is correct?

(a) The houses of Shobha and Geeta are less than 20 km apart
(b) The houses of Shobha and Geeta are 20 km apart
(c) Shobha and Geeta lives in the same street
(d) Geeta's house faces South.

132. A watch, which gains uniformly, is 3 minutes at 12 noon on Monday and is 5 minutes 36 second fast at 4 pm on the next Monday. At what time it was showing correct time?

(a) 12 am on Tuesday
(b) 12 pm on Wednesday
(c) 12 am on Thursday
(d) 12 pm on Thursday

133. A clock is set at 10 am, The clock gains 10 minutes in 24 hours. What will be the right time when the clock indicates 3 pm on the following day?

(a) 12.40 pm (b) 1.40 pm
(c) 2.40 pm (d) 2.48 pm

134. Pihu and Aayan are the children of Mrs. & Mr. Sharma. Riya and Shankar are the children of Mrs. & Mr. Kumar. Ayan and Riya are married to each other and have two daughter Mona and Shona. Shanker is married to Leena and they have two children Rohit and Ruchi. How is pihu related Shona?

(a) sister (b) mother
(c) aunt (d) mother-in-law

135. In a family, there are seven persons,comprising two married couple F1 is the son of F2 and the grandson of F3, F2 is a widower. F2 and F4 are brother and F5 is the daughter-in-law of F6, who is the mother of F4 and the grandmother of F7 How is F7 related to F2?

(a) brother (b) nephew or niece
(c) cousin (d) son-in-law

Directions (questions 136–140): *Read the following short passage and choose the best answer to the question that follow each passage.*

136. According to the last opinion poll in Bhadristan, most voters believe that the three problems government needs to address, in order of importance, are crimes; unemployment and capitalistic economy. Yet in election, candidates from political parties perceived as strongly against capitalism were defeated, while those elected were all from parties with a history of opposing legislation designed to curb anti-competitive practices. These result should not be taken to indicate that the polls was inaccurate, however, since................ ....

Which one of the following most logically completes the passage

(a) every candidate who was defeated had a strong anti- capitalism record.
(b) many of the people who voted in the election refused to participate in the poll.
(c) all the candidates who were elected were perceived as being stronger against both crime and unemployment than the candidates who were defeated.
(d) There were no issues other than crime, unemployment and capitalism in which the candidates had significant difference of opinion.

137. Natural Gas production units in Industan have recently been acquired in substantial number by investors from abroad. Industanian politicians are proposing legislative action to stop such investment, justifying the proposal by arguing that foreign investors, opportunistically exploiting a recent fall in the value of the Industanian currency were able to by Industanian assets at less than their true value.

Which on of the following. if true casts the most serious doubt the accuracy of the Industanian politicians' justification for the proposed legislation?

(a) In Bangania, a country broadly similar to Industan, the share of Natural Gas Production

Units that is foreign-controlled is 60 percent higher than it is in Industan.

(b) The true value of investment is determined by the value of the profits from it, and the low value of the Industanian currency has depressed the value of any profits earned by foreign investors from industanian assets.

(c) The Industanian government originally welcomed the fall in the value of Industanian currency because the fall made Industanian exports more competitive in international markets.

(d) Foreign investors who acquired Industanian production units generally did so with no intention of keeping and running those units over the long term.

138. Proposed new safety rules for Seashore City Port would Lengthen considerably the minimum time between departures from the port. In consequence, the port would be able to accommodate 10 percent fewer vessels than currently use the port daily. The city's operating budget depends heavily on taxes generated by tourist spending, and most of the tourist come by ships. Therefore, the proposed new safety rules. If adopted, will reduce the revenue available for the operating budget.

The argument depends on assuming which of the following?

(a) The response to adoption of the new safety rules would not include a large increase in the number of passengers per ship.

(b) There are no periods of the day during which the interval between ships departing from the port is significantly greater than the currently allowed minimum.

(c) If proposed safety rules are adopted, the reduction in tourist numbers will not result mainly from a reduction in the number of tourists who spend relatively little in Seashore city.

(d) Increasing the minimum time between departures is only way to achieve necessary safety improvements without a large expenditure by the city government on port enhancements.

139. The average amount of overtime per mouth worked by an employee in the design division of the Diva Corporation is 18 hours,Most employees of Diva Corporation work in the design division. Furthermore, the average amount of overtime per mouth per employee in the company generally does not fluctuate much from moth to month. Therefore, each month, most employees of the Diva Crop. almost certainly work at least some overtime.

The argument is most vulnerable to criticism on which of the following

(a) It confuses a claim from which the argument's conclusion about the Diva Crop. would necessarily follow with a claim that would from the argument's conclusion only with a high degree of probability.

(b) If overlooks the possibility that even of most employees of the corporation work some overtime each month, any one corporate employee may, in some months work.

(c) It takes for granted that the design division of the corporation with regard to the average amount of overtime its employees work each.

(d) It overlooks the possibility that even if, on average, a certain amount of overtime is worked by the members of some group, many members of that group may work no overtime at all.

140. Supporters of the recently introduced tax on sales of new luxury cars had argued that a tax of this type would be a equitable way to increase government revenues because the admittedly heavy tax burden would fall only on wealth people and neither they nor any one else would suffer any economic hardships. In fact, however, 30 percent of the workers employed by manufacturers of luxury cars have lost their jobs as a direct result of this tax.

The information given, if true, most strongly supports which of the following statements?

(a) Taxes can be equitable only if their burden is evenly distributed over the entire population.
(b) Because many people never buy luxury items, imposing a tax on luxury items is the kind of legislative action that does not cost incumbent legislators much popular support.
(c) The new tax would produce a net gain in tax revenue for the government only if the yearly total revenue that it generates exceeds the total of the year tax-revenue decrease resulting from the workers' loss of jobs.
(d) The market for luxury cars would have collapsed even if new tax on luxury cars had been lower.

MATHEMATICS

141. If $n = 1 + x$, where x is the product of four consecutive positive integers, then which of the following is true?

I. n is an even number
II. n is prime number
III. n is a perfect square
IV. n is odd number

(a) I, III (b) I, II
(c) I, IV (d) III, IV

141. Three wheels can complete 40, 24 and 16 revolutions per minutes respectively. There is a green spot on each wheel that touches the ground at time zero. After how much time, all these spots will simultaneously touch the ground again?

(a) 7 and ½ seconds (b) 7 seconds
(c) 7 and ½ seconds (d) 7 minutes

143. In a group of students in a class, 20 are in the debating club, 24 in the drama club and 27 in the recitation club If 12 like drama and debate, 10 like recitation and debate, 14 like drama and recitation and 7 like all the three activities, then the total number of student in class is

(a) 40 (b) 42
(c) 50 (d) 52

144. Class XII of XYZ International School has three sections –K, L and M. In Mathematics examination, the average marks obtained by these sections are 72, 60 and 50 respectively. The average ,arks of sections K and L taken together is 69 If the ratio of the number of student in sections L and M is 6 : 7, what is the average score of all the three sections put together?

(a) 65 (b) 64
(c) 63.4 (d) 64.7

145. Sheena's test had 75 questions i.e., 10 on English, 30 on Reasoning and 35 on Legal Aptitude. Although she answered 70% of the English,40% of the Reasoning and 60% of the Legal Aptitude question Correctly, she did not pass the rest because she got less than 60% of the question right. How many questions she would have needed to answer correctly to earn to earn a 60% passing grace?

(a) 7 (b) 6
(c) 5 (d) 4

146. Amrit wants to sell cars at 25% above the cost price. Due to a slump in the market his cost reduces by 5%. He thus offers a discount of 8% due to which the sales up by 25% Compute the change in Amrit's profit

(a) unchanged (b) 5%
(c) 4% (d) 3% 147.

147. A water tank has eight popes fitted into it. Pipes are of types : Green Pipe and Red Pipe.Green popes are used to fill the tanks and the Red pipes are used to empty the tank. Every Green pipe can fill tank in 12 hours and ever Red pipe can empty it in 36 hours, On opening all the pipes an empty tank is filled in 3 hours. The number Of red pipe is

(a) 5 (b) 3
(c) 4 (d) 2

148. Anju is waiting on the railway station for the arrival of her train. Two trains running in opposite directions cross each Anju on the platform in 27 seconds and 17 seconds respectively and they cross each other in 23 seconds. The ration of their speed is

(a) 2 : 3 (b) 1 : 2
(c) 3 : 2 (d) 2 : 1

149. Neeraj is going to Agra on his bike from Delhi. He overtakes a bus travelling from Delhi to Agra at 4.30 pm. Neeraj reaches Agra at 6 pm. After stopping there for an hour, He starts back towards Delhi and meets the same bus at 7.30 pm which was moving towards Agra at that time. If both the bus and the bike were traveling with uniform speeds on the same route, at what time would the bus reach Agra?

(a) 9.45 pm (b) 9.30 pm
(c) 9.15 pm (d) 9 pm

150. Sonam has a rectangular garden. If the length of the garden is reduced by 5 m and breadth is increased by 3 m, then the area of the garden gets reduced by 9 m^2. However, if we increase the length by 3 m and breadth by 2 m, the area is increased by 67 m^2. What is the length of the garden

(a) 16 m (b) 17 m
(c) 16.5 m (d) 17.5 m

ANSWER KEY

English

1. (b)	7. (c)	13. (d)	19. (b)	25. (a)	31. (c)
2. (d)	8. (b)	14. (c)	20. (b)	26. (d)	32. (b)
3. (c)	9. (a)	15. (d)	21. (c)	27. (b)	33. (a)
4. (a)	10. (c)	16. (c)	22. (a)	28. (c)	34. (c)
5. (c)	11. (d)	17. (c)	23. (b)	29. (b)	35. (b)
6. (d)	12. (b)	18. (d)	24. (a)	30. (d)	36. (a)

General Knowledge

37. (d)	42. (d)	47. (c)	52. (c)	57. (d)	62. (b)	67. (c)
38. (c)	43. (b)	48. (d)	53. (a)	58. (b)	63. (a)	68. (a)
39. (b)	44. (c)	49. (d)	54. (c)	59. (d)	64. (d)	69. (d)
40. (a)	45. (b)	50. (d)	55. (a)	60. (a)	65. (a)	70. (b)
41. (b)	46. (a)	51. (a)	56. (c)	61. (c)	66. (b)	

Legal Aptitude

71. (b)	76. (b)	81. (c)	86. (c)	91. (c)	96. (b)	101. (d)
72. (c)	77. (a)	82. (a)	87. (b)	92. (b)	97. (b)	102. (a)
73. (d)	78. (c)	83. (d)	88. (d)	93. (a)	98. (a)	103. (d)
74. (b)	79. (d)	84. (d)	89. (c)	94. (d)	99. (c)	104. (a)
75. (b)	80. (a)	85. (b)	90. (d)	95. (a)	100. (c)	105. (d)

Reasoning

106. (d)	111. (c)	116. (a)	121. (c)	126. (d)	131. (a)	136. (c)
107. (c)	112. (a)	117. (c)	122. (b)	127. (c)	132. (c)	137. (b)
108. (a)	113. (c)	118. (b)	123. (b)	128. (b)	133. (d)	138. (a)
109. (b)	114. (d)	119. (c)	124. (a)	129. (d)	134. (c)	139. (d)
110. (d)	115. (b)	120. (d)	125. (b)	130. (b)	135. (b)	140. (c)

Mathematics

141. (d)	143. (b)	145. (c)	147. (b)	149. (d)
142. (a)	144. (d)	146. (a)	148. (c)	150. (b)